# Social Paralysis and Social Change

## A CENTENNIAL BOOK

One hundred distinguished books
published between 1990 and 1995
bear this special imprint
of the University of California Press.
We have chosen each Centennial Book
as an exemplar of the Press's great publishing
and bookmaking traditions as we enter
our second century.

## UNIVERSITY OF CALIFORNIA PRESS

*Founded in 1893*

# Social Paralysis and Social Change

*British Working-Class Education in the Nineteenth Century*

Neil J. Smelser

UNIVERSITY OF CALIFORNIA PRESS
*Berkeley · Los Angeles · Oxford*

RUSSELL SAGE FOUNDATION
*New York*

University of California Press
Berkeley and Los Angeles, California

University of California Press, Ltd.
Oxford, England

© 1991 by
Russell Sage Foundation


Library of Congress Cataloging-in-Publication Data

Smelser, Neil J.
  Social paralysis and social change : British working-class education in
the nineteenth century / Neil J. Smelser.
      p.   cm.
  Includes bibliographical references and index.
  ISBN 0-520-07529-3 (alk. paper).
  1. Working class—Education—Great Britain—History—19th century.
2. Education, Elementary—Great Britain—History—19th century.
I. Title.
LC5056.G7S58   1991                                          91-6384
371.96—dc20                                                  CIP

Printed in the United States of America
9 8 7 6 5 4 3 2 1

# Contents

# Tables and Charts

Charts

# Preface

Writing this book was in one important respect a return to my youth. My first truly independent scholarly enterprise—my dissertation—was an application of sociological theory to changes in industry and working-class family life in nineteenth-century Britain with special emphasis on the cotton-textile industry.[1] Now I revisit Victorian Britain, this time with an eye to the development of a schooling system for the working classes. The era is the same, but the subject matters of this and the earlier work overlap only slightly, in chapter 8 below, where I explore the relations between education and the family economy. In addition, this book generates some new and different theoretical emphases and interpretations, which others are probably better able than I to fathom.

The book has been long in preparation, interrupted by many mid- to late-career involvements in other research, writing, and editing, and by several adventures in trying to defend, preserve, advance, and promote the institutions of social science in particular and higher education in general. The research began in earnest in 1977–79, when I was director of the Education Abroad Program for the United Kingdom / Ireland of the University of California. Those years provided an opportunity to return to the archival riches of the British Library in London, where I was based. In the 1980s I inched forward on a number of fronts, particularly the exploration of the comparative cases of Wales, Scotland, Ireland, and New York, and wrote a few articles on the nineteenth-century British family and education.[2] The final stages of research and writing were completed on a sabbatical leave in 1989–90, supplemented by a visiting fellowship at the Russell Sage Foundation in New York.

In many ways working on this volume was a solo operation, but I received many kinds of help from others along the way. An early grant from the Russell Sage Foundation launched the project in the late 1970s. In the early 1980s I profited from a grant from the National Institute of Education. These grants enabled me to bring several research assistants in on the project, each of whom helped push my investigations into new and more specific lines of research. These were Deborah Woods and Jo Fisher in England; Betty Lou Bradshaw, Sue Greenwald, James Lussier, Alanna Mitchell-Hutchinson, Kathy Mooney, Helen Schwartz, Ken Tucker, and Mary Waters at Berkeley; and Jennifer Parker at the Russell Sage Foundation, whose work in compiling the tables and charts and guiding the manuscript to final form was invaluable. In 1981–82 most of the research assistants—Bradshaw, Greenwald, Lussier, Mitchell-Hutchinson, Mooney, Schwarz, and Waters—and I held a weekly seminar on British and American educational development in the nineteenth century. Many of the insights of that seminar will have to wait for another book to be written; but the meetings were of extraordinary value for my own thinking.

The year at the Russell Sage Foundation was a kind of glorious capstone experience to the whole enterprise. It proved the essential condition for my completing several threads of research and writing the entire manuscript. Eric Wanner, the Foundation's president, was an ideal role model, providing a splendid blend of the work ethic and a relaxed style of leadership; my co-fellows and the foundation staff gave me the fullest intellectual, logistical, practical, moral, and emotional support. The Foundation's enlightened policy of providing housing at modest rent for its non–New York fellows solved most of my family's practical problems of living, which can be overwhelming in that magnificent city.

My longtime assistant, Christine Egan, was a mainstay during the entire project. In both the hunting-and-gathering and the digesting-and-formulating phases of the research, I dictated most of my research notes and thoughts on tape. Chris transcribed the mountains of material fully and accurately, and with no complaints about the many moments of boredom that that process must have entailed. She also processed all the grant applications, reports, and manuscripts associated with the project. During my year in New York, she remained in Berkeley and we established a high-tech communication system of faxes, bitnets, tapes, telephones, and even letters. Through these she continued to assist on the project and to manage, with characteristic efficiency and humor, my ongoing communications with students and colleagues in Berkeley and around the country.

## CHAPTER I

# General Considerations

Elementary education in society commands our attention for many reasons, not the least of which is the ambivalence with which it is often regarded. On the one hand, it is valued positively as a medium for instilling into coming generations the cultural ideals, values, and idols that its host society treasures. It is also the medium for establishing the fundamentals of rational thought—language and logic—that are believed to be essential conditions for intelligent participation in civilized society. On the other hand, it is often the target of negative emotions, primordial jealousies, and heated controversy. There are two reasons why elementary education should be simultaneously favored and unfavored. First, it shares its duties with two other social agencies—the family and religion—that are also jealous guardians of the primordial and the sacred. Second, education has a double potential—either reproducing and solidifying social inequalities by defining them as right and given or otherwise rationalizing them, or working to break them down by fostering social mobility or developing the fundamentals of social consciousness and criticism. Equality and inequality, moreover—like the family and religion—are not neutral issues in any society.

In the context of this general assessment, primary education in Britain in the nineteenth century is a subject of special interest. In the upper classes, much of it occurred in the family; in the lower classes, as we shall see, it both complemented and conflicted with family necessities and priorities. In addition, primary education was a resource that was claimed—unsuccessfully, as it turned out—by the Established Church.

And, finally, education in general and primary education in particular were probably as finely and self-consciously differentiated by social class as they have been at any other time and place. This is especially notable, since the idea of class hierarchy was—and had been, and is—central as a primordial principle and organizing basis in British society. Accordingly, primary education was a subject of exceptional discussion, heat, and primordial dispute in our era. This statement is especially true of the education of the working classes, the topic of this study.

Even further interest attaches to nineteenth-century Britain because it was in transition in so many fundamental ways. Of course, *every* society—even those that appear to possess stability—can be considered in transition from one state to another, especially if we look retrospectively at its history. In Britain, however, there was transitional movement along many of the most basic cultural and institutional lines. I list a number of these lines of transition, keeping in mind that while the trends mentioned were fundamental, none of them either began or ended in the nineteenth century:

The transition from a mainly agricultural toward an advanced industrial and urban society.

The transition from an oligarchic system of government toward a democratic one.

The transition from a religious system based on a state-established religion toward one based on denominational competition.

The transition from a system of allocating social positions on the basis of patronage and privilege toward a more meritocratic system.

The transformation of the social class system in accord with all these changes. Two-thirds of the way into the century, Matthew Arnold described England as a society of three classes: the *Barbarians*, the aristocracy, noted for their love of war and sports and their passion for personal liberty; the *Philistines*, the middle class, whose material values weaken human cultivation and narrow the spirit; and the *Populace*, the vast masses of the people in the working class.[1] The early part of the century might be regarded as a situation in which the Barbarians were firmly in control, with the Philistines battering at the gates and the Populace a source of fear and alarm. At the time of Arnold's writing, the Barbarians and the Philistines shared power, while the Populace, "raw and half-developed, has long lain half-hidden amidst its poverty and squalor . . . now issuing from its hiding-place to assert an Englishman's heaven-born privilege of doing what he likes."[2] Arnold's characterization is perhaps best regarded as an engaging literary oversimplification, but it is not a totally unacceptable account of the broad sweep of changing class relations.

I argue in chapter 2 that the educational arrangements of a society represent in many respects a microcosm of the cultural and institutional environment that impinges on them. For that reason we should expect the history of British primary education in the nineteenth century to embody—in one way or another—all these transitions, including the multiple tensions and contradictions they generated in the larger society.

The final justification for this inquiry—if another is needed—is that Britain is, on the face of it, a paradoxical special case. (This assertion must also be qualified by saying that *every* case may be regarded as a special case, depending on one's assumptions and comparative criteria.) The paradox is this: in many ways British society convincingly led the world along the road to modernization. However, its journey toward educational "modernization"—by which I refer to a universal, compulsory, secular, and free system—has appeared to many historians to have been sluggish and halting in comparison with the continental and U.S. cases.[3] John Pakington, a mid-nineteenth-century friend of educational reform, put this concern as follows:

> It is in my mind a most humiliating consideration that here in England, where we have attained a degree of knowledge and intellectual power, of civilization and of luxury, which has never been reached before—that in England, where we have attained such scientific pre-eminence as to have given the world the wondrous steam-engine and the miraculous telegraph—here in this same England we are surrounded . . . by a portion of the population, both in our towns and in our rural districts, steeped in a degree of ignorance, intellectual destitution, vice and crime, than which scarcely anything worse would be found in an uncivilized land, and the blackness and shame of which are rendered darker and more shameful by the civilisation which prevails around us.[4]

The actual historical story was much more complex than such a generalization suggests; but it is an engaging question to orient our study.

## SOME ORIENTING ADJECTIVES

The chapters that follow involve above all a *sociological* study of historical change. Several remarks follow from this characterization:

The presentation is not a chronological or narrative history, but rather a selected series of analytic interpretations of educational development framed in categories and frameworks appropriate to the explanation of general processes of social change. The general interpretative perspective is presented at the outset.

I focus on the institutional structure of education as the main outcome to be explained. This emphasis on structure means giving less attention to many other topics that have interested historians of education. These "ignored" topics include the influence of pedagogical thinkers (Jean-Jacques Rousseau, Johann Pestalozzi, Johann Oberlin, Robert Owen, Friedrich Frobel), the statistical tracking of literacy rates and attendance rates, and the history of curricula.

Part of the analysis, then, is an attempt to explain the structural outcomes in the primary education system by referring to the structural processes (class, religious, economic, and political) transpiring in the larger society. In addition, I give equal emphasis to the group processes (social movements, group conflict, political contests and compromises) that provided the mechanisms linking external structural changes in society to structural outcomes in education. By combining structural and group-process analyses, I hope to add to the efforts to join the macroscopic and microscopic levels of social analysis, an enterprise that has reemerged as an object of keen interest in the social sciences.[5]

From a theoretical point of view, this study is a *synthetic* one. As with many other subjects in the social sciences, the history of the writing of educational history has produced a number of distinctive approaches, perspectives, and even "schools of thought" on how best to interpret and explain that history. Most of these regard one set of determinants (for example, class or cultural domination) as more important than others. As often as not, the exponents of a preferred approach develop a polemic in favor of it and against others. In chapter 2, I review the main approaches that have appeared in the writing of the history of British working-class education. In the same chapter, I develop an alternate, more inclusive approach that incorporates some aspects of each of them—for none of them is without merit—into a more comprehensive explanatory framework for the analysis of educational change.

Finally, this study is a *comparative* one. On the surface it is not that, since it concerns only the British case. Even casual examination of the history of education in the United Kingdom reveals, however, that it presents not one case but many. I focus first on the overall development of educational arrangements in England and Wales (chapters 4 and 5). (Even this raises a comparative complication, because that evolution spilled over to influence Scottish developments between 1846 and 1872.)[6] Within the general pattern of development, Wales presents a sufficient number of differences—regional, economic, religious, and class—to have produced a different set of structural outcomes from England. Scotland, with the complication noted, had developed and continued in the nineteenth century to develop a separate set of educational institutions. Finally, education in Ireland, while financed mainly by the English Parliament and governed as its creature, manifested a set of educational outcomes that were vividly and distinctively its own. In connection with the Irish case, I look briefly at the educational history of New York City in the first half of the nineteenth century, in which the Irish Catholic minority played a central role in a largely Protestant city. The evident value of this kind of comparative analysis is to identify different combinations of the determinants of educational change in the different cases, and thus specify and enhance the general explanatory power of those determinants.

## TWO METHODOLOGICAL OBSERVATIONS

The history of British education in general and of that of the British working classes in particular produced a mountain of primary evidence. This is to be found in government documents, school records, the press, the papers and publications of religious societies and teachers' associations, and biographies and letters. The secondary literature is also enormous, despite the frequently registered complaints of historians about "neglected areas" and "unwritten chapters." Because that secondary literature is in many cases both deep and detailed, it is an essential part of our understanding. In this study I have made ample use of both primary and secondary sources, out of the conviction that it is proper to discover the facts of history and increase our understanding about it in all of the ways at our disposal.

A recurrent and inevitable difficulty in studying working-class history has to do with the source of its sources. Most of the things recorded about the working classes were written by representatives of other classes. This occurs in all societies, by virtue of the unequal distribution of literacy, power, wealth, and access to authorship. The problem has been given special salience in British history by the recent development of the intellectual position, championed by E. P. Thompson, that classes, and notably the working classes, make their own independent history.[7] Methodologically this behooves historians to consult sources produced by representatives of those classes themselves and perhaps to distrust sources produced by others. Such a stance is reflected among some recent British historians.[8] This intellectual position has served as a useful methodological corrective to naive interpretations of evidently biased materials. It should not, however, be pressed so far as to deny that any social group both makes its history and has it made for it by other groups. In addition, biases inhere in the other alternatives. For example, studies of working-class biographies are obviously skewed as sources toward the more literate—and, in all likelihood, the higher—levels of that class. This problem of the reliability of different historical sources does not admit of any definitive solution, but rather invites a practical and skeptical approach to all of them.

## THE ORGANIZATION OF THE VOLUME

As indicated, I begin chapter 2 with an examination of available accounts of the development of working-class education in nineteenth-century Britain and attempt to weld a more synthetic framework of my own. Chapter 3, also introductory, is a general examination of three central primordial dimensions of British society in that century—social class hierarchy, religion, and region. These dimensions constitute major parameters that conditioned conflict and change in the educational arena. In chapters 4 and 5, I lay out the major turning points in the evolution of working-class educational arrangements, analyzing each point as resulting from a confluence of forces identified in the general process model developed in chapter 2.

Chapters 6 and 7 are the comparative chapters; in them I attempt to account for the array of similarities and differences in educational outcome in England, Ireland, Wales, and Scotland (with that glimpse of New York City). Chapter 8 shifts gears abruptly, and works over the historical period once again, but this time from the standpoint of the family economy of the evolving school system's consumers. In chapter 9, I pick up and trace the emergence of three roles—pupil-teacher, teacher, and inspector—that evolved as parts of the educational system. Each of these roles is notable in that it involved the incumbents in crossing over delineated class lines in British society. Chapter 10, in conclusion, examines the results of the study in relation to some general processes (for example, secularization) and principles (for example, differentiation) of social change.

## CHAPTER 2

# Accounts of Educational Change

By all measures, English education in the nineteenth century produced a scene of interminable talk, conflict, and frustration, both on the part of partisans and observers in that century and among contemporary historians. In 1867 John Stuart Mill observed that education was "one of the most inexhaustible of all topics."[1] Several years later he described his age as one in which "education, and its improvement, are the subject of more, if not profounder study than at any former period of English history."[2] Throughout the century, members of Parliament worried and debated endlessly over the subject, intertwined as it was with their abiding concerns with class, religion, and economy. Partisans of all stripes were forever comparing English education—usually unfavorably—with systems in Prussia, France, Holland, the United States, Scotland, and sometimes Ireland.[3] In 1837 Thomas Wyse wrote of English education: "There is not, as in all Continental countries, a minister and council of instruction; nor as in Scotland a General Assembly; nor as in Ireland a Board of Education. [England] forms the one great exception to the entire civilised world."[4] Henry Brougham described English popular education as the worst in Europe and complained that the typical governmental response to proposed educational and other reforms was "to promise, pause, prepare, postpone, and end by letting things alone."[5] In 1852 Richard Cobden wrote that he had "for nearly twenty years been looking in all directions for an escape from our educational 'fix' and am more bewildered than ever."[6] The same preoccupations and moods are often reflected in the enormous mass of accumulated secondary literature on education in that century.

Most of these expressions concern only one part of nineteenth-century English education—that of the lower orders, the poor, the industrial classes, or the working classes, as they were variously characterized. Indeed, these accounts concern only one part of that part—the efforts of voluntary religious bodies and the state with respect to the elementary education of those classes. Although in this book I refer to the wider picture, like most other scholars, I focus on that sub-part, because it was the most important to those who made nineteenth-century educational history, and because it constituted the most important foundation for contemporary English primary education. However, it should be kept in mind that English working-class education in the nineteenth century, to say nothing of English education as a whole, covered much more than that part of a part.

In two centuries of concern, advocacy and counteradvocacy, reminiscence, and scholarly study of English working-class education in the nineteenth century, many accounts of why it developed the way it did have evolved and crystallized. Not all of these accounts are recognizable as "explanations" of the more or less dispassionate sort that historians and other social scientists have come to advance. They are sometimes only vague causal presumptions embodied in the contexts of ideologies of reform, resistance, and reaction, but nonetheless do constitute explanation-sketches. In this chapter I present a selective and distilled list of such accounts and develop a synthetic framework of my own.

## FOUR KINDS OF ACCOUNTS

### REFORM OR "WHIGGISH" ACCOUNTS

This kind of approach has been identified in American educational historiography, where it is associated mainly with the name of Ellwood Cubberly.[7] In its U.S. variant, as summarized by Carl Kaestle, the basic reformist impulse is perceived to be found in "native, Protestant ideology," whose spokesmen "deduced a need for government intervention at a time of rapid change, to regulate morals, develop institutions, and create a more homogeneous population."[8] In their more generic manifestation, such "Whiggish" accounts stress the transformative power of reformist impulses as articulated by ideological leaders, given force in social movements, and implemented by entrepreneurs and others in positions of power and influence. The approach has also been labeled "evolutionary idealism."[9]

Several variants of the change-as-reform approach appear in historical accounts of English working-class education. They may focus on important theorists or educationists such as Rousseau, Pestalozzi, Owen, and Froebel.[10] They may refer to more general intellectual movements, such as utilitarian middle-class radicalism and working-class radicalism;[11] to the classical economists;[12] or to institutional "movers" of educational reform, such as Brougham, Sir James Kay-Shuttleworth, and William Forster. A related approach points to the importance of the efforts of educational civil servants; John Hurt, for example, summarizes his own version of the educational history of the century as giving "[the] bulk of the credit for [educational] achievement . . . not to the voluntary societies as is commonly supposed, but to that much maligned figure the Victorian civil servant."[13] Hurt even singles out Robert Lowe, the perpetrator of the Revised Code of 1862, as facilitating future expansion by simplifying and secularizing the system of primary education, thus reversing the common historical verdict on Lowe as a retrograde influence on the march of popular education.

Accounts of educational progress through reform are not always advanced as a simple "reform-leads-to-change" story, but often contain a recitation of major obstacles that stood in the way of progress and frustrated it, at least temporarily. In the English context, the barriers to the reformers' schemes for popular education were Tory fears of social and political unrest stimulated by the education of the poor; laissez-faire doctrines that opposed government intervention; governmental paralysis occasioned by the jealousies of contesting religious groups (mainly Church of England and various Dissenting groups) who feared disadvantage to themselves;[14] and working-class families who were unwilling to send their children to schools.[15] An example of this kind of resistance is found in the assessment of the English scene in 1862 by Brougham:

> The progress of popular education has been grievously obstructed by the separate and often conflicting proceedings of its promoters, attached, and conscientiously attached, to different sects of religion, acting in opposition to each other, though if brought together, and to a clear understanding, they might, from their honest zeal for a common object, have been led to cooperate, or at least, not to conflict.[16]

The common ingredient of the "Whiggish" or reformist explanations of educational development, then, is that of a struggle between enlightened impulses to reform—from wherever derived—and the obstacles thrown up by those unenlightened or otherwise resistant to reform.

FUNCTIONAL ACCOUNTS

One of the assumptions underlying reformist accounts of educational progress is that knowledge is preferable to ignorance in human society, and that, correlatively, education has ameliorating, civilizing, and culturally uplifting effects. While that body of scholars who fall under the somewhat indistinct label *functionalist* do not necessarily share this positive evaluation, they do regard education, generally conceived, as *necessary* for society, in that it fulfills certain functions that are essential for its ongoing operation or survival. At a minimum these functions involve the need to inculcate society's cultural values, socialize the young for future roles, and generate and transmit knowledge.

One of the starting points of functional accounts of education is that the structures that address these several functions are multiple and variable. M. E. Shipman, for example, regards education as the more "planned and deliberate" part of the broader socialization process in society, noting that education itself can be shared among a variety of "religious, political, military, occupational and recreational institutions." [17] Schooling itself is in turn only one part of—or structural possibility for—the general process of education. A corollary is that the comparative study of education is, in large part, the systematic analysis of how different structures address the functions of socialization in society.

Functional analyses of educational change typically begin by noting that at a certain moment in a society's history, those institutions that have traditionally met educational needs cease to be adequate. In referring to the educational condition of Britain around 1800, for example, David Wardle argues that "[formal apprenticeship] was dying, and was often merely a polite euphemism for child exploitation, while the family either accepted no educational responsibility or wished to delegate its educational functions." [18] The reasons for this functional obsolescence, moreover, are often seen as originating in socioeconomic changes external to the educational system. Putting the case most generally, S. N. Eisenstadt argues that the onset of social conditions associated with modernity (the breakdown of homogeneous cultural traditions, the increase in occupational and social mobility) called upon education to "deal with problems of forging new national communities and their common symbols, access to which tended to become more widely spread among different strata."[19] The external changes most commonly cited for modern societies are economic and technological ones, which call for more diversified and higher-level skills on the part of the work force (and hence the need for more education).[20] From a source not known for its functional stress—G. D. H. Cole and Raymond Postgate—comes the following: "[As of the 1870s in England, industry] needed operatives who were able to read its rules and regulations, and an increasing supply of skilled workers able to work at drawings and to write at any rate a simple sentence."[21]

According to most functional accounts, the societal response to functional obsolescence is to generate more specialized—or differentiated—structural arrangements for education. These are, by implication, more effective in the changed socioeconomic environment. Shipman argues, for example, that modern schools, as "specialised education," serve "societies dominated by organisations."[22] The rise of more specialized roles in education can be explained in much the same way:

> As the needs of a developing industrial society were met through the growth of specialist groups like the engineers, chemists, accountants, civil servants and social workers, so one of the fundamental requisites for both the growth and continued existence of industrial society was met by the emergence of the elementary schoolteachers—the "teachers of the people."[23]

Functional accounts of educational change, then, are one kind of theory of adaptation, and treat the development of formal education as an adaptive response to a range of socioeconomic changes associated with the modernization of society.

## DOMINATION AND CLASS-CONFLICT ACCOUNTS

This range of accounts, the most frequently voiced in the interpretation of the history of English education, finds its clearest intellectual expression in works following the theories of Karl Marx. Within this scheme, the education of the working classes in capitalist society is regarded as a systematic effort on the part of the dominant economic classes to instill a false consciousness into the workers and the struggle on the part of the latter to resist that effort.[24] Engels's essay on the working classes in 1844 provides an example. His general interpretation of working-class education flows from the logic of class interest: "The bourgeoisie vouchsafes [the workers] only so much of life as is absolutely necessary; we need not wonder that it bestows on them only so much education as lies in the interest of the bourgeoisie; and that, in truth, is not much."[25] What little was given was either in the interests of ideological indoctrination or befuddled with sectarian "incomprehensible doctrines and theological distinctions."[26] Workers, moreover, struggled against this by initiating their own "proletarian education" through the trade-union, Chartist, and socialist societies, or, more generally, by subverting bourgeois purposes in developing a consciousness of their own interests through knowledge of their own circumstances.[27]

Few "class" historians of English education have attempted any wholesale application of Marxian theory in all its formality and complexity;[28] most have instead borrowed selectively from that theory, stressing mainly strategies of class domination, struggles against that domination, and the outcomes (victory, defeat, compromise) of those struggles. Early "Fabians" such as Sidney and Beatrice Webb, J. L. and Barbara Hammond, and R. H. Tawney belonged to this tradition, as do various more recent "radical" interpretations by Brian Simon,[29] Ivan Moorish,[30] Phillip McCann,[31] and, to some degree, Harold Silver.[32] Another variant, stemming mainly from the work of E. P. Thompson in the 1960s,[33] stresses the independent efforts of the working classes to articulate and develop their own culture.[34] A more or less explicit assumption accompanying this line of work is that, through their independent action, the workers were acting in defiance of the upper, controlling classes.

Some of Simon's accounts are illustrative of the domination-and-conflict approach. Much of the educational struggle from 1815 to the middle of the century was symptomatic of the ongoing struggle against the landlords by the middle classes, in which the latter employed identifiable strategies such as attacks on the grammar schools and universities and the formation of new institutions like the proprietary schools and the University of London. Prior to 1832, these efforts received some support from working-class radicals. After the Reform Bill of that year, however, the landlord and middle classes moved toward an alliance with each other against the politically menacing working classes (1830s–1840s). Accordingly, they generated educational reforms aimed at reducing crime and pauperism, establishing moral respectability and personal deference among the working classes, and instructing them in the principles of political economy. In the same period, the workers came to express a more straightforward class interest of their own through ideological defiance and the establishment of Owenite- and Chartist-inspired schools. The same kind of struggle continued between 1850 and 1870, though on somewhat different terms. According to Simon:

> A conscious effort was made to establish closed systems of schools; so to divide and differentiate the education given to different social classes that privilege could forever withstand the pressure of the working masses. This attempt could only meet with failure, whatever the temporary respite secured and the brakes put on educational advance. From the moment of the repeal of the Corn Laws [1846], the capitalist class could, in fact, take no step which was not conditioned by the attitude of the working class. To win the workers' support for their own ends, and curb independent action, it was also to make more concessions than they wished, in the educational no less than in the political field.[35]

In a similar spirit, McCann describes his approach to popular education in the nineteenth century as dealing with "its function as a means of countering social change and as an agent of the socialization of the children of the poor for life in a stratified, exploitative industrial society."[36]

One of the corollaries of the classical Marxian approach is that religious conflict over the control of the education of the young, overt espousal of and conflict over educational doctrines among philosophers and reformers, and struggles over curriculum all have a superficial aspect. These are symbolic manifestations of more fundamental, underlying struggles among economically based social classes. Not all class-domination interpretations of educational history embrace this point of view as a matter of theoretical principle. Nevertheless, a stress on class tends to downplay these political and religious phenomena as important or independent sources of educational content, structure, and change.

Domination-and-conflict accounts may overlap with functional accounts, depending on the vision of society that underlies them. Most functional theories posit that the maintenance of social order is among the essential functional prerequisites of society.[37] If so, education can be regarded as one of the structures that "specializes" in maintaining social control through socialization and discipline. Norman Morris's account of education in nineteenth-century England comes close to expressing this overlap of often-competing accounts. Morris argues that society was above all a system of social ranks, and that one of the state's major concerns was maintaining order through "control and regulation of the ranks of society." Schools were important agencies in this effort, and the state fostered them as a "legitimate state interest."[38] This illustration suggests that while the well-worn observation that Marxian-derived theory focuses on domination and conflict and that functionalist theory ignores or downplays those phenomena[39] is generally valid, this cannot be advertised as an absolute distinction.

## ACCOUNTS BASED ON COMPETITION AMONG STATUS GROUPS

Another account taking conflict as a central organizing theme is that ventured by Michalina Clifford-Vaughan and Margaret Archer in their study of the educational systems in England and France in the late eighteenth and early nineteenth centuries.[40] Clifford-Vaughan and Archer part with the classical Marxian approach, however, in that they move beyond the forces of economic production as the basis for structuring conflict groups. Their stress is on status groups as these were conceived by Max Weber. Such groups orient themselves to the control, even the monopolization, of values, knowledge, and other "ideal goods." Examples would be churches, denominations, and sects, as well as groups formed on the basis of ideologies such as utilitarianism or socialism. In order for a status group to maintain control, it must possess a monopoly of scarce resources relating to that control; erect constraints to assure that other groups acquiesce in its possession of, or cannot gain access to, those resources; and possess an ideology that legitimizes its monopolistic claims.[41] As this sketch shows, Clifford-Vaughan and Archer leave more room for autonomous processes—including conflicts—in the political and cultural "superstructure" than are envisioned in classical Marxian theory.

In their interpretations of nineteenth-century British educational history, however, Clifford-Vaughan and Archer focus not on a situation of cultural monopoly, but on one of competition. They identify the Church of England as the dominant group in the structuring of the primary education of the poor in the first half of the nineteenth century. They also identify several competing groups, each of which developed an ideology legitimizing its position to its own followers and to a wider audience, negate the ideology of the dominant group, and specify an alternative blueprint for action consistent with its ideological principles.[42] The three main challengers to Church of England hegemony were (1) middle-class

Dissent, which stressed doctrinal differences, rights of conscience, and religious parity in the control of education; (2) secularism, associated with the middle-class, utilitarian demands for education as practical preparation for prospective employment and economic productivity; and (3) working-class educational activity associated mainly with Owenism and Chartism, which ranged itself against Church, Dissent, and middle-class utilitarian radicals and strove for education as a means of self-improvement, class consciousness, and class power. After decades of conflict, the English educational system emerged in midcentury as

> An unstable situation . . . representing a new balance of forces. The middle class still fought to depose Anglican domination, without however being able to make dramatic interventions and to further devalue the church's monopoly. The voluntaristic principle had largely introduced a situation of stalemate between the two parties. At the same time, the disenchantment of the working class and its emergence as an assertive group in its own right constituted a major limitation on middle-class advance, both through reducing its facilities and discrediting its ideology.[43]

On the basis of this and other illustrations, Clifford-Vaughan and Archer construct an ideal-type sequence of four phases: assertion on the part of a competitive status group, transitional conflict, a new pattern of domination, and a new round of assertion. This kind of sequence never runs its full course in isolation, but continuously repeats itself in different variations and overlaps with other processes of social change. The sequence is complicated, moreover, when more than two groups are striving for hegemony at the same time.[44]

A variant of this group-conflict approach—which, however, has not been applied systematically to the educational scene—asks how the regional/ethnic/cultural conflicts in the United Kingdom shaped social arrangements. This approach, articulated by Michael Hechter,[45] portrays England as the core or dominant power, with Ireland, Scotland, and Wales as peripheral and subordinated. This perspective, labeled "internal colonialism," involves above all dominance relations between core and periphery with respect to commerce and trade, credit, and concentration of wealth and power. These are accompanied by discrimination against the peripheral groups with respect to language, religion, and other cultural forms.[46]

As in the Clifford-Vaughan–Archer model, the relations between core and periphery are not ones of simple domination-subordination, but involve the development of regional or ethnic identity, assertions and reassertions of cultural superiority on both sides, protest and conflict, and political compromise and accommodation. The internal colonial model is mentioned here because elements of it are clearly applicable to the regional histories of the United Kingdom in the nineteenth century.[47]

## SOME OBSERVATIONS ON THE ACCOUNTS

Each of these four approaches has been criticized as incomplete, limited, incapable of answering certain problems, and perhaps even incompatible with the others.[48] On the basis of examining their internal logic and appreciating the complexities of the history of British education, it is evident that (a) the accounts overlap with one another, (b) each has some relevance in explaining that history, and (c) any general explanatory model of the historical dynamics must take each into account and assign it to a more specific explanatory role.

With respect to overlap, I have already noted that insofar as the functional approach stresses the need to maintain stability through social control, it overlaps with the conflict models. Insofar as the status groups identified by Clifford-Vaughan and Archer overlap with economic class membership—as they are acknowledged to do—the status-competition and class-conflict models also overlap. Insofar as the functional/adaptive approach regards educational change as emerging from the adaptive compromise of the state and other agencies of social control in the face of group conflict, it overlaps with both the class-conflict and status-competition approaches. Finally, in a related observation, R. L. Schnell notes that the class-conflict model associated with Simon and others retains some of the analytic and evaluative elements of the reformist model.[49] Despite such overlaps, the tendency of exponents of each of the different approaches is to stress the relative advantage of their own, its antagonistic relations to other approaches, and its exclusivity. This tendency undoubtedly stems from the dynamics of academic competition and from the fact that the several approaches are embedded in larger philosophical and ideological positions that stand in polemical opposition to one another. Examining the internal explanatory logic of the approaches, however—as contrasted with their underlying ideological positions—yields a more promising view of the prospects for their synthesis with one another.

To regard the issue of overlap from another angle: a scholar often begins his or her study with a general statement setting out a preferred approach of the sort illustrated above. This statement of approach typically appears in an early chapter, and it is set off from other, presumably less valid, competitors. When confronted with the historical richness of the subject matter in question, however, the scholar may import, often in an unacknowledged or subterranean way, elements of the less favored approaches when the preferred one seems lacking. This phenomenon leads Douglas Sloan to observe that "in the course of historical inquiry, [the typology and models of a philosopoher-sociologist] can only be suggestive, and may have to be complicated, qualified, and refined out of recognition."[50]

As a corollary, it is evident that each approach captures some, but not all, of the complex reality of educational history, and thus falls short as a full explanatory account. For example, the appearance of formal schooling and its specialized roles (teacher, pupil, manager, inspector) is a result of a process of structural differentiation, but to establish that leaves out the complex mechanisms—social movements and counter-movements, group conflicts, compromises[51]—that produce that result. Functional accounts that trace the development of formal systems of schooling to the exigencies of industrial development also confront difficult cases—for example, why Ireland, an industrially "backward" country in the early nineteenth century, produced an "advanced" national system of education that was to appear in England only decades later. The class-conflict approach goes far in explaining how the curricula of working-class schools stressed deference to superiors and acceptance of one's lot in life,[52] and how closely the timing of the efforts of the ruling classes to expand and reform working-class education—in 1819, 1833, 1839, and 1843, for example—coincided with these classes' sense of alarm over outbursts of working-class protest. At the same time, the model of class conflict does not readily yield a very intelligible account of why certain religious groups—for example, the Methodists and the Catholics—engaged in a complex and shifting set of alliances with other religious groups on educational issues in the mid nineteenth century.[53] The dimensions of regional, ethnic, and religious conflict are indispensable for understanding the educational evolution of Ireland and Wales, for example, but in both cases these forces interact with distinctive patterns of class domination and conflict.[54]

The upshot of these observations is that an appropriate strategy in understanding a chosen phase of historical change is to develop a perspective that is synthetic in that it incorporates insights from approaches known to have usefulness but avoids shapeless eclecticism by setting these insights into some kind of systematic relationship to one another. Ideally, it should be sufficiently specific to be applicable to the distinctive historical case or cases chosen, but should also be sufficiently general to be of interest to those who focus on typical processes of social change. I now lay out the essentials of such an approach.

## A SYNTHETIC APPROACH

In taking up this task of synthesis, I shall first present some comments on the nature of education in society and then outline a process-model for educational change. The framework proposed is synthetic; it incorporates social-structural and social-psychological elements; stresses both functional adaptation and conflict; and makes central reference to both class and status groups.

### EDUCATION: A PROCESS

Consistent with a functional emphasis, education is taken as one part of the more general process of socialization. Socialization, including its educational aspect is, moreover, a process that applies simultaneously to several levels of analysis. Referring to the *individual,* socialization involves the acquisition of values, ideals, identifications, motivational commitments, interpersonal skills and styles, as well as information and cognitive skills. At the level of *society,* it refers to the resources allocated to the diverse activities, roles, and institutional structures that contribute directly or indirectly to the socialization of individuals. From the standpoint of *culture,* socialization is a mechanism by which societies transmit values, ideologies, meanings, and group identity from generation to generation, even though those ingredients of that social heritage are subject to change.

To define socialization at these different levels implies neither that the process is orderly at any of them nor that there is a continuity among the three. At the individual level, socialization sometimes fails, misfires, stirs rebellion, or is otherwise inadequate in relation to the expectations of the socializers. At the social level, a cohort of individuals, even if "adequately" socialized, may not match the demands for role performance in the institutional (for example, occupational) structures of adult life, particularly if those structures themselves are changing. And at the cultural level, the omnipresence of conflict and change in society suggests that the particular values, ideals, and so forth, transmitted to one generation may be inappropriate—or a matter of contention—for the next. Despite the omnipresence of failures and discontinuities in socialization, it remains the case that, from the point of view of the socializers, the object of the process is to reproduce cultural patterns in those being socialized.

In this study I concentrate on the educational aspect of socialization. According to conventional usage, education is the part of socialization that imparts and develops information, knowledge, cognitive skills, and critical abilities. While not incorrect, this should not be allowed to obscure the fact that education is never a solely cognitive process, but also attempts to shape the socializee's cultural values, ideals, and choice of heroes and villains, as well as normative expectations relating to personal ambition, attitudes toward authorities, cooperative and competitive behavior, and so on.

This view of education is consistent with the formulations of Emile Durkheim.[55] One point he stressed is that education always reflects the ideals of the home civilization, whether these be military valor, religious asceticism, aristocratic gentlemanliness, or economic productivity. It should be added that, particularly in times of rapid change, in no case is there a monolithic and well-integrated set of cultural ideals to be transmitted, but several sets in competition or conflict with one another. In addition, societies with specialized institutional structures—economic, legal, political, and so forth—will have produced groups (classes, estates, ethnic groups, etc.) that press their own values and interests with respect to the education of the coming generations. This cultural diversity constitutes one major source of potential conflict over education.

In this study I concentrate on the social-structural level of education, especially changes in schooling directed at the British working classes in the nineteenth century. To make such a choice is not to ignore that a great deal of education occurred outside those special social structures known as schools. The transmission of many agricultural and domestic skills occurs in families. Apprenticeship often occurs in an economic organization, such as a cobbler's shop or a newspaper's composing room. Basic training in the military, induction into a religious order in a monastery, and the retraining of government employees for transfer to other agencies are still other examples of education outside schools. The ways in which education is carried out through different structures is one focus of its comparative study.

## EDUCATION: A RESOURCE

While education, like socialization, occurs throughout life, the early years of childhood are crucial ones in this process. These are the years in which the basic motivational commitments (for example, trust and co-operation) develop, as do general cognitive skills (such as literacy and numeracy) and one's basic identities according to major social categories and groups (sex, regional origin, religion, and social class). The education of children in these years can thus be regarded as a *generalized resource* for society, capable of being shaped and channeled in different directions with respect to motivation, cognitive development, cultural commitments, and group membership and loyalty. For example, education is a resource for the military if ideas of valor and bravery and martial skills are stressed. It is an economic resource if scientific and technical skills take priority. It can be used to generate symbols of religious, national, or local identification and solidarity. It can be used to reinforce inequality by conferring status or cultivating deference, or to encourage social mobility. In contemporary societies, education is invariably called upon for most, if not all, of these purposes.

In our own society, education has been asked to help solve various kinds of social problems—such as labor shortages, low economic productivity, poverty, crime, and substance abuse—so that it has earned the label, "a sort of universal solvent for the problems of the polity."[56] In addition, the fact that education is an activity designed to shape children for the future means that it is a powerful instrument for investment in the future. For that reason, the young are "fair game" for competition among social groups who are pushing their own values, outlooks, and interests as part of the competitive struggle, and education is an arena where advantage in that struggle can be sought. Much educational conflict in society is among those competing for power and influence, who regard schools as recruitment grounds for their own ranks in the future. Part of such conflict is for material resources. In addition, it is conflict over ideologies and philosophies of education, which legitimize the allocation of those resources.

## OUTCOME AND PROCESS
## IN EDUCATIONAL DEVELOPMENT

Some students of change treat educational development according to a "convergence" point of view, pointing out that mass elementary educational systems are universal features of the complex process captured by the term *modernization*. Alex Inkeles, for example, has argued that

> [even] if they do not follow the same developmental sequences, industrial nations will converge at the same point on many dimensions. For example, in the United States, the extensive diffusion of primary schooling may have run well ahead of industrialization, whereas in England, the sequence was reversed. Nevertheless, in common with other modern systems, both countries came to have close to 100 percent of school-age children enrolled in primary schools.[57]

These educational outcomes produce mass public systems that establish basic cognitive skills, values, and beliefs in the populations served, and to share the basic socialization processes with the family and peer groups. Moreover, a reading of the historical and sociological literature on educational development yields a composite picture of a "modern" system of primary education. Such a system is, in ideal-typical form:

A comprehensive system, with universal, or near-universality of, coverage of the population; this is the "mass" aspect.

A "national" system, one administered by the state.

A literacy- and numeracy-producing system.

A system free of charge to its consumers.

A compulsory system with respect to attendance by its consumers.

A system that imposes values and beliefs that are believed to be common to the population served; these are mainly national values, but if it is believed that the society is culturally, ethnically, or religiously homogeneous, these kinds of elements may be present as well.

A system that is usually secular—that is, free from the imposition of the values, doctrines, ideologies, liturgies or rituals of *particular* religious, ethnic, cultural, or political groups in the society.

A system that enjoys more or less general acceptance among the population.

Such characteristics are not only after-the-fact assessments by modern scholars of developed educational systems. They are often ingredients of reform programs put forward by partisans in the process of educational development itself. For example, the National Educational League, a reform organization founded in the late 1860s, agitated for a program that would yield an "unsectarian, free, and compulsory" system.[58]

Because of the approximations to this ideal-type found in many developed and developing countries, it is tempting to regard it as an outcome of a typical, if not evolutionary, process associated with the exigencies of modernization (such as the requirements of technological and industrial change and the need to generate loyalty to the state). This view is wanting in several ways. For one thing, it does not account for apparent exceptions: decentralization of state support and the persistence of a significant private educational sector in the United States; the persistence of religion in modern educational systems, weakly in Britain, for example, and strongly in Israel; fragmentation or "pillarization" of educational education along religious, ethnic, and other cultural lines in some modernized systems—for example, Dutch society up to a few decades ago, French Canada, and the United States along black-white lines formally before 1954 and informally since. More serious, however, the ideal-type picture of common outcomes, even if generally accurate, does not reveal the *mechanisms* by which such outcomes were generated—the highly variable patterns of invention of ideas, group confrontation, political compromise, innovation, and implementation that constitute the historical process.

In keeping with this last observation, I intend to concentrate on the mechanisms and dynamics of change in interpreting the rise of popular education in Britain in the nineteenth century. While I shall keep in mind the ideal-type picture sketched above as a yardstick to measure its change, I want to account not only for its progress toward a "modern" system, but also for its moments of paralysis, "false starts," and incompleteness. In line with this intention, I shall now develop a framework, including a kind of process-model of educational change, to be applied in a general way to the relevant historical situations and events as they unfolded in the nineteenth century. As indicated, this framework incorporates and, it is hoped, integrates a number of the explanatory factors contained in the outline of available accounts.

## FIRST INGREDIENT: ESTABLISHING
## A MOMENT OF EQUILIBRIUM-IN-TENSION

Although this study focuses on the educational apparatus, a guiding assumption is that it is embedded in the society's sociocultural environment,[59] and that changes in that environment condition changes in the educational apparatus. A strategy for the study of educational change, then, is to identify a "starting point"—a selected historical moment—

and to sketch the character of the main forces impinging on education at that time. The selection of the starting point inevitably constitutes an arbitrary act[60] on the part of the investigator, though the occurrence of critical events (such as the passing of an educational law, a change of government) may provide certain guidelines for selection.

In the case of England around 1800, such a description would include the following illustrative ingredients:

The contours of the educational apparatus itself, including a description of the charity schools, the Sunday schools, and the dame schools.

The major features of the population and the economic/industrial structure.

The resulting social class situation, including a significant middle class and a nascent urban-based working class, neither of which was readily assimilable into the dominant rural/aristocratic class system based on paternalism and deference.

The religious situation, including the relative strengths of and balances among the Established Church, old and new Dissent, Catholicism, and so on.

Ideological forces arising from the above, including varieties of reformism and radicalism, conservative and reactionary positions.

Social movements and political mobilization relating to education and its environment.

As indicated by the term, *equilibrium-in-tension,* this description is intended to yield a picture of a balance of forces, but this balance is not static in any way, since the various forces may stand in tension or conflict with one another.

SECOND INGREDIENT:
TRACKING THE FORCES OVER TIME

Having established an admittedly arbitrary starting point, the next step is to "relax" the assumption of timelessness involved in positing that starting point, and to track the identified forces over time. The object is to determine how the constellation of forces is changing, and especially to identify cumulative imbalances among them as these are experienced by the relevant individual actors and groups of the time, and as they impinge on the educational process. Following the above illustration, the first two decades of the nineteenth century would produce the following kinds of changes:

The continuing development of urban population, especially the working classes.

The continuing manifestation of working-class radicalism through the Napoleonic wars and into the postwar period, accompanied by continuing apprehension among the ruling class, fed by the "counter-revolutionary" movement set off in Britain by the events of the French Revolution.

A repressive response to class protest.

The rise and spread of the Sunday school movement, notably among Wesleyan Methodists, new Dissenters, and the Evangelical wing of the Church of England, combined with a vigorous assault on the movement from Tory and High Church sources, attempting to lump together Dissent and radicalism, and to discredit both.

The limited effectiveness of the educational efforts of the Sunday schools, plus the continuing weakness of the charity schools and other educational efforts.

Inevitably, such changes create some imbalances, tensions, or contradictions—whichever term is preferred—and generate different kinds of psychological impact on the main historical actors and groups of the time. The most important of these impacts, moreover, are feelings of dissatisfaction, relative deprivation, or threat. Such feelings tend to generate new and activate existing ideological definitions of the historical situation, to induce actors to mobilize for political action on the basis of these definitions, and thus to engender group conflict.

The final task of this analytic step is to track those processes of ideological change, political mobilization, and conflict relevant to the educational process, and to identify a certain resolution of the sequence.[61] This resolution yields a new point of equilibrium-in-tension, which constitutes, in its turn, a new starting point for a next phase of change. With respect to the ongoing example, the early decades of the nineteenth century produced the following developments around 1820:

Mobilization on the part of Dissenters and Church of England moderates in a private educational effort and mobilization—provoked by this effort—on the part of the Established Church to provide similar voluntary schooling. The balance struck by these developments was a situation of private competition between the Church of England and Dissent.

Mobilization of a combination of radicals and Whigs to persuade Parliament to establish some kind of education for the poor, with efforts undertaken in 1802, 1807, 1819, and 1820 to secure legislation to that end; for a variety of reasons, these either foundered or were ineffective, so that the government did not become formally involved in the education of the poor.

The period around 1820, then, can be treated simultaneously as a point of resolution—a new equilibrium-in-tension point for education—and the starting point for a new period of change that continued to 1833, the year that saw the first formal involvement of the government in the education of the working classes. That involvement established yet another resolution and a new starting point. However, a few qualifying remarks about this perspective on educational change are in order.

First, it should be noted that each phase of educational change yields evidence of a certain drift or change of societal forces impinging on education that are meaningful—usually in a threatening way—to one or more involved groups. In many cases those drifts or changes manifest themselves in dramatic events that give both real and symbolic "testimony" to the societal forces they are perceived to represent. For example, the passage of acts of Parliament giving relief to Dissenters and Catholics in 1828 and 1829, followed by the Reform Parliament in 1832, marked a dire moment for the Establishment because they acknowledged and consolidated the forces both of Dissent and of middle-class radicalism. One consequence of these threats was to spawn a countermovement within the Established Church, of which the Oxford Movement, beginning in 1833, was a major part. The resulting revitalization of the Church of England accounts in part for its aggressiveness in the educational conflicts of 1839 and 1840 with the government over establishing normal schools and inspecting elementary schools.[62] Anglican "victory" in that conflict was, in its turn, a threat to Dissent and contributed in part to the mobilization of Dissenters to oppose educational proposals that favored the Church of England in Parliament in 1843.[63] Whether or not such dramatic moments truly reflected shifting social forces, they surely appeared to do so to actors and groups at the time.

In a line of analysis consistent with my own, P. W. Musgrave considers what I have called moments of "equilibrium-in-tension" to be "truce points." As a rule, these are "the end product of a bargaining process,"[64] certainly in societies that have the elements of a democratic polity.

Each new moment of equilibrium-in-tension involves a shift in the definition of the educational situation, a new alignment of institutional and political forces, and, very likely, an altered allocation of resources. As such it establishes for the educational system a new "gyroscope" or "program" for future change—more precisely, a new set of drifts and trends. For example, the solution of 1833, to offer limited state funds to "match" private religious societies' subscriptions for new schools was an equitable solution in that it rewarded the societies in accord with their own efforts. At the same time, it established an advantage or "tilt" toward the National Society of the Church of England because of its greater ability to generate subscriptions, and thus programmed future development in favor of the Anglican Church. This constituted a continuing threat to the competing forces of Dissent. It is essential, then, to ascertain how each new point of equilibrium-in-tension identified establishes a new gyroscope for future change.

Insofar as each new "truce point" creates a new allocation of resources, an altered institutional structure, and a new definition of the situation, the terms of orientation, negotiation, and conflict among interested parties are altered accordingly. As a result, subsequent phases of change are carried out in a new and different sociopolitical context. In that sense, educational change "builds on itself" because each new episode or sequence does not start anew but plays out in the context of inherited changes.

To treat educational history as a series of sequences of realignment of forces, group dissatisfaction, mobilization and conflict, resolution and the establishment of a new balance calls for the specification of the critical points. For the period under consideration, I have chosen the years 1807, 1820, 1833, 1839, 1843, 1846, 1846–61, 1862, and 1870. The reason for selecting these is that they marked significant shifts in the structure of the educational system, the reallocation of resources in some cases, and a new definition of the educational situation. In chapters 4 and 5, I analyze the transitions associated with each period.

EXTERNAL SOCIAL FORCES IMPINGING
ON EDUCATION

A central assumption underlying the approach sketched above is that any kind of educational development is explained in large part by referring it to the societal forces that impinge on it—those forces that demand, as it were, what education should do for society. To supplement the model of change, I now outline the general character of those external forces in this section.

In doing this I do not mean to suggest that these external forces always operate as permanent shaping or constraining parameters, though some of them—class and religion in nineteenth-century Britain, for example—may be especially salient. Typically, these external forces are embedded in other, semiautonomous sectors of society, and only sporadically does their influence spill over to influence the educational apparatus. To illustrate: it is frequently asserted that the demands of the economy for skilled labor give shape to society's educational system, and—closely related—that international economic competition gives urgency to those demands. With respect to the first assertion, it is difficult to argue that industrial and other economic demands for skills were a large part of the picture for British primary education in the first half of the nineteenth century. Most jobs in that phase of capitalist development were unskilled or semiskilled and required few workers with advanced technical expertise. The "demand for skills" factor emerged later in the century as the technological basis for industry became more complex and as the number of workers in the requisite service occupations (engineers, technicians, and clerks, for example) expanded. Similarly, only on certain occasions (in 1851 and 1867, for example, when international expositions revealed superior craftsmanship in other countries) did the international-competitive dimension surface. This factor did emerge mainly in the last three-quarters of the century, however, as British industry began to suffer visibly from U.S. and German competition.[65]

To choose another example, religious competition among denominations is essential to explain the patterning of educational growth throughout the period covered. However, this competition was variable over time, intensifying, for example, in 1823–1829 (prior to the measures of religious relief) and in 1839–1846 (a period of sectarian jealousies over the control of working-class education). After the direct entry of the state into the provision of schools in 1870, religious contests continued to be very salient, especially in certain localities, but receded relative to the organizational and administrative exigencies of the educational system. In its impact on educational policies and development, class conflict was also highly variable—very salient in the 1830s and 1840s, latent in the 1850s and 1860s, and rising to salience once again later in the century after the wider enfranchisement of the working classes and the rise of the Labour Party.

To generalize this point: society can be regarded as a congeries of sectors (economic, political, educational, familial) that exist in more or less continuous interdependence with one another but at the same time constitute semiautonomous arenas of activity. From time to time, effects emanating from the processes generated in the various sectors spill over into the other sectors, generate "problems" for them, and thus become active "determinants" in their functioning. This formulation has theoretical significance. It suggests how those factors contained in the different approaches outlined above can be treated as partial rather than general in their significance as determinants. More generally, the formulation expresses a view of society intermediate between the theoretical conception that regards societal interdependence and integration as a more or less continuous and normal feature of society[66] and theoretical conceptions of society either as consisting of more or less autonomous, but ill-integrated, layers[67] or as being in endemic tension or conflict.[68] With these qualifications in mind, I shall now proceed to list the principal societal forces that impinge on any educational system.

*Cultural Values and Other Symbols of Legitimacy.*     Commitment to general values such as individual liberty, democracy, and mastery and achievement have been central elements in the historical development of educational systems that stress mass access, technical training, and personal development. Such values—as well as the kinds of educational systems they call for—contrast with traditionalist, elitist, and theocratic values and beliefs. Cultural values of this type constitute the most general shaping factors for a society's educational apparatus. Special interest in these cultural determinants is created when the society in question experiences conflicts over basic cultural values—as England did in the early nineteenth century, as among traditional elitism, middle-class utilitarianism, and working-class radicalism. Under these circumstances, debates over educational institutions and policies tend to generalize into contests over basic values.

*Religious Organization and Conflict.*     Religious values overlap with the cultural values in general; however, religious organization can be treated separately. Different types of religious organization—established church, denominational competition, state repression of religious organizations—carry immediate implications for the structure and content of the education of the young. The religious element is especially important in the transition from "traditional" to "modern" modes of education. This transition often involves both tendencies toward secularization and strong resistance and reaction by established religious authorities. The British case in the nineteenth century is especially interesting, because the religious system was "mixed," involving the coexistence of establishmentarianism and denominationalism, as well as an enduring conflict between those two principles. Furthermore, since the state remained partially disengaged from the provision of mass education for much of the century, the dynamics of educational conflict and change closely reflected the dynamics of religious conflict and change.

*Family.*    Cultural expectations about, and the structural organization of, the family carry implications for how education is organized. For example, Victorian society in Britain and elsewhere stressed an extreme division of sexual roles for middle-class families. The husband-father was mainly responsible for generating income in an occupation and participating in community and public affairs, and the wife-mother was mainly responsible for work in the home and other domestic responsibilities, "representing" the family by maintaining a "respectable" home and sharing in the cultural-expressive aspects of family life. Since middle-class women could not and did not take jobs in the labor market (with exceptions, such as that of governess), they were thought not to require instrumental education. Accordingly, few institutions were dedicated to women's education until later in the nineteenth century, and those that were emphasized the expressive side of cultural life (music, dancing, learning of foreign languages, etc.). For working-class women, it was generally expected that they would be part of the paid labor force as well as responsible for work in the home. Accordingly, their educational preparation in primary schools was roughly parallel to that of boys, though their curriculum minimized technical subjects and stressed needlework and other skills that would fit them for employment as domestic servants and for maintaining a home.

*The Economy.*    Two aspects of the economic influence on education are especially salient. The first is demands for occupational skills. One determinant of the development of "technical" secondary instruction in late-nineteenth-century Britain was the apparent need for skilled workers in the chemical, metallurgical, and communications industries, as

well as in various service occupations. As noted, however, the demand
of the capitalist economy in the early part of the century was mainly for
low-skilled workers in agriculture and industry. Accordingly, the "need"
for numeracy and literacy was not immediate and apparent. Employers
themselves disagreed over whether educated workers were better
equipped for jobs and whether education tended to make them docile or
independent and defiant.[69] As late as the 1860s, the Rev. James Fraser,
assistant commissioner of the Newcastle Commission on the education
of the poor, cited only minimal skills of literacy and numeracy—such as
writing a letter, reading a newspaper, and understanding a shop bill—
as essential for members of the working class.[70] While such expressions
must be read in part as expressions of ideological opposition to working-class advances, it remains true that in the early stages of British capitalism (1770–1850), the economic demand for workers' education was
limited.

The second way the economy conditioned education was through the
patterning of work. For most in the working classes, survival required
that many of the family's members be wage-earners. The factory work
of children in the early nineteenth century, well documented and
roundly condemned by reformers, was only part of the story of child
labor, which was a regular feature of the economy. I document this in
chapter 8, recording something that was universally recognized at the
time: that the family's need for children's wages and the demands of
work on children's time constituted a major obstacle to their primary
education. This suggests that the "functional" relationship between
work and education was in large part a negative one, challenging the
functional postulate that industrial development imposes demands for
the development of education. My own argument is that if a connection between industrial/urban development and mass education existed,
it was based less on economic demands in the early phases of ur-
ban/industrial development than on the dynamics of class, community,
religion, and polity that were associated with that development.

*Social Differentiation and Class.*    The relations between these social
dimensions and education are among the most complex. On the one
hand, all modern—if not all—societies develop complex systems of inequality, and education is inevitably called upon to reinforce and rationalize those inequalities through differential socialization. This class-
socializing function was clearly evident in nineteenth-century Britain.
Accordingly, many conflicts among classes came to be expressed as

conflicts about education, as it was perceived—and embraced or rejected—as order-maintaining, unjust, or repressive, depending on advocates' ideological stances. On the other hand, education may constitute
an avenue by which individuals break out of their class and rise into
another. Finally, education may also be a vehicle for enlightening and
raising the social and political consciousness of classes, affecting their
capacity to challenge the existing class system. The balance between
class-maintaining and class-loosening effects of education is variable
and is invariably a matter of dispute among the actors in any stratifica-
tion/education system and among interpreters of its history.[71]

*The Polity.*     The first question to be asked about the polity and education in society is how the state becomes directly involved in its operation. One of the great regularities in the evolution of formal educational
systems is that sooner or later the state becomes the major provider of
education at the primary, secondary, and postsecondary levels, though
in different ways at each level. At the same time, this growth has occurred as part of an evolving balance—and conflict—between public
and private and between state and religious control of education.

As the state becomes involved, it influences the educational system in
two ways. First, it becomes the conduit for political forces relating to
education. To cite examples from the contemporary United States, the
issues of prayers in schools and schools' initiative in affirmative action
are primarily *political* issues, and the evolving policies and practices of
educational institutions with respect to these issues reflect political contests in the larger society. Second, the state inevitably develops a bureaucracy for administering education. This bureaucracy develops a life of
its own, usually insists on fiscal accountability as well as standardization of policies and procedures, and in these ways shapes the educational apparatus.

Chart 1 represents the several external influences on educational
systems. Two qualifications about that representation are in order.
First, the double arrows underscore that the influence between society
and education is not one-way but reciprocal. For example, the administrators, teachers, and students of an educational establishment may
become important actors that influence the polity. Similarly, while the
systems of inequality and class shape the contours of education, in its
turn, the educational apparatus's effectiveness in maintaining or loosening class boundaries constitutes a reciprocal influence on class and inequality. While this study treats the evolution of primary education in

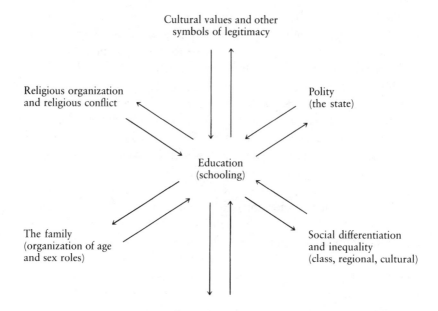

Chart 1.   External Forces Impinging on Education

Britain mainly as "dependent" on external influences, the reverse influence must also be acknowledged. Second, any educational system, once institutionalized, develops a certain autonomy of its own, maintaining complex sets of roles and relations among managers and administrators, certifiers and inspectors, teachers and pupils. Certain of its dynamics emanate from these quasi-autonomous processes.

A MORE FORMAL STATEMENT OF THE MODEL

Extrapolating from the foregoing observations, I now develop a more detailed statement of the kind of model of educational change informing my analysis, which will help explain the distinctive *outcomes* and *directions of change* in the British educational scene in the nineteenth century. This model is represented in general terms, applicable comparatively to different societies and different historical periods. In chapter 3, however, I specify some of the broad contours of British society in this period, thus indicating some parameters for the model's application. The model is represented graphically in chart 2, which summarizes the following exposition.

The first ingredient—that somewhat arbitrarily selected moment of equilibrium-in-tension—is a starting point for analysis and description of the existing structures and processes of change that are impinging on the society's educational apparatus. The guidelines for this description are the six sources of external influence listed above, plus any identifiable "internal" tendencies of the educational system ([1] in chart 2).

In and of themselves, these structural conditions do not initiate a sequence of social change. This begins only when meaningful actors and groups in society *witness* certain situations and events that signify something unsatisfactory, disharmonious, or dangerous, and *ascribe or assign* those phenomena to some aspect of the surrounding social context ([2]). To illustrate, a dramatic crime, series of crimes, or apparent rise in the crime rate in a community becomes significant for subsequent change only if it is referred to some offending institution—the family, schools, the police, or the public authorities generally. Another example is poverty. To qualify as a basis for initiating some kind of change, poverty must be explained as the result of some aspect of the social environment, such as the defects of market capitalism, or perhaps failures of socialization in family or school. If, however, poverty is explained as a result of personal failings of the poor, or as an unalterable aspect of social and economic life, it will not be "noticed"—that is, not assigned by significant groups to a social context capable of being changed. In that case, poverty becomes a "non-situation" therefore not the basis for calling for amelioration.

The process by which situations and events are referred to a social context presupposes an additional ingredient: some sort of *evaluative criterion or criteria* that render them problematical or unsatisfactory ([3]). For example, child labor had persisted for centuries in agriculture, crafts, and industry in Britain without being regarded as particularly noteworthy. As a rule, it was positively valued as a source of subsistence for the family and as a way of preparing a child for adult work. Certain humanitarian values, associated with the rise of Evangelicalism, and reference of those values to the situation of children, were required in order for child labor to be perceived as a social problem. Child labor is an apt example, because it illustrates both ingredients necessary for it to become problematical: it was referred to the conditions of early nineteenth-century capitalism ([2] in chart 2), which could be identified as evil because of the availability of humanitarian standards ([3]).

These points are important theoretically and methodologically. They underscore that the historical "situations and events" falling under heading [1] in chart 2 are not to be regarded as some objective historical

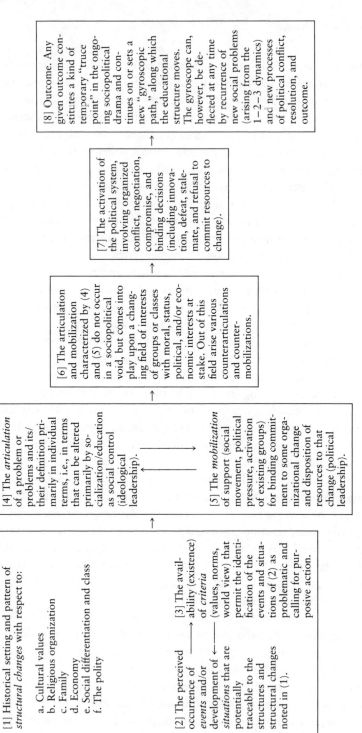

[1] Historical setting and pattern of *structural changes* with respect to:

a. Cultural values
b. Religious organization
c. Family
d. Economy
e. Social differentiation and class
f. The polity

[2] The perceived occurrence of *events* and/or development of *situations* that are potentially traceable to the structures and structural changes noted in (1).

[3] The availability (existence) of *criteria* (values, norms, world view) that permit the identification of the events and situations of (2) as problematic and calling for purposive action.

[4] The *articulation* of a problem or problems and its/their definition primarily in individual terms, i.e., in terms that can be altered primarily by socialization/education as social control (ideological leadership).

[5] The *mobilization* of support (social movement, political pressure, activation of existing groups) for binding commitment to some organizational change and disposition of resources to that change (political leadership).

[6] The articulation and mobilization characterized by (4) and (5) do not occur in a sociopolitical void, but comes into play upon a changing field of interests of groups or classes with moral, status, political, and/or economic interests at stake. Out of this field arise various counterarticulations and counter-mobilizations.

[7] The activation of the political system, involving organized conflict, negotiation, compromise, and binding decisions (including innovation, defeat, stalemate, and refusal to commit resources to change).

[8] Outcome. Any given outcome constitutes a kind of temporary "truce point" in the ongoing sociopolitical drama and continues on or sets a new "gyroscopic path," along which the educational structure moves. The gyroscope can, however, be deflected at any time by recurrence of new social problems (arising from the 1–2–3 dynamics) and new processes of political conflict, resolution, and outcome.

Chart 2.  A Model of Educational Change

reality, but must always be read in relation to both the interpretations of their social significance [2] and to the values of contemporaries [3]. Almost *any* situation or event is potentially interpretable as signifying something about the social structure or the social order and as morally charged. All three of the ingredients that initiate efforts at change must be imagined or posited as "real" by the individuals or groups who "see" them. For example, a troubling "event or situation" (such as prostitution on the streets) may be described by an interested group as "real" and assigned to the failure of the system of the family (also assumed to be "real"), which in turn may be referred to some "real" sacred value that legitimizes the family. Anything that becomes a "social problem" contains these three ingredients. Accordingly, debates about social problems include assertions about whether the situation exists or the event happened, what it signifies about society (if anything), and what cultural values are involved.

The ingredient that gives the model its distinctively "educational" flavor is the specific kind of articulation (situations and events, social context, and cultural values) found in the blueprints of educational reformers ([4]). These blueprints call for an amelioration of the identified social problems by transforming the ideas, outlooks, and behavior of present and future subjects or citizens through education. Such a diagnosis is ultimately a psychological or moral one because that is the kind of effect envisioned by reformers: changes in the values, attitudes, and social behavior of individuals. Even the radical educational reformer envisions a somewhat indirect avenue to social change—namely, enlightenment of those being educated and raising of their consciousness so that they may better effect reform or revolution.[72]

In any event, reformers must call upon, invent, or justify a "case" for educational reform as preferable to other kinds of action or reform. Such a case—an "ideology" of educational reform—invariably invokes some kind of psychological assertion or "theory" of how education affects people, and seeks to link that assertion or theory to some social effect. An example of an educational "case" is the arguments advanced by utilitarian writers early in the nineteenth century. The state, they said, should establish schooling for the poor at public expense—a view apparently at odds with the predominantly laissez-faire doctrines of the utilitarian school. The cost of providing schooling, which was thought to be a deterrent to crime, would be much less than that of incarcerating adult criminals. This apparently simple case invoked a whole range of assertions about the cost of education, the cost of crime, the effects of education, and the relation between the effects of education and criminal activity. Opponents of the utilitarians' educational solutions could, moreover, attempt to discredit the program by attacking any of these implied assertions.[73]

A further ingredient of the model is the social and political mobilization of individuals and groups in the name of the preferred ideological diagnosis and groups in the name of the preferred ideological diagnosis and blueprint ([5]). This mobilization takes a number of familiar forms —informal influence, direct action, demonstrations, generating a social-movement organization, producing pamphlets and other literature, putting pressure on politicians and political parties, or getting out the vote. The form that political activity takes is largely a function of the ways in which the society has institutionalized the processes of participation, access, and political influence.

The causal arrows in chart 2 represents the relations between elements [4] (ideology) and [5] (mobilization) as interactive. In some instances, ideological articulation may precede political mobilization: a new social movement makes its case and attempts to attract adherents. In other cases, mobilization may precede ideological articulation, as when existing groups (for example, religious denominations, political lobbies) become sensitive to new situations and problems and develop new ideological positions relating to them. In still other cases, articulation and mobilization may be concurrent, as when "watch-dog" groups continuously survey the sociopolitical scene for developments that may constitute "problems" for them and occasions for political activation of their constituents.

Proposals for educational restoration, redirection, expansion, or innovation seldom fall on uncontested ground and sail smoothly through to binding political commitments and implementation. In any society, certain lines of jurisdiction and control over the cognitive and moral development of the young constitute the preserve of established groups (families, religious denominations, private schools, governmental agencies, and the like). These groups develop vested interests and never greet proposals for change in the existing order neutrally. Even when jurisdictional jealousies are not salient, educational innovations invariably call for a commitment of financial resources, which are—or seem to be—drawn from the resources otherwise available to consumers, taxpayers, government agencies, and other interested parties. For these reasons, proposals for institutional change in education almost always become the occasion for a political contest among interested groups ([6]).

The competition and conflict defined in [6] may be institutionalized as "private" and thus develop and produce some outcome outside the polity. However, since education typically comes to involve the state—if not in its administration, then certainly in its support—conflicts over education usually become conflicts within the political apparatus ([7]). The possible outcomes of such conflicts are many—political repression of groups, unilateral decision in favor of one or another party, inaction. In societies with democratic values and institutions, conflicts usually take the form of conflict-management, influence, negotiation, and compromise. A key feature of a democratic polity, in fact, is the institutionalization of a range of conflict-managing agencies such as legislative bodies, regulatory agencies, hearing bodies, and courts.

As a general rule, conflicts involving direct competition for resources (institutionalized labor-management disputes, claims for subsidies, taxation policy) are amenable to solution in the polity because the relevant interest groups are often programmed, as it were, both to give and to take in the political arena. When conflicts involve sacred principles and rights (as many religious and ideological class conflicts do), compromise is often more difficult, because contending parties tend to frame their demands in either/or terms. As a result, any given outcome is likely to be experienced as an absolute "victory" for one party and an absolute "defeat" for the other. This is not to claim that groups representing sacred or moral interests are not prepared to, or do not, compromise from time to time. It remains true, however, that contests framed in terms of fundamental values and morals pose special difficulties for those who undertake to contain, manage, and resolve them by compromise.

Some kind of binding political decision completes the process ([8]). This also may take many forms: enacting a law, establishing a new agency, changing the policy and pattern of governmental support for education, expanding or contracting the educational apparatus, changing its pattern of administration, or political paralysis and inaction. Such a decision usually marks a temporary truce point, an effort on the part of the political authorities to affect institutional arrangements so as to attack some perceived problem and, it is hoped, to induce conflicting parties to cease or reduce their conflictful activities, at least about the issue at hand. The binding political decisions that occur at this point often have the effect of setting the educational system on a new course of change—a new gyroscope—under which it is anticipated that it may function more effectively and without generating the complaints and problems that initiated the change in the first place.

In describing the new truce point, the word *temporary* is essential.

The moment of political decision and hoped-for conflict resolution may create a situation of peace. It may, however, leave in its wake a situation in which a "victorious" group may be emboldened to press its advantage even further, or a "defeated" group may strive to seek revenge or to regain lost ground. Furthermore, the newly established gyroscope may push the system along a path that leads to a new perceived cumulative advantage or disadvantage for one or more interested groups, and thus create a new "problem" (ingredients [1], [2], and [3] of chart 2) and thus initiate new ideological articulation, mobilization, and pressures for change.

For this reason, the model I have generated does not tell a story of simple disequilibrium→conflict→resolution→equilibrium. In the historical process, we observe multiple processes of change occurring simultaneously in different sectors of society, which results in constant turbulence, efforts to adapt and stabilize, and the appearance of new sets of problems. The principal objective in generating and applying an abstract model to the historical process is to cut into the complexity and flux, isolate certain determinants, and elucidate general processes of change at work.

The most direct applications of the model of change are in chapters 4 and 5, which identify the critical moments—or temporary truce points—in the evolution of British education. In addition, the model is applied comparatively in chapters 6 and 7 to the special cases of Wales, Ireland, and Scotland.

## CHAPTER 3

# Primordial Imagery in the Nineteenth Century

In the preceding chapter I laid out several available accounts of educational development and generated a synthetic perspective that is both different from and inclusive of these accounts. That perspective will guide my accounts and interpretations of working-class education in the nineteenth century. This chapter is also introductory, but in a different way. In it I record several primordial dimensions of British life that constitute "givens" within which Britain's educational system evolved. These dimensions were not the sole determinants of that evolution; in chapter 8, for example, the direct impingement of the capitalist economy—especially its labor market—in shaping education will become apparent. But the dimensions of class, religion, and, in many respects, region framed all thought and debate about education, and were direct determinants of many of its institutional characteristics.

The first necessary assignment is to clarify the use of the term *primordial*. Its generic meaning is "constituting the beginning or starting point, from which something else is derived or developed, on which something else depends."[1] In its social version, the term refers to fundamental cultural values and beliefs that are the first premises for organizing and legitimizing institutions, roles, and behavior. Clifford Geertz gives an incisive characterization of the nature of primordial attachments:

> Congruities of blood, speech, custom, and so on, are seen to have an ineffable, and at times overpowering, coerciveness in and of themselves. One is bound to one's kinsman, one's neighbor, one's fellow believer, ipso facto; as the result not merely of personal affection, practical necessity, common inter-

est, or incurred obligation, but at least in great part by virtue of some unaccountable absolute import attributed to the very tie itself.[2]

Three specifying remarks about primordial groups are in order:

Geertz mentions kin, blood, religion, custom, and so on. He does not mention social class. There is no reason why that dimension cannot take on a primordial quality. In fact, it is helpful to regard class as such in nineteenth-century British society, though that was not its only significance.

Edward Shils argues that primordial ties are especially problematical with respect to social integration in less developed societies or relatively new states such as India.[3] To note this should not obscure the fact that primordial groupings are both salient and important in modernizing, modern, and even "postmodern" societies. This sociological truth has been underplayed by views of societal development that view the process as a progressive road to modernity, rationality, secularization, or *Gesellschaft*.

To identify such primordial cultural and psychological elements in society is not to make any claims about what has determined them. Formulations and debates on the structural bases for class are found, for example, in the work of Marx, Weber, Joseph Schumpeter, and Gaetano Mosca, and the ongoing literature on such theories. The following exposition does not address these debates. Furthermore, to identify first principles does not imply that these are items of consensus in society. An engaging aspect of studying Britain in the nineteenth century is that it was a period of lack of consensus, conflict, and continuous transition with respect to the primordial principles of class, religion, and region.

When social groups—social classes, religious parties, and national and ethnic groups, for example—form along primordial lines, they typically display the quality of *exclusiveness*. This appears in the following guises:

Membership in these groups is defined in categorical, mutually exclusive terms. One cannot be both upper-class and middle-class at the same time; insofar as gradations between these groups are made (upper-middle, lower-upper, for example), these, too, tend to be exclusive. Similarly, one cannot be Catholic and Protestant, or Irish and Welsh, at the same time.

Social interaction within such groups is more frequent than with groups outside it. This exclusiveness is never complete, but normative and other barriers tend to minimize cross-group interaction, and interaction with other groups is circumscribed situationally and ritually.

A primordial group typically becomes the basis for individual and collective identification, for the definition of individual and collective "interests," and for mobilization to defend, consolidate, or advance the group's position in society.

One additional qualification is in order. In this study, most of the exposition with respect to class and religion in the nineteenth century will be revealed from the perspective of actors involved in education—the advocates and opponents of its extension, those who administered it, and those who participated in it. As such, it is not an empirical account of the facts of class that might be determined by citing objective indices (for example, occupational composition) or by consulting other institutional actors and traditions. The major justification for this is that the descriptions and accounts given by those actors constituted the operative ideas in their cultural environment and the bases for their thinking and behavior. For these reasons, too, the descriptions ventured here are acknowledged not to be representative of beliefs in the entire society, but are skewed in the direction of those who in fact supported and controlled the culture and institutions of that society.

## IMAGERY OF HIERARCHY AND CLASS

The most evident and powerful organizing principle of nineteenth-century British society was that of social hierarchy,[4] a principle historically rooted in the monarchy, the feudal tradition, the peerage, and the agricultural squire system. Harold Perkin describes its ethic as that of "an open aristocracy based on property and patronage."[5] The core ingredients of this principle were privilege based on rank and paternalism in two of its aspects—expected deference from those below, and expected responsibility on the part of the privileged for the less privileged. Writing in 1836, Thomas Wyse, a member of the Catholic gentry in Ireland and educational reformer,[6] hailed the Scottish class system as an ideal manifestation of these ingredients:

> Clanship, though a relic of feudalism, has, in many instances, done as much for man and his interests, as the most enlightened liberalism. If it has kept up

the claims of the Aristocracy, it has combined with them the still higher claims of the People. It has retained all the rights, filial and paternal, of the earliest period of society. The proprietor is a father, not in privileges only, but in duty. He values himself, not on his acres, but on the devoted hearts and industrious arms which cover them. He is the same blood as the lowest of his herdsmen, and therefore governs with gentleness; his herdsman is of his blood, and therefore obeys, with zeal, the personification of his own power and importance. The numerous excellent habits derivable from this friendly recognition of mutual aid and mutual connexion, are everywhere visible in Scotch practice.[7]

Wyse was not only evoking an ideal and praising the Scots, but also scolding aristocrats in both England and Ireland for falling short of the ideal.[8]

### PHILANTHROPIC TRADITIONS

Given this ideal, it comes as no surprise that the educational heritage of nineteenth-century Britain was based on the philanthropy of the rich, powerful, and prestigious. In England the charity schools, and to a debatable extent the Sunday schools, emanated from the religious and class establishments and were justified mainly in terms of obligations on the part of the wealthier and more powerful.[9] The operative phrase in the eighteenth century was "the education of the poor," and books and pamphlets stressed its charitable dimensions.[10] The major innovation of the early nineteenth century was the formation of religiously based voluntary societies—the National Society and the British and Foreign School Society—that also strove to provide education "for the poor." When the state entered the arena of working-class education in 1833, this was justified as supplementing philanthropic activities. The Select Committee on Education in 1837 spoke of "[government] grants . . . made for the promotion of Education, through the medium of the [charitable] National and British and Foreign School Societies."[11] This principle of religious charity supported by government continued as the central principle of working-class education until the last third of the century. As will be demonstrated presently, the charitable motive almost always included the objective of maintaining order and stability among the classes. In any event, the charitable ideal, linked with the ideal of privilege and responsibility, was the main legitimizing argument for education in the eighteenth and most of the nineteenth century.

This philanthropic ideal did not go unquestioned, however, as new social classes rose to challenge the aristocratic order. In major outline,

the story of inequality in the nineteenth century is a story of assimilat-
ing and yielding power first to the middle and then to the working
classes. This story is told in many forms: the extension of the franchise
slowly and gradually downward through the classes; the assault on
privilege and patronage as mechanisms to allocate power, position, and
wealth, and the corresponding rise of meritocratic standards; reform of
institution after institution; and the rise of new democratic theories and
programs. In due course, inequality evolved from a system of "orders"
toward a system of "classes," and attitudes, consciousness, politics, and
even the language of inequality developed accordingly.[12] Even though
the class system was thus evolving, the principle of hierarchy retained
an important place. With respect to the organization of education, class
was perhaps the last parameter to be challenged. The division of education along strict religious lines was crumbling in the late nineteenth century.[13] Sex segregation was never as fully institutionalized in working-
class education as it was in middle- and upper-class education in the
nineteenth century.[14] The assumption of class-stratified education was
solidly reaffirmed as late as 1944 in the Education Act, however, and
still persists in some degree, despite the rise of the comprehensive
schools at the secondary level and further democratization of university
admissions.[15]

One of the major challenges to the aristocratic ideal of the combination of class deference and responsibility came from the commercial and
industrial middle classes. It is represented in the utilitarian conception
of the relations between persons as instrumental and contractual relations and not on status claims and obligations. The classic statement of
this drift is found in Henry Maine's work on the transition "from status
to contract"[16] and other classical works, and its evolution in England
was a preoccupation of both T. H. Marshall[17] and R. H. Tawney.[18] The
essence of the individualist drift was summarized by R. H. Gretton:

> Distaste [for aristocratic values] grew slowly into a more profound feeling
> as the quality of the relations between masters and men in industrialism be-
> came more apparent. The Middle Class had never had by nature any proper
> consideration for dependents, or any genuine sense of duty towards employ-
> ers. . . . The conviction of the masters of industry, developed later on into a
> regular economic theory, . . . was that the capital in his industry was his, the
> machines and buildings were his, and it was no concern of any other person
> what were the conditions of his business. It was the workman's own affair if
> he came to work in those conditions.[19]

Adherence to this ethos, moreover, entailed a corresponding decline of
commitment to aristocratic status-obligation ideals.

The surviving ideal of paternalistic obligation, however, continued to be expressed in educational legislation and in dialogues about working-class education. The factory legislation of 1802 and 1833, while oriented primarily to the regulation of the hours of labor of children, compelled the manufacturers themselves to provide schooling for children they employed—that is, to behave philanthropically. That the manufacturers conspired with working people to evade those requirements provided further ammunition for critics seeking to demonstrate that the manufacturers were not living up to their class obligations.[20] More generally, reformers and others concerned with the failure of voluntary education to reach the masses frequently laid the blame on uncooperative, irresponsible manufacturers. In his report for the Commission on Children's Employment in 1842, Thomas Tancred evoked an image of owners of collieries and iron works in the west of Scotland that was far from Wyse's ideal:

> That a capitalist should be allowed, as is now the case, to bring together a thousand or two of human beings, and to raise up a village on what was perhaps before a barren moor, without any obligation attaching to him to contribute one farthing to the regular means which our constitution has established for Christianizing and educating that population, is an anomaly which cannot but be productive of the worst consequences. Men thus left uncared for probably become, for the most part, sensualists and infidels, unless they join the congregation of a Dissenting minister.[21]

A year later, the commissioners found a few masters who took an interest in the amusement and recreation of their working people, but in general there was "an absence of any co-operation on the part of the great body of employers."[22] In 1858 Her Majesty's Inspector (of schools) Muirhead Mitchell listed among the causes of the "lack of efficiency of education" in his district "the indifference of the wealthier or chief inhabitants."[23] And the Newcastle Commission investigating working-class education in the late 1850s blamed the failure of education both in remote agricultural areas and in urban centers on absentee landlords and irresponsible merchants who would not provide resources for schools "for the poor."[24] Some commentators again turned to Scotland for a happier example. D. R. Fearon reported for the Taunton Commission that Scotland—with some exceptions in cities like Glasgow, where "purse pride" was appearing—had still not succumbed to the divisiveness and lack of responsibility of the English:

> *The wealth of the Scotch people has not yet out-grown their civilization*, as has been in the case in England. It seemed to me that in Scotland I seldom

met with those barbarians, those very uncultivated rich or substantial people, whom one sees every summer lounging at the Welsh and North country sea-side towns, or hurrying through the Continent. The average middle Scotchman has more humility and refinement than the average middle Englishman. Education has been more generally diffused; riches have been less rapidly and largely accumulated . . . [the Scottish middle classes] value [education] more than those in England do; and [they] have prevented the creation of that gulf which exists between men of cultivation and the middle classes in England.[25]

Some of this acrimony was an expression of the hostility of Tories to manufacturers, but the language demonstrates that the ideal of philanthropy still lived, and could be used as a basis for discrediting.

### SEGREGATIVE TENDENCIES

A corollary of the primordial assumptions that gave such a central place to hierarchy was that participation in society's institutions would be segregated along class lines. This is true of all societies, because all are organized into ranked classes to a degree. However, it is a variable phenomenon, which reached a kind of extreme in British society in the nineteenth century. In an address to a grand jury at Stafford, Justice Talfourd identified it:

It is so much a part of our English character that I fear we all of us keep too much aloof from those beneath us, and they are thus too much encouraged to look upon us with suspicion and dislike. . . . This arises from a species of contracted feeling—from a kind of reserve which is perhaps peculiar to the English character, and which greatly tends to prevent that mingling of class with class . . . if I were asked what is the great want of English society to mingle class with class, I would say, in one word,—it is the want of sympathy.[26]

Certainly that reluctance to mingle was reflected in the educational institutions in nineteenth-century Britain. "For each class of society," said the educational reformer and administrator Sir James Kay-Shuttleworth, "there is an appropriate education."[27] The ancient public schools catered to the children of aristocrats and the highest professional classes. Middle-class children attended a variety of endowed, private, and proprietary institutions.[28] The working classes attended mainly working-class day schools provided by charity and by the government. The pauper classes attended workhouse, industrial, and ragged schools.[29] This centrality of class was revealed when, in the 1850s and 1860s, parliamentary leaders launched a series of national investigations into the country's education. These followed class lines: the education of the upper classes was examined by the Clarendon Commission; of the working classes by the Newcastle Commission; and of the middle classes by the Taunton Commission. The separate commissions simply reflected the institutional realities they were asked to study.

Contemporaries described the fusion of class, age-grading, education, and future occupational destination as natural. In 1859, C. B. Adderley, the vice president of the Committee of Privy Council on Education (the government's administrative body for working-class education), characterized the system in these terms:

> General education for boys . . . extends over the first twenty-one years of life.
>
> Its first stage, that of childhood, is up to the age of ten. The instruction belonging to it is rudimentary, in reading, writing, and arithmetic, and it is alike for all classes of society. Boys of the upper class spend it chiefly at home; of the middle classes either at home or at preparatory schools; of the labourers' class, at national schools, and there *their* general education, for the most part, ends, and their apprenticeship to work begins.
>
> The second stage of general education is that of boyhood, from the age of ten to eighteen. Boys of the upper class spend this time at private schools or public schools such as Eton, Harrow, Rugby, and others; those of the middle class at private commercial schools or public[ly] endowed grammar schools; and here *their* general education, for the most part, ends, and their apprenticeship to business begins.
>
> Only boys of the richer classes, or destined for liberal professions, remain at the last stage of education, which they get at the universities.[30]

A decade later the Taunton Commission presented an almost identical, class-bound picture of English education; its statement was simultaneously descriptive and normatively approving.[31] About the same time, Mark Pattison, an assistant commissioner of the Newcastle Commission, observed that "class-education would seem to be as rooted an idea in the English mind as denominational religion."[32]

Not only were classes separated by institutional definition; there was also apparently little mixing by class in the respective kinds of schools. Matthew Arnold, responding to Talleyrand's judgment that the education received at the great English public schools was the best in the world, commented:

> How small a portion of the population does it embrace! It embraces the aristocratic class; it embraces the higher professional class; it embraces a few of the richest and most successful of the commercial class; of the great body of

the commercial class and of the immense middle classes of this country, it embraces not one.[33]

Social movements agitating for educational improvement also tended to develop along class lines. In the 1850s and 1860s, with working-class schooling increasing rapidly under the government subsidy initiated in 1846, complaints were heard from middle-class sources. In 1848, a pamphlet entitled *A Plea for the Middle Classes* appeared, arguing that both upper and working classes were well provided for, but not the middle.[34] In 1864, Lord Brougham reported that "the state of education for the middle classes has long been complained of."[35] Pressure of this sort was one factor that prompted the forming of the Taunton Commission on middle-class education in the 1860s.[36]

In its final report, the Taunton Commission reported on the problem of class mixing in middle-class schools. Private schools, they said,

> find it difficult, in some cases impossible, to resist the class feeling which compels the exclusion of boys of a lower rank than the rest. In a way, if private school be the only provision for education within reach, gross injustice is sometimes done. A boy of superior talents is not allowed, even if he be able to pay the school fees, to enter a school attended by children above him in the social scale. The parents threaten to withdraw their children, unless the social distinction is rigidly maintained, and the private school is often powerless to resist the threat. Thus parents in a lower rank . . . are discouraged by meeting with a barrier which they cannot pass.[37]

Not only were class barriers evident; some potential customers of the working-class schools chose not to attend them on class grounds. The commissioners added:

> Almost all private schools rest in some degree on social distinctions . . . private schools are powerless to ignore them. In fact the inferior private schools owe their existence to the unwillingness of many of the tradesmen and others just above the manual labourers to send their sons to the National or the British Schools. Rather than let their children mix with the class beneath them in a large well-fitted room where they would be taught by a thoroughly competent master, they will send them to an inferior teacher in a miserable room and pay twice or four times as much.[38]

Government policy limited institutions of working-class education to the classes for which they were attended. In 1857, Ralph Lingen, secretary of the Committee of Council, explained its rules for giving grants. He pointed out that the subsidized schools of the religious societies were intended for the "labouring classes who are dependent upon ordinary wages, and who do not employ capital." He went on to explain, however, that the schools could also be attended by "small farmers, small shopkeepers, small tradesmen . . . foremen and highly skilled artisans." Lingen referred to these as the "lower middle class" and suggested that they could "[maintain] their advantages in the future competition of life" by staying in school longer.[39] In the Revised Code for working-class education in 1862, Article 4 specified a kind of "means test" to prevent children not from the laboring classes taking advantage of subsidized government schools. The inspectors of schools commented on the difficulty of enforcing this provision, and in Scotland, where there was a stronger egalitarian strain than in England, Article 4 was odious to many.[40]

Despite efforts at exclusion, some children from that ambiguous band between the working and middle classes did attend the schools established for the working class.[41] This seems to have been especially true of the schools of the British and Foreign School Society. This religious society was multidenominational but dominated by some of the Dissenting churches, which were, above all, middle-class institutions.[42] When lower-middle-class children did attend, however, their mixing in sometimes created status problems. Matthew Arnold, an inspector of British and Foreign Society schools, noted, with irony,

> I must notice . . . that teachers do not always show perfect judiciousness in dealing with children [of the middle classes]. I have heard such children addressed by their teachers [who themselves were almost always from working-class backgrounds][43] with the title of "miss" and "master," an absurdity which would not for a moment be tolerated in English schools for the highest classes.[44]

Frederick Watkins, another inspector, complained about the "so-called 'middle class'" of students—whose parents paid higher fees. Such students, as a necessary consequence, received "more of the teacher's instruction and attention," which Watkins considered "unjust, unwise, and mischievous" because it placed "the children of the very poor at a great disadvantage."[45] Inspector William J. Kennedy remarked that in his estimation the middle classes of England would "always remain opposed to [a] system [of uniting children of the middle and labouring classes]." He said that when such a plan had been introduced, he "found it [in every case] to fail in consequence of the comparative neglect of the lower grade of scholars."[46]

The class at the upper range of the working classes thus showed a complex set of tendencies: some working toward their separation and some working toward their mingling, but not without uncertainty and ambivalence. The equally vague line at the lower range of the working classes was also exclusionary. The general rule was that the poorer the family of the child, the lower the rate and regularity of school attendance.[47] In the 1850s and 1860s, in particular, public attention turned especially to a sizable population of "street arabs," very poor children who were neither at work, at school, nor—as the label implies—at home.[48] A recurrent complaint was that the working-class schools did not reach this population.[49] The structural forces producing this destitute class were multiple and are difficult to unscramble.[50] It is probable, however, that some of the problem lay in segregative tendencies within the low-income classes themselves.

These tendencies were noticed by the inspectors of schools and other commentators. Matthew Hill, a barrister, spoke of "the very minute subdivisions of ranks which are maintained among [the lower classes]." Matthew Arnold said that small farmers, small tradesmen, and skilled mechanics were willing to pay from four to six pence a week to have their children educated. But at the same time "they often object as much as the classes above them to the contact, with their children, of children of the lowest class, of the class found in ragged schools."[51] Some managers, Arnold reported, conspired to cooperate with this feeling, because, desiring all the income they could generate, they preferred children who could pay high fees to those who could not.[52] Inspector J. D. Morell reported an interesting interaction between considerations of cost and considerations of class on the part of working-class parents:

> We find, as a matter of experience that in our districts [the parents' interest in education] is measured by from threepence to sixpence a week. If you go below threepence a week, the tendency is for the better class of work-people to withdraw their children from the school, because they do not think that the school is good enough, and they think that a number of dirty children with whom they do not like their children to associate go into it. If you charge above sixpence a week they withdraw the children from the school, too, because it is more than they think that they ought to pay for them, and then they probably send them to adventure [i.e., private] schools, where they can get taught a penny or too [sic] cheaper; and they would rather do that, though the instruction is inferior.[53]

The reluctance to mix was apparently a two-way street. Hill asserted that "respectable parents" would rather pay "at great sacrifice to themselves, than that their children should . . . mingle [with the street arabs]."[54] Inspector Watkins reported that many parents would not send their children to the government-supported working-class schools because they would come into contact with "what they call rough children."[55] Inspector D. J. Stewart believed that in town schools "the personal uncleanliness and the dirty clothes of the majority of the boys . . . are quite sufficient to shut out children used to cleanly habits and well-ordered homes."[56] But Mary Carpenter, the champion of the destitute classes, remarked that "not only do these [British and Foreign Society] schools for the labouring classes prove ineffective upon the lowest children but . . . the lowest children would not, if paid for at these schools, attend them."[57] Remarks such as these do not constitute quantitative evidence about the actual level of mingling of classes in the educational system and its consequences, but they do demonstrate that the issue was a part of the imagery of class in the nineteenth century.[58]

CLASS AND SOCIAL CONTROL

The promotion of class balance and harmony by the exchange of responsibility of the higher and deference of the lower proved to be an unstable formula. A class system is, above all, a mechanism for allocating the wealth, power, prestige, and privilege of the society unequally and for sustaining that inequality. A corollary of this is that those with less of all of those resources are more likely to be dissatisfied with the class system than those with more. An assigned task in any stratification system is therefore for those at the higher levels to devote part of their resources to convincing those at the lower levels of the legitimacy of the inequality. If effective, this reduces the likelihood of dissatisfaction and its accompanying individual and collective action, which is costly and/or politically threatening to the stability of the system. All class systems face this issue in some way, but because hierarchy and class were so primordial in British society, the problem of maintaining social control and stability was also salient and omnipresent.

Accordingly, the discussions, debates, and plans for educational reform were shot through with the language and imagery of social control, social stability, and social order. This symbolism will appear often in this volume; so, in the interests of minimizing repetition, I shall simply sketch here the main assertions and arguments that were heard.

*Education as Disruptive of the Social Order.* This argument was found mainly among Tory and High Anglican interests in the eighteenth and early nineteenth centuries—that is to say, among the greatest defenders of the view that the organic unity of society was most reliably preserved through the agency of the traditional hierarchy of the orders, privilege, and deference. The specific dangers of education (other than religious instruction, which was supposed to foster deference) were perceived as the following:

Education would make the poor dissatisfied with the meager material basis of their life and cause them to wish to improve their standard of living.[59]

Education would make the poor strive for occupational and class advancement. Those who learn to write, for example, would not "abide at the plough, but [would look] to a situation in some counting house."[60]

Education would foment sedition and revolutionary ideas. This was one of the bases for the conservative onslaught against the Sunday schools in the late eighteenth and early nineteenth centuries.

The strength of this view accounts in part for the defensiveness of Sunday school leaders when they themselves were attacked as politically disruptive.[61] They insisted that their objectives were only to teach reading and moral training. One promoter, Hannah More, wrote: "I allow of no writing for the poor. My object is not to make fanatics, but to train up the lower classes in habits of industry and piety."[62] The fear of writing, of course, was mainly the fear of seditious writing. This pessimistic view, antagonistic to most education of the poor, continued to be influential throughout the era of the French Revolution and the Napoleonic Wars, but appeared to lose force in the third decade of the nineteenth century.[63] It was countered by an array of opposing arguments, most of which, however, shared the emphasis on social control.

*Education as Promotion of Social Harmony.* John Roebuck, a utilitarian reformer active in the 1830s, expressed the view that education would lead to more constant and affectionate communication between the classes.[64] The mechanism by which this would occur was largely undefined, but the argument parallels the belief that realization of the principle of noblesse oblige would foster community and class integration. In this limited sense, Roebuck's argument for education presented a kind of functional equivalent of aristocratic *noblesse.*

*Education as Prevention of Social Disorder.* This argument is closely related to the two already advanced—a refutation of the first and a complement to the second.[65] One version of this argument was voiced by Hugh Tremenheere, an inspector of schools for a time in the early 1840s. The argument was that education, as a form of culture, controlled the spread of seditious ideas: "Secular education is more than ever needed as a means of temporal prosperity and advancement . . . socialism and a vast and dangerous flood of 'revolutionary literature' of the worst kind is occupying the ground left bare for its reception by the absence of all culture, secular or religious."[66] The mechanism by which education would stem the "dangerous flood" was seldom specified, but the opinion was nonetheless frequently uttered. Another version of the argument was that ignorance results in wrong and antisocial action. Kay-Shuttleworth argued that

> [there] are social disorders not attributable to defects in the physical condition of the people. The mobs of machine-breakers, which resisted every improvement in the inventions of our manufacturing industry, *ignorantly* attempted to destroy the chief sources of their own domestic well-being, and of the national prosperity.[67]

He added that trade unions' efforts to attain a minimum wage, standard wages, and limitations on recruitment to trades were similarly misguided. More generally, Kay-Shuttleworth believed that education was an integral part of assuring that "people should know how their interests are inseparable from those of the other orders of society."[68] His arguments are similar to those advanced by some political economists of the era: that proper knowledge of economic laws would induce in workers a proper knowledge of their situation and convince them of the pointlessness of industrial actions.

*Education as Preparation for Responsible Citizenship.*    This argument, based on the same rationalist premise as the one immediately foregoing, was heard especially in the late 1860s, when the franchise was being extended downward in the class structure. Robert Lowe's often-quoted aphorism on the wisdom of educating our future masters epitomizes the concern.[69]

*Education as Prevention of Pauperism and Crime.*    This argument, one of the most frequently heard in educational reform circles, had multiple appeal. The first was that crime was a threat to the system of private property that was so central to the economic and class order; education would reduce that threat. The second was that education would induce both paupers and criminals to become productively employed workers and respectable citizens—beneficial to both the economy and the social order. The third appeal was a utilitarian one of cost. It is easier to form good habits earlier than to break them later,[70] and schooling costs less than incarceration in prisons. Of more immediate utilitarian relevance was the assertion that these economies would ease the burden of the poor rates. Such arguments were frequently joined with empirical presentations showing that groups with little education (e.g., the Irish) had high crime rates and educated groups (e.g., the Scots) had low rates. It was seldom acknowledged that causality could not readily be established on the basis of such statistics. More systematic nineteenth-century studies on the connection between crime and education were incomplete and largely indecisive.[71] This did not, however, seem to stem the repeated appeals to the argument.

These last four arguments constituted perhaps the strongest positive driving force for the development of working-class education in the nineteenth century. Each is a variant of a "social order" argument. All are encapsulated in Kay-Shuttleworth's statement of his own educational philosophy:

> The central authority has a greater interest, collectively, in the intelligence and virtue of the people, than any fragment of the nation can have. On that intelligence and virtue depend respect for the law, the right discharge of civil functions and political franchises, the due subordination to authority, the harmony of classes, the development of the natural resources of the country and its power, the increase of commerce, wealth, comfort, and national contentment, the public spirit of citizens, the valour of armies and navies, and the national patriotism in sustaining the constitution alike against invasion and against internal corruption or revolution.[72]

The avenue to this utopia was the education of the people.

It was in connection with this abiding concern with social order that the forces of class, religion, and education merged. Many clergymen regarded teaching Scripture to the workers as a way of instilling into them a posture of social deference and other attitudes perceived as appropriate to their class. An extreme version of this attitude is found in a communication from the Reverend Baptist W. Noel, an Anglican clergyman, whom Kay-Shuttleworth commissioned in 1840 to report on working-class schools in the industrial districts. Noel envisioned the education of the poor in the following terms:

> Our Lord, by becoming a poor man, has taught us that lowly stations are honourable and connected with wisdom and with piety; and every day's observations may show us how much genuine happiness may be found in them. We have, then, to teach children, not that they should seek to raise themselves above the necessity of labour, but that labour which is the appointment of God, and while it secures the health also strengthens the understanding, is consistent with the greatest enjoyment of life; that, supplying a nation

with all its comforts, and being the source of its opulence and strength, it must be creditable to individuals; and that a man of intelligence, wisdom, and moral worth in a cottage has more true dignity than a sensual, selfish, ignorant, and irreligious man, though he should be the owner of a palace.[73]

Kay-Shuttleworth himself argued consistently that religious instruction was inseparable from secular instruction for the working classes.[74]

*Education as Avenue to Social Mobility.*    The primordial notions of hierarchy and class, as inherited in the early nineteenth century, implied a certain fixity and stability of that principle over time—that is to say, a certain castelike character of inequality. A further implication of the principle is that mobility between the classes would be rare (even though evidence of different kinds of mobility is evident in the historical record).[75] In addition, the more specific link between education and mobility—taken by some social scientists as one of the key features of industrial societies—was quite weak in nineteenth-century Britain. Certainly the structural fusion of class, education, and occupational target in the descriptions of Adderley and the Taunton Commission envisioned little intergenerational mobility. They assumed that formal education for each class stopped at the *same* class and occupational levels from which the students originated.

The early nineteenth century reveals some evidence of efforts to use education as a means of the social and intellectual improvement of the working classes—the friendly societies, the Mechanics' Institutes, and the mutual improvement societies. These were generally conceived, however, as fostering the self-improvement of a class as a whole through education, and not as providing avenues for mobility from that class.[76] The 1850s and 1860s witnessed the emergence of the "gospel of self-help" and social mobility, associated mainly with the widespread influence of the writings of Samuel Smiles.[77] This popular movement also revealed only muted connections between education and social mobility. Smiles himself explained it as follows:

> The education of the working-classes is to be regarded, in its highest aspect, not as a means of raising up a few clever and talented men into a higher rank of life, but of elevating and improving the whole class—of raising the entire condition of the workingman. The grand object aimed at should be to make the great mass of the people virtuous, intelligent, well-informed, and well-conducted; and to open up to them new sources of pleasure and happiness.[78]

Such a philosophy did not challenge the existing class structure, and it envisioned improvement rather than occupational movement.[79] Finally, we shall see in chapter 8 that the government-supported system of voluntary schools was not—with a couple of exceptions—envisioned as an avenue for working-class social mobility.[80]

*Education as Enlightenment and an Avenue for Social Change.* Overlapping with the mutual-improvement schemes of students were certain educational philosophies, found mainly in working-class circles, which presented images of education that ran directly counter to the dominant "social order" and "social control" imagery. In the first half of the nineteenth century, this imagery emerged in the Owenite and Chartist movements. The former, influenced by the educational optimism of the Enlightenment, depicted education as a road to personal liberation, truth and rationality, and social transformation. The Chartist leaders, William Lovett and John Collins, envisioned a national system of education that would be controlled by the people. The thrust of Chartist educational ideas was mainly, but not entirely, in the direction of universal and secular education. Their scheme included a wide range of educational institutions, run by popularly elected school boards, and stressed the values of democracy, citizenship, and "the organization of the people."[81] After 1848 the Christian Socialist movement, under the leadership of F. D. Morris, also developed a program of adult education.[82] These philosophies spawned a number of voluntary educational efforts by the movements themselves. They did not figure, however, as a legitimizing force for educational efforts undertaken "for" the working classes by religious and governmental leaders.[83]

## IMAGERY OF RELIGION

### THE CENTRALITY OF RELIGION AS SUCH

In regarding the primordial imagery of religion through the prism of education, we can note three fundamental contextual points. The first is the centrality of religion in the life of the society. The second is that the Church of England was "by law established" and intimately linked with the class hierarchy. The third is that this establishment was an incomplete one and was weakening in many ways throughout the nineteenth century.

During the preceding centuries, Britain had experienced a series of the deepest religious conflicts and turbulence: the rejection of Catholicism by Henry VIII; the reestablishment of the Protestant Church of England as a "middle way" between Catholicism and radical Protestantism; the radical Puritan experiment under Cromwell; the centuries of struggle between Anglicanism and Presbyterianism in Scotland, and between Protestantism and Catholicism in Ireland. All this had taken place, however, in the context of Britain as a "Christian nation." This commitment continued into the nineteenth century, despite the continuing denominational and sectarian contests, and despite the appearance of a small Jewish community and a number of secularist movements.

With respect to education, it was a seldom-questioned assumption that religion—Christian religion—had to be part of the education of the young. As late as 1868, the Taunton Commission would argue that "[religious instruction] is accepted by the people of England in the present day as an unquestionable good." Furthermore, "it is simply impracticable to exclude it from our schools." [84] (The requirement that religion be a part of elementary education survives minimally in English law to the present day.) That assumption guided the principles on which the Committee of Council operated. Harry Chester, an administrative officer with that body from 1839 to 1859, explained: "The Queen expressed her desire that the youth of this country should be religiously brought up." [85] He went on to say that "[it] was requisite that the Bible should be read daily in every school which received assistance from the Committee." [86] The Committee of Council held to this position. Secular schools approached it from time to time—for example, in 1853 and 1856—and asked to be included in its system of government grants. On both occasions, Ralph Lingen replied in the same language: "Their Lordships, in distributing the Parliamentary grant, have always required that religious as well as secular instruction shall be given in the schools receiving aid from the fund." [87] In 1859 Lingen reported that such applications were few, and from "representatives of single institutions." [88] In the early 1840s a music school at Exeter Hall came under fire and was ultimately excluded from parliamentary support on grounds that it gave no religious instruction and thus set a dangerous precedent for non-denominational training colleges. [89] In the early 1850s, Kneller Hall, a training institution for schoolmasters for the instruction of paupers, came under attack in Parliament and was eventually closed because it was too latitudinarian, if not secular, in its instruction. [90] Secularist education—that is, education without a religious component—appeared to be rare. More generally, while a number of educational movements advocated a secular system of education, [91] leaders of those movements were often thrown on the defensive and denied or minimized any anti-religious intent. [92] For example, the headmaster of the Manchester

Model Secular School—one of those who had applied unsuccessfully
for government support—argued that instruction in secular schools was
in fact religious in character, even though the Bible was not used.[93]

## THE CHURCH OF ENGLAND ESTABLISHMENT

One index of the centrality of religion was its establishment throughout the realm. The Church of England was the church of the state in
England and Wales, though often called "the Church in Wales" in the
latter.[94] Its sister Episcopal body, the Church of Ireland, was established
there, though shakily so, because of the large majority of Roman Catholics in the Irish population, many of whom, under Catholic Church
leadership, were hostile to the formal Anglican domination. The
Church of Scotland (commonly known as the Kirk) was established separately under Presbyterian principles.

Because of its established status, the Church of England enjoyed great
political, economic, and symbolic power. Its state representative was the
Crown, the "defender of the Faith." It was present at and gave legitimacy to the royal events of birth, marriage, coronation, and death. It
was one of the orders in the House of Lords. As late as 1870, Hippolyte
Taine could describe the social bases of the Church of England's institutional comfort in Britain in the following terms, albeit with considerable
exaggeration:

> The Anglican Church is most widely and best accredited. In its favour are its
> antiquity, its alliance with the State, its privileges and endowments, the pres-
> ence of its bishops in the House of Lords, its domination in the Universities,
> its middle position between two extremes; that is between the cult, dogma,
> and spirit of Puritanism, and the cult, dogma and spirit of Catholicism.
> Moreover, this church is an old and lawful compromise that suits the major-
> ity, which is attached to formal transactions, readily follows tradition, and
> lets itself be directed by statutes. Furthermore, the Church is rich, is one of
> the powers that be, has affiliations with the aristocracy, has splendid connec-
> tions, and is one of the great organs of the constitution. By these tokens it has
> the support of statesmen, conservatives, society and all who would be known
> as *respectable*.[95]

Two factors in particular cemented the Church of England's link with
aristocracy and wealth. First, its wealth was accorded by tithing, securing an income from the country's tax base for its institutions and
people. Second, in contrast to the Roman Catholic Church, which selected candidates from many ranks to staff its priesthood, many Church

of England clergymen were the younger sons of aristocrats, who—excluded from hereditary privilege—tended to go into positions in the military, the government, or the church.[96]

The Church of England also claimed a traditional monopoly on many rituals, including those associated with birth, marriage, and death. Not the least of these was its claim on the education of the nation, however eroded this had become after the restrictions on Dissenters' rights to teach were relaxed, beginning in 1718, and repealed finally in 1779. Dissenting schools and academies spread during the eighteenth century.[97] Taine's comment on the Anglican Church's "domination in the Universities" referred to the privilege of excluding Dissenters from admission and appointment, a privilege that was not to fall until the 1850s. Early in the century, church representatives either resisted or demanded to retain control over government-subsidized working-class education on grounds that the church had a monopoly of it.[98] In subsequent conflicts over the management of subsidized schools (the "management clauses" issue), and the requirement of the church catechism for non-Anglican pupils (the "conscience clause" issue), the church reasserted its privileges.[99]

EROSION OF THE ESTABLISHMENT

Taine's characterization was exaggerated because it was outdated. Dissent from the Church of England had gained force in the late eighteenth century in tandem with the Wesleyan and Evangelical forces and was a significant force in the British polity at the beginning of the nineteenth century. The strength of Dissent was especially great in Wales, establishing there a situation resembling the Irish case, in the sense that a majority of the population was non-Anglican by confession. The religious history of the nineteenth century was the story of successive relief of disabilities—such as office-holding, marriage, and burial rights—and corresponding gains for Protestant Dissent, Catholics, and Jews.[100] These gains, resisted at every stage by the Church of England, strengthened and emboldened these groups. The Anglican Church was disestablished in Ireland in 1869, and in Wales by 1914; England experienced a disestablishment movement as well throughout the second half of the nineteenth century.[101]

The struggles for religious parity on the part of Dissenters were enlivened by the fact that they overlapped significantly with class conflict. In general, the Church of England represented aristocratic interests, and the different kinds of Dissent represented middle-class interests. (This

statement, however, calls for so many refinements and qualifications
that it must remain a proximate assertion.)

T. H. Marshall observes that the increased power of the middle
classes in the industrial transition was manifested in large part in demands by the middle classes for equality and civil rights:

> Starting at the point where all men were free, and, in theory, capable of en-
> joying rights, [the demands of the middle classes] grew by enriching the body
> of rights which they were capable of enjoying. These rights did not conflict
> with inequalities of capitalist society; they were, on the contrary, necessary
> to the maintenance of that particular form of inequality. The explanation lies
> in the fact that the core of citizenship at this stage was composed of civil
> rights.[102]

The imagery of the Dissenters', Catholics', and Jews' striving in the
nineteenth century was similar, though clothed in religious symbolism.
Above all they legitimized their claims by appeal to considerations of
equity and freedom of conscience. Why should they, as citizens of the
realm, be subject to any categorical disabilities not suffered equally by
all? More positively, why should they not enjoy the same privileges? The
"rights of conscience" demands, rooted in the Protestant tradition,
proved a major weapon in resisting the Anglican Church's efforts to
impose its own doctrines, formulas, and rituals—all in the name of
its privileged position—on others. The logic of the case is found in
Brougham's presentation of a Unitarian petition relating to the marriage
ceremony in 1835. At that time, Dissenters could not have a formal registration of marriage unless they were married in the Church of England. Brougham reasoned as follows:

> [The Unitarians] complained of the Marriage-law; and urged that, in any
> change that was made, they should be put upon the same footing as Church-
> man; so that, with regard to both, marriage should be a civil, or a civil and a
> religious contract. . . . [Brougham's] opinion was that every measure was to
> be rejected on principle—as contrary to justice to the Dissenters—as con-
> trary to the policy of the law—as pernicious in itself—as pernicious with
> regard to all the relations of life—and as unjust both to the Churchman and
> the Dissenter—that should make any distinction in the marriage contract,
> declaring it to be of a nature civil only with respect to one class, and civil
> and religious with respect to another. [Parliament should make the marriage
> contract] purely civil, or civil and religious, as respected all denominations
> whatever.[103]

The period covered by this volume, then, was one of further transition from the principle of establishmentarianism to competitive denominationalism.[104] Moreover, since religion occupied such a central

place in British life, religious identification ran high, as did religious conflict. It was characterized by aggressiveness, defensiveness, and jurisdictional jealousies during that transition period. Furthermore, for several reasons, the kind of conflict generated in this conflict between establishment and equity had a peculiar, interminable, "unresolvable" quality. First, if one group possesses a permanent advantage (establishment) and another group suffers a corresponding disadvantage, no number of major or minor concessions to the disadvantaged will satisfy. The middle-class liberal reformer John Bright observed in an educational debate that "so long as the Church of England maintained its present national status a Dissenter was not in fact upon a par of religious equality with the Churchman." [105] Second, and closely related, was the principle of relative deprivation: a gain on one front (for example, equal access to civil registration of marriages) served to highlight dissatisfactions relating to *other* disabilities or rights, and renewed the struggle on another front. Struggles in this situation of mixed principles of legitimization (establishmentarianism and free denominationalism in this case) remind one of Tocqueville's general observation that struggles for equality are both inevitable and interminable so long as any vestige of inequality remains. [106]

The battles for the control of religious territory readily spilled over into battles for educational control. As indicated, the Church of England claimed, in principle at least, a monopoly, excluding both the state and other religious persuasions from that arena. Dissenters, Catholics, and secularists alike challenged that monopoly as fiercely as they did all the other privileges of the Established Church. Chapters 4 and 5 will demonstrate that this struggle between the Anglican Church and its challengers involved a kind of "repetition compulsion" of themes in the religious and educational debates. This led some to observe that the primary issue in the religious struggles over working-class education in the nineteenth century was not doctrinal—doctrines were seldom invoked—but the question of religious *control* over the schools. Such conflict was especially inspirited, since access to and religious training of the young was perceived as a principal way of maintaining, if not strengthening, a group's religious position in future generations. In any event, religious identity and membership—like class identity and membership, and overlapping with it significantly—was a sufficiently salient basis of group organization in nineteenth-century British society to merit the application to it of the term *primordial.*

As observed, conflicts among primordial groups pose special diffi-

culties for political leaders and administrators. Primordial assumptions
tend to take on a sacred, inviolable quality. As such, those who base
their arguments on them frequently adopt uncompromising "either/or"
postures, defining deviation from or compromise on them as a sacrifice
of fundamental values. To capitalize on primordial arguments and represent groups advancing them often constitutes a basis for political advancement for a politician. In addition, however, the motives of those
who govern—who must be problem-solvers and issue-settlers above
all—is to minimize the primordial elements and isolate them from conflict situations. Nassau W. Senior, a political economist and member of
the Newcastle Commission, asked Lingen if the Committee of Council
would supply grants to a Jewish school that professed to teach that Jesus
Christ was an imposter. Lingen replied, "The Committee of Council
does not enter at all into the question of the truth or falsehood of different religions."[107] Another evident tendency is for governments to seek
refuge in the ethic of "impartiality" to defend themselves against attack
from primordially based bodies. In defending the government plan to
expand subsidization to schools of a number of different religious societies, T. B. Macaulay remonstrated:

> Will any Gentleman say, that in that system or plan there is an advantage
> given to the members of the Church [of England], which is not given to those
> connected with the Baptists, the Presbyterians, the Wesleyans, and with the
> Church of Scotland? I can find no trace of the kind. The advantage of the
> scheme is intended for all in common.[108]

In addition, we shall discover that one strategy pursued by the government in the face of religious conflicts over education was to yield by giving each contending party its own territory—in this case, control over
its denominational schools—thus isolating the contending parties from
one another. This yielded a pattern of proliferation of educational institutions along primordial lines.[109]

## REGION AS PRIMORDIAL

The third background phenomenon is that of regionalism, with special reference to Ireland, Wales, and Scotland. In many respects, regionalism had a kind of primordial nature, most vividly in those three
regions, but also with respect to people from areas such as Cornwall,
Lancashire, Yorkshire, and Northumberland.[110] The bases of regional
differentiation include language and dialect, occupational (especially

agricultural/industrial) mix, religious composition, political culture, and social pretension, as well as local identification and pride.

With respect to the Celtic fringe, Ireland was most problematic in its relations with the English "core" during the nineteenth century. It experienced not only the greatest geographical isolation, but also a religious majority hostility to the Church of Ireland, subordination to absentee land-ownership, and an ethnic/cultural ambivalence, if not outright hostility to the English. The "Irish Question" was an unresolved running sore in the English polity throughout the century, dominating parliamentary debates, preoccupying state leaders (especially Peel and Gladstone) and producing political protests and contests on many fronts. That the question was unresolvable within the English polity was proved in the early twentieth century, when most of Ireland gained political independence from England.

The "Welsh Question" resembled the Irish one in several important ways: a religious majority (Dissent) hostile in many respects to the Established Church of England; English (or Anglophile) landlords and manufacturers superimposed on the large Welsh agricultural and industrial working populations; a different language; and an intense national pride. That question, however, unlike the Irish one, proved to be negotiable within the English polity in the nineteenth century, even though it was fraught with continuous tension and conflict. The Scottish situation was the least problematical, largely because Scotland had over the centuries gained a measure of constitutional autonomy. Religious conflicts with the Church of England were minimized by the fact that Scotland had a separately established church. Nevertheless, the distinctive political and religious dynamics of Scotland, as well as its partial incorporation into the English system of primary education, created a special "Scottish" situation that merits comparative attention.

It has been observed that one of the most revealing indices of the sociocultural life of a society is what strangers in that society want first to know about one another in order to establish a basis for identification and interaction. In nineteenth-century Britain, the answer to that question would include social class, religious affiliation, and region of origin, which parallel the three great primordial divisions outlined. Among the objectives of this study will be to understand how British elementary education proliferated so markedly along primordial class, religious, and regional lines; how different outcomes were thereby produced; and how counteracting forces pressed this evolution—not always successfully—in the directions of centralization, uniformity, and secularization.

## THE POLITY

To complete this sketch of the broad parameters that conditioned the evolution of education in the nineteenth century, it is necessary to mention that the polity itself was in transition from oligarchic rule to representative democracy. This transition involved successive extensions of the franchise to previously unenfranchised groups, the extension of personal liberties and democratic rights, and the evolution of more clearly identifiable political parties from a system of partylike cliques of ruling notables.[111] Thus, in transition, governments adopted a pattern of mixed strategies of governance that have been labeled "politics without democracy."[112] These strategies included the more or less familiar patterns of politicking and seeking the support of groups enfranchised at the time; responding to expressions of "public opinion" as voiced through petitions to Parliament as well as the activities of social movements and voluntary organizations; and reacting to "events" such as riots and demonstrations on the part of those who were neither enfranchised nor established in the organizational network that constituted—variably—the evolving civil society in that century.

## CHAPTER 4

# Truce Points and
# Moments of Change (1)

This chapter and the next present a history of British working-class education in the nineteenth century that is consonant with the perspective
developed in chapter 2. I identify a number of dates in the first seven
decades of the nineteenth century, each of which was decisive with respect to prolonging a stalemate, changing the definition of the educational situation, stimulating growth, or triggering an institutional innovation. (Making such identifications is scarcely an original act on my
part: some of these dates—for example, 1839, 1846, 1862—coincide
with those recognized by consensus among historians as the critical moments in British educational history.) I treat each moment as an "outcome" of the process-model represented in chart 2. For each outcome I
specify the main ingredients of that model by way of depicting the process that led to that outcome. In no case, however, does this involve a
formal, literal, or detailed imposition of the model on the historical flow
of situations and events. In each instance I begin with the wider cultural
and social-structural forces that conditioned the final outcome and then
move to its more proximate causes.

## A SIGNIFICANT MOMENT OF INACTION: 1807

Early in the nineteenth century, British society was still remote from
the modern urban, industrial, and relatively democratic society it was to
become during that century. Commercial development already had a
long history, industrial development was gaining a foothold in textiles

and a few other areas, and infrastructural development (mainly roads and canals) was under way. Yet the society and its population were still predominantly agricultural. The class system mirrored this transitional situation. It was built mainly on landed property and wealth. Redistribution of wealth was effected mainly through patronage, charity, and rates for the poor. It was also a castelike society of "orders," with little anticipated mobility.[1] The middle classes, with a long institutional presence, were mounting a serious political campaign for reform of Parliament and other institutions that embedded aristocratic privilege. The urban-industrial working classes, nascent in development, were the object of social and political concern. However, they were only beginning to be heard in the 1790s when radical ideologies, associated with the writings of Thomas Paine and others, found expression by activists in their ranks. The political structure, represented nationally by Parliament, did not yet reflect the presence of classes other than the aristocratic. Government was exercised through semiorganized groupings of conservative Tories and moderate Whigs rather than political parties of a more formal sort.

With respect to religion, the Established Church of England was dominant institutionally and numerically,[2] and it was closely affiliated with the ruling classes and fully incorporated into their politics of patronage. The Dissenters included a diversity of groups at variance with Church of England ritual and theology in various ways. Among those, the Nonconformists were fragmented into multiple groupings—the "old" denominations of Presbyterians, Independents, and Baptists; and smaller groups such as the Unitarians and Quakers. The Catholics were a small minority in England and Scotland but a very large majority in Ireland.

New Dissent included those remaining Protestant denominations that had arisen or received new life from the religious revival of the last half of the eighteenth century.[3] That revival was associated mainly with the rise of Wesleyan Methodism, which not only formed its organizationally separate church, but spilled over into and solidified the split in the Established Church between High Anglican and Low Evangelical. Ideologically and politically, both Wesleyanism and Evangelicalism occupied a position intermediate between the old Establishment and Nonconformity. In Elie Halévy's words, "If the Wesleyan sect, with its hierarchic constitution and frank political conservatism, constituted the High Church of Nonconformity, the new Low Church or Evangelical party was a species of Anglican Methodism."[4] Generally speaking, the eighteenth-century revival infused British religion with Calvinism and enthusiasm.

In the early nineteenth century, non-Anglican Dissent kept up its pressure to remove the disabilities it had suffered for centuries, and it achieved some successes in the first decade of the century.[5] At the same time, Dissenters and Wesleyans alike experienced a damaging political onslaught in the years of the French Revolution and the Napoleonic era (1790–1815) at the hands of Tories and Anglicans.[6] This assault arose in large part as a reaction against the French Revolution and the appearance of radical thought in England. In this period "Methodists, Dissenters, Sunday-school teachers, and village preachers" were denounced as Jacobins,[7] and as home secretary early in the nineteenth century, Lord Sidmouth attempted, largely without success, to implement new repressive measures against Dissenters.[8] All this served to polarize the relations of the Anglican Church and Dissent into a state of mutual distrust and antagonistic competition in the early decades of the century.

The educational picture for the poorer classes was a complex one.[9] In general, their education was limited in extent, voluntary or charitable in character, and outside the realm of government policy and expenditure. The charity schools constituted a limited philanthropic effort, mainly by the Church of England through the Society for Promoting Christian Knowledge (SPCK). Their educational aim was modest: in the words of Bishop Samuel Butler, "not in any sort to remove poor children out of the rank in which they were born, but keeping them in it, to give them the assistance which their circumstances plainly called for, by educating them in the principles of religion as of civil life."[10]

The appearance and rapid dissemination of Sunday schools in the late eighteenth century was a more dramatic but also limited educational effort. Originating with the work of Robert Raikes of Gloucester in 1781, these schools spread through the same ranks as did Methodism and the Evangelical revival. As suggested by their name, they gave instruction on the Sabbath only (in order not to interfere with the obligations of work during the week), and generally limited that instruction to reading Scripture. For a time in some localities, Sunday schools developed as an interdenominational effort,[11] but the forces of denominationalism began to reassert themselves early in the century.[12] In addition, many Sunday schools were attacked by gentry, Tories, and bishops as sources of religious and political sedition.[13] Two other forms of education, if they may be so designated, were the schools of industry, which aimed to teach pauper children the educational rudiments and prepare them for a trade, and the dame schools, which were modest, private establishments mainly run by women (hence the name), whose teaching sometimes included minimal reading lessons.[14]

This was the context in which Samuel Whitbread, a moderate Whig leader, introduced an education bill in 1807 that would have established schools in every parish to give children between the ages of seven and fourteen two years of education. Consistent with the Whigs' political approach, Whitbread justified his effort by arguing that "writing and arithmetic, so far as they tended to exercise and improve the understanding, tended also to improve morality."[15] Several other contemporary strands of thought were also favorable to the extension of education by the state. These were the educational ideas of Rousseau, as articulated in his novel *Emile,* which created a stir among those concerned with problems of science, industry, and public health;[16] the writings of some political economists, including Adam Smith and Jeremy Bentham, who exempted education from their general philosophy of governmental nonintervention in social life, believing that education was an economically feasible investment in social order and the prevention of crime;[17] and some social doctrines of the nascent working-class radical movement.

Two features of Whitbread's proposal presage themes that were to remain central in decades to come: the theme of religious jurisdiction over education and the theme of reform by accretion. Whitbread framed the legislation so that the parish schools would be under the direction of the parochial clergy.[18] In addition, he advertised the measure as a modest one, designed only to supplement existing efforts:

> It was not meant to supersede any parish schools for the education of the poor already established, it was not meant to increase unnecessarily the charges upon any district, where parish schools were already instituted for the education of the poor, by establishing therein additional schools; his object was, that in every parish where there was a number of poor who could not afford to pay for the education for their children, there should be a school established for their instruction.[19]

This proclamation that reform was an "add-on" that would not disturb existing arrangements was to become a standard litany of reformers for the rest of the century. This feature will also prove to be of general theoretical interest.[20]

Whitbread's bill—passed politely by the House of Commons but predictably defeated in the House of Lords—apparently did not excite significant attention or agitation outside the halls of Parliament. The parliamentary debates are notable, however, because they raised almost the whole range of arguments that were to become the common staple of educational debates throughout the century. As indicated, Whitbread advertised the bill as a means of promoting social order, a way of inculcating the virtues appropriate to a respectable lower class, and an antidote to revolution and crime.

> When a riotous mob was assembled, it was called an illiterate mob. . . . [In Ireland] the combinations were formed by the ignorant, when their ignorance made them the dupes of the wicked. In the three kingdoms, the excellence of the population would appear to be in proportion to the degree of information among the lower orders.[21]

In this connection, Whitbread pointed out that the majority of criminals executed in London were Irish, the next in order English, and the last Scots. He attributed these results to the different levels of education of these groups.[22]

Opponents of the bill raised a formidable range of objections:

That the kind of education proposed in the legislation would not have the desired effects of diffusing industry, religion, and morality.[23]

That the proposed system of schooling would be a drain on the public purse.[24] This argument was aimed at arousing the anxieties of ratepayers already feeling the burden of poor rates and the Revolutionary and Napoleonic Wars against France.

That the principle of compulsion was offensive. This argument, appealing to the values of individual freedom, resulted in a successful amendment to remove the compulsory clause.[25]

That the proposal would undermine the existing voluntary arrangements manifested in the charity schools and the Sunday schools.[26] This argument, which was closely related to the argument against compulsion, reasserted the values of philanthropy and voluntarism.

That education would raise unwanted expectations and political mischief on the part of the lower orders. William Windham argued that it was not right to teach reading beyond a certain point; Lord Petty, the chancellor of the exchequer, predicted that education would cause people to leave those positions of useful agricultural labor ("the Quakers were mentioned as a class universally educated . . . he never knew of an agricultural Quaker");[27] and, in a frequently cited passage,

Davies Giddy argued that education would make the laboring classes "factious and refractory," and "would enable them to read seditious pamphlets, vicious books, and publications against Christianity."[28] Such arguments, those of Tory paternalism, were commonly heard in the late eighteenth and early nineteenth centuries,[29] less so as the century progressed.

That the proposed scheme would remove instruction from the control of the clergy, thereby departing from "the great principle of instruction in this country"; this objection, voiced by the lord chancellor and the archbishop of Canterbury in the House of Lords,[30] invoked the ancient claim of monopoly over education by the Church of England. This claim was challenged by Lord Stanhope, speaking for Dissent, when he said it was not reasonable "that the children of Catholics, Presbyterians, Quakers, and all other innumerable sects of Dissenters . . . were to be debarred [from] all sources of public education . . . unless they were to become converts to our Established religion."[31] The fate of Whitbread's and many other proposals later in the century was to be attacked simultaneously by the Anglican Church, as eroding its authority, and by Dissenters, for impinging on personal freedom and strengthening the Established Church.

Virtually all of these arguments are notable for the fact that, whether favorable or unfavorable, they were hypothetical in character. Each argument selected some feature of the proposed legislation, erected a scenario based on a combination of invoked facts (the crime rate among educated Scots was low) and an assumed causal process (education reduces crime). The posited effect was then deemed favorable or unfavorable in light of some legitimizing cultural criterion (for example, Church of England monopoly, religious freedom, traditional class obligations of charity and deference). This structure of argumentation was a standard feature of educational debates throughout the century.

Historians have made little of this episode of 1807, probably because Whitbread's initiative was doomed from the beginning, and, as a result of that, "nothing happened" by way of advancing the educational cause. Given the context of the times, there appeared to be no compelling argument for a state program other than Whig accommodationalism, and a great array of arguments against it—reactionary Toryism, Established Church claims, the tradition of limited and unintrusive government, middle-class arguments against state intervention (the educational arguments of the political economists notwithstanding), and radical fears of governmental oppression and disregard of individual liberties.[32] Never-theless, the events stand as a kind of initial, if unsuccessful, foray on the part of the state in the field of education, and as a first instance of what was to prove to be something of a repetition compulsion of religious ar-gumentation, political paralysis, and minimalism in educational reform.

REVOLUTIONARY FEARS AND OPEN
RELIGIOUS CONFLICT: 1820

Most of the social forces identified at the beginning of the chapter persisted in the next two decades, changing little until the turbulent pe-riod of protest, reform, and renewed religious struggle in the 1830s and 1840s. However, a heightening of the religious and political tensions in the second decade of the century were to produce a second and also un-successful effort at educational reform.

The first development to note is a new line of religious and educa-tional activity outside the realm of parliamentary politics: the establish-ment of competing religious societies for the education of the poor. The first, the British and Foreign School Society, had its beginnings in the formation of a school by Joseph Lancaster, a Quaker, in 1798. He em-ployed the monitorial method (one master for as many as several hun-dred pupils, with older children as supervisors or monitors of smaller groups). His school was also nondenominational, admitting children of parents of all persuasions and requiring general but no special religious instruction or rituals. Lancaster proved a successful promoter initially but something of a mismanager and spendthrift in the end. He was able, with the help of friends, to secure the endorsement of aristocratic repre-sentatives, such as Lord Summerville and the duke of Bedford, and ulti-mately royal patronage for the Royal Lancastrian Institute (officially founded in 1811). The organization was also supported by William Wilberforce (an Evangelical reformer), Henry Brougham (an Anglican Scot and liberal reformer), Jeremy Bentham, James Mill, and Francis Place (political economists and utilitarian radicals), and Dissenting min-isters and philanthropists (Rowland Hill, William Allen, and Joseph Gloucester). This support was an amalgam of Low Church, Whig, and Dissent—thus overlapping[33] with the forces aligned behind, or at least not antagonistic to, the Whitbread proposal of 1807.[34]

The formation of the Lancastrian society aroused a reaction of alarm and opposition among High Churchmen and Tories. Their opposition began with a personal attack on Lancaster,[35] but in the end, the Anglican Church formed a parallel society, the National Society for Promoting the Education of the Poor in the Principles of the Established Church, in 1811. Both societies restricted their provision of education to the poor; both imparted secular training, religious education, and morality to their young;[36] and both used essentially the same monitorial method. As institutional forms, moreover, they seemed to avoid many of the criticisms that Whitbread's proposal drew: they were both voluntary and cheap. They differed, however—and contested one another— on basic religious grounds. The National Society insisted on the liturgy and catechism of the Established Church, as well as attendance at an Anglican Church.[37] The British and Foreign School Society was committed to scriptural instruction while leaving denominational explanations, commentaries, and rites out of consideration.[38]

The two societies competed nationally for funds to establish schools for the poor—here the Anglican-based National Society had a significant advantage[39]—and sometimes fought at the local level over which kind of school would prevail.[40] They also entered into a spirited and embittered, if somewhat meaningless, argument over the issue of whether the monitorial system had been "invented" by Andrew Bell (as asserted by the National Society) or Lancaster (as asserted by the British Society). The Lancastrians also attacked the National Society as elitist and dogmatic, and the latter attacked the former as a Dissenting plan, a Deist plot, and a heretical scheme.[41] For two decades, this kind of competition was superimposed on the ongoing struggle by Dissent to lessen religious disadvantages and gain religious parity. It helped to raise the levels of both emotion and intransigence on the part of those contending religious groups.

The second development was an intensification of a political threat from below. During the second decade of the century, radical political activity was frequent and sometimes violent—the Luddite destruction of machinery in the north (1812–14), the Blanketeers' March (1817), the Manchester spinning strike (1818), and the demonstration in St. Peter's Fields, Manchester, that eventuated in the Peterloo Massacre (1819).[42] This was also the decade of counterrevolution, government spies, vigorous repression of uprisings, and repressive legislation, such as the Six Acts of 1819, and later, in 1824, the repeal of the Combination Acts, directed against the nascent trade union movement.[43] All this generated an intense class fear among the ruling political authorities and a search by reform-minded leaders for solutions to class conflict more lasting than political repressiveness. In 1818 and 1824, for example, the government voted extra funds to the Church of England for the construction of new churches.[44] Another manifestation of this search was a renewed interest in education between 1816 and 1820.

The leadership of educational reformers in this period fell to Henry Brougham, who proved to be a remarkable force in British reform for half a century. The Whig party had been in opposition since 1807 and had disintegrated as a political force. With Whitbread's death in 1815, Brougham assumed the helm of a reformist group known as the Mountain.[45] He had strong ties with the utilitarians, and later spearheaded a large number of reformist efforts, including the movements for emancipation of slaves, religious freedom, and free trade, the establishment of the Mechanics' Institutes, and the formation of the University of London. His educational ideal was the Scottish parish school system,[46] and he believed that elementary education should be universal but not secular.[47] Brougham's parliamentary efforts began auspiciously, with the appointment of a committee to investigate the conditions of the education of the poor in London. The committee had representation from a wide political spectrum and included both Tories and Whigs.

In its 1818 report, the committee testified to a great thirst for education among the poor: "the anxiety of the poor for education continues not only unabated, but daily increasing."[48] The early age at which children were being put to work was undermining this desire in many places. This made for a high incidence of failure to attend school, irregular attendance, and early withdrawal.[49] With respect to religion, the committee reported great resistance on the part of Catholic priests in London to sending the children of their parishes to schools in which the Protestant Bible was read,[50] but a mixed picture otherwise. Some witnesses reported that parents of all religious persuasions willingly sent their children to National Society schools.[51] Others reported that when Dissenting parents objected to the teaching of the catechism, their children were excused from learning it.[52] Still others reported an uncompromising attitude on the part of Church of England schools, and that many Dissenters would not send their children to these schools.[53]

In 1817, Brougham suggested, without success, that Parliament provide subsidies to the National and British and Foreign Societies to aid their voluntary efforts—thus presaging the parliamentary "solution" adopted in 1833. In 1818 the committee reported again, noting the progress of the voluntary societies in the large towns, and further expressing the belief that religious difficulties would not be significant in populous areas because separate schools could be made available for members of the Anglican Church and Dissenters. For thinly populated areas, Brougham recommended establishing schools on the Scottish parish school system.[54] He recognized the religious complexity of the English situation, however, and acknowledged that the system in Scotland—where doctrinal differences were minor—could not readily be generalized to England. Accordingly, he recommended a kind of conscience clause, specifying that "the children of sectarians shall not be compelled to learn any catechism or attend any church other than those of their parents."[55] This kind of measure would "obtain the desirable objects of security to the Establishment on the one hand, and justice to the Dissenters on the other."[56] Despite these recommendations, no legislative bills directed to extending education were introduced between 1816 and 1818. Brougham aroused opposition in conservative circles, moreover, because he appeared to be raising questions about the role of the Church of England in national education, the state of the charitable endowments and trusts, and other controversial issues. Thus, while Parliament permitted the committee to extend its inquiry to the nation as a whole in 1818, it constricted its powers of inquiry.[57]

The religious difficulties came to a head in 1820, when Brougham introduced legislation for governmental extension of primary education. The bill attempted a compromise. On the one hand, it recognized the official and advantaged status of the Church of England and its own educational efforts. Brougham advertised his bill—as Whitbread had done—as seeking to establish schools only where there were none, or where they were insufficient, thus not disturbing existing arrangements. Schoolmasters were to be elected by the ratepayers, who were to support the schools in part. However, these masters were to be members of the Church of England, supervised—and ultimately dismissed, if it came to that point—by church officials. On the other hand, the bill would excuse children of Dissenting parents from learning the Anglican catechism and from attending Anglican services on Sundays. The catechism was to be taught, but only at specified hours, and religious instruction was to consist mainly in reading the Bible, with necessary explanations, but with no special formulary.[58]

The compromise satisfied few parties and gained little support. High Church spokesmen were disappointed because it fell short of their insistence on a compulsory catechism, liturgy, and creed. The most heated objections came, however, from the Nonconformists and the Roman Catholics,[59] who protested that they were being asked to pay for and send their children to government schools under the control of the Anglican Church, in which their members could not teach. John Bright, a young parliamentarian later to become a major voice of Dissent, claimed that "[the bill's] tendency and effect would obviously be, to throw the whole education of the country into the hands of the Established Church." [60] The Dissenters formed a Committee for the Protection of Religious Liberty, which maintained a persistent opposition. Even the more moderate British and Foreign School Society, of which Brougham was a founding and active member, objected. Finally, too, the Wesleyan Methodists, closer to the Anglican Church in doctrine and practice than most Dissenters, opposed the bill on grounds that it furthered the privileged position of the church.[61] Brougham himself attributed the bill's failure mainly to sectarian rivalry; "the Dissenters thought that the plan was too much connected with the Church . . . among a number of the churchmen an opposite fear prevailed." [62] Later he singled out the Dissenters as especially vehement in their criticism and the most important factor in its defeat.[63] With such a range of opposition, the failure of the bill seemed a foregone conclusion. Halévy observes that "it is doubtful whether Brougham introduced the motion with any other intention than to deliver a sensational speech." [64]

The year 1820 thus ended in a kind of religious stalemate, even though the sense of the political urgency of educational reform remained salient. Looking at the political-religious-educational situation of the 1820s, Henry Craik summarizes the forces making for that stalemate accurately:

> Most educational reformers still sought for the beginning of the work in the efforts of each separate locality. But to leave the decision of the religious question to the locality was to introduce . . . confusion and dissension—still more probably, as the Dissenters feared, a new and dangerous advantage for the Church. No means, however, was suggested for holding the balance between different religious communions; and still less possible did it seem to eliminate or even to restrain the religious element in instruction in any school. Yet the necessity of doing something was pressing itself upon attention more imperiously every day. The same movements that led to political reform in other directions also drew attention to the crying question of education. But the Church was alarmed at anything which seemed to trench upon what she naturally thought to be her appointed task. The Dissenters dreaded what might add to the impregnability of the Church's strongholds. All were conscious of the need; many were anxious to supply it; but none were able to propound a system to which the Legislature was prepared to give effect, or which offered any solution of the problem.[65]

Such a stalemate left the government quiescent for more than a decade to follow, and lay behind its policy of minimalism of reform at every turn throughout the century. While the events of 1816–20 did place a comprehensive scheme for educational reform before the country, its defeat seemed to discredit the Whig reformers and fed the scorn that some held for the "education-mad party." [66] The failure of Brougham's bill also no doubt resigned the ruling groups to the position that whatever amelioration of class conflict education might achieve would have to be limited to the efforts of the religious and philanthropic agencies.

## THE FAILURE OF MIDDLE-CLASS RADICAL SECULARISM: 1833

The quiescence of the state in matters of education did not mean that reformers were equally quiet. The 1820s registered notable efforts, if not spectacular successes, on a number of educational fronts. The two religious societies continued their voluntary work. In a series of admittedly inaccurate estimates, the National Society claimed 564 schools and 97,920 children in 1820; by 1829 the corresponding figures were 2,654 schools and 174,000 children. [67] Between 1811 and 1834, the National Society had laid out £105,000 to sponsored schools, with four times that amount raised locally. [68] In the meantime, the British and Foreign School Society struggled to gain funds, having applied unsuccessfully to wealthy companies in London in 1822 and to the government a year later. [69] In 1834 it was estimated that the British and Foreign School Society had 490 schools in operation, of which 90 were in London. [70] As was to be discovered by investigations in the 1830s, however, the schools supported by these two societies almost all operated on the "mass" monitorial method, applied by an ill-trained cadre of teachers, and were, to use the word of the day, very "inefficient."

In the meantime, a great deal of activity on behalf of secular education was proceeding apace. Brougham and others, inspired by the writings of the utilitarian political economists, launched the Mechanics' Institutes in 1825. These institutions of adult education aimed at promoting technical education among the working classes. The same group founded, on the same principles, the Society for the Diffusion of Useful Knowledge in 1827. Brougham and others from Scotland led in the formation of the University of London, free from the religious restrictions of the ancient universities. As to primary education, the interest in Robert Owen's educational experiment at New Lanark induced a benevolent group headed by Brougham to bring Samuel Wilderspin, a teacher from that school, to lead in launching a movement for infant schools in the 1820s. [71] These schools for very young children were opposed at first by the Church of England, but emulated through the efforts of the Home and Colonial Society in the 1830s.[72]

In the meantime, reformers and political leaders were taking note of education in other countries, especially Prussia (where in 1833 alone some £600,000 was voted for expenditure on education), France, Holland, and the United States. These countries appeared to be making great strides toward systems of national education and surpassing England in this regard.[73] Perhaps the most notable development, however, was closer to home, in Ireland, a society that had experienced decades of religious conflict over education (the Catholics resisting the efforts of Protestant-based educational societies). Popular discontent reached new heights in Ireland in the 1820s, culminating in the legislative relief of Catholic disabilities in 1829. In 1831 Parliament also established a "national" system of education in Ireland, over the vigorous opposition of many religious groups, including Church of England representatives, Scottish Presbyterians, and Wesleyan Methodists.[74] The feature of the Irish system that excited the greatest interest was its separation of the secular and religious aspects of education. Four days of the week were devoted to secular instruction for children of all religious persuasions, with special religious instruction reserved for the different churches and denominations on separate days of the week. In addition, the Irish "solution" dealt with several other issues that were later to prove contentious in England—issues such as the training of teachers, the mode of financing the system, and school inspection.[75] The Irish educational experiment was before the eyes of many English reformers and officials, and it was held up by some as a model.[76]

Three additional conditioning factors lay behind the legislative events of 1833. The first was the parliamentary reform of 1832, following years of agitation by middle-class and working-class groups of reformers.[77] This agitation had involved violence in the southern agricultural sectors in 1831,[78] and a genuine constitutional crisis in 1832. The reform eliminated many electoral abuses and enfranchised a portion of the middle classes. It ushered in what Halévy calls the era of "the triumph of reform, 1830–42." Brougham characterized the first reformed Parliament as composed mainly of "friends of sane and rational reform" amid groups in the larger society that were "unreasonable and expected too much."[79] The accomplishments of that Parliament included the emancipation of slaves in the colonies (1833), reform of the poor law (1834), and numerous commercial, banking, and legal reforms. The reform impulse also lay behind the effort to legislate a national system of education in 1833.[80] At the same time, a number of trends antagonistic to middle-class reforms developed, mainly in Tory and Anglican circles. Among these were the anticapitalist campaign on the part of some aristocratic groups to impose limitations on factory labor in the cotton-textile industry, and, indeed, the successful opposition to the educational project of the middle-class radicals in 1833.

The second set of forces was set in motion in 1828 and 1829 with the repeal of the Test and Corporation Acts, which brought relief for Dissenters, and the Catholic Emancipation Act, which eliminated prohibitions on office-holding by Catholics. Both these acts followed prolonged periods of religious and political agitation and debate. In combination with the reform of Parliament, these acts were correctly experienced as profound defeats for Tories and Anglicans. The apprehension of these groups increased in the first reformed Parliament in 1832–33, as radicals initiated a flurry of measures to reform, if not obliterate, many traditional Church of England privileges.[81] All these developments triggered a surge of aggressive activity and a reassertion of the Anglican Church's rights in the 1830s and 1840s. The acts of 1828, 1829, and 1832, plus the revitalization of the Church of England, also stimulated a season of both defensive and aggressive political activity on the part of Nonconformists. As we shall see, these developments escalated religious conflict, including its manifestation in the area of education of the poor.

The third contextual force was the continuing and urgent presence of the issue of the "condition of the poor"—and its linkage to education—in many quarters. In pressing the advantages of infant schools, Wilderspin mentioned first their promise to reduce juvenile crime among the working classes. The *Quarterly Journal of Education*, the utilitarian voice of the Society for the Diffusion of Useful Knowledge, asserted in 1831 that "a manufacturing population is peculiarly inflammable, and apt to be misled." It added that education was an indispensable instrument in instructing the laboring classes as to their real interests. Sound instruction, it pointed out, was "of the utmost importance . . . as respects the stability of our institutions, and the security of the middle and upper classes."[82] A report of the National Society in Manchester in 1830 argued that "the necessity of general instruction has become both more obvious and more urgent."[83] In the wake of the agricultural riots of 1830–31, the British and Foreign School Society advised that

> [the agricultural poor] need the steadying influence of a sound Scriptural education such as it is the Society's purpose to give the children of the labouring poor. Nor will they any longer be contented with the mere rudiments, once regarded as sufficient. Popular education must now take wider scope.[84]

The attempt to legislate educational reform appeared in the first reformed Parliament in 1833. Its initiation lay in a group representing
middle-class, utilitarian, radical interests.[85] The radicals had been heartened by their recent victory in the Reform Act, and found that the Whigs
sometimes had to rely on their support in Parliament. John Roebuck,
who introduced the proposal in July, promised that it would produce "a
people industrious, honest, tolerant and happy." [86] He put forth the argument, familiar in political economy circles, that a proper education
would yield a "thorough understanding on their [the people's] part of the
circumstances on which their happiness depended, and of the powers by
which those circumstances were controlled." [87] Roebuck also promised a
kind of utilitarian utopia if people understood their social condition:

> We shall have no more unmeaning discontents—no wild and futile schemes
> of Reform; we shall not have a stack-burning peasantry . . . a monopoly-
> seeking manufacturing class; we shall not have a middle class directing all
> their efforts to the repeal of a single tax, or to the wild plan of universal rob-
> bery; neither will there be immoral landlords wishing to maintain a danger-
> ous corn monopoly; or foolish consumers, who will suffer it to remain.[88]

Against the objection that government intervention would make the
people slavish, he asserted that under his plan, education would follow
the wishes of the people. Against the objection that government intervention would reduce private philanthropy and thus erode the relations
between the rich and the poor, he argued that private philanthropic
efforts had enjoyed only "imperfect success." [89]

Roebuck's scheme followed the Prussian model of compulsory secular education enforced by the state, covering the years between six and
twelve. He called for an omnibus set of institutions, including infant
schools, schools of industry, and normal schools for the training of
schoolmasters. He justified the cost of the schools by invoking the utilitarian argument that incarceration of criminals is more costly than the
prevention of crime. Finally, Roebuck proposed a central national officer for education, who was to be a cabinet member, and division of the
country into districts, with elected committees to govern the schools.

The proposed legislation never came to a vote; Roebuck withdrew it
after a storm of objections from both Whigs and Tories. Lord Althorp, a
Whig, argued that it would undermine the private efforts already undertaken. Sir Robert Inglis, a voice of High Anglicanism (jocularly labeled
"the Member from Heaven"), objected because the plan took educational responsibilities from the Church of England. Daniel O'Connell, a
Catholic, argued that such a measure would "unchristianize" the country through government domination, as it had done in France.[90] Even

Brougham opposed it, having moved from his earlier support for compulsory education, and now convinced that voluntary efforts were sufficient.[91] It was Sir Robert Peel's argument, however, made at the conclusion of the debate, that seemed finally to seal the measure's fate:

> Now, it would be necessary, in the first place, to decide whether national education would be in three countries which differed so much from each other, in many respects, as England, Scotland, and Ireland. . . . A compulsory system of education appeared to him to trench upon religious toleration; for it must, almost of necessity, interfere with religious opinion . . . if we were once to establish in this country an officer with power to superintend the education of children of all sects of religion, with power to select their books of instruction, we should excite apprehensions of general intolerance . . . we should create jealousy in every part of the country . . . in a country like our own, which was justly proud of its freedom, he doubted whether it ought not to be left free from control.[92]

Interestingly, Peel, a conservative and an Anglican, seemed to represent the voice of the Dissenters more than anyone else. If there was to be religious compulsion associated with state intervention, it would be the compulsion arising from the Church of England's insistence on the use of its formularies and rites. This argument against compulsion was to appear in other guises repeatedly throughout the century.[93] In effect, Peel was arguing that primordial loyalties of a regional and religious character held priority over other benefits that might accrue from a national system of education.

The failure of the 1833 legislation marked the third time in a quarter-century that reformers' efforts to involve the government in the education of the working classes had run aground. These failures occurred, moreover, in the face of acknowledged dangers from the classes below and an acknowledged commitment to the values of such education. The reasons why it had foundered were similar in all three cases. There was an inherited antipathy toward government intervention, which was reinforced by anti-state sentiments among political economists, middle-class spokesmen, and radicals on the left. More profoundly, the educational reforms failed because of the paralysis that resulted from the Established Church's claims to religious control over education on the one hand, and Dissenters' dread of such control and their suspicion that state control would entail Anglican Church control on the other. Or, as Brougham was to observe on a later occasion:

> Each and all of these various [religious] classes preferred to the extension of popular education one other object, and that one other object was a victory over each other. The Church was anxious to educate the people, but the

Church was still more anxious to get the better of the sects; the sects were anxious to have popular education, but the sects were still more anxious than this to overturn the Church.[94]

In the wake of the failure of Roebuck's bill, Lord Althorp ventured a modest suggestion on August 16 at 2 A.M. in Parliament, in the context of a miscellaneous discussion of estimates and budgetary affairs. Radicals apparently played little role in developing the measure—in all likelihood, it was the child of Brougham and Whig accommodationalism.[95] Althorp acknowledged that it was frequently mischievous for the government to interfere in educational matters, and that, in general, educational initiative was best left in private hands. He observed, however, that private subscriptions were frequently deficient. Considering that, he suggested that Parliament approve a sum of £20,000 annually, to be distributed by the Treasury in accord with applications put forward by "the two Great School Societies"—the National Society and the British and Foreign School Society. In common with other educational reformers of the day, he specified that the grants should be limited to the education of the poorer classes.[96] The measure stirred little debate. Joseph Hume, a supporter of the Roebuck bill, argued that the sum was too small to establish a national system of education. Inglis argued that he could not support any plan that did not accord with the principles of the Established Church. He added, in a providential, but not often cited, statement that "it was the commencement of a new system, the extent of which they could not know."[97] The radical traditionalist William Cobbett opposed Althorp's measure on the grounds that "education was [only] the knowledge necessary for the situation of life in which a man was placed," and that the main effect of the spread of education was "to increase the number of schoolmasters and schoolmistresses—that new race of idlers."[98] Without further ceremony, however, the proposal was passed by a vote of fifty to twenty-six.

Inglis was correct in asserting that the proposal introduced a "new system." It was the first time that Parliament had entered directly into the support of popular education. Yet it was a minimal measure. It was the act of a government under pressure to act (largely because of the uncertain and menacing aspects of the social-class situation) but simultaneously suffering from a seemingly intractable political paralysis (stemming mainly from the existing constellation of antagonistic religious forces). The main justifying arguments for Althorp's measure were negative and designed to avoid the objections to the more ambitious, but unsatisfactory, Roebuck initiative. It involved no compulsion. It was a boost to the voluntary efforts as they existed. It was equitable with respect to the major religious groups, and thus could not readily be accused of discriminating against either.[99] With respect to politics and administration, it passed as a financial measure, not a legislative act, and thus escaped a possible veto in the House of Lords; and it did not require any new administrative body, assigning the funds to the Treasury for disbursement.[100] Minimal as it was, however, Althorp's proposal was the first "truce point" that had ended in something other than a political standoff and governmental paralysis. The parliamentary action of August 1833 brought forward a new definition of the situation. It went beyond asking *if* the government should become involved and asked *how and under what conditions* support should be forthcoming.

## A VICTORY FOR THE CHURCH: 1839

The government began distributing funds through the Treasury to the two religious societies shortly after the 1833 provisions passed. The system, thus established, continued with little change until 1839. In 1834, the grant was supplemented by £10,000 for Scotland. In the same year, £10,000 was set aside for the support of model schools. While the National Society expressed some interest in those funds in 1835, they were not disbursed, and that portion of the grant remained unexpended up to 1839.[101] Spokesmen for the government described the system as evenhanded and acceptable; Sir James Kay-Shuttleworth (later to administer the government grants) depicted it as follows: "The Government recognised two principles—that of separate (Church) education, and combined (British and Foreign) education, and then left them to work themselves out."[102] In practice, however, the system yielded the greatest share of the funds to the Established Church. The shares distributed to the societies appear in table 1.

The skewed distribution was not lost on the British and Foreign School Society. In 1835 a delegation of its officials to the chancellor of the exchequer argued unsuccessfully that the government grant should favor groups least able to obtain assistance from other sources.[103] In late 1837 Brougham complained that while it was the initial understanding of the Treasury that half of the funds would go to support the efforts of each religious society, the actual result was far from equitable:

TABLE I    SHARE OF FUNDS DISTRIBUTED TO
RELIGIOUS EDUCATIONAL SOCIETIES, 1834–1838

|        | National Society | British and Foreign School Society |
|--------|------------------|------------------------------------|
| 1834   | £ 11,081         | £9,976                             |
| 1835   | 13,002           | 7,168                              |
| 1836   | 17,130           | 5,281                              |
| 1837   | 11,436           | 5,281                              |
| 1838   | 17,041           | 5,810                              |

SOURCE: *Parliamentary Papers*, 1837–38, 38, p. 328.

This [principle of equal division] was confined to the first year. The British and Foreign Society actually exhausted their funds during that year; it was therefore unable to make a proportionate advance in subsequent years, so that next year upwards of two-thirds or three-fifths, or even four-fifths of the Parliamentary grant went to the National Society, and necessarily so, because that society being richer, was able to make the required proportionate advance. It did not, however, at all follow, that because applications were not made from any given place, therefore there did not exist an equal want of assistance.[104]

This religious grievance was to continue for decades, playing a role in precipitating the withdrawal of some Dissenting bodies from the system of government subsidy to religious societies. The other serious religious grievance was that some groups—notably Roman Catholics and Wesleyan Methodists not affiliated with either society—were excluded from governmental assistance. O'Connell criticized the plan as favoring a "dictatorship in favor of the Established Church," and demanded "equality and justice," asking that the grant be "fairly divided amongst Protestants, Catholics and Dissenters."[105]

Dissatisfactions extended beyond the religious sphere. The voluntary efforts, combined with the extremely modest subsidies, were evidently failing to meet the country's educational needs. Brougham and others complained about this in public debates.[106] Some challenged the estimates of 1834 put forward by Lord Kerry as too generous in describing the extent of education of the poor. In independent examinations, they challenged the accuracy of that portrayal, especially for urban areas. The Manchester Statistical Society, for example, in a survey of schools in the borough of Manchester, concluded that one-third of the children between the ages of five and fifteen were receiving no instruction at all, even in Sunday schools. Voluntary research societies painted an even bleaker picture for other urban centers.[107]

Another range of dissatisfactions manifested the principle that once a government commits itself to an expenditure of public funds, questions about the *adequacy or quality* of the activities supported and the *accountability* of those spending the funds inevitably arise. The Treasury was scarcely a body to address these questions. It was mainly a conduit for funds, insisting on no statements of plans or deeds of trust as conditions for constructing schools. It tended to use the religious societies as go-betweens and did not directly supervise schools. It had no educational expertise or machinery to supervise the educational activities that were being supported.[108] Beyond this general concern, more specific complaints concerned the training and quality of teaching and teachers. The "mass-production" monitorial method was still the main one in use. Even though the religious societies engaged in modest efforts to train teachers, schoolteachers were widely regarded as incompetents who had gone into teaching because they could not succeed in other callings.[109] Much of the attention of parliamentary select committees from 1834 through 1838 focused on the quality of elementary teaching, and in general it was found wanting.[110] A second issue concerned the inspection of schools—a way of securing accountability. Under Treasury support, there was no machinery for inspection. This subject, too, was on the minds of those investigating the state of education of the country in the mid 1830s.[111]

The political and religious situations gave additional salience, urgency, and emotionality to the educational issues of the 1830s.[112] That decade saw the rise of the Chartists, who represented the new voice of the leaders of the working class who had supported parliamentary reform in 1828–32, but who were disappointed in its results and felt deserted by their former middle-class co-advocates. The Chartists not only wished to press constitutional reform to the point of universal suffrage. They also developed a scheme for universal education and initiated some educational enterprises of their own.[113] In addition, Chartism—especially its "physical force" segment—was a source of concern and alarm among the upper and middle classes. An ironic coincidence of the educational debates that occupied Parliament for three evenings—the 14th, 19th, and 20th—in June 1839 was that they were conducted at a climax of Chartist protest. On the evening of June 6th, for example, a question was raised in Parliament as to the degree to which the Char-

tists were arming. And in the very moments before the education debate
was to begin, Thomas Attwood placed the gigantic Chartist petition before the house.[114] It is difficult to imagine a more vivid sign of pressure
on Parliament to direct its attention to the condition of the poor. The
connection between this pressure and educational reform arose in the
debates. Most of the first two nights were consumed with tortured discussions of the religious aspects of the education question. Disraeli
scolded his colleagues for this at the outset of the third evening of
debate:

> The petition of upwards of a million of the people was not to be despised;
> and although hon. Gentlemen opposite might disapprove the prayer of the
> petitioners, yet let them remember that they were that night to decide upon
> the education of those by whom it had been signed. When, then, such was
> the grave and important issue which they had to decide, it certainly did not
> become them to act in the spirit of the Government, who had brought for-
> ward this proposition, and to allow the discussion to degenerate into a mere
> party struggle.[115]

Later, as though in answer, Lord John Russell, whose government was
the target of Disraeli's attack, acknowledged that it would have been
simple enough for his government to act out of alarm in the face of the
Chartist disturbances. Tory governments might have done so twenty or
thirty years before by suspending the Habeas Corpus Act and passing
new laws of coercion. By contrast, he held the belief that the improvement of the state of instruction of the people was the key to securing the
public peace: "The only permanent security for the country is to be
found in the general knowledge of the people, as well of their religious
duties as of their moral obligations, and of their fortunate state as subjects in this free country."[116]

The religious temperature of the country was also rising in the 1830s.
The Nonconformists, emboldened by the apparently greater powers extended to the middle classes by the reform of Parliament, assembled a
collective demand in 1833 for greater relief from disabilities and greater
equity: release from contributions toward any cost of Anglican worship;
the right to be buried by their own ministers; access to the universities,
the right to be married in their own chapels, and a general state policy of
neutrality toward all creeds.[117]

Many in the Church of England were alarmed not only by this increased militancy but by the ongoing accomplishments of the Dissenters
and Catholics: the Toleration Acts of 1828 and 1829; the establishment
of a national system of education in Ireland over the heated objections

of the Anglican Church in 1831; the reduction of the number of Anglican bishoprics in Ireland in 1833; the interest in confiscating the Church of Ireland property in 1834; the appointment of a royal commission to inquire into the revenues and patronage of the Anglican Church in 1836; and the passage of the Marriage Act in 1836. All these developments gave evidence of the steady erosion of the privileges and power of the Establishment.

The most visible reaction to this uneasiness, if not alarm, within the Church of England was the development of the Oxford, or Tractarian, Movement, beginning in 1833. This was prompted most immediately by the suppression of half the Irish bishoprics of the Church of England.[118] The movement had its distinctively theological side, reasserting the apostolic mission of the church as well as traditional High Church orthodoxy.[119] In addition, the Oxford Movement reinvigorated the Anglican Church as an institution and greatly increased its political assertiveness. On the other hand, to many Evangelical churchmen and Wesleyan Methodists—whom John Newman, the most visible leader of the Oxford Movement, regarded as heretical—and some other Nonconformists, the Oxford Movement smacked of a revival of Roman Catholicism. This sentiment, along with the prolonged anti-Catholic backlash that followed the Catholic Emancipation Act of 1829,[120] stimulated a growth of anti-Catholic sentiment in the country that was to reach a crescendo in the mid 1840s with the controversy over subsidizing the training of Irish Catholic clergy at the Maynooth seminary and again in the early 1850s with the "Papal Aggression," or attempt to establish a Catholic hierarchy in England.[121]

From this complex of social, political, and religious forces in the 1830s emerged a pressure for augmented governmental attention to the education of the poor, as well as a situation of heightened religious conflict, within which the accompanying debates over state policy in the educational arena transpired. Contemporaries identified the following lineup of religious opinions:

The voice of the Established Church, which claimed in the extreme case that education should be an ecclesiastical monopoly, sanctioned by divine calling and ancient religious law; and, in the less extreme case, that religious control ought to be maintained over educational efforts on behalf of the poor, even if these were subsidized by the state.

The voice of the Dissenters, who were calling for the establishment of a government system of support of education based on religion but under a policy of complete equality of the denominations; the British and Foreign School Society and independent Nonconformist groups represented this position.

The voice of the secularists, who argued that schools should be strictly civil institutions, and that education should be under the control of the government but confined to civil learning. This was the position of the Central Society for Education, formed in London in 1836, headed by Richard Cobden and incorporating some of the middle-class and utilitarian sentiments that had underlain Roebuck's efforts in 1833. Despite the evident unpopularity of the idea of compulsory attendance, the society endorsed it. It also called for an end to the inefficient monitorial system.

The voice of a party intermediate between the denominationalists and the secularists, who argued that the state should be in charge of secular learning, while the church would remain in charge of religious instruction. The two models that inspired this group were the Irish experiment in national education and the emerging American pattern, built on the constitutional provision of the separation of church and state.[122]

The Central Society for Education was a significant organization, boasting eighteen members of Parliament among its numbers. Its fortunes were damaged, however, when a number of prominent Anglicans, headed by the bishop of London, launched a spirited attack on its principles of secular, compulsory education as inimical to Christianity. In November 1837 the bishop introduced a petition from the town of Cheltenham protesting against the secular scheme. In this connection he asserted that any scheme that excluded the word of God from the education of the poor was "most erroneous, and . . . most unprofitable." Brougham was thrown on the defensive by the attack, pleading that "he did not believe . . . there could exist any intention of promoting any legislative measure, either for the purpose of making the education of the people compulsory on the people (God forbid! unless it intended to make education hateful to the people), or any system of national education which should exclude religious instruction altogether."[123] The bishop's attack also evoked denials by Lord Landsdowne that the government intended to introduce any scheme of education without religious instruction. Lord Denman, a member of the Central Society for Education, denied that members of that society had ever advocated such a position.[124] Under such attack, the society appeared to fall from favor, and by the late 1830s it had more or less passed out of existence.[125]

Despite the heat of educational discussion in the mid 1830s, few efforts at educational reform came forward.[126] The early reports of select committees on education in the 1830s limited themselves simply to presenting the evidence gathered.[127] In 1838, when a select committee submitted its final report, it prefaced its remarks by asserting that the education of the poor in England and Wales was "lamentably deficient" in quality, covering only "a small proportion of those who ought to receive it." The committee predicted that unless the government put forth "strenuous and persevering efforts . . . the greatest evils to all classes may follow from this neglect."[128] In its recommendations, however, it said meekly that "under existing circumstances and under the difficulties which beset the question" (an obvious reference to religious conflict), it was "not prepared to propose any means for meeting the deficiency beyond the continuance and extension of the grants which are at present made by Treasury . . . through the medium of the National and British and Foreign School Societies."[129]

In 1837 Brougham submitted a bill calling for the establishment of a board of education—constituted by ministers of the Crown—that would dispense funds voted by Parliament to areas of the country in need. Brougham denied he intended to introduce a totally general system; he sought only "to assist the further efforts of persons disposed to advance the good work, rather than supplant them."[130] He also ruled out government support of schools that did not have either a churchman or a Dissenter as a master; and he included a kind of conscience clause for Jews and Roman Catholics.[131] Finally, he invoked the argument, by then standard, that education was "the best safeguard against the commission of crime."[132] Without significant support from the Melbourne government's leaders, however, and with steady opposition from the Church, Brougham postponed the bill without a division.[133]

The Whigs' educational plans in 1839, according to Kay-Shuttleworth, were "to improve without altering the basis of popular education."[134] The first improvement was to establish better administrative machinery in the form of a committee of the Privy Council. This was a minimalist proposal. The fate of Brougham's initiative in 1837 indicated how unpopular the idea of a board or ministerial committee was, and how certain its defeat in the Lords was. The government adopted the strategy of creating the committee by an order in council, which did not call for formal parliamentary sanction.[135] Second, it suggested that subsidies would go to religious bodies other than the National and British and Foreign societies. Third, it proposed the creation of a normal and model school for the improved training of teachers. This proposal grew directly from the concern with the quality of teaching and teachers; reformers had pressed for funds for normal schools in the 1834 debates on extending the Treasury grant to Scotland.[136] Fourth, it suggested a plan for governmental inspection of schools. Taken together, the proposals seemed to attempt to meet the outstanding criticisms of the day by extending education further, establishing a body for administering it better, improving its quality, and making it more accountable.

The plan to extend the grants beyond the two societies ran into immediate difficulties. It drew fire from Bishop Blomfield in the House of Lords, who decried it as latitudinarian and irreligious: "if every sect was to have the same advantages as the Established Church, it might as well abdicate its functions."[137] One source of animus here was the "No Popery" alarm generated by the intent to assist Roman Catholic education by the extension of the grants. This played a role in the opposition of the Wesleyan Methodists, who stood to gain by the extension. They had taken a strong anti-Catholic stand during the Emancipation crisis of the late 1820s and were alarmed at the apparent Catholic overtones of the Tractarian Movement. Thus, despite their strained relations with the Anglican Church, the Wesleyans allied with it in opposing the government proposals of 1839.[138]

The plan for teacher training also created a religious uproar. The government had adopted a compromise strategy on religious education in these schools.[139] "General" religious instruction—defined as the teaching of the Protestant version of the Holy Scriptures—was to be given to all teachers-in-training by the masters of the school. "Special" religious instruction—defined as the catechisms and liturgies of the Church of England and the several Dissenting groups—was to be given by clergymen and ministers of the different communions at separate hours. The attacks on this scheme arose mainly from the Anglican Church—supported by the Kirk of Scotland and the Methodists—who opposed the "combined" nature of such religious instruction.[140]

The religious conservatives complained that the state was establishing ministers in the schools to controvert the truths of the Church of England. Furthermore, there would be no end to the process: "if permission were given to use the Popish version, it could not well be refused to the Unitarian version."[141] Sir W. James maintained that "if the Government applied any portion of the funds of the State" to the education of Roman Catholics, "they would adopt a course most hostile and unjust to the rights and interests of the Established Church."[142] And

J. C. Colquhoun predicted nothing but religious squabbling under the arrangement:

> Now what religion was the master to be of? If he were a member of the Church of England, all the other twenty-five sects would clamour against his appointment; and if he belonged to one of the twenty-five sects, the other twenty-four would clamour as loudly against him. If there were a man duly impressed with a sense of the religious principles of the sect to which he belonged, he would, of necessity, impress upon his pupils those religious principles which he himself conscientiously believed; and if he were a man of no religion, would the moral and religious people of England submit to have their children exposed to his tuition? [143]

Under such pressure, and with no major constituency pressing for the normal and model school suggested by the Melbourne administration, the government withdrew the proposal. The responsibility for establishing and operating teacher-training institutions was ultimately given over to the religious societies.

The issue of inspection ran even deeper, and conflict over it escalated further. The government's proposal was that it appoint inspectors to visit the schools periodically and report back to the newly created Committee of the Privy Council on Education. The National Society immediately voiced principled opposition to the scheme, insisting that any inspection that occurred should be under its exclusive control. Initially the society was divided over the best strategy for resisting the government's proposal. Lord Ashley argued for withdrawing immediately from cooperation with the government's subsidy program and proceeding independently. (This was the Voluntaryist strategy adopted by some Nonconformist groups in the 1840s.) The bishop of Exeter pressed for some kind of accommodation with the state. Kay-Shuttleworth and the Committee of Council remained adamant on the subject of governmental inspection, however, even though they continued to assure the Church of England that inspection mainly meant gathering information and affording assistance, rather than exercising control. Late in 1839 the National Society adopted a multiple strategy that ultimately brought the government to heel. First, it refused to accept government grants. This proved to be very effective. Of the 204 National Society applicants who had been promised government aid, only 49 accepted this aid, and of these 14 later withdrew their acceptances. Second, the Anglican Church began a grant scheme of its own, to help applicants who had refused government aid to establish schools independently. Third, it developed an independent inspection scheme of its own rather than submit to the control of "Russell's Pashas," as some labeled them.[144] Finally, at one point it broke off negotiations with the government altogether.[145]

In the middle of 1840 the government capitulated and signed a concordat with the archbishop of Canterbury. This agreement gave the Church of England the power to nominate inspectors of National Schools, to veto appointments when made, and to terminate the appointments of inspectors. It gave the archbishops the right to frame the instructions to inspectors regarding religious education. It required inspectors to send copies of their reports to the archbishop and to the local bishop. The settlement, a clear victory for the Anglican Church, left the British and Foreign School Society embittered. During the controversy, the society had demanded a scheme of inspection independent of the churches. But when the concordat with the Church of England was signed, the British and Foreign School Society did not receive parallel privileges. It had to fight for these until they were extended in 1843.[146]

The combination of a weak Melbourne-Russell administration and a reinvigorated and adamant Anglican Church (with some important allies) became apparent in the narrow margin by which the government escaped defeat on its remaining educational proposals. A motion to rescind the order of council establishing the Committee of Council was rejected by only five votes. The government's motion to pass the annual grant, now increased to £30,000, was passed by only two votes, 275 to 273.[147]

By one measure, the results of 1839–40 constitute a non-event. The government dropped its schemes for extending the grants to teacher-training altogether. It yielded almost total control to the Church of England with respect to inspection. It was barely able to take a single step toward the formalization of a government body to administer the educational grants. By another standard, however, those results were decisive. The initial Treasury grant of 1833 had raised the level of debate from "if" to "how" with respect to government involvement. The formation of the Committee of Council—with a secretary and tiny staff—elaborated the "how." It permitted the government to institutionalize procedures—for example, trust deeds to accompany grants—and records, themselves important instruments of control. The establishment of inspection, however humbling it was for the government, also changed the definition of the situation from one of "if" to one of "how." Any new discussions, debates, and conflicts with respect to these new arrangements would now be based on a different, more advanced platform than those that had gone before.

## A REPRISE OF 1820: 1843

The period from 1839 to 1843 was not noteworthy with respect to the growth of the subsidized voluntary system of education for the laboring classes. The education grant remained stable at £30,000 and was limited to support for the building of schools. Certain minor administrative advances and consolidations were, however, beginning to take shape. In 1840 the government quietly included the Wesleyan School Society among the groups who could apply for government grants and provided for inspection of its schools on the same basis as British schools.[148] The government appointed two inspectors, John Allen and Hugh Seymour Tremenheere, who began their work. Consistent with the concordat, the Committee of Council issued cautious instructions to the inspectors. It reminded them that "this inspection is not intended as a means of exercising control" and admonished them to refrain from any "interference with the duties peculiarly belonging to spiritual teachers," except when invited to do so by the local clergyman or a minister connected with the school. The committee asked the inspectors to report whether the Bible was being read in schools not connected with the two religious societies, however, and to inquire about due regard for rights of religious conscience.[149]

The inspectors were also requested to report on the monitorial system, on the numbers of teachers and monitors, and on the level of the children's accomplishments.[150] This opened the door for the inspectors to lend their voices to the criticism of the monitorial system, the quality of teaching and the qualifications of teachers. In doing this, they were to provide important arguments for the reforms of 1846.[151] The committee itself began issuing deeds of trust to new schools and laying down specifications for new buildings. It also formalized the criteria for preferring one application over another (e.g., whether there was a great deficiency of education for the poor in the district, whether the application contained provision for a conscience clause, etc.).[152]

The new system of inspection did not escape problems arising from religious sources. In the wake of the great struggle over inspection of 1839–40, the National Society remained guarded and suspicious about government inspectors. At one point, John Allen, the inspector for National Society schools, refused to present his reports to the Committee of Council, but he backed down in the face of strong committee pressure.[153] The aggravations of the leaders of the British and Foreign School Society were more severe. They rankled under the idea that Tremenheere, an Anglican, was inspecting their schools, and they were espe-

TABLE 2    SHARE OF FUNDS DISTRIBUTED TO
RELIGIOUS EDUCATIONAL SOCIETIES, 1839–1844

|  | National Society | British and Foreign School Society |
|---|---|---|
| 1839 | £ 5,369.17.0 | £ 5,556.10.0 |
| 1840 | 3,149.7.0 | 3,023.0.0 |
| 1841 | 20,197.18.4 | 10,945.10.0 |
| 1842 | 24,961.15.10 | 901.0.0 |
| 1843 | 22,105.0.0 | 2,384.0.0 |
| 1844 | 27,866.17.3 | 2,149.0.0 |

SOURCES: *Parliamentary Papers,* 1840, 40, pp. 1–19, and 1851, 43, pp. 126–39.
NOTE: In 1840 granting to the National Society was disrupted during the struggle over school inspection.

cially antagonistic to his negative reports on the condition of their schools. In the early 1840s they pressed for his removal.[154] They also felt deprived on grounds of parity. The government had been ready enough, in 1840, to extend the principles of the concordat with the Anglican Church to the Church of Scotland. It resisted going further, however, either in "signing on" the British and Foreign School Society on the same basis as the Church of England, or appointing inspectors in place of or in addition to Tremenheere. Under continued pressure for parity, and given a chance to break the deadlock when Tremenheere was appointed inspector of mines in 1843, the government extended to the society privileges relating to inspection enjoyed by the established churches of England and Scotland.[155] The running sore over inspection, plus their continuing disadvantage with respect to the share of the grant received (see table 2 for the years 1839–44), also fed the Nonconformists' sense of deprivation.

The "condition of the people" question reached perhaps its most critical point in the century in the early 1840s. The depression of 1841–42 created great distress throughout the country and the most serious levels of unemployment in the manufacturing districts.[156] Working-class protest ran very high, with the continuing activities of the Chartists, the Rebecca disturbances in Wales, the "Plug Plot" of 1842, and strikes against machinery in the manufacturing districts. These were also years of grim revelations about economic and social conditions by several parliamentary investigating committees on the mills and factories, mines, sanitary conditions, and the state of children.[157] The condition of the country was foremost in the awareness of political leaders. In 1843 Sir James Graham, home secretary in the Peel government, who was to present the educational measures of that year, spoke of "a social insurrection of a formidable character."[158] Kay-Shuttleworth, while stopping short of characterizing the Chartist and other convulsions as civil war, nonetheless said it was "likely that persons and property will . . . be so exposed to violence as materially to affect the prosperity of our manufacturers and commerce, to shake the mutual confidence of mercantile men and to destroy the stability of our political and social institutions."[159]

Graham, a conservative, came forth with the Whiggish view on the social and political role of education.[160] Speaking in March 1843, he said:

> The events of last autumn . . . have convinced us that not a moment should be lost in endeavouring to impart the blessings of a sound education to the rising generation in the manufacturing districts. . . . I am informed that the turbulent masses, who, in the course of last autumn, threatened the safety of property . . . were remarkable for the youth of the parties composing them . . . if some ten years ago we could have been so fortunate as to agree upon some . . . comprehensive scheme of education . . . my firm belief is that the outrages which took place last autumn . . . would never have taken place.[161]

Thus, in 1843, as in 1820, 1833, and 1839, the specter of class warfare gave urgency to the impulse for educational reform.

The class situation of the early 1840s also included a bitter antagonism between the manufacturing interests and the Tories, representing in large part aristocratic interests, stemming mainly from the agitation to repeal the Corn Laws. In their statements before Parliament, Graham and Lord Ashley, the latter a pioneer in the movement to restrict factory hours, repeatedly singled out the manufacturing districts as centers of the greatest distress, poverty, educational backwardness, and social disruption.[162] They cited the reports of parliamentary commissions and committees in this connection. In doing this, they excited regional, class, and religious antagonisms, by focusing on the industrial Midlands and north of England, which were also heavily populated with Dissenters. In response, Edward Baines, Jr., soon to appear as a militant religious and educational voice, wrote a polemic entitled *The Social, Educational, and Religious State of the Manufacturing Districts,*[163] which contained statistics refuting the findings of the commissions, attacking conservative critics, and attempting to restore the moral dignity of the urban Midlands and north. At the same time Baines issued an equally shrill attack on the pending educational legislation of 1843 as an example of Church of England and state interference with the religious liberty of Dissenters.[164]

The Peel government introduced its educational clauses of 1843 in the context of this regional-class-religious struggle. Long in preparation, the educational clauses were part of legislation, pressed by Lord Ashley, further limiting children's hours of work in the manufactories, thus seeming to single out the manufacturing districts.[165] The bill called for deductions from children's wages, supplemented by public funds, for the schooling of factory children in districts outlined in the Poor Law legislation.

The religious provisions of the bill provoked the greatest interest and public storm. Teachers in the factory schools were to be members of the Church of England. The Holy Scriptures were to be taught, and children of parents belonging to the Anglican Church would be instructed according to its catechism and liturgy. To accommodate possible objections, Graham wrote a conscience clause into the bill, giving children of non-Anglican parents the right to receive religious instruction separately, if the parents asked for it. The composition of school boards of trustees would be tilted toward, if not controlled by, the Church of England. Of the seven trustees called for, three were to be church officials, and the four others nominated by the local magistrates. Inspection was to be done by the clerical trustees.

Graham had done preparatory political work, having secured the support of Russell, Brougham, and Kay-Shuttleworth of the Committee of Council, as well as of Peel and the conservative cabinet.[166] In fact, he announced upon introducing the legislation that "he did not anticipate any objection to the principle of the bill from any quarter."[167] Subsequent events failed to justify this anticipation. An enormous outcry erupted in the Nonconformist press and elsewhere. Opposing petitions signed by millions, mainly Dissenters, flooded Parliament in the ensuing months. The Wesleyan Methodists, now more apprehensive than ever about the Oxford Movement and Roman Catholicism in the Church of England, also opposed the measure on grounds that it gave too much control to the Anglicans.[168] Roman Catholic spokesmen also opposed the bill. Finally, it excited criticism from the pocket of secularism that remained after the collapse of that movement in the late 1830s.[169] Later in 1843 Graham put forward an "olive branch" that contained a number of concessions to the Dissenting groups, but the opposition in the country continued, and the government was forced to withdraw the bill. Bitterness remained, as Ashley complimented the Anglican Church on its willingness to compromise and chided the Dissenters for "rejoicing that they had been successful in their efforts to defeat the measure." [170] Ashley had supported the Graham bill but was offended by its ultimate compromises, adopted to gain the Nonconformists' support. He gave up all hope of a denominationally mixed system of education with a common religious denominator. "Combined education," he wrote, "must never again be attempted; it is an impossibility and worthless if possible." [171]

In one respect the events of 1843 add up to a cipher, since nothing happened legislatively to advance the country's educational effort or to change its status. However, the controversy left in its wake a number of effects that were to alter the political and religious landscape and condition future developments in education.

First, the episode resembled that of 1820. A sustained effort to establish a state-supported educational apparatus under essential control of the Established Church failed, largely because of opposition by religious dissenters. Unlike in 1820, however, the defeat of the Church of England was permanent. No legislation based on formal religious principles other than religious parity was ever again brought forward.

Second, the episode marked a victory for Dissent that more than matched its subordination in 1839–40. Unified as the Dissenters were against the Graham proposals, however, the events of 1843 created an internal split among them that was to hobble their political and educational efforts in the next quarter-century. That split produced two distinct groups: (1) most Dissenters who opted to remain with the plan of government subsidy of voluntary educational efforts under the aegis of the British and Foreign School Society; (2) another group, headed by Edward Baines, Jr., which consisted mainly of Congregationalists and Independents who called themselves Voluntaryists. The name reveals their impulse. In the legislative fight of 1843 (and later in 1846), they became convinced that *any* government involvement in the education of the poor would end in domination by the Established Church.[172] The only way to guarantee religious freedom in education was to proceed voluntarily and create a system of schools completely independent of government support.[173] The movement, while it never seriously challenged the ongoing system of government-assisted voluntary education, had a meaningful impact in some areas such as South Wales.[174] The Voluntaryist movement also added strength to a broader associational grouping of the same name that was to have a visible political role as a quasi-party in the decade after 1843.

Third, the heightened religious competition generated by the struggle of 1843 gave an evident impetus to the voluntary efforts of many religious parties, both inside and outside the government system. The Voluntaryists began their work. The Church of England formed the Anglican National Society—with Peel heading the list of donors—to establish schools in the manufacturing districts.[175] The Anglican Church also launched an offensive in Wales, which the British and Foreign School Society countered.[176] In total the requests for building grants in the year following the controversy of 1843 more than doubled that of the preceding year. On the basis of this increase, Kay-Shuttleworth estimated that if that rate were to continue, the size of the parliamentary grant would have to multiply to nearly £180,000 for 1845–46.[177] These voluntary efforts were to continue through the decade, providing an impetus to growth in a system over which the government and religious bodies seemed locked in paralysis.

Fourth, there were other minor modifications that constituted significant openings for future growth. More or less immediately after the collapse of Graham's initiative, the Peel administration authorized the Committee of Council to extend the range of grants beyond constructing schools to providing houses for schoolmasters and schoolmistresses and for school furnishings. Also in 1843, the National Society began submitting requests for funds to take on pupil-teachers—assistants who were older than the children used in the monitorial system. Both these actions were signs that pointed toward expansions of the system in 1846. The scope of inspection and the number of inspectors were expanded.[178] In addition, the government approved the initiation of training colleges for teachers under the direction of the religious societies. Kay-Shuttleworth had himself been the principal of the normal school in Battersea for a number of years; in 1843 the management of this institution was transferred to the National Society.[179] Finally, the inclusion of the British and Foreign Society in the inspection scheme meant the appointment of an additional inspector—making a total of only three, however.

Fifth, the Committee of Council had set in motion a principle of support that was soon to become general. The effort to establish a multi-denominational normal and model school had failed in 1839, mainly through the opposition of the Church of England and its allies. The "way around" this opposition, realized in 1843, was to provide grants to teacher-training institutions initiated by the religious societies. The governmental capitulation to the British and Foreign School Society on the issue of inspection meant that inspection, too, was now organized along denominational lines. In these ways the principle of proliferation along religious lines, begun with the original grant in 1833, was becoming more firmly established as a government policy. The government's motives were largely those of desperation and defense. All *general* efforts to involve government in educational activities were foundering because of religious jealousies and the power of one or another set of religious groups to veto them. In this sense the government was doing the only thing it could under the circumstances: separating the religious combatants by giving money to them separately and inspecting them separately. The government was to carry on with this policy for almost two decades longer, at which time it became so expensive and unworkable that it required breaking.

## CHAPTER 5

# Truce Points and Moments of Change (2)

## THE CONSOLIDATION OF GROWTH UNDER PRIMORDIAL PROLIFERATION: 1846

The years 1843–46 were mixed ones for those pressing for an extension of working-class schooling. On the one hand, the heated competition among the religious groups, with the assistance of a few minor improvements under the Peel administration, gave an impetus to growth within the voluntary system, supplemented as it was by subsidization. The government began what was to become a steady program of annual increases in level of support. The grant, held at roughly £30,000 through 1843, was increased to £39,000 in 1844, £54,000 in 1845, and £58,000 in 1846—a doubling, though the amounts were still small in absolute terms. On the other hand, Kay-Shuttleworth and his reformist friends, mostly Whigs, were living through Peel's conservative government, which was generally unfriendly to major educational reforms. Kay-Shuttleworth had supported Sir James Graham's proposals of 1843, while pressing for greater toleration for non-Anglican minorities in their provisions.[1] In light of the irreducible denominational jealousies, however, the decisive defeat of Graham's proposals seemed to negate the possibility of a national system that gave religious education a central place. Kay-Shuttleworth pressed for other reforms, but those that the Peel government was willing to concede were only minor. The level of Kay-Shuttleworth's frustration can be measured by his jubilant communication to Lord John Russell when the latter was invited to assume power in 1845:

I am now able to restore into your hands the Education Department not only I trust uninjured, but, though not advanced by legislation, developed from being a mere whim of the Privy Council Office to a public department requiring reorganisation. I've remained in this office in the hope that, on your Lordship's presumption of power, there might be no insurmountable difficulty to the completion of the structure of a truly national education, and that you would be disposed to finish the work you began [referring to 1839].[2]

These hopes were momentarily dashed, inasmuch as Peel soon returned as prime minister, but Kay-Shuttleworth's aspirations must have been even higher in the summer of 1846, when Russell formed a Whig government, with a badly divided conservative opposition.

The transition from a reluctant government to one friendly to educational change was only one of the economic, religious, and political forces shaping the important educational reforms of 1846. In England between 1843 and 1846, the most visible evidence of economic and class conflict was the climax of the long struggle between the agricultural and the manufacturing classes over the Corn Laws, which were finally repealed in 1846. The great improvement of trade from 1843 to late 1846 and the strong agricultural performance of 1843 and 1844 helped to calm the working-class unrest that so alarmed the ruling groups in 1843. In the educational debates of 1846, expression of fears of insurrection and civil disorder was conspicuously absent. Economic disaster struck in Ireland with the famines, however, and the political situation there once again became critical.

As indicated, 1843 had produced both solidarity and a sense of victory among almost all Dissenters, the Wesleyan Methodists, and the Roman Catholics in their opposition to the educational clauses and the Anglican Church. This unity proved momentary, however, as the religious picture was becoming more intense and complex in the few years leading up to 1846. Within the Church of England, the division between the High Church party and the Evangelicals was greatly exacerbated by the conversion of John Newman and others to Roman Catholicism. This brought the Oxford Movement to an extreme conclusion and apparently confirmed the worst prejudices of its antagonists.[3] Newman's conversion fanned the anti-Catholicism of the Wesleyan Methodists and deepened the division between them and the Church of England, but without, however, driving the Wesleyans fully into the arms of Dissent.[4] The Dissenters themselves were split between those who were more or less content with the religious status quo—that is, an Establishment combined with religious freedom—and two overlapping militant wings: the Voluntaryists, whose position consolidated in 1843 and who opposed all state involvement in education, and a group that favored the general disestablishment of the Church of England. The latter coalesced into the British Anti–State Church Association in 1844, which became the Society for the Liberation of Religion from State Patronage and Control in 1853.[5] In Scotland, 1843 was the year of the Disruption, the political culmination of a long struggle over authority within the Scottish religious Establishment. This break produced the Free Church of Scotland, which proved to be a political competitor with the General Assembly of the Kirk of Scotland in many fields, education being among them.[6]

This complicated religious picture was clouded even more by the Maynooth controversy of 1845, which produced a new mix of both religious and political allies and antagonists. That controversy, to be revisited in chapter 7, stemmed from Peel's general policy of conciliation as a way of dealing with the explosive Irish situation in the early 1840s.[7] Peel's specific initiative was to provide a large augmentation of the annual government subsidy to the Maynooth Seminary, the central institution for training Catholic priests in Ireland. This was to be a gesture of goodwill toward Ireland, which would provide superior training for priests, and would, it was hoped further, generate a more loyal attitude toward the English government. Peel's reasoning was as follows:

> The Lord Lieutenant tells us that the real enemies of the government and the really powerful incendiaries are the young priests . . . the College of Maynooth as it is at present governed and scantily provided for, is a public nuisance. . . . We educate Priests, more than half of the number for the yearly supply of all Ireland, and the wit of man could not devise a more effectual method for converting them into sour, malignant demagogues, hostile to the law, . . . living by agitation, inclined to it and fitted for it by our eleemosynary but penurious system of education.[8]

Though the Maynooth subsidy had existed since 1796, and had been the target of attacks by Anglicans from time to time in the interim, Peel's proposal set off an enormous controversy in 1845.

The groups favoring the Maynooth augmentation were mainly Roman Catholics in both Ireland and England—whose reasons were straightforward—and moderate Anglicans, including Peel himself, Russell, and Brougham,[9] who believed the augmentation to be a politically appropriate response to the Irish situation. Formidable opposition developed immediately among the Presbyterian and Anglican minorities in

Ireland, who feared any measure that might benefit the Catholic majority. This antagonism spread to some Scottish Presbyterians[10]—especially the new, Evangelical Free Church of Scotland—and to some
Anglicans in England. The latter opposed any gesture that seemed to
establish or endow any church other than their own; the Maynooth
issue also appeared to excite their traditional animosity toward Roman
Catholicism. Representatives like Inglis and Ashley spoke out vig-
orously in Parliament.[11] (The Church of England position was undoubtedly intensified by the bitter defeat dealt the church by the religious
coalition of dissenting groups opposing the educational clauses in
1843.) The Anglican Church was joined by the Wesleyans, also ani-
mated by a strong anti-Catholic sentiment. Some Dissenters were also
opposed, because they had never enjoyed anything like the kind of
"concurrent endowment" apparently now offered to the Catholics in
Ireland.[12] This Dissenting opposition was especially strong among the
Voluntaryists, who opposed the grant as part of their general antagonism to the role of the state in education.[13]

   This coalition of Anglican churchmen, Wesleyans, and many Dissenters differed greatly from the alignment in 1843. The irony was not lost
on Graham, who commented on it, and attributed the anti-Maynooth
religious alliance to a shared anti-Catholic animus.[14] One parliamentarian G. Bankes, labeled Inglis, normally a predictable voice of militant
Anglicanism, the new "representative of the English Dissenters."[15] Both
Russell and Brougham lamented the destructive religious passions that
underlay the sectarian split over the Maynooth issue.[16] The controversy
divided the conservatives along much the same lines as it split the Anglican Church. In that respect, it served as a kind of religious prelude to
the political split of 1846, when Peel went over to the side of those
favoring repeal of the Corn Laws, thus alienating the Tory-agriculturalist
wing of the Conservatives, and occasioning its split from the Peelites.[17]
Aside from this political effect, the Maynooth controversy heightened
religious passions, and contributed to the growing anti-Catholic sentiment in Britain.[18]

   Such was the kaleidoscope of religious opinion in 1846 when Russell
and Kay-Shuttleworth brought forth new educational minutes. These
reforms called for expanding the operations of the Committee of Council in several ways. The main change was the introduction of the pupil-
teaching system and the expansion of support to teacher-training institutions. These measures were in large part a response to the long-standing
concern over the poor quality of teachers and teaching and dissatis-

factions with the monitorial system, fed by the inspectors' reports and acknowledged by the religious societies.[19] Under the new minutes, qualified teachers were to receive an augmentation of salary for taking on pupil-teachers (assistants of adolescent age). The pupil-teachers themselves were to receive a modest stipend, and made eligible to compete for admission into and support under a queen's scholarship at the teacher-training institutions for professional training. This also entailed expanding the number of training institutions and the number of inspectors. In addition, the minutes proposed funding an educational apparatus for learning trades in the workshops and in the fields. Finally, the minutes provided for a pension scheme for teachers who served fifteen years or more in approved schools.

These proposals are noteworthy in that they did little to disrupt the existing *structure* of funding. This was to continue as a system of private subscriptions by religious bodies, combined with government subsidies. The formula was the familiar one of improving and expanding within the existing parameters. It reflected both the strong reformist motivation of Kay-Shuttleworth and his allies and the realistic limits established by the events of 1839 and 1843.[20] These limits were that neither any general solution that gave official favor to the Church of England nor any principle other than formal equity among religious competitors was feasible. The religious and political paralysis of the past decade had taught reformers that the only way to engineer change through the maze of interests was to respect all of them and defend reforms on the grounds that they were honoring the principle of equity and disturbing no one group's interests.

The government's campaign for the proposals, such as it was, began with the publication by Walter Farquhar Hook, vicar of Leeds and a High Churchman, of a pamphlet on educational reform that Kay-Shuttleworth had assisted in preparing.[21] In it Hook praised the clergy for spreading education and raising its esteem throughout society. He argued further, however, that the existing voluntary system was hopelessly inadequate in both quantity and quality: "It is impossible for voluntary associations to meet the wants of the nation by a sufficient supply of school-rooms and competent masters."[22] Any effort to establish a state-supported educational system on a religious basis was, furthermore, impossible because of religious jealousies. The "practical English mind," he asserted, could not think of religion without simultaneously thinking of *what* religion was intended:

The Churchman asks, is education to be based on *my* religion? if it be I am ready to sacrifice everything in order to work with the State. But no; this cannot be; for this would exclude a large and influential portion of the community, the Protestant Dissenters. And then comes the question from the Dissenters; will you base education upon Protestantism, or the admission of every species of doctrine and opinion except those which are peculiar to the Church of Rome? This cannot be; because it would lead to the rejection of the Roman Catholics. Will you base religion, then, on the Bible, and the Bible only? The difficulty now occurs as to the version to be used, whether the authorised version, the Roman Catholic version, or the "Unitarian" version.[23]

If religious instruction were presented in special denominational terms, it would trigger insoluble conflicts. If it were presented as a common denominator of religious beliefs, it would appear as no religion, also unacceptable to the "English mind." Having set up these premises, Hook could conclude only that the state should supply "literary or secular instruction," leaving religious education to the denominations.[24]

Hook's pamphlet set off a flurry of controversy. The High Church attacked it because of its heterodox rejection of its monopoly over the people's education.[25] This objection was somewhat muted, however, because the Church of England generally favored expansion of a system in which it maintained a continuing advantage. Moreover, the relations between the Committee of Council and the Anglicans had not yet been soured by imminent conflict over the management of schools.[26] The strongest voice of opposition that emerged in the war of words that Hook's pamphlet touched off was that of the Voluntaryists, headed by Edward Baines, Jr. In a series of pamphlets, Baines laid out argument after argument against the minutes—their unconstitutionality and their increase of government expenditure, influence, power, and interference. The main animus, however, was religious. The minutes should be opposed mainly because of

[the] new religious Establishment formed in the country, as an appendage to the Church, and the new legislative sanction given to the teaching of the Church Catechism . . . the fearful amount of influence and patronage given to the Parochial Clergy . . . the shameful injustice to Dissenters, in taxing them for a new religious Establishment. . . . The certain effect of the measure to destroy the schools of the Dissenters.[27]

Admiring as he was of American education in its separation of church and state, Baines nevertheless opposed it as a state system; he called for a system of completely "free and voluntary Education" in England.[28] Kay-Shuttleworth himself wrote an anonymous pamphlet in 1847 entitled *The School, in Its Relations to the State, the Church and the Congregation,* in which he attacked the Voluntaryist anti-state position, and defended the minutes' equitability, helpfulness, and "[conduciveness] to the interests of civil and religious liberty."[29]

The Dissenters remained split on this matter. The British and Foreign School Society, having separated from the Voluntaryists in 1843 by staying with the government system, supported the minutes of 1846, standing to gain continued general support and the opportunity to expand its training colleges in particular.[30] The Methodists played a unique and interesting role. Dissociated from the Church of England, and unable to have their members teach in their schools, the Wesleyans formed an independent religious party. For a time, they proceeded to establish day schools on a voluntary basis (sometimes receiving assistance through the British and Foreign School Society).[31] Their progress, however, was slow. In the years of denominational competition after 1843, the Methodists expanded from 290 day schools in that year (20,804 scholars) to 395 in 1847 (37,341 scholars).[32]

In 1846 the Committee of Council expressed a willingness to include the Methodists in the government funding scheme on terms identical to those of the other religious societies.[33] The issue had been raised before, but the Peel government had vetoed the proposal in 1843.[34] The invitation caused a rift in the Wesleyan body. The moderates were eager to benefit from the government support, but the militants were apprehensive on anti-Catholic grounds. If the Evangelical churches accepted state aid, "there would be no logical reason why Roman Catholics should not also secure State pecuniary help in running their schools."[35] (A few Catholic efforts to secure Treasury grants had stalled, and no funds had as yet been given to Catholic religious societies or schools, except for one group that accommodated to British and Foreign School Society policies.)[36] As an indication of this concern, the Methodists asked that all schools supported by the government should use the Authorized Version of the Bible.[37] The government apparently handled the issue with the Wesleyans by assuring them that they would have the same privileges as the other religious societies—including partial control over inspection—and that the Roman Catholics would not gain access simultaneously with them.[38] The government gave an indication to the Catholics, however, that they would be brought in on the same basis later.[39] By these assurances the government secured agreement from the Methodists and the Catholics that they would not oppose the minutes.

Given the emerging lineup of religious groups, the overall response to the minutes was scarcely in doubt. The Church of England, many Dissenters, the Wesleyan Methodists, and the Roman Catholics supported or acquiesced in them, as did the Unitarians. The Society of Friends and the Free Church of Scotland took no denominational action.[40] The Voluntaryists, virtually isolated in opposition,[41] were able to mobilize some 4,068 petitions containing 546,343 signatures against the minutes, pale in comparison with the 113,369 petitions containing 2,068,059 signatures against Graham's educational clauses in 1843.[42] A handful of Anglo-Catholics, who still opposed state control of the Anglican Church in the area of education, joined the Voluntaryists in opposition to the minutes, but by this time they were a weakened force.[43]

Within Parliament itself, the debate was relatively calm and brief. John Bright represented the opposing position of Voluntaryism with a secularist expression of sentiment favoring the U.S. model. Some questions from the floor dealt with the place of the Methodists and the Catholics in the scheme.[44] Peel and Graham supported the measure,[45] and Gladstone had earlier indicated that he would "like to try a larger extension of the present [educational] system before altering it fundamentally."[46] The final vote was an overwhelming majority of 372 to 47 on behalf of the government.

With these minutes, the government set into place an educational system, the fundamental parameters of which were not altered until 1870, even though the Revised Code of 1862 was to have some major redirecting influences. The measure was significant in several respects:

It marked the end of an earlier debate about the fundamental role of government. Hook was correct when he wrote: "[We] live in an age when the question is not *whether* but *how* the poor are to be educated."[47]

Despite the minimalist character of the minutes—adding to the existing system without altering its basic defining parameters—the provisions opened the door to an enormous expansion of governmental expenditure, particularly for the payment of teachers and their pupil-teacher assistants, and for the support of colleges for the training of teachers.

It stabilized political relations among the contending religious parties. Ashley had observed that the defeat of the educational clauses of 1843 established that both Anglicans and Dissenters now had their own separate spheres of influence and that, formally and legislatively, neither could gain ground at the expense of the other.[48] With the inclusion of the Methodists and the Free Church of Scotland in the scheme, and with the promised inclusion of the Roman Catholics, this generalization could now be extended to other religious groups as well.

The ultimate basis for the religious solution of 1846 was the "religious difficulty" as Hook had sketched it. Education had to be religious, but the religious parties would not tolerate formal government sponsorship of or inclusion of particular religious doctrines or rituals in state-financed or state-administered schools. Faced with these difficulties, the government responded by creating a system that, in Robert Lowe's words, "offended no honest prejudices, but left every sect free to teach its religion as it understood it, and merely gave the assistance of the Government in that good work."[49] This was the consolidation of the system of proliferation along primordial lines that was to characterize working-class education during the quarter-century between 1846 and 1870. The subdivision of primary education invaded all facets of the Committee of Council's educational efforts—schools, training colleges, and the inspectorate—and even the schools provided by the manufacturers under the factory legislation were subdivided along religious lines.[50] The political solution of 1846 had a paradoxical result with regard to state involvement. On the one hand, the government expanded its operations enormously. Simultaneously, however, it solidified a range of religious groups with vested interests—vested because they secured resources from the subsidized voluntary system. Archdeacon George Denison, the High Church warrior of the 1850s and 1860s, called 1846 the year of the "introduction of bribery-power."[51] The grain of truth in this embittered description is that the agreements associated with the minutes made the denominations parties to the system and created a symbiotic relationship between them and the state. The constellation of forces that resulted constituted, in effect, an obstacle to independent government development of schooling. In fact, it was mainly because the Voluntaryists in particular and the Nonconformists in general continued to operate at such a disadvantage under the arrangements established in 1846 that they began to abandon that system and press for full state involvement.


RAPID EDUCATIONAL GROWTH AND
POLITICAL PARALYSIS: 1846–1861

The "truce point" established by the minutes of 1846 was to be a stable one in that the growth of working-class education proceeded along existing institutional tracks for a sustained period without major "constitutional" change. The elements of the truce point were the decisions (a) to continue the voluntary system with government subsidy; (b) to expand the scope of government; (c) to confirm the compact among government and the religious groups that the former would prefer none of the latter formally, but would be guided by the criteria of evenhandedness and equity; and (d) to permit the educational system to proliferate along religious lines, each group maintaining essential control over religious instruction and a great deal of control over the management and inspection of the schools. By 1862 there were nine types of schools supported: Church of England, British and Foreign, Established Church of Scotland, Wesleyan, Free Church of Scotland, Roman Catholic, Jewish, Episcopal Church (Scotland), and undenominational (schools belonging to none of the previous classes, but in which the Bible was read daily from the authorized version).[52]

By all measures the system of education for the poor grew significantly on these denominational tracks. The contours of this growth will be traced presently. The growth took place, however, in the context of some continuing tension and conflict between the state and its constituencies. Over time, it generated anomalies and imbalances that set the stage for the changes of the 1860s. Side by side with growth, moreover, apprehension persisted that the educational system was failing to provide comprehensive and adequate educational coverage of the children of the working classes. Finally, the larger religious conflicts continued to spill over into the educational scene. In Parliament, reformers launched effort after effort to alter and expand the system by government action, but religious and political conflict stymied all of these. The period was thus one of several separate dramas. In this section I shall fill out this complex picture.

GENERAL FEATURES OF THE PERIOD

The years 1846–61 overlap with the high Victorian period of prosperity and stability in British society. This period is commonly seen as extending from 1851, the year of the triumphant Crystal Palace Exhibition, to 1867, that of the passing of the second parliamentary reform bill.[53] Asa Briggs calls the period "The Age of Improvement."[54] Among other labels, W. L. Burn considered Walter Bagehot's epithet "The Age of Discussion" (so called because there was interminable talk on many subjects, including elementary education, leading to no tangible results), but finally chose *The Age of Equipoise* (referring to the fine balance among social institutions and classes) as the title of his study of it.[55] Briggs describes the era as interweaving the themes of thought, work, progress, a common moral code, and a strong faith in institutions, as well as smugness and dullness resulting from a national sense of self-satisfaction.[56] At the same time there were some signs of uncertainty and ugliness: the ripple of self-doubt about Britain's international economic competitiveness at the time of the Great Exhibition of 1851 and, more seriously, the Paris Exhibition of 1867;[57] religious and ethnic bigotry, especially the anti-Catholic hysteria dramatized by the "Papal Aggression" of establishing a regular Catholic hierarchy in England;[58] and a subterranean preoccupation with sex and sexual perversions.[59]

Economic activity rose steeply in the period, despite short-lived depressions such as that of 1857–58. Exports, having reached a record high of £60 million in the boom year of 1845, soared to £136 million in 1860, and doubled again in the following decade. J. R. T. Hughes attributes this extraordinary prosperity to the fruits of free trade; gold discoveries, especially in California; investment opportunities; and war (no fewer than five military undertakings from 1848 to 1860).[60] Agriculture continued to prosper, in a kind of honeymoon period from the repeal of the Corn Laws in 1846 to the disastrous effects of competition from American and Russian grain beginning in the 1870s. By and large, industrial peace reigned, with unions consolidating themselves organizationally and bidding to share in the prosperity.[61] The working classes were generally quiescent, despite the last significant episode of Chartist protest in 1848. Several strands of radicalism continued, especially in the industrial cities of the north, but failed to coalesce.[62] A new mobilization of labor developed before the Reform Act of 1867 and the political role of the working classes grew rapidly thereafter. G. Kitson Clark describes this "high noon of Victorianism" as follows:

> It was not . . . likely that either the class struggle, or for that matter, the battle for popular radicalism would decide the shape of politics in the early years of the Victorian interlude. After 1848 the pressures behind both of them died away. Chartism flickered out, the agitation for factory reform died down, . . . and the attack on the new Poor Law ceased.
>     . . . As conditions became easier, the tension between the middle class and the working class seems to have slackened and they appeared to live together in the great cities which they had formed. Meanwhile popular radicalism was at a discount. When the Corn Laws were repealed the Anti-Corn Law League was dissolved and though John Bright was still anxious to lead the assault on the battlements of privilege he could never get enough determined followers to give him much chance to make any impression.[63]

Yet the assumptions of class and the language of class continued to be the main organizing basis of society. Most institutions and organizations were segregated along class lines—education in particular—and this seemed to be more or less taken for granted as the correct way of organizing things. One feature of the period was the increased talk of the possibilities of social mobility by political and intellectual leaders such as Palmerston, Bagehot, and Mill;[64] the books of Samuel Smiles and the popular press sounded the gospel of success through self-help.[65] The rigidities of class were also muted by the growing difficulty of drawing precise lines between the classes, and of internal gradations within classes.[66] Many of the empirical facts of the life of class—the actual levels of social mobility, the degree of class antagonism—are not adequately known, but by comparison with the 1830s and 1840s, the 1850s and 1860s were years of relative balance and peace among the classes.

G. I. T. Machin suggests that religion in the 1850s displayed "something of the equipoise visible in other spheres," but adds that the situation was one of "tense equilibrium."[67] The religious census of 1851 confirmed the very high percentage of Dissenters in the population, and apparently emboldened that group. They were relatively quiet politically, however, until the 1860s.[68] Despite this, the march of religious liberalism continued, with concessions to Dissenters and Roman Catholics, and later to Jews and Tractarians; so, too, did the government's extension of control over marriage and poor relief, domains previously controlled by religious bodies.[69] At different times, religious parties pressed for disestablishment of the Church in Ireland, Wales, Scotland, and England; and the expansion of social and religious freedoms continued apace.[70] In the early years of the period, politics was marked by the eruption of anti-Catholicism during the "Papal Aggression" in 1851 and the election campaign of 1852, mainly over Maynooth.[71] In the late 1840s and early 1850s, the Voluntaryists—one branch of Dissent—played an aggressive political role in electoral campaigns. That force was gradually spent, however, as Nonconformists began to align with the emerging Liberal Party, and increasing numbers of Nonconformists began to be returned to Parliament.[72]

EDUCATIONAL GROWTH

The minutes of 1846 and subsequent extensions of the activities of the Committee of Council brought a whole new range of educational

TABLE 3    GOVERNMENT EDUCATIONAL
OUTLAY, ENGLAND AND WALES,
1846–1861

| | |
|---|---|
| 1846 | £  58,000 |
| 1847 | 62,000 |
| 1848 | 83,000 |
| 1849 | 110,000 |
| 1850 | 193,000 |
| 1851 | 164,000 |
| 1852 | 189,000 |
| 1853 | 251,000 |
| 1854 | 326,000 |
| 1855 | 370,000 |
| 1856 | 424,000 |
| 1857 | 560,000 |
| 1858 | 669,000 |
| 1859 | 723,000 |
| 1860 | 724,000 |
| 1861 | 834,000 |

SOURCE: J. M. Goldstrom, *The Social Content of Education, 1808–1870* (Shannon: Irish University Press, 1972), pp. 193–94.

expenditures. Among these were the provision of materials such as books and maps; salary augmentations for certificated teachers; building, sustaining, and enlarging training colleges; and paying stipends to pupil-teachers and queen's scholars. The growth of total expenditures in these categories from 1846 to 1861 is shown in table 3. In 1853, in an evident move to increase attendance in rural schools, the Committee of Council initiated the system of capitation grants, payments to schools per child on the basis of attendance and examination performance. It extended the principle to urban schools in 1856, and by 1859 some £186,230 had been expended in such grants.[73] These expenditures combined with a steadily increasing number of grants for the building of new schools. Inspection costs grew, too, as the government appointed new inspectors to accommodate the system's growth and the incorporation of new religious societies, each of which required their own kind of inspection. This figure grew from £11,990 in 1847 to £43,565 in

1861.[74] The administrative apparatus of the Committee of Council grew to one of the largest civil staffs in the country, reaching a total of 127 employees by 1860. In 1856, by an Order in Council, the government established an Education Department, with a vice president appointed by the party in power, providing a closer link between the House of Commons and the state's educational efforts.[75]

In general this growth could occur in relative isolation from the religious conflicts in the larger society, because, one by one, the religious groups became part of the operation itself. They benefited from the state's assistance and were given much autonomy, especially in religious instruction. This resulted in a unique symbiosis between state and religion. Matthew Arnold, himself an inspector of schools, noted this anomaly. Pointing to France, where the state recognized only the three religious orders of Catholics, Protestants, and Jews, he added that in France the state "does not divide itself in order to meet them." In England, by contrast,

> the State makes itself denominational with the denominations. It offers to them no example of the civil unity in which religious divisions are lost; in which they meet as citizens, though estranged as sectaries. It makes its inspectors Anglican with the Anglicans, Roman Catholic with the Roman Catholic, Orthodox Presbyterian with the Old Church of Scotland, Free Church with the New.[76] It does not hold itself aloof from the religious divisions of the population; it enters into them.
>
> What has been the result? By dint of concession to the denominational spirit, by dint of not maintaining an impartial and nonsectarian character, the State, in England, has been betrayed into a thousand anomalies.[77]

Arnold maintained that this system was "far more irritating to sectarian susceptibilities than if it had regarded none of them." That view, however, is surely subject to challenge. The cementing effect of the symbiosis with respect to religious conflict was probably more powerful than the aggravating effect, at least in the short term.

A significant part of what aggravation there was came from the religious groups that had opted *not* to be part of the system: the Voluntaryists. They continued their war on the system in their active, quasi-party period from 1847 to 1852 and fought every parliamentary effort to expand the government's role in education. Edward Miall, an arch-enemy of established religion, and Goldwin Smith submitted a minority report of the Newcastle Commission in 1861, calling for a voluntary approach to popular education.[78] However, the progress of the Voluntaryists without government help was modest, and over time some of that group defected to the secularist National Public School Association.[79] In 1867 Baines renounced the Voluntaryist principle and endorsed the idea of government support of secular education.

Within the system there were some abrasions based on religious sensitivities. Shortly after the minutes of 1846 were instituted, the Committee of Council expressed concern that Congregationalists who were receiving government grants (i.e., those who were not Voluntaryists) might be failing to guarantee religious instruction to pupil-teachers and scholars. After a brief skirmish, the government backed off and took the position that to be a religious congregation was a sufficient condition for a claim to a government grant.[80] The British and Foreign School Society objected to a provision of the minutes that demanded religious certification of teachers. After the society registered a protest in 1847, the Committee of Council ruled that where managers expressed scruples of conscience, no such certification would be required.[81] In 1847 the Wesleyan Education Association expressed alarm that inspectors of their schools had to be sanctioned by an archbishop of the Church of England. Kay-Shuttleworth assured the association that the apprehension was a "delusion" and that "schools connected with the Wesleyan association would not . . . ever be entered by a Church of England inspector, or by any inspector who did not enjoy the confidence of the Committee of Privileges [of the Wesleyan association]."[82]

The government had more serious brushes with the National Society over the long-standing question of the control of schools. This had been the main issue in the conflict over school inspection in 1839–40, and again in the fight over the education clauses in 1843. The issue emerged again in 1846. This time it had to do with the management clauses for the schools. The government ceded to religious societies control over the content of religious education and a large measure of control over inspection. However, it began to insist on increased representation of subscribers and lay people on local management boards. While potentially offensive to all the religious societies, these measures drew the heaviest fire from the National Society, which wished to maintain exclusive clerical control. (In 1849, however, the government and the Roman Catholic Poor School Society clashed over the management clauses, the main issue being the society's sensitivity about control of the religious and moral dimensions of education).[83]

About 1850 the conflict between the Committee of Council and the National Society over the management clauses became more brittle and intractable because of two circumstances: first, the resignation of Kay-

Shuttleworth as secretary of the Committee of Council in 1849, midway in the conflict, and his succession by Ralph Lingen, who was to gain a reputation for rigidity in dealing with many of his constituencies; second, the emergence of Archdeacon George Denison as spokesman for the militant wing of the Church of England on this issue. Denison labeled the government's intent in the management clauses as being "to get the parish school out of the hands of the parish priest." He insisted on absolute ecclesiastical control, with no representation of the laity.[84] The Church of England was actually divided on the issue between a Low Church group interested in a negotiated settlement and Denison's stronger-line group. The conflict became sufficiently serious that some militant managers defied inspection. In 1852 the Derby government attempted to mollify the National Society by relaxing the demands in the management clauses. The battle lines were drawn in the following year, however, when the Whigs revoked that effort and took a firmer line once again. The conflict finally ended not in resolution but in a kind of "agreement to differ."[85] The government would issue the management clauses, but the National Society would refuse to recommend them to its school promoters. The conflict erupted periodically in the 1850s, inasmuch as Denison continued to challenge the clauses.[86]

The second note of conflict in the relations between the government and the Anglican Church was the conscience clause. I discuss this issue briefly here, as part of the educational politics of the 1850s. It will arise again later in this chapter and in chapter 6 on Wales, where conflicts over the conscience clause were common. The essence of the conscience clause issue is as follows. In a society with a commitment to include religion in educational instruction *and* with a heterogeneous religious population, the question of what to do about religious instruction in schools with a religious mix of pupils naturally arises. The British and Foreign School Society "solved" this problem from the time of its foundation by adopting a policy that no doctrines, formularies, or rituals specific to any denomination would be required in its schools, even though it called for the reading of the Scriptures and general religious instruction.[87] The Church of England, however, while internally divided, insisted through its National Society that the church catechism be a part of religious instruction and that its pupils attend Anglican services. The issue of the conscience clause was what to do about non-Anglican pupils (mainly Dissenters and Roman Catholics in the English context). Should it insist on the specific Anglican instruction for all or isolate or exempt the children of non-Anglicans from it, thereby honoring their parents' principles of conscience? The issue of the conscience clause was thus above all one touching the Church of England.

In addition, the conscience clause was largely a small-community issue.[88] In large urban areas there were usually enough children of the different denominations to provide separate schools for each. This obviated any question of conscience in both religiously homogeneous and religiously permissive (e.g., British and Foreign Society) schools. In small communities that could support only one school, this solution was not available. The alternatives thus became:

To build two or more very small schools (the solution adopted in some Welsh and English communities in the 1850s); this solution, however, raised questions of economy.[89]

To insist on specific religious instruction and thus violate the principles of conscience of Nonconformist parents; this was the "strong" solution adopted by the National Society.

To honor those principles of conscience by some kind of exemption; this was the conscience clause proper.

To remove specifically denominational religious instruction altogether; this was the intent of the Cowper-Temple provision in the Education Act of 1870.[90]

To remove religious instruction from the schools altogether; this was the "American" solution.

The Church of England itself had incorporated the conscience clause in the practices of the schools it sponsored in Ireland in the late eighteenth century. In this case, the accommodation was mainly to Catholics, the majority in most regions.[91] In 1818 Brougham's committee recommended that children in Anglican parish schools "not be compelled to learn any catechism or attend any Church, other than those of their parents." This solution, the committee felt, would "obtain the desirable objects of security to the Establishment on the one hand, and justice to the Dissenters on the other."[92] A conscience clause for Dissenters was written into some of the subsequent legislative proposals, including the amended education clauses in 1843.[93]

In 1839 the Committee of Council adopted the proviso that applicants for school building grants who were not connected with the two religious societies had to explain why they did not incorporate a conscience clause. Furthermore, the committee announced its intention to give preference to schools that "do not enforce any rule by which the children will be compelled to learn a catechism or attend a place of Divine worship, to which their parents, on religious grounds, object." [94] In 1846 the committee made it a "requirement" for a grant that National Society schools not enforce the catechism and requirement of church attendance on persons outside the Anglican confession. In 1847, however, the committee seemed to indicate that the issue was still unresolved. It mentioned the subject again, noting only that some National Society schools observed the conscience clause, but that others did not. On this occasion, the committee went no further than to express its "regret that the children of Dissenters are not admissable [*sic*] into Church-of-England schools without these requirements [for a conscience clause], . . . [members] would rejoice in a change in the regulations of such schools, providing for [Dissenters'] admission." [95]

In 1852 Lingen attempted to secure an agreement that local conflicts over the conscience clause be referred to the bishops (who tended to be more liberal than the local priests) for final decision. In the same year the committee began entering conscience clauses into some of its grants. [96] The National Society opposed that policy, and in the early 1850s its opposition was intensified when Denison made the issue into a special cause and defined it as stridently as he did the issue of the management clauses. He withdrew from the scene for a number of years in 1855, however, after his own militant position on the conscience clause was defeated at a diocesan board meeting. [97] The conflict over the conscience clause was eased by Denison's departure, as well as the fact that the Committee of Council encouraged expansion above all in the 1850s. It often permitted more than one school in small communities, even though this practice was acknowledged sometimes to produce "inefficient" schools. [98] In the 1850s, then, the issue of the conscience clause seemed to exist as a kind of low-grade infection affecting the relations between the National Society and the government. The dispute reerupted in the 1860s, however, when the Education Department began to withhold grants from applicants who refused to accept one, and when the Church of England stiffened its opposition to this policy once again.

In addition to these developments in the state-subsidized system, a number of other trends affecting working-class education should be mentioned. These mainly concerned other types of schools. The Sunday schools continued as a permanent element on the scene, especially among Dissenters and especially in Wales, though the rapid growth of day schools was eclipsing their general educational role. [99] Dame schools also persisted as partly child-minding, partly educational institutions for very young children. Most contemporaries regarded them adversely because of their low educational quality.[100] Overlapping with the dame schools were the infant schools, to be discussed in chapter 8.

Some children of the working classes also attended private schools, but the total numbers of such schools and of scholars in them are elusive, as are the quality of their schooling and the motives of parents for sending their children to them.[101] Three other types of schools accommodated mainly pauper and criminal children, namely, the "ragged schools," reformatories, and workhouse and district schools:

Ragged schools, begun around 1840 and consolidated into the Ragged School Union in 1844, were a special cause for Shaftesbury and Mary Carpenter.[102] These schools were designed for the "perishing and dangerous classes" [103]—the children of criminals, vagrants, orphans, runaways, and others thought to be outside parental care. Henry Mayhew and others interested in the condition of vagrants and delinquents were skeptical about the effectiveness of the ragged schools.[104]

Reformatories for juvenile criminals were initiated in the 1840s on a voluntary basis and were supported mainly by the landed classes and religious organizations. The Committee of Council began to subsidize them in 1856. These schools were designed for children from the "criminal and abandoned classes." [105]

Workhouse and district schools were designed for the industrial training of pauper children. These were administered through the Poor Law districts and supported from 1846 on under grants from the Committee of Council.[106] The terms of support were converted into a capitation grant in 1852, but few grants were made.

The Mechanics' Institutes, dating from 1823, had by the 1850s evolved into mainly middle-class institutions, little attended by members of the working classes, whom Working Men's Colleges were beginning to serve.[107] I discuss schools established by the Factory Acts, and adult and evening schools for the working classes in chapter 8.

PUBLIC MOVEMENT
AND PARLIAMENTARY INACTION

The dominant strand of public opinion in the 1850s appeared to be a kind of status quo denominationalism. This entailed commitment to a religious component in working-class education, but subdivision of that education along denominational lines. This also appeared to be the consensus among those religious societies who were receiving subsidies. The Committee of Council was part of this consensus; it pursued a policy of freely granting funds to the religious societies and steadfastly refusing to support applications from secular groups.[108] Another segment of opinion, the Denominationalists, differed in detail from the dominant position. They favored financing education from local rates, to be distributed to the religious societies in much the same way that the Committee of Council was doing centrally.[109]

More serious opposition to the dominant view emanated from two kinds of Voluntaryists: first, a minority of the High Church faction who argued against state interference with the Anglican Church's claimed educational monopoly; second, the Voluntaryists proper, Dissenters who pressed for a completely private system, fearing that any form of state support entailed domination by the Church of England. The first view proved hopelessly outdated, even among most churchmen. The second proved futile, because the Voluntaryists could not secure the resources to compete successfully with the subsidized religious societies.

Interest in a government-financed and government-administered system of secular education also revived in the 1850s, first appearing in Manchester in 1847 among the forces represented in the Anti-Corn Law League and liberals who wished to extend parliamentary reform.[110] The organization representing these interests was the Lancashire Public School Association, indicating its region of origin. This became the National Public School Association in 1850 after its support became general. Spokesmen for the association argued that the voluntary system was inadequate to cover the country, especially the poorer districts. The voluntary system, moreover, excluded everyone not connected with a religious denomination. The positive program included imposing taxes for educational purposes in large local areas; excluding all catechisms and creeds so that no one would be barred from participating; limiting religious instruction to selections from the Scriptures; and forming county boards of education, which would control day schools, evening schools, industrial schools, and normal schools.

The LPSA drew some inspiration from the continental and Irish systems, but the principal model was the Massachusetts system of public education, which had recently made great strides under the leadership of Horace Mann. Richard Cobden, a leader of the association, praised the American model as early as 1835, and intensified his enthusiasm later after a visit to the United States. He claimed it to be as superior to the English system as the English system was to that of Naples. What appealed to him was its local financing and administration and its non-sectarian religious instruction.[111] In an enthusiastic moment he wrote:

> I call for the American system. I do not want to have my Bible read in the schools, because, if so, the children of 60,000 must go uneducated. I am neither for the Bible as a schoolbook nor for its exclusion as a schoolbook. I am for the American system precisely as it stands.[112]

Given Cobden's position, it is not surprising that those who attacked the association accused it of being Irish, godless, and anti-Scriptural. Its program drew the fire of Kay-Shuttleworth, who said it threatened to minimize religious instruction and separate day schools from the religious societies. He argued that England was a country of such "religious sympathies" that it would not abide excluding religion from education: "Every system of combined education [i.e., one that separated secular from religious instruction like Irish and U.S. systems] which has been proposed, whether on a purely secular basis or on that of toleration, or on that of religious equality, has been rejected promptly, if not indignantly, by the religious communions of England." [113]

The association also came under attack from the Denominationalists and the religious societies, who stood to lose control over education if its program were enacted. The Tory radical Sir Joseph Rayner Stephens emerged from political retirement to denounce the plan as one enabling a self-elected board to levy taxes and to construct a new Bible.[114] In 1850 the LPSA itself experienced an internal split on the religious issue. The debate was on whether it should describe its educational purposes as *secular, non-sectarian,* or *public.* The latter term finally won out as a neutral compromise.[115]

W. J. Fox brought the association's program forward as a parliamentary bill in 1850. He argued that the religious-voluntary system was languishing. He justified his claim for educational reform with the familiar arguments that education was an antidote to crime, and that England had fallen behind other countries educationally.[116] John Roebuck, a supporter, said that, if enacted, the bill would produce a system like that of education in Massachusetts, which had created "the most moral and the most religious people upon the face of the globe." [117] The proposal, he added, entailed no restraints on the religious societies, which could still erect and endow denominational schools, and receive state grants on the basis of results in secular education. He also called for free tuition.

Fox's bill drew a predictable attack from the High Church representative, Inglis, on the grounds that it was a secular scheme.[118] In addition, Russell and other moderates attacked its secular character and its principle of gratuitous instruction.[119] Fox went on the defensive, arguing that the bill did not deny religious education but permitted religious instruction if desired by parents, and that he was not attempting to drive religion from education.[120] Despite some countrywide agitation in favor of it, the bill failed by a large majority on the second reading.

Early in 1851 a second group—the Manchester and Salford Committee on Education—formed in opposition to the Lancashire Public School Association. Supporting it were a number of Church of England clergymen and laymen, Wesleyan Ministers, and Kay-Shuttleworth. It wished to preserve the religious system of education, which, the committee felt, was threatened by the LPSA. At the same time, it insisted that there should be no compulsory attendance at the teaching of any distinctive religious doctrine. The committee's legislative proposal, the Manchester and Salford bill, came before Parliament in 1852. It proposed free education for working-class children financed by a rate in aid of existing schools, no change in management, and the requirement that an authorized version of the Bible be read, but with a conscience clause. Joseph Brotherton, who introduced the bill, argued that it was badly needed in Manchester and Salford to reduce crime and related evils in that urban area.

Criticism of the Manchester and Salford bill came from several different quarters. Inglis objected on grounds that the Church of England should be responsible for education.[121] Gladstone opposed using local rates as a source of financing the plan.[122] Others indicated that Roman Catholics, Jews, and Quakers were antagonistic to the bill because its provisions offended their religious sensibilities.[123] Outside Parliament the LPSA attacked the bill because it covered only elementary day schools, was limited to one urban area, and would extend the supremacy of the Established Church in education. Finally, Cobden sounded the most common argument of the 1850s by criticizing the bill as "a proposal by which everybody shall be called upon to pay for the religious teaching of everybody else."[124] With both High Church and most of Dissent opposed, the bill failed.[125]

After an unsuccessful attempt in 1853 to introduce a borough bill that would finance voluntary efforts through local rates, the Manchester and Salford bill came up again in 1854. It called for the ratepayers of Manchester to contribute to a common fund, to be distributed to the elementary schools in the area.[126] An extended parliamentary wrangle developed over the status of the bill—whether it was a private or a public measure. The main debate, however, revealed that the principal objections to the bill were the same religious ones, advanced by the same groups, for the same reasons, as in 1852.[127] Russell summarized the liberal and Dissenting opposition by noting that though the legislation contained a clause excluding religious creeds, it was futile to try to include all denominations in a system of management that laid down religious rules.[128] This second Manchester and Salford bill also failed.

Three additional legislative efforts appeared in Parliament in the 1850s. Sir John Pakington introduced an educational bill in 1855. He prefaced it by citing Horace Mann's educational census of 1851, which showed a great deficiency of education in the country. Pakington attributed the findings of the census to the fact that "the voluntary system has broken down." [129] He represented his bill as modeled on the American system, which he regarded as an effective one.[130] The proposed schools would be funded through local rates, with a managing board for schools elected by the ratepayers. There would be religious instruction combined with complete toleration—"perfect religious liberty and perfect and equal regard to the feelings of all religious denominations, and complete liberty of conscience." [131] To attain this, Pakington specified that religion would be taught in accordance with the views of the majority of the persons in the localities where schools were established, but that there would be no imposition of any religious creed.[132] The main attack on the bill was that it was too secular. J. W. Henley objected by raising the same argument that Pakington had used to advertise it—that it *was* like the American educational system, which "has sunk down into a purely secular system, and has produced results which . . . are not of a very favourable character." [133] Thus, while Pakington contended that the bill would simply extend the existing system and retain religious education, it failed because it appeared to threaten religious interests.

In 1856 Russell made a try. He acknowledged the risk in introducing any legislation on education. It was, however, necessary to enter those dangerous waters because of the insufficient spread and low quality of education in England, as the Mann census had proved.[134] Russell's bill was omnibus, calling for an expansion of the inspectorate, establishment of educational districts, and new powers for the commissioners of the charitable trusts. Its key proposals, however, were financing by rates in districts where education was deficient, and the formation of a committee to appoint teachers and regulate the schools. The bill also called for reading the Scriptures, but exempted the children of any parent or guardian who objected on grounds of conscience.[135] In debate, critics argued that the proposals would not reach the poorer classes and that they contained elements of compulsion. The main attacks were against the rating clauses, which, it was argued, were unworkable in the English religious situation. They would generate unmanageable religious conflict among the Church of England, the Nonconformists, and the Roman Catholics. Such conflict, moreover, would drive the system in a secular direction because it would exclude the religious principles specific to all of them.[136] Both Gladstone and Disraeli spoke against the bill. In a final, unsuccessful effort, Russell raised the familiar minimalist argument that "it is a proposal to continue [the plan of 1839]—to extend it very considerably, and to add some matters to it which would only make it more complete and efficient."[137]

Finally, in 1857 Pakington introduced a bill that he hoped would avoid the weaknesses in Russell's attempt—that it contained too many ingredients, and that it compelled some districts to establish schools. Pakington's proposal was permissive in this respect, as well as in regard to religious instruction. This was to be left to the districts, with the proviso that there should be no violation of conscience.[138] The familiar objections surfaced. While permissive in principle, the system would ultimately be supported from the rates; it would stir religious controversy and sectarian bitterness; Roman Catholics would not attend Protestant schools.[139] This bill failed as well.

Historical interpreters have noted that the great accomplishment of the unsuccessful reform efforts in the 1850s was to advance all of the ideas eventually incorporated into the Education Act of 1870.[140] Be that as it may, the country seemed to be mired in a swamp at the level of national politics. Free from the immediate pressure of working-class protest—so evident in most of the earlier parliamentary actions—political leaders perhaps indulged themselves in the luxury of even more doctrinal, sectarian, and jurisdictional rigidity than before. Pressure for reform was present, because evidence suggested that the subsidized voluntary system was far from general in its coverage. The great trap, however, was religious. Almost all groups, including those attacked as secularist, insisted that religion had to be a component of working-class education. Yet any proposal calling for religious education was attacked because it violated some groups' conscience. Any proposal that minimized religious content to avoid conflict was condemned as irreligious. There seemed to be no acceptable middle ground between these two arsenals of criticism. Finally, the religious societies were wary of proposals to initiate direct governmental involvement, because such proposals threatened to diminish their claim on the educational system. The repeated failures occasioned a flagging of reformist zeal—the National Public School Association folded its tents in 1862—and a pervasive sense of frustration in Parliament. It was in this context that Pakington was able to persuade Parliament in 1858 of the necessity of launching a major national commission that would gain information about, examine the condition and needs of, and, it was hoped, generate nonpartisan recommendations for major reforms of the British educational system.

## ECONOMIZING, STREAMLINING, STANDARDIZING, AND SECULARIZING: 1862

The religious stalemate was not the only source of dissatisfaction with working-class education leading to the appointment of the Newcastle Commission. As noted, promoters of educational reform cited the voluntary system's limited coverage of the country's children. Mann's statistics showed that 41 percent were at school, 12 percent at work, and over 46 percent neither at school nor at work.[141] In pressing for the appointment of a commission in the summer of 1857, Pakington underscored these deficiencies, both on absolute grounds and in relation to other countries.[142] The main need was to provide schools in poor and apathetic districts.[143] Accumulating evidence from the school inspectors' reports and elsewhere confirmed, moreover, that in districts with schools, the quality of education was impaired by irregular attendance and withdrawal of children from school at an early age. Both problems were traceable to the fact that children were so heavily engaged in the work force. These attendance problems were among the most intractable facing the schools and the educational reformers.[144]

As table 3 shows, the government's educational outlay had spiraled during the fifteen years following the adoption of the minutes of 1846. These costs were becoming the object of increasing concern, explicable not only in terms of the absolute amounts expended but also in the context of three other factors. In the first place, the mounting cost of education rankled because the system appeared not to be covering the country and educating working-class children adequately. Secondly, despite the increasing prosperity of the country, reflected in the revenues the state received, the government was under financial strictures in the 1850s, principally because of the tremendous economic burden of the Crimean

War and other British military adventures in that decade,[145] and one response was to search for budgetary savings. And, last but not least, there was the influence of William E. Gladstone, who played a special role in the area of finance. By the 1850s, Gladstone had become one of the most powerful figures in English politics, serving brilliantly as chancellor of the exchequer. In that decade and in the 1860s, he established himself above all as an economy-minded leader.[146] Also, while Gladstone was prepared to compromise on many occasions, he was a strong Establishmentarian,[147] committed to an education based on religion, and without enthusiasm for educational reform involving the extension of state power.[148] His concern over rising educational expenditures in the 1850s was no secret,[149] and his concern for economy was supported by voices like that of Bright,[150] who represented traditional liberal apprehensions about government interference in economy and society. Additional concerns about cost derived from the belief of some members of Parliament that the House of Commons did not monitor and exercise sufficient control over expenditures on education.[151] Concerns about costs were at the center of Pakington's arguments justifying the appointment of the Newcastle Commission.[152] They were also one of the main considerations motivating the adoption of the Revised Code in 1862.[153] Finally, they were the decisive factor in the Committee on Council's insistence on enforcing the conscience clause in small communities in the 1860s.[154]

Some of the reasons for the increasing educational costs were obvious: the continuous increase in population of working-class children during those years;[155] the many new types of expenditures initiated by the minutes of 1846, especially the payment of teachers, pupil-teachers, and teachers-in-training; and the capitation grants paid after 1853.[156] The cumbersome administration of the grants was a fourth source of dissatisfaction with the existing system. The London office of the Committee of Council dealt with every school individually, and this entailed preparing deeds of trust, correspondence, and a constant flow of money transactions.[157] Other complaints flowed from the fact that the system had proliferated along denominational lines. Lowe noted the multiplication and waste:

> If . . . the schools were founded upon exclusive [religious] principles, so that the people of other denominations were obliged to come to the Board, and say "Here are fifty of our children whose consciences are violated" they made out a case for another school, and two schools were built where one would suffice. Although it was said to be a blessing to make two blades of grass

grow where only one grew before, yet this saying could not fairly extend to men who built two schools where one would be sufficient. He feared the country was somewhat retrograding in this matter, for the deeds . . . were for the most part more exclusive than they were thirty years ago, and were now formulated with the greatest precision and accuracy, from the circumstance, as he believed, that as people's attention was drawn to these matters, they looked more narrowly than formerly to the boundaries of their denominations. The British and Foreign schools were open to all classes of Christians except Roman Catholics, who did not use the Protestant version of the Bible. It was found, however, that these schools were now replaced by denominational schools, especially Wesleyan, so that the system was growing more wasteful rather than more economical.[158]

Such was one kind of cost stemming from Arnold's complaint that the state had made itself "denominational with the denominations." The same point could be made with respect to the inspectorate. Table 27 reveals how rapidly those costs had risen. By virtue of the agreements with the Church of England in 1840, the British and Foreign School Society in 1843, and other schools thereafter, the inspectorate had proliferated along much the same lines as the schools. There were separate inspectors for National schools, British and Foreign schools, Wesleyan schools, Roman Catholic schools, Established Church schools in Scotland, Free Church schools in Scotland, and Church of England schools in Scotland. A similar exclusivity applied to the inspection of the training colleges. This arrangement tended to multiply inspectors and to involve additional travel and other costs as they criss-crossed the country on separate tours of inspection. In introducing the Revised Code of 1862, Lowe identified the difficulty in a somewhat gingerly manner:

The number of inspectors is far larger than it need be at this moment, because each denomination has its own inspectors, and it often happens that three or four gentlemen are sent to the same town to inspect the schools in it. That, of course, involves an enormous waste of time and money, and some good might be affected by making the same gentlemen inspect all classes of schools, with the exception, perhaps of those belonging to the Roman Catholics. However, we propose nothing of the kind; I merely point out what might be done.[159]

A fifth source of dissatisfaction had to do with the status of teachers in the state-supported system. As chapter 9 will show, teachers were the object of ambivalence in many quarters—including in the minds of Lowe and Lingen—in the years before 1860. Critics believed them to be overeducated and overpaid for the simple tasks of educating working-class children in the basics, and socially pretentious. These beliefs appeared to play a role in the formulation of the Revised Code.

The Newcastle Commission thus began its work in the presence of two sets of institutional and political "givens." First, an already substantial system of state-supported voluntary education was in place institutionally by 1858. Second, this system was subject to a range of dissatisfactions and criticisms. As a result, the commission scarcely operated in a wide-open environment, with all options possible. By formal charge it was bound to produce suggestions for a "sound and cheap" system of instruction, a charge reflecting dissatisfaction with the effectiveness and cost of the existing arrangements. As A. S. Bishop notes, however, there were also constraints "to reduce the pressure on the Department [reflecting concerns about administrative complexity], to foster local interest in education [reflecting concerns about centralization and inadequate subscriptions under the voluntary system] and to preserve the denominational character of the system [reflecting the general antipathy to secular education in Britain at the time and the vested interests of the religious societies]."[160] Bishop might have made explicit one more constraint: to improve the regularity and duration of attendance at the schools. All these constraints reduced the likelihood that the commission would produce many bold, revolutionary suggestions. Its own composition further reduced that likelihood. Although a diversity of political positions were represented on the commission,[161] only one member—Pakington himself—championed an enlarged role for the state in popular education.

The Newcastle Commission produced a mountain of evidence and opinion on the contemporary condition of working-class education, to be cited in these pages from time to time. For the moment it will serve to note a few of its recommendations in light of the constraints mentioned. The major recommendations were the following:

To support the existing plan of voluntary education as subsidized by the Committee of Council. This "was a sort of compromise between the admitted necessity of promoting popular education and the difficulty of devising any general system for that purpose which would be acceptable by the country."[162] The commission affirmed that the country opposed a fully secular system of education, as well as any kind of formal split between religious and secular instruction (as in Ireland and the United States). The main problem the commission saw with the existing system was that its administration was too costly and cumbersome (echoing the complaints of Lingen and Lowe).

To establish elected boards of education by county. The Court of Quarter Sessions would elect up to six members from the ranks of the

Justices of the Peace and the Boards of Guardians, and these electees would elect up to six additional members. The number of ministers of religion on any board would be no more than one-third of the total membership. The boards were to be empowered to levy rates. The choice of larger areas was apparently designed to minimize the religious intolerance and jealousies if rates were exacted in small localities. The limitation of religious representation on the boards apparently had the same motive of reducing religious controversy.[163]

To establish a system of "payment by results" as the main form of board grants to schools. This meant that children would be examined with respect to their proficiency in the basic subjects (the "three R's") and the amount of the grant would be dependent on the numbers of children who passed the tests. This would be substituted for the complex combination of payments in the existing system.

For all its monumental efforts in gathering information, reflecting, and recommending improvements, the commission saw its recommendations rewarded mainly with indifference and hostility. Kay-Shuttleworth attacked the recommendations as subverting the existing system and undermining the religious basis of education.[164] Shaftesbury charged that its inaccuracies impugned the Ragged Schools. Arnold[165] attacked it for its exaggeration of the numbers of schools and scholars.[166] The National Society warned that its recommendations posed a danger to religious teaching, and some Dissenters complained of the injustice of the recommendations. Like so many of the proposed reforms of the 1850s, the commission's recommendations seemed to satisfy no party.[167]

The sole suggestion adopted by the government was the system of payment by results, the one most clearly directed to the problems of administration (one possible reading of "soundness") and economy ("cheapness"). This principle was the foundation of the Revised Code of 1862. The method of rewarding for examination results had a number of precedents earlier in the century. It was also a feature of the capitation grants of 1853.[168] The idea accorded well with the prevailing popularity of examinations, which developed in the 1850s and continued throughout the century.[169] Payment by results was also consistent with the utilitarian values of political economy espoused by Lowe,[170] its principal proponent, who stressed the themes of efficiency and economy— "Am I getting what I want, and the most of it possible for my money?"[171]—in his defense of the Revised Code.[172]

The Revised Code was apparently drafted without extensive consultation with the major constituencies of the educational system. (This may account in part for the extreme hostility that its introduction provoked.) Lingen and Lowe were the main framers; the latter was its main presenter and defender in Parliament. The code's major provisions were relatively simple. All grant monies were to go directly to the school managers, with no direct salary payments to teachers. A single grant would replace the augmentation grants, the salaries of student teachers, and attendance-based capitation grants. The amount of the grant would take into account three considerations: the numbers of students passing examinations in reading, writing, and arithmetic; the number of students in attendance; and whether the school was superintended by a certificated teacher. In introducing the measure, Lowe advertised its economy and its minimalism. It was a measure in accord with the recommendations of the Newcastle Commission, and it would not disturb the existing system:

> So long as it is the opinion of those who contribute to the maintenance of the schools that the present system is the right and the best one so long will the present system continue . . . it is not the intention of Government to infringe on the organic principles of the present system—namely, its denominational character, its foundation on a broad religious basis, its teaching religion, and the practice of giving grants from the central office in aid of local subscriptions, the propriety of those grants to be ascertained by inspection.[173]

As we shall see, the promise of minimalism proved wrong, as the effects of the code were to permeate almost all aspects of the system.

The code's publication in July 1861, however, drew a broadside of protests. The National Society attacked it on the grounds that basing grant support on the three R's would diminish attention to religion,[174] and that it would diminish voluntary educational activity in the country. Lowe's statement that the government stood "impartial among the sects" also infuriated some Anglicans, who felt that language reduced the Church of England to the status of a mere sect.[175] The British and Foreign School Society opposed the code as educationally unsound; it also argued that it would discourage the valuable pupil-teaching system.[176] Other religious societies joined in protest. Associations of schoolmasters petitioned against the code. Managers and principals of the teacher-training colleges expressed apprehension that their revenues would fall.[177] The inspectors of schools objected through the bishop of Oxford against the idea of examining students individually.[178] Kay-Shuttleworth argued that the code would limit the recruiting of teachers, lower the standard of instruction, and fail to reach those areas really in need of schools.[179]

Opposition also arose in Scotland, on grounds that the Revised Code was especially incompatible with its system of education.[180]

In the face of this chorus of objections, the government suspended the code until after March 1862, and in the meantime it made a few concessions. It delayed the withdrawal of grants to training institutions. Children under six could earn a capitation grant without being examined, and age-grading was also abandoned as the basis for examination. Scotland was exempted from the operation of the code. The main provisions were preserved, however, and the principle of payment by results was to endure for several decades.

Presently I shall review the consequences of the code as a buildup to the Education Act of 1870. In a more immediate sense, it can be assessed in terms of its relation to the constraints facing the educational system in general and the Newcastle Commission in particular in the late 1850s. By cutting through the different kinds of payments, the government was attempting both to simplify the system's administration and to reduce its cost—even though the exact outlay under the code was not accurately predictable at the time of its enactment.[181] By restricting examinations to the three R's, the government removed itself even further from the arena of religious education by the denominations. This measure seemed to pave the way for disbanding the denominational system of inspection. The code is also notable for what it did not do. The new method of payment remained a centralized one and avoided the paralyzing political issue of levying rates in religiously diverse localities. The code did not alter the fundamental contours of the voluntary/religious system, which possibly explains why the objections of the religious societies, despite their apprehensions, were less passionate than they had been on other occasions—for example, in 1839 and 1843.[182] Finally, the act amounted to a devaluation of teachers by removing them from their quasi-civil servant status and by making them more like technicians, training children in the basics and turning them out as "results."[183]

## DIRECT STATE PROVISION OF EDUCATION: 1870

In chapter 9 I examine the impact of the Revised Code on pupil-teachers, teachers, training colleges, and the inspectorate. In the meantime, a word should be said about its apparent economic, class, and religious consequences, each examined in relation to the conditions leading to the legislation of 1870.

ECONOMIC AND CLASS CONSEQUENCES

The effect of the code on government expenditures was as hoped: it reduced them substantially. Table 4 shows the educational grants in the first five years of its operation. The reductions are the more remarkable because the numbers of children in school continued to increase modestly between 1862 and 1866. (After 1867 expenditures began to climb again, when the government raised the maximum payment per child examined from 12s. to 13s. 4d. and restored payments for pupil-teachers.) Disaggregating these figures, Norman Morris discovered that the main sources of reduction in the mid 1860s were in expenditures for teacher-training and new building grants.[184] The second factor could partly be treated as an indirect effect of the Revised Code in the sense that it depressed interest in teaching and discouraged potential applicants, and at the same time, the government itself was shifting its granting policy for building new schools "by declining to support more than one school in a single catchment area, taking the view that it was unreasonable for the public purse to provide two or more small and possibly inefficient schools just to justify the desire of rival religious denominations each to have a school of its own." [185]

The general decline in government grants occasioned a shift in the sources of income for the elementary schools. In 1869 Parliament published a summary of expenditures on public education over the past decade. Three sources were identified—parliamentary funds, school pence

TABLE 4    REDUCTION IN PARLIAMENTARY GRANTS,
1860–1866

|  | Average Attendance | Parliamentary Grants |
|---|---|---|
| 1860 | 803,708 | £724,403 |
| 1861 | 855,077 | 813,441 |
| 1862 | 888,923 | 774,723 |
| 1863 | 928,310 | 721,386 |
| 1864 | 937,678 | 655,036 |
| 1865 | 1,016,558 | 636,806 |
| 1866 | 1,048,489 | 649,307 |

Source: *The Final Report of the Commissioners Appointed to Inquire into the Elementary Education Acts* (1888), p. 18, cited in D. W. Sylvester, *Robert Lowe and Education* (Cambridge: Cambridge University Press, 1974), p. 82.

TABLE 5    SOURCES OF SUPPORT FOR EDUCATIONAL
DEVELOPMENT, 1859-1868

|  | Parliamentary Funds Expended | Sum Derived from School Pence | Sums Derived from Subscriptions | Sums Derived from Other Sources | Total Non-parliamentary Funds |
|---|---|---|---|---|---|
| 1859 | £609,072 | £229,474 | £458,151 | £100,835 | £788,460 |
| 1860 | 615,377 | 263,529 | 497,051 | 108,920 | 869,500 |
| 1861 | 664,382 | 279,617 | 486,116 | 122,905 | 888,638 |
| 1862 | 700,700 | 286,217 | 476,868 | 134,255 | 897,340 |
| 1863 | 668,120 | 296,367 | 436,206 | 132,877 | 865,450 |
| 1864 | 584,822 | 322,508 | 419,759 | 132,961 | 875,228 |
| 1865 | 533,537 | 356,946 | 419,394 | 129,095 | 905,435 |
| 1866 | 527,362 | 376,093 | 398,012 | 135,627 | 909,732 |
| 1867 | 582,964 | 400,291 | 462,989 | 107,143 | 970,423 |
| 1868 | 583,794 | 430,279 | 499,782 | 91,121 | 1,021,182 |

SOURCE: *Parliamentary Papers*, 1868-69, 57, "Copies of Accounts of the Sums Extracted out of the Monies Voted by Parliament for Public Education in England and Wales between the 31st Day of March 1858 and 1st Day of April 1868."

(i.e., fees charged to parents of students), and subscriptions (i.e., donations by individuals in localities). The results appear in table 5. Government grants to schools rose until 1862, the year of the Revised Code, declined sharply to 1864, and stabilized between £550,000 and £600,000 from 1864 to 1868. Private subscriptions remained virtually stable, with some year-to-year fluctuations, over the period. Sums derived from school pence rose by 54 percent between 1861 and 1868, however; this contrasts with the rise of less than 20 percent in average attendance figures. The figures thus demonstrate the shift of the educational burden toward consumers in the years following the enactment of the code.

The precise dynamics underlying this shift are not discernible from the figures themselves. Evidence provided by school inspectors and others, however, indicates a probable rise in school fees and, closely related, a probable upward shift in income level and social class of the parents of children in schools. In summarizing inspectors' reports for 1865, Granville and Henry A. Bruce of the Committee of Council reported that "there is a tendency to charge higher fees . . . than formerly." They added that "[this higher charge] is often no more than just, and, so long as the poorest are not excluded, is advisable."[186] One year later the committee noted the same tendency, and suggested that it be watched, out of concern for the very poor.[187] The exact effects on attendance of these apparently rising fees are not known. Insofar as fees made any difference in parents' decisions to keep children in school,[188] it would affect the poorest parents most. HMI W. Scoltock, referring to the British and other Protestant schools in his Midlands district, put the case directly:

> If a master farms a school for his own profit, he is liable to the temptation of raising the fees to at least six pence for the upper classes, and thus debar the child of the working man from the advantages of instruction in higher arithmetic and other subjects; for even "fourpence" is stated by a most competent authority "to be a great strain upon those who earn small wages, and the poor."[189]

Other, more informal processes also probably tended to skew the income- and class-composition of the schools upward. One effect of the code was to alter the incentive structures of managers and teachers. Much of their income now depended on the numbers of pupils passing examinations at various levels. The evident temptation under these circumstances would be to attend more to those students who would or could pass. In 1869 HMI D. J. Stewart summarized this situation as follows:

> If teachers, from choice or from necessity, are led to give undue importance to the purely commercial aspect of school, a strong temptation will be created to keep down its expenses and to get rid of those pupils who pay badly, that is to say, to avoid as far as possible the employment of pupil-teachers *and the admission of the very poor children*. . . .
> If a teacher becomes as it were a large share-holder in a school it will be at once an important object with him to keep down the teaching staff as low as he possibly can, and he will have the same inducements to get rid of poor or backward children, because they are the most troublesome to teach and the most uncertain under examination.
> It cannot be denied that this kind of temptation must be extremely powerful in certain cases.[190]

Two years earlier HMI H. M. Cabel had taken note of the publications of the Manchester and Birmingham Education Aid Societies, which indicated that large numbers of children were neither at school nor at work. He attributed part of this problem to the working of the Revised Code:

> There is some truth in the assertion that the Revised Code, while improving greatly the quality of the eduction, which the thoughtful and respectable artizan obtains for his children, is an injury rather than a benefit to the very poorest class in towns. In the smaller town-schools, the master, who cannot get a pupil-teacher, and whose salary depends in a great measure on the Government grant, is exposed to too great a temptation to keep his numbers below an average of 90. And in many of the larger parishes, it can hardly be expected that the teacher whose rooms are almost full, should not give a preference to the child who will attend regularly, pay regularly, and bring credit, and an examination grant to the school, over the poorer child who is unlikely to do either.[191]

In parliamentary discussion of a school endowments bill in 1869, George Melly called for a select committee on education in the large towns. Citing similar figures from investigations of children not at school in Liverpool, Manchester, and Birmingham, he also put part of the responsibility on the Revised Code: "The master, paid by results, prefers the well-dressed regularly attending children of a more respectable class, and the cold shoulder is not unfrequently given . . . to the very children for whom [the national schools] are endowed and maintained."[192]

This phenomenon is related to two other concerns of the time, both of which would affect the apparent class-upgrading of the elementary schools. The first is that apparently because of the poor quality of the lower-middle-class private schools,[193] some children from those classes were shifting to working-class schools. Acknowledging the difficulty of securing statistics, Melly nevertheless claimed that "the national primary schools have been invaded, and in some instances even monopolised, by classes [well-to-do artisans and shopkeepers] for whom they were [not] intended."[194] Clause 4 of the Revised Code actually *excluded* from government-supported schools children of parents in classes above those earning their livelihood by manual labor. The impact of this provision of the code on the schools' social class composition was no doubt mixed. On the one hand, HMI C. H. Anderson reported that managers and teachers, eager to recruit children who would pass examinations, ignored the clause and took in numbers of middle-class children.[195] On the other hand, HMI W. W. Howard reported that because the Revised Code neglected the "fancy subjects" of geography, mathematics, and history, pupils who were "generally better mannered, neater in dress, and cleaner in person than the children of the very poor" were now going to private schools that offered these subjects.[196] On balance, however, the accumulated evidence suggests that the government-supported schools for the working classes experienced a marginally upward shift in class composition that resulted from the effects of the Revised Code.[197]

The second concern had to do with the apparently mounting numbers of destitute and poor children—the "street arabs"—in the 1850s and 1860s. This problem was not new, having been a part of urban poverty since the beginning of the industrial revolution. But in these decades the preoccupation with this class of children and young persons appeared to grow. It was mentioned repeatedly in parliamentary debates in the 1850s.[198] School inspectors reported that such children were not being caught in the net of the denominational schools.[199] Visitors to England were also struck by this aspect of the urban scene.[200] Mary Carpenter maintained that the British and Foreign School Society schools served the upper ranges of the working classes and did not reach the destitute.[201] It was this class of very poor children, who were neither at school nor at work, whom the industrial, ragged, and reformatory schools were seeking to reach but scarcely covering.[202]

If this destitute class of children was expanding, the sources of its growth were no doubt multiple. One source was the decrease in demand for the labor of young children associated with the growth of factory legislation. In the cotton-textile industry alone—which was the first affected by factory legislation in 1833—the percentage of children under thirteen in the labor force dropped from 13.2 to 4.6 between 1835 and 1850, about fifteen thousand in absolute numbers.[203] Evidence taken in the 1851 census and by investigating commissions confirmed that fewer young children were employed in industry; accordingly the number of children in factory schools was low.[204] Estimates based on the education census of 1851 suggest that it was around 3 percent of the national total enrolled in day schools.[205] The numbers of children employed in industry began to decrease further in the 1860s as more industries came under the umbrella of factory legislation. One estimate is that two hundred thousand children were relieved of employment as a result of the factory legislation of 1867 alone.[206] It was also estimated that by 1868 fewer than eighty thousand children were in compulsory schools established by factory legislation.[207] J. S. Hurt concludes that "by the 1860's the exploitation of the labour of the very young was the exception rather than the rule."[208] This meant that the net of compulsory schooling for factory children caught only a small proportion of the young. It also meant that the unemployed young probably contributed to the class of children who were neither at work nor at school.[209] The evidence reviewed above suggests that the arrangements established by the Revised Code also worked to discourage the attendance of the very poor at the schools.

Whatever the structural sources of the class of children not reached by the subsidized voluntary system, that class was very large in the 1860s. The Birmingham Education Aid Society's survey of 8,044 children in Birmingham between the ages of three and twelve revealed that 887 were at work, 3,972 were at school, and 3,185 were at neither. An earlier survey by the Manchester Education Aid Society showed that of 11,086 children between three and twelve in that district, 762 were at work, 4,537 were at school, and 5,787 were neither at work nor at school.[210] Both surveys were seen as correctives to the Newcastle Commission's apparent underenumeration of children not reached by schools. The surveys created a public stir. They were followed by government-ordered surveys of Liverpool, Leeds, Manchester, and Birmingham, which showed a similar pattern of nonattendance.[211] Hurt argues that this failure to cover the young was the main motive in the minds of reformers pressing for governmental reform in the late 1860s, and that the "gaps" to be filled by William Forster's proposals in 1870 referred mainly to the "social and educational outcasts" of the day.[212]

RELIGIOUS CONSEQUENCES

Recent historical interpretations have taken different views of the religious impact of the Revised Code. Hurt argues that it was decisive:

> The religious monopoly . . . was breached by the state not in 1870, as is commonly supposed, but in 1862 when the Revised Code was introduced. By emphasizing the secular element in education at the expense of the religious, it forced Anglican schools to subordinate the paramountcy of their former function to the needs of an industrial society. This code, in turn, was the outcome of a closer and more detailed control that had been growing since 1839.[213]

Hurt's conclusion appears to rest mainly on the restriction of payments to the basic secular subjects, which would turn the managers and teachers toward them and away from religious instruction, since they were the subjects that mattered in the reckoning of grants. The National Society objected to the Revised Code on this basis. In the years following, inspectors of Church of England schools reported a decline in the "religious and moral aspect of the school" because of pecuniary interest in the basic subjects,[214] and that religious knowledge had "fallen off."[215] Such comments were not frequent, however, and a consensus on the matter was not evident to the Committee of Council in its report of 1868. On the basis of this and other information, D. W. Sylvester concludes that "[there] is no statistical evidence to show whether there was a decline in the amount of religious instruction during the period of the Code."[216] Granting the uncertainty, it may be assumed safely that the code did not *increase* the stress on religious instruction, and that, consistent with Hurt's interpretation, it gave explicit priority to secular education, while remaining officially silent on religious instruction.

A more important alteration in the definition of religious instruction did not arise directly from the Revised Code, but nonetheless flowed from the same efforts to economize. That alteration concerned the conscience clause in the 1860s. For many years the Committee of Council had been trying to persuade the National Society to accept a liberal arrangement. In 1860 it began to demand that, in small communities with many Dissenters, the Church of England exempt their children from instruction in its doctrines and catechism.[217] The National Society reacted negatively, and this began a running conflict between the society and the committee in the 1860s, especially in Wales, where many small communities had a majority of Dissenters.[218] Archdeacon Denison entered the contest, assuming as militant a stance as he had on the management clauses a decade earlier. The Anglican Church was divided, however, many, having become reconciled to the conscience clause and other retrenchments, adopting the policy that in order to maintain its established position, it must concede strategically.[219] In 1863 the committee demanded the insertion of a conscience clause in every deed of trust. The National Society balked, and in the following year Lingen agreed to insist on the clause only for small communities. This accommodation did not satisfy the Church of England either, and the matter ended in stalemate. The committee insisted on the conscience clause and the National Society refused to support schools that accepted one.[220] This conflict no doubt contributed to the decline in the number of building grants in the 1860s.[221]

The committee, caught in conflict with the Anglican Church, never issued an official minute on the subject; it handled the matter informally, but with increasing firmness during the 1860s.[222] In 1867 the committee acknowledged that the issue was still unresolved.[223] A conscience clause seemed to become inevitable, however, after the Gladstone government had concluded in 1868 that the Church of England could no longer assert its exclusive claims and after the church gave ground on rates and disestablishment in Ireland.[224] Most witnesses testi-

fying before the Select Committee on Education in 1865 acknowledged
that the multiplication of schools in small communities was uneconomi-
cal, and that the motive for the conscience clause was an economic
one.[225] Lowe laid out the priorities clearly: "The conscience clause was
not my end; my end was to see that the public money went only as it
ought to go; it was merely to protect the public purse and the rights of
conscience that I refused the grant, and I was quite as well or better
pleased that public money should be saved, as that the conscience clause
be adopted."[226] In earlier testimony Lingen had said the reasons for insisting on the conscience clause were to economize and to avoid injustice to those who conscientiously objected to doctrinal instruction
and liturgy.[227]

The issue of the conscience clause was an unwelcome one for the
state because any solution to it seemed to generate conflict with one or
another religious group. Not to insist on it would raise objections by
Dissenters and Catholics, and to insist on it would—and did—create a
fight with the Anglican Church. This difficulty helps explain both the
inability of the state to reach a final solution on the issue in the 1860s
and its justification of its insistence on it by falling back on an external,
neutral reason—the need for economy. Be that as it may, to insist on
such a clause was government policy by the mid 1860s, and this was
endorsed by the Select Committee on Education.[228] Its policy, moreover,
marked a shift in the definition of the religious situation. The Church of
England was, in effect, now treated as one of many sects, because it was
being asked, along with the others, not to impose its doctrines and rituals on those unwilling to receive them. Once the conscience clause became official state policy, moreover, it became more or less impossible to
adopt anything less when the state addressed elementary education officially in 1870.

## EDUCATIONAL EFFORTS IN THE 1860S

After the legislative failures and the political stalemate in the
1850s,[229] leaders apparently became discouraged. In July 1867, when
Bruce introduced an educational measure, he noted that more than a
decade had passed since Pakington's and Russell's efforts had failed.[230]
Bruce explained that his motives for pressing for legislation were that
too small a proportion of the nation's children were in schools and that
schools were unevenly distributed.[231] His proposal was permissive, allowing districts to levy rates, and he called for inspections and manage-

ment committees that would not interfere with religious or secular instruction. His proposal provided for a conscience clause, and for free attendance for children of parents who could not afford to pay school fees.[232] Bruce compared his proposals closely to the Irish system, which he described as originally a national system, which had evolved to a denominational system with a conscience clause.[233] His bill was attacked by J. W. Henley as being as inimical to the Church of England as the Irish system was, and by J. G. Hubbard, who argued that the bill's permissiveness would not guarantee coverage of those areas "where poverty and ignorance existed."[234] The bill was withdrawn shortly after brief debate.

In 1867 the Conservative Derby administration prepared a bill for presentation to Parliament that would centralize and rationalize the administrative authority for education. It did not call for local rates, which Conservatives traditionally opposed on grounds that they would encourage "democratic" control of education by ratepayers and diminish the position of the Anglican Church. Instead, the bill proposed an increase in state aid within the existing system. It is notable that it also called for a conscience clause in single-school communities, indicating that the Conservatives accepted the idea. The bill never came before Parliament, partly because the Conservative and Liberal leadership was passing to Disraeli and Gladstone respectively, and neither was enthusiastic about the Derby proposal's centralizing tendencies.[235] In 1868 Bruce introduced a bill similar to his proposal the year before, but with machinery for compulsory enforcement. He withdrew the bill, however, in hopes that a similar measure would be introduced after the election of 1868. These failures of 1867–68 were reminiscent of those of the 1850s and revealed the same paralysis. They reflected fears of support from the rates by both the Church of England and Dissent (the one fearing erosion of the Anglican Church, the other fearing dominance by it). None of the measures came close to fruition, despite the increasing acknowledgment that the existing system was not reaching the nation's educational goals.

## OTHER RELIGIOUS AND POLITICAL DEVELOPMENTS

The 1860s witnessed continuing efforts on the part of the Society for the Liberation of Religion to disestablish the Church of England. Gladstone orchestrated the church's actual disestablishment in Ireland in

1869. Edward Miall introduced bills for its general disestablishment in 1871, 1872, and 1873, but without success. The Anglican Church experienced defeats with the opening of the grammar schools to Dissenters in 1860 and the abolition of the church rates in 1868. In a letter to Lord John Russell in 1868, the earl of Clarendon guessed that the Anglican Establishment in England would "perhaps last until the end of the century."[236]

With respect to education, the 1860s witnessed the coalescence of Dissenting groups, which had been badly divided since the middle 1840s, when Voluntaryism emerged and the Wesleyan Methodists were coopted separately into the state system of support. The decisive event was Baines's and Miall's desertion of the Voluntaryist principle in 1867. Baines indicated that the Congregational Board would now be prepared to accept government money for secular education only (which actually ruled out Committee of Council aid, restricted as it was to support of recognized denominations offering religious instruction.) More important, the former Voluntaryist leaders called for a *state* system of *secular* education. Baines and Miall offered several reasons for their conversion, but mainly it was a matter of not being able to sustain schools on a private, voluntary basis without imposing excessive school fees on parents.[237] The emphasis on secular instruction derived from the Voluntaryists' conviction that any state-supported religious system would ensure Anglican domination.[238] By thus altering their position, the Voluntaryists could now make common cause with the British and Foreign School Society, which, although receiving in state support, had also continued at a disadvantage in relation to the Church of England. Hostility between the British Society and the National Society had increased in the 1860s because of the latter's apparently intransigent stand on the conscience clause. In fact, the British and Foreign School Society supported the Liberals' efforts to set up a state system in 1869 and 1870, approving of their stand on religious toleration in particular.[239]

This Nonconformist coalition was able to weld at least temporary alliances with other groups. Among these were the secularists. This group survived from the National Public School Association and were represented in the education aid societies in Birmingham, Manchester, and elsewhere. The coalition found friends among leaders of the trade unions and skilled artisans, who joined the call for "free, compulsory and unsectarian education" in the late 1860s and organized meetings of workers to support the Education Act of 1870.[240] This support was qualified, however. Education occupied a low place on the agenda of the emerging labor union movement in the 1860s.[241] In addition, the labor groups were themselves divided with respect to stressing the secular or the religious element in education (the latter finding favor in labor organizations with heavy Catholic memberships).[242]

These were the interest groups that came together in the Birmingham Education League, later the National Education League. Their program called for universal coverage of the young, support of schools from rates supplemented by government grants, inspection, unsectarian education, free schools, and compulsory attendance. From the very beginning, however, the league was haunted by a religious conflict, arising from differences between those favoring a completely secular state system and those favoring a model along British and Foreign School Society lines. The league settled on the compromise term *unsectarian*, but as the secretary and historian of the league observed, the compromise seemed to accomplish little good, because it did not lessen Tory and Church of England attacks on the league as "the enemies of religion, of government, and of morals."[243] The league's leaders were almost all supporters of the Liberal Party and they included all shades of religious opinion except High Church and Catholic.[244]

In this period, the Church of England was thrown on the defensive, both by the continuing assaults on its established position in the 1860s and by the unity among the Nonconformists and others in the league. Throughout the campaign preceding the Education Act of 1870, the Anglican Church assumed what might now be termed a posture of "damage control"—to protect what it enjoyed out of fear of losing altogether to secularist opponents. As the campaign proceeded, the National Society surrendered on the conscience clause issue, but fought against rate-support and lay management of its schools, and for the continued funding of Anglican schools.[245] In 1870 the Anglicans took the lead in forming the National Education Union, a counterorganization to the league. This group advocated continuing denominational education and increasing the level of support for voluntary schools. The union gained the support of Wesleyan Methodists, whose joining of the government system in 1847 had reallied them with the Church of England at least in this regard.[246] The union was also supported by the Catholic hierarchy, who shared with Anglicans the desire to retain the religious dimension and clerical control of education. (Interestingly, the Catholics supported the Nonconformist/Liberal position on the disestablishment of the Church of Ireland, but parted company with it on the question of elementary education.)[247] The union also experienced some internal splits, with moderates willing to accept the conscience clause and the High Anglicans opposing it, and the Anglicans and Roman Catholics favoring more religious doctrine and worship in education.[248] Kay-Shuttleworth generally supported the union; his *Memorandum on Popular Education* favored in expansion of the denominational system and continuation of the religious emphasis in education.

Historians have identified several additional factors that gave an impetus to the extension of state involvement in elementary education in the 1860s. Briggs notes the return of radicalism after its retreat in the high Victorian years, a return conditioned by the death of Palmerston, the conversion of Gladstone to liberal causes such as parliamentary reform, and the lull in economic prosperity in 1866 and 1867.[249] Others have mentioned the success of the Prussians in the Austro-Prussian War and of the North in the American Civil War. British observers attributed both events to those countries' highly developed educational systems, remembering, perhaps, the mediocre British performance in the Crimean War.[250] The Paris Exposition of 1867, publicized by Leon Playfair,[251] touched the growing sensitivities of Englishmen to competition from presumably better-educated artisans and laborers abroad.[252] Finally, much has been made of the effect of the Reform Act of 1867, which enfranchised a portion of the working classes and converted Lowe to the idea of state education out of the necessity of "[prevailing] on our future masters to learn their letters."[253] Recently, however, several historians have downplayed the centrality of that concern.[254] It is difficult and probably fruitless to attempt to assess the precise role of these factors, beyond noting that central historical actors of the time, such as Gladstone, Lowe, Forster, and Baines, stressed them and made them salient in the political consciousness of the time.

When Gladstone's Liberal government assumed office in 1868 with a huge majority, it was widely expected that educational reform would be at the top of its agenda. The cabinet included Forster, a Quaker, a friend of educational reform, and a co-sponsor of the Bruce proposals of 1867. An education bill was delayed mainly because of Gladstone's and Parliament's attention to the land question and disestablishment in Ireland. When Forster introduced his bill on February 17, 1870, he acknowledged that public opinion was divided "more or less, into two camps"— the league and the union. He denied the charge that the bill was any kind of compromise; it was "a measure too important to be dealt with in such a manner."[255] He began by citing statistics from the education aid societies, plus some of his own, to prove that the existing system was falling short, because some 1,500,000 children were receiving only "imperfect education." By way of further introduction, Forster appealed to the principle of minimalism, that apology for almost every educational reform previously introduced:

> We must take care not to destroy in building up—not to destroy the existing system in introducing a new one. In solving this problem there must be . . . the least possible expenditure of public money, the utmost endeavour not to injure existing and efficient schools, and the most careful absence of all encouragement to parents to neglect their children. . . . Our object is to complete the present voluntary system, to fill up gaps.[256]

In addition to protecting existing institutions and observing economy, Forster gave three additional, also familiar, justifications for expanding the system:

Increasing the competitiveness of British industry: "[Upon] the speedy provision of elementary education depends our industrial prosperity."

The working of democracy: "[Upon] this speedy provision depends also, I fully believe, the good, the safe working of our constitutional system." Forster argued that he was among those who believed that good education should have preceded the extension of the franchise, but in any event, "now that we have given [the people] political power we must not wait any longer to give them education."

National power: "If we are to hold our position among men of our own race or among the nations of the world we must make up for the smallness of our numbers by increasing the intellectual force of the individual."[257]

The provisions of the bill were to divide the counties into school districts; to grant a year of grace to denominations to establish schools in districts found wanting; to establish elected school boards, with powers of rating to construct and support schools; to eliminate denominationally based inspection (because of its cost and cumbersomeness); to enforce a conscience clause to protect parents who protested against doctrinal education; to remit school fees for children in poverty; to remove restrictions against supporting secular schools; to permit school boards to compel attendance; and to empower school boards to assist existing (including denominational) schools with funds from the rates.

The initial debate was calm and friendly. No one challenged the principles and justifications that accompanied Forster's introduction of the

bill. George Dixon, the representative of the Birmingham League, expressed general satisfaction. In the question period, Forster said that
"there were many hard-working clergymen of the Church of England, of
all schools of thought, who on the whole supported the plan." [258]

The peace was short-lived, however; almost immediately public opposition to the bill appeared. In the debate, which resumed on March
14, a great range of challenges and amendments arose. Almost all of
these came from the league, and most concerned provisions that, it was
felt, left too much power in the hands of the Church of England. Dixon
objected to the year of grace; he argued that school boards should be
extended to every district, and elected by ballot; most important, he
argued that the power of local boards to regulate religious instruction
should be further restricted. [259] Forster was thrown on the defensive. In
response to repeated attacks that the bill favored the Anglican Church,
he enunciated the complex principle of legitimization within which the
government had by this time come to operate:

> I have seen it stated very often in the public press . . . that [the bill] gives
> more assistance to the Established Church than to any other denomina
> tion . . . I can only say that I am innocent of any such attempt, and of all
> belief that such a result would be produced. My object . . . has been educa-
> tion and education alone. We determined that nothing we might do should
> discourage religion . . . we were also determined that . . . we would not treat
> one religious sect with greater indulgence than another. [260]

The defense was not successful; debate of an intense and sometimes
bitter sectarian character continued for several days, the most aggressive pressure being applied constantly by the representatives of the
league and its allies. The prolonged and acrimonious debate prompted a
cynical remark by Lowe, now chancellor of the exchequer and friend of
the Forster bill: "Is it not a pitiable sight? It reminds me of a fine herd of
cattle in a large meadow deserting the grass which is abundant about
them [the extension of popular education] and delighting themselves by
fighting over a bed of nettles [religious sectarianism] in one corner of the
field." [261]

In the ensuing months the conflict and efforts to achieve compromise
continued. These developments will not be reviewed here [262] except to
indicate the compromises reached. The period of grace to permit denominations to "fill the gaps" by new applications was reduced to six
months. The school boards were to be elected popularly by ratepayers
and burgesses, instead of by town councils and vestries as originally suggested. Religious instruction was to be limited to certain fixed hours

(the time-table clause) to facilitate the withdrawal of children from that instruction if their parents desired to do so. Finally, Parliament approved an even stronger version of the conscience clause than that earlier proposed. The amendment was the one devised by W. F. Cowper-Temple: "No catechism or religious formulary [that] is distinctively of any particular denomination shall be taught" in schools established from local rates.[263]

Virtually all the compromises represented concessions to the left, in this case the coalition represented by the Nonconformists and the league.[264] Late in the day, Gladstone pointed out that all the concessions had been made by the Church of England and the Roman Catholics, and he chided the Nonconformists for not being as agreeable.[265] Still, the government stood firm on the most fundamental issue and left the denominational system intact, side by side with the new board system.[266] Gladstone summarized the government's final position:

> It was with us an absolute necessity—a necessity of honour and a necessity of policy—to respect and to favour the educational establishments and machinery we found existing in the country. It was impossible for us to join in the language, or to adopt the tone which was conscientiously taken by some members of the House, who look upon these voluntary schools, having generally a denominational character, as admirable passing expedients, fit indeed to be tolerated for a time, deserving all credit on account of the motives which led to their foundation, but wholly unsatisfactory as to their main purpose, and therefore to be supplanted by something they think better.[267]

In this explanation Gladstone endorsed the principles of accretion and proliferation that had dominated the scene of primary education of the working classes since the formation of the religious societies at the beginning of the century. The decisive difference in 1870, however, was that the government itself became one of those layers blistered onto the patchwork system that had accumulated over six decades.


EPILOGUE

This completes the account of the decisive moments of change and truce points in the history of working-class education in the nineteenth century. Needless to say, the system did not stabilize when the state entered, formally and unequivocally, into the administration of the elementary education. The Education Act of 1870 was only one step in the long march toward conquest of the elementary system by government. As might be expected, the resources of the government—relying on rates rather than contributions—quickly came to outstrip the voluntary impulse in terms of numbers of schools established and pupils served.[268] The state accomplished the general enforcement of compulsory attendance in 1876 and subsequent years, made attendance free in 1891, and established a whole new and systematized framework by the legislation of 1902. On many other fronts the rationalization and bureaucratization of the system continued.

Yet the competitive religious impulse continued for decades to come. In the immediate wake of the act of 1870, the Church of England and the Catholic Church led a surge of 1,332 new applications for denominational schools (about one-third of which were subsequently withdrawn) before the six-month grace period had expired. The normal rate had been about 150 applications per year.[269] The Nonconformists and the league, having secured many compromises during the course of debate over the legislation of 1870, nevertheless emerged from the contest bitterly disappointed with the educational result and with the Liberal Party. Before the dissolution of the league in 1876, it initiated a prolonged personal attack on Forster[270] and sought repeatedly to amend the act of 1870. It also joined with workingmen's groups in a six-year assault on Section 25 of the Education Act, which permitted public funds to be allocated to denominational schools to aid children of poor parents. Elections to the newly created school boards also turned into bitter sectarian contests, with a coalition of Nonconformists and sectarians lined up against Church of England, Roman Catholic, and sometimes Wesleyan groups. The method of preferential voting was also a bone of contention, because it appeared to give an advantage to better-organized religious groups such as the Church of England and the Catholics. The conscience clause issue persisted as a matter of controversy in rural and Anglican schools. In many urban areas, debates continued as to how much religion was to be taught in the schools.[271] And, finally, the administrative transition from school boards to local educational authorities in 1902 was plagued by prolonged controversies over the supposed advantages and disadvantages that might accrue to the different denominations as a result of the reform.[272] As was the case with so many features of traditional British society, the primordial bases of religious organization were slow to erode with the rise of "modern" social institutions.

## CHAPTER 6

# The Case of Wales

For the student of comparisons, Wales holds a special fascination as one of those "near cases"—near to, even an integral part of, England in many cultural and social-structural respects, but different in others. It was also near to Scotland and Ireland in that it shared Celtic influences, but had distinctive features of its own and differed from the other two in its relations with England.

To commence, then, it is helpful to note some ways in which Wales presents a distinct picture in comparison to England, Ireland, and Scotland in the nineteenth century.

With respect to polity, Wales had been officially coterminous with England politically and administratively for centuries. By contrast, Ireland had a dual system of administration, and Scotland enjoyed significant autonomy in many administrative respects.[1]

With respect to religion, Wales was also officially under the Church of England, though contemporaries occasionally spoke of the "Church in Wales" to indicate, perhaps, that the Anglican Church's position there was not quite the same as in England.[2] Demographically, however, the Anglican Church commanded a minority of communicants, as in Ireland and Scotland. The majority in Wales was Nonconformist/ Wesleyan by perhaps a 4:1 ratio over the Church of England.

With respect to social class, Wales possessed what was almost a two-tiered system, consisting of a small elite of landowners and a small number of manufacturers on the one hand, and large numbers of farmers and tenants and industrial workers on the other, with a smallish middle class, again in contrast to England. The upper classes contrasted with the lower with respect to language (English versus Welsh), religion (Anglican versus Nonconformist/Wesleyan), and cultural orientation (England versus Welsh identification). In these regards the Welsh situation resembled the Irish one and contrasted with that of Scotland, which had a resident landed class and a larger middle class.

With respect to economy, Wales had a mixture of industrial workers, miners, and agricultural tenants and laborers, and in this regard resembled several other regions. The southern counties, however, became highly industrialized, whereas industrialization in the north was much more limited.

The Welsh case presents some peculiarities with respect to educational outcomes as well. Considered in comparison to England, Wales displayed:

A consistently lower level of educational development according to all—admittedly imprecise—measures.

A greater vitality with respect to the development of Sunday schools.

A certain sluggishness in the establishment of day schools on the part of voluntary religious bodies.

A notable fusion of educational conflict with conflicts over religion, class, region, culture, and language, with resulting intensity, polarization, and "primordialization" of that conflict.[3]

A stronger tendency to "undenominationalize" or secularize primary education in the second half of the nineteenth century.

My objective in this chapter is to link the general structural conditions with the distinctive educational outcomes, using the model of structural pressures, conflict, and change to connect them. I shall proceed by several stages. First, I shall identify certain historically inherited contours of Welsh society within which change in the nineteenth century played out. Second, I shall outline some demographic, economic, and religious trends that continued into that century and conditioned educational developments. Third, I shall identify those educational changes themselves. Fourth, I shall describe the ferment of the 1840s and the clash of forces affecting Welsh education at that time. Fifth, I

shall trace the pattern of "situations and events" in the 1850s and 1860s
that propelled Wales toward its radical and secularized political stance
in the late nineteenth century.

## RELEVANT CONTOURS OF WELSH HISTORY

While Wales, like the other Celtic regions, possessed sufficient cultural and linguistic distinctiveness to be considered a "nation" separate
from England, this separateness was scarcely acknowledged in a formal
sense until disestablishment, new language policies, and other changes
in the twentieth century. The political union of England and Wales was
effected in 1536. The cultural boundaries between the two remained indistinct over the centuries,[4] and Wales never developed a regional capital like Edinburgh or Dublin. This union implied a centuries-long policy
of more or less uniform application of statutes, administration, and
practices to England and Wales:

> The union with England had been followed by a systematic process of ad-
> ministrative uniformity down to the abolition of the court of Great Sessions
> in 1830, itself a creation of the Act of Union. From Tudor times, it had been
> governmental policy to extinguish the language and cultural expression of
> the Welsh people for official purposes, in the interests of centralisation, al-
> though in fact by authorising the use of Welsh in church services the Tudors
> themselves had helped to insure the survival of the native culture. In
> Scotland, an independent legal profession had become the "bearers and de-
> fenders of nationality." In Wales, pastors had to make their way on English
> circuits. In Ireland, a dual system of administration between Westminster
> and Dublin Castle testified to the separate role of Ireland in public policy. In
> Wales, the Home Office and the Court of Chancery made no distinction be-
> tween Welsh and English problems. In Scotland, the Kirk remained a repre-
> sentative assembly community.[5]

This virtual ignoring of Welsh peculiarities found a parallel in the
policies and practices of the Church of England. The Anglican Church
never developed a "Church of Wales" parallel to the Church of Ireland,
which acknowledged—in name at least—the religious peculiarities of
that largely Roman Catholic island. Between 1715 and 1870 not a
single bishop in Wales was a Welsh-speaking Welshman. Assignment to
religious duty in Wales appeared to be unattractive for English clergymen, a fact traceable, no doubt, to the disdainful attitude that many
educated English had for the Welsh and to the cultural and religious remoteness between Anglican clergymen and their potential Welsh flocks.[6]

As late as 1886, the bishop of St. David's reflected that "Wales is at present nothing more than the Highlands of Scotland without a Highland Line: it is a geographical expression."[7]

For centuries, then, Wales experienced a tension, if not contradiction, arising from the disinclination of English officialdom to recognize its cultural distinctiveness. This tension was to prove a political and administrative problem at times in dealing with the Welsh situation during the nineteenth century. What were the components of Welsh distinctiveness? It included historical identification with an ancient Welsh separateness, if not statehood, symbolized by national warriors and other heroes such as Llewelyn and Glyndwr. The Welsh also identified with their Celtic language, which symbolized their own unity and separateness as well. In the eighteenth century especially, Welsh distinctiveness became associated with religious Dissent, which was greatly stimulated by the Methodist and Evangelical revivals, during which Dissenters came to constitute a large majority.[8]

Whatever the ingredients of Welsh distinctiveness, the coincidence of certain social-structural trends early in the nineteenth century served to consolidate it. Wales had retained its geographical and economic isolation from England. In the late eighteenth century, however, capital, consumer products, and English (and Irish) immigrants began to flow into Wales as industrial growth took off in the ore-extracting, ore-processing, and coal industries. Even though economic activity had been stimulated in the wars of the late eighteenth century, many of the early canals in South Wales served only to link its mines and industries with the sea. North Wales was more isolated than the Highlands of Scotland with respect to roads.[9] The persistence of the Welsh language was both effect and cause of this isolation, and the domination of Methodism and Dissent also served to accentuate Welsh localism, patriotism, and incipient nationalism.

Welsh class relations also worked to isolate and polarize. Wales had participated in the great enclosure movement that preceded the industrial revolution, and in some respects that movement reached more extreme lengths there. In the 1870s, on the eve of the fragmentation of the estate system into a more widespread freehold system, estates of more than one thousand acres covered 60.6 percent of the cultivated land in Wales, as compared with 53.5 percent in England.[10] In addition, farming was carried out largely under tenancy-at-will arrangements, renewable on a year-by-year basis—in contrast with lease-holding—making the tenant more vulnerable to eviction and increases in rent.[11] These arrangements tended to homogenize tenants and laborers at the bottom of the agricultural class spectrum.

> The small Welsh farmer worked the land alongside his labourers, and scarcity of farms meant the farmer's sons often became labourers of the indoor servant type on neighbouring farms. Labourers, for their part, frequently achieved their ambition of becoming tenant farmers, for the small Welsh holdings could be taken with only little capital. . . . Thus, farmers and labourers shaded imperceptibly into one another. . . . This general absence of class cleavage in Wales contrasted markedly with the situation in most areas of England, where the two classes were separate and distinct and where the larger farms meant that the prospects of an agricultural labourer becoming a farmer were remote.[12]

The relations between Welsh landlords and their workers was thus intermediate between those of Scotland and Ireland. The Scottish lairds were mainly a resident Scottish class. Many Irish gentry were both English and absentee. Most Welsh landlords were Welsh by ancestry and name, and they were largely resident in Wales.[13] But over time these landlords had become more or less anglicized. They had adopted the English language, identified with the English aristocracy in style, manners, and outlook, embraced Tory politics, and affiliated with the Anglican Church[14]—all in contrast to, and making for remoteness from, their workers. This situation was aggravated by the facts that many landlords employed English and Scottish agents, who dealt with tenants and laborers in the English language,[15] and that the administration of justice was in the hands of magistrates who came mainly from the anglicized gentry and conducted their sessions in English.[16] Finally, prior to the 1867 Reform Act and the election of 1868, few in the Welsh population enjoyed the franchise, and representatives in Parliament were almost exclusively gentry and largely Tory.[17]

When it is noted further that largely rural Wales had a negligible middle class,[18] the class system at the beginning of the nineteenth century appears as an extreme one. At the risk of oversimplifying, it can be argued that it was almost a two-class system, with overlapping cleavages along many dimensions of social life—wealth, political power, administration of justice, religion, cultural aspirations, regional identification, style of life, and language. All class systems overlap in these ways to some degree, but the Welsh case was, along with the Irish, exceptional.[19] When such overlapping occurs, the potential for class consciousness, antagonism, and conflict is usually high. When conflict breaks out, moreover, it is generalized, with one dimension fusing with or turning into another, since all types of conflict rest on the same social-structural foundations.[20]

Although Wales was already notable for its Nonconformity before the nineteenth century,[21] Dissent established itself more firmly there in that century. Tables 6 and 7 document the fact that all Dissenters' places of worship accounted for about one-third of the total in both North and South Wales in 1800 and show that by midcentury the percentage had nearly doubled. Nonconformity marched forward as dramatically as population and economic growth in Wales in both agricultural and urbanized counties. The figures also reveal the strength of the Congregationalists or Independents in the south and the Methodists in the north, as well as the inactivity of the Church of England during the first third of the century.[22]

With respect to numbers of adherents, the picture is even more striking. While the 1851 census showed almost half of the Welsh population unclaimed by denomination, among those who were, three-quarters were to be found among the Independents, Baptists, and Methodists (see table 8). The dominance of Dissent is even greater when measured by "attendants" on a given date in 1851 rather than "sittings" (seats).[23] These facts express a conclusion that will also apply to educational growth in Wales: that the Church of England had been better able to cover that principality with its institutions than it had been able to secure the participation and loyalty of its people.

Welsh Nonconformity received further impetus from the great religious revival of 1859. The second half of the century saw the development of an outspoken Nonconformist press, the enfranchisement and increased political involvement of Nonconformists by the Reform Act of 1867, its marriage with the Liberal Party in the early Gladstonian years, and its subsequent involvement in the tithe wars and the struggle for the disestablishment of the Church in Wales.[24] In education, Nonconformity struggled with both the Anglican Church and the British government especially in the 1840s and afterwards, involving itself in the politics of the Education Act of 1870 and in local election struggles and other conflicts after that time. This Nonconformist influence will appear in my accounts of Welsh educational developments throughout this chapter.

TABLE 6   GROWTH OF CHURCHES AND CHAPELS IN
SOUTH WALES, TO 1851

| | Before 1801 | 1801–11 | 1811–21 | 1821–31 | 1831–41 | 1841–51 | Not Stated | Total |
|---|---|---|---|---|---|---|---|---|
| *Protestants* | | | | | | | | |
| *Church of England* | 497 | 1 | 0 | 5 | 18 | 30 | 64 | 615 |
| *Independents or* | | | | | | | | |
| *Congregationalists* | 90 | 34 | 30 | 58 | 64 | 77 | 13 | 366 |
| *Baptists* | 55 | 16 | 31 | 52 | 61 | 74 | 7 | 296 |
| *Society of Friends* | 3 | 2 | 0 | 0 | 2 | 0 | 0 | 7 |
| *Unitarians* | 10 | 3 | 2 | 2 | 2 | 3 | 2 | 24 |
| *Wesleyan Methodists* | 15 | 23 | 30 | 33 | 40 | 42 | 26 | 209 |
| *Calvinist Methodists* | 91 | 28 | 31 | 46 | 62 | 39 | 6 | 303 |
| *Brethren* | 1 | 0 | 0 | 0 | 0 | 0 | 0 | 1 |
| *Isolated congregations* | 3 | 0 | 1 | 1 | 1 | 5 | 1 | 12 |
| *Other Christian Churches* | | | | | | | | |
| *Roman Catholics* | 0 | 0 | 0 | 0 | 0 | 5 | 1 | 6 |
| *Latter-Day Saints* | 1 | 0 | 0 | 0 | 3 | 4 | 10 | 18 |
| *Jews* | 1 | 0 | 0 | 0 | 0 | 1 | 0 | 2 |

SOURCE: *Parliamentary Papers*, 1852–53, 89, census of religious worship, p. ccl.

TABLE 7   GROWTH OF CHURCHES AND CHAPELS IN
NORTH WALES, TO 1851

| | Before 1801 | 1801–11 | 1811–21 | 1821–31 | 1831–41 | 1841–51 | Not Stated | Total |
|---|---|---|---|---|---|---|---|---|
| *Protestants* | | | | | | | | |
| Church of England | 272 | 7 | 2 | 2 | 15 | 25 | 47 | 370 |
| Independents or | | | | | | | | |
| Congregationalists | 29 | 18 | 34 | 79 | 57 | 49 | 7 | 273 |
| Baptists | 21 | 16 | 20 | 32 | 27 | 19 | 11 | 146 |
| Society of Friends | 1 | 0 | 0 | 1 | 0 | 0 | 0 | 2 |
| Unitarians | 1 | 0 | 0 | 1 | 0 | 0 | 0 | 2 |
| Wesleyan Methodists | 5 | 39 | 25 | 91 | 101 | 55 | 28 | 344 |
| Calvinist Methodists | 82 | 42 | 72 | 122 | 90 | 53 | 17 | 478 |
| Brethren | 0 | 1 | 0 | 0 | 0 | 0 | 0 | 1 |
| Isolated congregations | 2 | 0 | 5 | 0 | 2 | 5 | 2 | 16 |
| *Other Christian Churches* | | | | | | | | |
| Roman Catholics | 1 | 0 | 0 | 1 | 1 | 0 | 2 | 5 |
| Latter-Day Saints | 1 | 0 | 0 | 0 | 1 | 3 | 2 | 7 |

SOURCE: *Parliamentary Papers*, 1852–53, 89, census of religious worship, p. ccl.

TABLE 8   RELIGIOUS COMPOSITION OF WALES AND
MONMOUTH, 1851 (%)

| | Church of England | Independents | Baptists | Methodists | Roman Catholics | Jews | Others |
|---|---|---|---|---|---|---|---|
| *North Wales* | | | | | | | |
| *Attendants* | 22.3 | 14.8 | 7.9 | 53.2 | 0.5 | 0 | 1.4 |
| *Sittings* | 29.7 | 24.4 | 16.6 | 26.3 | 0.4 | 0.02 | 2.6 |
| *South Wales* | | | | | | | |
| *Attendants* | 21.2 | 29.3 | 20.8 | 25.8 | 0.9 | 0.02 | 2.1 |
| *Sittings* | 31.1 | 12.8 | 25.3 | 26.8 | 2.4 | 0 | 1.6 |
| *Monmouthshire* | | | | | | | |
| *Attendants* | 24.6 | 15.2 | 27.0 | 27.7 | 4.0 | 0 | 1. |

SOURCE: *Parliamentary Papers*, 1852–53, 89, cclxxvi–vii.
NOTE: Only those who specified a confession are included. "Sittings" = seats.

INDUSTRIALIZATION
AND RELATED DEVELOPMENTS

South and North Wales both experienced great economic activity beginning in the last part of the eighteenth century, though the regional
differences were striking. In the north, the iron, copper, and lead industries prospered during the French and American Wars, and these in turn
stimulated mining in Flintshire. But a slackening of demand, the ex-
haustion of ores, and competition from South Wales and elsewhere led
to a falling-off in these industries by mid nineteenth century. The slate
industry, after remaining stagnant in the war period, grew rapidly in
Carmarthenshire between 1820 and 1840. Woollens developed in north
central Wales during the first four decades of the century, but both domestic and manufacturing production declined thereafter in the face of
competition from England. The net effect was that, after a few decades
of marked industrial activity, North Wales reverted to an economic condition more dominated by agriculture.[25]

The south, by contrast, experienced an industrial revolution. The
iron industry was slow to develop in the eighteenth century, largely because of Wales's economic remoteness. But the demand occasioned by
the wars and the opportunities arising from an improved steam engine
and the invention of the puddling process produced a great expansion of
the iron and tin-plate industries along the coalfields in the south. After

TABLE 9    POPULATION CHANGES IN SOUTH WALES, 1801–1871

|            | 1801    | 1811    |           | 1821    |           | 1831    |          |
|------------|---------|---------|-----------|---------|-----------|---------|----------|
|            | Total   | Total   | % Change  | Total   | % Change  | Total   | % Chan   |
| Brecon     | 32,325  | 37,735  | 17        | 43,826  | 16        | 47,763  | 9        |
| Cardigan   | 42,956  | 50,260  | 17        | 57,784  | 15        | 64,780  | 12       |
| Carmarthen | 67,317  | 77,217  | 15        | 90,239  | 17        | 100,740 | 12       |
| Glamorgan  | 70,8⁄ )  | 85,067  | 20        | 102,073 | 20        | 126,612 | 24       |
| Monmouth   | 45,568  | 62,105  | 36        | 75,801  | 22        | 98,126  | 29       |
| Pembroke   | 56,280  | 60,615  | 8         | 73,788  | 22        | 81,425  | 10       |
| Radnor     | 19,135  | 24,417  | 7         | 22,533  | 10        | 24,743  | 10       |
| Total      | 334,460 | 397,416 | 18        | 466,034 | 18        | 544,189 | 17       |

the wars, the iron industry continued to grow, largely in response to demands for railway construction, first in Britain and later abroad. Copper smelting also developed, using first domestic and later Cuban and Chilean ore. All these developments created more demand for coal, which became a product for export as well as domestic consumption later in the century. To gain an idea of the pace: the combined output of the blast furnaces in South Wales was 2,550 tons in 1806; in 1823 it was 223,520 tons, and in 1839 it was 453,000 tons.[26] The South Welsh industrial revolution was itself a response to the needs of the larger industrial revolution's needs for metals and energy. It occurred later than England's, but it transformed the southern part of the principality rapidly.

The magnitude of these economic developments is also seen in the demographic transformation of Wales. The figures for North and South Wales respectively appear in tables 9 and 10. North Wales showed considerable increases in the first two decades of the century, reflecting the industrial and mining activity stimulated by the French revolutionary and Napoleonic Wars. Thereafter depopulation occurred in some places, as industrial life stagnated and laborers migrated southward and eastward to the great centers of industrial activity. The growth of the southern iron and coal regions, particularly Glamorgan and Monmouth, was rapid and steady during the first half of the century. John Clapham notes that between 1800 and 1831, the population of Lan-

| 1841 | | 1851 | | 1861 | | 1871 | |
|---|---|---|---|---|---|---|---|
| Total | % Change | Total | % Change | Total | % Change | Total | % Change |
| 5,603 | 16 | 61,474 | 11 | 61,627 | 0.2 | 59,901 | −3 |
| 8,766 | 6 | 70,796 | 3 | 72,245 | 2 | 73,441 | 2 |
| 6,326 | 6 | 110,632 | 4 | 111,796 | 1 | 115,710 | 4 |
| 1,188 | 35 | 231,849 | 35 | 317,752 | 37 | 397,859 | 25 |
| 4,368 | 37 | 157,418 | 17 | 174,633 | 11 | 195,488 | 12 |
| 8,044 | 8 | 94,140 | 7 | 96,278 | 2 | 91,998 | −4 |
| 5,458 | 3 | 24,716 | −3 | 25,382 | 3 | 25,430 | 0.2 |
| 9,753 | 19 | 751,025 | 16 | 859,713 | 14 | 959,827 | 12 |

CE: *Parliamentary Papers*, 1831, 18, 332–65; 1841, 2, 57–61; 1851, 43, ccii; 1871, 59, 6.
OTE: Monmouth is not normally listed as in South Wales, but is included here because of its
aphical contiguity and economic continuity with Glamorgan. The commissioners on education
les included Monmouth in their investigation (*Parliamentary Papers*, 1847, 27).

TABLE 10    POPULATION CHANGES IN NORTH WALES,
1801–1871

|  | 1801 | 1811 | | 1821 | | 1831 | |
|---|---|---|---|---|---|---|---|
|  | Total | Total | % Change | Total | % Change | Total | % Cha |
| Anglesey | 33,806 | 37,045 | 10 | 45,063 | 22 | 48,325 |  |
| Carmarvon | 41,521 | 49,655 | 20 | 58,099 | 17 | 66,818 | 1 |
| Denbigh | 60,299 | 64,249 | 7 | 76,428 | 19 | 82,655 |  |
| Flint | 39,469 | 45,937 | 16 | 53,893 | 17 | 60,244 | 1 |
| Merioneth | 29,506 | 30,854 | 5 | 34,382 | 11 | 35,315 |  |
| Montgomery | 48,184 | 52,184 | 8 | 60,245 | 15 | 66,844 | 1 |
| Total | 252,785 | 279,924 | 11 | 328,110 | 17 | 360,201 | 1 |

cashire, the home of the cotton-textile industry and the fastest-growing of the English counties, increased by 98.5 percent, but Monmouth grew by 117 percent. While the industrial counties of the West Riding of Yorkshire grew by 74 percent in the same period, Glamorgan grew by more than 100 percent.[27]

Changes of this magnitude depended in large part on internal migration. Much of this was over short distances within Wales, as people left their agricultural pursuits and sought employment in the iron, tin, copper, or coal industries. This movement accelerated after 1841–51, as much domestic industry that had supplemented agricultural income declined as a result of competition with cheaper factory production.[28] Some migrants came from the western English counties, and the population of English origin in eastern Wales was considerable.[29] In addition, Irish immigrants came into the mining and agricultural areas, especially after the famine of the 1840s.[30] One striking characteristic of the Welsh industrial labor force in this era was its high proportion of unskilled laborers. A. H. John estimates the percentages of unskilled laborers as of midcentury at 80–85 in the copper industry, 70–80 in coal mining, 75 in tin-plate manufacture, and 60–70 in iron production.[31]

Another peculiarity of South Wales was that in the late 1700s and early 1800s, most of the capital and entrepreneurial talent came from outside, mainly from London, Bristol, Gloucester, Birmingham, and Cornwall. Later there was some domestic capital accumulation in the

| 1841 | | 1851 | | 1861 | | 1871 | |
|---|---|---|---|---|---|---|---|
| Total | % Change | Total | % Change | Total | % Change | Total | % Change |
| 50,891 | 5 | 57,327 | 13 | 54,609 | −5 | 51,040 | −7 |
| 81,093 | 21 | 87,870 | 8 | 95,694 | 9 | 106,121 | 11 |
| 88,478 | 7 | 92,583 | 5 | 100,778 | 9 | 105,102 | 4 |
| 66,919 | 11 | 68,156 | 2 | 69,737 | 2 | 76,312 | 9 |
| 39,332 | 11 | 38,843 | −1 | 38,963 | .3 | 46,598 | 20 |
| 69,607 | 4 | 67,335 | −3 | 66,919 | −1 | 67,623 | 1 |
| 396,320 | 10 | 412,114 | 4 | 426,700 | 4 | 442,796 | 4 |

ɔURCE: *Parliamentary Papers*, 1831, 18, 332–65; 1841, 2, 57–61; 1851, 43, ccii; 1871, 59, 6.

iron and copper industries that spilled over into investment in coal and tin-plate.[32] This peculiarity reinforced the semicolonial character of Welsh society, and inhibited the development of indigenous middle classes—which had formed, for example, in centers like Manchester and Birmingham. Also, perhaps, it accentuated the distance between capitalist and worker in industrial Wales just as the Anglicans and partial absenteeism of the landlord class had done in the countryside.

## IMPLICATIONS OF THESE CHANGES
## FOR WELSH EDUCATIONAL DEVELOPMENT

These inherited and ongoing changes in Welsh society in the nineteenth century produced a number of social forces that impinged on the development of the elementary education of the working classes during that period:

The very rapid growth of population, particularly in urban centers, generated a need for a great increase in educational places, even if the proportion of children in attendance remained the same. Since the general aim of educational reformers throughout the kingdom was to increase that proportion, the pressure to grow was even greater. This problem posed by an increasing population was not unique to Wales; it was shared by many parts of England and Scotland. But because the rate of population growth was so striking, especially in South Wales, this factor must be stressed.

As in England, the involvement of children in labor constituted an obstacle to their involvement in education, for both boys and girls in both agriculture and industry. As a result, Wales also experienced the "twin evils" of early withdrawal and irregular attendance.[33]

Because of the distribution of wealth in Wales, the only classes who could readily provide subscriptions for day schools were the landowning classes and the manufacturers. These classes, however, being sometimes nonresident and not locally oriented, were often not motivated to attend to the educational needs of their localities.[34] When landlords, themselves Anglican, did help to support schools, they worked through the National Society, which often insisted that children learn the catechism in the schools and attend an Anglican church or Sunday school.[35]

Because the majority of religious communicants in the majority of communities were Dissenters of various sorts, the establishment of Anglican schools raised the specter of community tension and conflict. The pattern of this tension and conflict varied, but it usually included several components: religious conflict between Establishment and Dissent; conflict between "English" and "Welsh" cultural identification; linguistic conflict, since instruction was usually in English; and class conflict, which was often virulent in the bifurcated class system of both agricultural and urban-industrial Wales.[36]

As part of this conflict, Dissenters tended either not to attend the Anglican day schools or did so halfheartedly, for instrumental purposes only, or perhaps with hostility. In addition, non-Anglican Protestants were motivated to establish competing Wesleyan or Dissenting Protestant schools more congenial to their religious persuasions. But because Dissenters were poorer, they were often unable to raise the subscriptions necessary to support day schools and had to rely on private subscription schools or on Dissenting Sunday schools for their children's education.

On the positive side, Dissenting Sunday schools provided an important source of limited education for adults and children. Being self-supporting, they escaped dependence on the wealthy classes and the Established Church. They also constituted a powerful basis for class, regional, religious, and language cohesion. Finally, limiting their religious instruction to Sundays, they did not interfere directly with the work commitments and economic interests of scholars and their families.

These diverse social forces manifested themselves both in the general trends of educational development and in the patterns of educational competition and conflict in Wales.

## PATTERNS OF DEVELOPMENT OF PRIMARY EDUCATION

Many of the factors just identified suggest that elementary education for the Welsh working classes would be slow to develop: the geographical, economic, and cultural isolation of the principality; its lesser wealth;[37] the alienation of the wealthier classes from their local communities; the alienation of the majority of the population from Anglican religion and schools; and the inability of that majority to provide day schools for its children.

Most observers in the nineteenth century voiced the opinion that Wales was educationally backward. This view appeared especially in the 1840s, in the wake of episodes of social turmoil—the Rebecca Riots, the Newport uprising, and the appearance of strong Chartist sentiment in Wales. While those who commented on those disturbances acknowledged the legitimacy of many grievances underlying them,[38] the deficiencies of the working classes' education were also mentioned as contributing conditions. In the wake of the Monmouthshire disturbances of 1839, James Kay (later Kay-Shuttleworth), secretary to the Committee of Council, dispatched a newly appointed inspector of schools Hugh Tremenheere to investigate the scene. As might be expected, his report stressed the deplorable state of popular education there.[39] Subsequently Kay himself described the workmen of the region as "the prey of low moral habits, to a large extent without religion, and consequently the easy victims of the disaffected and of the emissaries of disorganising doctrines."[40]

In 1844 a Commission of Inquiry for South Wales complained that the children of both farmers and workers were "almost beyond the state of any moral improvement" because of the scantiness of schooling in the region. "How greatly such a state of things is calculated to minister to those prejudices and misconceptions to which so much of the recent excitement of the country may justly be attributed," the report of the commissioners commented.[41] In calling for a Crown Commission in 1846, William Williams acknowledged the same state of educational destitution. However, he blamed the government for that condition (and the associated political disturbances), arguing that since 1839 the Committee of Council had spent £438,000 on education for the poor in En-

gland, whereas the five counties of South Wales affected by the Rebecca
riots had received only £2,176. Staffordshire, with a population not
larger than the whole of South Wales, had received seven times as much
in educational grants.[42] The 1847 Commission on Education in Wales
complained of low rates of literacy, the sparseness of schools, the low
qualifications and low pay of teachers, and the difficulties in teaching in
English to Welsh-speaking students—all of which made for serious educational deficiencies in the principality.[43]

It is difficult to evaluate these indictments, because most of them
were impressionistic, given by outsiders who were possibly biased, and
frequently put in absolute terms, without reference to educational conditions elsewhere in the United Kingdom. In addition, global assessments of this sort generally neglect local variations. The limited quantitative evidence available does, however, suggest that Welsh progress
with respect to establishing certain types of educational arrangements,
especially day schools, was halting in comparison with most of England.

The earliest estimates of day schooling appear in the parochial returns gathered in 1819 by the Brougham Committee on the education of
the poor. Parish clergymen prepared digests from the surveys they conducted. These surveys were not complete, and for parishes not reporting, the committee estimated averages based on those parishes that
did. For England, the population in 1811 (the most recent census) was
9,543,610. The number of children in English free schools in 1819 was
322,518, with 321,764 in fee schools, for a grand total of 644,282. For
Wales, the 1811 population was 622,719. According to the 1819 returns, there were 13,318 Welsh children in free schools and 17,283 in
fee schools, for a total of 30,601. The number of scholars at the time of
the survey was 6.7 per 100 of population in England, and 5.0 scholars
per 100 in Wales. When the same calculation for unendowed schools is
made—thus excluding grammar and other schools catering to the
higher classes—the ratios are 5.0 per 100 of the population for England
and 3.75 for Wales. These figures are imprecise; about the only thing to
be said is that they point in the direction suggested by commentators of
the time.

As an additional exercise, the returns of 1819 may be compared with
the age-specific census figures of 1821. Table 11 shows the percentage of
children aged between five and fifteen who were not in school in each of
the counties of Wales in 1821. The aggregated percentage is 85.5. A
similar calculation for all English counties yields a figure of 70.7, and
the difference between the two figures points in the same direction as the
calculation in the preceding paragraph. (Returns from Scotland yield a

TABLE 11    ENROLLMENT IN DAY SCHOOLS,
WALES, 1818

| | Total Population, 1821 | Population Aged 5–15, 1821 | Population in Day Schools, 1818 | % Aged 5–15 Not in Attendance |
|---|---|---|---|---|
| *Anglesey* | 43,715 | 11,077 | 1,401 | 87.4 |
| *Brecon* | 42,904 | 10,102 | 1,353 | 86.6 |
| *Cardigan* | 57,745 | 15,222 | 2,111 | 86.1 |
| *Carmarthen* | 90,137 | 23,010 | 3,060 | 86.7 |
| *Carnarvon* | 57,958 | 14,647 | 2,054 | 86.0 |
| *Denbigh* | 75,063 | 18,607 | 3,748 | 79.9 |
| *Flint* | 74,782 | 18,577 | 4,148 | 78.7 |
| *Glamorgan* | 96,977 | 23,923 | 4,594 | 81.2 |
| *Merioneth* | 33,877 | 8,072 | 901 | 88.8 |
| *Montgomery* | 56,653 | 13,680 | 2,203 | 83.9 |
| *Pembroke* | 74,023 | 18,299 | 4,091 | 77.6 |
| *Radnor* | 22,503 | 6,959 | 1,027 | 85.2 |
| *Total* | 726,337 | 182,175 | 26,543 | 85.5 |

SOURCE: *Parliamentary Papers*, 1822, 15, 471–523; 1820, 12, 359.
NOTE: The figures for 1818 include scholars of all ages at endowed and unendowed day schools. Percentages are counted as a ratio between day-school figures in 1818 and census figures in 1821 (the nearest available date for census figures).

figure of 60.2 percent not in attendance, which provides crude quantitative confirmation of the widely stated opinion that the Scottish educational system was more extensive than those of the other regions).[44]
Two additional calculations were performed, with an eye to determining whether the differences might be owing to "Welshness" or to other factors. For example, the differences might have resulted from the sparseness of population of the Welsh counties (and, by extension, from their rural character). Many Welsh counties were among the least populated, according to the 1821 census. Among the twelve English counties with the smallest populations,[45] the average percentage of persons five to fifteen years not in school was 68.1, substantially less than the corresponding figure of 85.5 for the Welsh counties. This at least suggests that "rural outlyingness" was not the major factor in accounting for the English-Welsh differences. Again, when the Welsh counties adjoining England[46]—and presumably more subject to "English" influences— were compared with the rest,[47] the figure was 80.0 percent for the former, 84.9 for the latter. The difference is small, but consistent with a cultural interpretation.
The education returns submitted in 1833—themselves subject to evi-

TABLE 12    ENROLLMENT IN DAY SCHOOLS,
WALES, 1833

|  | Total Population, 1831 | Infant and Day Scholars, 1833 | Enrollment as % of Total Population |
|---|---|---|---|
| Anglesey | 48,325 | 3,303 | 6.8 |
| Brecon | 47,763 | 2,601 | 5.5 |
| Cardigan | 68,780 | 4,152 | 6.1 |
| Carmarthen | 100,740 | 6,005 | 6.0 |
| Carnarvon | 66,448 | 3,766 | 5.7 |
| Denbigh | 83,629 | 5,748 | 6.9 |
| Flint | 60,012 | 6,100 | 10.2 |
| Glamorgan | 126,612 | 8,776 | 6.9 |
| Merioneth | 33,315 | 1,900 | 5.7 |
| Montgomery | 66,482 | 4,667 | 7.0 |
| Pembroke | 81,425 | 6,318 | 7.8 |
| Radnor | 26,651 | 1,474 | 5.5 |
| Total | 810,182 | 54,810 | 6.8 |

SOURCE: *Parliamentary Papers,* 1831, 18, 332–65; 1835, 43, 398.

dent underenumeration and other methodological difficulties[48]—can be compared to the census figures of 1831. Since these returns included scholars from different classes, and the census figures do not provide breakdowns by age, the comparisons must be even cruder. In any event, the relevant county figures for Wales are shown in table 12. The aggregated Welsh figure of 6.8 percent compares with an English figure of 9.0. Those counties adjoining England show a percentage of 7.1, those not adjoining a percentage of 6.8.

In 1847 the Commission on Education in Wales also produced some educational returns. The comprehensiveness of its survey cannot be known, but some care was apparently taken in recording information about schools.[49] These figures were compared on a county-by-county basis with the numbers of children between five and fifteen as recorded in the census of 1841. The results are shown in table 13. While obviously approximate, and lacking any comparative base for England, the county averages do not differ significantly from results obtained in the educational census in 1851, the aggregated percentages for Wales in the two surveys being almost identical (see table 14). In the 1851 educational census, also flawed by incompleteness,[50] the figures can be compared to the population of children between ages five and fifteen collected in the general census of the same year. The Welsh figure of

TABLE 13    ATTENDANCE AT DAY SCHOOLS,
WALES, 1847

|  | Total Population, 1841 | Population Aged 5–15, 1841 | Population in Day Schools, 1847 | % Aged 5–15 Not in Attendance |
|---|---|---|---|---|
| Anglesey | 50,891 | 12,233 | 3,150 | 74.3 |
| Brecon | 55,603 | 12,215 | 3,559 | 70.1 |
| Cardigan | 68,766 | 16,440 | 3,703 | 77.5 |
| Carmarthen | 106,326 | 26,154 | 6,266 | 76.0 |
| Carnarvon | 81,093 | 18,614 | 5,275 | 71.7 |
| Denbigh | 88,866 | 20,796 | 7,052 | 66.1 |
| Flint | 66,919 | 15,968 | 6,818 | 57.3 |
| Glamorgan | 171,188 | 38,121 | 12,604 | 66.9 |
| Merioneth | 39,332 | 8,802 | 2,855 | 67.6 |
| Montgomery | 69,219 | 16,846 | 4,488 | 73.4 |
| Pembroke | 88,044 | 20,847 | 6,834 | 67.2 |
| Radnor | 25,356 | 6,145 | 1,275 | 79.3 |
| Total | 911,603 | 213,181 | 63,879 | 70.0 |

SOURCE: *Parliamentary Papers,* 1847, 27, pt. 1, reports of the commissioners of inquiry into the state of education in Wales.

TABLE 14    ATTENDANCE AT DAY SCHOOLS,
WALES, 1851

|  | Population Aged 5–15 years, 1851 | Number in Attendance, March 31, 1851 | % Not in Attendance, March 31, 1851 |
|---|---|---|---|
| Anglesey | 9,910 | 2,413 | 75.7 |
| Brecon | 12,876 | 3,484 | 73.0 |
| Cardigan | 23,405 | 6,610 | 71.8 |
| Carmarthen | 23,173 | 7,119 | 69.3 |
| Carnarvon | 22,019 | 7,785 | 64.7 |
| Denbigh | 22,491 | 7,676 | 65.9 |
| Flint | 10,320 | 3,569 | 65.0 |
| Glamorgan | 53,489 | 16,156 | 69.8 |
| Merioneth | 11,980 | 3,064 | 74.4 |
| Montgomery | 18,071 | 4,933 | 72.7 |
| Pembroke | 20,483 | 6,606 | 67.8 |
| Radnor | 7,164 | 1,901 | 73.5 |
| Total | 235,381 | 71,316 | 69.8 |

SOURCE: *Parliamentary Papers,* 1851, 43, ccii; 1852–53, 90, 464–65.

TABLE 15    ENROLLMENT IN DAY SCHOOLS,
WALES, 1858–1861

| | Population Aged 5–15 years, 1861 | Numbers Attending Day Schools, 1858 | % Not in Attendance |
|---|---|---|---|
| *Anglesey* | 12,854 | 10,005 | 22.2 |
| *Brecon* | 13,658 | 5,598 | 59.0 |
| *Cardigan* | 16,574 | 6,555 | 60.5 |
| *Carmarthen* | 26,125 | 13,455 | 48.5 |
| *Carnarvon* | 23,025 | 8,543 | 62.9 |
| *Denbigh* | 22,712 | 11,100 | 51.1 |
| *Flint* | 16,236 | 10,153 | 34.5 |
| *Glamorgan* | 70,518 | 31,278 | 55.7 |
| *Merioneth* | 8,680 | 4,298 | 50.5 |
| *Montgomery* | 15,058 | 7,203 | 52.2 |
| *Pembroke* | 21,584 | 11,467 | 46.9 |
| *Radnor* | 5,845 | 2,277 | 61.1 |
| *Total* | 252,869 | 121,932 | 51.8 |

SOURCES: *Parliamentary Papers*, 1861, 21, pt. 1, 612–16; 1871, 59, 6.

69.8 percent not attending school corresponds with a figure of 55.0 calculated for all English counties.

Comparable estimates are available, finally, for the period 1858–61. The Newcastle Commission produced returns of numbers attending public day schools and private day schools.[51] As before, these figures were compared, county by county, with census figures for 1861 on the population between five and fifteen years of age. The results are in table 15. The aggregated percentage of Welsh children not in attendance was 52.2, whereas the corresponding figure for all English counties had fallen to 39.1.

The summary results of these several surveys appear in table 16. For comparable surveys, the differences between England and Wales remained of approximately the same magnitude (12–15 percent) over the four decades from 1820 to 1860 with respect to the spread of day schools. (The 1831–33 figures, while not comparable with the others, show a similar difference.) In general, the picture is consistent with the expectations derived from examining religious, class, and political patterns in Wales during these decades.[52]

When the religious denomination of day schools is examined, and when day scholars are compared with Sunday school scholars,[53] we arrive at several other insights regarding the structure of Welsh education.

TABLE 16 SUMMARY OF
PERCENTAGES OF CHILDREN AGED
FIVE TO FIFTEEN NOT IN DAY
SCHOOLS, ENGLAND AND WALES

|  | Wales | England |
|---|---|---|
| 1819–21 | 85.5 | 70.7 |
| 1847 | 70.0 | — |
| 1851 | 69.8 | 55.0 |
| 1858–61 | 52.2 | 39.1 |

SOURCES: Wales, tables 11, 13, 14, and 15; England, figures calculated from sources cited in tables 11, 14, and 15.

In 1858 the Newcastle Commission requested that religious societies submit returns for their day schools and for the number of scholars in them. The returns for day schools in Wales are shown in table 17. What appears is discrepant representation of the Church of England and Dissent in relation to the Welsh population as a whole. The Anglican Church still dominated the school scene. This situation held, despite the facts that the British and Foreign School Society had launched a campaign to spread schooling in Wales a decade earlier and that certain Nonconformist groups had turned their voluntary efforts to the same end.[54] The National Society sponsored four-fifths of the day schools and served more than two-thirds of the scholars in all Welsh day schools. Yet three-quarters of the Welsh church-going population were Dissenters at the time. The distribution of day schooling as reported to the Newcastle Commission reversed this ratio in favor of the Anglican Church. These differences are consistent with the pattern of a greater Anglican presence in eastern Wales. The British and Foreign School Society and various Dissenting bodies sponsored only 15.6 percent of the schools and commanded only 22.9 percent of the scholars in the Welsh counties bordering on England. The corresponding figures for the western Welsh counties are 23.6 and 33.7 percent respectively.

An examination of the relations between day schools and Sunday schools in Wales completes this anomalous picture. The 1847 Commission on Education in Wales enumerated the scholars in different kinds of schools. The survey was admittedly inadequate, particularly for the Sunday schools,[55] so the returns must again be interpreted with caution. This qualification noted, the results in table 18 indicate that Sunday

TABLE 17   SCHOLARS IN PUBLIC DAY SCHOOLS, WALES AND MONMOUTH, 1858

| | Estimated Population, 1858 | Total Number of Day Schools and Scholars | | Number of Schools and Scholars, Anglican Day Schools | | Number of Schools and Scholars, Dissenting Day Schools (including British and Foreign)* | | Schools of Dissenters as % of Total Schools | Scholars in Dissenting Day Schools as % of Total |
|---|---|---|---|---|---|---|---|---|---|
| | | Schools | Scholars | Schools | Scholars | Schools | Scholars | | |
| Anglesey | 62,253 | 60 | 4,139 | 45 | 2,451 | 15 | 1,688 | 25.0 | 40.9 |
| Brecon | 65,888 | 60 | 3,403 | 50 | 2,565 | 10 | 838 | 20.0 | 24.6 |
| Cardigan | 72,186 | 92 | 4,216 | 72 | 2,776 | 20 | 1,440 | 27.7 | 34.2 |
| Carmarthen | 113,645 | 121 | 8,438 | 84 | 4,619 | 34 | 3,819 | 30.6 | 45.3 |
| Carnarvon | 92,862 | 113 | 8,543 | 85 | 5,671 | 28 | 2,872 | 24.8 | 33.6 |
| Denbigh | 95,481 | 109 | 6,904 | 92 | 4,870 | 17 | 2,034 | 15.6 | 29.5 |
| Flint | 68,972 | 106 | 6,141 | 100 | 5,543 | 6 | 598 | 5.7 | 9.7 |
| Glamorgan | 286,429 | 159 | 15,067 | 119 | 10,886 | 40 | 4,201 | 25.2 | 27.9 |
| Merioneth | 38,843 | 53 | 2,758 | 40 | 1,792 | 13 | 966 | 24.5 | 35.0 |
| Monmouth | 175,705 | 158 | 13,551 | 122 | 7,666 | 36 | 5,885 | 22.8 | 43.4 |
| Montgomery | 67,335 | 81 | 4,610 | 72 | 3,933 | 9 | 677 | 11.1 | 14.7 |
| Pembroke | 98,566 | 103 | 6,975 | 88 | 5,954 | 15 | 1,021 | 14.6 | 14.6 |
| Radnor | 24,716 | 35 | 1,402 | 31 | 1,165 | 4 | 237 | 11.4 | 16.9 |
| Total | 1,262,881 | 1,250 | 86,147 | 1,000 | 59,871 | 250 | 26,276 | 20.0 | 30.5 |

SOURCE: *Parliamentary Papers*, 1861, 21, pt. 1, 612–16.
*Twenty-two Roman Catholic and thirty-nine Calvinist Methodist schools are excluded. The latter are represented by 2,474 scholars' records in the 1851 educational census.

TABLE 18    DAY AND SUNDAY SCHOLARS, WALES AND MONMOUTH, 1847

| | Population in 1841 | Scholars in Day Schools | Scholars in Anglican Sunday Schools | Scholars in Dissenting Sunday Schools | Sunday School Scholars as % of Total Scholars | Dissenting Sunday School Scholars as % of Total Sunday School Scholars |
|---|---|---|---|---|---|---|
| *Anglesey* | 50,891 | 3,404 | 709 | 12,998 | 80.1 | 88.4 |
| *Brecon* | 55,603 | 3,985 | 2,409 | 11,245 | 77.4 | 82.4 |
| *Cardigan* | 68,766 | 3,885 | 4,074 | 23,057 | 87.5 | 85.0 |
| *Carmarthen* | 106,864 | 7,191 | 2,777 | 24,371 | 79.1 | 89.8 |
| *Carnarvon* | 86,093 | 5,867 | 1,455 | 23,308 | 81.5 | 90.8 |
| *Denbigh* | 88,866 | 7,405 | 3,145 | 20,661 | 77.0 | 86.7 |
| *Flint* | 68,191 | 7,586 | 3,841 | 11,469 | 66.9 | 67.0 |
| *Glamorgan* | 171,188 | 15,659 | 5,832 | 24,371 | 68.0 | 82.4 |
| *Merioneth* | 39,332 | 3,006 | 884 | 16,075 | 66.7 | 94.8 |
| *Monmouth* | 86,079 | 6,652 | 3,193 | 14,337 | 72.5 | 81.8 |
| *Montgomery* | 69,219 | 4,765 | 1,857 | 16,852 | 79.8 | 90.1 |
| *Pembroke* | 87,506 | 7,698 | 3,403 | 14,013 | 69.4 | 80.5 |
| *Radnor* | 25,356 | 1,381 | 1,146 | 1,163 | 63.6 | 50.4 |
| *Total* | 1,004,682 | 78,484 | 34,725 | 217,920 | 76.2 | 86.2 |

SOURCE: *Parliamentary Papers*, 1847, 27, reports of the commissioners of inquiry into the state of education in Wales.
NOTE: Population taken on a decennial basis (1841, 1851, 1861, for example) only; 1841 figures were used for comparison base.

TABLE 19 DAY AND SUNDAY SCHOLARS, WALES AND MONMOUTH, 1858

| | Estimated Population, 1858 | Scholars in Day Schools | Total Number of Sunday School Scholars | Scholars in Anglican Sunday Schools | Scholars in Dissenting Sunday Schools* | Sunday School Scholars as % of Total Scholars | Dissenting Sunday School Scholars as % of Total Sunday School Scholars |
|---|---|---|---|---|---|---|---|
| Anglesey | 62,253 | 4,139 | 7,645 | 2,003 | 5,642 | 64.9 | 73.8 |
| Brecon | 65,888 | 3,403 | 6,692 | 1,933 | 4,759 | 66.3 | 71.1 |
| Cardigan | 72,186 | 4,216 | 7,456 | 2,557 | 4,899 | 63.9 | 65.7 |
| Carmarthen | 113,645 | 9,438 | 10,819 | 3,495 | 7,324 | 53.4 | 67.7 |
| Carnarvon | 92,862 | 8,543 | 11,164 | 3,829 | 7,335 | 56.6 | 65.5 |
| Denbigh | 95,481 | 7,081 | 12,771 | 4,312 | 8,459 | 64.3 | 65.2 |
| Flint | 68,972 | 6,586 | 10,878 | 4,210 | 6,668 | 62.3 | 60.1 |
| Glamorgan | 286,056 | 16,056 | 29,724 | 9,396 | 20,328 | 65.0 | 68.6 |
| Merioneth | 38,843 | 2,758 | 4,231 | 1,528 | 2,703 | 60.5 | 63.9 |
| Monmouth | 175,705 | 13,551 | 24,459 | 5,713 | 18,746 | 64.3 | 76.6 |
| Montgomery | 67,335 | 4,610 | 10,731 | 3,975 | 6,756 | 70.0 | 60.9 |
| Pembroke | 98,566 | 6,975 | 11,377 | 4,384 | 6,993 | 62.0 | 61.0 |
| Radnor | 24,716 | 1,402 | 1,622 | 1,134 | 488 | 53.6 | 29.5 |
| Total | 1,262,881 | 88,758 | 149,569 | 48,469 | 101,100 | 62.8 | 67.6 |

SOURCE: *Parliamentary Papers*, 1861, 21, pt. 1, 612–16 and 625–27.
* Excluding Roman Catholic scholars.

scholars (76.2 percent) greatly outnumbered day scholars (by about three to one). In addition, Dissenting Sunday scholars (86.2 percent) greatly outnumbered those in Church of England Sunday schools (almost seven to one). Eastern and western Wales showed a pattern consistent with these differences. For counties adjoining England, Sunday school scholars were 71.9 percent of the total, and Dissenting Sunday school scholars were 82.5 percent of the total number of Sunday school scholars. The figures for the western counties were 80.5 and 89.6 percent respectively. Thus, while the religions' populations in day schools was in reverse ratio to the Welsh population at large, the Sunday school population mirrored that ratio.

The Newcastle Commission also requested the religious societies to submit estimates of day and Sunday scholars throughout England and Wales. The figures for Wales are shown in table 19. The same preponderance of Sunday school over day school scholars and of Dissenting Sunday school over Anglican Sunday school scholars appears. In both cases, however, the differences are less pronounced than those reported in 1847. It is difficult to press comments and interpretations on these methodologically vulnerable figures too far. Two comments are possible, however. First, the apparent increase in numbers of day scholars is intelligible given the building efforts undertaken in the late 1840s and the 1850s by two major religious societies.[56] Second, the extreme discrepancy between the two surveys with respect to the number of scholars in Dissenting Sunday schools (217,920 in 1847 and 101,100 in 1858–61) suggests a substantial overenumeration in the former or an underenumeration in the latter, or both. Internal examination of the 1858–61 data confirms the strength of the Sunday school movement—and, within that, the strength of Dissent—in Wales. For England, Sunday scholars were 58.4 percent of the total as compared with 62.8 in Wales. The percentage of Dissenters among English Sunday scholars was 49.9, as compared with 67.6 in Wales.

Despite the unsatisfactoriness of the survey materials, it appears that the efforts to establish educational arrangements for the poor in Wales separated into two distinct tracks. These reflected the religious, cultural, linguistic, and class cleavages that were so pronounced in that principality in the first half of the nineteenth century. The Church of England dominated the modest spread of day schools. In relative terms, however, the Anglican Church had considerably more difficulty in raising subscriptions for National Schools in Wales than in other districts; the National Society report of 1843 indicated that the number of persons per pound sterling collected was among the highest in Wales and Monmouthshire.[57] Judging by their attendance, moreover, those day schools seemed to have been remote from the great mass of Dissenters in the Welsh population. The Dissenters dominated the second, much larger track of Sunday schools. For them, the Sunday schools, while typically less effective in imparting secular education, nevertheless engaged the common people and found a warmer place in their hearts.

Contemporary observers perceived and frequently commented on the close relations among Welsh culture, Dissent, and the Sunday school movement. Instructing the Commission on Education in Wales in 1847, Kay-Shuttleworth asked the commissioners not to overlook the Sunday schools' "character and tendencies," adding that the Sunday school "must be regarded as the most remarkable, because of the . . . zeal of the Christian congregations for education. Its origin, organization, and tendencies are purely religious."[58] Ralph Lingen, one of the commissioners, described them as "almost the sole . . . still the main and most congenial, centres of education."[59] And Henry Vaughan Johnson, commissioner for North Wales, contrasted the Welsh Sunday schools with the day schools:

> In the week-day schools all profess to learn English, in the Sunday schools (speaking generally) all learn Welsh; the object which the poor desire from the former is secular knowledge; the end to which they devote their whole attention in the Sunday-school is religion, to the exclusion of every other study. . . . The humble position and attainments of the individuals engaged in the establishment and support of Welsh Sunday-schools enhance the value of this spontaneous effort for education; and, however imperfect the results, it is impossible not to admire the vast number of schools which they have established, the frequency of the attendance, the number, energy, and devotion of the teachers, the regularity and decorum of the proceedings, and the permanent and striking effects which they have produced upon society.[60]

In promoting Sunday schools, the Dissenters showed more vitality, according to Jeliger C. Symons, the third commissioner, who found the routine of hymn, reading verse by verse, and the repetition of Collect and catechism to be "spiritless and monotonous" in the Anglican Sunday schools. He judged the Dissenting institutions to be "decidedly more effective for the purposes of religious instruction."[61] A decade later, the Newcastle Commission noted that—except for the Established and the Roman Catholic Churches—Sunday schools predominated over day schools in Wales as the preferred means of instruction. The commissioners also noted the widespread and vigorous development of Sunday schools in that principality.[62]

Spokesmen for the Church of England and Dissent frequently clashed with one another over educational policies affecting Wales in the nineteenth century. However, the two educational tracks appear to have existed side by side there, largely in effective ignorance of each other and influencing each other little culturally. Except for some factory and pauper schools, midcentury Britain had almost no compulsory attendance. Thus there was no enforced mixing of children of different religious persuasions.[63] Those Dissenting parents who decided to send their children to Anglican day schools for secular education and to learn to read and write English perhaps regarded the religious requirements of those schools as a troublesome but meaningless façade. Symons commented:

> Churchmen can derive no benefit, and Dissenters no injury, from the utterance of doctrines by their respective children in words unintelligible to both. . . . I have found many dissenting children innocently repeating what their godfathers and godmothers did promise and vow in their names, who never had either the one or the other, and who were utterly unconscious of what they were saying.[64]

Others, as Johnson observed, may have taken advantage of a day school for their children's secular education and then made use of a Dissenting chapel or Sunday school as a religious "corrective" to Anglican instruction.[65] More important, however, the Dissenting Sunday schools, being voluntary, were free from intervention by state or Establishment authorities. Being self-supporting, they were not accountable to any subsidizing authority either. Since the Dissenting Sunday schools were thus politically and economically independent of government, administration, and religious officialdom, they had limited occasion to come into direct conflict with these agents. A basic principle underlies this observation: the potential for open conflict is less when opposed groups are not implicated in the same authority system or the same pool of scarce resources. Later, in the 1850s and 1860s, when the Dissenters and the Anglican Church did become thus implicated in small Welsh communities, open conflict over educational arrangements erupted.

## DRAWING THE BATTLE LINES: THE 1830S AND 1840S

For education in Wales, Thomas Evans identifies 1833–47 as years of "intolerance and a disposition not to compromise" on the part of the interested parties—mainly religious. He also identifies 1843 as the year in which an "all-pervading interest" in education crystallized. This year witnessed the struggle over Graham's educational clauses, in which the Nonconformists became deeply embroiled and ultimately emerged victorious. It was also the year in which Hugh Owen wrote his letter to the Welsh people calling for a renewed dedication to education.[66] This emergence of education as a salient issue in Wales in the early 1840s was conditioned by the cleavages and conflicts outlined above,[67] but its timing was affected by the onset of both rural and industrial distress and by a series of associated political protests and disturbances. As indicated, the latter were interpreted as emanating in part from the ignorance of the Welsh people.

Wales had seen significant political protest earlier—including a season of political/religious radicalism during the French revolutionary/ Napoleonic period—but the late 1820s, the 1830s, and the early 1840s were noted for their intense political activity in that principality.[68] Economic riots erupted in 1818, 1825, 1826, 1830, and 1831, triggered by a combination of economic distress and an interest in parliamentary reform. The 1820s witnessed the development of the violent and anonymous "Scotch Cattle" movement, directed against industrialists, contractors, landlords, and "black legs" (workers willing to work for lowered wages). The Rebecca riots of 1839–42 expressed mainly rural discontent, and were focused primarily, but not exclusively, on the despised toll gates. Welsh Chartism was strongest in South Wales, where it had a more urban/industrial base, and rose to a climax in the Newport rising of 1839.[69]

The grievances underlying these disturbances were many: wage cuts, unemployment and general economic hardship, especially during periods of economic depression; hardships and injustices imposed by the Poor Law legislation of 1834; the tolls imposed by the turnpike trusts; the system of justice, including high salaries for magistrates' clerks; and the tithe and associated religious grievances felt by the Nonconformists, to name the most evident. The responses of the authorities to the disturbances were a complex combination of repression, relief, and reform. The protests were put down by strong reactions by the local authorities and the police, and many of the protest leaders were imprisoned or transported. At the same time the government responded more positively, for example, by the dispatching of commissions of inquiry, correcting many abuses of the turnpike system in 1844, reforming the enclosure procedures in 1845, and, more generally, repealing the Corn Laws in 1846 and establishing the Poor Law Board in 1847.[70] The authorities' concerns also revealed the belief that deficiencies in education

were among the causes of the unrest. This belief lay behind the dispatching of HMI Tremenheere to investigate the educational conditions of
South Wales in 1839. In addition, those who pressed for an investigation of Welsh education in 1846 tied the Newport and Rebecca Riots to
educational deprivation in Wales, and those sympathetic to the Welsh
cause deplored the apparent stinginess of the government in promoting
education there.[71] Finally, the appointment of the Commission on Education in Wales of 1847 itself rested on the same assumptions connect-
ing educational destitution and political unrest.

The impulse to expand working-class education also extended to religious groups, whose efforts appear to have been motivated both by a
desire to allay political unrest and by competition with one another.
The National Society became more vigorous in its educational activities
in the late 1830s. The number of pupils in Church of England schools
had remained constant—around 25,000—until 1837, when the Anglican Church launched a campaign to increase it, raising approximately
£12,000 and doubling the number of schools over three years. In a petition submitted in 1839, representatives of the Anglican clergy in North
Wales complained of the inadequate Church of England coverage there,
and demanded more support.[72] Also in 1837, Hugh Owen, who was to
become a vigorous organizer of Nonconformist educational efforts in
Wales, was attempting, albeit without notable success, to mobilize support for education among the Nonconformist churches. By 1843 the
Anglican Church claimed to have schools in districts including 327,000
of the total population of North Wales (396,000), whereas the British
and Foreign School Society had been able to establish only two schools.[73]

As Church of England success mounted in Wales, Nonconformist
efforts to compete grew accordingly. The Dissenters were heartened by
their unity—even with the Methodists—in the fight against the educational clauses in 1843. Nonconformists also united, but without Methodist support this time, in opposing the minutes of 1846 on the grounds
that they gave a continuing advantage to the Anglican Church.[74] They
were split, however, between those who wished to benefit from government subsidies (mainly the British and Foreign School Society and those
sympathetic to it), and the Voluntaryists, who campaigned against co-
operation between religious groups and the state in education. The events
of both 1843 and 1846 also galvanized Nonconformists' educational
efforts in Wales. Their enthusiasm (and anger) was increased in 1847,
the year of the report of the Commission on Education in Wales. Nonconformists condemned the report as the "Treachery of the Blue Books,"

and regarded it as an insult to the morals of the Welsh, the Welsh language, and Dissent by the English/Anglican ruling authorities.[75]

The competition for educational development thus intensified in the early 1840s. Owen's letter to the Welsh people fueled that competition. In 1845 a Nonconformist South Wales Education Committee formed, and in 1846 an Anglican Welsh Education Committee also appeared.[76] By the time of the Newcastle Commission's inquiries, British and Foreign Society Schools were more strongly represented in Wales than in most other parts of the country.[77] Yet for all its fervor, Nonconformity was hobbled in Wales. Its long-standing disadvantage in raising subscriptions—in contrast to the Nonconformists' much wealthier Anglican counterparts—continued.[78] In addition, Wales was especially affected by the Voluntaryist split. In South Wales the Independents and Baptists were strong; accordingly, Voluntaryism was also strong there. Vigorous efforts to establish schools without the assistance of government began in the 1840s. In 1860 John Jenkins observed that "in no district in the Kingdom were such vigourous and well-combined efforts made for education extension by voluntary means as in the manufacturing and agricultural districts of South Wales."[79] At the same time he noted the insufficiency of those efforts, largely because the Voluntaryists lacked financial resources, especially in comparison with the National Society, which was better endowed and was receiving governmental subsidies.

Such was the strength of Voluntaryism, however, that Jenkins sensed hostility in South Wales to those who capitulated and took state aid "as a submission to existing arrangements rather than an unhesitating concurrence with them."[80] In North Wales, by contrast, while the Independent and Baptist bodies were in evidence, Calvinist Methodism was dominant. "This denomination never took up the attitude of *opposition,* or even of *indifference* to the Government Minutes," HMI J. D. Morell observed.[81] Accordingly, when Owen and the British and Foreign School Society initiated their campaign in 1843, the response was greatest in the north. In November of that year, when the society appointed an agent in the north to foster schooling under its aegis, it refrained from appointing one in the south out of deference to Voluntaryist feeling there. Not until 1853 was an agent appointed in the south.[82]

As of midcentury, then, Wales showed the following picture with respect to working-class education:

Energetic efforts on the part of religious groups to expand day schools for working-class children.

TABLE 20     VOLUNTARYISM IN WALES
AND MONMOUTH, 1858

| | British and Foreign School Society | | Congregationalists and Baptists | | Congregationalists and Baptists as % of Total | |
|---|---|---|---|---|---|---|
| | *Schools* | *Scholars* | *Schools* | *Scholars* | *Schools* | *Scholars* |
| *Anglesey* | 12 | 1,483 | 3 | 205 | 20.0 | 12.1 |
| *Brecon* | 5 | 555 | 5 | 283 | 50.0 | 33.8 |
| *Cardigan* | 11 | 994 | 9 | 446 | 45.0 | 31.0 |
| *Carmarthen* | 21 | 2,970 | 16 | 349 | 43.2 | 22.2 |
| *Carnarvon* | 26 | 2,776 | 3 | 96 | 10.3 | 3.3 |
| *Denbigh* | 13 | 1,747 | 4 | 287 | 23.5 | 14.1 |
| *Flint* | 3 | 390 | 3 | 208 | 50.0 | 34.8 |
| *Glamorgan* | 19 | 2,701 | 16 | 973 | 45.7 | 26.5 |
| *Merioneth* | 10 | 852 | 3 | 14 | 23.1 | 11.8 |
| *Monmouth* | 22 | 4,086 | 14 | 1,339 | 38.9 | 24.7 |
| *Montgomery* | 5 | 493 | 4 | 184 | 44.4 | 27.2 |
| *Pembroke* | 4 | 441 | 11 | 580 | 26.7 | 56.9 |
| *Radnor* | 1 | 97 | 3 | 140 | 75.0 | 59.9 |
| *Total* | 152 | 19,585 | 94 | 5,704 | 38.2 | 22.6 |

Source: *Parliamentary Papers*, 1861, 21, pt. 1, 612–16.

Continuing, vigorous competition between the National Society on the one hand and the British and Foreign School Society and the Voluntaryist bodies on the other. The British and Foreign schools were more successful in the north, and the Voluntaryist schools in the south, as table 20 indicates.[83] The National Society had an advantage over both Nonconformist bodies with respect to resources and numbers of schools,[84] but many parents of Welsh children shunned National schools on grounds of religious conscience. As a result many areas were supplied with Church of England schools that were half-empty.[85] The British and Foreign School Society day schools tended to charge higher fees (2*d*.) than the National Schools (1*d*.) and seemed to be attended "by children of a more respectable or higher grade of the working classes, than the latter."[86] This suggests that British and Foreign School Society schools compensated for their difficulties in raising and sustaining subscriptions by charging higher fees.

Continued vitality, especially among Nonconformists, of the Sunday school movement—an educational movement in the first instance, but with elements of protest against the English/Anglican presence in Wales.

There were also some private-subscription Nonconformist schools as well, opened as alternatives to National Society day schools, but these were low in quality and suffered in comparison to British and Foreign School Society schools.[87]

The elevation of the educational question to one of wider public concern, and the further fusion of educational conflict with the *general* economic, religious, and cultural/regional conflicts in Wales.

## LLANGEFNI, 1850–1852: A MICROCOSM OF EDUCATIONAL CONFLICT

The creeds were in competition with one another at two levels in Wales: first, they were striving for the moral, religious, and educational guardianship of the young people of Wales,[88] and second, they disagreed on the religious principles under which this education should be carried out. Open political conflict seldom erupted, however. When it did, it was in debates in Parliament over educational policy and in the Committee of Council over questions of educational administration. The latter conflicts centered on small communities with heterogeneous religious composition but with populations too small to support more than one school. I focus on these community conflicts in the remainder of this chapter because of their frequency in Wales and their general significance for the evolution of British educational arrangements in the 1860s and 1870s.

In opposing the minutes of 1846, the Nonconformists in Wales and elsewhere expressed their apprehension that the denominational system with government support would continue to operate to the advantage of the Established Church. The Nonconformists and other Welsh groups envisioned, instead, arrangements more permissive of religious freedom and autonomy. In May 1848 the Welsh Education Committee of the National Society appealed to the Committee of Council to establish National schools in Wales, adding that the inspectors of these should be required to be able to speak Welsh. At the same time Dissenting groups submitted two memorials asking the council to rule out establishing any schools that did not forbid religious tests.[89]

Also in 1848, William Williams, a Welsh partisan, wrote an open letter lamenting the relative lack of government support for working-class education in Wales. In this letter he expressed doubt that the voluntary principle could work in Wales, because of the lack of means in most communities. In order to sustain a comprehensive system of education in Wales, he argued, cooperation rather than competition among the denominations was essential:

> All religious denominations should unite and cooperate, which is the more indispensable in consequence of the most destitute districts, which form a very large extent of the country, being, from their mountainous character, but thinly-populated,—this renders the maintenance of schools for different sects an impossibility. That such a union may be affected, I fervently pray; I will not spare that, in promoting a work which cannot but be acceptable in the sight of the beneficent Creator, sectarian prejudices and worldly-mindedness will be laid aside, and, that influenced by Christian benevolence, all will unite to raise our Countrymen from that lamentable condition, from which nothing can rescue them but the liberal help of their affluent and more fortunate fellow-men; I pray that their hearts and minds may be so righteously directed—then will the Welsh people at no distant day take their stand on inequality with their brethren, the people of England and Scotland; but if, unhappily, sectarian prejudices and interests should be permitted to mar this righteous work, then will they inevitably rank far below any portion of the people of the United Kingdom.[90]

One would expect such expressions from Dissenters and Welsh regionalists. But other, less partisan observers pointed to the difficulty of applying the voluntary, denominational principle as well. HMI H. Longueville Jones reminded the Committee of Council of the Nonconformists' difficulty in raising subscriptions.[91] Reflecting on the situation in South Wales in the mid 1850s, HMI J. W. Bowstead spoke of the impossibility of adopting the denominational system in that region. He pointed out that the Anglican Church's friends had established many facilities for the training of teachers. Because the Church of England insisted on the use of its catechisms and formularies, however: "Many stand aloof altogether from such institutions, and either leave their children entirely untaught, except in the Sunday schools, or obtain for them elsewhere an education which is at once more costly, and in a secular point of view, less effective."[92] Bowstead concluded that some modification of the existing system was absolutely unavoidable, because Nonconformists would never submit to the Establishment. However: "They are for the most part ready, in school affairs, to act with the Church on terms of perfect equality, and to support combined schools, basing their highest teaching upon the Bible, but rejecting all catechisms and denominational peculiarities."[93]

HMI Morell underscored the same contradictions in his report of 1856, but narrowed his focus to small, outlying communities in North Wales:

Most of the towns and all the villages of North Wales are far too small to render two schools necessary or desirable. Where they do co-exist, accordingly, they become easily the occasion of infinite rivalry and opposition, the final result being, that one good school is spoiled for the sake of keeping up two sickly ones. As far as I have had the opportunity of speaking with the managers of British schools, they all express themselves ready to join in any united system, where the managing power is equally balanced, and the religious instruction is given from the Bible alone. It only needs, I conceive, a willingness on the part of the clergy in Wales to co-operate with others on equal terms, to give the Principality one united system of national education.[94]

Morell concluded that the British and Foreign system, with its permissive religious provisions, was best for the peculiar situation of the Welsh population.

Despite this deep religious and political conflict over education in Wales at midcentury, neither the Committee of Council nor Parliament showed any inclination to alter the subsidized denominational system that was consolidated by the minutes of 1846. The reasons for this were several. First, in 1839, 1843, and 1846, the government had weathered a series of conflicts that gave evidence of the unacceptability (to one religious party or another) of arrangements *other than* the government-supported voluntary system. The year 1846 represented a kind of "truce point" acceptable to most parties, even though the minutes were a thorn in the side of many Nonconformists, especially those who became Voluntaryists. The Church of England was supportive of the 1846 arrangements, as were the British and Foreign School Society, the Wesleyan Methodists, and the Roman Catholics. Second, the Committee of Council felt the pressure of the late 1840s and early 1850s to expand the government-supported voluntary system. As Lingen explained retrospectively, the "early years of administration" (1840s and 1850s) were years "when there was a great scarcity of schools throughout the country, and when the object was to get them built with no more inquiry than was absolutely forced upon the Committee [of Council]."[95] In keeping with this policy, the Committee of Council tended to encourage all legitimate efforts, even if these might result in cost-ineffective arrangements in places.

The tensions cited by Morell erupted into conflict in 1850 in the small parish of Llangefni, in the county of Anglesey, in North Wales.[96] This conflict lasted for eighteen months before it was resolved. Llangefni is worth a detailed examination, since that tiny parish constituted a microcosm of many of the social, religious, and political tendencies that were to play themselves out in Wales and more generally in the ensuing two decades.

In June 1850 the office of the Committee of Council received a request from a number of signatories in Llangefni for resources to establish a school under the auspices of the National Society. The school would house 100 boys, 100 girls, and 100 infants of both sexes, to be taught by a master and two mistresses.[97] The initiator of the request was evidently Henry Owen, an Anglican clergyman who had arrived on assignment to Llangefni only two months before the request was submitted. On arriving he had found the local church "very thinly attended" and its school in "a very low and neglected state." According to the request, Owen had proceeded with vigor to improve the state of both church and school; he had hired a qualified master and increased the attendance of the school. The signatories believed that this progress justified the request for support from the Committee of Council.[98] In any event, the Privy Council office received the request routinely, and the initial disposition of Lingen, the secretary, was favorable.

Within a matter of days, however, a communication came from a second group of signatories requesting resources to establish a British and Foreign Society school in the same parish. The evident point of competition was one that was by this point a familiar one: National Society schools insisted that their pupils learn the Anglican catechism and attend a Church of England service on Sundays; the British and Foreign School Society rejected particular denominational rituals, calling instead for instruction in the Scriptures without special interpretation or comment.

The Committee of Council remained silent for a period, but on October 1, Lingen wrote to the promoters of the British and Foreign school. He explained that while there was no objection in principle to supporting two schools in one parish if it needed them, "their Lordships [of the Privy Council] would not, however, feel at liberty to assist in founding merely rival schools. Under these circumstances, therefore, of the present application, the Committee of Council required to be further informed."[99]

The phrase "merely rival" apparently struck a nerve, since both sets of promoters responded immediately to that issue in communications dated October 4. Owen asserted that the projected British school was a rival in every respect; it could not serve the population it claimed it could. Furthermore, he argued that the National School's requirement that its pupils attend a Church of England service on Sundays did not constitute an infringement on religious liberty. To show further evidence of rivalry, Owen claimed that the occasion for the British and Foreign School Society's application arose from a dispute between him and several former promoters of the National Society school. This concerned the level of fees to be charged parents of pupils in the school (Owen argued for a fee of 1d. per week, his critics for 2s. 6d. per quarter). When he refused to accede, Owen said, the others withdrew their subscriptions and began to promote the rival school. The supporters of the British and Foreign school denied all rivalrous intentions, maintaining that they simply wished to serve the local population, 80 percent of whom were Dissenters by religious conviction. The smallness of the parish's population, they argued further, was not a problem, since their school would be available to six adjoining parishes, containing at least 3,500 inhabitants (the parish of Llangefni itself, according to the most recent census, had 1,754 inhabitants).[100]

In an effort to ease the situation, Lingen wrote Owen on October 5. He reminded him of the British and Foreign School Society's principles, and requested him to join with the competing group to establish a school on that basis. On October 7, Owen rejected the request, explaining that his school had been in existence for thirty-two years, and had served all denominations. He argued further that because the school had now become "efficient" (i.e., eligible to apply for government funds), there was no need for another school in the parish.

With the passage of another week, the conflict developed into an explicitly religious one. In a series of stinging letters to Owen, the signatories of the British and Foreign petition complained that he had unjustly applied the term "latitudinarian" to the British and Foreign School Society:

> You intend to insinuate that there is . . . infidelity or laxity of religious principle in [the British and Foreign School Society's] educational plan. How that can be asserted when the Society place the Word of God supreme, to the exclusion of mere human dogmas and conceits, they cannot understand. On the contrary, they feel confident that the system they have adopted is, in fact, the golden mean between that "latitudinarianism" you allude to on the one hand, and religious bigotry and intolerance on the other; two extremes which they equally dislike, and both of which they consider highly pernicious in their tendency.[101]

They also accused Owen of publicly denouncing the act of a Dissenting schoolboy who had been caught stealing apples "as an instance of the depravity of the child of a Dissenter."[102] In response Owen wrote to Lingen complaining of the proceedings and reiterating that he and his promoters would not cooperate in establishing a school on British and Foreign principles.

In a renewed effort, Lingen indicated to Owen on October 20 that if the National Society school would set aside the requirement that pupils attend Church of England services on Sundays, the committee would agree that a second (British) school was not necessary for the parish. Owen again resisted the request, stressing the efficiency of the National Society school and claiming again that the attempt to establish a British and Foreign school "has its origin in rivalry and opposition," and expressing the hope that "their Lordships will not attempt to impose upon us as a condition . . . of our receiving aid from the national Treasury, the renunciation of principles which we conscientiously hold, and to which we consider it our sacred duty to adhere." [103]

In response, Lingen tried to minimize the personal and sectarian dimensions of the conflict. He made an effort to define it not in religious terms, but as reflecting issues of economy and toleration. In a letter of October 28, he explained that the parishes (Llangefni and its neighbors) did not require two schools. If another were built, they would constitute an excess, providing places for nearly one in every four of the population, which "considering the state of other parts of the country . . . would certainly be disproportionate." [104] Noting the religious composition of the parishes, Lingen continued to press for compromise on the part of the Anglicans. With his letter of the 28th, he enclosed a minute of the committee containing the following language:

> Their Lordships cannot but hope that the clergy and laity of the Church of England will admit that the view they take of the obligations resting upon them, as to the inculcation of religious truth, must be limited by their duty to recognise the state of the law as to the toleration of diversities in religious belief, and especially in those who, on the basis of the Apostles Creed, approach so nearly as the Wesleyan communions do in doctrine to the Church of England. [105]

On this basis Lingen attempted to persuade Owen that pupils' parents who objected to Church of England requirements should be freed from participating in them without losing the benefits of schooling. In the same letter he tried to limit the conflict to more manageable dimensions: "The Lord President thinks it to be most desirable, in a case of this kind, to narrow the question as much as possible and to avoid all topics which are merely personal." [106]

Despite Lingen's efforts, matters remained at an impasse. After a few weeks' delay, the Committee of Council moved beyond persuasion, and threatened to withhold educational resources altogether from Llangefni if the conflict were not resolved satisfactorily. On November 16, Lingen wrote to Owen, with a copy to the competing group, that the Committee of Council had determined that two schools were not necessary to the parish. Somewhat surprisingly,[107] he said that the committee had determined that *neither* a British and Foreign school, in which the position of the Established Church was not recognized, *nor* a school compelling children of Dissenting parents to receive the religious instruction of the Anglican Church was appropriate for the parish. In light of that determination, the Committee of Council had suspended *both* applications, "in order to give the several promoters an opportunity of coming to a common understanding."[108]

Lingen's efforts to press the local parties into compromise did not succeed. Instead, within a week, the issue began to escalate to the level of national politics. Sir Richard Bulkely, member of Parliament from Anglesey, wrote Lingen criticizing the Committee of Council's conclusion that there was no place for a British and Foreign school in the parish. He urged the committee to reconsider. Two days later, the promoters of the British and Foreign school also protested the decision to suspend both applications and indicated that they had called upon Sir Richard. In response, Lingen wrote to the British and Foreign School Society promoters, admonished them not to begin any building, and assured them that Sir Richard's letter would be given consideration. Two weeks later, Lingen wrote to Sir Richard, reiterating that the committee would support only one school, a school on which all parties in Llangefni could unite. If such a school could be constituted, the committee would not approve a second school. The conflict appeared to be locked in a stalemate.

Matters took a new turn on January 8, 1851. Sir Richard forwarded a communication from the promoters of the British and Foreign school objecting to a proposed compromise whereby Church of England scholars would be catechized in a separate classroom. The promoters claimed that Dissenting bodies would demand the same right, and that several catechisms in one school would create confusion and religious rivalry.[109] On Febuary 7, the same promoters wrote to Lingen again in response to the proposal for governing a projected single school, saying that it gave the Church of England commanding power. In a neighborhood where the majority of Nonconformists was so great, ministers and deacons of other denominations ought to be included.[110] In the same letter the promoters chastised the committee for its decision to withhold funds:

> It would certainly be felt in this country as matter of great surprise and disappointment to be deprived of this grant of public money specially voted by Parliament towards the education of the people, more particularly so soon after the well-known reports of the Commissioners appointed to inquire into the state of education in Wales, of the great wants of the country in that respect.[111]

Lingen responded on February 15 and reminded the promoters of the British and Foreign school that the parish should have only one school, and that the parochial clergyman should have a place of influence in it. He repeated the committee's position that unless a satisfactory proposal could be fashioned, it would continue to withhold funds.

The record is silent for a few months, but on May 20 the promoters of the British school registered some objections to a sample trust deed suggested to them by the Committee of Council. That deed, evidently an attempt at compromise, specified a number of conditions. First, the management committee of the school should include the first officiating minister of the parish (Owen), his curate or curates, the church wardens (all Anglicans), and four other persons elected from those subscribing at least 20s. a year to the school. Second, the Bible should be read daily, but there would be no requirement for any child to learn any particular catechism or to attend any particular Sunday school. Third, the minister would catechize and give religious instruction in the schools, but only to those choosing it, and in a separate room for one hour a day.[112] The promoters objected to the power given to churchmen in the management committee. Instead, they suggested making the rector *ex officio,* thus providing for a larger number of elected members on the management committee. They also suggested reducing the necessary subscription level to 10s. for elected members and asked that the third clause providing for separate religious instruction be omitted.

On May 29, Lingen wrote the British and Foreign school promoters, regretting that they objected to the compromise, but adding that, considering the circumstances of the parish, the committee would be prepared to accept their modifications. He said, however, that the committee would review the matter with Owen. If he still insisted on compulsory and exclusive religious instruction, the committee would be inclined to support the arrangements as modified by the promoters of the British and Foreign school. On the same day, Lingen asked Owen to cooperate in establishing and maintaining a common parish school, thus resolving the conflict and negating the demand for a second school.

Owen's reply was negative and strident. He complained that the revised proposal was not consistent with "fairness and justice toward the Established Church."[113] He objected particularly to the composition of the management committee, which would be controlled by Dissenters with the reduction in the number of Anglican members, the increase in elected members, and the lowering of the subscription to 10s.[114] Then, generalizing the terms of the conflict, he offered the following complaint:

> It has surprised us much that the promoters of the British school should have considered it consistent with propriety, or the most ordinary consideration for the rights and feelings of others, to propose a coalition of parties, upon terms so utterly destructive of the influence of the Church, and so pointedly setting at naught the authority of the clergy.
>
> But we are still more surprised and grieved to find that the Lord President . . . expresses his disposition to concede to their unreasonable demands, and to accept the draft-deed as amended by them, as the basis on which to make them a grant. . . .
>
> We would respectfully ask, why Churchmen should be required to forego their principles any more than Dissenters? And is it fair and just that, upon their declining to do so, the Church is to be superseded by Dissent in the education of the poor? . . .
>
> We cannot regard this as an individual case. It embraces a principle which, if generally acted upon, must materially injure and cripple the Church in Wales, now slowly, but decidedly, emerging from a state of long-continued depression.[115]

In this seemingly disadvantaged position, Owen and his supporters apparently decided to raise the conflict to a higher political level. On June 20, the lord bishop of Bangor wrote to Lingen taking Owen's side in the dispute and requesting support for a school based on National Society principles. He concluded with a kind of political threat: he hoped that the agitation caused by the issue of the management clauses[116] had quieted, but he feared that if the Committee of Council persisted in its position, it would "excite feelings of sympathy and alarm in the minds of Churchmen."[117] Lingen acknowledged the bishop's letter and indicated that he would bring the correspondence to the attention of the committee.

During early July, Lingen continued his efforts to persuade Owen to reconsider his position. After Owen met with his fellow-promoters, he finally and reluctantly agreed to insert a clause into the trust deed that would provide "against enforcing upon children, whose parents or guardians shall object, the learning of the catechism, or attendance at the services of the Church."[118] He thereby submitted on the issues of compulsion and exclusiveness on which he had insisted so steadfastly up to that point. In response, Lingen quickly forwarded a new trust deed, revised in line with that concession for Owen's completion, and assured him that no grant would be given for a second, British and Foreign school.

Even this compromise could not bring matters to rest. As Lingen had promised Owen, he wrote to the promoters of the British and Foreign school on August 7, saying that in light of the rector's new position, a second school could not be supported. In response, on August 9, the promoters asked to see the exact plan for the management of the school that Lingen had provisionally approved.

Several months then passed without significant action. On November 29, however, Henry Dunn, the national secretary of the British and Foreign School Society, wrote a strongly worded letter to the Committee of Council. He reviewed the history of the conflict and concluded that because six hundred persons had pressed for a British and Foreign school in the autumn of 1850, and because Sir Richard Bulkely had intervened, there should be a second school in Llangefni. His concluding paragraphs were frankly menacing:

> The committee [of the British and Foreign School Society] cannot but feel that the course adopted in reference to Llangefni will, if pursued more extensively, be fatal to any combination of Government aid with voluntary effort for the spread of education among the people.
>
> The promoters of schools, whether British or national, will only subscribe their money towards the support of institutions in harmony with their own views and principles; and if these are interfered with, they will separate themselves altogether from the Government, and either erect schools irrespective of public aid,[119] or abandon the promotion of education altogether.
>
> So strongly do the committee feel this, that they have no hesitation in saying, that if the principle adopted in the Llangefni case is in future to be acted upon, they will be obliged, in a great measure, to abandon further efforts for the promotion of education in North Wales. They have appointed, at considerable expense, an agent expressly for the purpose of awakening the Welsh to the importance of extending and improving popular instruction, and through his exertions, aided by the Committee of Council, 73 schools are at the present time affording daily instruction to 8,000 or 10,000 children;[120] but so great has been the discouragement felt by those friends of education who have hitherto been willing to co-operate with the Government in the promotion of education, by the correspondence in reference to Llangefni,

that all similar undertakings in the country will speedily be abandoned, under the mistaken impression that the Government is hostile to the establishment of British Schools.[121]

Dunn ended with a plea that the Committee of Council support a British and Foreign school in Llangefni. He also demanded that it make explicit the conditions under which it would refuse to aid more than one school in a small community in the future.

On December 23, Lingen explained to Dunn that the Committee of Council was opposed in principle to "the multiplication of schools viewed without reference to each other," [122] and that limiting the expenditure of public money to a single school was the correct policy. At the same time, he added, the committee did not wish to incur the risk of discouraging the promoters of the British and Foreign school. In light of that consideration:

> The Lord President authorises me . . . to state that he has advised the committee to release the rector from the condition on which a grant was offered to the national school, and to allow a grant at the ordinary rate to the promoters of the British, as well as those of the national school, on fulfillment of the usual conditions.[123]

In early January 1852, Lingen executed these decisions, and eventually agreed to supply £229 10s. to the National Society school and £179 15s. to the British and Foreign school. Both parties accepted the grants, but after a few months both groups asked for augmentations, which were denied by the committee. Dunn wrote a letter of gratitude, in which he indicated that the action would encourage the British and Foreign School Society to continue its efforts to spread education in Wales.

The Llangefni episode holds out much intrinsic interest, largely because of its complexity and duration, both of which resulted from the passion and intractability of the parties involved. It is a single case, of course, and one cannot generalize to the whole of Wales, much less to British society as a whole, from it. Nevertheless, the episode contains in microcosm a number of general features relevant to the educational situation in both Wales and England, outlined below.

*The Salience of Religious Principles and Religious Jurisdiction.* Owen referred to "the authority of the clergy" and "the violation of our consciences and the abandonment of our principles." The Dissenters referred to freedom of religious choice and conscience. Both of these references invoked the religious groups' claims to legitimacy and advantage with respect to control of resources and access to the young of the community's poorer classes. That the dispute flared so readily into religious language shows how prepared the conflicting parties were to call up these fundamental principles of religious commitment.

*Government Discomfort with Disputes over Religious Principles and Jurisdiction.*  Lingen, as representative of the government bureaucracy, was as reluctant to invoke religious considerations as the warring parties were ready to do so. He seldom discussed and never challenged either the Anglican Church's claim to establishment and its derived authority or Dissent's claims of freedom of conscience and demands for equitable treatment. His strategy seemed to be to give explicit deference to the religious principles of both, while simultaneously attempting to persuade first one, then the other, to compromise those principles in ways that would appear minimal to the compromising group and acceptable to its contender. The state, personified in Lingen, was more comfortable with influencing and appealing to reasonableness than with entering into religious debates.

*Obstacles to Compromise Presented by Fundamental Principles of Legitimacy.*  If one regards the negotiations between the religious parties and the government as a game, it is apparent that each side continuously attempted to play its strongest suit. The religious groups found advantage in advancing religious arguments that invoked notions of the absolute and the sacred, and on which compromise was unacceptable in principle and difficult in practice. By calling up such arguments, the religious parties were engaging in a species of moral blackmail of the government—attempting to move its representatives by appeals to absolute principles. The government, on its side, ignored sacred considerations as much as possible (Lingen politely scolded the religious parties for raising them) and put forth practical arguments. Lingen first resisted the demands of both parties by appealing to criteria of economic and administrative efficiency: two small and inefficient schools were not economical or practical in the thinly populated parish. Failing in these, the government "caved in" in the face of escalating pressure from the religious societies and permitted the establishment of both schools on a government-supported basis, justifying this collapse by invoking considerations of equity. The government's response to this conflict also illustrates one of the main mechanisms by which the educational pattern of "proliferation along primordial lines" evolved in midcentury:[124] if parties claim rights and resources on sacred grounds, provide some to each and thereby attempt to keep them separated from one another.

*Class and Regional Cleavages Underlying the Conflict.*   The whole conflict in Llangefni was infused with class considerations, because the issue concerned a school *for the poor.* It reflected the era's taken-for-granted assumption that their education was to be supplied by and conducted separately from that of the higher classes. Also, the contest between Dissenters and Anglican Church was a conflict between classes. The dispute over the subscription rate (20s. or 10s.) necessary for membership on the management committee reflects the fact that the higher rate would tend to exclude Dissenters, often lower in the class hierarchy, less wealthy, and less able to subscribe than Anglicans in Welsh communities. Welsh-English tensions never became explicit in the conflict, but the Dissenting impulse in Wales was always infused with an antagonism toward the English. From the standpoint of the promoters of the British and Foreign school, they constituted a part of the Welsh "periphery" dealing with the English "core" in Whitehall. It is also difficult to imagine that the fact that Lingen himself had been one of the "treacherous" commissioners in 1847 was lost on the Welsh Dissenters.

*The Difficulty of Containing the Conflict.*   Structurally, the decision-making apparatus for working-class education was highly centralized in this period. Beginning in 1839, the Committee of Council dealt with every local request to establish schools, and it had not delegated this responsibility. In addition, the committee dealt on a continuous basis with the National Society and the British and Foreign School Society (and subsequently others), through which requests had to come. Both these societies were national organizations. Finally, while enjoying a large measure of independence from parliamentary supervision, the Committee of Council was subject to intervention on the part of members of Parliament. Given these centralized arrangements, a local conflict became central when some complaint flowed upward through one of the religious societies or through the formal political structure. In the Llangefni conflict, much of the political heat experienced by Lingen and the Committee of Council is traceable to the fact that nationally significant representatives of the conflicting parties entered the fray periodically. (This contrasts with the situation of the school board districts established by the Education Act of 1870, which insulated religious conflicts in communities by institutionalizing local election of board members.)

*The Symbiotic Relationship between the State and the Religious Societies.* Despite the heat and duration of the Llangefni conflict, it must be kept in mind that it transpired in a context in which all its principals—the Church of England, Dissent, and the state—were motivated to spread elementary education among the poor. In addition, both religious parties had entered into many "matching funds" arrangements with the state that bound each to the other. The state was reluctant to withdraw from such arrangements because this would undermine its efforts to encourage education (it could not at that time establish and sustain schools on its own, independent of the religious societies). The religious parties were reluctant to withdraw because they would lose resources and experience difficulty in establishing and sustaining schools on their own (as the Voluntaryists discovered).[125] At the same time, this symbiosis supplied each side with a political weapon. The religious societies could threaten not to accept funds, and carry out that threat. The Church of England did that during the conflict preceding the concordat of 1840 and during the management clause conflicts of 1848–52, and the Dissenting Voluntaryists had been doing so since the mid 1840s. The British and Foreign School Society's threat to join the Voluntaryists during the Llangefni conflict constituted a significant political component in the Committee of Council's final decision to permit two government-supported schools. The Llangefni conflict thus reflected the fact that the relations between the religious societies and the state resembled a less-than-happy marriage without the realistic possibility of divorce.

## THE WELSH SITUATION TO 1870

In many respects the story of Wales through the 1850s and 1860s continues the same themes and dynamics that characterized the heated conflicts in the 1840s. The Sunday schools, particularly among the Nonconformists, remained a vital force.[126] The Nonconformist initiative in establishing day schools retained its vitality,[127] though South Wales, where the commitment to Voluntaryism remained strong, struggled to keep the pace without the benefit of state funds. Nonconformist difficulties in raising subscriptions also persisted, because those denominations were not as wealthy as Anglican-landowning groups.[128]

There were also continuing signs of growing tension between localities and the central educational authorities, some of which took on a special "Welsh" cast. In the late 1840s, the proposal was made that inspectors of Welsh schools know the Welsh language.[129] In 1857 Lingen circularized principals of schools to enter a G (Gaelic) or W (Welsh), so that teachers with those language skills could be assigned to appropriate schools.[130] In 1861, Jenkins complained that because of special agricultural conditions in Wales, the requirement of 176 days' attendance in order to receive capitation payments was unrealistic. He also believed that the construction requirements for both schools and masters' residences were inappropriate for Wales, because of the impecuniousness of many of the districts there.[131] Several years later, HMI B. J. Binns reported difficulties in Welsh schools because of their inability to cope with the standardized examinations (in English) imposed by the Revised Code.[132] These local-central tensions added yet another note of discord in the Welsh educational situation.

The most striking developments of these years, however, was the extension of the "small-community" problem exemplified in Llangefni, and, along with it, the problem of the conscience clause. Wales, especially rural North Wales, would be expected to contribute disproportionately to these problems, because of the many localities in that region that had a large majority of Nonconformists. The history of the 1850s and 1860s bears out this expectation. Before detailing this history, however, we should notice that there was also some evidence of accommodation to religious conscience and religious heterogeneity. In 1857 HMI H. Longueville Jones reported that of 19,949 children on the books of 168 Church of England schools in his area of Wales, only one-third (6,130) were of parents belonging to the Establishment. The remainder were children of fee-paying parents of other denominations. Jones concluded that "[no] accusation of exclusiveness or bigotry can therefore be sustained against the schools in question."[133]

Be that as it may, applications for multiple schools for thinly populated districts increased in these decades, as did conflicts over the conscience clause and conflicts between religious groups and the state educational authorities. The Newcastle Commission noted the severity of these problems in Wales,[134] and its assistant commissioner for Wales underscored this, claiming that "in many instances the result of this [religious] antagonism has been to keep all education in a neighbourhood in abeyance, and not unfrequently to leave it for years without any educational provision, each party singly being unable . . . to establish a school without the cooperation of the other."[135]

In 1862, the Committee of Council published extensive correspondence between itself and various religious parties in Llanelly, Nevin, Towyn, and Beddgelert, all districts in Welsh counties. Each conflict was reminiscent of the Llangefni dispute, involving either multiple applications from thinly populated communities or committee pressure on a National school to adopt a conscience clause.[136] Also in 1862, a prolonged controversy over the same set of issues arose in Llanelly in Carmarthenshire.[137] One result of these conflicts was that Wales seemed to be multiplying schools unduly along religious lines. As late as 1869, HMI Bowstead claimed:

> This is a serious waste of educational resources, and that is not the only evil. The schools destroy each other's discipline, and it thus becomes impossible for either to be a thoroughly good one. The competition between them is not altogether of a wholesome kind, for much of it must consist in a rivalry between the teachers as to the most effectual means of humouring the children and their parents.
>
> This seemingly unnecessary multiplication of different classes of schools is very common in Wales . . . it . . . divides the inhabitants from their earliest infancy into different, if not hostile, sects.[138]

Then, on a more personal note, he complained that it meant sending "two, and sometimes even three, of your Lordships' officers [inspectors] to a remote locality in order to execute separate portions of a piece of work which could easily be done in its entirety by any one of them in the course of a few hours." [139]

By 1867, this type of conflict was recognized as significant. The Education Department submitted a special report dealing with conflict situations in which local (National Society) schools had capitulated to demands for a conscience clause, and those in which grants were refused because a local school would not accept such a clause. Between January 1, 1861, and March 31, 1867, the Education Department awarded 954 grants *in toto*, 867 to National schools, 87 to others.[140] In 829 cases there was no conflict and no need to insist on a conscience clause (presumably in larger communities). In 68 cases there was an initial refusal and then subsequent adoption of the conscience clause; most of these (59) were in small English communities. In those 37 cases where the department denied grants to build National Society schools, they were denied because the National Society would not accede to the government demands; half (18) of these were in Wales. In all, about one-quarter of the conscience clause cases occurred in Wales. In addition, the large number of refusals to make grants there underscores the fact that religious intransigence in Welsh communities was probably greater.[141]

When the Select Committee on Education reported in 1866, it singled out Wales. It noted the enormous Dissenting population there, and the "much and not unnatural jealousy of any predominant influence of the Church in the schools" on the part of Dissenters. With respect to small communities, the committee suggested one of two solutions: schools should be established either on the British and Foreign principle but with the parish's Anglican clergyman *ex officio* chairman of the committee or by the National Society with a conscience clause. They left the Education Department to judge which would be more appropriate and recommended that the minister of education have power to suspend grants if there was exclusion or undue restraint placed on Nonconformists. The committee also called for a general plan of education for Wales, without specifying the details of such a plan.[142]

The principal reason for the increasing severity of the conscience clause problem was that the government's position on multiple schools in small communities had hardened. The Newcastle Commission asked Lingen how he would handle a (hypothetical) district in Wales in which there were only a half-dozen families adhering to the Church of England. He said he would challenge an application from a clergyman in such a community, explaining: "For several years the great object was to have schools built; there was a crying deficiency of them. I believe that want has now been to a very considerable extent supplied, and in the case of any parish, such as you mentioned, undoubtedly attention would be paid to that fact."[143]

Lingen mentioned that in the Welsh community of Towyn a rejection had been sent to the promoters of a Church of England school, because a British and Foreign school had already been approved. The reason behind this stiffening of attitude was probably not, as Lingen suggested, because there was such an ample supply of schools. Rather, it was because the Education Department had been under such pressure to economize from the middle 1850s on.[144] One response to this pressure was to insist that there not be too many schools for too few children. This led the government (a) to insist on a conscience clause if the single school in the small community were a Church of England school (or to reject the application for a National school if the Anglican Church would not go along) or (b) to choose an alternate religious society that had long been permissive with respect to religious conscience (i.e., the British and Foreign School Society). It is notable that the Select Committee on Education of 1866 did not even envision the policy of multiple schools in small districts (the Llangefni solution). The effect of the committee's position was to further erode the lingering claims of the Church of England to a religious monopoly over education and to hasten the progress of nondenominational education well before the Education Act of 1870 and its extension in future years.[145]

## EPILOGUE

Beginning with the Parliamentary Reform Act of 1867, Welsh politics took a new turn, and so did the pattern of religious and educational conflict. That act extended the franchise further down the class lines, and more shopkeepers and small farmers were brought in. For Wales, this meant a great boost to Nonconformists, long excluded from the parliamentary scene by the landlord/Tory/Anglican grip on Welsh politics.[146] Already Wales had shown a steady drift toward the Liberal Party throughout the 1850s and 1860s.[147] Expectably, the newly enfranchised voters embraced Gladstonian liberalism; in the election of 1868, twenty-one Liberals and eight Conservatives were returned.[148]

In the period of political agitation preceding the passage of the Education Act of 1870, the Welsh were especially active.[149] In that agitation, the Welsh Educational Alliance, formed in January 1870, threw in its lot with the progressive National Education League. Many of the Welsh, carrying forward the tradition of Voluntaryism, stood on the radical side of the league's program, rejecting any kind of conscience clause and insisting on a completely secular system of day schools.[150] After the 1870 legislation, the politics of school board elections became especially heated in Wales, both in urban areas, where the Nonconformists were not altogether successful,[151] and in rural areas, where "school boards formed with great political enthusiasm to oust the influence of the English landowning classes and the Anglican church quickly lapsed into educational apathy in many villages."[152] As the school-board era developed, Wales was notable for its high proportion of districts where boards adopted a nonsectarian policy and paid for pupils in denominational schools only rarely.[153] Given the background of decades of polarization of conflicts in Welsh politics and the fusion of regional, language, religious, class, and educational issues in those conflicts, these political developments in the period around 1870 and afterward were expectable and understandable.

## CHAPTER 7

# The Cases of Ireland and Scotland

To deepen the analysis of elementary education in nineteenth-century Britain, I now turn to two other facets of it, Ireland and Scotland. Both were under the rule of the British Parliament in London but had either a degree of autonomy or separate administrative arrangements in several institutional areas, including education. As a case for study, Ireland represents a more extreme version than Wales of cultural (including religious), institutional, and political differences from England. These included antagonism to and religious alienation from the established Anglican Church of Ireland; a fusion of social class with religious and ethnic differences; and a developed national identity and nationalist movement. By contrast, Scotland had its own established religion, separate from the Church of England, and its upper class was largely indigenous, but while Scots had a strong sense of national identity, this did not develop into an advanced cultural and nationalist movement in the nineteenth century. The educational outcomes in the two societies, moreover, reflect these different patterns of determinants. To supplement these two cases, I take a brief comparative look, midway in the chapter, at the Irish in New York City in the early nineteenth century.

The accounts that follow are not intended to be general histories of elementary education. I present the selected historical materials with a conscious comparative intent—to identify decisive determinants and outcomes that differ from the English pattern. Methodologically, this exercise approximates John Stuart Mill's method of difference. This involves comparing cases that bear evident similarities—stemming mainly from the legal and governance structure of the United Kingdom—but also manifest significant differences. These points of difference carry a special explanatory significance for differences in educational outcomes.[1]

## IRELAND

### GENERAL BACKGROUND TO THE
### EDUCATIONAL REFORMS OF 1831

While the same general cultural and institutional forces operate in all cases of educational development,[2] these assume a distinctive constellation in different national settings. I have noted Wales's semicolonial status and the fact that it was given little official acknowledgment. That status implied a fusion of the ethnic, economic, religious, and regional dimensions. Accordingly, most issues that arose, including educational ones, had significance for all these dimensions. The same observations—in more extreme form—apply to Ireland.[3] In 1836 Thomas Wyse wrote a tract urging a national system of education on England.[4] Wyse himself was Irish, a member of Parliament, and among the leaders of the middle-class radicals who pressed for educational reform unsuccessfully in the 1830s.[5] In this pamphlet he produced a vignette of the fusion of many social dimensions in the Irish class system:

> [In Ireland the] Upper and Lower orders have neither the harmonious blending of the English, nor the friendly subordination of the Scotch. They are hostile armies; and, through the comparative insignificance of the Middle class, they have repeatedly come into collision. . . . the aristocracy [are] absentees, if not from their country, from their estates. . . . [in Ireland] to the common hostility between high and low, rich and poor, was conjoined the far deadlier hatred arising from national and religious distinctions. England never thoroughly subdued Ireland, and had the folly always to war against her. She contented herself with merely *garrisoning*, when she should have *incorporated* her. . . . England governed her . . . not in the sense of an integral empire, but as a dangerous rival. . . . She set up an opposing creed, an opposing property, an opposing code, all English; and made the rich and the exclusive enjoyers and guardians of all. No wonder, then, the functionary was hated with the same hatred as the system; that the Aristocracy was confounded with the hereditary enemies of the country . . . the Aristocracy on their side were not less hostile to the People. They hated and despised; but it was not the scorn of real superiority, it was the spurious pride of sect and party.[6]

Wyse's account is no doubt a caricature, subject to many qualifications according to locality. It does, however, touch that important overlapping of cultural, social, economic, and political dimensions that proved so important in understanding Welsh educational development.[7]

The history of education in Ireland in the eighteenth and early nineteenth centuries is mainly a story of the unsuccessful efforts of English Protestants—sometimes aided by government—to gain religious and cultural hegemony over the largely Roman Catholic Irish population, and the more or less successful efforts of the latter to resist the former. As part of this effort, the Church of England and other Protestant bodies attempted to provide religiously based schools for the poor, while the state enacted penal laws against Catholic education. Catholic priests, teachers, and pupils often undermined these efforts by boycotting Protestant schools and establishing their own "hedge schools."[8] These were often conducted outdoors behind hedges or hedgerows to avoid detection. As England relaxed the penal laws in 1782, 1792, and 1793, the hedge schools evolved into private, informal fee-paying schools, with masters conducting classes in local huts and houses.

The Protestant campaign developed mainly through educational societies for the poor, all with some kind of proselytization on their agenda. The following were the principal ones:

The Incorporated Society for Promoting English Protestant schools in Ireland, founded in 1733 with an avowedly proselytizing aim. It never enrolled more than a few thousand students.

The Association for Discountenancing Vice and Promoting the Knowledge and Practice of the Christian Religion, founded in 1792. This was at first a voluntary society, then received parliamentary monies up to 1831. These grants grew to £9,000 in 1823 and were discontinued around 1830. The Anglican Church controlled the association. It served a multidenominational population of pupils—about half Catholic—until around 1820. By way of accommodation, the association did not require Catholic children to attend instruction in the catechism. After 1820, however, the association's teachings became openly proselytizing; gradually Catholic priests and parents became alienated from it, and its numbers of Catholic pupils dwindled.[9]

The London Hibernian Society, founded in 1806. Its aim was to promote the diffusion of religious knowledge in Ireland, mainly through distributing the Scriptures and establishing elementary schools. Avowedly nonproselytizing, it nevertheless evoked hostility among Catholic clergymen because its schools called for the reading of the Protestant Scriptures. Under this criticism, some Catholic teachers and children withdrew from its schools. Nevertheless, by 1823 it had opened some 653 day schools, of which 326, with 31,702 scholars, were in Ulster.

The Sunday School Society for Ireland, founded in 1809. Sunday schools began in the 1780s in Ireland, but after a burst of enthusiasm, waned in the last decade of the eighteenth century. The society's schools grew from 22 in 1810 to 2,091 in 1820. Completely voluntary, these drew criticism not only from Catholic clergy, because of their proselytizing, but also because of the general association of Sunday schools with popular political protest at the time.[10]

The Baptist Society for Promoting the Gospel in Ireland, founded in 1814.

The Irish Society for Promoting the Education of the Native Irish through the Medium of Their Own Language, founded in 1818.[11]

Despite their number and variety, these societies failed in their attempts to cover the Irish population. A survey of such schools in 1810 showed a coverage of only 23,000 pupils. A similar report in 1823 yielded a figure of 36,000 pupils, of whom fewer than half (15,000) were Roman Catholic. For a population of more than 6,000,000, of whom four-fifths were Catholic, the figures were very small.[12]

The most notable educational society in the early nineteenth century was the Society for Promoting the Education of the Poor in Ireland (also known as the Kildare Place Society, after the site of its headquarters). Joseph Lancaster visited Dublin in 1811 and helped establish it. Expectably, the new society employed the monitorial method. More important, it explicitly disavowed proselytizing and adopted the religious-educational philosophy of its parent, the British and Foreign School Society. This called for multidenominational sponsorship as well as the practices of reading the Scriptures without note or comment and excluding catechisms and controversial religious books. The intent of the society appeared as follows in its tenth annual report:

> It is hoped, that in such Seminaries the labouring classes may obtain suitable instruction, without any attempt being made to disturb their religious opinions; and that the children of the poor being thus associated together without distinction, may thereby learn to regard each other without prejudice, and to indulge a charitable feeling for their neighbours, of whatever religious persuasion they may be.[13]

The experiment began auspiciously.[14] It secured the approval of the Catholic clergy; a minority of Irish clergymen served on its board of directors; and Catholics were patrons of individual schools. Parliament began giving grants in support of the society in 1812. It voted £7,000 for its first building. The annual grant was £10,000 in 1817, and it had grown to £30,000 by 1831. It was finally phased out in 1833. (The sums are not enormous, but notable in light of the fact that in 1833 the parliamentary grant to religious societies for all of England and Wales was only £20,000.) In two decades of support, the Kildare Place Society received some £216,000 from Whitehall. It provided cheap books for school libraries, and by 1825 it was supporting some 1,100 monitorial schools. A former pupil of Lancaster's served as a trainer of teachers and school inspector.[15]

Despite its favorable beginning and favored status, the Kildare Place Society ultimately fell on difficult times. From the beginning, Catholics were suspicious about the Protestant majorities on the general managing committee and the reading of the Scriptures without comment. (Catholic tradition called for priests' interpretations as an essential element of religious worship and education.) In the 1820s, however, Catholic alienation from the society mounted. Part of this was linked to the larger Irish agitation of the time, which included popular demonstrations against tithes for the Church of Ireland, for Catholic emancipation, and for parliamentary reform.

The Catholic bishops' specific criticisms of the Kildare Place Society focused on local Protestant clergy in its schools, whom they charged with giving doctrinal interpretations of the Bible. In addition, the society began giving some of its funds to frankly proselytizing societies—the Association for Discountenancing Vice and the Hibernian and Baptist societies. Daniel O'Connell, the leading Irish Catholic activist of the day, who had been a member of the managing committee of the society, became a vocal critic of it. Also in the 1820s, the Catholics began forming religious societies of their own—the Irish National Society for the Education of the Poor in 1821 and the Catholic Education Society in 1828. These societies applied unsuccessfully to Parliament for grants in aid. If they had succeeded, and if the Kildare Place Society's funds had not been discontinued, the Irish situation would have paralleled the subsidized denominational arrangements that governed the English system between 1833 and 1870. After Parliament declined to support them, the Catholic educational societies turned to the religious orders for help.[16]

In the meantime, Parliament had grown increasingly uneasy about the religious/educational situation in Ireland and carried out a series of investigations in the early part of the century. The first, a royal commission established in the year of the Act of Union (1800), reported in

1806. The commission took cognizance of the religious peculiarities of Ireland and acknowledged the unworkability of the traditional policy of entrusting education to the Church of Ireland. It adopted as its first principle that "no attempt shall be made to influence or disturb the peculiar religious tenets of any section or description of Christians." [17] The commission asked for a state system of education, in which general scriptural extracts would constitute religious education, with specific doctrinal instruction offered by ministers of religion. With these recommendations, the commission confessed that Ireland could not be regarded as subsumable—as it was assumed Wales could be—under a general educational system of Great Britain. A commission of inquiry in 1812 came up with similar recommendations.

Under renewed Catholic pressure, Parliament established another commission of inquiry in 1824, which called for an eventual abolition of grants to the proselytizing societies. It also recommended a state-supported denominational system with lay teachers of different denominations, according to the population served. Religious instruction would be provided separately. The commission drew up a system of extracts from both the Authorized Version of the Protestant Bible and the Roman Catholic version, but these proved objectionable to Catholic spokesmen.[18] Catholics objected further because the commission's recommendations provided for religious education by Protestant clergymen but only by Catholic laymen, which would have locked Catholic priests out of the system.[19] Despite the apparent consensus that Irish education should be national and multidenominational—with controversies over implementation, however—the English government initiated no major changes after the commission reported.

The decisive parliamentary report came from the select committee of 1828, which affirmed the inadequacy of existing efforts, stating that some 150,000 Irish children were untouched by the efforts of any of the educational societies.[20] (A select committee on the poor in Ireland put the figure at 280,000 two years later).[21] As with the other investigating bodies, the religious issue stood paramount. The committee's object was "to discover a mode in which the combined Education of Protestant and Catholic may be carried on, resting upon Religious instruction, but free from the suspicion of Proselytism." [22] Its solution was along the lines already suggested: "To bring together children of the different religious persuasions in Ireland, for the purpose of instructing them in the general subjects of moral and literary knowledge, and providing facilities for their religious instructions *separately,* when differences of creed render it impracticable for them to receive religious instruction together."[23] The mechanism envisioned was to distribute parliamentary grants to a governing board, and to impose no religious criteria in hiring teachers. The committee suggested scheduling four days for "moral and literary instruction" and two days for the separate instruction of Protestant and Catholic children. It also recommended a national governing board of educational commissioners, to be appointed without religious distinction. The board would edit and print all books for the literary instruction of the pupils. It would also print and distribute books for religious instruction, but only as approved by the authorities of the Church of Ireland and the Roman Catholic bishops.

The Irish educational debates of the late 1820s reveal both the political pressure on the English government and the limited number of options available to it. The ingredients of its political dilemma were the following:

Ireland was in a state of great political protest, with revolutionary overtones.[24] In July 1832 Lord Stanley, the author of the legislation establishing the Irish national system,[25] spoke of "the entire disorganization of society" in Ireland,[26] and of the need for pacification there.[27] Immediately after the debates on Irish education in 1832, the House of Commons debated whether to suppress public meetings in Ireland.[28] A measure to this effect passed the following year. The idea that popular education was one means of pacifying unrest was voiced in later debates, both by those who thought the new national system was working[29] and by those who thought it was failing.[30]

Education controlled by the Church of Ireland and taught under its principles could not achieve the desired educational objectives. Many in Parliament branded the existing efforts—including those of the Kildare Place Society—as part of a long, unsuccessful policy of attempting to make Ireland "English."[31] Proselytizing under any guise could not be effective.[32] Various members of Parliament, including Brougham, spoke of the injustice of imposing Protestant principles on Catholics.[33] Both Catholics and Protestants were reluctant to attend schools based on the religious principles of the other.[34] The Irish clergy, for their part, discouraged children from attending the Protestant-sponsored schools, including those of the Kildare Street Society,[35] and encouraged them to attend schools of the Catholic voluntary societies or hedge schools. The reason given was that priests and parents objected to the reading of the Protestant Bible and reading it without interpretation.[36]

It followed that any system that would reach the people—and thus achieve the political goal of pacification—required the support of the Catholic clergy and laity. James Doyle, an Anglican minister in Ireland, asserted that he did "not see how any man . . . can think that the peace can ever be permanently established, if children are separated at the commencement of life on account of their religious opinions."[37] This apparently irreducible fact led all investigatory bodies to call for a "combined system"—common secular education combined with separate religious instruction. Such a solution gained further favor from the fact that the Catholic prelates approved the essentials of the select committee's report of 1828.[38]

## THE SOLUTION OF 1831

Despite the fact that the logic inherent in these social/religious forces dictated some kind of national system, its implementation proved difficult. Parliamentary action stalled in 1828, and only after the formation of the first Whig cabinet of 1830 was the passage of a bill assured. Even so, the debates leading up to its passage revealed a profound religious struggle. The Catholic Church in both Ireland and England strongly supported the recommended combined system.[39] The Anglican establishment opposed it equally strongly, defending its claim to monopoly over the education of the poor. Representatives of the Established Church in Parliament held out the apprehension that without instruction in the Protestant Bible, the dangers of godlessness and the destruction of the English religious system were immanent.[40] Supporters countered that to require the Protestant Bible in Irish schools would (as it already had done) drive the majority of the Irish parents and children away from the schools.[41] The Anglicans also argued that Catholics would inevitably seize control of a national system, which would in effect create an establishment of the Roman Catholic Church in Ireland.[42]

Protestant Dissenting groups divided on the plan for national education. The Presbyterians in Ulster opposed it, largely because of their fear of Catholic domination of such a system.[43] They were joined by their Presbyterian brethren in Scotland, many of whom shared their antagonism to and fear of Roman Catholics.[44] Other Dissenters were ambivalent on the issue, for the same reasons that later caused them to divide over the augmentation of the government subsidy to the Maynooth seminary.[45] Insofar as the measure weakened the role of the Established Church in education, Dissenters were in favor of the Stanley plan. Insofar as they shared the Anglican apprehension that Catholics would take over a national school system, effectively creating a Catholic establishment, they were opposed. This ambivalence probably accounts for their relative lack of public visibility—except for the Presbyterians—in their petitions and in representing a position in Parliament. The Wesleyan Methodists, themselves engaged in an uphill campaign of proselytism in Ireland, opposed the national scheme because, according to one interpretation, "they would not share any government gift with Roman Catholics or Protestant 'heretics.'" [46]

Opponents of the Stanley proposal advanced several alternatives to it. The first was the status quo, of government support for some Protestant educational societies but not for Catholic ones. This was the position of many in the Anglican hierarchy, a position that would preserve the Church of England's position. All other solutions appeared to entail a loss for the Anglican establishment. The second was to subsidize all the religious dominations (including the Catholics)—a variety of the "1833 solution" that was to develop in England. This was the implied solution in the Irish educational societies' plea for assistance in the 1820s. That position was advanced in the educational debates on Ireland in 1827 and 1831. [47] Such a solution—and the antagonism to it—presaged the debate in the 1840s on the subsidization of Maynooth, also originally proposed as a measure of political pacification. [48] The Maynooth subsidy was attacked at the time of the debates on Irish education as not efficacious, [49] and as constituting a concurrent endowment—a form of establishment—of Roman Catholicism. [50] This same apprehension surfaced in the debate over the subsidy of voluntary Catholic schools in Ireland.

The third solution was to remove the state completely and allow the voluntary religious societies to proceed on their own. The earl of Roden, a spokesman for the Anglican hierarchy, [51] suggested this out of fear of anything resembling a Catholic establishment in Ireland. His argument paralleled that of the Voluntaryists in England, who feared that any state religion would lead to Anglican domination. The corresponding argument about Ireland in 1830–31, such as it was, was that of Anglicans who feared the same result if the government supported religious education. This Voluntaryist diagnosis had an element of truth for both countries, [52] though in neither did that alternative show much promise of producing a comprehensive educational system.

In the end, the Stanley proposals won the day, bolstered largely by arguments that political concessions to the Catholic Church—which supported those proposals—would pacify the Irish population. These arguments overcame a sizable religious opposition, mainly on the part of Anglicans. (In this regard, the political dynamics of 1830–31 and the 1845 Maynooth crisis were almost identical, except that the Whigs led in the first and the Conservatives in the second.)[53] From another angle the outcome can be regarded as a compromise. If Ireland had been independent of English domination and the Anglican establishment, the Catholics, with their enormous numerical majority, would most likely have instituted a state-supported system of Catholic religious instruction. The compromise represented by the national system—which essentially separated *all* sectarian religious instruction from the general system—took into account the facts of the political strength, *in England,* of the Anglican Church and the Presbyterians. These groups opposed the national system, but that system, by ruling out mixed secular and religious instruction, kept them from being swamped by Catholic strength in Ireland.

According to the legislation of 1831,[54] the lord lieutenant of Ireland, while answerable to Parliament, had the authority to appoint commissioners to the Irish Board of Education. (From 1831 to 1837 there were three commissioners from the Established Church and two each from the Roman Catholic and Presbyterian churches.) The board could authorize the building and support of schools in localities where groups of residents (usually a denomination) could raise one-third of the necessary financial support. Any Christian group could apply, and the board especially encouraged multiple-denomination applications. (The Irish system thus retained a voluntary, denominational element.) The board was to establish a model school, appoint inspectors, reward and discipline teachers (though local managers could hire them), and edit, print, and distribute textbooks. Schools were open to children of all denominations. The legislation circumvented any need for a conscience clause by eliminating all denominational materials from the four days of secular schooling. Religious education would transpire on the two remaining days of schooling, and the clergy of the different denominations of the school districts were to be responsible for it.

The legislation is remarkable in several respects. In a country remote from economic and institutional "modernization," the Irish national system "solved," in a radical way, the problem of religious conflict in education by a structural separation of the spheres of religion and the state. As such, the Irish system approached the "American" solution. The legislation is also striking as a rehearsal of solutions to issues that were to develop over the next four decades in England—for example, the balance between central and local control, inspection, and teacher-training. The most important rehearsal was for the Education Act of 1870, which established state (local board) schools for secular and general religious instruction and in large part avoided the need for a conscience clause by isolating religious instruction temporally and ruling out denominational content and rituals.

A key question is: Why was this "modern" solution put in place in Ireland at a time when England was managing (in 1833) only the barest subsidy to the religious societies without imposing any state control? The answer appears to lie more in the politics of religious conflict than anywhere else. The English government confronted a threatening political situation in both England and Ireland in the late 1820s and early 1830s. Furthermore, the idea of education as conciliation and pacification was in the air as a legitimizing device in both countries. These general conditions pressed for *some* kind of educational reform in both. The specific *form* it took, however, followed the line suggested by the patterns of religious composition and conflict.

The politics of Ireland in the first third of the century dictated that a state system of education based on the Church of Ireland was not a viable alternative for that country. The Catholic Church and its people would vote with their feet, as it were, and successfully boycott and raise political opposition to such a system. In that respect, adoption of the national system in Ireland seemed to follow from the fact that any other form of religious mixing was politically impossible with the Established Church in such a fragile position in a society so fraught with primordial conflicts. Similar impossibility was not evident in England in 1833. The Dissenters were a smaller proportion of the population and were less homogeneous in outlook and less well organized than the Roman Catholics in Ireland, despite, or perhaps because of, that country's situation of quasi-colonial denomination. Accordingly, in England, it was possible to segregate religious from political conflict in another way: to provide separate and (in principle) equal treatment by the government and partially isolate the contending religious parties from one another.[55] In the 1840s and 1850s, religion outside the Church of England witnessed several fragmenting tendencies. These were with the rise of Voluntaryism, the vacillation of the Wesleyan Methodists, and the independence of English Catholicism from (if not outright antagonism to) English Protestant Dissent. It took the renunciation of the Voluntaryists, the conversion of other Nonconformists to the idea of a secular state educational system, and the union of these parties with the secularists and trade union leaders to build a political coalition that could impose an "Irish solution" on the new English coalition of Anglicans, Catholics, and Wesleyans in 1870.[56] As it turned out, the act of 1870 created only a partial, layered-on system that left voluntary denominationalism undisturbed in principle, but unsupported by the school boards and local rates. The full "Irish" solution applied only to the board schools.

Wales falls between Ireland and England on this comparative dimension. Between 1830 and 1870, its proportion of Dissenters was almost as high as that of Roman Catholics in Ireland, and the level of Welsh antagonism to the Anglican/English/upper-class complex was also strong. Yet the Welsh—like the English—Dissenters were divided with respect to both religious persuasion and the politics of education. Furthermore, Voluntaryism split the Welsh Dissenters more than the English. Accordingly, the Welsh "solution" was intermediate between the Irish and the English. The Welsh Dissenters partially succeeded in "leaving empty," through disinterest and boycott, many Anglican day schools in their principality. They also competed, with limited success, with the Anglicans for the state subsidy (mainly in North Wales) and on a voluntary basis (mainly in South Wales). They did not, however, render the English system of denominational support totally unworkable in Wales, even though Welsh progress in elementary education lagged behind that of England. The Welsh-Dissent break with Anglican domination became more effective only after 1870, when Dissenters could impose their political preferences in those localities they dominated; even then, the dethronement of the Church of England in Welsh primary education was only partial.

## THE EVOLUTION OF THE IRISH NATIONAL SYSTEM, 1831–1870

By many measures, the Irish national experiment began auspiciously. The general landscape of Irish politics from the mid 1830s to the early 1840s was calm; Russell referred to "that sweet sleep in which Irish agitation slumbered from 1835 to 1842."[57] The number of pupils in Irish schools expanded steadily after 1831, and education was funded handsomely. These advances are recorded in table 21. An inspectorate and a model school were installed in 1832, and by 1845 training colleges for both males and females were in place. Ireland, with about one-half the

TABLE 21    GOVERNMENT EXPENDITURE ON
ELEMENTARY EDUCATION IN IRELAND, 1831–1870

| | Expenditure | Number of Pupils Registered in Day Schools | Population (thousands) |
|---|---|---|---|
| 1831 | £ 25,000 | 137,639 | 7,769 |
| 1832 | 30,000 | — | |
| 1833 | 37,500 | 107,042 | |
| 1834 | [45,000] | — | |
| 1835 | | 145,521 | |
| 1836 | 35,000 | 153,707 | |
| 1837 | 38,500 | 166,929 | |
| 1838 | 50,000 | 169,548 | |
| 1839 | 50,000 | 192,971 | |
| 1840 | 50,000 | 232,560 | |
| 1841 | 50,000 | 281,849 | 8,197 |
| 1842 | 50,000 | 319,792 | |
| 1843 | 50,000 | 355,320 | |
| 1844 | 50,000 | 395,550 | |
| 1845 | 72,000 | 432,844 | |
| 1846 | 75,000 | 456,410 | |
| 1847 | 85,000 | 402,634 | |
| 1848 | 100,000 | 507,469 | |
| 1849 | 120,000 | 480,623 | |
| 1850 | 120,000 | 511,239 | |
| 1851 | 125,000 | 520,401 | 6,574 |
| 1852 | 135,000 | 544,604 | |
| 1853 | 165,000 | 550,631 | |
| 1854 | 182,000 | 551,110 | |
| 1855 | 193,000 | 535,905 | |
| 1856 | 215,000 | 560,134 | |
| 1857 | 228,000 | 776,473 | |
| 1858 | 213,000 | 803,610 | |
| 1859 | 223,000 | 806,510 | |
| 1860 | 249,000 | 804,000 | |
| 1861 | 271,000 | 803,364 | 5,799 |
| 1862 | 285,000 | 812,527 | |
| 1863 | 290,000 | 840,569 | |
| 1864 | 306,000 | 870,401 | |

TABLE 21   (*continued*)

|        | Expenditure | Number of Pupils Registered in Day Schools | Population (thousands) |
|--------|-------------|--------------------------------------------|------------------------|
| *1865* | 317,000     | 922,084                                    |                        |
| *1866* | 326,000     | 910,819                                    |                        |
| *1867* | 336,000     | 913,198                                    |                        |
| *1868* | 302,000     | 967,563                                    |                        |
| *1869* | 380,000     | 991,335                                    |                        |
| *1870* | 394,000     | 998,999                                    |                        |
| *1871* |             |                                            | 5,412                  |

SOURCE: J. M. Goldstrom, *The Social Content of Education, 1808–1870* (Shannon: Irish University Press, 1972), pp. 193–94.

NOTE: Grants to the Irish commissioners and the Kildare Place Society only. On number of pupils on register, figures up to 1831 are for the Kildare Place Society schools only. Figures from 1833 are for Irish commissioners' schools only. In the early years, the figures underestimate the number of scholars, but in later years they probably overstate it, since a child's name had to appear on the register for only one day to be included in the figures. After 1850 there were very few schools that did not come under the supervision of the commissioners.

population of England and Wales,[58] received an absolutely larger grant right up to 1850, when the enthusiastic period of English growth began. In 1838, a select committee in England could find no recommendations other than to continue an admittedly inadequate system of subsidization.[59] In the same year a parallel Irish committee submitted a plan for improving, systematizing, and expanding the system with respect to financing, administration, fees, and provisions for teachers.[60] The main argument employed for the Irish national system was that it was growing and working effectively.[61] In its second report for the year ending in March 1835, the Commission on National Education in Ireland concluded "that the new System of Education has proved generally beneficial and acceptable to Protestants and Roman Catholics, according to their respective wants."[62] Horace Mann gave the Irish system a very positive review in 1846, citing its growth, its effectiveness of teacher-training, and its stability: "Not withstanding the novelty of the subject [of national education], and the number and delicacy of the questions to be settled, as between opposing parties in religion and politics, not a single protest had been entered upon its records, nor had any schism disturbed the harmony of its members."[63] In the 1850s, Harriet Martineau contrasted the efficiency of the national elementary schools in Ireland with the failing system of middle-class education there.[64]

Despite this outward evidence of institutional health, other signs indicated early on that the national system, as designed, was being taken over and undermined by denominational forces. The original understanding was that the commissioners would show preference to multidenominational applications for grants. If an application came from persons of only one denomination, they would investigate it before awarding a grant.[65] In practice, however, the board tended to ignore these provisions and to supply grants to individuals and groups of good standing in a community. Given the divisions and hostilities among the major denominations in Ireland—Roman Catholic, Church of Ireland, and Presbyterian—this virtually assured that the applications would be denominational. From the beginning, national schools tended to minister to children of their own denominations. A typical situation, with the Church of Ireland as example, was the following:

> A local Anglican clergyman could become manager of a school and receive a generous government grant, then appoint an Anglican teacher, and run a school almost entirely of Anglican children. In that school, an Anglican teacher could have interpreted the moral material inherent in the general literary texts in terms consistent with Anglican attitudes; and in the time set aside for religious instruction at day's end, the minister himself, or a deputy, could come into the school and catechize the children in Anglican doctrine.[66]

By midcentury, the typical manager of an Irish national school was the local clergyman of one of the denominations.[67] A survey in 1852 showed that only 175 of the 4,795 national schools—about 3.5 percent—were under joint management; in 1867 only 10 percent had teaching staffs that were religiously mixed.[68]

Several other trends accentuated the drift toward de facto denominational control. The Presbyterians, a minority clustered mainly in Ulster, had opposed the legislation of 1831. In Ireland a significant wing of that church displayed a fundamentalist religious temperament. They rankled under the prohibition of the Bible as a means of instruction and ridiculed the multidenominational "Scripture lessons" approved by the commissioners. This fundamentalist wing also resented separated religious instruction, which meant that Roman Catholics more or less completely controlled the exposure of their own children to religious thought.[69] In 1833 the Synod of Ulster initiated a campaign for denominational, state-supported education, demanding that local managers control religious instruction in their schools. After failing in this attempt, the Presbyterians broke off their relations with the board for a time.[70] They did not desert the system permanently, however. It did, after all, contribute two-thirds of the support of the schools they operated. Instead, by a steady exercise of political pressure they were able to bend the national system's policies in a denominational direction. They gained rulings that enabled them to relax the strictures on hours set aside for religious instruction, to discourage clergymen from other faiths from entering their schools, to give religious instruction on the same day as secular instruction, and to permit children of other faiths to receive their religious instruction if their parents so wished. These concessions succeeded in large part in isolating Presbyterian schools as a kind of self-governing religious cocoon in receipt of government aid.[71] The board, on its side, appeared to be willing to make these concessions in order to keep the Presbyterians participating. The relaxations, granted initially because of Presbyterian agitation, gradually became general.[72]

The Anglicans took a different route of noncooperation with the national system. The 1830s witnessed a number of significant defeats for the Anglican Church—the imposition of the national educational system over their opposition, the reduction of bishoprics in Ireland in 1833, the reduction of tithes (and revenues) by the tithe act of 1838. All of these measures were Whig initiatives, and solidified the Church of Ireland's support of the Tory and anti-Catholic parties.[73] After 1831 the Anglican Church's opposition to the national system continued. A survey of Anglican clergy at midcentury revealed that only one-quarter of them were in favor of participating in the national system.[74]

Throughout the 1830s, Anglican spokesmen in Parliament attacked the national system, especially in the annual budgetary debates. The charges were that the system gave power to the Catholics, that it was a corruption of the Protestant basis of British society, and that it was a disguised system of Roman Catholic establishment in Ireland.[75] Critics also noted that the government grant for Ireland was larger than it was for the religious societies in England and Wales.[76] Graham claimed that the system was ineffective, because it evidently had not created religious peace in Ireland.[77]

The mid 1840s brought another defeat to the Church of Ireland when Peel pushed through the augmentation of the grant to the Maynooth seminary. This controversy was reviewed in chapter 5 in the context of the alignment of political and religious forces building up to the minutes of 1846.[78] Here I would remind readers of its significance in the context of the Irish situation. The Maynooth issue was a thorn in the side of Anglicans long before the crisis of 1845. Throughout the 1830s, the vote on the annual grant was accompanied by vitriolic attacks on the subsidy on the part of Anglican spokesmen.[79] (Their sensitivities on Catholic issues were heightened by dissensions within their own ranks and attacks from Wesleyans and others on the "Catholic" tendencies of the Oxford Movement.) The criticisms sounded the same themes that arose in the debate on elementary education in Ireland. These were that the government was, in effect, establishing the Roman Catholic Church in Ireland, and that the Protestant principles of the United Kingdom were being correspondingly eroded.[80]

The political lineups on Maynooth were much the same as those in the Irish elementary education debates. Anglicans and Presbyterians in both Ireland and Scotland were opposed.[81] Other Dissenters were divided between their antagonism to Catholics and their disposition to grant the Catholics (as Dissenters of a sort themselves) the independent right to train their clergy.[82] (The dominant *political* impetus for the augmentation, it will be recalled, was Peel's conviction that the Irish political crisis could best be managed by a policy of securing Irish loyalty by conciliation and concession.) The Maynooth controversy, finally, occurred in the context of continuing Anglican hostility to the Irish national system.

The Church of Ireland had reservations about the national system that resembled those of Presbyterians. Anglicans were a minority on the original board. They feared that the system would, in effect, become a Catholic system. They resented the separation between religious and literary education and the restriction of the Bible to separated religious instruction.[83] Their political strategy in the 1830s was to influence the Tories in Parliament to abandon the system or at least provide the Church of Ireland with a separate subsidy. (The second would have meant making explicit the kind of denominational subsidization that, de facto, existed in the national system.) The Tory leadership, including Peel were not, however, moved into legislative action by these appeals.[84] Despite its lack of success, the Anglican strategy evinced a certain logic. The Anglican Church was in a preeminent institutional position on the English educational scene at the time;[85] it was thus reasonable on the part of Anglicans in Ireland to believe that they could influence conservative forces in the English Parliament.

Having failed in its parliamentary efforts, the Church of Ireland took a voluntaryist turn. In 1839 a religious society known as the Church Education Society was organized in Dublin. Its leaders were Church of

Ireland officials and lay nobility and gentry. The society organized local groups throughout the country to raise subscriptions and open schools. These voluntary schools were open to non-Anglican children but required the reading of the Authorized Version of the Scriptures. In deference to other faiths, however, these children were not required to learn the Anglican catechism or doctrines. For a decade the society enjoyed considerable success. Between 1839 and 1849, its schools grew from 825 to 1,870, and enrollments in them from 43,627 to 111,877. About half of the children were from Anglican families. By the late 1840s, the Church of Ireland was spending between £50,000 and £60,000 annually on primary education in that country.[86] (Structurally, this strategy resembled that of the religious societies in England and Wales before 1833 and the Voluntaryists in England between the mid 1840s and 1867).

Still hoping that help might come from Parliament, the Church Education Society launched a campaign to secure subsidies for its independent Protestant schools. Hard economic times, culminating in the famine of the 1840s, made a strictly voluntary system even more difficult to support. Appeals for subsidization began to reach Parliament in 1842,[87] and the campaign reached a height in 1844–45. In one respect the appeal could not have come at a worse time. It coincided precisely with the Maynooth crisis, in which Peel was pressing a policy of pacification in Ireland despite Anglican opposition. In 1844 he told Parliament:

> Her Majesty's Government had not been inclined to propose a vote of money to the Established Church system in Ireland, because they found that by so doing they would be practically creating three different systems of education in one country—a Roman Catholic system, a system in connexion with the Established Church, and, no doubt a Presbyterian system, which would also be demanded. The effect of this would be that the youth of Ireland would be brought up under different systems, and that union which it was so desirable to promote among the subjects of Her Majesty in that country would not be promoted.[88]

Under pressure from Anglican officials, Peel apparently wavered, but he decided finally to continue with the national system and not to subsidize the religious societies.[89] (Ironically, with that decision, Peel rejected the very system of proliferation along religious lines that was shaping in England and would be consolidated a year later in the minutes of 1846.)

Despite their defeats on both counts in 1845, Anglicans did not relax their opposition to either the Maynooth grant or the national system in Ireland. They spoke mainly through R. Spooner, who had replaced Inglis as the voice of High Anglicanism in Parliament. Almost every year Spooner challenged the vote on the Maynooth grant and moved for its repeal.[90] He argued each time that Roman Catholicism was an idolatrous religion and that Catholics were disloyal to the British way. From time to time, opponents were able to force a close vote on the Maynooth grant.[91] Attacks also continued on the elementary school system. Until the English grant began to spiral upward in the 1850s, opponents complained that the Irish grant was disproportionately large.[92] Anglican spokesmen also resented that they could not read the Scriptures in the Irish schools. This was particularly grating because in England Catholics could read their Scriptures in *their* schools.[93] Some charged that the national system was being taken over by the Catholics.[94] Other charges were that the system was irreligious[95] and that it had failed in its mission to unite the Protestants and Catholics in Ireland.[96]

In addition to the partisan charges, the debates from approximately 1850 on reveal that people understood that the national system had in fact become a denominational one. In proposing to Parliament in 1850 that Anglican Church schools be permitted to resume scriptural education, G. A. Hamilton compared the English and Irish systems as follows:

> Formerly education was considered to belong exclusively to the clergy; and a system of church education was the only one encouraged by the State. Now, State education in both countries is denominational. In England avowedly so. In Ireland practically so. In England, the only indispensable requirement now is a religious basis; formerly it was church education; then, in deference to Dissenters, a system was permitted, as regards them, based upon the Scriptures, without requiring the distinctive doctrines of the Church. And now, in deference to the Roman Catholics, the use of the Scriptures is dispensed with as regards them, and the only requirement is that their education shall be based upon religion. . . . In Ireland the national system, though intended to be united, is now really a denominational system also.[97]

Hamilton added that in the Irish national system, 2,505 schools were under the patronage of Roman Catholic clergymen, 384 under ministers of the Presbyterian religion, and 96 under clergymen of the Established Church of Ireland. A decade later Adderley concluded that the "system of National education had broken down as a combined system in Ireland . . . the Irish system was like those of England and Scotland, a denominational one."[98] In 1870 George Dixon, the voice of the Birmingham League, asserted that the denominational impulse had ruined the intended Irish system of education.[99] Anglicans accompanied this acknowledgment with its demand that if the system was indeed denominational, the government should face that fact and directly subsidize the contending religious groups.[100]

Despite all appeals, parliamentary channels for help remained closed throughout the 1850s and 1860s. In Ireland, meanwhile, the Anglican Church was continuing to experience difficulties in securing subscriptions. After leveling off in the early 1850s, the income of the Church Education Society began a downward trend around 1855. The fortunes of the Anglicans, competing privately in a heavily government-supported system, thus paralleled the efforts of the Voluntaryists in England. Their respective responses to their difficulties differed, however. The Voluntaryists, convinced of inevitable Church of England dominance under any system of state aid, refused to join the system, and later disbanded and called for a secular state educational system.[101] The Church of Ireland, with the prospect of two-thirds support for its schools under the national system, felt the pressure to join it on grounds of expediency. In 1860 Archbishop Beresford circulated letters to patrons of schools and explained the problems of low teachers' salaries, poor conditions of schools, and even shortages of books and supplies. He concluded by advising the patrons to seek support from the national education system.[102]

In the meantime, the Roman Catholics were inheriting the national system almost by default. The Presbyterians had arranged for an isolated niche in which to educate children of their own faith. The Anglicans first tried to dismantle the system through Parliament, then took a voluntary road, next attempted to seek independent subsidies for their schools, and, finally, failing in all these, opted for the Presbyterian mode. Greeted with these strategies of aloofness and self-isolation by the Protestants, the Catholic clergy were able to apply for and secure most of the available grants to educate a clientele of almost exclusively Catholic children.

It is not surprising, then, that most Catholics did not publicly challenge the system. A general meeting of the Catholic bishops approved the system in 1838. Along with this policy of quiet acceptance, however, Catholic representatives attacked its details, and the Sacred Congregation of Propaganda tried unsuccessfully to secure Catholic control over the appointment of teachers and in other areas. In 1849 a struggle broke out between Catholic prelates and the commission over the required use of certain books in the normal and national schools. The Catholic Church organized a campaign by parents, and the commission relented under the pressure. Archbishop Whately, one of the strongest Anglican supporters of a truly mixed system, resigned from the commission over this struggle, and this generally weakened its authority.[103] In the late 1850s, the Catholic bishops launched a campaign for a number of additional changes that would enhance clerical control, and in 1859 they secured a reconstitution of the commission that made it half-Catholic, half-Protestant in membership.

The Catholics' general strategy is revealed in a communication to Rome, written shortly after the archbishops met in 1858 to draw up a policy on primary education in Ireland. The author was Paul Cullen, archbishop of Dublin from 1852 to 1878. He explained:

> Although we desire to see the Catholic Youth of the country educated apart from Protestants, we do not consider it expedient to call for a separate grant for that purpose at the present time, because the National Schools are for the most part exclusively Catholic, but, tolerating the system for fear of greater evil, content ourselves for the present with seeking the following modifications of the system, namely, the appointment of a Catholic Resident Commissioner, of a Catholic Resident Head-Inspector, of a suitable number of Catholics among the District and other Inspectors, and of a fair proportion of Catholics on the Board of Commissioners of whom two at least should be Ecclesiastics.[104]

The most important word in this communication is *expedient*. The Catholics rankled at the heavy Protestant representation in the administration of the national system, but under it 70–85 percent of the teachers and pupils were theirs. In addition, they received the lion's share of grants generated from taxes other than those they paid. A fully denominational system would give them little additional advantage. Bishop David Moriarty summarized in a letter to Cullen in 1859: "While the united system of secular education gives us the great advantage of getting all the money—we can never be exposed to the dangers of a mixed system in a country where they have nothing to mix—where all are Catholic."[105] Throughout the 1860s the Catholic Church continued to criticize the working of the system and to seek ways that would increase its real and symbolic presence in it. It did not, however, campaign to alter the constitutional principles on which it was founded.[106]

In 1869 the government appointed a commission—the Powis Commission—to investigate the Irish national system. Its recommendations included the discontinuation of publication of textbooks by the National Board, state aid for denominational teacher training, and the model schools. These tended to weaken the power of the commissioners and strengthen the denominational groups, thus propelling the system even further in a denominationalist direction. Presbyterians in particular interpreted the Powis Commission and its recommendations as a concession to Catholic pressure.[107]

The recommendations of the Powis Commission were not adopted immediately, but the system gradually evolved in the indicated directions. In 1880 the commissioners abolished the rule that forbade the use of national schools as places of religious worship. During the 1880s they permitted greater use of religious pictures and symbols such as crosses to adorn the buildings. In the late nineteenth century, the pressure to introduce bilingual education made further headway (the national schools had excluded the teaching of the Irish language until the late 1870s).[108] Making the sign of the cross in school became a usual practice, with the commissioners making no effort to enforce the rule that prohibited it. In addition, the Catholic Church continued to consolidate its control. By 1900 7,636 of the 8,684 national schools had clergymen as managers. This clerical control was by far the strongest in the Catholic schools, with 85 percent of the schools under clerics (against 32 percent for Anglican and 62 percent for Presbyterian schools).[109]

From its initial adoption of the national system, however, Parliament continued to endorse its fundamental constitution. It followed this policy despite the relentless pressure from Anglicans, sometimes joined by Presbyterians, to scrap it, alter it, or give supplementary grants to them, and despite the evidence that the growing denominationalism reinforced rather than diminished the country's religious divisions. Defenders of the national system denied that denominationalism was taking over,[110] praised it for avoiding the wastefulness of competitive English denominationalism,[111] and asserted that it was not an avenue for proselytizing by Roman Catholic priests.[112] Graham acknowledged that Ireland posed such intractable religious problems that it was necessary to separate religion from literary or secular education.[113]

Graham was probably right in one respect. Irish religious divisions were of such a primordial character that an educational system formally controlled by a single religious group—which many Anglicans *and* Roman Catholics eyed as a remote ideal—was an impossibility.[114] Furthermore, to reach a common denominator for religious instruction was more difficult in Ireland than in England. Catholic-Protestant doctrinal differences and antipathies were more fundamental than Protestant-Protestant ones. In addition, the Irish national system, as constituted, seemed to generate less conflict about itself than other arrangements might have done. It was pacifying in the sense that the Catholics in Ireland accepted its fundamentals by joining and profiting from it, attempting only to change its particulars in their favor. For the government to have altered it in any "Protestant" direction would have stirred Catholic antagonisms both in Ireland and in England, where Irish Catholics were becoming more numerous and—after the parliamentary electoral reforms of 1867 and 1884—stronger politically.[115] Finally, the state retained a strong political position in relation to the Church of Ireland's demands that it alter the system's fundamentals or provide supplementary support. The national system always permitted Anglicans to join and benefit from it on their own terms. The national system thus seemed the line of least political resistance for the British government. It followed a policy of insistence on the principle of national education but of compromise in the face of demands from the religious groups in practice. Peace was thus maintained, but some saw a negative side to the compromising as well. In 1870 Alexander Sellar, a Scottish critic, wrote:

> Nothing could have been conceived in a more tolerant spirit than the Irish National System. And if it were possible to unite the various sections of the churches on the matter of education by gentle means, their union would have been effected long ere this in Ireland. But . . . the very opposite spirit has been developed. Instead of harmony, we have had discord—a sulky discord on part of the Episcopalians; and aggressive, dangerous discord on part of Roman Catholics. And, instead of an efficient system of education, we have had the schools degraded to the lowest level. . . .
>   The Irish system was founded on compromise; it was undermined by concession; and it has gone to ruin.[116]

Such global judgments are difficult to accept uncritically, but some insight is gained from it on how institutions evolve when they are populated by militants and governed by compromisers.

The evolution of the English and Irish educational systems from the 1830s to the 1870s presents a picture of fascinating counterpoint. Put simply, Ireland began in 1831 (state-supported, nondenominational education) where England ended in 1870 (nondenominational board schools). England began in 1833 (state-subsidized, denominational education) where Ireland in effect ended. Furthermore, the two systems met along the way, as it were, going in opposite directions. Both countries manifested class and/or regional conflicts that demanded some educational effort that promised to ease them and promote social harmony. In both countries, moreover, the religious culture was such that a totally secular system was not possible.

In England in the 1830s, the following conditions contributed to the institution of primary education that proliferated along primordial denominational lines:

The inability of the Established Church to claim its religious monopoly, excluding both the state and other denominations. Dissent was too powerful a political force by the 1830s to permit that solution.

Closely related, the capacity of the Dissenting minorities to insist on the principle of equity.

The prior existence of contending religious educational bodies in the form of the National Society and the British and Foreign School Society.

The existence of ideological and institutional forces antagonistic to state interference in economy and society.

The government took account of all these conditions, and, in a series of discrete political adaptations between 1833 and the early 1850s, created a structurally separated system that was denomination-controlled but state-subsidized.

In Ireland an overlapping, but different, set of conditions lay behind the implementation of the national system in 1831:

The impossibility of either a Church of Ireland monopoly or any other Protestant-dominated solution to popular education given the large Catholic majority and militant Catholic opposition to Protestants. The long history of undermined and unsuccessful voluntary Protestant efforts documented that impossibility.

The impossibility of finding a religious common denominator along the lines fashioned by the British and Foreign School Society because of the depth of doctrinal and institutional religious divisions.

A weaker institutional and political position of the Anglican establishment there than in England.

The weakness of viable voluntary educational societies among the Catholics in Ireland, only a few of which had emerged in the 1820s.

Less reluctance on the part of the British government to intervene in Irish institutions than in English ones. Despite the Union of 1800, Ireland was above all perceived as a semicolonial society that had to be governed.

Because of these more extreme religious and political conditions in Ireland, the British government attempted to solve the "religious problem" by a policy of extreme separation along the lines of the developing American system. The solution of 1831 was something of an "un-English" solution, at least for those who boasted that England, unlike other countries, did not try to invent institutions anew, but rather built incrementally on its existing traditions.[117] In the long run, however, the same political-religious forces that demanded the national solution in Ireland undermined that very solution. Whether aggrandizing and/or defensive, the denominations ultimately cannibalized the system and converted it into a state-supported denominational system.[118] H. A. Bruce described this evolution in a nutshell in 1867: "The national system of education in Ireland was, at its foundation, a system of united secular and separate religious education. This had been gradually and partially superseded by a system which might be fairly called denominational, *plus* a conscience clause."[119] He need only have added that that denominational system was, in most important respects, a Catholic system, because 70–80 percent of the schools were Catholic, and at least that large a percentage of those schools were managed by Catholic clergy.[120] Despite this erosion of its original purpose, the national system endured because it "worked," in that it covered much of the country— mainly because the Catholics embraced it and were aided by it—and because it was not a running sore for most of the Catholic clergy and for the British government.

In England, by contrast, the state, while largely driven by the same motive of conflict-minimization, reacted to a different set of forces. It created a system that tended to grow by "blistering"—that is, by adding on schools and related educational arrangements along the lines of religious and class division in the society. Yet that system, too, was fraught with competition and conflict; moreover, it was so relatively unsuccessful in covering the country, and so costly economically, that it gave way, by increments, to a nondenominational system that separated secular from religious education in large part, as did the original Irish national system.

## THE IRISH IN NEW YORK

The Catholic issue did not play a central role in English educational history in the nineteenth century, but at several points it entered into it significantly: in the impact of the "Catholicism" of the Oxford Movement, especially on Evangelicals in the Anglican Church and the Wesleyan Methodists; in the delicate matter of incorporating Roman Catholics into the denominational system in 1847–48; and in the merging of Anglican and Catholic interests in 1870 and in the ensuing decades.[121] In Wales the role of the Catholics was minimal, mainly because of their small numbers. In Ireland the Catholic Church was pivotal and in some ways dictated the evolution of primary education in that country. As we shall see later, the Catholic presence in Scotland posed unique issues, especially in the large cities. To add another comparative twist, I shall cross the Atlantic briefly and examine an episode of conflict in New York City in the 1840s in which the Irish Catholics figured prominently. Interest attaches to this episode because it occurred about a decade after the introduction of the national system in Ireland, and on the eve of the incorporation of the Catholics into the English scheme of subsidization.

## CONTEXTUAL AND HISTORICAL BACKGROUND

Any comparison between British and U.S. education in the nineteenth century should note some contextual differences between the two countries:

The principle of "separation of church and state" was an element of the U.S. federal constitution and was echoed in state constitutions as well (as we shall see, however, the issue was far from settled in the 1840s). This principle put the burden of proof on those who sought to *include* religious considerations in government concerns, education among them. In Britain the establishment of religion and the fusion of religion and education were long-standing traditions.

New York City was a city, not a country or region. The federal government did not enter the educational picture of the city, though the city was subject to the laws of the state of New York and influenced by its politics.

Since colonial times, British North America had experienced religious heterogeneity (mainly among Protestant sects) and had accommodated to this by imposing taxes to support common schools that minimized sectarian religious teaching.[122] In England in the 1840s, the imposition of local rates for education lay several decades in the future.

Popular democracy was more advanced in the United States than in Britain.[123] By the 1840s, white male suffrage was the rule. Diverse political groups entered the political process through parties and electoral politics. In New York, Irish Catholic immigrants were involved through enfranchisement, party, and machine.[124] By the 1840s in New York, the Irish vote was a matter of concern to both Whigs and Democrats.

All these factors were to shape the contours of educational conflicts and outcomes in New York City.

In the early nineteenth century, New York City was a rapidly growing port and urban center, reflecting the dynamic commercial and industrial development of the young nation. Its population grew from around 120,000 in 1820 to 200,000 in 1830, then to 270,000 in 1835 and 300,000 in 1840. Immigrants played a great role in this growth. Aliens in the city's population increased from 11 percent in 1825 to 35 percent in 1845. A decade later the figure was more than 50 percent; among these, more than half were Irish-born.[125] Almost all the Irish were Roman Catholics.

This flood of immigration created a surplus labor force in New York, and workers faced both declining real wages and high unemployment in the 1830s and 1840s. Indigence increased during periods of economic depression, especially in 1837–39. In 1847 almost 25 percent of the population were in receipt of some kind of charity. Rich and poor also grew further apart geographically with the development of slums and ghettos. In the early part of the century, charitable associations to relieve orphans, the sick, widows, black people, and others began to grow correspondingly. In the early 1840s, there were a total of three dozen separate charitable associations. Movements for prison reform and temperance also appeared.[126]

Public concern with education in New York was scarcely distinguishable from problems associated with class and poverty. (The dominant motive for early educational efforts thus resembled that in Britain.) In 1795, when the state of New York established an annual fund of $50,000 for schools in cities and towns, Governor De Witt Clinton justified this on class grounds. "[Academies] are principally confined to the children of the opulent, and . . . a great portion of the community is excluded from their immediate advantage."[127] The bill stipulated that the money for New York City be allocated to charity schools. A subsequent "rate bill system" inaugurated in 1812–14 called for fees in common schools, but specified that indigent parents were excused if they declared their poverty. In New York City the statements of the early charitable societies underscored the urgency of reaching the poor, and they linked vice, crime, and education in their messages. In 1808, Clinton, then president of the Free School Society in New York City, made those connections:

> A number of benevolent persons had seen, with concern, the increasing vices of the city, arising, in a great degree, from the neglected education of the poor. Great cities [are], at all times, the nurseries and hotbeds of crime . . . there can be no doubt that hundreds . . . in this city, prowling about our streets for prey, the victims of intemperance, the slaves of idleness, and ready to fall into any vice, rather than cultivate industry and good order. How can it be expected that persons so careless of themselves, will pay any attention to their children? [128]

William Seward, the governor of New York who was at the center of the struggles of 1840–42, stated repeatedly that New York City's schools were not reaching the poor, especially the poor Catholics.[129]

The educational efforts of the better-off in New York City went through several phases up to 1840, each turning on religious contests not closely involving the Roman Catholics. When New York State voted to provide school funds—on a matching basis—in 1795, the Common Council of New York City voted to allocate these to the six charitable schools in the city. These were all Protestant in the beginning and all provided free education primarily for children of their own denominations. They were modeled on the English tradition of church-based charity education. While the Common Council experienced some pressure to initiate new public schools, it opted to provide funds to existing ones.[130] (New York City thus instituted, for a brief historical moment, an educational system that paralleled that of British denominationalism between 1833 and 1870.)

In 1805 some citizens of New York formed the Society for Establishing a Free School in the City of New York, and petitioned the legislature for support. Inspired by Quaker leadership, the society called for "[inculcating] the sublime truths of religion and morality contained in the Holy Scriptures," without including specific denominational materials. It secured a grant from the legislature in that year and launched a campaign for public support, arguing that "early education" was preventative of crime, irreligion, and vice. In keeping with the general "English" orientation of New York's charity school education, the society employed the Lancasterian monitorial method in its schools.[131] Experiencing success and growth, it opened new, larger quarters and changed its name to the Free School Society in 1808. To supplement its non-denominational religious instruction, the society arranged for children to assemble at its schools on Sunday morning and proceed to their Sunday schools for worship and denominational religious education.[132]

The Free School Society operated in competition with the existing denominational charity schools. A conflict developed in 1821–22 when the Bethel Baptist Church tried to extend its educational activities on behalf of the poor. In this effort the trustees of the Bethel church were able to secure privileged access to legislative funds as its numbers increased. The Free School Society and other religious groups objected to this, and petitioned the legislature to repeal the privilege. They appealed to the logic of equity: "Why has a right been given to one religious society which is not imparted to another? And why has a privilege been granted that not only vitiates the principles of equality, but perverts a part of the school fund intended—and wisely and humanely intended—to be expended to the last cent in the wholesome education of poor children?"[133] The Baptists' activities also generated a flurry of petitions by other denominations such as the Congregational, Grace, and Dutch Reformed Churches to expand their schools and gain equal status with the Baptists.

In the context of this sectarian competition, the Free School Society brought a different principle for allocating school funds to the legislature in 1824. It argued that the "rivalry . . . between existing sects" would "disturb the harmony of society" and "infuse strong prejudice in the minds of children taught in the different schools."[134] The society first secured the support of the Common Council of New York City. In response to the Free School Society's pressure, the legislature delegated the distribution of all legislative funds to the council. Then the society argued before the council that the sectarian system failed to reach the children of the poor, and that, accordingly, education should be made civic and unconnected with religious denominations. The society put forth a distinctively "American" argument: "It has been left to the experience of this country to show—what appears problematical in the eyes of Europe—that religion requires no aid from the civil arm; she needs no resources drawn from the treasury of the State, but her resources consist of the willing contribution of hearts subjected to her influence."[135] It also proposed that it change its name to "Public School Society" and sponsor nondenominational common schools. (The society asserted in this connection that education was essential if suffrage were to be further extended.) Finally, the society proposed that it receive all public funds, and that other schools transfer into it. The Common

Council accepted these arguments, and agreed that families sending their children to the society's schools should pay a fee. In approving the fee, the council quoted a British and Foreign School Society publication to the effect that free education isolated and pauperized the very poor.[136] The legislature approved the plan in 1826, and the Public School Society began operating under its new, favored status.

This sequence of events in 1825 and 1826 constitutes a familiar example of secularizing education in the face of sectarian conflict. The mechanism is to "water down" the religious component and thereby reduce sectarian bickering. Similar instances in Britain were the implementation of the Irish national system (which separated secular and denominational religious instruction), the imposition of the conscience clause, and the Cowper-Temple provision of 1870 prohibiting special denominational formularies.[137] The "New York" solution of 1825–26 was unique in that it gave an educational monopoly (over receipt of state funds) to a private, religious, but nondenominational society. (An English parallel would have been to turn over the entire subsidy to the British and Foreign School Society.)

After 1826 the Public School Society expanded its day school operations. Its efforts overshadowed the private fee-paying schools,[138] and the Bethel Baptist schools disappeared. The tuition fees proved unpopular, however, and after an actual decline in attendance, the society abolished these in 1832 and relied on campaigns to increase public funding through taxation. Its reports and campaign statements indicated, however, that many poor children were still not being educated by the system.[139] Moreover, the religious solution of 1826 proved to be unstable. In 1831 the Common Council heard appeals from the Roman Catholic Orphan Asylum for support. Despite remonstrances by the Public School Society, the Board of Aldermen of New York approved the petition. About the same time, the Methodists sought to include their schools as recipients of public funds. The Public School Society strongly opposed this appeal. It put forward a "floodgates" argument that paralleled that of the Church of England in connection with the proposal for multidenominational training schools in 1839:

> Methodists, Episcopalian, Baptist, and every other sectarian school, must come in for a share of this fund. And the Common Council cannot stop here. If charity schools are founded in which the doctrines of an Owen and a Wright are taught, or in which the "Age of Reason" or the Khoran is adopted as a standard work, they will stand on the same footing as other religious

schools. Should such a course be pursued, it will be a violation of the liberal principle established by the Common Council in 1825, of denying admission to all schools and institutions which were considered as sectarian.[140]

The society went on to argue that support of denominational bodies would lead to an "unnatural union of Church and State . . . a union destructive of human happiness and subversive of all liberty."[141] By this argument, used by the Church of England to protect the union of church and state in the British Establishment,[142] the Public School Society sought to protect privileges deriving from the supposed separation of church and state. The establishment of a nonestablishment generates the same jealousy of privilege and the same structure of justifying argumentation as the establishment of a church.

ACTIVITIES OF THE CATHOLICS
IN EDUCATION

The Catholics were a small part of the New York population in 1800, numbering an estimated 1,300. This figure had risen to 100,000— about 19 percent of the population—by 1850. The main influx was Irish, though about half the German immigrants were Catholic. The first Catholic church was built in 1785, and in 1802 its trustees opened a day school. This was one of the denominational schools that received state funds. (Cultural memory in the early 1840s could, then, produce a precedent for denominational subsidization.) A second Catholic school opened in 1815; and it also applied for and received state aid as a denominational school.[143] In 1825, just prior to the consolidation of the Public School Society as the sole recipient of public funds, Catholic churches were petitioning for aid to their schools. Their successful campaign for support of the Catholic orphan asylum rested on the argument that a similar Protestant association was already receiving funds.[144] However, in 1834, when Bishop Dubois of New York asked the society to support a school with a Catholic teacher, who would use books approved by the bishop, the society declined on grounds that such a school was sectarian.[145] Denied public funds, the Catholics continued to educate a portion of the Catholic youth in their own parish schools.

Before turning to the events of 1840–42, several aspects of the New York scene in the 1830s should be called to mind:

The issue of the uneducated poor remained active as an item of public concern. The Public School Society's annual report in 1831 expressed concern about nonattendance at school, particularly among immigrant children. Later a committee of the society recommended a system of visitors to certain neighborhoods to urge parents to send their children to the schools. The committee also recommended a system of mandatory public schooling for children found idle and uninstructed.[146] This continuing dissatisfaction lent legitimacy to parties who advanced schemes to extend education.

The Public School Society maintained its strict stance against sectarian schooling. In its report of 1838, it reaffirmed that it endorsed religious education, but argued that nondenominationalism was the only method compatible with the ideal of the common school.[147]

The economic depression of 1837–39 generated high levels of unemployment, accentuated the city's poverty problems, and overtaxed the limited facilities for charitable relief of the poor.[148]

The city, like others in the United States,[149] witnessed a flurry of nativism. The Native American Democratic Association, a Protestant group that adopted stands against further immigration and against office-holding by foreigners, formed in 1835. The association was overtly hostile to the Catholic Church. In the 1837 city elections, it threw its support behind the Whigs, who were victorious in that year.[150]

The main parties were the Whigs and the Democrats. The former relied mainly on the wealthy and the conservative for support and under the expanded suffrage were concerned to expand their base of support downward. The Democrats were more the party of the working people. In New York immigrants were linked to the Democratic party mainly through the Tammany Hall machine.[151]

THE ERUPTION OF CONFLICT

Two main political events appeared to precipitate the initiative seeking public funds for Catholic schools in 1840. The first was the evident interest of the Catholic hierarchy in the issue of children's education. At the Provincial Council meeting of 1840 in Baltimore, the bishops expressed apprehension that children in common schools were being exposed to Protestant religious exercises and to textbooks that vilified Catholics. At the same time the Catholic Church recognized that it could scarcely supply enough schools to serve its children. At their 1840 meeting, the bishops resolved to "educate as many Catholic children as they could in Catholic schools while striving to protect the faith of those who were in public schools."[152] The second event was the public stand taken by Governor Seward, a liberal Whig elected in 1838. Early in 1839 he called for improvement of the public school system. After a visit to New York in 1839, he concluded that many Catholic parents were boycotting the schools of the Public School Society for religious reasons. Seward's response was to call publicly for the establishment of schools satisfactory to the Catholic minority. This would place—and finance— Catholic schools in the state's common school system, but permit administration by Catholic officials. His stand evoked attacks from conservative Whigs and the Protestant press.[153]

Both the Catholic Church's position and Seward's stand emboldened New York City's Catholics, who petitioned the Common Council for a share of the common school fund in February, 1840. The Catholics had a strong leader in the person of Bishop John Hughes, an aggressive churchman known for his opposition to the common schools as sectarian Protestant institutions and as abusive to Catholics. The Public School Society opposed the petition, as did the Protestant churches— especially the Methodist, Episcopal, Baptist, Presbyterian, and Dutch Reformed churches. Immediately after the Catholic petition, the Scotch Presbyterian Church and the Jews submitted petitions asking for *their* share of public funds if the Common Council acceded to the Catholics' request. The Jews, however, were the only religious group that did not speak out openly against the Catholics.[154]

This unfolding of this political/religious situation in New York provides a microcosm for comparison with Ireland and England as of 1840. In New York, as in Ireland, the Irish Catholics believed themselves subordinated and beleaguered by a Protestant Establishment. A major difference was, however, that the Catholics were a majority in Ireland and a minority in New York. Another was that the Irish in Ireland were virtually disenfranchised, whereas the Irish Catholics in New York had greater access to the polity as voters and as supporters of machine and party. In addition, the Anglican Church was fully established in Ireland, whereas the New York religious "establishment" was a nondenominational collection of Protestant churches that had accommodated to Protestant nonsectarianism. Finally, the Catholics' status in the educational structure differed. In Ireland, the Catholic Church was already "in" the national system, and profiting from it. Its main options were either to remain in and influence, if not control, the system or to seek an independent, denominational subsidized status.[155] In New York, the options were to make public schools more palatable for Catholic children, to fight to get their schools into the system of support, or to take an independent path.

Carl Kaestle classifies the Catholics' objections to the common schools as "textual, catechetical, and cultural." First, they argued that the King James version of the Bible was not legitimate for Catholics, and that the Douay version was the only acceptable form. Second—as in Ireland—the Catholics argued that reading the Bible without note or comment was foreign to the Catholic tradition of priestly interpretation. They maintained that simple reading represented a Protestant bias. Third, they argued that Protestant teachers and overtly anti-Catholic texts demeaned Catholic children and undermined their faith.[156] Bishop Hughes said that as a result many Catholic children would not be educated at all because "illiteracy was preferable to infidelity."

Hughes also objected to a "double taxation" on Catholics—paying for public schools to which they could not in conscience send their children and paying for sending them to their own schools.[157] The Catholics also used liberal arguments, asserting that the common schools offended their "rights of conscience."[158] They promised, if supported, to honor others' rights—to limit Catholic religious instruction to times outside regular school hours, and to prohibit any materials derogatory to other religions.[159] In one statement they activated a theme of class conflict:

> They [the Protestants] finally got themselves nominated "the Public School Society of New York," and from that time labelled *their* schools, as if they belonged to the community at large, "Public Schools" . . . they were merely *called* "public schools," but they belonged to a private corporation, who have crept up into high favor with the powers that be, and have assumed the exclusive right of monopolizing the education of youth.[160]

The Catholic position was not entirely monolithic. One Catholic newspaper, closely allied with the Democratic party, opposed Seward's position and proposed a more or less complete split between secular and religious education. The common schools would be responsible for the former and the church and home for the latter. A second Catholic daily criticized this position and reiterated the Catholic Church's stand against the nondenominational system and for a subsidized system of church schools.[161]

On their side the Public School Society and Protestant groups appealed to the legitimacy of nondenominationalism as the American way; attacked the constitutionality of the Catholics' appeal for public money for secular education; denied the Catholic charges of Protestant bias in texts and teaching; and predicted wastefulness, inefficiency, and decline in quality of education, inasmuch as other denominations would rush to appeal for support. The symbolism of social class and "the foreigner" also crept into the Public School Society's memorial to New York City officials:

> [Your memorialists] operate under a firm conviction that the sooner [the oppressed of other lands] abandon any unfavorable prejudices with which they may arrive among us, and become familiar with our language, and reconciled to our institutions and habits, the better it will be for them, and for the country of their adoption. If this be true, the best interests of all will be alike promoted having their children mingle with ours in the public seminaries of learning.[162]

The Methodist Episcopal Church, apparently sharing the anti-Catholicism of its British brethren,[163] issued a strong attack on the Catholic position. It predicted a chaotic struggle if the city permitted a denominationalist competition for funds. It also accused the Catholics of demanding "unqualified submission, in all matters of conscience, to the Roman Catholic Church." Furthermore, if censorship in schools were permitted to the Catholics, it would be the "censorship of a foreign potentate."[164] In counterattack, Hughes asserted that the Methodists had "done as little for mankind as any other denomination" and had forsaken the Dissenters in their struggle against the Test and Corporation Acts of 1828 in England.[165]

There were some efforts to conciliate and compromise. In March 1840 the trustees of the Public School Society agreed to meet with Catholic officials to expurgate materials derogatory to Catholics from texts. Some of this was done.[166] The Board of Aldermen attempted to exact a series of pledges from both the Catholics and the Public School Society that would assure fairness, fiscal responsibility, and adherence to the law.[167] Theodore Sedgwick, a lawyer representing the Public School Society, sought neutral ground, pointing to the Irish national school solution of selecting extracts from the two versions of the Bible as one possible route. In this context, Sedgwick put forth a diagnosis of the impossibility of combining state support with sectarian education. His words were almost identical to those written by Walter Hook in England in 1846:

> So long as you give a secular education combined with moral instruction alone, and steer clear of all doctrinal or sectarian principles, all are satisfied;

but the moment an apprehension exists that a part of this great fund goes to increase the numbers and power of *one* particular sect, that moment the others will early strive to check what they believe a pernicious influence, and to check it in the same way.[168]

The Protestants claimed that they had solved this problem in New York City by offering "moral instruction alone" without sectarian content. The Catholics claimed that vision was limited: it was a common *Protestant* school, and therefore not common for them. Such is the fate of an assumed consensus when a different set of fundamental premises arises to challenge the assumed ones. In that part of the debate, the Catholics were correct. The nondenominational solution *was* a sectarian solution, a compact among Protestants. On the other hand, the Catholics made the search for new common ground difficult by insisting on traditional Catholic religious controls, teaching, content, and rites in their schools.

### COURSE AND RESOLUTION OF THE CONFLICT

Throughout 1840 and into 1841, Catholic appeals to the government of New York City met a series of rebuffs. In late February 1840, the Board of Commissions of School Money denied the Catholics' request for school funds, and in September of that year, they carried the appeal to the Board of Aldermen of New York. They also placed it before the Common Council, which scheduled a debate for the end of October. After further investigation and debate, both the Board of Aldermen and the Common Council denied the Catholic request early in 1841.

During the October debate, the lawyers representing the Public School Society argued that the city of New York should not even be hearing the Catholic appeal. The state legislature had passed the law denying funds to religious organizations in 1824, and only the state could repeal it.[169] Aware of this possibility, Catholics from New York City presented a petition to the state legislature in the spring of 1841. The legislature postponed the matter until 1842. In the meantime, in the elections of January 1841, Governor Seward's margin of victory decreased because of a combination of Whig defections and the reluctance of Democrats to cross party lines. In April 1841 the Democrats swept the city elections in New York. In the period leading up to the November 1841 elections, the political controversy over the schools heated. The debates between Hughes and various Protestants continued. The

Public School Society continued its agitation in Albany against the Catholic appeal. On July 8 a riot broke out after a bitter debate among religious leaders on the education issue. A nativist organization, the American Protestant Union, with Samuel F. B. Morse as president, took up the anti-Catholic cause. Though divided, the Democratic Party voted to support the Public School Society's claim. The Catholics refused to endorse Democratic candidates who supported that position, and in the November elections, all those candidates lost.[170]

In these elections the Catholics thus established themselves as a political force. Their influence was seen in the legislature when it turned to the New York City schooling issue in 1842. The most influential proposal emerging at that time came from John C. Spencer, New York secretary of state and *ex officio* superintendent of schools. He based his proposal on the facts that the Public School Society's system did not reach enough children and—in Spencer's judgment—was a sectarian system. Spencer proposed to extend the state principle of district schools to New York City. He suggested electing ward commissioners, who would sit as a governing board for the city's schools. Management and the decisions on the character of religious instruction would, however, be determined at the district level. This proposal was clearly a gesture to the Catholics, since it envisioned an end to the society's monopoly. In addition, in those districts where Catholics were a majority, they could be the determining voice. Such districts did exist, since the Catholic and especially the Irish population lived in ghetto areas in New York at that time.[171] Critics charged that the Spencer proposal would erode uniform standards for schooling and would set the stage for bitter sectarian conflicts in the districts.[172]

Partisan feelings continued to run high in New York City in 1841. The state assembly passed a district bill on April 9, 1842. Two days later, angry mobs of nativists and Catholics clashed on the streets of the city, and Bishop Hughes's house was stoned.[173] The state senate, more evenly divided, ultimately passed the bill by a vote of only thirteen to twelve. The bill followed the Spencer recommendations, but a critical amendment to it provided that schools could not receive funds if they taught sectarian religion. This was a blow to the Catholics. Salt was thrown on that wound in 1844 when the first New York Board of Education, dominated by anti-Catholic forces, ruled that reading the Bible without comment did not constitute sectarian education.[174]

Diane Ravitch summarizes the legislative outcome as follows: "The Catholics did not win, but the Public School Society lost."[175] Without a monopoly, the latter's schools mostly became absorbed into the new system. The Catholics retained an influence in the New York City school system, and, in keeping with the growing Irish political power in the city, gained their share of Catholic teachers in the system. In general, however, Catholics in New York City and elsewhere in the country could not secure a direct share of the public purse to finance Catholic schools. In that situation, they turned increasingly to a policy similar to English Voluntaryism, establishing their own parochial schools at their own expense. In many communities, they left the public schools in effective control of the Protestants. The Catholic position became official at the Third Council of Baltimore in 1884, which adopted the principle "Every Catholic child in a Catholic school." [176]

The Catholic adaptation was thus tailored to the distinctive religious and political setting in the United States, and for that reason contrasts with the Catholic Church's experience in England and Ireland. In New York, the Catholics first enjoyed a position of subsidized denominational education (1809–26) that resembled the English mode between 1833 and 1870. They were excluded during the period of non-denominational monopoly (1826–42), and in 1840 they launched an offensive to return to the earlier system. Rejected in that effort, they moved to proceed independently.[177] In England, in 1869–70, Catholics fought to remain in the subsidized denominational system, but, along with the Church of England, failed, inasmuch as Parliament voted not to fund sectarian schools in its district scheme.[178] In Ireland, Catholics were excluded *as a church* from receiving funds from the state, but with their numerical supremacy and organized efforts were able to "re-sectarianize" the national system in their favor. In Scotland—as we shall see—the Catholic Church was excluded from the established parish system. It enjoyed a period of state support during the period when parliamentary grants covered Catholics in Scotland (1848–72), but the Scottish Education Act of 1872 excluded Catholic schools from state aid. Facing an "American" type of political situation, Scottish Catholics took the same route as U.S. Catholics, establishing parochial schools.

## SCOTLAND

### HISTORICAL BACKGROUND

The most striking difference between Scotland on the one hand and England and Ireland on the other lies in the kind of educational apparatus that each inherited at the beginning of the nineteenth century. Working-class education in England consisted of a limited number of religious charity schools and Sunday schools. Both were private, and state intervention, beginning in 1833, "grew more or less continuously from nothing."[179] Ireland inherited a variety of schools operated by Protestant religious societies, many of them proselytizing and a few subsidized by Parliament; a modest number of Sunday schools; and the Roman Catholic religious society and hedge schools. Most of these were superseded by the national system in 1831. Scotland, by contrast, had evolved a comprehensive parish school system over several centuries. As a result, "Scotland came closer to the continental pattern in that it had a relatively uniform national system whose parts were linked to each other."[180] This system provided a structural starting point onto which adaptations were "blistered" in the nineteenth century up until 1872, when the Scottish Education Act reconsolidated it.

The Scottish scientist Leon Playfair characterized Scottish education up to 1646 as a "purely ecclesiastical" phase, in which "the Church did everything and the State nothing for the education of the people."[181] After the Union of 1603, Scotland experienced prolonged religious struggles over religious hegemony between Episcopalians and Presbyterians. These were resolved only with the Glorious Revolution of 1688, when Scotland regained its Presbyterian liberties. This ended the effort to force the episcopy on Scotland. Presbyterianism was restored as the established religion of that country in 1690.[182] The decisive legislative acts that consolidated the Scottish parish system were those of 1638, when Parliament reaffirmed the Presbyterian policy of having a school in every parish; 1646, which made this resolution into law, and provided for taxation to support parish schools; 1690, which imposed a religious test—subscription to the Confession of Faith—for all schoolmasters; 1693, which placed schoolmasters and teachers under the control of the presbyteries; and 1696, which repeated the provisions of 1646 and consolidated the system.[183] The system received theoretical and practical guidance from the Scottish theologian John Knox[184] and expressed reformers' visions of "an educated flock in every parish."

The eighteenth century witnessed the flowering of the parish system under conditions of relative religious homogeneity and relative demographic and social stability.[185] Under it the literacy of the population increased greatly, and Scotland became the principal model of educational success for English reformers in the early decades of the nineteenth century.[186] Financing of the system was based on the taxes of heritors, or proprietors of charitable properties. Pupils' families paid fees, but these were waived for the very poor. Heritors were responsible for appointing schoolmasters for parish schools, with the approval of the presbytery. Schoolmasters received a salary and a house, along with payments of fees for keeping parish records, and an increment of additional income at an annual ceremony. After a probationary period, most school-masters, like ministers, were assumed to have a life appointment. The heritors stressed religious commitment, college education, and literary and arithmetical skills for schoolmasters.[187] The curriculum included reading, writing, arithmetic, and religion, with scientific subjects be-coming more important in the eighteenth century.[188] The parish schools were supplemented by "burgh schools" in the towns. These were consti-tuted on the same principle as the parish schools, but operated by town councils. Subsequently the burgh schools tended to evolve into a kind of urban secondary school sector.

Two principles of the parish system were its community inclusiveness and its egalitarian and meritocratic foundations. These were notable when compared to the more stratified English system:

> In Scotland [English] social divisions were absent. . . . Traditional provision was for parish schools in the countryside and "burgh schools" in the towns, but both were expected to serve the whole local community and meet a wide range of educational needs. Although the main task of the parish schools was elementary education, their masters normally had some university training and could teach Latin, allowing them to prepare the sons of the local middle class, or the occasional talented "lad of parts," for university entry. In smaller towns the burgh schools did much the same, but in larger ones these developed into middle-class schools, leading to both the universities and commercial careers.[189]

Thus rooted in the religious, class, and community life of Scotland, the parish system was not very receptive to the educational develop-ments that were stirring in England in the late eighteenth century.[190] The Lancaster monitorial movement enjoyed only a brief popularity in the cities and scarcely penetrated the Highlands.[191] The Sunday school movement, initiated in 1787, made little headway in Scotland, largely because religious and educational neglect was rarer there. Its early suc-cesses were in Glasgow, where many children were already employed in industry and could not attend day schools. Most Scottish Sunday schools were under Church of Scotland auspices, but for a period in the late eighteenth century, the Kirk, religiously moderate, strongly opposed them on the grounds that they were expressing a more radical Evangelical impulse. As the movement grew in the first part of the nineteenth century, it retained its Evangelical flavor.[192]

Despite the apparent integration of the schooling system into Scottish social life, certain strains had developed by the late eighteenth century. Heritors were not always willing to sustain their payments, especially in difficult years, and tension between them and the church courts became evident. Some secessionists, such as the groups that developed after the expulsion of Thomas Erskine and others opposed to the Kirk's patronage system in 1840, made claims to the right to control the morals and education of their people.[193] More generally, the "constitutional" provisions of the parish system proved to rest on an unworkable assumption of community and demographic stability. The acts of 1638 and 1646 called for one legal school and one schoolmaster for each parish. But parishes varied greatly in size and density of population. Even in the early eighteenth century, parishes in Stirlingshire ranged between 73 and 1,082 children from five to twelve years of age, and "[one] kirk and one school could not possibly be adequate for both extremes."[194] By late in the century, the Scottish industrial revolution (taking off in the 1780s)[195] and the associated demographic relocations in Scotland rendered the one-school-one-parish system even more archaic. The growth of the textile industry transformed Glasgow. Glasgow had a population of 31,700 in 1755. By 1801 this had risen to 83,700, and by 1821 to 147,000. The figures for Paisley, also a great textile center, were 6,800 in 1755, 31,200 in 1802, and 47,000 in 1821.[196] Even more striking increases occurred in the mid nineteenth century in metal-working towns such as Coatbridge and Motherwell.[197] These urban developments overwhelmed the cities' capacity to expand their educational efforts to meet the needs of their populations.[198] At the end of the nineteenth century, Graham Balfour looked back at some of the inevitable deficiencies of public education in Scotland:

> The [Scottish] system was excellent as far as it extended, but it practically did not affect the large towns, and it fell especially short in the Highlands and Islands. The county parishes were very large, for in Scotland there were less than a thousand parishes in all on an area of 20 million acres, whereas the thirty-seven million acres in England and Wales comprised 15,000 parishes. The towns, on the other hand, relied chiefly on burgh schools and academies, which were to a great extent secondary, and relied on voluntary effort, which proved inadequate.[199]

Industrial and demographic realities, in short, were running ahead of the parish system's structural rigidities.

Political and religious leaders did not respond to these anomalies by altering the fundamental contours of the parish system. Instead, supplementary schools spread—some sponsored by the Kirk—and heritors and religious leaders attempted to accommodate to them. The schools were of the following types:

In the countryside the Kirk tried to supplement the parish schools by relying on the efforts of the Scottish Society for Propagating Christian Knowledge and other, smaller philanthropic societies. Their schools were placed in outlying, difficult-to-reach areas,[200] in such a way as not to compete with the parish schools. The Presbyteries continued to have control over the schoolmasters of the SSPCK schools.

In the towns "sessional schools" began to develop in 1813 and expanded thereafter. These were also controlled by the Kirk.

Endowed schools were established mainly by bequest but also relied on fees. These remained sufficiently low, however, that these schools, too, could cater to students from different social classes.

Miscellaneous charity schools were supported by subscriptions, and private schools were established by landowners and industrial managers.

Private "adventure schools" attracted the greatest attention and criticism. Educational entrepreneurs started them, and they survived on the basis of school fees. They tended to segregate along class lines, because they operated on the basis of ability to pay. As such, they were criticized as incompatible with Scottish democratic predilections. Educational experts criticized their quality; Kay-Shuttleworth judged "the condition of the great majority of the 'Adventure Schools' [to be] an opprobrium to civilization."[201] Some religious authorities regarded them with suspicion because they did not guarantee adequate religious instruction.[202] By and large, however, the Kirk tolerated the private adventure schools as supplements to the parish system.

In 1818 Brougham's committee presented a classification of Scottish schools and scholars. The survey was incomplete and otherwise flawed,[203] but produced an array of figures shown in table 22. The "ordinary day schools" figure probably inflates the development of private schools, because it included SSPCK and other religious society schools. Nevertheless, the table reveals the increasing diversity of the educational arrangements in Scotland. (Despite this, William Boyd claims that for the half-century ending in 1839—when the Committee of Council was

TABLE 22   SCOTTISH SCHOOLS AND SCHOLARS, 1818

|                      | Schools | Pupils  |
|----------------------|---------|---------|
| Parochial schools    | 942     | 54,262  |
| Endowed schools      | 212     | 10,177  |
| Dame schools         | 257     | 5,560   |
| Ordinary day schools | 1,111   | 106,627 |
| Total day schools    | 3,633   | 176,525 |
| Sunday schools       | 807     | 53,449  |

SOURCE: R. D. Anderson, "Education and State in Nineteenth-Century Scotland," *Economic History Review*, 2d. ser., 36 (1983): 522.

formed—"the Church [of Scotland] was at its zenith" in Scottish education; the Education Act of 1803 had put the parish schools on a sounder financial basis, and the Kirk still maintained its religious authority over much of the system.)[204] The Kirk was also showing signs of adaptation. In 1825 its General Assembly formed an education committee to deal with shortages of schools in the Highlands, and "assembly schools" began to appear there and in the islands, to parallel the sessional schools in the cities. By 1843 there were 146 assembly schools, with 13,000 pupils.[205] Despite all these adaptations, the effectiveness of Scottish elementary education, the object of both congratulation and self-congratulation at the beginning of the nineteenth century, was imperiled. By 1834 a Scottish clergyman, George Lewis, had written a book entitled *Scotland, a Half-Educated Nation*,[206] which, notwithstanding that it was a polemic, provided disturbing documentation.[207] In the same year, J. C. Colquhoun introduced legislation in Parliament to provide for the expansion of the Scottish parish school system, which, he argued, had been completely outgrown by increases in population.[208]

PROBLEMS BUILDING TO 1843

Ongoing social changes, combined with the rigidities of the parish system, continued to produce problems in the first half of the nineteenth century. First, the contradictions between the growth and shift of population and the parish system's structural rigidities persisted. Second, under fixed rules that had remained unchanged over a century, teachers' salaries in Scotland's schools underwent a long and serious decline. They gained some relief from the Parochial Schoolmasters (Scotland) Act of

1803, which doubled the statutory minimum salary, but schoolmasters' income still lagged.[209] The situation in the Highlands was especially severe.[210]

More important, the further industrialization and urbanization of Scotland began to generate the same educational problems that England was experiencing. Many of these had to do with the chronic problems of irregular attendance and early withdrawal of working-class children. The continuing patterns of seasonal labor in the agricultural areas— and their implications for attendance—drew the attention of inspectors of schools.[211] Attendance problems also plagued the industrial districts.[212] In 1846, 54 percent of Glasgow's children were not in schools, and in the poverty-stricken Gorbals district, it appeared that 93 percent were attending no school at all.[213] The problems of attendance were especially severe for Catholics, who lived in the greatest poverty and who lacked voluntary schools.[214] The most frequently given reasons for non-attendance were the demands of children's employment.[215] Thus in Scotland, previously thought to be well covered educationally, serious problems of coverage were developing. Perhaps more serious, according to Halévy's assessment, was the fact that "[parishes] were swamped in a chaos of houses and factories, and like the church, the school ceased to be a centre of social life."[216]

An additional problem associated with the industrial working class lay in its increasing number of Roman Catholics. Glasgow represented the most extreme case. Its industrial development brought a heavy Irish immigration. By 1831 there were 35,554 Irish in Glasgow, mainly Catholic and mainly in the ranks of unskilled labor; the figure was nearly 70,000 in 1846. There were no Catholic schools in Glasgow, however, until after 1817, when a new Catholic Schools Society established four schools over several years to accommodate Catholic children.[217] The proportion of Catholics was greater in Scotland than in England in the nineteenth century. In 1841, the percentage was 4.8 (1.8 in England); in 1851, 7.2 (2.9 in England); and in 1861, 6.7 (3.0 in England).[218]

Schooling for Catholics in Scotland posed three special problems. First, there were many very poor families among the Irish Catholics, and this class of families tended generally to show the highest rates of nonattendance and irregular attendance. Second, especially during bursts of rapid population growth (as in Glasgow after 1847), Catholic efforts to provide schools for their children lagged far behind the need for them.[219] Third, Catholics posed more serious problems of educational integration than other Scottish Dissenters, who "differ little, if at all, in doctrine from the Establishment."[220] In 1818 a clergyman from Ayr reported that "amongst the Irish inhabitants education is scarcely known, and they will not send their children to school, although they may be able to afford it."[221] In 1856, J. F. Maguire registered a complaint about reformatory schools in Scotland that struck a note familiar in England and Ireland:

> I distinctly state that the treatment of Irish Catholic children in these [reformatory] schools . . . is unmanly, bigoted, and unchristian. . . . what provision is there made for the religious teaching of those children? When Catholic children are committed to these schools, they are compelled to receive Presbyterian teaching—they are compelled to become or profess themselves Presbyterians—they are given over, without any protection whatever, to the undisputed authority of men whose open and public boast it has been, that they would never be satisfied until Popery was extirpated from the land.[222]

The situation for Catholics in Scotland was probably eased by the fact that the Kirk adopted a conscience clause early. In 1829 the education committee of the General Assembly ruled that its schools were open to both Protestants and Catholics and directed its teachers "not to press on the Catholic children any instruction to which their parents or their priests may object, as interfering with the principles of their own religion."[223] Still, the doctrinal, liturgical, and political differences between the Catholic and Presbyterian churches constituted a basis for mutual antagonism. Scotland experienced bursts of anti-Catholicism during the Maynooth crisis of 1845 and the Papal Aggression of 1851.[224]

Developments with even greater implications for Scottish education were taking place within Protestantism. The small minority of Anglicans in Scotland grew in numbers in the nineteenth century with the increasing anglicization of the upper classes, some of whom were sending their children to English public schools.[225] A few migrants from Ireland were members of the Church of Ireland. Scottish Anglicans opened their own schools in Scotland. In addition, there were some 350 schools operated by the Independents, Baptists, and Methodists.[226] The Presbyterians themselves had experienced several secessions in the eighteenth century.[227] The first to secede were the Erskine group, who formed an associate presbytery, which itself split into four groups on the basis of doctrinal differences over predestination and the taking of oaths before civil authorities. A realignment of these groups produced the United Secession Church in 1820. The second secession dealt with objections to

Kirk patronage and led to the formation of the Relief Church in 1752. In 1847 the Relief and the United Secession Church merged into the United Presbyterian Church. Also in the eighteenth century, an ancient schismatic group evolved into the Reformed Presbyterian Church. These seceders differed little from the Church of Scotland doctrinally, but in the 1830s they repudiated Chapter XXIII of the Westminster Confession of the Kirk and distanced themselves further by adopting the Voluntary principle.[228] They thus became dissenters from the Established Church in much the same sense that English Dissenters were.

The most serious challenge to the Kirk accompanied the development of Evangelicalism. Wesleyanism and its English evangelical offshoots did not take root in Scotland,[229] but a similar indigenous movement arose. The Scottish Evangelical movement was a kind of resurgence of Puritanism, which had experienced a long decline in the Kirk during the eighteenth century.[230] The Evangelicals were Calvinist-Fundamentalist in theology, adhered to a strict interpretation of the doctrine of predestination, and on the political front were antagonistic to the Kirk's traditional patronage over ministerial and other church positions.[231] After the Disruption of 1843, this group launched vigorous campaigns on Sabbatarian issues, such as the running of trains on Sunday, temperance, and popular entertainment. The Evangelicals also pressed for franchise reform and for the extension of the Kirk's activities into poor relief.[232] Different as these emphases were from those of the more moderate Church of Scotland, the Evangelicals' decisive challenge to the Kirk was not on doctrinal or social conscience issues. The split came over church patronage and authority: the right to appoint ministers. In 1834 the Evangelicals gained control of the General Assembly of the Kirk and succeeded in passing a veto act that gave congregations the right to refuse a patron's (heritor's) nominee. This event began what is called the Nine Years' Conflict, which consisted in the Evangelical-controlled General Assembly taking action after action, many of which were invalidated by the Court of Session.[233] The impasse came before Parliament in November 1842, but the conflict was not actively taken up by either Peel or Russell.

In 1843 the Evangelicals lost their majority in the General Assembly, and in May of that year the Disruption took place. David Welsh, a leader of the Evangelicals, declared that the assembly was not free, and that he could not accept the benefits of the Establishment under the conditions it imposed. He left the assembly, taking more than four hundred ministers with him. Four hundred and seventy clergymen ultimately left

the Establishment, giving up both stipends and housing, and shortly
thereafter established the Free Church of Scotland.[234]

## THE DISRUPTION AND ITS IMPACT:
## DENOMINATIONALISM

The conflict that produced the Free Church had a social-class dimension. The secessionist body appealed mainly in isolated Highland communities suffering the greatest economic distress and in the urban,
middle-class areas of Glasgow and Edinburgh. Its social support was
drawn from "the lower middle class, notably shopkeepers, and tradesmen, and from the artisans and peasantry."[235] The main sources of loyalty to the Established Church came from the lowland rural regions,
where the lairds retained the greatest influence. The Free Church and
other Scottish Dissenters fought to abolish all religious tests and to end
annuity tests—in short, to erode the privileges of Establishment in
Scotland.[236]

A remarkable feature of the Disruption was the magnitude of its
effects. With that event, and with the amalgamation of other secessionists into the United Presbyterian Church in 1847, Scottish Presbyterianism divided into three parts. The religious census of 1851, only
a few years after these decisive events, showed how equal these parts
were. The figures for total attendance were as follows:

| | |
|---|---|
| Church of Scotland | 566,409 |
| Free Church | 555,702 |
| United Presbyterian Church | 336,412[237] |

These numbers also reveal the size of the majority of Presbyterians not
affiliated with the Establishment. Presbyterian Dissenters were more
than 60 percent of all Presbyterians. To be sure, Presbyterian Dissent
was "political" (that is, dealing with the authority of the church) rather
than "doctrinal" dissent. This made for less militancy among Scottish
Dissenters than among their brethren in England, but the political implications of their numerical dominance could not be ignored.

The Disruption spread immediately to questions of education. Many
parish, General Assembly, and SSPCK schools broke away and joined
the seceders.[238] In 1843 the Free Church began an educational campaign. This included an effort to duplicate the parish system, and to
cover the country with Free Church schools. This movement was given
an added emotional dimension—and a supply of teachers—by the fact

that the Established Church dismissed several hundred schoolmasters who had declared for the Free Church.[239] Almost immediately, however, it became apparent that they could not realize their ambitions on the basis of private support. As early as 1844 some Free Church schools were experiencing difficulties in meeting their payment obligations.[240]

The minutes of 1846 emerged mainly from a religious-political impasse in England, and had little to do with Scotland.[241] However, they came as a boon to the struggling Free Church. Despite a Voluntaryist minority in their ranks, and despite some "Methodist-like" fears that accepting aid would encourage "Popery or Socianism," the Free Church immediately took advantage of the government subsidy. Many of its applications met the Committee of Council's approval because of the high qualifications presented. By 1850 the Free Church covered some sixty thousand pupils in its subsidized schools. Faced with this competition, the Established Church also began applying for government grants. As a result "education [became] a battlefield for the two churches, and they sought to overbid each other in the provision of educational opportunities."[242] Shortly thereafter the Church of England and Roman Catholic schools in Scotland followed suit. The Committee of Council's principle of assigning denominationally approved inspectors to each type of denominational school spread to Scotland as well.[243] The Free Church schism also affected the teaching colleges. David Stowe and all but one of the teachers of the normal college joined the Free Church, and were obliged to leave the Establishment. The Established Church had set up teaching colleges in Glasgow and Edinburgh, and these remained with it. By 1845, however, the Free Church had "matching" colleges in both cities, so that by that year, Scotland had four training colleges, split along denominational lines.[244]

The educational fallout from the Disruption of 1843 thus superimposed a new system of education on the inherited parish system. Playfair designated the phase beginning in 1843 as the third, "denominational" phase of Scottish education, following on the "ecclesiastical" (pre-1646) and "national" (1646–1843) phases.[245] In 1867 the Commission on Scottish Education (Argyll Commission) described the situation as follows:

> The position of education in Scotland . . . is peculiar. We have found, on one hand, a National Institution, consisting of Parochial, Side, and Parliamentary schools, established by law, maintained by local assessment, and designed to be commensurate with the educational wants of the country. . . . On the other hand, we find a supplementary system, forced into existence

partly by denominational rivalry, but mainly by the deficiencies of the National System, which furnishes more than two-thirds of the education of the rural districts of Scotland, and on which that of the towns of Scotland mainly depends.[246]

The accumulated attempts to meet new population demands, to deal with a pauper class, and to accommodate denominational demands had yielded a cross-patch of ten different kinds of schools in Scotland by midcentury: the old parochial schools; burgh schools (mainly for secondary education); parliamentary schools (special schools established in 1838, in which teachers' salaries were paid by Parliament); sessional schools; assembly schools; Free Church schools; SSPCK schools, mainly in the Highlands; other church schools such as United Presbyterian, Roman Catholic, and Episcopal schools; philanthropic schools, such as ragged schools and reformatory school; and private schools.[247]

In 1869 the duke of Argyll described the grants of the Privy Council as a "foreign element altogether to the ancient constitution of the parochial schools of Scotland." He then added a characterization of Scottish history since 1843 that could, with appropriately changed words, be said to describe the English system of the time:

> There were in Scotland special circumstances which undoubtedly brought out into very full relief the peculiar defects of the Privy Council system of grants. In the first place there was, at the very time these grants were introduced into Scotland, a very great excitement, and what I may call an exacerbation of the rivalry of ecclesiastical sects. . . . local subscriptions in Scotland for particular schools were produced not merely with reference to the wants of the locality, but with regard to the desire of particular religious bodies to outstrip and rival each other in the educational management of the country. The consequence was that, to some extent, encouragement was given to schools erected out of mere denominational rivalry, and not with reference to the existing wants of the locality.[248]

In view of the great range of schools resulting from changes in the early nineteenth century, however, the denominational schools were only one of the many "foreign elements" that had barnacled onto the side of the ancient, neat parochial system.

There were two respects in which the denominationally based, state-subsidized schools did not dominate the Scottish scene as much as they did the English in the 1850s and 1860s. First, despite the Argyll Commission's stress on denominational competition, there remained an impulse among the educators "to use [schools] for their primary educational purpose, and not with a view to their secondary object, of

upholding the influence and powers of the Churches."[249] One manifestation of this impulse was that the Scottish schools tended to wel-
come—and not proselytize—all denominations. The major religious
bodies in Scotland—Established Church, Free Church, Roman Catholic
Church—had long been committed to the principle of the conscience
clause.[250] Playfair claimed that "the freest conscience right prevails in all
[Presbyterian] schools," and sectarian teaching was at a minimum.[251]
An assistant commissioner of the Argyll Commission reported that in
the country districts, "[religious] differences between the parents and
managers of schools do not . . . have any effect in keeping the children
from school."[252] In 1846, in the heated aftermath of the Disruption,
HMI John Gordon reported on the religious heterogeneity in the town
of Airdrie. He counted no fewer than "ten distinct religious parties" in
Airdrie: two congregations of the Established Church, three of the Free
Church, and one of each of the United Secession, Roman Catholic, Baptist, Independent Relief, Wesleyan Methodist, Congregational and Reformed Presbyterian churches. With respect to projected plans for a
new school, to be established by a free-standing committee of citizens
and supported by the Committee of Council, Gordon commented: "In
any circumstances, the children here, like those of most other places,
would probably have been admitted without reference to their religious
denominations; but the rule becomes the more necessary where much
division prevails in the matter of religious opinion."[253] Gordon might
have added that despite the religious heterogeneity of communities in
Wales, Ireland, and England, the assumption of multidenominational
attendance was more difficult to make in those regions than it was in
Scotland.

Additional, more systematic evidence for this multidenomination-
alism in Scottish education appears in the Argyll Commission Report.
Surveys covering four-fifths of Scotland showed a high level of cross-
attendance of children in different denominational schools. The figures
are given in table 23. Beyond these results, the commission reported
only 1,919 Episcopalian students in Episcopalian schools. Of the 5,736
scholars in Roman Catholic schools, 5,229 were of that faith, but the
commission pointed out that there were more than 7,000 Catholics in
Protestant schools.[254] The commission found the results "remarkable"
and "satisfactory," and inferred that "the situation of the school and the
merits of the teacher weigh more in determining the school which children attend in Scotland than religious differences."[255] While such statistics must be regarded with skepticism, they do indicate that conscien-

TABLE 23    RELIGIOUS PERSUASIONS OF PUPILS IN
SCOTTISH SCHOOLS, 1864

|  | National Parish Schools | General Assembly Schools | Free Church Schools | Undenominational, Others |
|---|---|---|---|---|
| *Church of Scotland* | 47,161 | 18,000 | 10,000 | 39,000 |
| *Free Church of Scotland* | 14,486 | 8,000 | 28,000 | 19,000 |
| *United Presbyterians* | 7,462 | 2,700 | 3,000 | 12,000 |
| *Episcopalians* | 521 | 200 | 313 | — |
| *Roman Catholics* | 1,243 | 1,000 | 974 | 2,898 |
| *Other denominations* | 1,644 | — | — | — |
| *Not known* | 3,976 | — | — | — |

SOURCE: *Parliamentary Papers*, 1867, 25, pp. ix–xx.

tious objections appeared not to run as deep in Scotland as they did in England and Wales. That statement was especially true for the relations between the Church of Scotland and Scottish Presbyterian Dissent.

The second dampening effect on denominationalism was that many Scottish educators did not care for the kind of denominational education that the Committee of Council imported from England into Scotland. Objections arose about the pupil-teacher system; it was claimed to be foreign to a country that valued the scholarly teacher.[256] Some regarded the normal schools as "cramming institutions"[257] that turned out "teaching machines rather than intelligent educators of youth," who fell short of university-trained teachers.[258] It was the threat of the Revised Code, however, that drew the strongest objections in Scotland. Robert Buchanan summarized it as a "deteriorating influence." The specifics of this objection were the following:

The certification system for teachers ignored the higher subjects—so central to the Scottish academic traditions—and dragged qualifications down because of the minimal standards of certification.

Managers discouraged those higher branches because their payment depended on performance in the basic subjects only.[259]

The code, by emphasizing basic subjects, discouraged attendance at school of all children above the age of eleven.

The code discouraged the recruitment of young men of "superior talents and character" into education because of the debased quality of primary education.

Most important, a provision of the code called for identifying students from a certain social class ("a sort of pauper class") and setting them apart from those in social grades above them as a condition of their entry. This was especially offensive to Buchanan, who felt that the best feature of common schools in Scotland was "that they blended different classes together."[260]

Buchanan was speaking of Article 4 of the code, which prevented children above the class of manual labor from earning any portion of the parliamentary grant. This provision had caused concern in England,[261] but it was anathema to many Scots. The Argyll Commission discussed it at some length, indicating that it was considered an "obnoxious regulation" by many. In the country districts, it was reported that "both managers and parents regard [the inquiry into the class background of children] as inquisitorial and as repugnant to Scotch feeling."[262] The regulation might well apply to England, which had no provision for community education in every parish—that is, no national system—but not to Scotland, where "the public duty is recognized of supplying education to the whole people." Since 1696 and even earlier, the commission argued, all rural parishes in Scotland had enjoyed "what may be truly termed, a National System." They had "submitted to be taxed for schools open to all classes of community and the effects of this system are as satisfactory as they are instructive."[263] Rev. Sir H. Moncreiff summarized the situation by saying that "[the] principle, even of the Old Code, is not exactly suited to Scottish educational habits, but the Revised Code is still more adverse to them."[264] Article 4 thus brought to life the tension between the English values of class hierarchy and the Scottish values of community democracy.

This opposition to "English" denominationalism, educational methods, and class assumptions helped excite the movement for national education in Scotland in the 1850s. In 1850 and 1851, Lord Melgund introduced bills in Parliament aiming at a national system in Scotland, but these were opposed successfully by the Established Church, eager to preserve its control over the parish schools.[265] Denominational growth and even more the Revised Code appeared to excite a certain measure of general Scottish nationalism, which, however, when compared to the

Irish and Welsh cases at the time, was relatively dormant.[266] In parliamentary debate on the code, J. Whiteside took note of the fact that both the Established Church of Scotland and the Free Church had petitioned against it as "an insult offered to the Scottish nation."[267] Buchanan also appealed to "Scottish" values in attacking the code, saying:

> The history, the habits, and the ideas of the Scottish people, in reference to common education, are . . . so different from those of England, that a system of education, framed with a view to England, and administered according to English notions, can hardly be ever made to work either smoothly or satisfactorily among us. . . . If we are ever to have an educational system that will work well in Scotland, it must be both framed and administered by men who understand this,—a thing which Englishmen never do.[268]

Sensitive to the opposition, the government delayed the application of the Revised Code until March 1864, and even then it remained in existence for only a few months before it was suspended—to await the report of the newly appointed Argyll Commission—except for the examination of individual children in the basic subjects.[269] The Scottish Education Department finally adopted a payment-by-results scheme in 1873, but this was tailored to take account of the traditional Scottish emphasis on the higher subjects.[270]

## OBSTACLES TO AND PRESSURES FOR REFORM, 1850–1870

Several considerations thus indicate that Scotland was friendlier to the idea of a national system of education than England was. "National" implied two things: first, a state-supported system that would cover the country systematically and in a more or less uniform way; and, second, a national system that was Scotland's national system, not England's. There were two main stumbling blocks to the formation of a new national system that would not be controlled by the Established Church and heritors. Both were based on religion, but were of a different character.

The first stumbling block was an apprehension of secularism. It was a commonly voiced opinion that both Wales and Scotland had a strong passion for religion. In introducing a bill to reform the Scottish system in 1854, J. Moncreiff, the lord advocate, attempted to pinpoint the "religious difficulty" in Scotland by comparing it to Ireland. If, as a Protestant in an Irish parish that was entirely Roman Catholic, he were to open a school and propose to teach the Bible and Anglican catechism, he would find "that the children refuse to learn either . . . and that [his] school is deserted." With respect to Scotland, however:

The religious difficulty in that country takes altogether another shape. Your difficulty begins, not by introducing religion, but by excluding it, and for one child that may be excluded by the teaching of religion, a hundred would be shut out by the refusal to teach it. In short, nothing is more certain than this, that if it were attempted to establish in Scotland a system of education purely secular, from which religion should be excluded, it would, in the first place, be impossible to induce one tithe of the population to make use of the schools, and, in the second place, the proposition would raise a flame of agitation throughout Scotland more general and more violent than any we have witnessed. . . . It would therefore . . . be a very great mistake to propose a system of secular education in Scotland.[271]

The apprehension associated with such a spirit was that a government anxious to avoid religious conflict might exclude religion altogether.[272] At the same time, two groups were pressing for such an exclusion. In 1847 the United Presbyterian Church had "gone Voluntaryist," taking the position that religious training belonged to the parents and church, not to the state.[273] The second group was a coalition of secularists. Colquhoun referred to this group as a collection of "Unitarians, educational secularists, and the adherents of an advanced liberal party in education."[274]

The second stumbling block was fear of any religious monolith. In the same debate, Moncreiff added that "by some a strong Presbyterian feeling of Scotland is deplored. They think it narrow and bigoted, and would like to see its influence diminished." Paradoxically, he added, it was from that Presbyterian tradition that Scotland derived her "love of civil liberty" and "resistance to religious oppression"—those very features that found a religious monolith offensive.[275] The Established Church still posed an obstacle in this regard. Along with other denominations in Scotland, it observed a conscience clause. However, the Kirk had discharged several hundred teachers who had joined the Free Church at the Disruption, and it still required its own teachers to be members of the Established Church. In reciting the difficulties facing a national system in Scotland, James Begg, a Free Church leader and Scottish nationalist, singled this out as *the* obstacle:

The parochial schools are under the control of the ecclesiastical establishment, and those who are not members of the Established Church are excluded from the office of teacher. In a country like Scotland, where such a proportion of the population are now Dissenters, such a constriction is alike unjust and impolitic. It prevents the schools from obtaining a choice of all classes of successful teachers and it prevents the national system of education from being developed to meet the needs of a growing population.[276]

The most sensitive group in Scotland with respect to religious indoctrination was the Catholic Church. Its doctrines were at odds with those of the Presbyterian majority, and it insisted on Catholic control of religious education.[277] Colquhoun, writing in 1859, pondered "[how], by any surrender, Roman Catholics and Protestants can be united in one school I confess myself unable to divine."[278] Even though government support was available under the minutes of 1846, most Catholic elementary schools remained outside the system of government aid and inspection, "mainly because of their apathy and groundless fears of government control."[279]

All the while, however, people concerned with inadequate educational coverage were pressing—as they were in England—for some kind of comprehensive reform. Moncreiff pointed out in 1854 that "the poorest places are those that stand most in need of additional schools," and that the denominational system would not reach the poor, the destitute, and the ignorant.[280] The Argyll Commission reported that almost a fifth of the child population did not attend any school. These problems were severest among the fishing, crofting, weaving, and mining occupations, and, among the cities, in Glasgow.[281] In a later debate, the duke of Argyll explained that the main defects were that the cities and towns had entirely outgrown the capacity of the parochial system and that both densely and thinly populated districts were neglected. The parochial system was thus "wholly inadequate for the proper education of the people." Argyll added, however, that the denominational system, in addition to other difficulties, implied that "you give to the richest part of the country and withhold from the poorest." As a result, the Committee of Council system, while "useful in supplementing" the parochial system in some cases, did not reach the poorest, especially in the Highlands and the Hebrides.[282]

In the 1850s and 1860s, then, Scotland, like England, faced social and economic problems that pressed for educational development, but at the same time lived with a complex religious impasse that threatened to block that development. Legislative failures in those decades underscored this difficulty. In 1854 Moncreiff introduced his bill as a way of improving the low salaries of schoolmasters. In actuality, the bill called for boards that would govern schools through the collection of rates, improve the salary conditions of masters, and improve and extend

schooling in very poor areas.[283] Schools would hold open competitions
for hiring schoolteachers without regard to religious denomination
(clearly a red flag to the Established Church). The bill provided for Protestant religious instruction, but with a provision excusing Catholic children from attending during the hours of such instruction. The bill drew
criticism from a Roman Catholic representative, who argued that
Moncreiff exaggerated the religious uniformity of Scotland.[284] In addition, a contest between the Free Church and the Establishment emerged
during the course of the debates. The earl of Dalkeith praised the work
of the parochial system and its educational results, and asked whether it
was not unwise "to destroy a system which had worked so well, for the
purpose of substituting in its stead a plan founded entirely on theory."[285] Bruce summarized the range of support and opposition to the
bill: "As to the Free Church of Scotland, he believed they were almost
unanimous in favour of the Bill. . . . On the other hand, the Bill was
opposed by the Established Church, by nearly the whole of the landed
proprietors of Scotland—at least 2,000 of the most important of them
had signed a petition to that effect—and also by those who held what
was called 'the voluntary principle.'"[286] He added the opinion that "if
the Free Church never had existed the present Bill would never have
been brought forward."[287] Several others attacked the bill as an assault
on the Established Church of Scotland and as a threat to destroy what
had proved valuable.[288] After a long debate, the lord advocate summed
up the paralysis in the following terms:

> The alternatives set before the House were clear and distinct. They must ei-
> ther have a national system of education based upon religious instruction
> combined with secular instruction; or a national system of secular instruc-
> tion disconnected from religion; or the system commonly called denomina-
> tional. . . . [As for secular schooling separated from religion], the people of
> Scotland would not adopt such a system. . . . Then there was the denomi-
> national system. They had the denominational system already in Scotland.
> It had been tried and proved, and had been found most unquestionably
> wanting.[289]

In the end the debate revealed a struggle between English (R. Cobden,
W. Ewart) and Scottish Dissenters on the one side, and English (R.
Spooner, Lord J. J. R. Manners, C. D. W. Sibthorp) and Scottish Estab-
lishmentarians on the other. The bill failed by the narrow majority of
193 to 184.

In considering the bill to raise the salaries of schoolmasters in 1855,
the House of Lords, evidently under pressure from the Church of

Scotland, removed the provision that ruled out religious tests for school-masters.[290] Legislation for a variant of a national system was introduced in 1855 and again in 1856; it failed on both occasions because of op-position from the Church of Scotland. Not until 1861 was Parliament able to secure increases in teachers' salaries. That bill did weaken the Kirk to a degree by shifting the responsibility for examining new teach-ers from the presbyteries to university boards.[291]

All legislative efforts to extend Scottish education in the 1850s and 1860s thus proved abortive, in that respect resembling developments in England.[292] Both countries were locked in a kind of political/religious paralysis. After the various unsuccessful efforts, Moncreiff despaired, charging that the English members of Parliament regarded Scotland as "a provincial exotic" and concluding that it was useless "to go knock-ing at the doors of Parliament."[293] His frustration was probably fueled by the fact that the Scottish education bills introduced in 1850, 1851, 1854, and 1855—each with a systematizing, nationalizing intent—had all been supported by the Scottish M.P.'s, the last two by substantial ma-jorities. The movement toward national education could thus have been regarded, with some justification, as thwarted by the English.[294] In any event, just as the Newcastle Commission (1858–61) was born of the frustration of Pakington and his co-reformers with parliamentary pa-ralysis, so the Argyll Commission was formed out of Scottish reformers' frustration.

Like the Newcastle Commission, the Argyll Commission gathered a vast amount of information. It documented the past successes of the parish system and its present inadequacies; the problems of irregular at-tendance and nonattendance; the mixed quality of private schooling; the failure of the denominational system to supplement the system to reach the poor; the wasteful duplication occasioned by the competition among denominations; and the same irrationalities associated with the denominational inspection system. With respect to religion, the Argyll Commission noted that 85 percent of the Scottish population was Pres-byterian (in one or other of Presbyterianism's three likenesses), and that, except for Catholics, schools were attended by different denominations. For these reasons, the commission saw no true obstacle to a uniform system of education.

Also like the Newcastle Commission, the Argyll Commission was conservative and made patchwork recommendations. Part of this may trace to its composition. As Argyll explained, it included both liber-als and conservatives, as well as representatives from the Established

Church, Free Church, United Presbyterian Church, Episcopal (Anglican) Church, and a group committed to secular education.[295] (Interestingly, there was no Roman Catholic representative.) The recommendations called for the preservation of the parish school system. The main reforms were to be supplementary. Denominational schools were to be adapted to a national system, but were to be allowed to maintain their religious managements; the commission recommended some new schools— on the principle of "filling the gaps." These would be governed by elected boards and supported by local rates.[296] The commission also recommended more centralization—a central board of education. And consistent with Scottish predilections, it recommended the application of the Revised Code, but not of its despised Article 4.[297]

Argyll himself introduced legislation, following directly from the work of his commission, in February 1869. His bill called for a board to initiate and regulate new educational ventures in Scotland. The board would include representatives of proprietors of land, the burghs, higher education (with representatives from the universities), the schoolmasters, and the Crown.[298] The bill ended denominational inspection on grounds that there was so much "crossing-over" of denominational lines in attendance.[299] At the second reading there were complaints that the suggested composition was unjust, particularly to Catholics. "What chance had any Roman Catholic of being elected by this Board?" the earl of Airlie asked, for example. In addition, "it appeared to him monstrous that the Universities should have two members on the Board, when counties and the parishes had only the same number." The earl of Denbigh, also picking up the Catholic interest, charged that "this bill was drawn up by a Presbyterian for the benefit of Presbyterians, for assuredly both the Episcopalians and Catholics will alike suffer under it."[300] In the House of Lords, various members attacked the mode of selecting the board; the archbishop of Canterbury wished to maintain the principle of denominational education, and the duke of Richmond argued that the bill discriminated against minorities. In the end the Lords amended the bill to give more consideration to voluntary schools. Various other amendments, including the effort of the duke of Argyll to expand the board's membership so that more interests could be represented, were attempted, but ultimately the bill foundered, mainly under sectarian attack.[301]

Thus, despite the extended efforts of Argyll's Commission and Argyll himself, Scotland still seemed paralyzed by a version of religious conflict that, as in England, reflected its mixture of Establishmentarian and denominational principles, with the political dominance of neither. Alexander Sellar would complain in 1870:

> Since 1843, and prior to it, a struggle has been going on between the church and the political parties in Scotland upon [education], and now, after the lapse of more than quarter of a century, the motive of the struggle remains unchanged, and the bitterness of the combatants is undiminished. The tactics by which the Scotch Education Bill of 1854 was defeated were almost identical with those by which the bill of 1855 was defeated, and almost identical with those by which the bill of 1869 was defeated. The arguments of 1854 were repeated in 1869. The same feelings were aroused; the same prejudices fostered; the same animosities embittered.[302]

Another bill, introduced by the lord advocate, C. Young, in 1871, failed largely because it provided for a Scottish Education Department located in London, a provision that raised an outcry among Scottish interests.[303] In 1869, however, a significant change in position on the part of the Church of Scotland had opened the door for more advanced legislation. The synod of the Kirk ruled that it would not object if parishes agreed to apply state funds to religious education. This paved the way for adoption of a national system of parish support.[304] In 1867 some United Presbyterians, already on record as opposing religion in state education, declared—along with the English Voluntaryists in the same year—in favor of a national system of secular education along American lines.[305] In addition, the parliamentary reforms of 1867 had extended the franchise and shifted the balance of electoral power away from the Scottish religious and class Establishment and strengthened the Liberal Party in Scotland.[306]

The Education Act of 1872, which has been regarded as a Scottish version of the Education Act of 1870 for England and Wales, went further than the recommendations of the Argyll Commission. It provided for compulsory education for children between the ages of five and thirteen (with some exceptions possible). It also provided for a system of public schools governed by popularly elected school boards, to be integrated under a coordinating authority, the Scottish Education Department. The critical "advance" over the Education Act of 1870 was that the system *subsumed*—not coexisted with—the parish schools and many of the denominational schools.[307] The new boards assumed wide powers, including control over school buildings, finance, attendance, the appointment and payment of teachers, and arrangements for religious education. As for religious instruction, the act specified that it should occur at the beginning or the end of the school meeting. Inspectors were not to examine pupils in religious subjects or religious knowledge.[308] By this act the Scottish system moved closer to the American common school tradition in most structural respects, the main difference being the greater emphasis on religious education.

In the succeeding years the new public system grew rapidly. Even though compulsory after 1872, it suffered from continuing attendance problems, especially among very young children. The school fees were also experienced as burdensome, as they were in England, until their remission in 1891.[309] Those denominational schools not absorbed—as well as private institutions—tended to fall by the wayside. Roman Catholic schools were the most significant exception to this pattern. (A few Episcopal schools, also more sectarian in character than those of Scottish Presbyterians, also did not join.)[310] The Catholic hierarchy could not accept the loss of its control over curriculum and religious education, which the new Scottish system demanded. As a result, the Catholics declined to join the state system, and launched a campaign to support a school system built, staffed, and operated on a parochial basis. Despite their voluntary efforts, however, the Catholics could not keep pace with subsequent development under the new national system.[311] The act of 1872 thus created a turning point for the Catholics similar to that encountered by their coreligionists in New York City in 1842. In the circumstances, they moved in a similar direction: toward establishing a parochial school system separate from, and at a disadvantage to, the state system.

## CHAPTER 8

# The Family Economy and Working-Class Education

## THE DEMAND FOR EDUCATION: GENERAL CONSIDERATIONS

Until now the analysis has taken the perspective mainly of those pressing for or providing working-class education: reformers, the ruling classes, the religious societies, community subscribers, and the state administration. This emphasis has concerned the supply side of education, with little consideration of its impact on its recipients or their interest in it. I have touched on the ways in which conditions of supply facilitated the spread of education—for example, sectarian competition among religious groups and sustained pressure on the part of the state. I have also noted how educational progress was impeded, for example, by difficulties in raising voluntary subscriptions and political paralysis in the face of sectarian conflict. In this chapter the focus shifts to the demand side. This means taking note of the interest of working-class parents in the educational attainment of their children, their attitudes toward the schools, constraints on their ability to participate in these schools, and their resulting behavior.

It can be argued that a *direct* demand for education by the working classes did not play a large role in shaping those institutions. It was more a matter of a political dialogue among the classes above them that affected education directly. The working classes did not make many collective educational demands on their own behalf throughout the century. Their direct political pressure and action were felt more through demands for better wages, protests against machinery, demands to organize into trade unions, demands for political enfranchisement, demands for an end to the privileges of the classes above them, and movements to revolutionize the society. Working-class leaders stressed the need for education for their classes, but these demands were for educational content—and were based on principles of democratic participation—that the ruling classes were not prepared to grant.[1] Only later in the century, when the working classes became a more integral part of British constitutional life, did their interests in the educational system itself acquire articulate political expression.

For most of the nineteenth century, the supply-demand relationship was thus a more *indirect* one. Many dominant groups in society became interested in education as a possible response to *other* working-class demands. To recapitulate what has already been noted, early in the century the Tory position was that education would stimulate the wrong kinds of demands among the poor, especially demands for a better standard of living and for work above their class, or perhaps seditious ideas. The Whig position was that education would diminish such demands by instilling moral and civic values in the lower classes. Some political economists believed that instruction in the laws of their subject would bring workers to understand their place in society and forsake strikes and other actions inimical to the economy and public order. Most reformers believed that education was a cure for or an antidote to crime, idleness, and pauperism. Few reformers and politicians indicated that their activity in the educational field was in response to a direct demand for education by the working classes. It is evident from these views that England occupied a somewhat unusual position among nations with respect to mass education. As R. H. Tawney put it, English educational policy was made, except for brief intervals, "by men few, if any, of whom have themselves attended the schools principally affected by [those policies], or would dream of allowing their children to attend them."[2] Not too much weight should be placed on this observation, however, for in other countries at the time governments were organizing education for their people—for example, in Prussia, France, and Holland. Even in the "democratic" United States, leadership for educational development came from reformers, clergymen, politicians, and civic leaders.[3] The British situation was merely an extreme case: education was stratified by class in the extreme; it was organized in the first instance by strata-within-community rather than community as such;[4] and the upper classes explicitly and self-consciously organized education for the combined control and presumed benefit of the lower classes.

In addition to focusing on those who provided education, it is essential to consider the demand side proper—the attitudes of the working classes toward it and how they accepted, accommodated to, or rejected it. Two features of the working-class situation bear directly on this: first, the pattern of working life in workers' families, especially the work of their children, because nothing affected their schooling more than the exigencies of work and income; and, second, their class attitudes and aspirations as these related to education.

Some additional introductory remarks on educational demand are in order. First, it is an error to conceive of the working classes as an entity consuming education. The differences in the conditions of agricultural and urban labor, for example, demand that a distinction be made between them for the purpose of any analysis. Classified by a combination of labor-market position and educational aspirations, the urban scene produced at least four different groupings:

The highly skilled, decently paid "labour aristocracy,"[5] including spinning operatives and others, many of whom regarded schools as an avenue to respectability, self-improvement, and perhaps social mobility.

The mass of ill-paid semiskilled, low-skilled, and unskilled workers, who were employed much of the time but could harbor few expectations beyond sustaining themselves and their families in the capitalist wage economy; many in this class valued education, but mainly as a means of securing the essentials of literacy and numeracy.

The unemployed, often pauperized, "underclass," who had few contacts with education or any other institution, save for the poor law machinery.

That minority of articulate leaders who represented the voice of the working classes and who developed many ideas about education for the working classes and for people generally.

Finer gradations than these are possible—for example, by industry, region, and ethnic group. Representatives of and commentators on the working classes themselves recognized such distinctions. It is therefore important to keep the heterogeneity of the working classes in mind throughout the analysis, even though contemporaries also spoke freely of the tripartite division of British society into upper, middle, and working classes.[6]

Second, the use of the labor of children, including even very young children, in economic activity was an ancient one in Britain (as elsewhere).[7] That tradition resided in agricultural customs (the "peasant family"), in the apprenticeship system, and in domestic industry, including the "putting-out" system of the eighteenth century.[8] As the commercial and industrial transformation of Britain quickened in that century, the principle of child labor continued, though in altered form. The statutory seven-year apprenticeship weakened as crafts declined in competition with mechanized production, and the low-skilled jobs that proliferated requiring little training. In the first half of the nineteenth century, child labor continued in agriculture; in new works associated with the industrial revolution, such as mining, ore-processing, potteries, and the infamous cotton-textile manufactories; in domestic industries such as weaving; in miscellaneous trades such as tobacco-processing,[9] and in low-skilled services such as errand-running. Children were, finally, widely employed in unpaid domestic work, including child-minding.

Third, the timing of the development of the British working classes and of the rise of schooling affecting them was unique. By the time the state entered the arena of popular education even minimally in Britain (the 1830s and 1840s), the industrial revolution was at hand, and with it a socially and politically visible working class. This industrial development, including its pattern of labor-force participation, was an institutional "given" for British educational reformers. Many European countries—notably Prussia, France, and Holland—had national educational systems in place prior to industrial and urban development. In the period of great activity in primary education in the United States (the 1830s and 1840s), the country was still predominantly agricultural, and urban-industrial conditions common in England were emerging only in centers such as New York, Boston, and Philadelphia.[10]

## ECONOMIC CONDITIONS AFFECTING WORKING-CLASS CHILDREN AND SCHOOLS

### THE GENERAL PATTERN: IRREGULAR ATTENDANCE AND EARLY WITHDRAWAL

From its inception, working-class education in Britain bore a relation to the labor of that class that was partially complementary but often competitive. Work called for minimum skills, which schools could impart, but provision of these seems to have been secondary to education's social-control functions. Work was frequently competitive with schooling, moreover, because it threatened continually to take children away from school.

The charity schools of the eighteenth century, organized by the Society for Promoting Christian Knowledge (founded in 1699), were not designed primarily for the children of the working poor, but rather for the pauper classes, many of whose members were on relief. One aim of these schools was to make those children literate and to motivate and fit them for work appropriate to their class. Critics of these schools feared, however, that they "unfitted" them for such work by instilling unreasonably high ambitions into them.[11] When the Sunday school movement arose in the late eighteenth century, Robert Raikes, a founder, explained that one of his motives was to control throngs of children, who, on the Sabbath, "spend their time in noise and riot, playing at chuck, and cursing and swearing in a [horrid] manner."[12] Pioneers of the movement also took for granted the inviolability of work by offering instruction on Sundays, the only day on which their potential students—both children and adults—would not be at work. The Sunday school movement thus avoided the competition between work and schooling, except that its clientele might be exhausted on the Sabbath and prefer rest and play to additional disciplined activity.

When day schools under the auspices of the religious societies began to spread in the early nineteenth century, the competition between schooling and work came plainly into view. In 1818 a select committee on the education of the poor sent questionnaires to clergymen in every parish in Britain asking about the education of youth. The clergymen appended additional comments on the condition of their parishes. The repetition of the statement that the economic exigencies facing the poor discouraged the education of their children is remarkable. Consider only a few examples:

For the county of Bedford, parish of Pertenhall: "The boys are taken in to husbandry work at 7 or 8 years old, and the girls are put to the lace pillow at an early age, so that the time for education is short; and after the children are sent to work, they depend chiefly on the Sunday school."

For the county of Lancaster, parish of Ashton-under-Lyne: "The poorer classes . . . being generally weavers, are most desirous of obtaining instruction for their children, but being compelled to put them to labour at an early age, the only means they can avail themselves of, are the Sunday schools."

For the county of Gloucester, parish of Stapleton: "The extreme indigence of parents compels them to procure employment for their children as soon as they can get the most trifling wages."

For the county of Cornwall, parish of Illogan: "Many of the poor classes have not the means of educating their children, nor do they seem desirous of possessing them, as their time could not be spared from the mines, whither they send them to work at a very early age."[13]

The same themes appear in parliamentary inquiries into education in 1834, 1835, and 1837–38, even though those committees focused more on the quality of schooling and the qualifications of teachers.[14] The new factory inspectors and others reported that workers in the cotton-textile industry were indifferent or hostile to the factory legislation of 1833 because its provisions for compulsory schooling deprived them of their children's potential earnings.[15] The parliamentary inquiry into children's employment in the mining districts in 1842 documented that the early employment of children drew them from the day schools. This limited the educational experience of many to the Sunday schools, "which in no way atones for the early removal of children from the day schools."[16] The same pattern appeared when the commissioners on trades and manufactures reported on calico making, straw plaiting, card setting, and other industries in 1843. The commissioners concluded: "Such is the neglect of the Children and Young Persons employed in Trades and Manufactures, that in some districts, out of the whole number of Children employed in labour, scarcely more than one-half are receiving instruction either in day or Sunday Schools; in others, two-thirds, when examined, were found unable to read; and in one, the great majority are receiving no instruction at all."[17]

When inspection of state-aided voluntary schools began in 1840, the inspectors reiterated the themes of irregular attendance and early withdrawal. Commenting on the schools of London, HMI Frederick Cook complained:

> We not only lose our children at a very early age, without any systematic means, or indeed, for the most part, without any kind of means of keeping up an intercourse with them after leaving school, but . . . a fearfully large proportion of poor children either do not enter our schools at all, or remain in them so short a time, that any expectation of their receiving real benefit from the instruction therein given must be a mere illusion.[18]

This pattern of early withdrawal persisted. Official figures for inspected schools indicated that in the late 1850s and 1860s about 70 percent of all pupils were under ten years of age.[19]

Seldom was irregularity of attendance or early leaving mentioned without noting its economic causes. HMI H. W. Bellairs enunciated the principle simply: "The demand for juvenile labour being great, it follows that a large proportion of juveniles will be withheld from the day school." [20] HMI John Morell said the main reasons for keeping children from school were the need for girls to care for younger children or to help their mothers in other ways, and the ability of boys to earn money very early.[21] Economic opportunities always appeared to be at the center of the problem. For Wales, HMI H. Longueville Jones reported:

> [The difficulty in attendance], which probably is met with more or less in all districts, has been increased during the last year . . . by the scarcity of adult labour, which certainly has not been equal to the marketable demand. In many localities I have found boys of twelve years old earning from 3s. to 3s. 6d. a week; in some towns and mining districts from 5s. to 6s.; and in a peculiar instance, in Flintshire, the managers informed me, last winter, that lads of this age were gaining no less than 9s. a week in colliery operations. Under such temptations as these, it is no wonder that children should be drawn away from school at a premature period of their physical as well as their mental development.[22]

These kinds of statements continue to appear in the inspectors' reports throughout the 1850s.[23] The Newcastle Commission reiterated the negative relationship between the work and schooling of the young.[24] Kay-Shuttleworth testified that the higher the children's wages, the more likely parents were to take them out of school.[25] Finally, a recent study of the quality of childhood in working-class families in the nineteenth century as reflected in autobiographies of working people indicates "the subordination of education to the demands of the family economy." [26]

The problem of work's interference with children's education seemed so intractable that many observers were pessimistic about it. HMI Henry Mosely said in 1850 that the withdrawal of children from school at an early age was "the *great* discouragement of the friends of education; it is the *hopeless* side of the question. No other obstacle appears to them altogether insurmountable but this." [27] And in 1858 W. F. Kalper, speaking on the early commencement of labor as the chief cause of absenteeism from school, said simply, "I am not sanguine enough to expect that this hindrance will ever be removed." [28]

The general evidence gathered up to the middle decades of the nineteenth century thus seems consistent. The involvement of the working-class family in wage-earning activities created strong countertendencies to the efforts of the reformers and the wealthy to deliver education to the working classes. It is difficult to establish exact secular trends in this tug-of-war between work and schooling. However, a few observations are possible. With the extension and consolidation of factory legislation, especially in the 1860s, managers in the affected industries discharged children to conform with the law or to avoid the cost and inconvenience of guaranteeing the education of their young employees. As a result, the interference of work with schooling receded as a problem. (A new problem tended to rise in its place—namely, an increase in the number of children who were neither at work nor at school.)[29] This also meant that the average age of children in school appeared to rise. Comparing its work with that of the 1843 Children's Employment Commission, a parallel commission in the 1860s reported that the age at which children were being put to work "is now a little advanced." Earlier, "instances occurred in which children began work 'as early as 3 and 4 years of age; not unfrequently 5, and between 5 and 6.' Instances of children being employed below 6 appear now to be comparatively rare, except in the straw-plait schools, where children of 3 and 3½ years old were found at work for many hours together."[30]

## VARIATION BY LEVEL OF ECONOMIC ACTIVITY

It follows from the general evidence on the negative relationship between children's involvement in work and in their education that conditions of briskness and dullness of economic activity should also have affected school attendance. According to the available evidence, those effects were visible, though they varied according to the circumstances of the community and the parents.

The most general relationship is that attendance fell off when trade was brisk and rose when it was poor. In the silk district of Spitalfields in 1816, for example, a schoolmaster reported that "the silk trade at present is very dull, and does not afford much employment for children." He added that in times of greater demand, parents kept their children from school and put them to work.[31] A schoolmistress in the Wolverhampton manufacturing district estimated that if trade were to improve, "in a fortnight half the school would leave."[32] The prosperity of the early 1850s drew consistent comments to the same effect. HMI Frederick Watkins reported that the strong economic activity and the wonders of the Great Exhibition of 1851—"both of them causes of rejoicing on other accounts"—were taking children from Yorkshire schools.[33] Similar comments were heard in the prosperous year of 1853.[34] In the following year, HMI Josiah Blandford reported that in the schools for the laboring classes "the attendance is in an inverse ratio to the prosperity of the locality in which they are situated." HMI Matthew Arnold complained of the same effect in the British and Foreign Society schools.[35] When prosperity also brought inflation (as in the Crimean War years), the motive for removing children from schools became a double one. Demand for their labor was high, and the rising cost of provisions made the family's need for their wages greater.[36] In 1861, which was a year of "greater unalloyed commercial success than any previous year in the memory of man," there were "irresistible" opportunities for employment for children, and more frequent complaints than usual from teachers about attendance.[37]

There is also evidence that attendance increased when trade was sluggish. HMI J. S. Laurie hinted at this relationship when he said that "even when the labour market is glutted by redundant supply, or somewhat depressed by slightness of trade, attendance does not decline." The more provident parent, he added, acknowledged that schooling might be of some future material benefit and "prefers to renew or prolong the term of his children's schooling, at least till the avenues of employment be again fairly open."[38] HMI William Kennedy provided the most dramatic evidence in 1862 when the cotton famine—which arose when the North blockaded the South's ports during the U.S. Civil War—struck Lancashire:

> Hundreds of thousands are unemployed and penniless. [A year ago] the difficulty was to get persons to fill the schools. Now, schools have been thrown open freely, and the difficulty is to find rooms to hold the scholars, and teachers to instruct them. The contrast is one of the most striking that could be imagined, and especially impresses those who, like me, have it daily thrust upon their observation wherever they go. Most of the schools I go to are either crowded by scholars taken very obviously from the unemployed classes, or are partly turned into sewing schools, or into store-rooms for clothing, or into soup kitchens.[39]

He added that the invasion of these unemployed children—"strange, undisciplined scholars"—disrupted the progress of ordinary pupils.

These relations between the level of economic activity and rates of attendance appeared in both manufacturing and agricultural districts.[40] They were also witnessed in the workhouse schools, which catered to the most destitute children. During the 1850s, the inspectors reported that these schools emptied in times of prosperity, so that the workhouse teacher was sometimes "left with a small number of minute and illiterate children, but little removed from the grade of infants."[41] In 1859 HMI Edward Tufnell, a workhouse inspector, noticed a decrease of about 20 percent in attendance. He attributed this to the lowered price of provisions and the diminished need for parents to apply for support from the poor rates and turn their children over to the schools.[42]

The bulk of the evidence argues in favor of the negative relations between economic prosperity and attendance. There appear to have been a few countertendencies as well. For families in or on the margin of poverty, the schools' fees (ranging from 2*d.* to 4*d.* per week) made a significant difference. Hardship stemming from unemployment would only magnify the difficulty of paying fees. Such reasons as "the want of clothes" as a by-product of poverty also might have induced parents to keep their children home in bad times.[43] HMI Kennedy reported in 1855 that a six-month lockout in Lancashire the year before had produced a double effect. Many of the parents thrown out of employment were "unable to pay the school fees." In some places, however, school managers suspended fees in recognition of parents' difficulty in paying them. In these cases the schools were "[flooded] with young people thrown out of employ," so that they were "[kept] out of harm's way" and enabled to receive "some amount of instruction."[44] A related effect was that when parents were discharged in sluggish times, many would leave the area to seek other work, taking their children with them and away from school.[45] Finally, one inspector reported that good times benefited the education of children. The parent "begins . . . to feel more *ambition* for his family; he demands an instruction for them which goes beyond the bare elements; and if he cannot get it at one school, he feels no hesitation in paying twice as much to get it at another."[46] I shall return to this theme of parental ambition later.

VARIATION BY INDUSTRY AND REGION

To supplement further the case for the importance of labor-force involvement in the education of children, I now present a few illustrations of how attendance and withdrawal varied by industry and trade.

Lancashire offers the clearest case, because children there worked extremely long hours in the textile mills and stayed out of school altogether. The factory legislation of 1833, moreover, explicitly linked hours of work with education, requiring manufacturers to establish schools for children between the ages of eight and thirteen working in their mills, or certify that they were attending school elsewhere. This legislation had a limited effect, however, because many masters simply dismissed children, thus avoiding the nuisance of the educational requirements.[47] In addition, many masters and workmen conspired to continue the overworking of young children by falsifying their ages.[48] In 1850 HMI Kennedy expressed the view that the educational difficulties of children in Lancashire were perhaps the greatest in Britain, because "[the children's] labour is, unfortunately, so useful to the mill-owner and so profitable to their parents!"[49] In 1856 HMI Morell judged that the required half-time education for mill children was not working:

> Although [the child] *does* go to school, yet the time is shortened one-half; . . . the mind is divided between the prosecution of his industry and the attention due to his elementary studies; . . . he gets mixed up with a miscellaneous class of work people of both sexes, not always or perhaps *generally* disposed either to good habits or decent language . . . the atmosphere of the mill puts precocious ideas into his head, and gives him a distaste for all learning.[50]

A number of other, unregulated industries were noted for their demands on children's labor and the resultant diminution of their school attendance: lacemaking,[51] pottery and hardware manufacture in South Staffordshire,[52] bleaching and printworks,[53] and straw plaiting.[54]

The mining and ore-processing industries also posed problems. Coal mines were among the most notorious for their exploitation of child and female labor, and legislation regulating its employment was passed in 1842. Yet an assistant commissioner found many children still at work in the pits in the late 1850s.[55] There were important differences according to type of mining. In 1843 the Children's Employment Commission reported a "gratifying contrast" between children in tin, copper, lead, and zinc mines and those in coal mines. The main reasons given were that "mining labour commences at a considerably later age than colliery labour, and that in its own nature is less oppressive."[56] In both coal and iron mining, children were drawn from school during the working day. In addition, "the fatigue produced by the labour is in general so great, that they cannot, with any advantage, attend School after the work of the day is over."[57]

Inspectors' complaints of irregular attendance and early withdrawal in the agricultural districts were also frequent.[58] Problems in those areas focused on irregular attendance associated with the seasonal demands on children's labor. Visiting districts of Scotland, HMI Edward Woodford explained the very low attendance of his remote agricultural schools by noting that his annual visit occurred in autumn: "[It] is only in the winter and spring quarters that the country schools, and more especially those in the Highlands, are well attended. This arises primarily from the presence of many at this season, who, in summer, are engaged in farm or other work." [59] For counties in the West of England, HMI Bellairs recited a kind of desperate, month-by-month series of demands on young people: preparing hop poles, bark stacking, grain seeding, working the hop ground, wheat hoeing, hop harvesting, fruit harvesting, and cider making. In certain years this yielded "a twelve-month's cycle of harvest from the beginning to the end of the year." [60] In some agricultural areas, children also worked in nonseasonal cottage industries, such as making pillow lace, straw plaiting, and gloving. [61] In the 1850s and 1860s, public attention turned to a special variant of educational problems: the agricultural gangs, or "public gangs." In some of the eastern counties, employers conscripted children of both sexes between six and thirteen for agricultural work. A parliamentary commission complained in 1867 that these gangs were corrupting the morals of the young and added that "the gang system, where it prevails to any important extent, is a great obstacle to education." [62] The 1867 Gangs Act laid down regulations governing the size, sexual composition, and age of these agricultural groups.

While agricultural employment had an adverse effect on attendance, [63] its effect on early withdrawal was apparently less than in manufacturing areas. Ralph Lingen, a Welsh education commissioner in 1847, noted this relationship in Glamorganshire (heavily industrialized), Carmarthenshire, and Pembrokeshire (less so). In all three counties, more than half the scholars were between five and ten years of age. However, in Glamorganshire the percentage of the children over ten was smaller than in the other two. He accounted for this fact by noting that "in Glamorganshire labour very soon becomes valuable (a boy of 11 or 12 can earn from 5s. to 7s. per week), and manufacturing employment is not suspended by the vicissitudes of the seasons, so as to afford more leisure at one time of the year than at another for a person to go to school again." [64]

VARIATION BY SEX

The effects of the labor market are further elucidated by evidence of sex differences in families' sending children to school or keeping them out. In 1816 the master of a Lancasterian school in Spitalfields indicated that in good times all family members who were able to work did so, and that under those conditions, "one at least in most large families is necessarily detained at home." [65] The likely implication is that this would be either the mother or an older daughter, to keep the household and

TABLE 24  PROPORTIONS OF VARIOUS COHORTS OF
STUDENTS IN AGRICULTURAL AND INDUSTRIAL MINING
POOR LAW UNIONS, WALES, 1858

| | Age (years) | | | | | | | | | | | | | |
|---|---|---|---|---|---|---|---|---|---|---|---|---|---|---|
| | Under 3 | 3–6 In-clusive | 7 | 8 | 9 | 10 | 11 | 12 | 13 | 14 | 15 | Over 15 | Total Number of Children |
| *Agricultural Unions (58 schools)* | | | | | | | | | | | | | |
| Males | .79 | 12.7 | 10.5 | 11.3 | 13.1 | 12.7 | 10.9 | 9.0 | 8.4 | 5.0 | 3.4 | 2.1 | 1,772 |
| Females | 1.1 | 16.2 | 11.1 | 11.1 | 13.0 | 12.2 | 9.6 | 9.5 | 7.0 | 4.8 | 12.0 | 2.2 | 1,346 |
| *Industrial Mining Unions (59 schools)* | | | | | | | | | | | | | |
| Males | 3.0 | 23.1 | 13.8 | 16.6 | 13.1 | 11.2 | 8.3 | 4.6 | 3.1 | 2.1 | 1.3 | 1.3 | 3,535 |
| Females | 3.8 | 26.1 | 11.2 | 12.9 | 10.3 | 8.4 | 8.9 | 6.5 | 5.6 | 3.5 | .92 | 2.1 | 3,137 |

SOURCE: *Parliamentary Papers*, 1861, 21, pt. 2, p. 469.

tend to those "who may not be old enough to work." In 1837 a witness before a select committee on education pointed to the problem of early withdrawal for both sexes, but noted a difference: "[parents send their children to] dame schools until they are six or seven years of age, and then they have them home to nurse, or they send them to a neighbour to assist in nursing, or they get them employment as errand-boys." [66]

Beryl Madoc-Jones analyzed the records of one National Society school in the 1830s to determine "reasons for leaving" and found that 57 percent of the boys, but only 10 percent of the girls, gave work as the reason; 27 percent of the girls and 2 percent of the boys gave "service" or "helping at home and child-minding" as reasons. [67]

The reports of the school inspectors noted the early withdrawal of girls to mind younger children, [68] though sometimes other lodgers or grandparents did this when the mother worked. [69] After analyzing attendance figures drawn from the census of 1851, Horace Mann concluded that "girls are taken away from school in very great numbers at a very early age to attend to various household avocations." [70] The Newcastle Commission commented on the same pattern, noting, however, that the practice also applied in certain cases to boys. [71] Girls were kept out of school both to assist in household chores and to work as nursemaids at 6d. per week plus food. [72] In some industries, such as lacemaking, girls were more commonly sent out to work, but this, too, constituted an interference with their education. [73]

Evidence showing the combined effect of sex and type of work appears in a report on conditions in Wales submitted to the Newcastle Commission. The investigator (Assistant Commissioner John Jenkins) secured educational data on several agricultural Poor Law Unions in North Wales (Corwen, Dolgelly, Bala, and Ffestiniog), a mixed mining/manufacturing and agricultural section (Neath), and a mining and manufacturing section (Merthyr Tydfil). Jenkins compared the agricultural unions with the other two with respect to the proportion of students of each age in school. The results are given in table 24. The manufacturing and mining unions showed a large proportion of the very young in school, as well as a tendency for children to fall out rapidly around nine and ten years of age. In the agricultural unions a higher proportion of the children stayed on to eleven, twelve, thirteen, and even fourteen years of age. This result is consistent with Lingen's report a decade earlier. In the agricultural unions, the differences between the sexes are not significant, whereas in the manufacturing areas girls appear to have been pulled out between the ages of seven and ten (presumably to tend to younger siblings and assist the mother at home). For older children, the sex proportions change in the manufacturing districts, with more boys leaving and more girls staying in school through the ages thirteen and fourteen. (As a rule, farm girls, the main source of supply for domestic service in the nineteenth century, did not go into service until after age fifteen).[74]

With respect to daily attendance, there was little difference between the agricultural and manufacturing/mining unions. The figures fluctuated between 70 and 77 percent of enrollment in both types of districts. Jenkins describes the reasons for nonattendance:

> [Absence arises] either from the withdrawal of the child from school for a continuous period of greater or less duration, or from irregular attendance carried over the year or throughout the whole school period. The former is most generally the case in North Wales, where children are withdrawn from school at the most pressing seasons for agricultural operations, and the latter in the manufacturing and mixed districts.[75]

### CONTEMPORARY ACCOUNTS OF THE PROBLEM

The apparent inability or unwillingness of much of the working class to participate in the educational system loomed large in the minds of those who were promoting it. Their frustration with this situation produced efforts to explain what the problem was and to assign responsibility and blame for it. However, little consensus emerged among contemporaries as to the causes of the failures of education on the demand side. Without attempting initially to evaluate the diverse and competing explanations, I merely present a sample of them.

Some observers commented on how unfriendly the culture of the working classes was to the education of their children. The traditional hostility to "learning" in isolated rural communities is well documented.[76] Commentators on the urban working classes noted a similar suspicion of education, as well as the drawing power of work, which parents and peers alike saw as a sign of independence and maturity.[77] This cultural resistance, if it can be so termed, entered some of the inspectors' "explanations" of attendance problems. Some of these accounts were little more than moral condemnations. HMI Morell spoke of "the *apathy or cupidity of parents,* who have no interest in seeing their children instructed, or would rather put their little earnings into their pockets at the week's end."[78] In a similar vein, HMI Bellairs argued that "juvenile labour and the indifference of careless and dishonest parents are the causes of our schools being so imperfectly filled." [79] HMI John Norris suggested that of all of the hindrances to teachers' efforts to secure regular and prolonged attendance, the greatest was "the want of cooperation of the children's parents." [80]

HMI Frederick Watkins evoked a generational argument, arguing that children's earnings and independence enabled them to rebel successfully against parents:

> What the [bread-winning] child wills, *that* the parent must do, and in fact *does;* and where there are three or four of these little tyrants in the family, who know their own value, and are determined to act upon it, the confusion that ensues is most miserable and degrading. Does the parent wish the child to be punctual at its half-school time? to attend the Sunday-school? not to remain in the streets after dark? to go to bed betimes? to give up the company of wicked disreputable children? He may command all this, but the truth is, that the child will not obey him; and, moreover, glories in his disobedience. [81]

Watkins added that the peer culture of work also drew youths away from the school scene:

> The young child at 11 or 12 years of age (not infrequently at 9 or 10) is launched, rudely enough, into the world of labour. The boy finds himself surrounded by big boys, whose manners he admires, and whose example he follows. I need not say what sort of a model he generally has before him. Perhaps he becomes a satellite of some bigger, rougher, more lawless lad than the rest, who is a hero in his own eyes. He imitates his dress, and repeats his slang. He looks up to him as his teacher, and is his scholar; not, as at school, a listless uninterested learner, but giving him all his attention. . . . Nor does it fare much otherwise with the girl. . . . She, too, imitates, naturally enough, the dress and the manners, the new bonnet, and the idle talk of those who are older than herself. She unlearns from them what she has learned at school and soon becomes such as they are. [82]

Others put the onus for poor attendance not on the clients but on the teacher. Many witnesses before the parliamentary commissioners between 1834 and 1837 characterized the teacher—whether accurately or not—as ignorant, as one who had failed in other callings, and as one incapable of commanding the respect of parents and children. [83] Kay-Shuttleworth maintained that the superior class of teachers to be created by the normal schools authorized in 1846 would command the respect of the poor: "To make every elementary school a scene of exertion, from which the highest ranks of teachers may be entered by the humblest scholar, is to render the profession of school masters popular among the poor, and to offer their children the most powerful incentives to learning."[84] He promised that the resulting efficiency of the schools would "increase the period of school attendance for the children."[85] Yet a decade later HMI W. J. Unwin was concerned about early removal and urged "that the office of the teacher ought to be raised in public estimation, in order that his influence might be rendered more powerful than it has hitherto been."[86]

Other inspectors regarded the problem as arising from necessity, especially on the part of the poorest among the working classes. Certainly many working people themselves viewed the matter that way. When he was asked by a parliamentary committee in 1857 about sending children to work, a bleacher replied simply that "[when] a father of a lot of children cannot get bread, he is willing to send them to work young."[87] HMI Watkins wondered "what can fairly be expected" other than defective education when "the mill, or the mine, or the loom, the 'care of younger children,' or 'assistance in the parents' labour,' carry away the child?"[88] James Mitchell, reporting to the Commission on Mines, acknowledged that with the poverty of the parents and the demand for boy labor in South Staffordshire, "I fear that it would not be practicable to restrain boys of 10 to 14 from going down into the mines."[89]

Still others suggested the problems arose not from morality or natural necessity but, rather, from systemic features of the capitalist labor market. Inspectors frequently referred to the impossibility of regular attendance as arising from two sorts of irregularity in family life. The first was the periodic unemployment of the parents, which meant increased pressure on the children to take on work and leave school. The second was the migration of parents and their children from community to community to change jobs.[90] HMI Bellairs, however, identified a range of larger *structural* constraints that crippled the struggle to secure attendance on the part of working-class children:

> I have never yet seen it laid down with sufficient clearness that there is this antagonism between the material interests of the poor, the laws of political economy in a mere productive point of view, and the objects of educationalists. Political economy would seem to require the greatest possible amount of goods at the least possible expense. Experience shows that, in some branches of industry, children are less expensive agents in production than men. Hence their selection by the producer. The earnings of the adult operative are insufficient to support himself and *children* up to fourteen years of age, hence the removal of them from school in order to meet the wants of his household. Compel them to go to school, and you drive the family to the workhouse.[91]

To put this antagonism in slightly different words, mid-nineteenth-century British society appeared to face four "givens":

The reluctance of the government to intervene in the market for labor.

The governing classes' traditional dread of pauperism and its supposed consequences (crime, idleness, destitution, and increased poor rates).

The structure of the labor market of the time, which called for the labor of many children and young people.

The drive on the part of working-class families to survive economically.

With such a combination it was impossible to expect any other result than the withdrawal of many children from school when economic opportunity presented, and consequent failure to attain the educationalists' goals of spreading elementary schooling among the masses.

A few years after Bellairs made his observation, the Newcastle Commission commented on the same issue. The commissioners made a distinction between "the independent poor" on the one hand and "paupers" and "vagrants and criminals" on the other, acknowledging that different considerations applied to the two. In referring to the independent poor, the commissioners reiterated the range of facts reported by the inspectors. They indicated "but little conflict of opinion" about the motives of parents in removing their children from school at an early age. All agreed "that the children are removed for the sake of the wages which they earn, or of their services at home." [92] These motives operated in different ways in agriculture, manufacturing, mining, and various urban occupations, but the general theme was the same.

Moreover, the Newcastle Commission confronted the contradiction that Bellairs had identified, and attempted to resolve it. In priority, the commissioners observed, "[independence] is of more importance than education; and if the wages of the child's labour are necessary, either to keep the parents from the poor rates, or to relieve the pressure of severe and bitter poverty, it is far better that it should go to work at the earliest age at which it can bear the physical exertion than that it should remain at school." [93] In the words of Bellairs, the "material interests of the poor" should take priority over the "objects of educationalists."

The commissioners went on to reject any scheme of general compulsion (on the Prussian model), which they believed would come into collision with "the constitution of English society and habits and feelings of the people."[94] Finally, they rejected any compulsory education imposed by employers, unless it was contractually agreed upon by both employers and employees.[95] In these statements, the commissioners were proclaiming that the "principles of political economy" (including the noninterference of government in contractual arrangements) should also take precedence over the objects of the educationalists.

In voicing these priorities, the Newcastle commissioners reaffirmed that the capitalist wage structure and the freedom of the family to determine the activities of its own children were inviolable parameters. Educational changes should take place *within* those parameters. It can be argued, moreover, that the government's policy was based on a paradox from the outset of its support for voluntary education in 1833 until the legislation relating to compulsory attendance in the 1870s.[96] It encouraged the "supply side" of educational development—that is, building schools, training teachers, and supplementing teachers' salaries. At the same time, it offered educational services to the poor under labor-market and other institutional conditions that it was not willing to change, and within which, it was known, many of the poor would refuse, or partake minimally of, those services.

## PRIMARY EDUCATION AND SOCIAL MOBILITY

In the observations above, among the most frequently mentioned points was that the parents of working-class children did not value education, that they were indifferent to their children's education. As HMI Watkins's remarks in 1845 indicate, such statements often constituted little more than a direct moral rebuke:

> We blame masters, and we blame monitors, and we punish children; we find fault with methods and systems, and rooms and situations; but we often leave untouched the tap-root of all the evil—the parent. This is sadly true. And I am not now speaking of the bad example too often set at home by the uneducated father or mother to children rightly trained in school. I do not now allude to the daily unteaching of that which is carefully taught there; but I state the *indifference* of the parent as the cause of the child's irregularity and want of punctuality at school.[97]

In one respect, the accusations of indifference of Watkins and others are unsatisfactory explanations, because they do not move beyond mere rebuke and pose the question, why should that indifference—if it existed—prevail? The labor-market deterrents just explored yield part of the answer: the family's economic survival did not allow it the luxury of being other than indifferent. We should also ask, however, if and how parents and their children envisioned primary education as an investment in the children's future. This question leads directly to the issues of material and social improvement and social mobility.

Even acknowledging the phenomenon of social mobility and class restructuring over the centuries in Britain, we must recognize the castelike character of that country's inherited class system. We observed this in the educational ideologies espoused in the late eighteenth and early nineteenth centuries. Both Tory apprehensions (that education would fire unwanted ambitions among the poor) and Whig assurances (that education would encourage the poor to be content with their place) reveal the preoccupation with "station." Politicians, clergy, and educational leaders argued that a religious basis for education was important because it instilled the virtues of humility and deference. Throughout the century, the insistence on only the basics of literacy and numeracy—and moral and religious instruction—implied an education for a station. Finally, the corresponding suspicion of "fancy subjects" and of "overeducated" teachers who would "overeducate" poor children added to the endorsement of the idea of a class order that maintained itself over the generations.[98]

At the same time the nineteenth century showed many signs of greater opening up, especially at the upper levels. Wealthy merchant families had long been able to move into the aristocracy by marriage and the purchase of land over generations. The widespread adoption of competitive examinations, beginning in midcentury, stressed advancement according to talents rather than position.[99] Slowly, also, the elite universities became more permeable as class and religious barriers to entry began to erode. In the early industrial revolution many of the inventors and entrepreneurs came from artisan backgrounds. And the "success" literature of the Victorian period, epitomized in the writings of Samuel Smiles, stressed the self-improvement of, and some mobility for, the poor.[100]

All these complexities considered, it remains true that education as such did not hold out much promise for economic and social mobility for the working classes in nineteenth-century British society. The Taunton Commission's statement correlating class, age of school leaving, curriculum, and occupational targeting was a clear endorsement of class fixity in education and class immobility.[101] It was appropriate that an American, Horace Mann, was the one who reminded his British hosts in 1851 that indifference toward education was all they could reasonably expect from their working classes. The reason for this was that education led them nowhere:

> The great fact that seems to be intruded on our notice is that the children's absence from, or a very brief continuance at, school, is *mainly* owing to the slight esteem which parents have for the education itself . . . [this indifference] principally flows from an idea prevalent amongst the labouring classes, that instruction *beyond a certain point* can never be of any practical utility to those of their condition; for in general a parent, in whatever station, takes himself or his own social *status* as the standard up to which he purposes to educate his offspring. . . . It is hardly . . . a matter for surprise . . . that the working classes—seeing that the purely mental training which their children pass through in the present class of schools can rarely exercise an influence upon their future temporal prosperity, and having for some generations past been tutored not to look *beyond their station*—should esteem a thorough education of this character to be not worth the time and money needed for its acquisition.[102]

Inspectors and others wrote along the same lines in the 1850s. HMI Edward Tinling observed that "the character of instruction given in our schools is not such as to bring back an immediate return; and little or no reward is held out in the way of prizes in afterlife to the better trained and educated children." [103] HMI Watkins summarized the views of parents in Yorkshire: "As soon as the child can read a little, and write a little, and count a little, as they call it, he is good for work in life." [104] In a similar vein, HMI John Norris said that the parents in his rural parishes "do not want contented labourers to be made into discontented scholars, but they want bad labourers to be educated into good labourers." He regretted that the young were not exposed to "*schooling such as will 'pay.'* " [105] The Reverend J. P. Hastings spoke of the fact that "our [working-class] schools lead nowhere" as an "almost insuperable difficulty":

> When a son of working parents has had his little day of success at the top of National school, suppose him to know geography, grammar, arithmetic and even political economy better than many a poll-man of Oxford or Cambridge, where does it lead him? As a plowboy or artisan . . . wherein is he benefitted?[106]

To note these comments is to make no assertion about the actual level of occupational mobility in Britain in the mid nineteenth century. It is to say, however, that most parents and children of the working classes perceived no realistic connection between schooling and social and economic betterment.

Two aspects of the educational scene in the mid nineteenth century, however, touched the issue of schooling and advancement directly. The first was the opportunity for a working-class child to move through an elementary school, become a pupil-teacher, go on to a teacher-training college, and then become an elementary school teacher. I shall return to this special line of advancement in greater detail in the next chapter. The second example is a kind of running problem that affected the supply of pupil-teachers in the 1850s. This stemmed from the call for educational skills necessary for employment opportunities in other, competing lines of work.

As a rule the inspectors endorsed the pupil-teacher system as a beneficial educational device providing an opportunity for bright young children, mainly from the working classes, to improve themselves.[107] Matthew Arnold called the pupil-teachers "the sinews of English primary instruction" and "the grand merit of our English State-system."[108] Writing in 1848, HMI Morell saw the pupil-teacher system as a kind of counterforce to the apathy and cupidity of parents, "who either have no interest in seeing their children instructed, or would rather put their little earnings into their pockets at the week's end." He regarded the pupil-teacher system as "opening an hounourable sphere of effort and remuneration" for the working classes. Then, in a burst of enthusiastic hyperbole, Morell asserted that "[there] is no parent, however poor, whose child has not the chance of being *apprenticed* to the worthy and honourable profession of a *teacher*." And in a final, hopeful comment, he wrote: "The time, we trust, is not far distant when no parent, however ignorant himself, shall be insensible to the importance of education to the temporal as well as the moral advancement and respectability of his own family."[109] Lingen reported on the general popularity of the pupil-teacher system among parents of schoolchildren.[110]

Given this general popularity of the teacher-apprenticeship system, it is understandable that alarm was expressed when it came under threat. This alarm was most visible when the Revised Code of 1862 began to reduce pupil-teachers' recruitment and remuneration.[111] In addition, however, the prosperity of the 1850s and 1860s also posed problems for the pupil-teacher system. As early as 1848, HMI Henry Moseley reported that "the total number [of pupil teachers] apprenticed this year would have been much larger but for the increased demand for juvenile labour." [112] A few years later, HMI Frederick Cook warned that the education being received by pupil-teachers would push boys toward places in the "mercantile and industrial community" and girls to "those branches of business which require skillful accounts and intelligent, well-trained, and trustworthy agents." [113] In the same year, HMI Watkins reported evidence of some pupil teachers being "withdrawn from the apprenticeship" for employment elsewhere. [114] In 1854, HMI Kennedy complained of the drawing power of employment in offices in Lancashire. [115] Two years later, he reiterated his complaint, noting that the demand for boys in offices and other employment was increasing because youths were being drawn off into the militia. [116] In the meantime, HMI D. J. Stewart noted that in the same northern counties, boys were going into telegraph work in railway offices. Such employment gave earlier certainty to a life career than did an apprenticeship to teaching, even though in adult life a schoolmaster made a higher salary. [117] In 1858, HMI Arnold reported that in the London districts, children "can earn so much, and can earn it so young, and in so many ways," that "parents [are] unwilling to permit their engagement as pupil-teachers at the present rates of remuneration." [118] HMI Thomas Marshall wrote in the same year that "pupil-teachers are about the worst paid class of labourers in the country." [119]

The complaints about the recruitment of pupil-teachers in the face of competing demands were repeated in 1860 and 1861. [120] As the Committee of Council's economy measures were beginning to take effect in 1861 (the number of pupil-teachers per master or mistress was limited to four), a number of inspectors objected. HMI Moncreiff said: "As to *pupil-teachers*, I do not see how any reduction can be made, either in their stipends, or in the number allowed. The former are (for boys at least) as low as they could be put in these parts, too low indeed to compete with the labour market." [121] The Revised Code aggravated the continuing difficulty of drawing children into training because of competition with better paying opportunities elsewhere. [122]

The pressure on the pupil-teacher recruitment stemming from market forces was by no means uniform. The north and the industrial areas in general felt it more than other regions. [123] In addition, the competition affected boys more than girls. HMI Cook pointed out in 1857 that, especially with the growth of infant schools (taught almost exclusively by women), "the future prospects of female teachers certainly exceed what any of them could anticipate in other employments." On the other hand, "the parents of a clever and good lad make a real sacrifice when they consent to his apprenticeship." [124] A year later, Arnold spoke of the

TABLE 25    PUPIL-TEACHERS BY GENDER,
            SELECTED YEARS

|        | Males  | Females |
|--------|--------|---------|
| 1849   | 2,424  | 1,156   |
| 1850   | 3,070  | 4,660   |
| 1851   | 3,657  | 1,950   |
| 1852   | 4,011  | 2,169   |
| 1853   | 4,308  | 2,604   |
| 1854   | 4,500  | 3,096   |
| 1855   | 4,910  | 3,614   |
| 1856   | 5,800  | 4,445   |
| 1857   | 6,773  | 5,449   |
| 1858   | 7,673  | 6,351   |
| 1859   | 8,219  | 7,005   |
| 1870   | 6,384  | 8,228   |
| 1880   | 10,822 | 21,137  |
| 1896   | 7,737  | 28,137  |

SOURCES: *Parliamentary Papers*, 1861, 21, p. 638; Pamela Horn, *Education in Rural England, 1800–1914* (Dublin: Gill & Macmillan, 1978).
    NOTE: The years 1849–59 are for England, Wales, and Scotland; 1870, 1880, and 1896 are for England and Wales only.

difficulty of getting boys to serve as apprentices, but the same did not apply to girls; "their labour being less valuable, and the field of employment open to them less wide, it is easy to obtain girls in sufficient number as apprentices."[125] In 1859, when Moncreiff was considering ways of economizing on pupil-teachers, he suggested reducing the stipends of female pupil-teachers, indicating that their numbers were ample.[126] The sex differential in supply continued through the 1860s.[127] The general drift in proportions of male and female pupil-teachers from 1847 to 1870 is depicted in table 25. The steady increase in females reflects both the increase in demand for schoolmistresses, and the diversion of males into other service occupations. The market for juvenile labor, as reflected in these figures, thus appears to be one factor that contributed to the feminization of the teaching profession in the late nineteenth century.[128]

    In this section I have dealt with two "exceptions" to the rule that working-class education had little connection with higher job aspirations and social mobility for the working classes. The movement into schoolteaching and industrial service jobs in industry did constitute a case of upward mobility from blue-collar to white-collar positions. Three concluding observations on this topic are in order. First, when such opportunities became available, many working-class parents availed themselves of them, sometimes at some short-term financial sacrifice to themselves. In general, however, those pupils who continued their education through pupil-teachership and became available for education-related upward mobility came from the upper levels of the working classes.[129] Second, even in these two areas, short-term economic and security considerations often took precedence over longer-term career opportunities. Third, education-related service occupations grew at a rapid rate in the last half of the century and thereafter.[130] More young pupils could avail themselves of the education necessary, and, as a result, the functional connection between education and economic opportunities became much stronger than it was in the earlier development of English capitalism.

## ANTIDOTES FOR IRREGULAR ATTENDANCE AND EARLY WITHDRAWAL

If the diagnosis of the Newcastle Commission expressed a consensus of the ruling groups of the time, those groups would appear to have been reluctant to alter the major structural conditions that generated the "twin evils" of irregular attendance and early withdrawal. These conditions were, first, a capitalist labor market that dictated the employment of large numbers of women and children as workers; second, perceptions of the legitimacy of employing many family members as a way of keeping families "independent" (that is, off the support of the poor rates); and third, the unacceptability of any principle of compulsory attendance. To describe this situation as bluntly as possible, the Newcastle Commission admitted defeat in handling the "twin evils." As long as the underlying structural conditions remained unchanged, these evils would persist. Given those conclusions, all that could be done was to scratch away at the problems in ways that were necessarily limited in their effectiveness. In this section I shall describe these antidotes.

### INFANT SCHOOLS

The idea of the infant school—education and care of very young children—traces to the name of Jean Frederic Oberlin of Strasbourg in the late eighteenth century. In England it made its appearance in the New Lanark experiment of Robert Owen. A school based on Owenite principles was opened in London in 1818, with James Mill and Brougham among its leading sponsors. The London experiment generated an enthusiastic movement, with Infant School Societies springing up around the country.[131] This movement received further impetus from the work of David Stowe in Scotland, who developed a system of training and established the Glasgow Infant School in 1826,[132] and in England from the work of Samuel Wilderspin (1791–1866) in the 1820s. The latter advertised his schools as a means for preventing crime among the young by instilling into them principles of obedience, order, "delicacy, cleanliness, and kindness," as well as the rudiments of arithmetic, reading, and religion.[133]

In the infant schools of the 1830s, the average age of entrance was two years; that of leaving, seven.[134] These schools overlapped in clientele with the dame schools, whose proprietors viewed them with some hostility.[135] The Manchester Statistical Society and the parliamentary select committee on education of 1835 both regarded infant schools as much superior to the dame schools, and recommended the displacement of the latter by the former.[136] James Kay, close to the Manchester surveys, also came out strongly for increasing the number of infant schools in his testimony before the select committee on education in 1837. He argued that they were important for employed mothers of infants, and that they "[separated] the children from the contamination of the street playground."[137] Within the infant school movement, however, a swell of criticism arose in the 1830s, mainly concerning the quality of the schools and the level of education imparted.[138] In 1836 the Evangelical wing of the Church of England started taking an interest in infant schools. The Home and Colonial Society supported them, and they began to be adopted as adjuncts to National Society day schools and Sunday schools. As a result, many of them fell under the government's funding and inspection scheme. Despite these institutional supports, the infant schools continued to present some problems. They were usually taught by unqualified women teachers who suffered under both low pay and low status. Some evidence indicates that they were not especially popular among the poor, and that they, like day schools, suffered from irregular attendance because of the parents' residential and occupational mobility and their low interest in schooling.[139]

As time went on, interest in infant schools increased among educational reformers. The basic cause for this interest, moreover, was the knowledge that day schools were most attended by very young children, and that when they reached nine or ten years of age, many were taken from school and put to work. HMI J. Bowstead made the connection in his 1854 report. He noted the aggravation of attendance problems by "every fresh demand for juvenile labour" and the unwillingness of parents to sacrifice their children's wages and "purchase education." From this he concluded that the "only practicable remedy" was to be found "in multiplying infant schools and evening classes."[140] The Newcastle Commission praised the infant schools, and endorsed them as the only feasible answer to attendance problems.

> To keep at school a boy who might be earning wages, or a girl who might help the mother in household work, must always be a sacrifice; but children under seven can earn little or nothing. . . . Infant schools, therefore, are free from competition with the employers of labour and with the requirements of the family. . . . Infant schools are also comparatively cheap, as they are usually taught by mistresses.[141]

Following on this positive recommendation, the Revised Code offered favorable terms of compensation for schools with scholars under six years of age in attendance.[142]

The movement for infant schools, which became associated with, and was displaced in some degree by, the kindergarten movement in the 1850s and thereafter, was part of a larger movement that led to the consolidation of the age of entry into full-time compulsory education at five.[143] From the standpoint of this study, the efforts to extend infant schools in the 1850s and 1860s are best understood as part of British society's rearguard battle against the overwhelming structural conditions that produced limited demand for, irregular attendance at, and short duration of elementary education. It was one of several limited attempts to overcome those intractable problems without modifying the conditions that created them.

### NIGHT SCHOOLS

Bowstead's remedies also included night schools, which can be treated in part—but only in part—as arising from the same circumstances as the infant schools. The idea of night education was not new, having been part of some of the adult education programs of religious societies and working-class scientific societies in the eighteenth century and of the Mechanics' Institutes since the 1820s.[144] However, in the mid nineteenth century, there developed a kind of night-school movement. By 1850 the National Society was speaking of the "great advance made in the number and importance of Evening Schools for adults, both in towns and rural districts." [145] The inspectors of schools noticed this development and welcomed it as a way of compensating for the withdrawal of juveniles from day schools.[146] In 1858 a minute of the Committee of Council permitted certificated teachers to superintend night schools and extended the capitation grant to them. The Revised Code further facilitated their support. Thus stimulated, night schools boasted a growth of the number of scholars in National Society schools from 54,000 in 1856 to 149,000 in 1866.[147] Yet in the latter year, the Committee of Council could describe them as "as yet in their infancy." [148]

Despite the increase, there is evidence that night schools were limited as a means of compensating for interrupted attendance at and early withdrawal from day schools.[149] The commissioners on children's employment reported in 1842 that attendance at night schools was negligible in the mining districts. They considered the experiment a doubtful one because "the children, who come home fatigued from the mines, get drowsy by the fire, and feel reluctant to go out." [150] The Newcastle Commission reported that they were difficult to establish and maintain in country districts.[151] The main limitation, however, was in the clientele they reached. HMI Kennedy reported in 1861 that night schools catered to three classes of students: first, very young persons (aged eight to twelve) who were employed during the day; second, adults whose early education had been neglected, and who attended "to pick up the rudiments of reading, writing, and arithmetic"; and third, young persons (aged thirteen to twenty-five) who wished to augment the education they had previously received at day school.[152] Helpful as schooling might have been for all these classes, it constituted a direct offsetting of labor-market interference with day-school attendance mainly with respect to the first class. So, while the Newcastle Commission endorsed the night schools, it recognized the limitations of this expedient as an antidote for the fundamental difficulties facing the elementary education of the working classes.[153]

## PRIZE SCHEMES

Some inspectors and manufacturers made efforts to devise prize schemes as a reward for school attendance and performance. Beginning around 1840, schemes of these sorts began to appear, mainly in the mining and industrial districts.[154] A plan of this sort was initiated in 1851 in South Staffordshire, and some organized efforts to institute such incentive schemes were seen in Wales and elsewhere in the 1850s.[155] Leslie Evans has gathered evidence in Wales of certain scattered efforts at mid-century in day schools supported by industrial firms. All aimed at encouraging more education among children employed in their works. Among the strategies were appointing schoolchildren to certain attractive posts, such as office clerkships, on the condition that they remain in school for a certain number of years; apprenticing promising pupils to special trades or processes in industrial works on the condition that they improve their skills through schooling; and using an educational test as a condition for employing children of ten to twelve years of age.[156] Evans gives no general assessment of these schemes except to note that they were limited in number and that they seemed to appeal to the self-interest of parents. (Incidentally, they mark another, minor "exception to the rule" in that they attempted to establish a direct link between education and occupational advance.) In mentioning prize schemes, the Newcastle Commission commented that they did good, but were very costly and were not "likely to produce much effect on the great mass [of pupils]."[157] Little more was made of prize schemes in educational commentaries and discussions, however, and HMI Cook seems to have summarized their significance accurately in 1857:

> The truth is that the parents remove their children because they contribute to the support of the family, instead of being a burden upon its resources; and the employers take them because their labour is much cheaper, and, in some respects, more valuable than that of adults. I cannot see that either of these facts is likely to be affected, or the results materially modified, by the distribution of merely honourary rewards [to school children].[158]

These schemes are significant mainly because they constituted yet another limited antidote to the problems of attendance in the 1850s.

CAPITATION PAYMENTS

In the early 1850s, the Committee of Council was enjoying general support and was asked to extend schooling as much as possible within the framework of the minutes of 1846.[159] In this context, it initiated a scheme in 1853 to grant additional payments to schools on the basis of the annual attendance of pupils. Lingen acknowledged that the intent of the scheme was to prevent the bankruptcy of some schools. (The policy thus falls into the same category as supporting more than one school in religiously divided small communities even though doing so might not be the most "efficient" policy.)[160] The scheme was called "capitation" (an appropriate name because it was a system of awards based on student head-count) and is mentioned here because of its evident objective of attacking problems of irregular attendance and early withdrawal.

Parliamentary action also influenced the introduction of capitation grants. In 1853 an education bill was introduced to provide machinery for establishing and using returns on rates for education in urban areas. In anticipation of this, the Committee of Council devised the policy of helping rural areas by capitation grants. As it turned out, the bill ultimately failed in Parliament, but the policy of capitation remained. In the beginning, then, grants were directed at small schools in agricultural districts and unincorporated towns (communities with no more than five thousand inhabitants). These localities were in any case known to have high rates of seasonal absence from school because of rural employment patterns.[161] The capitation payment was to be six shillings to boys' schools and five shillings for girls' schools with fewer than fifty pupils, with smaller payments for larger schools. The formula called for four days' attendance a week for forty-eight weeks, or 192 days per year.[162] Shortly thereafter, the Committee of Council relaxed the rule to permit 16 days of absence, or 176 days of attendance. In 1854 the provision was further modified, extending capitation grants for boys over ten for 88 instead of 176 days of attendance. The committee advertised the modification as encouraging a "system of half-time" education for schools in the affected districts.[163] (The structure of incentives reveals that the original measure was intended to address problems of irregular attendance, whereas the 1854 modification sought to address problems of early withdrawal.)

In the period immediately following the implementation of the capitation grant system, some inspectors began to question its usefulness. In 1855, HMI Josiah Blandford reported that the scheme was having little impact on agricultural districts in the Midlands because of "the small number of children whom the managers are able to return as having attended the required number of days"[164]—a symptom of the very evil that the measure was intended to alleviate. Two years later, HMI Bowstead criticized the scheme on grounds that the communities for which it was intended were often poor and struggling, and could not take advantage of it.[165]

In response to such concern, the Committee of Council extended the capitation grant system to all kinds of communities in England and Wales.[166] In the following year, the inspectors for Middlesex (Cook) and Lancashire (Kennedy) both reported that the extension was a boon to corporate areas and populous towns, and that its positive effects were already in evidence.[167] Their judgment seems to have been valid, because the sums spent on capitation grants tripled from 1856 to 1859,[168] "rising more rapidly than any other grant."[169] The Newcastle Commission feared that if the capitation grants were to increase according to their existing pattern, they would reach some £300,000 or more, and be "wastefully increased" in some respects.[170] Thus, when concerns about economy appeared in the late 1850s, the capitation grants were the first type of expenditure targeted for reduction.[171] Such grants soon vanished as part of the Revised Code's assimilation of many payments into the "payment by results" scheme. The code continued the principle, however, by making payments contingent on both examinations and attendance rates.[172]

No systematic attempts have been made to estimate the impact of the capitation grants on attendance. The persistence of complaints throughout the 1850s indicates that their impact could only have been marginal. Several other aspects of the scheme, however, command interest.

The incentive structure of capitation grants reveals that the scheme looked in the direction of compulsory attendance, because its evident intent was to spur masters and teachers to increase children's attendance. It fell short of compulsion, however. It merely held out the "carrot" of increased payment to schools rather than the "stick" of compulsion with some kind of punishment for truancy. How well that sanction worked was a matter of disagreement. Kay-Shuttleworth believed the capitation grants should never have been adopted, largely because they did not require schools to improve themselves, as the pupil-teacher provision had done.[173] HMI Frederick Temple went further, saying that capitation grants constituted a kind of gift for schools and were a disincentive inasmuch as they "diminished the proportions . . . of [private] subscriptions."[174] During his testimony before the Newcastle Commission, Lingen was implicitly criticized for extending the capitation grant system beyond small communities, because it led to supporting schools "which would be perfectly capable of continuing their operations without them." In responding, he acknowledged that in the extension "the more liberal rate [spread] to cases for which it was never meant."[175] HMI Moncreiff complained that the scheme actually backfired in some cases:

I fear that the capitation grant is sometimes injurious to discipline. Managers are afraid to insist on punctuality, cleanliness, submission to rules, &c., for fear of reducing numbers. It would be well if "a day" for capitation purposes were defined as not less than (say) five hours actually in school. Many children come in a morning not much before 10, and leave on different pretexts considerably before 12.[176]

HMI Watkins recommended to some managers that they give "some small portion of [the capitation grant]" to the children who showed regular attendance, and indicated that this "inducement and encouragement had worked to increase attendance."[177]

It is difficult to know how general such effects may have been, but the inspectors' observations permit one additional speculation. It was noted above that a likely impact of the Revised Code was to bias the class composition of elementary schools upward.[178] The mechanism was that managers and teachers paid closer attention to those scholars more likely to pass, because their institutional livelihood depended on examination results. Such scholars, moreover, were more likely to come from the higher social-class ranges of their pupils. As a corollary, the code motivated managers and teachers to neglect unreliable, shiftless, sporadically attending students because they could not be brought up to the pass level. Insofar as the capitation scheme had an impact on managers and teachers, it probably worked in the same direction. It motivated them to encourage the attendance of those pupils most likely to attain 176 days annually, and perhaps to ignore those who had no chance of doing so. This would also have an upward-biasing effect with respect to social class. Whether this speculation has historical validity probably cannot be determined with certainty, and the historical data required to assess it are probably not available. Nonetheless, the issue of the impact of different incentive schemes remains one of enduring importance. Furthermore, the topic of capitation grants touches the issue of incentives for pupils' participation in the school system and leads logically to the next items for consideration.

## ATTENDANCE FEES
## AND COMPULSORY ATTENDANCE

Two final factors that affected attendance were the direct cost of fees imposed on families with children in school,[179] and legal compulsion for children to attend school under pain of some kind of punishment. The issues surrounding these factors were not finally "solved" during the period covered by this study (1800–1870). The Education Act of 1870 gave districts the discretion to compel attendance; this provision became mandatory in 1876 and was finally made operative in 1882.[180] Fees for attending elementary schools for the working classes were not abolished until 1891. Both fees and compulsion, however, were issues of continuing concern throughout the nineteenth century.

From an early period, the two issues were linked in the minds of educational reformers and politicians. That connection seemed to develop in the following way. One argument against compulsion that appeared early concerned the independence of the family and its authority over its children. This was the most frequent argument advanced against parliamentary legislation affecting children's employment in factories in 1802, 1819, and 1833: the family should determine whether and how much its children should work.[181] The argument carried over into educational debates as well. Sturges Bourne invoked the sanctity of parental authority in opposing the compulsory features of Whitbread's proposed legislation in 1807.[182] John Roebuck's argument for compulsion in 1833—that if parents failed in their obligation to educate their children, the state should make them do it—also failed under attack.[183] As late as 1860, when the principle of noncompulsion had already been compromised in factory and pauper education, Kay-Shuttleworth posed the central issue as follows:

> The first question which meets us is, whether education ought in all cases to be regarded as a sacred function of the parent, with which none are to interfere? Is the parental authority an individual moral force which, even in the immoral, the ignorant, or those otherwise without a sense of parental obligation, may not at least be subject to the natural influence of religion, charity, the commonwealth, and of the whole of these embodied in law as the protector of childhood?[184]

The idea of the independence of the families of the poor had a double connotation. The first implication, just mentioned, was the family's power to determine its own economic and educational fate. The second was that the poor should be independent of—that is to say, not dependent on—the richer classes. More concretely, "independence" meant not making demands on the poor rates. The problem of the rates was often on the minds of the British ruling groups in the nineteenth century, and their upward spiral was a major motivating force behind many reform efforts, including the Poor Law of 1834. The implications of government support of education for the level of rates was an issue in parliamentary debates on the subject from the beginning.[185] The argument that more and better education would relieve pauperism and crime—and the rates that were required to deal with them—was a standard ingredient in educational reformers' repertoire of arguments.[186]

This idea of independence, as espoused by the ruling groups, included the assumption that the poor themselves wanted to be independent in both senses—free in decisions about themselves and their families and free from dependence on the rates. This assumption led to a number of arguments concerning the payment of school fees. The first was that the poor felt more respectable, worthy, and dignified if they paid for their education. The Reverend William Gurney expressed this sentiment in 1818 in commenting on the advantages of fees:

> From the parents [the fee] removes the unpleasant feeling of receiving charity . . . if they were in the habit of receiving even gratuitous education for their children, they might by degrees become very willing to receive pecuniary aid for the support of their families. . . . It appears also that they maintain a sort of superiority in their own minds . . . they feel, and they express frequently, that they belong to a superior class to those who are called parish children . . . this sort of pride . . . is rather desirable than otherwise, because it makes the lower classes of people aim to keep themselves in a considerable degree independent of the higher orders.[187]

Gurney argued that paying fees actually increased attendance according to school records. The principle was that "everybody values that which costs them something, more than that which costs them nothing."[188] Testimony before parliamentary bodies in the 1830s endorsed the payment of fees by invoking the same kind of arguments.[189] After 1840, the inspectors of schools argued consistently that poverty and fees were not the main deterrents to attendance. The tendency of parents to put their children to work was a much stronger force.[190] Horace Mann discounted the influence of fees except for the very poorest:

> [The inability to pay fees is] scarcely satisfactory [as an explanation] to any great extent beyond the purely *pauper* class; and indoor pauper children are already educated by the State. . . . The condition of . . . many of the *free* schools, where *no* payment is demanded of the scholar, seems to show that "poverty" is not an adequate explanation of the children's absence; for in many *free* schools, though located in the midst of populous neighbourhoods, the attendance of scholars is less numerous and much less constant than in schools which require a fee.[191]

Matthew Arnold observed that high fees brought "a better and more instructed class of children coming to schools." He noted the associated disadvantage, however, that parents who paid high fees were more likely to interfere in the work of the teacher.[192] In 1861 the Newcastle Commission reiterated the value of fees, using the familiar argument that paying them encouraged independence on the part of the poor.[193] So did the Taunton Commission in 1868, arguing that "people will learn the value of education by being perpetually urged to make the sacrifices necessary to procure it for their children."[194]

Mann was correct in noting that school fees were a deterrent to attendance for the poorest families. The inspectors noted that fees were a factor in times of high unemployment.[195] HMI Kennedy recommended against raising them, because of the negative impact it would have on the poorest families, especially in agricultural districts.[196] The inspectors' reports gave evidence that some school managers either lowered fees or remitted them altogether for the poorest children.[197] The practices of remitting fees for the very poor and charging different fees according to means persisted in the decades following the Education Act of 1870.[198]

The assumption that paying fees encouraged independence and respectability produced arguments against free education for the poor on grounds that it would pauperize them. In 1833, Roebuck attempted to deal with such arguments by asserting that if the whole educational system of education for the poor were free (as he proposed), this would remove the stigma on those currently receiving gratuitous education.[199] In a debate on the Pakington bill in 1855, J. W. Henley argued that free education would "stamp upon the education of the country the brand of pauperism."[200] The Newcastle Commission expressed the belief that gratuitous education offended "the sentiment of independence" among the working classes; parents were thus "inclined to pay as large a share as they can reasonably afford of the expense of the education of their children."[201]

Such views on independence and the value of fees can be read, with merit, as rationalizations by the wealthy of the exploitation of the poor and of the kind of educational system that the former were foisting on the latter. Be that as it may, they constituted a component of the social psychology of those in control of the educational system. These arguments, along with concerns for economy, remained the basis for charging fees—even increasing them after the Revised Code—until almost the end of the century.[202]

As is the case with other factors, the degree to which fees were a deterrent or impetus to attendance cannot be established with certainty, given the lack of systematic information. For what it is worth, however, the general consensus of the day was that, whatever the precise impact of fees on attendance, that factor was less important than the drawing power of the market for children's employment.

The arguments against compulsory attendance went beyond those emanating from the idea of parental independence. Three additional considerations came into play. The first, closely related to the idea of independence, was the assertion that compulsory education would induce poor families to take their children from work and expose them to the possibility of pauperism and dependency on the poor rates. This view was a minor extension of the Newcastle Commission's dictum that, if it came to a choice, "independence" was more important than "education."

The second consideration was a religious one. At various times we have noted the sensitivity of Nonconformists and other non-Anglican confessions about the rights of conscience. Several legislative efforts—notably in 1819 and 1843—failed because those groups feared that the proposed arrangements permitted the Church of England too much control over religious education. The many efforts to expand educational coverage by calling on local rates in the 1850s and 1860s also failed. Many religious groups objected that levying common rates raised the specter of unwilling parents paying for, and having their children exposed to, unwanted religious teaching if they attended rate-supported schools. In addition, a central feature of the battle over the conscience clause in the 1850s and 1860s was that Dissenters would, in effect, be coerced into receiving Church of England doctrine and rituals if the sole school in a small community was an Anglican one.[203]

The proposal for compulsory attendance was an item on the agenda of the National Education League in the late 1860s. The provision for compulsion on a local, discretionary basis in the Forster bill of 1870 brought the conscience issue to a point of crisis. It had to do so, because that bill contained rate-support, religious teaching, and compulsion in one package. That crisis was resolved—or, rather, relieved to the point where the bill could be passed in Parliament—by several compromises. These included provision for nondenominational teaching in rate-supported board schools, the timetable conscience clause, and the prohibition of rate aid for denominational schools.[204] Even after this legislation passed, the problem of conscience persisted. Article 25 of the Education Act permitted boards to pay the fees of needy children in denominational schools. Nonconformists objected because that rate money was financing denominational teaching. Some district boards dominated by Nonconformists refused to make such payments.[205]

The third argument arose from the general concern over government intervention—strengthened by the doctrines of laissez-faire—and assertions about the "character" of English people and English institutions. Many educational partisans looked to Prussia as a model at various times during the century, but their view of it was often tinged with ambivalence. On the one hand, they admired the Prussian system for its comprehensiveness, effectiveness, and mode of dealing with religious conflict.[206] On the other hand, they regarded its compulsory features as somehow "un-English." Speaking in 1834, the lord chancellor balked at the notion of compulsion:

> Suppose the people of England were taught to bear [compulsory education], and to be forced to educate their children by penalties, education would be made absolutely hateful in their eyes, and would speedily cease to be endured. They who have argued in favour of such a scheme from the example of a military government like that of Prussia, have betrayed, in my opinion, great ignorance of the nature of Englishmen.[207]

The Newcastle Commission also rejected the idea of compulsory education because it was incompatible with English ideals and institutions. And in 1867, Matthew Arnold, who favored compulsion, nevertheless commented on its difficulties in practice. In Prussia, he observed,

> education is not flourishing because it is compulsory, it is compulsory because it is flourishing. Because people there really prize instruction and culture . . . they have no difficulty in imposing on themselves the rule to get instruction and culture. In this country people prefer . . . politics, station, business, money-making, leisure and many other things [to instruction and culture]; and til we cease to prefer these things, a law which gives instruction the power to interfere with them . . . cannot be relied upon to hold its ground and to work effectively.[208]

To recite these diverse arguments against compulsion is not to ignore the fact that the principle was imposed many times in the nineteenth century. The Health and Morals of Apprentices Act of 1802 compelled factory owners to provide and pay for secular and religious instruction for their apprentices.[209] The Factory legislation of 1833—which Halévy called the "first victory [of the] 'Prussian' principle of compulsory education"[210]—required that the factory owner either provide schools or certify that children were attending an approved school. This provision was compulsory, and inspection was provided to enforce it. However, it applied only to children in the cotton manufactories. Furthermore, the legislation did not oblige factory owners not to discharge the children— which they did in great numbers—and thus undercut the provision for compulsory education.[211] Subsequent factory legislation had similar educational provisions. Compulsion was also a feature of education in workhouse and reformatory schools. Once children joined the ranks of poor-rate recipients or convicted juvenile offenders, they were required to receive secular and religious instruction.

In none of these cases, however, was the fundamental principle of family independence thought to be violated; rather, "exceptions" to it were being made. The strongest argument against factory legislation in the first third of the nineteenth century was the independence of parents and their right to control their children's destiny. Factory legislation, proponents argued, did not renounce this principle, but only subordinated it to the issue of the physical and moral evils of factory labor. These were presented as being so severe that they demanded an exception to the principle of parental independence.[212]

The education of the pauper child and the juvenile criminal was also regarded as something of an exception to the rule. Mary Carpenter acknowledged in 1852 that English law considered children "incapable of guiding themselves"; they were therefore "entirely submitted to the guidance of their parents" with respect to employment, control of earnings, and other matters. She added, however, that some situations justified the intervention of the state:

> The father is . . . considered as responsible for [the child's] maintenance; if he neglects to provide him with the proper food, the child can appeal to the parish, who will punish the father for so neglecting him. But the moment the child shows he is really incapable of guiding himself by committing a crime, from that moment he is treated as a man. The expense to the country is exactly the same as if he were a man. He is tried in public, and all the pomp and circumstance of law is exercised towards him as a man, while his father is from that moment, according to the present law of the land, released from obligation to maintain him.[213]

In both cases—destitution and crime—the family had failed, and children could therefore be removed from its responsibility and custody. The value of independence remained intact in principle; it was a matter of redefining the circumstances to which this value applied.

Such was the "overdetermined" opposition to compulsion in general and compulsory education in particular. In this light, it is not difficult to understand England's delay in adopting it, even though school inspectors and others, despairing of limited and ineffective antidotes, called for some kind of compulsion.[214] In light of the British values, religious sentiments, and legal provisions just reviewed, a few observations are in order about the changes in structural conditions under which the compulsory principle came to be adopted.

Recall that the program of the coalition of Dissenters, secularists, and working-class leaders called the National Education League, which crystallized in the late 1860s, envisioned a universal educational system that was "unsectarian, free, and compulsory." Every feature of the league's program—near-universal coverage, nondenominational instruction, compulsory attendance, and no fees—was, in fact, either a reality or advancing by the beginning of the twentieth century. I would like to argue, however, that these features did not constitute a simple list, but, in the context of late-nineteenth-century British society, stood in a systematic relationship to one another.

The league appears to have been correct in assuming that universal schooling called for nonsectarianism, compulsion, and abolition of fees as necessary conditions for its realization. In addition, however, it can be argued, first, that compulsion required nonsectarianism, and, second, that compulsion, once established, demanded that schools be free of charge. With respect to the first, analysis of the conscience clause shows that a single Anglican school without such a clause was untenable in a small community in the 1850s and 1860s. It was untenable because that arrangement combined quasi-compulsion (because it was the only school available) and sectarianism (because the Church of England insisted on its doctrines and rituals). Analysis of the Education Act of 1870 reveals that the provision of discretionary compulsion for rate-supported board schools depended on the presence of some mechanism for nonsectarian religious instruction. A corollary was that state funds should not go to denominational schools if they were allowed—as they were—to teach their special religious doctrines. With these prior religious issues set on one side, compulsion became more nearly acceptable.

Once compulsion was in place, the pressure to reduce or remove fees became evident. For one thing, to compel attendance meant that families with school-age children were under pressure of law to take or keep them from work and put them in school. As commentators in the nineteenth century observed, this was a great sacrifice in many instances. This remained true, even though the proportion of parents affected during and after the 1870s was smaller than in earlier decades. (This resulted, in turn, from the diminution in child labor occasioned by fewer demands for children in industry and the inconveniences of hiring children imposed by factory legislation.)[215] In addition, compulsion put pressure on children from the poorest families to attend school. That was the part of the population for whom fees were known to constitute

an economic hardship. This reasoning lies behind John Morley's assertion that if education is to be compulsory, it follows that it must be
free.[216] The view expressed by working-class representatives in the National Education League was that compulsion would bring the poorest
families enormous difficulties if schools were not free.[217]

Economic hardship resulting from school fees was, in fact, felt by the
working classes in the years between 1870 and the general abolition of
fees in 1890. The average annual fee in voluntary schools rose from 8s.
4½d. in 1870 to 11s. 3½d. in 1891; fees for board schools were on
average 9s. 1¼d. per annum in 1891. This burden was aggravated by
the reluctance of school boards, poor law guardians, and voluntary
school managers to pay school fees for the neediest children.[218] The final
abolition of fees thus appears as a kind of historical resolution of the
pressures arising from the solution of the issues of sectarianism and
compulsion.

## POSTSCRIPT

In this chapter I have traced the difficulty and irregularity with which
the structural conditions for a "universal, compulsory, free, and unsectarian" system of primary education inched toward realization during
the nineteenth century. Some of these conditions were on the "supply"
side, especially resolution of the paralyzing effect of sectarian conflict
and the inability of the promoters of education to make elementary
schooling compulsory. Other conditions involved the "demand" side:
the interest of parents and children in securing education as it became
available. To summarize the conditions affecting demand and their at-
tenuation later in the century, consider first an assessment of English education—while looking at midcentury America—put forth by Edward
Baines in 1846. After mentioning the egalitarian and anti-aristocratic
traditions in America, and the necessity for education to maintain a free
people, Baines turned to the economic side:

> The principal cause of the general education of the [American] people is
> doubtless the state of unparalleled comfort and ease in which the population
> are placed. Four-fifths of them are engaged in agriculture,—a very large pro-
> portion of whom have land of their own. Commerce, navigation, mining,
> manufactures, and handicraft and retail trades, are, generally speaking, so
> prosperous as to afford good profits and high wages. Labour is in such re-
> quest as to obtain a large remuneration. Parents have not the same need of
> assistance from the labour of their children, as in England. Nor is there any-
> thing like the same demand for juvenile labour. Agriculturists in that country

have little occupation in the winter months. It is not compulsory on parents to send their children to school; but they send them because they can afford it, and because they appreciate, at least in some degree, the importance of education.[219]

Historical evidence indicates that Baines's view was oversimple in several respects. Real wages were generally higher in the United States, but the differentials varied from occupation to occupation.[220] Child labor in both agriculture and industry was also common in America, though certainly not as widespread in industry as in Britain. Baines might also have added that employment of women in the American population—immigrant families excepted—was lower in the United States than in Britain. As a result, fewer dame and infant schools developed, and the pressure to remove children from school for child-minding and other domestic duties was less.[221] Attendance problems in the United States were attenuated in rural areas because short winter and short summer school terms accommodated seasonal work patterns. In urban-industrial areas such as Lynn and Lawrence, Massachusetts, however, the "British" problems of irregular attendance and early withdrawal made their appearance.[222]

Oversimplified as Baines's view was, it is consistent with a more general observation—that is, that the evolution of a national educational system is profoundly affected by the timing of its introduction in relation to the urban and industrial development of the country. In Britain, industrial capitalism had developed significantly by the time that efforts to expand mass education materialized. The reverse was the case in the United States, which meant that competing demands for the employment of children did not interfere as much with U.S. education at the early stages of its educational development. When such problems did arise in the United States, they could be confronted more readily because an educational system was already more nearly "in place" institutionally. In England, by contrast, the fundamental features of early capitalism—including the need for semiskilled and unskilled labor and the great use of female and child labor—were "in place" and constituted more serious obstacles for primary education. This observation does not account for the whole story of comparative educational development in the two countries, but it indicates something about the variable significance of the economic factor in that development.

Baines's observation also brings to mind some of the economic developments in Britain in the late nineteenth century that facilitated the universalization of education:

The continuation and ultimate completion of the removal of children from the labor force, accomplished through technological changes, the generalization of factory legislation, and enforcement of compulsory school attendance by local authorities.

The gradual economic changes that came to provide more service jobs for both men and women, making educational skills more relevant to children's future occupations. For males, this meant more jobs of the sort that distracted pupil-teachers in the 1850s and the 1860s—industrial office work and clerical work in the private service and government sectors.[223] For girls it meant the growth of clerical and sales roles as alternatives to domestic service, which was already declining.[224]

The continuing rise in the real wages of the working classes. Using 1900 as the base year of 100, real wages for full-time work were 60.1 in 1868, 69.9 in 1873, 74.9 in 1879, and 82.5 in 1886. Compensating for unemployment, real wages were 56.4 in 1868, 70.9 in 1873, 76.6 in 1879, and 76.0 in 1886.[225] This rise can be seen as compensating in part for children's wages forgone by withdrawing them from the labor force.

The beginning of a decline in the fertility of the British laboring classes. Such a decline had become observable in the middle classes around the 1880s and began to generalize downward on the economic scale toward the end of the century.[226] Smaller families resulted, easing the economic pressures on the working classes and making education correspondingly more affordable.

These trends, combined with abolition of fees, interacted to affect the demand side for education in a favorable direction. In addition, they interacted with increases in supply made possible by the religious and political "solutions" of 1870. All these forces worked toward the goal of universal elementary education envisioned by reformers for nearly a century.

## CHAPTER 9

# New Roles: Pupil-Teacher, Teacher, Inspector

One feature of the institutional structures that appear in the "modernization" process is their new and more specialized roles. Industry, for example, generates new managerial and supervisory roles, as well as engineering, sales, personnel, counseling, and other staff roles. Modern schooling systems are no exception. The system of British working-class education produced managers, full-time male and female schoolmasters and schoolmistresses (including mistresses of infant schools), monitors, pupil-teachers, teachers-in-training, inspectors, assistant inspectors, and numerous roles in the growing bureaucracy of the Committee of Council and the Department of Education. Some of these, such as manager and teacher, were not new, but they took on a new definition in the nineteenth-century context. Each role generated the usual sociological components—expectations for behavior, rewards for performance, punishments for deviance, cultural values and the beliefs that legitimized them, role ambiguities, and role conflicts.

In this chapter, I examine three of these roles, those of pupil-teacher, teacher, and inspector. One reason for selecting these is that each, in a different way, "crossed over" class lines in a society with a class system in which little crossing was normally expected.[1] Pupil-teachers were working-class adolescents recruited as assistants to teachers in working-class day schools. Subsequently they could gain training in a college, and in adulthood they could move into full-time teaching. On the surface, this was social mobility—elementary school teachers were of working-class origin but now occupied a kind of white-collar, middle-class role. It will become apparent, however, that there was ambiguity about the class position of teachers in working-class schools. The inspectors crossed lines in that they were in the professional classes—almost all had university educations from Oxford or Cambridge—but their round of life involved interaction with teachers and pupils, both below them in social status. In each case this crossing-over component created complications for incumbents of the role.

## PUPIL-TEACHERS

### ORIGIN AND NATURE OF THE SYSTEM

The minutes of 1846 officially created the role of pupil-teacher. The origins of the scheme lay in feelings of both despair and hope. The despair concerned the apparent failure of education in working-class schools in the 1830s and early 1840s. Critics blamed the low quality of teaching, the poor qualifications of teachers, and the monitorial system. In chapter 4, I pointed to these dissatisfactions, which preoccupied both the investigating committees and educational reformers.[2] The dissatisfactions prompted Lord Melbourne's administration's unsuccessful effort to establish training institutions in 1839 and the efforts of the religious societies to do the same. Kay-Shuttleworth summarized the teaching situation in dreary terms:

> While the condition of the master is one of such privation and uncertainty, he has by the existing system of school instruction been placed in the situation, the difficulties of which are insuperable, éven by the highest talent and skill, much less by men struggling with penury, exhausted with care, often ill-instructed, and sometimes assuming the duties of the most responsible office, only because deemed incompetent to strive for a livelihood in the open field of competition.[3]

To improve teaching by training students from the elite of the scholars educated in elementary schools and training them further in teaching colleges was the vision that informed the minutes of 1846.[4]

The major complaints about the monitorial system were that a single master could not possibly teach such large numbers effectively, and that the monitors themselves were poor assistants. They were often under twelve years of age and, in Kay-Shuttleworth's estimation, "very ignorant, rude, and unskillful."[5] The early inspectors' reports further discredited the use of monitors. HMI Alexander Thurtell judged them to be young and poorly trained. There were also some problems about their supply. Thurtell said some parents were averse to the employment of their children as monitors, especially when they were unpaid.[6] Kay-Shuttleworth regarded the monitorial system as having "practically failed" because of "the early period at which children are required for manufacturing and agricultural labour."[7] The initial issuance of the minute creating the pupil-teacher system connected difficulties in retaining monitors directly with the need for pupil-teachers:

> Their Lordships had further under their consideration the Report of the Inspectors of Schools, memorials from certain Boards of education, and letters from the clergy and others, representing the very early age at which the children acting as assistants to schoolmasters are withdrawn from manual labour, and the advantages which would arise if such scholars as might be distinguished by proficiency and good conduct were apprenticed to skillful masters, to be instructed and trained, so as to be prepared to complete their education as schoolmasters in the Normal School.[8]

The corresponding advantages of the pupil-teacher scheme were that assistants would be older (between thirteen and eighteen) and more mature; that they would be apprentices to and under the direct tutelage of teachers; that they would receive daily instruction in "a higher class of studies" than other students received in elementary schools;[9] and that they could move on to teacher-training colleges and prepare for a career in teaching. (Up to that time many teachers were hired long after they had finished their education and had worked in some other line, such as a craft or in domestic service.)[10] Kay-Shuttleworth was familiar and positively impressed with the pupil-teacher system as it had worked in Holland, and modeled his plan in large part on it.

A notable feature of the proposal was that pupil-teachers (and future teachers) would "for the most part belong to families supported by manual labour."[11] The reasons for this lay deep in assumptions about social class in mid-nineteenth-century Britain. Kay-Shuttleworth suggested two such reasons. First, teachers who had risen from the ranks of manual labor would be a source of inspiration to their pupils: "To make every elementary school a scene of exertion, from which the highest ranks of teachers may be entered by the humblest scholar, is to render the profession of schoolmaster popular among the poor, and to offer their children the most powerful incentives to learning."[12] The second reason was that others might not be willing to teach in working-class schools. "It cannot be expected that members of the middle class will, to any great extent in this country, choose the vocation of teachers of the poor."[13]

In any event, the new apprenticeship system was advertised as an avenue of social mobility. Through it a child could "enter a profession at every step in which his mind will expand, and his intellect be stored, and, with the blessing of God, his moral and religious character developed."[14] In 1848 HMI Thurtell reported glowingly that children who were chosen to be pupil-teachers experienced a "growth in the tone and bearing suited to their new calling," and that "they had arrived at another, and higher, position in the scale of civilised and educated people."[15] HMI Morell believed that for a youth selected as a pupil-teacher in a normal institution, "if he be persevering and accomplished, there is no precise limit to set to his future advancement."[16] A journal called *The Pupil Teacher* claimed that the system had established a "distinct class in society":

> [The pupil-teachers] are the apprentices of the nation . . . many a country boy, whose highest ambition, 10 years since, would have been to be the village innkeeper or the village blacksmith . . . will now aspire to a profession . . . he has [now] at least a fair chance of raising himself in the social scale . . . many a country girl now, by becoming a pupil-teacher, may be the first in her family, for many generations, to be accounted of a higher grade than that of peasants and domestic servants.[17]

Later we shall observe that the class position of adult teachers was more ambiguous and complicated than this vision indicated.

Great care was taken in selecting and training pupil-teachers. Inspectors were instructed to evaluate the moral training as well as the character and conduct of children considered for apprenticeships. In 1849 the Committee of Council admonished:

> Every expedient should be adopted likely to improve their habits and manners, to promote a sense of order and decorum, respectful obedience to their parents, teachers, and superiors, to cultivate an intelligent disposition to fulfill the duties of their station in life, and to enable them to see how their interests and happiness are inseparable from the well-being of other classes of society.[18]

In 1854 the committee ruled that pupil-teachers could be trained only under certificated teachers (i.e., graduates of training colleges) or by teachers over thirty-five who were qualified for registration by the committee.[19] This concern with socializing pupil-teachers appears to have been a corollary to the mode of their selection: if they were chosen from a class about whose morals and decorum the upper and middle classes were apprehensive, then it seemed imperative to see that they were socialized properly in the values they were to impart to future generations.

The system worked as follows. In most cases, teachers and inspectors identified boys and girls as candidate pupil-teachers at about the age of twelve, and they began their apprenticeship the following year. In the beginning, the ratio of scholars to pupil-teachers was 25 : 1, but as early as 1848 this ratio appeared to be too expensive, and it was revised to 50 : 1 in 1851. The norm remained around 40 : 1 or 50 : 1 until 1890, when it was set at 30 : 1.[20] In many small rural schools, where head teachers were often not certified to apprentice pupils, "stipendiary monitors" were hired as a kind of inexpensive substitute for pupil-teachers. The apprentices remained in training for five years. The Committee of Council paid schoolmasters a stipend for each pupil-teacher supervised, beginning at £10 and rising to £20 in the fifth year.[21] The committee attempted to assure that male pupil-teachers did not teach female children, except in the presence of a master, and that masters did not apprentice female pupil-teachers except in the presence of a mistress. Under no circumstances would a school assign a female pupil-teacher to a master who was both young and unmarried.[22] At the end of the five years, most pupil-teachers sat for examinations and, if successful, qualified for a queen's scholarship at one of the training colleges.

Progress from the role of pupil to pupil-teacher, queen's scholar, and, finally, certificated teacher was thus "a closed system, both socially and educationally, with recruitment of teachers taking place from among the most able of the elementary scholars themselves."[23] It was a closed system with respect to religion as well. In the minutes of 1846, the government assumed financial support for the training colleges. Over time these proliferated along the same religious lines as schools and inspectors—Church of England, British and Foreign School Society, Wesleyan, and Roman Catholic.[24] As was the case with schools, inspectors visited only those training colleges under their appropriate religious jurisdictions.

THE SOCIAL ORIGINS OF PUPIL-TEACHERS

The logic of the pupil-teacher system implied, almost inevitably, that candidates would come disproportionately from the upper reaches of the working classes, and especially from that ambiguous band separating the working class from the lower middle classes. If the finest pupils were to be chosen, this meant those pupils who were in most regular attendance at school. Because of poverty and the demands of the family economy, failure to attend, irregular attendance, and early withdrawal became more severe as one moved down through the levels of the working classes.[25] It followed that fewer candidate pupil-teachers would appear at the lower levels. HMI Watkins observed this in his comment on the difficulty of recruiting pupil-teachers in Durham and Northumberland, which contrasted with Yorkshire:

> Throughout the whole of the great Northern Coal-field . . . only two [schools] which can be considered as connected with coal-working, have obtained the apprenticeship of pupil-teachers in them. . . . The children are taken at such an early age to the pit, that it is not uncommon to find in the colliery schools not a single boy of the age required for the apprenticeship; or, if there be any, they are, in general, unintelligent lads, who attend at school very irregularly, and are occupied during a great part of the year in the agricultural operations of the district.[26]

Beyond the labor-market effects, inspectors felt that pupil-teachers *ought* to possess those intellectual and moral qualities they associated with the higher, more respectable levels of the working classes. HMI Henry Moseley acknowledged in 1850 that some of the best pupil-teachers were the children of laborers. However, he made a point of determining, as a condition of their appointment, that "the abode of [the pupil-teacher's] parents is not wanting in that which belongs to the proprieties and decencies of life." He added that "where other things are the same," the choice of pupil-teachers is best made "from the class of tradesmen, small farmers, and shopkeepers." Not surprisingly, he said that "young persons of this class of life . . . constitute the majority of the pupil-teachers in my district."[27] HMI Frederick Cook laid down as an essential condition for appointment that "the character of the parents must be certified as respectable, and is generally represented to be exemplary." His inquiries along these lines were "even stricter and more searching" with reference to girl apprentices.[28] Cook reported that he had taken pains "to ascertain [the] character and position in life [of the parents of pupil-teachers]." He reported a condition of "respectability in the best sense of the word." If any fault could be found, he added, it was that "hitherto they have belonged to a class rather higher than was apparently contemplated in your Lordships' Minutes."[29] HMI Edward Tinling commented on pupil-teachers' "knowledge, religious training and generally high, respectable moral tone."[30]

In stressing such criteria, the inspectors were no doubt responding to their own class preferences about morality and respectability. In addition, they may have been responding to the concern, "frequently heard" by Cook, that teachers . . . selected from the lower orders, as they are called, are not likely to be endowed with the principles and habits, or to possess that degree of influence, which are requisite in order to raise the moral and intellectual condition of children in National schools. It is asserted that, although they may be intelligent and well-informed, their manners will of necessity be less cultivated and their character probably more liable to be affected by sensual temptations than is the case with those who have been educated with the children of a higher station.[31]

Whatever the mix of supply (availability of superior students with steady attendance) and demand (the criteria imposed by inspectors and others), the evidence indicates that recruitment was from the class levels implied by these criteria. In 1848 Cook surveyed the 192 pupil-teachers in his area in and around London. In the country districts, he found only two from families of agricultural laborers; most were children of "small tradesmen, yeomen, or the upper servants in gentlemen's families." In the towns, and especially in London, they came mainly from the "better and higher division of the operative classes," which meant respectable artisans, silk weavers, cabinetmakers and "children of widows reduced in circumstances."[32] Other inspectors submitted reports consistent with this.[33] The Newcastle Commission heard that most pupil-teachers came from the families of "the artizan class" and "labourers and skilled artizans of the superior class; a few, children of small tradesmen."[34] Surveys of students in several training colleges indicate that the majority of them were the children of shopkeepers and artisans, with many fewer from families of servants, farmers, and laborers.[35] The evidence thus indicates that the social mobility experienced by most children selected as pupil-teachers and prepared for a career in teaching was of an incremental sort. Few appear to have leapt from the lower levels of the working class into the ranks of this new occupation that was finding some indeterminate place in the middle classes.

TURBULENCE IN THE "CLOSED SYSTEM":
THE REVISED CODE

Several considerations suggest that the system, including the pupil-teacher program and the training colleges, must have been unresponsive to market demands and difficult to administer. First, the condition for admission to a training college was the completion of five years of apprenticeship; the period spent in such colleges was usually two years. Administrators' decisions to meet an increased demand for teachers by increasing the number of pupil-teachers would take years to implement because of the long period of training. Efforts to reduce the supply of teachers would also take a long time because of the existing numbers of pupil-teachers and teachers-in-training already "in the pipeline." [36] Second, the recruitment, retention, and placement of pupil-teachers in the training schools did not occur in a vacuum but within a larger economy that both constrained and distracted its participants. Both these factors help account for the buffeting that the system experienced from its beginning up through the 1870s.

We have seen that recruiting pupil-teachers was sometimes difficult for the same reasons that recruiting monitors was difficult: children left school to work at an early age. We also saw that many pupil-teachers sought other avenues of employment—primarily office employment—in the prosperous years of the 1850s and 1860s. [37] The Newcastle Commission found that only 76 percent of the pupil-teachers tried for a queen's scholarship, the remainder moving mainly into office work. [38] This drain was greatest in the urban-industrial regions. In the 1860s, however, when the provisions of the Revised Code reduced pupil-teachers' stipends, the competition from other kinds of juvenile labor was felt in country districts as well. [39] In addition, there was concern about how to accommodate pupil-teachers who did not pass the examination for the queen's scholarship. In the early years they could enter positions in the lower ranks of the civil service. The government closed off this option in 1852, however, when it created the position of assistant teacher, which unsuccessful candidates for the queen's scholarships could fill. In the mid 1850s the Committee of Council tried to revive the possibility of unsuccessful candidates entering junior clerkships at the Board of Inland Revenue, but this civil service avenue closed finally in 1858. [40]

Throughout the 1850s the Committee of Council intervened in the pupil-teacher system when supply problems and exigencies of economy appeared. The minute of 1851 changing the ratio of pupil-teachers to pupils from 25 : 1 to 50 : 1 had an immediate impact on numbers. One year after its issuance, HMI Cook reported a decline in pupil-teachers from 416 in 1851 to 408 in 1852 in his district, and he feared a further decline to below 400 in the following year. He believed the drop was "owing entirely to the change made in the Minutes." [41] Cook claimed further that the decline was disrupting the system by forcing teachers back to the inefficient monitorial system. He also felt that the concern with oversupply of teachers, in the air at that time, [42] was unfounded. Apparently it was, because in 1854 the committee relaxed the limit on admissions, improved the instructions and renewed scholarships for the second year in the training colleges. The problems of reduced numbers for the training colleges reappeared in 1857. Students who had finished their apprenticeships but had not yet sat for the examinations were being "easily induced to accept offers of immediate employment." In that year the committee relaxed the scholarship and examination criteria in teaching colleges further. It also opened the queen's scholarships to "assistants in private schools, untrained schoolmasters and schoolmistresses desirous of improving their attainment, Sunday school teachers." [43]

In May 1859, reacting to the pervasive concerns for economy in the late 1850s, the Committee of Council cancelled all exceptions to the ratio of one pupil-teacher for every forty scholars and set an upper limit of four pupil-teachers for each schoolmaster or schoolmistress. This minute disturbed teachers, who had come to rely on larger numbers of pupil-teachers. [44] It also led to a drop in the number of pupil-teachers in large schools and forced their managers to consider hiring assistant teachers or additional full-time teachers, both more expensive expedients. [45] All these adjustments reflected the Committee of Council's struggle to balance the need for economy with maintaining an adequate supply of pupil-teachers in the face of outside competition.

It was the Revised Code of 1862, however—also inspired in large part by concerns for economy—that imparted the greatest shock to the pupil-teacher and training college system. When the code was issued, Kay-Shuttleworth reacted negatively to this threat. He maintained that it would cut off much of the income of the training colleges and create "an inferior class of Queen's Scholars." [46] The basis for this apprehension was that the code reduced the stipend from £15 to £10 and would reduce the training time for apprentices from seven and a half to five hours per week. This provision affected both the incentive structure for schools and the demand for pupil-teachers. Lowe explained:

> Of course there are fewer pupil-teachers, and so there ought to be. Under the old system we were paying the whole salary for every pupil-teacher, and only part for other teachers—giving a bounty for every one of them—and of course all school managers got as many as they could. But afterwards, a grant was given to the managers to spend as they pleased and as they naturally spent it as economically as they could, fewer pupil-teachers were employed. [47]

Earlier he had boasted that "we got rid of the enormous incubus of 15,000 pupil teachers who were receiving grants." [48]

Another provision of the Revised Code removed the direct stipend previously paid to teachers for superintending pupil-teachers; it subsumed that under the "payment-by-results" scheme. The evident effect was that "[the] schoolmaster . . . does not care to have pupil-teachers, because he gets no pay for teaching them." [49] One result of these changes was an apparent deterioration in the ratio of pupil-teachers to scholars; Kay-Shuttleworth calculated that in 1866 the ratio was 1:54, up from 1:36 in 1861. "[It] is preposterous," he added, "to conceive that a pupil-teacher even in the fifth year of his apprenticeship could keep order, much less teach fifty-four scholars." [50] Furthermore, the fact that teachers were now directly responsible for setting the stipends of their pupil-teachers depressed those stipends. The minutes of 1846 called for a stipend of £10 in the first year of the apprenticeship. In 1869 a survey revealed that 10 percent of first-year male pupil-teachers and 19.9 percent of first-year females were receiving less than £5, and that 80.4 percent of the males and 79.5 percent of the females were receiving between £5 and £10. The surveys revealed similar reductions for the later years of the apprenticeship. [51] Finally, cuts in the support of queen's scholarships constituted a disincentive for young people to enter the role of pupil-teacher, which prepared them for those scholarships. [52]

The impact on the supply of pupil-teachers in the next few years was dramatic. From 1861 to 1862, the number of new recruits was down by only 58, and the number admitted in 1863 was actually up by 208. However, the total number of pupil-teachers dropped by 525 from 1861 to 1862, and by 1,572 from 1862 to 1863. This was because many were leaving the ranks of the very large cohorts admitted in the late 1850s. [53] This situation did not yet alarm the Committee of Council, and in its 1864 report, Granville and Robert Lowe stated confidently that "[we] see no reason to believe that the system of pupil-teacher will fail under the Revised Code." [54] However, in 1864, the school inspectors registered an alarm over the decline of pupil-teachers. They made statements like "the supply of candidates . . . to take the place of those whose apprenticeship expires is diminishing" and "the reduction of the staff of pupil-teachers is proceeding rapidly." [55] Rural areas, traditionally less vulnerable to recruiting difficulties, now began to report them. [56] HMI C. H. Alderson commented both on the declining numbers and the falling spirits of the pupil-teachers:

> Both [the pupil-teachers'] written exercises and their practical skills seem to me to show deterioration. Their demeanour in school has been marked, in many cases, by a languor and want of interest which have . . . been rarely

noticed til now. It is probably to be accounted for by the fact that many of them have intended to quit the profession of a teacher at the end of their engagement. With regard to the future supply of pupil-teachers, I have found comparatively few eligible candidates ready to take the place of those whose time of service has expired.[57]

HMI B. M. Cowie reported that teachers, themselves exhibiting a "lachrymose and peevish tone" because of their situation under the code, were discouraging pupil-teachers from going into teaching. As a result, a situation of "faint-heartedness and despondency" had set in among the young people.[58] In 1866 Matthew Arnold complained of the lower quality of apprentices who were applying to the teacher-training colleges.[59] The inspectors' reports of 1865, 1866, and 1867 continued to note the diminished supply of apprentices, worse training, lower performance, and poor morale.[60]

Statistical results confirmed these impressions. Table 26 summarizes these. The total numbers between 1861 and 1867 show a drop of more than one-third for males and about one-fifth for females. Initial admissions, however, fluctuated little. The decrease is found more in attrition. For years after the first, the percentage increase or decrease of the cohort in each year is shown in parentheses. This can be traced for each cohort by reading diagonally downward and to the right. The attrition rate is much higher for males than females. This is consistent with other evidence showing the greater sensitivity of males to other employment opportunities.[61] The table also confirms the Committee of Council's observation that "the [reduction] is not due so much to deficiency in the number admitted as to removals in the course of apprenticeship."[62] Referring to boys, the committee explained that two factors seemed to be at work. The apprentices themselves were tempted by higher wages in other jobs, and managers were readier to let them go because they became more expensive as they reached the later years of apprenticeship.[63]

The slight upward movement in the number of new pupil-teacher recruits in 1866 and 1867 (see table 26) probably reflects a response to short-term economic conditions. In 1867 the Committee of Council noted the "severe commercial distress" of 1866, and attributed the lower number of new schools established in that year to it.[64] By the same measure, the sluggishness of trade eased the competition for pupil-teachers from other trades. (As if to confirm this, the committee reported in 1869 that one of the sources of difficulty in procuring pupil-teachers was "the general rise of wages.")[65] HMI Charles F. Routledge reported an increase in the numbers of new pupil-teachers in the West

Riding area in 1866. This occurred despite the persistence of competition from mill jobs that would pay a boy £18 to £22 a year in contrast to the £10 or £15 available as a pupil-teacher. The increase in numbers, however, was apparently accompanied by a decrease in quality and a lowering of the class-level of applicants: "Schoolmasters complain that the pupil-teachers do not come now from so high a class as they formerly did; and if this be so it is a very serious thing, for children cannot be expected so readily to respect and obey those whose parents are living in the same alley and working at the same trade as their own."[66] Routledge's observation confirms that pupil-teachers had traditionally been drawn from the higher ranges of the working classes. As the competition from other lines of work drew these boys away, the vacuum tended to be filled from lower ranks, particularly when other lines of employment were not as available.

The inspectors observed how schools were adapting to the shrinking population of pupil-teachers. In some cases they returned to employing monitors.[67] This was apparently not widespread, however. Parents were not interested in having their children work as unpaid monitors, and to pay a monitor now cost the school as much as it did to pay a pupil-teacher.[68] The more important trend was to substitute assistant teachers for pupil-teachers. The former were usually young people who had not passed their examinations for queen's scholarships and had gone directly into that job. Assistant teachers were similar to pupil-teachers in that they were supervised by fully certificated teachers. According to the provisions of the Revised Code, an assistant teacher counted for two pupil-teachers as staff. The committee had actually suggested the use of assistant teachers on grounds of economy. For one thing, their appointment was for a shorter term, and could be terminated more easily than that of a pupil-teacher contracted for five years. Other advantages were that "[such] substitution checks the too great increase of pupil-teachers; brings the experience gained during apprenticeship to bear at once upon elementary education under skilled guidance; and adds a valuable stage to the course whereby future teachers are prepared."[69]

Schools around the country apparently responded, as school inspectors reported the frequent substitution of assistant teachers for pupil-teachers.[70] The Committee of Council recorded that the numbers of assistant teachers were 401 in 1863, 608 in 1864, 933 in 1865, and 1,040 in 1866.[71] This increase might have been greater had it not been for the fact that teachers in many cases had to pay the assistants out of their own pockets.[72] The increase in assistant teachers was both effect and

TABLE 26   PUPIL-TEACHERS, 1861–1867

| | First Year | Second Year | Third Year | Fourth Year | Fifth Year | Total |
|---|---|---|---|---|---|---|
| | | | *Males* | | | |
| 1861 | 1,521 | 1,653 | 1,799 | 1,768 | 1,654 | 8,395 |
| 1862 | 1,454 | 1,593 (+4.73%) | 1,522 (−7.92%) | 1,712 (−4.84%) | 1,682 (−4.86%) | 7,963 (−5.15%) |
| 1863 | 1,160 | 1,431 (−1.58%) | 1,521 (−4.52%) | 1,375 (−9.66%) | 1,556 (−9.11%) | 7,043 (−11.55%) |
| 1864 | 884 | 1,077 (−7.16%) | 1,281 (−10.48%) | 1,242 (−18.34%) | 1,241 (−9.75%) | 5,725 (−18.71%) |
| 1865 | 1,212 | 885 (+.11%) | 929 (−13.74%) | 1,106 (−13.66%) | 1,075 (−13.45%) | 5,207 (−9.05%) |
| 1866 | 1,311 | 1,169 (−3.5%) | 792 (−10.51%) | 799 (−13.99%) | 961 (−13.11%) | 5,032 (−3.36%) |
| 1867 | 1,711 | 1,291 (−1.53%) | 1,013 (−13.3%) | 709 (−10.48%) | 650 (−18.65%) | 5,374 (+6.8%) |

*Females*

| Year | | | | | | |
|------|------|------|------|------|------|------|
| 1861 | 1,571 | 1,586 | 1,558 | 1,704 | 1,463 | 7,882 |
| 1862 | 1,480 | 1,672 (+6.43%) | 1,484 (−6.43%) | 1,526 (−2.05%) | 1,627 (−4.5%) | 7,789 (+1.18%) |
| 1863 | 1,155 | 1,521 (+2.77%) | 1,619 (−3.17%) | 1,411 (−4.92%) | 1,431 (−6.23%) | 7,137 (−8.37%) |
| 1864 | 1,011 | 1,198 (+3.72%) | 1,383 (−9.07%) | 1,489 (−8.03%) | 1,355 (−3.97%) | 6,436 (−9.82%) |
| 1865 | 1,143 | 1,063 (+5.14%) | 1,152 (−3.84%) | 1,272 (−8.03%) | 1,384 (−7.05%) | 6,014 (−6.56%) |
| 1866 | 1,409 | 1,324 (+15.84%) | 1,000 (−5.93%) | 1,073 (−6.86%) | 1,133 (−10.93%) | 5,939 (−1.25%) |
| 1867 | 1,735 | 1,462 (+3.76%) | 1,236 (−6.65%) | 922 (−7.8%) | 957 (−10.81%) | 6,312 (+6.28%) |

SOURCE: *Parliamentary Papers*, 1867–68, 25, p. xc.

TABLE 27    NUMBERS OF PUPIL-TEACHERS EXAMINED,
PASSING, AND ADMITTED TO TRAINING COLLEGES,
1861−1867

|      | Number Examined | | Number Passing | | Number Admitted | |
|------|------|--------|------|--------|------|--------|
|      | *Male* | *Female* | *Male* | *Female* | *Male* | *Female* |
| *1861* | 1,174 | 1,299 | 869 | 858 | 821 | 770 |
| *1862* | 1,128 | 1,385 | 990 | 993 | 913 | 842 |
| *1863* | 789 | 1,042 | 691 | 791 | 594 | 694 |
| *1864* | 592 | 904 | 518 | 810 | 501 | 697 |
| *1865* | 608 | 947 | 521 | 785 | 508 | 707 |
| *1866* | 616 | 968 | 450 | 757 | 436 | 685 |
| *1867* | 599 | 879 | 454 | 706 | 445 | 676 |

SOURCE: *Parliamentary Papers*, 1867−68, 25, p. xc.

cause of what was happening to the pupil-teachers. To employ assistant teachers was one way to make up for the diminished supply of pupil-teachers; and one reason why pupil-teachers left their apprenticeships was to become assistant teachers.[73]

Closely related to the diminishing supply of pupil-teachers was a falling-off in admissions to the training colleges. In 1868 the Committee of Council presented figures on pupil-teacher candidates who took training-college examinations as well as on those who passed. These results are shown in table 27. Inspectors commented on these downward trends in their reports.[74] The committee reported that in 1868 there were 922 male students, with unfilled places for 747, and 1,335 female students, with room for 201 more in the teacher-training colleges.[75] In his report for 1867, HMI J. Bowstead concluded that "the pupil-teacher system has in fact been seriously damaged for a time, if not permanently endangered."[76] The depletion of the training colleges appeared to justify a similar assessment.

Reacting in part to the decline in male pupil-teachers and teacher-trainees in the colleges ("the supply of school-mistresses is sufficiently well-maintained"), the committee issued a minute on February 20, 1867, to the effect that "a male pupil-teacher, who gets to the middle of his apprenticeship, represents an extra grant of £5, £10, £13, £15, or £18 to his school, if he completes his apprenticeship, and gains admission into a training college—the amount varying according to the proficiency which he has acquired and maintains."[77]

The committee described this as a "counterpoise" and, quoting several inspectors' reports, attributed the rise in the number of pupil-teachers in 1867 to its effect.[78] In 1869 the committee was even more optimistic. It reported another slight rise in the number of residents in the training colleges. It noted that there were fewer pupil-teachers among the applicants to training colleges in 1868 than in 1867, and that the quality of the male candidates was lower. It hastened to point out, however, that the candidates in that examination class were those admitted in 1864 and 1865. These were the years, the committee explained, in which the "panic about the effects of the Revised Code was still prevalent," and during which the numbers of pupil-teachers were reduced by 2,019 in 1864 and 940 in 1865. It pointed to the continuing increase in new pupil-teachers that had begun in 1867—see table 26—and commented that "the tide is now steadily rising again" as a result of the 1867 minute.[79]

Earlier I observed that the new arrangements set in place by a "truce point" constitute a new gyroscope that initiates a cumulative set of trends as activities associated with those new arrangements work themselves out.[80] This principle is well illustrated in the cases of the pupil-teachers and the teachers' colleges in the 1860s. The Revised Code of 1862 was such a truce point.[81] In introducing "payment by results," it altered the incentives of pupil-teachers and students in training schools, who were, in any event, subject to market distractions and opportunities. The trends set in motion are seen in tables 26 and 27—drastic declines in the case of both roles. The minute of 1867 was an effort to equilibrate, which began to have a reversing effect in the late 1860s. In these instances the trends were in large measure planned and hoped for by the planners. The intentions of the framers of the Revised Code were to economize by reducing the supply of teachers and teachers-in-training. The framers of the minute of February 1867 wanted to reverse that process. In other cases the trains of events that "truce points" set in motion were neither intended nor anticipated.

The occupation of teaching in England and Wales in the 1860s adds a special wrinkle to the general principle. The Committee of Council pointed to a kind of anomaly in 1868: a continuing decline of the candidates admitted to training colleges. It read that as a shock-effect felt four or five years after the "panic" years of 1864 and 1865, even though recruitment of new pupil-teachers was showing signs of vitality in 1868. The anomaly underscores the difficulty in articulating supply and demand when there was a substantial lag (seven years) between initial commitment (recruitment of a pupil-teacher) and ultimate employment (entering the labor force as a teacher). When the moment for employment arose, the demand might be very different from the conditions that had determined the initial commitment to training.

## TEACHERS

The history of the use of children in teaching in the first three-quarters of the nineteenth century can be summarized by identifying three overlapping phases. The first, the monitorial system, extended roughly from 1810 to 1846. It was marked by the religious societies' use of very young children, recruited haphazardly, trained informally, not paid or ill-paid, and involved in an educational system based on mechanical learning. The second, from 1846 to 1861, inaugurated the pupil-teacher role, and was something of a golden age, despite problems of recruitment stemming from competition with other lines of work. The pupil-teachers were older children, with better supervision and training, paid throughout their apprenticeship and teacher-training college years, and with the promise of a definite career line. The third, beginning with the Revised Code, was a kind of depression period, with lower pay, thinning ranks, diminished quality, and low morale for pupil-teachers. Apprenticeship and teacher-training reached a nadir between 1864 and 1866, and began to recover slowly after government intervention in 1867.

The history of teaching falls into roughly the same phases: (a) an informal and anomalous calling of low status (before 1846); (b) the spectacular but uncertain beginnings of institutionalization and professionalization (1846–61); and (c) a decade of institutional bleakness and depression (1862–1870), from which the profession emerged when the system began a new course of rapid development in the last third of the century. Observers of the time acknowledged such phases. The Newcastle Commission remarked on the ambiguity, low status, and institutional precariousness of the teachers' position before 1846, with a rapid improvement thereafter.[82] HMI Morell, reflecting in 1865, spoke of the ten or fifteen years after 1846 as a period of great educational enthusiasm, which, however, "has undoubtedly in great measure died away." Morell attributed the change partly to "the natural decay of enthusiasm," and partly to "the sudden change which has taken place in the government system of school grants [i.e., the Revised Code]."[83] In any event, this rough division provides a convenient device for tracing the vicissitudes of the role and social status of teachers in working-class schools.

## WORKING-CLASS TEACHING BEFORE 1846

Prior to the nineteenth century, most education of the poor was in apprenticeships and in charity schools organized for the very poor and orphans.[84] Teachers in the latter were by and large ill-qualified. Some schools in London, however, did have full-time teachers, and rudimentary teacher-training and pupil-teaching made an appearance.[85] The qualification for Sunday school teachers was mainly an ability to read the Scriptures; these teachers, moreover, were almost always volunteers and amateurs.[86] The dame schools were primarily child-minding institutions, though sometimes they imparted the barest reading skills. The British and Foreign School and National Societies ushered in a small measure of professional institutionalization early in the century, however paltry that may appear by later standards. Joseph Lancaster started a teacher-training department at his school in Borough Road in Chelsea in 1805, and after 1812 the British and Foreign School Society carried on some work of teacher training. The National Society established a training college in 1812. These institutions usually taught their students the rules and procedures of the monitorial method. In the 1830s a Scottish influence became evident, mainly through David Stowe's academy in Glasgow. This occasioned modest flows of Scottish "trainers" to England and English students to study in Glasgow. The Home and Colonial Society, founded in 1836, was also a training institution. Its managers made a deliberate effort to break from the mechanical methods of monitorial education and work toward the broader cultivation of teachers.[87]

Teachers became an object of public interest in the 1830s when attention turned to the quality of education. The parliamentary investigatory bodies of the 1830s gathered many facts and opinions about teachers and teaching. Much of what they heard revealed a largely negative stereotype that echoed Bernard Mandeville's unkind characterization of charity school teachers in the eighteenth century: "starving wretches of both sexes that, from a natural antipathy to working, . . . think themselves qualified to become masters and mistresses of charity schools."[88] Cobbett had referred to teachers as the "new race of idlers."[89] The select committee on education heard in 1834 that the recruitment of teachers "is left to mere chance, and those who can get nothing else to do, are often resorted to."[90] Most of them were said to "have previously tried other professions or callings,"[91] while some came from "very respectable stations in life, in which they have not been successful."[92] The witnesses also spoke consistently of the low status of the schoolteacher.

"The elementary schoolmaster is . . . so much despised that men of respectable attainments will not undertake the office of schoolmaster"; [93]
the position "is not viewed [with a right state of public feeling] at
present." [94] Teaching was generally regarded as being of low quality, [95]
and teachers as having little training. [96] Needless to say, almost all of the
witnesses called for an improvement in the training and status of
teachers. [97]

As for their actual social origins, many teachers were mechanics who
had "evinced a taste for teaching" by working in Sunday schools. A few
came from private schools. [98] Tropp summarized the evidence on origins
by listing "semi-skilled craftsmen, shopkeepers, clerks or 'superior' domestic servants, all occupations which either required a knowledge of
reading and writing or offered opportunities to acquire such knowledge." [99] The entrants of the training college at Battersea were "sons of
small tradesmen, of bailiffs, of servants or of superior mechanics." [100]
Salaries were around £60 or £70 per year on the average. Salaries in the
National Society day schools were between £50 and £100 a year for
masters and £35 and £70 pounds for mistresses trained at the society's
central school. [101] These levels were seen as too low to draw qualified
people into teaching. "If teachers are to have the wages of porters or
ploughmen, you will never get fit persons for teachers," J. T. Crossley
observed. [102] Managers provided some teachers with housing, which
would add £7 to £10 a year to their salaries, but the practice was not
general. [103]

THE PERIOD OF ENTHUSIASM, 1846–1861

The Melbourne government tried to respond to the concerns of the
1830s by establishing state-supported model and training schools. This
project went down to defeat in 1839 after a prolonged squabble over
the character of religious instruction to be offered in them. [104] For the
next few years the government gave limited support to the training
schools of the religious societies. The minutes of 1846 expanded this
support and made it more official. In effect, the minutes provided for the
training and certification of teachers, thus endowing them with a position something like that of the civil servant. They stopped short of
providing that status, however, because the state did not actually pay
the basic salaries of teachers (managers of schools did this). It supplied
them with a salary supplement (£10 to £30 for men, £6 13s. to £20 for
women) if they became certificated. In addition, they did not normally
qualify for pensions and other benefits of civil servants. The clear intent

of the minutes was to improve the quality of teaching by setting up a system of recruitment and training, and to give teachers a greater measure of professional recognition. The minutes also held out the promise of improving the pay, status, and self-esteem of teachers. Shortly after the minutes were issued, HMI Bellairs gave voice to that promise:

> Schoolmasters will at length find a position, and their importance in the social system will be recognised. The possession of a certificate of merit will of itself confer on its possessor not only an honourable badge of distinction, but will give him an authoritative professional rank, and that from a very high source of honor, which under the most favourable circumstances has hitherto been denied him. Another benefit will be produced by the pecuniary advantages held forth to such as choose to fulfil the conditions upon which they are offered. This will prove an immense boon, and destroy that wretched system by which a master was made to be dependent upon the weekly pence of his scholars for his salary, a system which produced a miserable trade of petty huckstering with the parents for payments, of truckling to the children from fear of giving offense; and of simulation in the masters themselves towards the managers, lest their income should be thought too much, and their salary reduced.
> Another great point will be the increase of professional skill which must necessarily follow.[105]

The developments of the late 1840s and 1850s were to justify Bellairs's hopes only partially.

Instituted in 1846 and involving a seven-year training cycle, the system could not begin to yield a supply of fully trained, regularly certificated teachers until the early 1850s. The government coped with this situation by authorizing inspectors to examine teachers who had not trained in or completed courses at teaching colleges.[106] Thurtell described the standard as "not easily attainable" but within the reach of "most respectable schoolmasters . . . not far advanced in years . . . with a reasonable sacrifice of time and effort."[107] Because the period immediately following 1846 was a transitional one, moreover, some of the income and status problems of the teachers remained. Salaries of teachers, as reported by inspectors in 1846 and 1847, were in the same ranges as those reported to the investigatory commissions a decade before.[108]

The salary increment that accrued to those fully in the new governmental system is suggested in HMI Watkins's report in 1853 on teachers' salaries in Yorkshire. For uncertified teachers in schools without pupil teachers, the average salary was less than £48. Certified teachers' salaries reached almost £60, however, and in schools with pupil teachers, £86 5s. 2d. Watkins found the pay of uncertified teachers, especially in agricultural areas, unacceptably low—"lower than the wages of an uneducated agricultural labourer, and not equal to half the earnings of a fairly skilled mechanic." In a country like England, he added, "where money is often the test of excellence, such a stipend must be fatal to the success of a school-teacher." [109] In 1850 Kennedy struck the same note:

> We must look forward to having a more highly educated body of head teachers before adequate results can be expected from our schools. . . . [Teachers] are, in my opinion, decidedly underpaid; they are often very inadequately accommodated in the houses or apartments assigned to them; they have little or no suitable society; and they are frequently left without proper support and encouragement. [110]

The salary problems of the uncertificated teacher, especially women, continued to persist into the 1850s. [111] Even under the new system, some managers continued to seek economies. Watkins complained in 1850 that when teachers' salaries were improved by certification and by compensation for taking on pupil-teachers, some managers would then lower their base salaries. [112]

The teachers' ambiguous occupational status was underscored by the issue of retirement pensions. The minutes of 1846 gave the Committee of Council the power to arrange such pensions. Most managers and inspectors (to say nothing of the teachers themselves) favored some kind of provision. Consistent with Lingen's position, however, the committee balked. In 1852, Lingen circularized the inspectors, insisting that the government had not pledged itself to such a scheme, and that pensions were not a right: "I am to repeat the caution, that it has not been their Lordships' intention to make provision, by the establishment of a general system of pensions, for persons who have had average means of providing for themselves, or to offer a premium upon removal which might with strict justice be simply enforced." [113]

The most Lingen would permit were strictly defined and limited exceptions. Lingen's posture was that teachers should lay aside a portion of their income for retirement or join private assurance societies. To arguments that teachers could not afford to do either, the committee replied in 1858 that teachers received "liberal payment" in their "comfortable and honourable profession," payment that began early in life and continued through a long period of service. [114] The committee also insisted that the state could not properly provide pensions to employees with which it had no direct relationship: "The Government neither appoints nor dismisses these officers, nor does it recognise them, except as employed by the independent managers of schools under inspection." [115] The Revised Code abolished all pensions for teachers, and only in 1865 was a superannuation scheme consistent with the minutes of 1846 admitted.[116]

The phasing-in of the pupil-teacher, teacher-training, and certification system was complete by the early 1850s. In addition, that decade witnessed vigorous competition among religious groups for new schools and very rapid expansion of the government grant.[117] All these factors worked to improve the teachers' situation significantly. The inspectors' reports of the 1850s noted shortages of schoolteachers in various regions;[118] schoolmistresses were singled out especially.[119] Accompanying these reports were indications of improving salaries for both mistresses and masters.[120] In reminding the teachers that they should put money aside for their own retirement, the Committee of Council reported the level of teachers' salaries for 1857, a year characterized by "demand in excess of supply" for teachers. Certificated masters received about £90 a year on the average in salary and supplementary government grants, and mistresses about £60, plus housing. In 1860, the committee noted that the average schoolmaster's salary (including government grants, which constituted about 25 percent of it) had risen from £90 1s. 7d. in 1855 to £94 3s. 7d. by 1859. For schoolmistresses, the figures were £60 11s. 5d. in 1855 and £62 13s. 10d. in 1859.[121] The continued rise of salaries up to the early 1870s is seen in table 28. For 1859–60, the Newcastle Commission estimated the average salary of uncertificated

TABLE 28    SALARIES OF CERTIFICATED TEACHERS,
1860–1872

|            | Males      | Females    |
|------------|------------|------------|
| *1859–60*  | £94.3.10   | £62.13.10  |
| *1861–62*  | 94.10.3    | 62.15.5    |
| *1863–64*  | 93.17.6    | 61.7.10    |
| *1864–65*  | 90.4.6     | 58.8.9     |
| *1865–66*  | 86.10.9    | 55.2.1     |
| *1866–67*  | 87.3.0     | 55.0.2     |
| *1867–68*  | 88.18.5    | 55.11.0    |
| *1868–69*  | 91.5.11    | 56.1.7     |
| *1869–70*  | 93.5.7     | 57.1.0     |
| *1870–71*  | 95.12.9    | 57.16.5    |
| *1871–72*  | 98.5.6     | 58.11.9    |

SOURCE: D. W. Sylvester, *Robert Lowe and Education* (Cambridge: Cambridge University Press, 1974), p. 111.

masters to be £62 4s. 11d.; that of uncertificated mistresses £34 19s. 7d.[122] The differential between certificated and uncertificated teachers was apparently considerable. The news of brisk demand and improving salaries was accompanied by complaints of high turnover of teachers[123] and of trainees in teacher-training colleges leaving to assume positions before completing their course of study. This phenomenon, too, was especially pronounced for schoolmistresses.[124]

THE SOCIAL ROLE

The 1850s, then, were years of economic good times for schoolteachers, if not absolutely, then certainly in relation to their situation before the system established by the minutes of 1846. There was also general consensus that the fledgling profession was gaining respect in the public eye. An assistant commissioner of the Newcastle Commission wrote: "As the cause of education itself rises (and it is every day rising) in popular estimation, so are those who are its able ministers rising in social position; and, so far as I have been enabled to judge, there is no profession which has made of late years so rapid a stride in asserting for itself due consideration and respect."[125] The Newcastle Commission entered a more cautious positive assessment of the social position of the teacher:

> A schoolmaster is sure of a good income, a great deal of leisure, and moderate labour as long as his health lasts. If his prospects are not so extensive as in some other walks of life, they are more secure. He is never out of work. He is affected only casually and indirectly by the vicissitudes of trade, and he fills a position, which if not socially all he could wish, is universally recognised as respectable and useful.[126]

The cautious and labored wording of this assessment suggests what was in fact the case—that the schoolmaster occupied a status in society that was both ambiguous and ambivalently regarded.

Evidence compiled by inspectors and others in the 1850s suggests that schoolteachers were not very satisfied with their lot. Some of this dissatisfaction stemmed from economic circumstances, but a great part rested on status considerations. In 1855 HMI Kennedy remarked that "[teachers'] qualifications have been universally raised, but their status has not been raised proportionately."[127]

Given the special features of the British class system in mid nineteenth century, and the special place of the teacher in it, the basic conditions that produce status-discrepancy were present. Those conditions followed from the character of the British class system. As observed in chapter 3,[128] descriptions of the class system were not completely consistent in the high Victorian period. Some characterized it as castelike, others stressed the possibilities of self-improvement and mobility.[129] Despite this mixed message, the general expectation for the working class was that it was a "station" within which one might improve and become more respectable, but out of which mobility was rare. One significant and promising exception was the avenue leading through the pupil-teaching system into schoolteaching.[130]

Such mobility had to be read in a special context, however. Teaching was an occupation with a past of ambivalent, if not low, status. In 1852 Tremenheere reflected this fact indirectly by a comment on American schoolteachers after his visit to the United States: "Anyone from England visiting those schools [in America] would be . . . greatly struck with the very high social position, considering the nature of their employment of the teachers, male and female."[131] Within the American system itself, teachers did not experience their social standing as particularly high, and they strove in midcentury to improve their income and status.[132] Nevertheless, Tremenheere's observation indicates their comparatively low status in England. Working-class teaching was an occupation into which men and women of the middle classes would not enter until later in the century, when its professional status became more secure.[133] By design the training system targeted children of the working classes almost exclusively for the career-line leading to teaching in working-class elementary schools. This imparted to elementary teaching an unmistakable working-class aura. At the same time, teaching required skills that prepared young people for lower-middle-class, white-collar jobs. ("A schoolmaster is always a tolerably efficient clerk," Lingen said.)[134] When the trained teacher took employment, however, he or she—an educated person—dealt mainly with working-class children and parents in the daily round of life. The position, in short, was a thoroughly marginal one. "[Schoolmasters'] social position is equivocal. They are isolated both from the class above and the class below them," HMI Watkins remarked.[135] Such a role invariably excites ambivalent reactions from others and uncertainty and dissatisfaction on the part of the incumbents themselves.

The available evidence is thus consistent with the interpretation of marginality and status-discrepancy. The themes that emerge from that evidence are outlined below.

*Relative Deprivation.*    Observing schoolteachers in 1855, HMI W. J. Kennedy gave a classic and accurate rendition of the principle of relative deprivation:

> I have long perceived that there was some feeling of dissatisfaction with their position and prospects, but never so strongly as during the past twelve months. And, indeed, considering the excellent and high education which they are now receiving, one might have foreseen that they would not remain content with the condition their class has hitherto occupied.[136]

HMI Frederick Watkins also spoke of this discontent to the Newcastle Commission, and attributed it to the same motive:

> I certainly think that the school masters . . . are not content with their social position. . . . It is a sort of morbid feeling that they are not quite in the position where they should be, that they are educated men, and that they are not received by the world at large as gentlemen. It is a rather morbid desire to be a gentleman too soon, I think.[137]

HMI H. Longueville Jones reported his observation that "the prevailing tendency of the minds of masters *coming from training schools, and especially of such among them as hold certificates of merit,* is to become dissatisfied with what is called their 'social position,' and to consider themselves worthy of something much higher." [138]

If accurate, these descriptions are consistent with the kinds of responses expected when a low-status occupation is advertised as an opportunity for upward mobility and when incumbents from backgrounds of modest status sense they are not receiving the rewards that have been held out. One of the more militant teachers' periodicals of the 1850s expressed their disappointment vividly:

> It is no strange thing that men who in education, tastes and habits have all the qualifications of "gentlemen" should regard themselves as worthy of something much higher than the treatment of a servant and the wages of a mechanic.
>
> What in short the teacher desires is that his "calling" shall rank as a "profession"; that the name of "schoolmaster" shall ring as grandly on the ear as that of "clergyman" or "solicitor"; that he shall feel no more that awful chill and "stony British stare" which follows the explanation that "that interesting young man is only the schoolmaster." [139]

*Preoccupation with the Symbols of Status.*    Watkins reported that a widespread criticism of young schoolmasters was that they went into debt. "They fancy that their position requires certain social luxuries,— furniture, books, dress, society,—which they cannot really afford, and in obtaining which they exceed their limited incomes." [140] Taking that criticism into account, HMI Bellairs admonished schoolmasters not to incur debts to improve their social positions. [141] In 1860 Watkins reported that at a large meeting in Bradford of the National Association for the Promotion of Social Science "a rather sweeping charge was brought against [schoolmasters] of coxcombry and pretentiousness. Seals, with crests engraved on them, and visiting cards were the chief points of accusation." [142] In this area, as in others, it is difficult to sort out objective descriptions from exaggerated charges coming from those experiencing status envy and antagonism toward teachers. A focus on the symbols of status, however, is a frequent concomitant of status uncertainty.

*Feelings of Frustration and Stagnation.*    Observers in the 1850s often described the schoolmaster's position as both unenjoyable and unpromising. The principal of Battersea Training College pointed out to the Newcastle Commission that from an economic point of view, the occupation of teaching showed "almost no progress; it does not advance." [143] The increase in earnings in the early years was not sufficient to provide for a wife and two or three children. Watkins felt that the schoolmaster, besides earning a precarious income, "has little or no professional prospect. . . . The scholastic profession in elementary schools is almost a dead level, at the best a dull table-land, which, when you have once surmounted you have no other rise before you, and look forward only to going down wearily at its end." [144]

HMI J. P. Norris suggested in 1858 that the government establish secondary schools to which the most promising teachers of the working-class elementary schools could advance. Such schools would "open a career for our older certificated teachers; promotion to the charge of such a school would be a natural and most suitable reward for ten or fifteen years' service in a successful elementary school." [145] In the following year, Matthew Arnold, noting that "almost every teacher under my inspection is now certificated," proposed a revision of the teachers' promotion scheme to permit accelerated promotion "when the teacher has given proof of distinguished excellence of some sort." [146] All these observations indicate a perceived problem of status-frustration and blocked mobility in a professional role in transition. [147]

*Restlessness and Status-Striving.*    After pointing out the lack of opportunities for further advancement, Watkins drew the conclusion that if society were to "open to them an honourable career, . . . they will speedily and rightfully avail themselves of it."[148] In the middle 1850s, some managers complained that schoolmasters thought themselves "above their work, . . . using the school only as a stepping-stone, not as a resting place, and of their being actuated by a morbid restlessness to leave their occupations, and to 'better their positions.'"[149] HMI Edward Tinling gave instances of how schools were disrupted when, after a period of disappointment with the actual conditions of work, teachers "speedily lose heart, become dissatisfied, and . . . seek to change by escape from [the trials of everyday life]."[150]

This interest in further mobility was manifested in several ways. In the early 1850s, pressure developed on the part of teachers' organizations to permit the appointment of schoolmasters into the ranks of the inspectorate. The class differences between inspectors and teachers were evident.[151] This pressure was resisted by the Committee of Council, but when the post of assistant inspector was created in 1862, it was opened to teachers. The salary was between £100 and £250 per annum, and a few teachers were appointed to these positions. A second possibility for mobility, affecting National School teachers, was to take holy orders and enter the Church of England as clergymen. This had special symbolic significance because in most cases, clergymen, as managers of local National schools, often were the direct superiors of schoolmasters. In the late 1840s and 1850s, some training colleges came in for criticism because they were thought to encourage this kind of mobility.[152] Pamela Horn reports a number of examples of this transition, but indicates that problems of low social origin continued to bedevil those who became clergymen.[153] A trickle of teachers found positions in secondary schools, but the more common avenue of exit was to positions as secretaries, accountants, and clerks in commercial undertakings.[154]

*Public Ambivalence.*    An improvement of status experienced by a socially visible group inevitably excites envy and antagonism, particularly in a society as preoccupied with class as mid-nineteenth-century Britain was. Schoolteachers did not escape public ridicule and scapegoating. Several instances of hostility to their "uppitiness" as a group have already been noted. Apparently this was a common charge, as HMI Frederick Temple's defense of them in 1864 suggests:

> The teachers of National schools are peculiarly liable to be judged according to the worst and not the ordinary specimens of their kind. Very foolish letters are sometimes written in educational periodicals, and very foolish speeches

are sometimes made at Associations, and these catch the ears and eyes of the world without, and not unnaturally "the folly of schoolmasters" becomes a popular topic, whereas, in fact the perpetrators of these follies are very few, and the work of the great majority of teachers is honestly and carefully done.[155]

Much of this hostility came from middle-class educators, whose fears of status-competition were part of the general resentment of the middle-class educational establishment over the public resources going into working-class education and the apparent improvement in its quality.[156] In particular, elementary school teachers were criticized for having been elevated by government support—rather than having succeeded on their own—and as therefore not deserving. Hugh George Robinson summarized this mentality before the Newcastle Commission:

> [Schoolmasters] naturally think more of what education has made them than of what it first found them. They easily lose sight of the fact that they have risen from a very humble social position, and they crave for that status which education seems generally to secure. I think too that in some cases they are apt to forget that they owe the culture they have to the public provision made for them.[157]

Trygre Tholfsen argues that a major motive in the formation of the Newcastle Commission itself was middle-class antagonism toward schoolteachers of working-class origin, who were perceived as becoming overeducated, overpaid, and socially pretentious. "The middle-class reaction to Kay-Shuttleworth's [system under the minutes of 1846] was plain: working-class education should be cheaper and less ambitious."[158] Lingen's relations with managers and schoolmasters were mainly antagonistic, and some of his language and style was condescending.[159] Lowe believed that elementary schoolteachers were overeducated. He regarded them as craftsmen, whose education and duties should be limited to the teaching of the basics necessary for the working class.[160] Some have interpreted the effect, if not the actual intention, of the Revised Code, the creation of Lingen and Lowe, as being "to put an end to the 'overeducation' of the pupil and teachers . . . it pleased many who disliked the independence and self-assertiveness of the 'government man.' . . . It was an attempt to confine the elementary school and the elementary schoolteacher within narrow limits."[161]

Speaking to the teachers' association in Gloucestershire in 1855, HMI Bellairs seems to have captured the ambivalence about the teacher's status. He assured his listeners that they were worthy to be called "gentlemen"—a point of some concern for some schoolmasters—but that they should not pretend to positions held by "persons born in certain grades of society, and possessed of certain pecuniary and other considerations." Above all, Bellairs counseled good behavior and patience:

> Little gain will result from these complaints of the neglect with which the public treats the profession; less from those deprecations of the calling, as if it were in itself low and unworthy of a man of education; less, still, from attempts to obtrude themselves into spheres of society to which society is not yet prepared to admit them. . . . There is nothing to prevent your advancement to any place or grade to which God may be pleased to call you. You live in a land where the highest offices are open to you. Let this be sufficient. Do not attempt to thrust yourselves where people are not willing to receive you. Do your duty, and bide your time.[162]

*Social Isolation.* Many commentators regarded the life of the teacher, especially in a rural community, as an isolated one. One assistant commissioner of the Newcastle Commission found it "difficult to point to the class with whom they can associate at all."[163] In a teachers' periodical, an anonymous author characterized the teacher's position as follows:

> The schoolmaster is far too frequently . . . the solitary bee, or wasp of place . . . it is, usually, a rare thing to see the good man with a companion, or to hear of his having any friend with him. . . . You do not find he visits his neighbours, or being visited by them . . . when he has quitted the scene of his daily toil, entered his little dwelling, and pocketed his latch-key, he is left completely alone, without any human being to break the social monotony of his existence for weeks together. Even if married, blest with children . . . his wife and children are, herein, partakers with him of the same difficulties in regard to social life. They cannot force themselves upon the courtesy of others, or associate with every one, anymore than himself.[164]

Such descriptions, however typical they may be, are consistent with a position of social marginality. The schoolmaster was educated and perhaps middle-class to pupils and parents, but was of working-class background to managers,[165] clergy, and other middle-class residents. As such, he could find little common ground with either, and his presence perhaps constituted a source of discomfort for both.

The situation of schoolmasters differed from that of schoolmistresses in these dimensions of social marginality. About the time the minutes of 1846 were taking effect, HMI Joseph Fletcher surveyed some 301 British and Foreign Society schools. He reported that schoolmistresses generally came from a slightly higher social background than male teachers. "[Owing] to the want of employment for unmarried [middle-class] women in England, they are, as a whole, derived from a somewhat more educated class than the masters." [166] He reported that many married female teachers were the wives of masters of boys' schools on the same premises. In later years, inspectors estimated that about half of the married schoolmistresses' husbands were masters.[167] In such cases the couple sought appointments "where the husband can take charge of the boys', and the wife of the girls' school." [168] A small number of women left elementary school teaching "to better their position" as teachers in middle schools or as governesses.[169] Women's concern about social status, however, was probably less than that of men. Watkins remarked that "the school masters, more than the school mistresses, are not content with their social position." [170] One possible explanation for this is that their slightly higher social origins gave them a greater sense of continuity with their past. Another is that a woman's social status depended heavily on the status of her husband, so that women teachers' status concerns may have been more intermingled with concerns about marriage than those of males. Despite these qualifications, the immediate difficulties of a marginal class position were no doubt experienced. This was no doubt what Kay-Shuttleworth had in mind when he wrote, sympathetically, in the preface to an article on "ladies in elementary schools":

> A real lady may have some [trials] to bear from the vulgar prejudices of ignorant persons, who know of no standard by which to judge their fellows but their own mean measure of worldly position . . . what is worse, she will find such persons among those who should know better, even in the family of her clergyman, or among the surrounding gentry.[171]

Many women teachers remained unmarried, possibly for the reasons of marginality and isolation that characterized the occupation of teaching in general. HMI Frederick Cook commented:

> The social position of the schoolmistress is a very peculiar one; it separates her very much from the class to which she originally belonged, while it does not bring her into contact with a different class, and therefore she is very much isolated. She would not marry a labourer, she would not marry an artizan who was not an educated man, and she is not, very likely, generally speaking, to marry a person very much above herself; she does so sometimes.[172]

At the same time, Kay-Shuttleworth attributed part of the shortage of schoolteachers to the fact that "we are educating the most eligible wives

for the middle classes . . . not merely among the higher class of mechanics, but amongst even the shopkeepers and tradesmen the school mistresses are selected as the best wives." [173]

The first collective association of teachers was the Committee of
Metropolitan Church Schoolmasters. This group agitated successfully
throughout the country for the repeal of an 1852 minute of the Committee of Council that gave the clergy the right to dismiss teachers for
giving unsound religious instruction or on other moral and religious
grounds. In the early 1850s, two separate associations of teachers
formed. One was the United Association of Schoolmasters (UAS), a
London-based association of teachers and training-college tutors from
National, British and Foreign, Home and Colonial, Congregational and
some "middle-class" schools. A more country-based and exclusively
Anglican body was the General Associated Body of Church Schoolmasters in England and Wales (ABCS). The UAS concerned itself mainly
with "professional interests" shared by members. While proclaiming
that it was not a union, the ABCS nonetheless turned almost immediately to questions of the promotion of teachers to the subinspec-
torships, pension schemes, and examination for certificates. [174] The
ABCS excluded teachers of other denominations from its association
right up to 1870. It also excluded clergymen, despite the arguments of
some members that their inclusion would add to the association's
status. [175] (Religious divisions, so pervasive in the educational establishment, affected the occupational associations of teachers as well.) As the
government was preparing to issue the Revised Code of 1862, both
teachers' organizations joined inspectors and managers in unsuccessfully opposing it.

THE IMPACT OF THE REVISED CODE

In chapter 5, I reviewed the Revised Code from the standpoint of its
economic, class, and religious consequences, and observed how it
hastened some of the tendencies that produced the Education Act of
1870. [176] Earlier in this chapter, I noted its temporarily crippling effect
on the pupil-teacher system. It remains to assess the diverse consequences of the code's policies—and of the 1860s in general—on the
situation of teachers in the working-class elementary schools.

The features of the Revised Code that most affected teachers were the
following:

In keeping with a recommendation by the Newcastle Commission, the code abolished the capitation grant and the augmentation grant to teachers and made their full salaries payable by managers.

Payments to schools by the government depended on a combination of attendance and the results obtained from the examination of pupils in the basic subjects. Religious instruction and higher subjects such as science, history, and geography were omitted from consideration.

Payment of pupil-teachers' stipends became the responsibility of managers and teachers. This discouraged schools from employing them; it also reduced their stipends.

Grants to training colleges were converted to a system of payment by results; the code also revised the curriculum of the training colleges to stress instruction in the basic subjects.

The first two provisions affected teachers' short-term situation the most; the second two, affecting the supply of teachers, were more likely to be felt in the longer term (from four to seven years) because of the long period between recruitment as an apprentice and certification upon completing the training college.

As indicated earlier, a principal motive for the Revised Code was to achieve economies. Years later Lowe was to describe it as "more a financial than a literary preference."[177] Most of these economies were to come from abolishing supplementary grants, changing the principle for granting to payment by results, and reducing grants for pupil-teaching and teacher-training. Lowe boasted that he had succeeded with respect to teaching: "[The Revised Code] swept away the vested interest of some 10,000 teachers, who had begun to consider themselves government *employés,* having a claim to augmentation grants for the rest of their life."[178] Another of Lowe's motives, noted above, stemmed from his view of teachers as "over-educated" and the curriculum of the teacher-training colleges as too academic. In the 1850s, the colleges had been criticized as "pretentious" and too much influenced by college principals and school inspectors who were university graduates.[179] The *Edinburgh Review* made that charge in 1861. In introducing the Revised Code, Lowe announced that "a lower kind of teacher must be employed."[180]

The evidence from the 1860s indicates that the code was indeed creating its intended effects. Table 28 shows the movement of average wages of certificated schoolmasters and schoolmistresses. The salaries of both dipped in the middle of the decade and began to recover around 1867. The decline is attributable to the loss of supplementary grants for teachers and the drive for economies imposed on managers suffering from decreased government grants. The rise in salaries later in the decade probably reflects the cumulative effects of the great drop in pupil-teachers between 1862 and 1866, which manifested itself in a smaller supply of certificated teachers around 1870.[181] Inspectors commented on the loss of income of teachers between 1864 and 1867,[182] and it was noticed in the debates on education in Parliament in 1867.[183]

The impact on status and morale is not so easily measured, but all evidence points to a decline in these as well in the early and middle 1860s. Observers agreed that the loss of the quasi-civil-service status implied by direct government payments had an adverse effect on morale. Matthew Arnold attributed part of the decline of schools to the fact that the code had "withdrawn from teachers all character of salaried civil servant."[184] Bellairs suggested how this might have been experienced:

> [The Revised Code] has removed from them that quasi protection of the State which enervated their character and withdrew them from those general conditions of employment which assign merit and reward to those who earn it. Under the old Minutes a man who had gained a first-class certificate secured for himself with tolerable certainty a prize in his profession, which he maintained to a great extent independent of the state of his school, provided it passed a decent inspection.[185]

The complete transfer of the teacher to the employ of managers removed that protection and status.

Teachers' morale also appeared to sag. Inspectors' reports in 1863 reveal a sense of apprehension, if not panic, among managers and schoolmasters.[186] The reports up to 1866 gave instances of teachers departing for other kinds of jobs when they could find them.[187] Kennedy gave the following account of morale among the teachers in his district in 1866:

> If I were to say that the teachers of schools were carrying on their work with the same zeal and heartiness now as they did a few years ago, I should say what is not true. They themselves are fully conscious that they do not now work so much *con amore* as was the case a little time back, and among other facts which prove this is the number of teachers who leave our National and Church schools for the purpose of setting up private schools or for some other employment. The present drift downwards was perhaps inevitable, and may in time again right itself.[188]

Both economic pressure and diminished morale affected the school-masters' organizations. Several had exhausted their funds in the fight against the Revised Code, and went more or less into institutional abeyance. The ABCS experienced a bitter fight between its rank and file and the leadership shortly after the campaign against the code, and efforts to rebuild the association proved unsuccessful. In 1867 Kennedy reported that the schoolmasters' association in Manchester was "dis-solving," which he read as "one sign of the depressed spirit prevailing in the body." [189] Schoolmistresses' associations, however, though never so numerous or active as males, remained in existence during these years. [190] Educational publications by teachers' associations also dropped off in the first few years of the code. [191] In 1867 and 1868, with conditions easing slightly, and with hopes for a general education bill from Parlia-ment in the air, the political activity of teachers revived.

In sum, the years 1862–67 appear to illustrate the kind of outcome that is typical when a marginal and low-status group is propelled into a phase of exceptional support and improvement—accompanied by ris-ing expectations, euphoria, frustration, and militancy—and then de-pressed by a precipitate withdrawal of support that generates reactions of passivity, bitterness, and morbidity. After returning to England in 1867, Matthew Arnold drew a grim comparison with his impressions after an earlier return in 1859. "I find in [the English schools], if I compare them with their former selves, a deadness, a slackness, and a discouragement which are not the signs and accompaniments of progress." [192]

Extreme as these signs of withdrawal were, the system survived, and inspectors and managers, as well as most teachers and pupil-teachers, stayed and coped with it under the new circumstances. To focus on teachers and managers, the code altered most of their important role-relations significantly. Above all, it imposed changes in the incentive sys-tem for schools. The minutes of 1846 created what we would now call "institutional grants" from the state—block grants based on the general adequacy of *institutional* performance. The code based grants on the year-by-year performance of *individual* students. The measure of this was a series of highly standardized examinations in the three R's, con-ducted by the inspector on his annual visits. Many school managers re-acted to this system by attempting to protect and maximize their finan-cial support under conditions of reduced resources.

The most visible reactions of managers and teachers were to adapt to the altered method of calculating the annual grants. First they placed a higher premium on preparation in the basic subjects. In 1865 HMI J. G. Fitch reported that teachers were "disposed to narrow their sense of duty to the 'Six Standards' [the levels of examination under the Revised Code], or to what they sometimes call, with unconscious sarcasm, 'the paying subjects.'"[193] Textbooks especially adapted to the requirements of the Revised Code appeared. The accompanying effect was neglect of grammar, history, and geography,[194] and in some cases needlework, in favor of arithmetic.[195] National Society school inspectors and some clergymen complained that teachers neglected religious instruction as well, because it did not pay.[196] In addition, the approaching examination day became a subject of heightened preparation and anxiety. Pamela and Harold Silver uncovered the following entries in the logbooks of St. Mark's National School in Lambeth:

> In October, 1863 [Harriett Gibbs, the schoolmistress] examined the children who were to be presented to the inspectors: "Result not very encouraging." The Rev. C. H. Wychag "examined the children for the new Code. Result most disheartening." Walter Cornell, master of the boys' school . . . "changed organisation for arithmetic. . . . Intend to try the same classes reading and writing, on account of new Code." . . . In September [of 1863] he recorded that "We are spending much time in arithmetic, in which subject many boys will fail." . . . In 1863 the master "commenced the plan of keeping late schools half an hour beyond the school hours so as to fulfill the requirements of the New Code.[197]

Inspectors reported instances of deviant and near-deviant adaptations, which occurred—as Morell observed—"when the interpretation of rules comes into collision with self-interest."[198] Examples were "packing"— bloating attendance on examination days—bringing sick children in for examination, cheating by copying results, misrepresenting children's ages, manipulating the definitions of standards so that more children would pass, and making false entries in school registers.[199] Morell reported instances of holding older students back so that they could pass the lower standards more easily, or giving them more advanced work but having them examined at lower levels.[200] Some schools neglected infant education because these young scholars were not eligible for examination, or held on to infant scholars as long as possible so they could pass the first standard.[201]

This range of reactions is intelligible in light of the facts that the school managers and teachers were struggling for economic sustenance, if not for survival, under the code, and that their government income depended on the number of passes. Matthew Arnold wrote that "on the examination day [scholars and teachers] have not minds for anything else [than the benefits and losses for the school]." [202] As a result, education was administered with the knowledge that "the object is attained if it be done *well enough to pass*." [203] The motive of maximizing the number of passes also lay behind the frequent observations of inspectors that the method of instruction was dull, routine, standardized, and mediocre. It was so because that was what was required if students were to pass standardized, minimal examinations. [204] Arnold summed up the critics' reactions in a reflection in 1867:

> In a country where everyone is prone to rely too much on mechanical processes, and too little on intelligence, a change in the Education Department's regulations [the Revised Code], which, by making two-thirds of the Government grant depend upon a mechanical examination, inevitably gives a mechanical turn to the school teaching, a mechanical turn to the inspection, is and must be trying to the intellectual life of a school. [205]

The emphasis on results spilled over into the relations between managers and teachers. Some managers were reported to have made the teachers' pay partly dependent on the number of passes. The relations between teachers and pupil-teachers also had to take into account that the main aim was to strive for the maximum annual number of passes. Later it will be noted that the code altered the relations between teachers and inspectors, too. [206] HMI George French suggested that the code aggravated sometimes already antagonistic relations between teachers and parents:

> Oddly enough, it takes a very small matter indeed to cause parents to keep a child from school. They are vexed perhaps at something the teacher has done or left undone as regards their children. He may have been too harsh or not harsh enough. He may have hurt the mother's feelings by sending back a child who has come to school unkempt and unwashed. . . . Then the child is kept away to spite the teacher, as it is expressed. And if the child or children be eligible for the grant, the revenge is sweeter, more satisfactory, and severe, as their place is sure to be vacant on the day of examination. [207]

The alteration of the teachers' situation with respect to welfare, role relations, social status, and morale during the 1860s demonstrates how deeply the manipulation of economic incentives affecting institutional survival can penetrate the social fabric.

In a "re-equilibrating" minute of February 1867, the Committee of Council reintroduced examinations on the "higher subjects," which had been neglected because of emphasis on the three R's. It also permitted credit for infant-school teaching not connected with the payment-by-results system. The committee's sensitivity to these problems is seen in its explanatory note to the inspectors' reports of 1867: "[The] greater part of [these] reports were written before the publication of the Minute of 20 February 1867. It meets the objections and embodies the suggestions which many of the inspectors make."[208]

### EPILOGUE

The payment-by-results system continued until 1895, and many of the problems associated with that incentive system persisted after its initial application.[209] But the passage of the Education Act of 1870 and the subsequent burst of growth of primary education revitalized the associational life of teachers. They reunited in a National Union of Elementary Teachers in 1870, just before the final passage of the act. This new organization was multidenominational, replacing the sectarian groups of earlier decades. The appearance of nondenominational schools, the adoption of the conscience clause, and the end of denominational inspection in 1870 contributed to the diminution of sectarian rivalries among the teachers. (Just as proliferation along primordial lines was the rule under conditions of unresolved sectarian conflict and religious paralysis, so it could recede when those conditions diminished in force.) The teachers' concerns in the decades following 1870 were controlling entry into the profession (including certification) under its condition of rapid growth, recruitment into the inspectorate, pension schemes, salaries, and conditions of work. Some advances on all these fronts occurred, and by the 1890s the relationship between the professional teachers' association and the Education Department had advanced to one of consultation.[210]

### INSPECTORS

When the system of inspection of government-assisted schools for the working classes began in 1840, the idea of visitation to ensure quality was already an established practice. The Church of England had long used visiting clergymen to keep the activities of its local churches up to standard. In the eighteenth century, the Society for the Propagation of Christian Knowledge used Anglican clergymen to inspect the charity schools. These inspectors assumed a multiplicity of auditing, appointing, and advising roles—including the overseeing of examinations. Ministers and volunteers approved by ministers inspected and advised denominational Sunday schools. Inspection had long been a feature of continental school systems. The National Society established inspectors and visitors for its monitorial schools, with the clergy taking the main responsibility. The British and Foreign School Society developed a system of traveling "agents" in the 1820s, which became regular in the following decade. In Scotland, the presbyteries of the Kirk were responsible for school inspection, and after a long struggle, the Irish experiment incorporated a system of inspection. The Factory Act of 1833 involved the government directly in the creation of factory inspectors. These men, who received a good salary (£1,000 a year), visited factories and submitted regular reports on the effectiveness and enforcement of factory legislation, and on other conditions, including the working of factory schools. The New Poor Law of 1834 also built in a system of inspection.[211] Thus by the 1830s the country had firmly established the idea and the role of inspection.

The select committees of the 1830s inquired especially about the inspection system in French schools and the National Society's scheme.[212] They also learned of the Anglican Church's opposition to government inspection, when Wigan, the secretary of the National Society warned:

> It must be remembered that many of the . . . Church of England schools . . . are supported by gentlemen of property of the country, who would feel considerable jealousy at any inspector from Government being sent around. Of late in certain cases gentlemen have reduced the scale and extent of the school which they intended to establish, and borne all the cost of establishing it themselves, because they did not choose to subject themselves to what they apprehended might produce some kind of interference.[213]

In 1838 the Treasury gave some £500 to each of the voluntary societies for inspecting schools built from government grants. The National Society asked for more, but was rejected, so some of its schools went uninspected in that year.[214] The grant, while not calling for government inspectors, nevertheless established in a minimum way the concept of government interest in inspecting schools. By taking the money, the religious societies also gave acquiescence to that concept.

Earlier we noted the initiative of the Melbourne government to introduce inspection; the prolonged struggle of 1839–40 resulting in substantial Church of England control over inspection; the government's caution in instructing the early inspectors, especially with respect to religious education; the incremental incorporation of religious societies other than the National Society into the inspection scheme; and some initial jurisdictional struggles over inspection between the government and the religious societies.[215] The religious issue will reemerge, but now the main focus will be on the role, role relations, and role conflicts of the inspectorate as it developed to 1870.

The first decade of inspection was an interesting combination of official minimization of the inspectors' powers, and a substantial growth in their involvement, influence, and power. In commenting on the minutes of 1846, Kay-Shuttleworth itemized the areas to which the authority of inspectors did *not* extend: selecting and dismissing masters; influencing the curriculum or methods of teaching; dismissing pupil-teachers; and directing or even advising their management committee, unless invited. Kay-Shuttleworth stressed usefulness, helpfulness, and guidance—and all of these on request, not on initiative.[216] The minutes instructing the inspectors in 1840 were consistent with his cautious approach.[217]

The inspectors' actual role contrasted sharply with the official line of passivity. They became reformers, in effect, by criticizing the schools they inspected. They underscored the low quality of teachers and teaching, and described many infant schools as "a miserable caricature" of Samuel Wilderspin, the promoter of infant schools. Hugh Tremenheere suggested closing most of the monitorial schools he visited, much to the chagrin of the British and Foreign School Society.[218] The inspectors went beyond mere agonizing, however, and consistently attributed the poor quality of the educational apparatus—buildings, teachers' qualifications and motivations, monitors, educational books—to the scantiness of the resources devoted to them.[219] Such communications were harbingers of the improvements of 1846 and became an important basis for justifying them.

After 1843, when Kay-Shuttleworth worked out a plan for more systematic inspection, the inspectors appeared to expand their concerns and comments. The documentation of poor quality under the monitorial system continued. Inspectors' reports contain an extended array of additional suggestions, such as discontinuing corporal punishment; combining separate boys' and girls' schools into mixed schools, mainly on grounds of economy;[220] encouraging the separation of infant schools from day schools to relieve the latter of the burden of very young children; delegating mechanical work to monitors; improving the quality of books; and proposals for arranging desks, heating buildings, and designing cloakrooms.[221] All these comments were advisory, but they nonetheless carried messages to local schools and to the central administration.

An increasing workload accompanied the expanded range of concerns. As training colleges developed, inspectors included them in their assignments. They also set, supervised, and marked the examinations of teachers, teachers-in-training, and pupil-teachers. They were responsible for certifying teachers and for recommending on eligibility for pensions. In documenting his workload in 1852, HMI Watkins also complained about travel time and about his huge correspondence, dealing with "inquiries, complaints, advice, applications from schoolmasters and schoolmistresses, notices of new books, requests for assistance from the public purse, and communications from your Lordships' secretary." [222]

The number of inspectors increased substantially during the late 1840s (see table 29), but apparently not rapidly enough for them to be able to do what was asked of them. After 1846, the visits of inspectors to most schools were cut to one every two years. [223] The inspectors also proved to be an expensive budget item. They were paid £600 a year at first, but in the face of evident pressures for economy in 1850, the Committee of Council reduced the salary to £400 for the first year. Also in 1850, the committee appointed a number of assistant inspectors, who had, as "nearly as possible," the same rank and attainments as the inspectors, but with salaries of around £250. Even with these economies, the costs of inspection continued to climb. The costs from the beginning of government inspection in 1839 to 1861, just before promulgation of the Revised Code, appear in table 29.

The evident reasons for the appointment of assistant inspector in 1850 were the costs of inspection and the complaints of the inspectors about their workloads; possibly, too, it was a gesture to schoolmasters, who had been campaigning unsuccessfully for the right of appointment to the inspectorate. [224] The Committee of Council minute announcing the appointment of the assistants reveals the germs of several associated problems:

Of the sixteen existing inspectors, eleven were Anglican clergymen, reflecting the continuing dominance of the Established Church in the educational establishment.

If current needs were to be met, the system required nine new inspectors; the increase in numbers of schools was the principal reason for this. In addition, the workloads of inspectors varied greatly. HMI Watkins (most vocal in commenting on conditions of overwork) had a total of 184 Anglican schools under his jurisdiction in York, whereas HMI Thomas Marshall had only 39 Catholic schools—the total in-

TABLE 29    NUMBERS OF INSPECTORS AND ASSISTANT
INSPECTORS AND INSPECTION COSTS, 1839–1861

|            | Number of Inspectors | Number of Assistant Inspectors | Total Payments |
|------------|----------|----------|----------------|
| 1839–40    | 2        |          | £    186.15.6  |
| 1840–41    | 3        |          | 1,234.2.1      |
| 1841–42    | 4 [a]    |          | 2,200.10.11    |
| 1842–43    | 3        |          | 2,019.3.2      |
| 1843–44    | 5        |          | 2,163.19.5     |
| 1844–45    | 8        |          | 5,492.7.5      |
| 1845–46    | 8        |          | 5,979.5.4      |
| 1846–47    | 13       |          | 6,747.8.9      |
| 1847–48    | 19       |          | 11,990.3.6     |
| 1848–49    | 21       |          | 15,055.5.10    |
| 1849–50    | 22       |          | 17,183.5.11    |
| 1850–51    | 23       |          | 18,678.0.10    |
| 1851–52    | 23       | 2        | 19,870.1.5½    |
| 1852–53    | 24       | 9        | 20,793.15.2½   |
| 1853–54    | 25       | 10       | 26,574.12.6½   |
| 1854–55    | 29       | 10       | 30,939.3.7½    |
| 1855–56    | 30       | 12       | 30,526.18.9½   |
| 1856–57    | 30       | 12       | 31,131.8.9     |
| 1857–58    | 30       | 16       | 36,052.5.6½    |
| 1858–59    | 36       | 18       | 39,753.5.3½    |
| 1859–60    | 36       | 19       | 41,890.2.6     |
| 1860–61    | 36       | 25 [b]   | 43,565.9.1     |

SOURCE: *Parliamentary Papers,* 1861, 158, p. 2.

[a] This included one inspector who was "employed on a Special Commission, to inquire into the condition of education in Birmingham and the Cotton districts of Lancashire, 63 days, at £2 2s. per day."

[b] By the summer of 1861 the number of assistant inspectors had been reduced to twenty-four.

spected in Britain. This was an early sign of the administrative anomaly stemming from the proliferation of schools along religious lines.

As if in recognition of that anomaly, the committee made an effort to realign the workloads of inspectors by reassigning some schools, but without, however, crossing denominational lines. The committee acknowledged that this would ease the immediate pressure of work, but noted: "It will, however, fall short of meeting the public demand for inspection."[225]

This issue of allocation of inspectors by religious denomination is another illustration of how a "truce point"—here 1846 and its subsequent denominational elaboration—creates a gyroscopic effect that generates results that subsequently become a social problem.[226] This problem of cumbersomeness for the inspectors continued to develop throughout the 1850s. The government grants were extended to Jewish schools in 1852 (with some limitations),[227] and to the Episcopal Church in Scotland in the same year.[228] In 1859 the Committee of Council recorded the complexity that had emerged. There were now:

> The Inspector of Schools connected with the Established Church; the Inspector of Schools organised on the British system; the Inspector of Wesleyan Methodist Schools; the Inspector of Roman Catholic Schools; the Inspector of Workhouse Schools; while in Scotland four Inspectors are, in like manner, everywhere crossing each other, those, namely, who visit the schools of the Established, of the Free, of the Protestant Episcopal, and of the Roman Catholic, Churches.[229]

The committee acknowledged how "unfavourable such an arrangement necessarily must be for purely administrative purposes." It argued that this was compensated for by the fact that "we receive reports from several witnesses [i.e., inspectors] acting quite independently of each other in every part of the country."[230] The administrative cost and unwieldiness of the denominational inspectorate were part of the concern for simplification that motivated the adoption of the Revised Code, but the government could not bring itself to alter the anomalous system.[231] Nondenominational inspection had to await the Education Act of 1870.

The class origins of the inspectorate were clearly the upper ranges of the middle classes. Of sixty-four inspectors about whom David Roberts was able to secure reliable information, more than one-third came from landed families, about one-third from the clergy, law, and medicine, and the remainder from various kinds of involvement in higher education.[232] In many respects, the role of inspector was attractive. From the perspective of the Church of England—which supplied most inspectors, many of whom were clergymen—the inspectorate was a well-paying career: the salary of even an assistant inspector was approximately double that of a young curate.[233] The inspectorship thus appears to have fallen into the tradition under which the Anglican Church provided "positions" where the children of the wealthy could be placed securely. The political economist Nassau Senior, a member of the Newcastle Commission, actually characterized the inspectorate as a kind of jobbery for well-to-do people or those who had delayed a choice of profession.[234]

The class dimension of the inspectors' role calls for further comment. The schools they inspected were, above all, working-class institutions, and as such largely insulated from the broader society. The students in these schools were working-class children, and their teachers were largely of working-class origin; teachers from higher classes apparently did not choose to teach in them.[235] The class of those responsible for the *control* of the schools, however, contrasted sharply. The managers of elementary schools for the poor were drawn predominantly from the ranks of the local clergy, landowners, manufacturers, and merchants.[236]

The inspectors thus enjoyed a class position similar to that of the managers. This was consistent with the idea that education was to be organized for the working class from above, and, accordingly, controlled from above. At the same time, the role of school inspector may have acquired a tinge of lowered status from its attachment to a lower-status enterprise. Their income was lower than that of inspectors of the factories and the collieries. School inspectors, unlike factory inspectors, could not prosecute, and managers affronted by them could complain to the Committee of Council.[237] In 1843 HMI Tremenheere was under fire from the British and Foreign School Society for his negative accounts of their schools. He remarked that "it was necessary for [the government] to provide me with some other employment which should be a promotion" before the inspection arrangements affecting the British and Foreign School Society could be changed. That "promotion" was to an inspectorship of mines.[238]

Be that as it may, the school inspector was lodged in a role that crossed class lines. He interacted with many different constituencies, and sometimes became a negotiator among them. Inspectors maintained relationships with the central educational office of the government, school managers, teachers, other inspectors, and, more in passing, with pupil-teachers and (especially after the Revised Code) pupils. Such a role typically involves its incumbents in role conflicts; the inspectorship was no exception to this rule.

The relationship between inspectors and school managers was necessarily a delicate one, because the inspector could affect the reputation of a school, and, in the extreme, its grants. The inspectors also were conveyors of the rules and regulations of the Committee of Council. This role was not eased by the bad relations that developed among Lingen and the managers, teachers, and inspectors during the 1850s and 1860s. Much of the early uneasiness over inspection arose either from sensitivity about religious inspection or, as in the British and Foreign School Society's running conflict with Tremenheere, about the negative quality of inspectors' reports. Over time, however, inspectors began to take on the role of outside helper in disputes among managers, between managers and teachers, and sometimes between managers and parents.[239] The Revised Code altered this role. It put the inspector in a position to directly affect a school's income, inasmuch as he determined how many children passed in examination. One Lincolnshire teacher complained of the effects of the code:

> The teachers have been defrauded. The time of Inspectors is wasted on comparatively trivial details; the ordinary working of the school is so entirely cast aside that the Inspector cannot form any opinion respecting either the general character or discipline. The Managers are led to look upon the inspection as merely a scheme for raising money, and the inspector as a necessary evil or nuisance invented by Government to enhance the value of cash.[240]

Managers denied the charge, but it remains true that the code moved inspectors to a central place in the funding decisions, a place that they had not occupied before. Generally speaking, however, the relations between inspectors and managers—cemented by membership in the same general social class—remained generally cooperative during the difficult years of the Revised Code.[241]

The class differences between inspectors and teachers framed all their relations. The situation is underscored in an exchange between HMI John Allen and Kay-Shuttleworth. The former had asked whether he should dine together with a manager and a schoolmaster. Kay-Shuttleworth replied,

> About your dinner-party, I am not sure what your clergy would think. . . . We very much need to have different classes brought together; but although I have met with several instances of the schoolmistress being received at the clergyman's table, I scarcely recollect an instance out of London . . . of a clergyman's shaking hands with, or even talking familiarly with, the parochial schoolmaster.[242]

If some schoolmasters wanted to be addressed as gentlemen, the inspectors did not oblige. Only one inspector—a Scot and a former schoolmaster himself—referred to schoolmasters as "gentlemen" in the reports; the others referred to them as "persons."[243]

There were tensions other than those stemming from class differences. The schoolteachers were dependent on inspectors in many respects—for certifying their pupil-teachers and thereby enabling them to
receive the augmentation grant; for recommending their promotion and
placement; for certifying their pupil-teachers for advancement to training colleges; and, in extreme cases, for helping them retain their jobs. If
anything, the Revised Code increased this dependency. It put the inspector in a position to evaluate teachers' worth in detail by examining their
pupils. More generally, the code created an atmosphere in which it was
more difficult for inspectors to be supportive.[244] The alteration of the
relations among inspectors, teachers, and pupils occasioned by the Revised Code is revealed in a characterization of examination day by a former pupil in a National Society school:

> Two inspectors came once a year and carried out a dramatic examination.
> The schoolmaster came into school in his best suit; all the pupils and teach-
> ers would be listening til at 2 o'clock a dog-cart would be heard on the road,
> even though it was 80 yards away. In would come two gentlemen with a de-
> portment of high authority, with rich voices. Each would sit at a desk and
> children would be called in turn to one or the other. The master hovered
> around, calling children out as they were needed. The children could see him
> start with vexation as a good pupil stuck at a word in the reading-book he
> had been using all year, or sat motionless with his sum in front of him. The
> master's anxiety was deep, for his earnings depended on the children's
> work.[245]

On their part, some teachers resented the inspectors' lack of famil-
iarity with and alienation from the teaching situation:

> [The] experienced teachers . . . bitterly resented these young men who had
> never been in an elementary school before, and had to learn it all from the
> teachers they were paid to control. They came in, so the teachers felt, by
> favour, and were just another manifestation of the injustice of the service.[246]

Despite the tension and conflict, many inspectors came to identify with
the schoolteachers and to represent them sympathetically. Their reports
described the teachers as underpaid, undersupported, and underap-
preciated. They supported teachers' efforts to obtain a regular superannuation scheme. Most of them supported teachers' attempts to achieve
an associational life, much as this offended their superiors, Lowe and
Lingen. HMI W. Warburton felt that associations permitted the exchange of common interests, and compensated for the "want of sympathy," "misunderstandings," "slights," and "craving for the compan-
ionship of others" that characterized a teacher's life.[247] Even after the
adoption of the Revised Code, which soured the relations between

teacher and inspector in some respects, the inspectors continued to champion the teachers in many ways.[248]

The relations between the inspectors and the Committee of Council (after 1856 the Department of Education) in some ways resembled those between "line" and "staff" in any formal organization. The secretary and staff of the committee constituted the authority system of the educational establishment. They carried out the policies of the committee, approved and distributed grants, issued directives, assured compliance with them, established and implemented procedures, and kept the paperwork flowing. The inspectors formally had a reporting and advisory relationship with the committee, but they also enjoyed potential influence because of their social status. Moreover, their knowledge of the educational system gave them claims to expertise, the opinion of some teachers to the contrary notwithstanding.

The educational bureaucracy and the inspectors had overlapping, but different, constituencies. The main forces in the lives of the secretary and staff of the Committee of Council were the committee itself (and, more indirectly, members of Parliament), the religious societies,[249] and school managers. The inspectors also interacted with many of these groups, but had closer working relations with managers, teachers, pupil-teachers, pupils, and, in rare cases, parents. This different range of involvements suggests that inspectors' views would sometimes conflict with those of the bureaucracy.

In the early years of the inspectorate, many of the relations between the committee and the inspectors were open, informal, and collegial. Kay-Shuttleworth's personal style and the smallness of the inspectorate made this possible.[250] As the inspectorate grew—inspectors and assistant inspectors numbered thirty in 1853—and Lingen and later Lowe brought a chillier and sometimes more officious tone to the Committee of Council, relations became more formal and more conflictful in several ways.[251]

The first bone of contention was the association of inspectors with one another. In 1846 Kay-Shuttleworth initiated the custom of an annual meeting of inspectors to exchange information and discuss educational matters. The practice continued after Kay-Shuttleworth retired in 1849, evolving into a medium for inspectors to express their collective mind on educational matters. From time to time they would even put controversial issues to a vote and go on record, sometimes expressing opinions contrary to committee policy. This activity constituted a thorn in the side of the committee and its secretariat. In 1858 C. B. Adderley (its vice president) and Granville (its president) forbade the practice as inappropriate to civil servants, whose role did not permit criticism of official policy. In 1859 Lowe, as vice president, banned the annual conferences altogether. This weakened the collective voice of the inspectorate. Annual meetings did not resume until around 1880.[252]

The independence of inspectors in preparing their reports—which were published—was another point of conflict. After the religious struggles accompanying the establishment of the inspectorate (the major confrontation with the Church of England in 1839–40 and the skirmish with the Wesleyans in 1847),[253] Kay-Shuttleworth was reluctant to appear to interfere with their reports. As he explained to the Newcastle Commission,

> Great delicacy was felt in the Committee at that time [the late 1840s] in interfering with the reports of the inspectors, inasmuch as the controversy with the Church of England and with the religious bodies, as to the mode of appointing the inspectors, had been so recent, it was thought desirable to give inspectors a larger amount of discretion in the form of their report than would have been permitted if they had been officers appointed solely by the Government and without the power of withdrawal and sanction by the archbishops or by a religious body.[254]

Kay-Shuttleworth only reviewed the inspectors' reports informally and suggested emendations. In 1845 the dean and archbishop of Canterbury persuaded Kay-Shuttleworth to excise a portion of HMI John Allen's report critical of the Chapter of Canterbury, but when Allen complained, the language was restored.[255]

The issue of censorship erupted into a serious controversy at the time of the design and implementation of the Revised Code. The inspectors were "as a body . . . averse to the Revised Code."[256] They regarded it as harmful to the education of the young and personally demeaning to managers, teachers, and themselves. The initial issue of censorship arose not over the code but in a different context. In the late 1850s, Adderley had returned some reports to inspectors for correction. The report that precipitated the crisis was one by HMI Morell, the inspector of Catholic schools. In it he cited statistics that purported to demonstrate that illegitimate births and capital crimes were higher in Protestant than in Roman Catholic countries—a reflection on the morality of the former. Lowe maintained that this report "was too offensive a document to be laid on the table of the House and to be printed at the public expense."[257] He promulgated a minute in January 1861 specifying that:

> Inspectors must confine themselves to the state of the schools under their inspection, and to practical suggestions for their improvement; if any report, in the judgment of their Lordships, does not conform to this standard, it is to be

returned to the Inspector for revision; and if on its being again received from him it appears to be open to the same objection, it is to be put aside as a document not proper to be printed at the public expense.[258]

Morell was ultimately dismissed in 1864, ostensibly on grounds of complaints about the performance of his duties.[259] In addition, six other inspectors' reports—including one by Matthew Arnold—were withheld from publication in 1862 and 1863. After HMI Watkins questioned the practice of actually marking the offensive passages, Lowe ordered that the practice of marking be discontinued. Rather, the reports were returned to the inspectors for them to determine which were the offensive paragraphs. However, HMI H. Longueville Jones's report for 1862–63 was felt to be so hostile to the Department of Education that passages were again marked. Several inspectors testified before a subsequent select committee that the "offensive" passages were consistently those critical of the Revised Code.[260] Among the passages excised was the following from one of Henry Bellairs's reports:

> [Under the Revised Code the] Inspector's position will unquestionably, for some time at least, be a very difficult one. The grants in very many schools will be very considerably reduced . . . the faults of schools will frequently be laid to the Revised Code and its administration. In some instances, "packing" will, no doubt, be attempted. In others, the higher branches of study, e.g., geography and history, will be excluded, in order to insure a safe mediocrity which will ensure grants.[261]

The practice of excising offended many inspectors, including the influential Watkins and Arnold. On April 5, 1864, Lord Cecil demanded to know why HMI Morell had been suspended; Lowe referred him to the relevant correspondence.[262] One week later, on April 12, Cecil entered a resolution stating that the exclusion of statements from inspectors' reports violated the understanding of their original appointment. The resolution passed by a vote of 101 to 93. Lowe defended himself in the Commons on that day and again on April 18, but Granville announced in the House of Lords on the 18th that Lowe had resigned as vice president of the committee.[263]

The issue remained alive, however, and in the following month Parliament established a select committee to look into the issue. Lowe defended himself before that committee:

> It is not [the Inspector's] duty, indeed it is contrary to it, to enter avowedly into a controversy with the Department; it is not his duty, in my opinion, to write in a manner which displays a decidedly hostile *animus* towards the Department. I think that there needs no Minute to lay aside such reports as

those; it is a mere matter of common official subordination, that they should not be printed.[264]

In all the parliamentary discussions, speakers went to some lengths to deny that any specific criticism of Lowe was intended. In June 1864, Palmerston moved that the house rescind the vote of April 12, thereby exonerating Lowe, and this motion passed over the objections of Cecil.[265]

The controversy over censorship shows all the earmarks of an intra-departmental political struggle. In 1859, no doubt impatient with criticisms of the budgetary reductions under way, Lowe had suspended the annual meetings of the inspectors and substituted no form of consultation for them. The inspectors were not consulted during the planning and drafting phases of the Revised Code.[266] The inspectors' reports, even those not censored or withheld from publication, were sharply critical of the Code in its first years of existence.[267] One of their objections—as Bellairs's censored report indicates—was that the code demeaned the inspectors themselves. The overt issues were inspectors' freedom and the discharge of an inspector on those grounds. On the legitimate grounds of opposition to censorship, the inspectors were able, through Parliament, to launch an attack on Lingen and Lowe, and to secure Lowe's resignation.

In terms of their actual work, the 1860s constituted a somewhat dismal era for the inspectors, as they were for teachers and pupil-teachers. It is as much an exaggeration to suggest that the Revised Code was motivated by revenge against inspectors as it is to attribute it to a like motive against teachers.[268] It did, however, have a degrading effect on both. We have noted that in the eyes of some managers and teachers the inspectors gained power under the code because they had a greater role in determining the schools' income from grants. The inspectors themselves complained that it buried them in a mass of routine, trivialized their role, and discouraged any attention to larger educational matters. Matthew Arnold conceded that the new examination system was less exhausting than the old, because it did not demand "spirit and inventiveness" on the part of the inspector. It was, however, tedious and demanding:

> Few can know till they have tried what a business it is to enter in a close-ruled schedule, as an examination goes on, three marks for three different things against the names of 200 children whom one does not know one from the other, without putting the wrong child's mark in the wrong place. Few

can know how much delay and fatigue is unavoidably caused, before one can get one's 600 communications fairly accomplished, by difficulty of access to children's places, difficulty in seeing clearly in the obscurer parts of the school-room, difficulty in getting children to speak out,—sometimes of getting them to speak at all—difficulty of resisting, without feeling oneself inhuman, the appealing looks of master or scholars for a more prolonged trial of a doubtful scholar.[269]

The Committee of Council seemed to acknowledge this change in the inspector's role in its report of 1864. First it abolished the role of assistant inspector on grounds that in all important respects there were no longer any differences between them and the inspectors. Then it announced a series of economy moves. Reports for schools were to be submitted in alternate years only under a new system of districts.[270] The committee also created a new class of officers (inspectors' assistants) who "under the inspector's own superintendence and orders, [might] do a specified amount of the work which, if done wholly by the inspector himself, would be needlessly expensive."[271] The inspector's assistantships were open to schoolteachers by examination and inspectors' recommendation. Their work, however, dealt mainly with the mass of routine involved in the examination system under the Revised Code.

The Education Act of 1870 rationalized the inspectorate by abolishing the concordat of 1840 and subsequent agreements that had linked inspectors to religious denominations. The act also divided the country into new districts, and inspectors reported on all schools, board and voluntary, in their districts. The government attempted, with partial success, to systematize inspection standards and the relations between inspectors and their assistants. Above all, the inspectorate grew at an extraordinary rate in parallel with the growth of the school system itself. In 1870 there were 75 full inspectors and 23 assistants; by 1885 the number of inspectors was 121, while the numbers of assistants had increased sixfold, to 152. The changing ratio reflected the Department of Education's continuing preoccupations with economy, as well as the vast amount of routine work—readily delegated to subordinates—associated with the continuing system of payment by results.[272]

## FINAL COMMENT

The three roles examined in this chapter give evidence of the kind of rockiness that is frequently experienced when a new institution with a new and not altogether familiar set of roles arises. Some ambiguity and

ambivalence accompanies their creation, and new relations with existing roles have to be established. For these reasons a season of anxiety,
jealousy, striving for status, and antagonism on all sides is to be expected. The roles of pupil-teacher, teacher, and inspector in nineteenth-
century Britain were probably special in this regard, because each of
them involved—in different ways—crossing over class lines in a society
that was extremely conscious of class and status.

## CHAPTER 10

# Conclusion

From time to time in this study, I have interspersed remarks and interpretations that touch on the general historical and sociological points embedded in the story of British educational development. In this brief concluding chapter, I shall make some of these points more explicit.

## THE GENERAL PROCESS OF CHANGE

In chapter 2, I laid out the components of a general framework for the analysis of social change, qualified to apply to educational development. The model involves the specification of certain starting and ending points in historical sequences (labeled *moments of change* to signify their transient character and *truce points* to underscore that they are usually established as the result of a political process). The movement from one point to the next is characterized by a number of analytic steps:

Describing the main parameters of the institutional structure under analysis—in this case, primary education in nineteenth-century Britain. These parameters were found to lie mainly in the economic, political, religious, and class environments of education.

Identifying ongoing trends affecting the educational structure, many of which are perceived by the relevant historical actors as unbalancing, menacing, evil, or otherwise unsatisfactory. Such perceptions are inevitably referred to and given valence by reference to some legitimizing criterion, usually a cultural value or belief.

Tracing the development or activation of ideologies relating to the "problems" thus identified; tracing the processes of group formation and mobilization aound these ideologies.

Following the political process generated by the group mobilization and activity and identifying the new "truce point" established by some kind of political outcome. This new point may be a "non-event" or stalemate, but even this kind of outcome provides a new definition of the situation for the historical groups involved.

Repeating the above operations taking the emergent "truce point" as the new starting point—the new "equilibrium-in-tension"—on which a new set of structural forces are superimposed and play out, culminating eventually in another structural resolution.

The process-model, thus summarized, has a kind of dialectical element, but it is not intended to be an evolutionary model, leading to some definite end point. The sheer variety of educational outcomes identified in this study—to say nothing of the variety if the comparative scope were expanded—should dispel any impression of linearity or directionality. Finally, as indicated, the process-model is a synthetic one, attempting to incorporate a number of the social forces identified in a number of available accounts of educational change.

The repeated and more or less explicit applications of this process-model are found in chapters 4–7. By way of summarizing that analysis, I have extracted the most evident truce points in the five cases I have considered in this study—England, Wales, Ireland, Scotland, and New York City. These are noted and briefly described in chart 3. Several clarifications and qualifications of chart 3 are in order.

First, in some cases the same "truce points" appear in several of the cases. The year 1846, for example, when Parliament authorized an expanded system of support for the educational activity of religious denominations, was relevant as a critical moment for the English, Welsh, and Scottish systems—encouraging educational developments in all three. That year was not relevant to the Irish system, however, because it was institutionalized on a basis more or less separate from that of the rest of the United Kingdom; and, of course, it was not directly relevant for New York. The reason for the multiple significance of events like the minutes of 1846 is that England and Wales were under the same

Chart 3. Truce Points and Moments of Change

| | England | Wales | Ireland | Scotland | New York City |
|---|---|---|---|---|---|
| 1800 | | | | 1800s–1830s: Continued growth of supplementary and private schools | 1805: Establishment of the Free School Society |
| | 1807: Failure of Whitbread's legislation for parochial schools | 1807: Same as for England | | | |
| 1810 | | | 1811: Formation of the Kildare Place Society | | |
| 1820 | 1820: Failure of Brougham's legislation for government schooling for the poor | 1820: Same as for England | 1820s: Catholic alienation from the Kildare Place Society | | 1822: Effort of Bethel Baptist Church to secure subsidy for its schools |
| | | | | | 1826: Grant of monopoly for public funds to the Public School Society |
| | | | 1828: Report of Education Commission | | |
| 1830 | | | 1831: Establishment of national system of education | | |
| | | | 1830s: Concessions for denominational control to Presbyterians | | |
| | 1833: Failure of Roebuck's bill for national school system | 1833: Same as for England | | | |
| | 1833: Beginning of state subsidies for religious societies | 1833: Same as for England | | | |
| | | 1837: Beginning of educational campaigns of religious societies | | | |

Chart 3  (continued)

|  | England | Wales | Ireland | Scotland | New York City |
|---|---|---|---|---|---|
|  |  |  |  |  | 1839: Governor Seward calls for public support of Catholic schools in New York City |
|  | 1839: Formation of the Committee of Council on Education | 1839: Same as for England | 1839: Beginning of Anglican Voluntaryism |  |  |
| 1840 | 1840: Government inspection system begins | 1840: Same as for England |  |  | 1840: Catholics launch campaign for support of parochial schools |
|  |  |  |  |  | 1841: Catholic appeals denied by various public agencies in New York City |
|  |  |  |  |  | 1842: New York State establishes district system in New York System prohibits funds for denominational schools |
|  |  |  | 1844–5: Failure of the Church of Ireland to gain parliamentary subsidy | 1843: Disruption of the Church of Scotland and formation of the Free Church of Scotland |  |
|  |  |  | 1845: Augmentation of Maynooth Seminary subsidy |  |  |
|  | 1846: Minutes establishing government-supported pupil-teacher system, training-colleges, etc. | 1846: Same as for England | | 1846: Minutes of government providing for support of denominational schools; onset of denominational period |  |
|  |  | 1847: Report of Commissioners on Education in Wales ("Treachery of the Blue Books") |  |  |  |
| 1850 | 1850–68: Repeated failure of government to establish national system in face of religious conflict | 1850–68: Same as for England | 1850s: Incremental evolution of denominationalism and Catholic control of national system | 1854–71: Repeated failure of government to establish national system in face of religious conflict |  |

| | | | |
|---|---|---|---|
| 1860 | 1862: Adoption of Revised Code | 1862: Same as for England<br>Early 1860s: Strict enforcement of conscience clause | 1862: Exemption of Scotland from Revised Code<br><br>1867: Argyle Commission's recommendations for national system of education |
| | | 1869: Powis Commission and further denominationalism | |
| 1870 | 1870: Provision of state board schools, end of state support for denominational schools, end of denominational inspection, etc. | 1870: Same as for England | 1872: Scottish Education Act establishing the essentials of a new national system |

governmental and administrative system, and Scotland was partially under that system. Both Scotland and Wales each had additional or different critical moments (for example, 1872 in Scotland), however, because of their semiautonomous status as regions within the kingdom.

Second, the listing of truce points is arbitrary in several senses,[1] not the least of which is that it is not exhaustive. For example, it would have been possible to enter every one of the dozen or so unsuccessful legislative efforts of reform for England[2] and Scotland[3] in the 1850s and 1860s, but the operation would have been tediously repetitive, and since all of them failed, they generated no structural changes in the educational system. Taken as a period of structural "paralysis," those decades were significant as a kind of truce point—more accurately, a truce situation—but it is necessary to go into only so much detail to demonstrate that.

Third, another way of expanding the entries in chart 3 would be to specify events and situations "external" to the educational system but that had a direct impact on the alignment of forces affecting educational development. For example, 1833 could be entered as the beginning of the Oxford Movement, and 1845 as the conversion of Newman to Catholicism. The former was directly connected with the increasing aggressiveness of the Church of England in educational affairs between 1839 and 1843. The latter affected the posture of both the Anglican Church and Wesleyan Methodism in 1846, as well as the building anti-Catholic sentiment in England that affected denominational-government relations in 1846–48.[4] In a similar spirit, the political crises stemming from class conflict in 1816–19 and 1842–43 could be included as critical shaping forces for the legislative initiatives in 1820 and 1843. In addition, the special effect of the Reform Act of 1867 on Welsh politics—and on educational developments in Wales—could also be included. As a matter of strategy, however, I have omitted these "external developments" from chart 3, largely because to enter them would end by incorporating almost all the materials presented and analyzed in chapters 4–7.

Finally, it is in principle possible to specify critical points in the evolution of the working-class family economy from the competition of their labor with the schooling of working-class children to the increasing structural separation between family demands and educational demands. Such moments would include 1833 and 1867, which were important moments in limiting child labor and requiring schooling in its place; 1861, when the Newcastle Commission enunciated the illegitimacy of compulsory education because of its interference with children's labor; 1870 and 1876, which marked points in the making of education compulsory; and 1891, which made it free. The significance of these and other moments in family-education relationships in Britain is analyzed in chapter 8.

## SEPARATE BUT CONNECTED HISTORICAL DRAMAS

Extracting from the analysis above, it is possible to identify at least five arenas of social change that affected the evolution of working-class education in the nineteenth century. The first is the drama of class hierarchy, class consciousness, class conflict, and the attempts to contain that conflict. While these dimensions were more or less permanent fixtures in nineteenth-century England, tensions and conflicts reached dramatic proportions at certain times—1816–19, 1830–33, 1839–43, and to a lesser extent, 1867–70—in the history of class relations during the century. And while class relations were a pervasive influence on education in Britain—the whole system was structured by class—class conflict constituted a special influence in these critical years.

The second drama, closely connected with class, is that involving the influence of economic forces as they affected the behavior of parents and children, the clients of working-class schools. These economic forces constituted a complex pattern of discouragement and encouragement of children's schooling.

The third drama is the religious one, told in the complex evolution from the situation of the Established Church challenged by Dissent to that of denominationalism in the context of a weakened Establishment. Throughout this drama every group experienced victory and defeat, and each employed an array of aggressive, defensive, accommodative, and retreatist strategies. The education of working-class children was a major component in these recurrent religious contests, and virtually every turning point in educational development was simultaneously an expression of the religious struggle.

The fourth drama is the political one, with reformers, Parliament, and the government bureaucracy pursuing a periodically renewed mission of pressing educational development, but at the same time attempting to keep the peace with their diverse constituents and among them. On many occasions these two missions were at cross-purposes with each other, and the resulting paralysis accounts in large part for the irregular and halting pace of educational change in Britain throughout the century.

The final drama is that internal to the educational system: the processes by which new roles—pupils, pupil-teachers, inspectors, managers, civil servants—arose and were incorporated into it. This process
was also irregular and was marked by the ambivalence, competition,
uncertain relations, and conflicts associated with the rise and consolidation of a new institution. This drama is the subject of chapter 9.

The complexity of the evolution of education lies in the fact that
these several dramas were *both* independent of one another *and* interde-
pendent. The story of religious change, for example, has a dynamic of
its own, and only a part of that dynamic concerns the history of primary
education. The same can be said of the evolution of market capitalism
and class relations. Furthermore, as these separate dramas played themselves out, they touched primary education *irregularly, in different
ways, and only from time to time.*

To illustrate this general principle: the more or less chronic tension
between the Anglican Church and Dissent meant that whenever an issue
dealing with the control of education arose, it would be inflamed by jurisdictional religious warring. That religious presence varied from time
to time, however. The heightened competition associated with the esca-
lation of religious conflict between the late 1820s and the mid 1840s
meant that practically any educational issue was supercharged with religious energy and conflict. By contrast, the period of religious "equipoise" in the 1850s meant that the religious factor was less salient and
operated as a more passive, but at the same time still paralyzing, force.[5]
The tide of class conflict rose and fell as well, and the urgency attached
to the agenda of educational reform varied with those vicissitudes. The
issues of the irregular attendance and early withdrawal of children were
more or less continuous throughout the nineteenth century. They assumed special salience, however, when new and dramatic information
about their damage to education came forth, as in the educational census of 1851 and in the reports of the Education Aid Societies in the
1860s. Budgetary support for the primary educational establishment
operated always to set upper limits to it, but under exceptional circumstances—the national indebtedness generated by England's wars in the
1850s, for instance—that factor rose to greater salience.

One general lesson to be drawn from this is that a proper explanation
for any episode of change—or, indeed, a longer developmental sequence—will invoke a different *combination* of explanatory factors.
This is true even though the same *categories* of factors have repeated
and general significance. This formulation, while perhaps not as theo-

retically determinate as one might like, is the one that is forced upon the scholar by the complex patterning of the historical process. It also cautions against singling out any "most important factor" as a determinant of that process.

The observation also suggests a lesson for sociological theorists interested in social integration and the genesis of social change. One reading of the theme of integration in both functionalist and Marxist theories of society uncovers a notion of "fit" among the major institutional complexes of society. Functional theorists often posit a kind of "strain toward consistency" or stress how institutions contribute to one another or to society as a whole.[6] Marxist theories stress the dependence of a whole range of class, political, legal, and cultural institutions on the economic structure of society; that formulation also implies a certain fit.[7] Neither of these conceptions of integration is precisely appropriate as an interpretative framework for this study. I read functional integration as consisting of those historical moments at which the semi-independent processes of routine functioning, change, or crisis in one institutional arena create *problems or crises* for other arenas, both of which demonstrate the interdependence among institutional arenas. This formulation acknowledges the integration of society and the mutual influence among institutions, but regards this coupling as looser, more sporadic, and not necessarily either stable or unstable.

## "INDUSTRIAL SOCIETY" AND EDUCATION

Both functional and Marxist theorists also regard schooling as functionally related to the economies of industrial societies, and trace the evolution of the former to the requisites of the latter. Again, the emphases differ. Functional theorists have interpreted modern education as developing to take the place of a family outmoded by the demands that the industrial economy makes, and to generate the skills required in an increasingly complex industrial structure. This formulation is not far from one Marxist interpretation of education. According to the labor theory of value, the capitalist must pay the amount of wages necessary to reproduce the capitalist labor force, both on a day-by-day basis and in the longer term. The wages paid workers must be sufficient to keep them fed, clothed, and housed—all at the level required to prevent the deterioration of the labor force through malnutrition, disease, and death. This logic applies to the coming generation as well. One of the costs of guaranteeing the appearance of that generation is provision for its socialization—including acquisition of the relevant skills required for work. This would include as much education as capitalists believe necessary. Engels stressed this point,[8] and another distinctively Marxist one as well: the indoctrination of the workers with ideologies that work to develop a false consciousness about their position and interests in a capitalist economy.

The findings of this monograph raise doubts about the link between primary education and ability to participate in the labor process. That link was attenuated in the British case by four factors:

At that phase of British capitalism, the level of skill required for participation in the labor force was, as a rule, minimal. This fact weakens the argument for the necessity of formal schooling.

Because of the low level of skills required, and because of the low wage outlay, employers hired children on a mass basis from very early ages. This interfered with their schooling rather than calling for it.

Given the rigidity of the British class system, the link between formal schooling and social mobility was weak, tangential, and observable only in a few corners of the class/economic system.

Working-class families seemed to be aware of all of the above, and in many cases needed the wages of their children for economic survival. Consequently they limited the duration and amount of their children's education and put them to work as soon as they could contribute to the family purse.

Later in the century, as the technical needs of industry expanded, as the service sector became more salient, and as signs of loosening of the class structure began to appear, the functional link between formal education and the labor force became more evident. Accordingly, secondary and technical education began to expand toward the end of the century. Even this functional argument should not be carried too far, because many jobs in the service sector—sales, delivery, and custodial and security services, for example—require few skills. The functional argument seems to hold best for technicians, engineers, and a variety of highly skilled and high-status professional employments. Even in these cases, the idea of a weaker functional link is often more realistic: the completion of a certain level of schooling is regarded as "evidence" that a candidate is capable of disciplined work and responsibility, but not necessarily that specific, job-related skills have been acquired. In any event, the case of British working-class education in the nineteenth century raises serious doubts about the direct tie between the functional needs of an industrial economy and formal education.

That tie is better regarded as an indirect one. That is to say, the development of an urban industrial economy generates the kinds of social problems that civic and political leaders *perceive* education to be able to ameliorate or solve. Among these problems are crime, vice, social disorganization, deterioration of old class relations and the rise of new ones, and new forms of social protest—all of which are threats to property, safety, and social order. The link between these concerns and social reformers' and governments' efforts to establish schooling systems is evident in all the cases analyzed in this study. It would be instructive to determine how generalizable this formulation is to other developing industrial societies. Be that as it may, the results of this monograph underscore the need for more precise attention to the *mechanisms* by which formal education is determined by, or otherwise linked to, economic development.

## "NATION-BUILDING" AND EDUCATION

To compress the foregoing argument about industrialization and education into its essence: the British case casts doubt on the simple functional assertion that education can be regarded as a resource for industrial development. The relationship between industrialization and primary education through most of the nineteenth century appears to have been negative in some ways, and, when positive, mediated through the kind of class system and the kinds of social problems that industrial capitalism generated in the nineteenth century.

A different kind of functional analysis of education and schooling has appeared in the sociological literature more recently. This approach often goes under the heading of "nation-building." Its central tenet is that modern economic, political, and social development—of both Western nations and newer arrivals—is traceable to the strategies of states seeking to establish themselves competitively in the international arena, or, alternatively stated, in the world system of nations.[9] Needless to say, the dynamics of leadership and followership among nations are central to this perspective. So is the state; it is the manager of nation-building, and its principal strategies are the fashioning of the complex and distinctive institutional structures that constitute the modern nation. Mass education is one of these structures; it is one of the principal resources for building the nation, mainly through the inculcation of the values, attitudes, and behavior associated with citizenship.

In an application of the nation-building perspective, John W. Meyer, David Tyack, Joane Nagel, and Audri Gordon have analyzed the development of mass educational enrollments in the United States in late nineteenth and early twentieth centuries.[10] They first attempted to rule out the exigencies of industrialization, bureaucratization, state mobilization, and urbanization as distinctive causal factors. These forces were weakly represented in rural areas, where educational enrollments grew most rapidly, so instead, Meyer et al. treated a nation-building social movement as the principal engine of educational development:

> We need to take seriously the millennial ideology by which 19th-century Americans, especially in the North and West, blended their religious and political faiths and which provided a potent unifying force for collaborative action. It is this Protestant-Republican millennial view of the polity, coupled with a particular view of the nature of capitalism, that we take to be central to the expansion of the common school.[11]

The analysis of Meyer et al. supports the idea that mass education was a resource for creating a citizenry and a polity consistent with the cultural ideals of early American capitalist society, but in the American case in this era, organized collective action through a social movement, rather than the state, was the key agency.

Subsequent work within the nation-building perspective has stressed the modern state as the agency for the worldwide building of rationalized institutions in the name of general cultural ideals such as progress and justice. With respect to education in particular, Meyer, John Boli, and George M. Thomas advance the thesis that "the dominance of this institution is part of the reconstruction of society around the authority of the nation-state via the political expansion of individual membership through citizenship."[12] More specifically, education provides a crucial link between the ideology of the state as the vehicle for societal development and ideology of the individual as the fundamental unit of social action. That link is the ideology of citizenship, "in which the individual is seen as both a contributor to the national development project (as a producer and a loyal supporter of state programs, laws, and regulations) and as a beneficiary of state organizational action (as a consumer and as a 'citizen' in the pure sense who enjoys certain protections and guarantees underwritten by the state)."[13] Within this framework, the authors develop an explanation of the explosive growth of mass education systems around the contemporary world, which do not appear to be otherwise explicable.

Of special interest is Francisco Ramirez and John Boli's account of educational developments in England in the nineteenth century.[14] They describe England as the "core," meaning that it was dominant politically and economically among nations in that century. Because of its advantaged position, the English state was not pressed to intrude itself into the building of education. Ramirez and Boli appeal to this factor, plus the principles of voluntarism and laissez-faire, to account for the failure of Whitbread's efforts in 1807: "The principle of voluntarism that had shaped the private, religious, elitist schools of England would not be overturned, especially in light of the global success to which it was believed they had contributed."[15] In subsequent decades, they argue, the church-controlled voluntary system could continue because "no conflict was seen between church control of education and state aid to the schools." This possibility rested in turn on the traditional link between aristocracy, state, and church.[16]

Beginning in the 1860s, however, two circumstances contrived to make the state more aggressive in the educational sphere. The first was enfranchisement of segments of the working classes, which underscored the need to cultivate the qualities of citizenship among them (Lowe's defense of the Education Act of 1870).[17] The second was the appearance of the United States and Prussia as international economic rivals, and the need to cultivate labor as a competitive resource (one of Forster's defenses of the 1870 act).[18] At that time the factors of national assertiveness, educational institution-building, and citizenship converged and imparted the late-nineteenth-century impetus to educational development in England.

This line of argument has a certain plausibility at one level. Just as the link between the need for education and industry was probably weakened by a sense of complacency bred by Britain's economic lead, so was its need for more general assertiveness and mobilization *as a nation*. As an explanation of British educational development, however, the nation-building perspective is wanting on several counts. First, like other functional explanations, it is cast at such a general level that it misses altogether the complex network of mechanisms—especially social movements, group conflicts, and political processes—that reveals the actual history of that development. Second, Ramirez and Boli's sketchy account contains some gross gaps and errors. For example, the "voluntarism" that entered into the education of elites was so different from the philanthropic "voluntarism" that fostered charity and religious-society schools for the poor that the two can in no way be equated. Again, to assert that "no conflict was seen between church control of education and state aid to the schools" appears to ignore the century-long struggle between the Anglican Church and Dissent over that issue, which was probably the single most salient feature of working-class educational history.

Third, even when the factor of international competition became salient in the late nineteenth century, it could not be isolated from—and certainly not regarded as dominant over—the array of domestic religious, class, regional, and economic changes that worked to accelerate economic development. And, fourth, with respect to the first half of the century, it could be argued that educational efforts were mainly directed *against* active citizenship on the part of the working classes rather than *for* it. The major justification for promoting education on the part of the reformers and Whigs was that it would make for respectability, responsibility, and orderliness on the part of the working classes, *but in the context* of preserving a social order that relegated these classes to a non-citizen, unprivileged position. Early British educational efforts might thus better be regarded as "nation-saving" and conservative rather than "nation-building" in the citizen-participation and citizen-mobilizing sense.

## SECULARIZATION AND PRIMORDIALISM

In the nineteenth century and the first half of the twentieth, sociological theory generated a series of dichotomies between "modern" and "traditional"—*Gesellschaft* and *Gemeinschaft*,[19] organic solidarity and mechanical solidarity,[20] rational and traditional,[21] and urban and folk.[22] An assumption that often accompanied the employment of these dichotomies is that the march of modern history involves an increase of the former and a corresponding decline of the latter, or perhaps even the "replacement" of the latter by the former.[23] This process entails the decreasing significance of primodial establishments such as family, community, tribe, religion, and ethnicity. In connection with religion, secularization is a part of the general process.

The dichotomies between modern and traditional—and the pattern of social evolution implied by them—have long been a target of criticism by some students of modernization.[24] More recently, a surge of research and criticism, mainly but not exclusively by anthropologists, has challenged "the expectation that secularization is normal and inevitable" and reasserted the centrality of primordialism and religion in developed and developing societies.[25] Evidence for this assertion is the visible religious presence in contemporary politics (for example, in the creationist movement, the anti-abortion movement, and the issue of prayers in schools in the United States), the vitality of ethnic/nationalist movements in Western Europe (e.g., the Basque, the Celtic) and throughout Eastern Europe and the Soviet Union, and the renewed role of religion in Latin America and the Middle East. The final answers about the persistence or vitality of primordialism in contemporary society are certainly not in. Since religion and the issue of secularization had such a central role in nineteenth-century British society in general, and in its education system in particular, I shall now develop some observations on those phenomena.

As a matter of general belief, the people who spoke about the matter in the nineteenth century regarded Britain as a religious society, and within that a Christian society, and within that a Protestant society. Certain parts of the British Isles, such as Scotland and Wales, were described as especially zealous. A corollary of this was a certain abhorrence of secularism, except within the confines of a few social movements. At the same time, the century was marked by an advance of "rationalist" ideologies such as utilitarianism and socialism, which were nonreligious in content and sometimes antireligious in sentiment. In addition, the reputed religiousness of British society was in part a class matter. The enthusiasm of Wesleyanism, Nonconformity, and Evangelicalism was in large degree a middle-class phenomenon (though seeping both upward and downward), often resisted by more complacent or moderate establishments in the Churches of England and Scotland. In addition, commentators remarked frequently on the indifference or hostility of many in the working classes to religion, especially that variety served up to them by the religious societies in the schools for the poor.[26] In any event, the religious picture was a mixed one, and it is difficult to document any kind of definite long-term trends with regard to secularization of religious sentiment.

In that corner of education examined in this study—the provision of elementary schooling for the working classes by the classes above them—a certain paradox emerges. On the one hand, it was a canon that religious instruction ought to be part of that education. Any person or group that suggested otherwise was opposed, ridiculed, and thrown on the defensive. On the other hand, by almost all measures—assumption of control over education by the state, administrative requirements for religious instruction, curricular emphasis, and so on—the trend was toward secularization.

The historical causes of religious change in the nineteenth century are so complex that a full account cannot be developed here. The study of education, however, offers a suggestion about the *mechanisms* by which secularization occurred despite the avowed commitment of the society to religion.

The essence of the Protestant cause during the Reformation was a revolution against the Catholic Church's authority. The Protestant fathers of that revolution insisted on direct communication with God as authority, without the intermediation of Rome, the bishops, and the priests. Both Lutheranism and Calvinism were explicit on this point. The Protestant break with Catholicism in sixteenth-century England was also a challenge to papal authority, but the moderate resolution effected by Elizabeth I was to leave Anglicanism midway between the authoritarianism of Catholicism and the anti-authoritarianism of radical Protestantism.[27]

Two consequences followed from these circumstances. The first was that the Anglican Church emerged both officially established in the authority system of the state and proximate to Catholicism in doctrine, ritual, and assumptions about authority (though still anti-papal and anti-Catholic in sentiment). As a result, the Anglican Church, like the papacy, though in lesser degree, was vulnerable to further "Protestant" assaults, even though it was nominally Protestant. Such attacks were a large part of the story of Nonconformity, which resisted submission to Anglican doctrines and rituals and assaulted the privileges associated with the Establishment. The victories of Dissent and defeats of the Church of England marked the long transition from a predominately Establishmentarian system to a predominantly denominational one.

The second consequence arose from what has historically proved to be the frailty of radical Protestantism—its predilection to schism. In a way, this is an inevitable concomitant of its antiauthoritarianism. If a first principle of religious life is the rejection of authority, then any attempt to institutionalize that principle in an organized church creates the very conditions for opposing and undermining that attempt. Organization entails authority, and even the gentlest assertion of that authority arouses "protestant" suspicions. Furthermore, because Protestantism was itself a product of a schismatic break from Catholicism, it found itself less well armed ideologically to insist on unity and to resist secession.

The picture of British Protestantism in the nineteenth century is consistent with this diagnosis. One part of that picture is the unending parade of Nonconformist (as well as Catholic and Jewish) assaults on the authority and the privileges of the Church of England. The second is the myriad of non-Anglican denominations and sects that were precipitates of a long history of schisms. In a kind of ridicule of that history, Brougham counted the sects as follows in 1855:

> [The sects of Dissent] are five and thirty—twenty-seven British and eight foreign; there are divisions and subdivisions: thus, when we speak of Methodists as a sect, we are speaking of nine sects; for there are two great divisions of Arminian and Calvinistic, and the Arminians are subdivided into seven, the Calvinists into two. So the Baptists are five sects, not one; and thus, when we speak of Methodists and Baptists as if they were two sects, we, in fact, are speaking of no less than fourteen, which, with the Roman Catholics, the Presbyterians, the Independents, Unitarians, and others, make in all five and thirty different persuasions.[28]

Scottish Protestantism was equally susceptible to schismatic tendencies in the eighteenth and nineteenth centuries.[29] None of that history, however, implies a decline in religiousness or a rise of secularism. It could even suggest the opposite. Schism along religious lines meant that religion occupied such a place in people's consciousness that they chose it as a basis for organizing and defending their collective lives. In addition, most Dissenters were noted for their religious zeal, not their irreligion, despite accusations of the Establishment to the contrary.

Throughout the eighteenth and nineteenth centuries, moreover, this religious kaleidoscope of Dissent increasingly entered the political process. Part of this resulted from its impressive increase in numbers. Its entry was also facilitated by the slow but definite increase in the democratization of the English polity. Even before the Reform Act of 1832, which enfranchised many Nonconformists, their political presence was felt through petition, demonstration, and agitation through the press. Further extensions of the franchise increased their numbers among both voters and their representatives in Parliament. The rise of Gladstonian liberalism in the 1850s and 1860s reflected in part the support given it by the Nonconformist voice.

These religious and political developments constitute the background for several comments on the problem of secularization in education. Both when the state attempted unsuccessfully to assume a role in the education of the poor (1807, 1820, 1833, and 1843) and when it augmented that role (1833, 1840, 1846, 1870), it inherited the religious struggles of the day, because the major religious groups were competitors in the educational arena. The Church of England continued to assert at most its monopoly and at least its right to control, and all stripes of Dissenters opposed these claims and insisted on their rights, freedoms, and equity as legitimate religious parties. Both sides bolstered their assertions with doctrinal and political claims, and—in a way befitting religious groups—typically referred these claims to sacred first principles.

Several times I have noted that political leaders find religious and other primordial conflicts unwelcome. This derives from the circumstance that political leaders are, by virtue of their positions, interested in and responsible for conflict management and assuring order and stability in society. Those pressing religious claims frequently present them as inalterable and beyond compromise (because they are sacred), and this justifies their postures of intransigence and emotionality. Confronting this kind of conflict, political leaders' preferred tendency is to back away, to appeal to conflict-diffusing criteria such as "fairness" and "equity," and to isolate themselves from the combatants and the combatants from one another. The following governmental strategies in dealing with religious-educational conflict—all of which were suggested or attempted solutions during the nineteenth century—are understandable in this light:

Persuading the Established Church not to impose its monopoly (the conscience clause). This was, in effect, requesting the Anglican Church to avoid conflicts of principle with Dissenters.

Striving for some kind of religious instruction that would be acceptable to all religious parties. This is the "common denominator" strategy, intended to eliminate conflict on matters of principle, but difficult to implement in the context of combative sectarian groups and anti-secularist sentiments.

Separating "secular" instruction from "religious" instruction. This was the essence of the Irish solution—an extreme form of conflict-insulation, presumably called for by the severity of religious conflict in that setting.

Removing religious instruction altogether from the secular educational process. This was difficult in Britain but was the main form of adaptation in the early days of the American Republic, culminating in the imperfectly realized separation-of-church-and-state formula in U.S. education.

Distributing resources and administrative control among the competing claimants on the basis of evenhanded treatment. This was the sustained British solution in the middle of the nineteenth century, resulting in the proliferation of education along religious lines.

The main dynamics that led to the secularization of the primary education of the working classes, then, appeared to be (a) the reluctance of the state to deal with religious conflict, and (b) its efforts to insulate such conflict from the educational system, in which it was becoming increasingly involved as financial supporter, administrator, and direct provider. All these strategies added up to secularization, because they had the effect of muting or excluding the religious component. Ironically, however, the state accomplished this secularization at the same time as it was claiming to honor, respect, and respond positively to the pressures and demands of religious parties.

A second mechanism leading to secularization was an economic one. It can be observed in two contexts. The first is the enforcement of the conscience clause. By the 1850s, the idea had been available for a century or more. It had been incorporated in numerous legislative proposals for educational reform, and suggested, pressed, and feebly enforced by the Committee of Council for about two decades beginning around 1840. One motive for the conscience clause was political: to minimize religious conflicts in the religious societies' schools. The principal motive for *enforcing* the conscience clause—and risking political conflict—however, appeared in the late 1850s and early 1860s. These were the years of the great budgetary squeeze that was a factor in the imposition of the Revised Code of 1862 and other cost-saving devices. The connection between considerations of economy and the conscience clause appeared in thinly populated communities. State officials, under pressure to economize, heightened their sensitivity to the duplication, waste, and inefficiency involved in supporting two or more small schools (each for a religious constituency) in such communities. These officials were explicit in referring to budgetary considerations in their decision to enforce the conscience clause instead of allowing it to ride as a kind of running, unresolved conflict among them, the Anglican

Church, and the Dissenters. The conscience clause was above all a move toward the secularization of education. The motive for its enforcement, however, was not an antireligious one but a combination of economic and political ones.

Second, the guiding motive for excluding other religious ingredients from the educational system was to achieve economies and administrative simplicity. The standardization of the examination system under the Revised Code to include only secular subjects by grade levels—and excluding religious instruction as a basis for examination—was consistent with the impulse for administrative simplification. That impulse was bred in part from civil servants' frustration in dealing with so many schools on a one-to-one basis. Similarly, the "undenominationalizing" of the inspectorate as part of the Education Act of 1870 grew from a long history of concern with the cumbersomeness and waste associated with separate denominational inspection. In these cases, too, the secularization of the schooling system developed more as a by-product of concerns with economy and administration than as a direct assault on religion.

A general upshot of this line of interpretation is that religiousness and secularization need not always be formulated as opposed principles. The attempt to insulate or remove religious conflict (and, indirectly, religious content) from the schools did not mean that religiousness was diminishing. It is more nearly correct to say that the religious impulse was now more likely to be working itself out *in structural settings different from the educational one.* More generally, the illustration supports the notion that an increase in "modern" or "rationally purposive" structures in the process of development need not lead to a diminution of the primordial impulse. It may result in the diminution of that impulse in those agencies where it previously was manifested, but primordialism may reassert itself with equal strength in more new, less familiar, and possibly less manageable, arenas.


STRUCTURAL DIFFERENTIATION

In chapter 2 I noted a recurrent feature of the functionalist approach to education: the belief that the development of modern schooling marks a differentiation of the educational process *from* other, functionally diffuse agencies (family, church, neighborhood) and *toward* the institutionalization of new, more specialized agencies (schools). The latter, moreover, are perceived as structurally separate from those previously fulfilling educational functions. Many functionalist theorists argue further that specialized schools are more effective in their new environment (industrial, urban, "modern" societies) than the agencies they superseded. Leaving the latter claim aside, I shall comment on the logic of the former.

Consider once again the formula put forward by the National Education League in 1869 as its slogan for educational reform. Schooling, it demanded, should be "universal, free, compulsory, and unsectarian."[30] Several of the ingredients of this goal can be regarded as pressing the system to move in a more *differentiated* direction with respect to education's linkages with other institutional structures:

*Unsectarian* implied a shedding of those aspects of religious education that were connected with specific religious denominations, and thus differentiating education from the religious arena; the next step in this process is "secularism," or the exclusion of *all* religious ingredients from education.[31]

*Universal,* in its generic meaning, implies the coverage of everybody in society, without respect to other characteristics, such as religion, ethnic group, and class. (As of 1869, *universal education* meant universal for the working classes.) Universality implies more generally that education (more particularly, educational attendance) should not be discriminatory with respect to any other social category; it should be differentiated from them.

*Free* also means access without economic cost to the consumers (parents and children). Even within the restricted reference to the working classes only, the term implied that the educational system should not discriminate by subclass. Fees for the very poor (the lowest range of the working classes) were a long-standing issue in the educational debates, and continued as a burden after 1870 and until they were abolished in 1891.[32] *Free,* then, was differentiated from "having the ability to pay," which in turn meant differentiated from economic and social class.

Insofar as the British system moved toward realization of the reformers' goals by passing the Education Act of 1870 and adopting subsequent measures, then, it became a more differentiated institutional structure. The dimension that remained, of course, was class; only in the twentieth century was the stratification of education by class challenged, and then only partially. In these ways the perspective of differentiation is relevant to the evolution of primary education in Britain.

As a general rule, the development of a differentiated system of education is facilitated if its host society has already experienced a number of other, prior lines of differentiation. Several remarks on this score apply to the British experience, viewed in comparison with the United States, especially Massachusetts.

From the standpoint of religion, multireligious, nonsectarian schooling had existed on a district basis in the American colonial era. This had been stimulated mainly by the difficulty of contending with multiple sects in the same community. The U.S. Constitution, which forbade an established church, and thus separated church and state—as did the state constitutions that followed suit—established a social "gyroscope" that *formally* insulated religious matters—including religious conflicts—from the polity. The New York situation in the first half of the nineteenth century demonstrates how imperfect this principle was, as do other cases. It still survives, as the perennial conflicts over prayers in school illustrate. The development of American primary education in the antebellum period was therefore eased, so to say, by the prior differentiation between church and state. In England this differentiation was accomplished only over centuries of struggle and evolution, and has not been completed to this day, despite the eclipsed position of the Church of England. This book has confirmed, above all, that the development of British primary education was shaped, and probably inhibited, because religion and the state had not extricated themselves from each other structurally, and were in conflict over this matter throughout the century.

With respect to the economy, the widespread presence of child labor in early British industrial capitalism meant that age had not been effectively differentiated from economic performance. (Arrangements like the prohibition of child labor and enforced retirement make this kind of differentiation.) Neither had that differentiation been made in the United States in the early nineteenth century. But because American educators scheduled rural education to fit the rhythm of agricultural life, and because industrial development (and the child labor it demanded) was less advanced in the United States, this fusion of childhood and work was not as pronounced and did not constitute as great an obstacle as it did in Britain.[33]

Finally, the logic of differentiation yields some insights with respect to class as well. Through its rejection of the principles of monarchy, aristocracy (inherited titles), and established religion, the Constitution differentiated the stratification system of the young American Republic from various ascribed foci, especially kinship and privilege based on religion. That circumstance, plus the fact that the former colonies had adopted a variant of the egalitarian ideology of the French Enlightenment and some English philosophers, provided a cultural setting on which education could be organized more nearly on a *community* rather than a *class* basis. (One meaning of "common school" is that it was meant to be common to everyone in the community.) This judgment is a relative one. Even in the early nineteenth century, education in New England, especially in the cities, was stratified by class.[34] The common schools themselves were in some respects institutions of class control.[35] And in the subsequent educational history of the United States, public schools themselves have been segregated (by race), and have lived in tension with private (class) and parochial (religious) schools. As a relative matter, however, American schooling was not subordinated to a primordial class structure (race excepted) to anything like the same degree as was Britain's. The exact effects of this class factor on the development, effectiveness, and quality of education are not known. Surely, however, the class factor was decisive in shaping the differing educational *structures* of the two countries.

## "MUDDLING THROUGH"

Like many societies, Britain has had a way of generating and collecting special stereotypes about itself. Among these are "fair play," "an Englishman's home is his castle," and "the rights of Englishmen." Another, meant to characterize the country's style of political leadership and social change, is "muddling through." Among other things, this stereotype suggests a certain lack of entrepreneurship, even passivity, on the part of leaders; a principle of incrementalism; a tendency to rely on tried and true traditions and institutions rather than invent or adopt them wholesale; a confrontation with obstacles; a lack of deliberation and planning; but, in the last analysis, the exercise of practical intelligence and the attainment of results.[36]

Like all such stereotypes, this one demands skepticism and a non-literal reading. Nevertheless, it can be argued that if any sequence of social change manifested the principle of muddling through, the one I have studied in this volume is a good candidate. The title of the book is intended to capture part of the story: "social paralysis *and* social change," indicating that both were omnipresent in the dynamics of educational development. The idea of "muddling through" does not in itself explain much. However, the analysis in this study has revealed at least

one historical feature of British social structure that suggests the historical and social origins—and perhaps the partial correctness—of that
stereotype.

That feature has to do with the special pattern of primordialism in
British society. I singled out social class, religion, and region as fundamental dimensions of this primordialism in chapter 3. One connotation
of primordialism is that its objects should not be touched or altered;
they are in the category of the sacred. Political leaders who initiated or
engineered change, therefore, had to walk a careful path through a
maze of primordial groups who regarded their own presence as inviolable and their interests as not to be violated. In examining the plans for
reforms, the debates, and the legislation on primary education in the
nineteenth century, one discovers a remarkable regularity. Almost every
proposal, whether ultimately successful or not, was accompanied by a
series of disclaimers. These were that past good work in the area would
not be dishonored; ongoing efforts would not be disturbed; what was
being added would be no more than a helpful supplement to cover certain gaps; and the claims, rights, and sensibilities of interested parties
would not be offended. I read these disclaimers as taking into account
complex patterns of primordial claims and loyalties; the aim was to
squeeze limited increments of social change by and through them without disturbing them. The results of the effected changes were often
much more than proponents claimed in their modesty. And in the long
run, the policy of "incremental change in the context of the protection
of primordial claims" revolutionized the educational system. The road
to that end was marked, however, by a great deal of muddling through
the obstacle course of primordialism and the sentiments of territoriality
it nurtured.

# Notes

In the following notes, "P.P." stands for *Parliamentary Papers* and "P.D." stands for *Parliamentary Debates*.

## PREFACE

1. Neil J. Smelser, *Social Change in the Industrial Revolution* (Chicago: University of Chicago Press; London: Routledge & Kegan Paul, 1959).
2. Neil J. Smelser, "The Victorian Family," in R. N. Rapoport, M. P. Fogarty, and R. Rapoport, eds., *Families in Britain* (London: Routledge & Kegan Paul, 1982), pp. 59–74. Neil J. Smelser, "Vicissitudes of Work and Love in Anglo-American Society," in N. J. Smelser and E. Erikson, eds., *Themes of Love and Work in Adulthood* (Cambridge, Mass.: Harvard University Press, 1980), pp. 105–19. Neil J. Smelser, "Evaluating the Model of Structural Differentiation in Relation to Educational Change in the Nineteenth Century," in J. Alexander, ed., *Neofunctionalism* (Beverly Hills, Calif.: Sage Publications, 1985), pp. 113–29. Neil J. Smelser, "The Contest between Family and Schooling in Nineteenth-Century Britain," in J. C. Alexander and P. Colomy, eds., *Differentiation and Social Change Theory: Comparative and Historical Perspectives* (New York: Columbia University Press, 1990), pp. 165–86. Neil J. Smelser, "Biography, the Structure of Explanation and the Evaluation of Theory in Sociology," in H. M. Blalock, Jr., ed., *Sociological Theory and Research: A Critical Appraisal* (New York: Free Press, 1980), pp. 23–30.

## CHAPTER 1

1. Matthew Arnold, *Culture and Anarchy: An Essay in Political and Social Criticism* (London: Smith, Elder, 1869), pp. 104–5.
2. Ibid., p. 105. In an aside, Arnold describes the class situation in the

United States as "just ourselves, with the Barbarians quite left out and the Populace nearly" (ibid., p. xxx); see also Matthew Arnold, *Civilization in the United States: First and Last Impressions of America* (Boston: Cupples & Hurd, 1888), pp. 80–85.

3. This view has not been without challenge. See, for example, E. G. West, *Education and the State: A Study in Political Economy* (London: Institute of Economic Affairs, 1965), esp. pp. 130–49.

4. J. S. Pakington, "Address on Education," *Transactions of the National Society for the Promotion of Social Science* (London: John W. Parker & Son, 1858), p. 37.

5. See Jeffrey Alexander et al., eds., *The Micro-Macro Link* (Berkeley: University of California Press, 1988).

6. This was the period when the pattern of governmental subsidization of religious societies' voluntary efforts was extended to cover the denominational efforts in Scotland. See the section on "The Disruption and Its Impact" in chapter 7.

7. E. P. Thompson, *The Making of the English Working Class* (London: Gollancz, 1963).

8. Two examples: Richard Johnson, "'Really Useful Knowledge': Radical Education and Working-Class Culture, 1790–1848," in John Clarke, Chas Critcher, and Richard Johnson, eds., *Working-Class Culture: Studies in History and Theory* (London: Hutchinson, 1979), pp. 75–102; David Vincent, *Bread, Knowledge and Freedom: A Study of Nineteenth-Century Working Class Biography* (London: Europa Publications, 1981).


CHAPTER 2

1. John Stuart Mill, "Inaugural Address at St. Andrews," in F. A. Cavenagh, ed., *James and John Stuart Mill on Education* (Cambridge: Cambridge University Press, 1931), p. 132.

2. John Stuart Mill, *Autobiography* (London: Longmans, Green, Reader & Dyer, 1873), p. 1.

3. See the sections on "A Significant Moment of Inaction" and "The Failure of Middle-Class Radical Secularism" in chapter 4.

4. Thomas Wyse quoted in Donald K. Jones, "The Movement for Secular Elementary Education in Great Britain in the XIXth Century," in Willem Frijhoff, ed., *The Supply of Schooling: Contributions to a Comparative Study of Educational Policies in the XIXth Century* (Paris: Institut national de recherche pédagogique, 1983), p. 84.

5. Henry Brougham, 1st baron Brougham and Vaux, quoted in Francis Adams, *History of the Elementary School Contest in England*, edited, with an introduction, by Asa Briggs (Brighton: Harvester Press, 1972), p. 108.

6. Richard Cobden, letter to George Combe, quoted in Donald Read, *Cobden and Bright: A Victorian Political Partnership* (London: Edward Arnold, 1967), p. 181.

7. Ellwood P. Cubberly, *Public Education in the United States: A Study and Interpretation of American Educational History* (1919; rev. ed., Boston: Houghton Mifflin, 1934).

8. Carl F. Kaestle, "Ideology and American Educational History," *History of Education Quarterly* 22, no. 2 (Summer 1982): 128.

9. R. L. Schnell, "Childhood as Ideology: A Reinterpretation of the Common School," *British Journal of Educational Studies* 27, no. 1 (February 1979): 14.

10. As found, for example, in W. H. G. Armytage, *Four Hundred Years of English Education*, 2d ed. (Cambridge: Cambridge University Press, 1970).

11. For example, Harold Silver, *English Education and the Radicals, 1780–1850* (London and Boston: Routledge & Kegan Paul, 1975).

12. For example, E. G. West, "The Role of Education in Nineteenth Century Doctrines of Political Economy," *British Journal of Educational Studies* 12, no. 2 (May 1964): 161–72.

13. John Hurt, *Education in Evolution: Church, State, Society and Popular Education* (London: Rupert Hart-Davis, 1971), p. 9. See also H. Holman, *English National Education: A Sketch of the Rise of Public Elementary Schools in England* (London: Blackie & Son, 1893).

14. In referring to the work of the Committee of Council in the 1850s, for example, Holman noted that "it is almost amusing to notice how the Committee of Council managed to introduce into the actual working of the system of schools most of the principles and regulations advocated by the more advanced thinkers of the time, discussed and rejected in Parliament, and resented and resisted by the Church party" (*English National Education*, p. 154).

15. See the section on "The General Pattern" in chapter 8.

16. Henry Brougham, 1st baron Brougham and Vaux, "Address," *Transactions of the National Association for the Promotion of Social Science* (London: John W. Parker, Son & Bourne, 1862), pp. 10–11.

17. M. E. Shipman, *Education and Modernisation* (London: Faber & Faber, 1971), p. 33.

18. David Wardle, *The Rise of the Schooled Society: The History of Formal Schooling in England* (London: Routledge & Kegan Paul, 1974). For the argument that a decline in the family's educational effectiveness contributed to the rise of formal schooling in colonial America, see Bernard Bailyn, *Education in the Forming of American Society: Needs and Opportunities for Study* (New York: Vintage Books, 1962).

19. S. N. Eisenstadt, *From Generation to Generation: Age Groups and Social Structure* (New York: Free Press, 1956), p. xvii.

20. David Gottlieb, John Reeves, and Warren D. TenHouten, *The Emergence of Youth Societies: A Cross-Cultural Approach* (New York: Free Press, 1966), p. ix; Shipman, *Education and Modernisation*, 33–34. For another standard statement of the industrial bases for the rise of educational systems, see T. L. Jarman, *Landmarks in the History of Education: English Education as Part of the European Tradition*, 2d ed. (London: John Murray, 1963).

21. G. D. H. Cole and Raymond Postgate, *The Common People, 1746–1938* (London: Methuen, 1938), p. 356. One of the reasons why technical schooling was so late in developing in England is that such a large proportion of the roles in the industrial labor force called for only minimal technical skills. See Gordon W. Roderick and Michael D. Stephens, *Education and Industry in the Nineteenth Century: The English Disease?* (London and New York: Longman, 1978), pp. 6–10. Roderick and Stephens attribute Britain's weakness in the

competitive international economic arena late in the century to its inadequacies in technical education.

22. Shipman, *Education and Modernisation*, p. 36.

23. Asher Tropp, *The Schoolteachers: The Growth of the Teaching Profession in England and Wales from 1800 to the Present Day* (London: Heinemann, 1957), p. 2.

24. In his historical observations on English capitalism, Marx himself treated reform movements for legislation about working-class education—mainly associated with factory legislation—as manifestations of working-class agitation to relieve the exploitative conditions of factory life and to improve the workers' situation. See Karl Marx, *Capital: A Critique of Political Economy* (1867; reprint, London: Penguin Books, 1976), pp. 613–14.

25. Friedrich Engels, *The Condition of the Working Class in England*, edited, with an introduction, by Victor Kiernan (1845; reprint, London: Penguin Books, 1987), p. 139.

26. Ibid., pp. 139, 202.

27. Ibid., pp. 244, 141.

28. An example of a more or less formal application of Marxist theory, which, however, scarcely deals with educational topics, is found in John Foster, *Class Struggle and the Industrial Revolution: Early Industrial Capitalism in Three English Towns* (New York: St. Martin's Press, 1974).

29. Brian Simon, *Studies in the History of Education, 1780–1870* (London: Lawrence & Wishart, 1960).

30. Ivan Moorish, *Education since 1800* (London: Allen & Unwin, 1970).

31. Phillip McCann, ed., *Popular Education and Socialization in the Nineteenth Century* (London: Methuen, 1977).

32. Harold Silver, *English Education and the Radicals, 1780–1850* (London: Routledge & Kegan Paul, 1975). For an assessment of the work of "class" and "conflict" historians writing about American educational history, see David Tyack, "The Common School and American Society: A Reappraisal," *History of Education Quarterly* 26, no. 2 (Summer 1986): 302–6.

33. E. P. Thompson, *The Making of the English Working-Class* (London: Gollancz, 1963).

34. For example, Richard Johnson, "'Really Useful Knowledge': Radical Education and Working-Class Culture, 1790–1848," in John Clarke, Chas Critcher, and Richard Johnson, eds., *Working–Class Culture: Studies in History and Theory* (London: Hutchinson, 1979), pp. 75–102.

35. Simon, *Studies in the History of Education, 1780–1870*, pp. 366–67.

36. Phillip McCann, "Popular Education, Socialization and Social Control, Spitalfields, 1812–1824," in McCann, ed., *Popular Education and Socialization in the Nineteenth Century*, p. 2.

37. Talcott Parsons, *The Social System* (Glencoe, Ill.: Free Press, 1951).

38. Norman Morris, "State Paternalism and *laissez-faire* in the 1860's," in Morris, ed., *History of Education in Society, Studies in the Government and Control of Education since 1860* (London: Methuen, 1970), pp. 15–16.

39. Ralf Dahrendorf, *Class and Class Conflict in Industrial Society* (Stanford: Stanford University Press, 1959).

40. Michalina Clifford-Vaughan and Margaret Scotford Archer, *Social Conflict and Educational Change in England and France, 1789–1848* (Cambridge: Cambridge University Press, 1971).

41. Ibid., pp. 24–25.

42. Ibid., pp. 31–32.

43. Ibid., pp. 34–35.

44. Ibid., pp. 21–23.

45. Michael Hechter, *Internal Colonialism: The Celtic Fringe in British National Development* (Berkeley: University of California Press, 1975).

46. Ibid., pp. 33–34.

47. See chapters 6 and 7.

48. See, for example, Clifford-Vaughan and Archer, *Social Conflict and Educational Change,* pp. 4–15, for a critique of both the functionalist and the Marxist approaches; for a commentary on the variety of Marxist and revisionist approaches in the history of education, see Harold Silver, "View from Afar: An Afterword," *History of Education* 2, no. 3 (October 1978): 237–42.

49. Schnell, "Childhood as Ideology," p. 15.

50. Douglas Sloan, "Knowledge, Values, and Educational History: Once More unto the Breach, Dear Friends," *History of Education Quarterly* 25, nos. 1–2 (Spring–Summer 1985): 9.

51. See Neil J. Smelser, "Evaluating the Model of Structural Differentiation in Relation to Educational Change in the Nineteenth Century," in Jeffrey C. Alexander, ed., *Neofunctionalism* (Beverly Hills, Calif.: Sage Publications, 1985), pp. 113–29.

52. See the section on "Education as Prevention of Pauperism and Crime" in chapter 3.

53. See the sections on "A Reprise of 1820" in chapter 4 and "Direct State Provision of Education" in chapter 5.

54. See the introductory pages of chapter 6 and the section on "General Background to the Educational Reforms of 1831" in chapter 7.

55. Emile Durkheim, *Education and Sociology* (1903; reprint, Glencoe, Ill.: Free Press, 1956); Durkheim, *Moral Education* (1925; reprint, Glencoe, Ill.: Free Press, 1961).

56. Joseph Adelson, "What Happened to the Schools," *Commentary* 71, no. 3 (March 1981): 36.

57. Alex Inkeles, "Convergence and Divergence in Industrial Societies," in Mustafa O. Attir, Burkhart Holzner, and Sdenek Suda, eds., *Directions of Change: Modernization Theory, Research, and Realities* (Boulder, Colo.: Westview Press, 1981), p. 6.

58. Taken from a pamphlet issued by National Education League ca. 1870, reproduced in J. M. Goldstrom, *Education: Elementary Education, 1780–1900* (New York: Barnes & Noble, 1972), pp. 141–42.

59. Lawrence Stone has asserted that the contours and history of any educational system can be understood in terms of its having been shaped by forces emanating from seven identifiable "external" institutional complexes: "social stratification, job opportunities, religion, theories of social control, demographic and family patterns, economic organization and resources, and finally

political theory in institutions" (Stone, "Literacy and Education in England, 1640–1900," *Past and Present*, no. 42 [February 1969], p. 70).

60. The term *arbitrary* is used to indicate that identifying a moment, freezing it in time, calling it a moment of "equilibrium-in-tension," and describing it in terms of balance of social forces ignores the fact that at any given moment the historical process is an ongoing flow, incapable of being described in static terms.

61. To use the term *resolution* here does not imply any kind of return to any kind of static state, but refers to a significant realignment of historical forces, usually achieved by some kind of political action, such as government decree or legislation.

62. See the section on "A Victory for the Church" in chapter 4.

63. See the section on "A Reprise of 1820" in chapter 4.

64. P. W. Musgrave, *Society and Education in England since 1800* (London: Methuen, 1968), p. 2.

65. See A. Abbott, *Education for Industry and Commerce in England* (London: Oxford University Press, 1933), pp. 23–24; William Ashworth, *An Economic History of England, 1870–1939* (London: Methuen, 1960), pp. 33–34; George Haines IV, "German Influence upon Scientific Instruction in England, 1867–1887," *Victorian Studies* 1, no. 3 (March 1958): 215–54.

66. This view is articulated most consistently in the works of Talcott Parsons. See, for example, *The Social System* (Glencoe, Ill.: Free Press, 1951); and Talcott Parsons and Neil J. Smelser, *Economy and Society* (Glencoe, Ill.: Free Press, 1956).

67. This view has been articulated, with respect to classical China, by Wolfram Eberhard, *Conquerors and Rulers: Social Forces in Medieval China* (Leiden, Holland: E. J. Brill, 1965), pp. 2–11.

68. See, for example, Lewis A. Coser, *The Functions of Social Conflict* (Glencoe, Ill.: Free Press, 1956), and Dahrendorf, *Class and Class Conflict.*

69. Assistant Commissioner Josiah Wilkinson reported to the Newcastle Commission in 1860, for example, that "[all] employers of labour with whom I have conversed stated that the educated is superior to the uneducated workman, but I fail to discover an instance in which higher wages are paid for a specific duty to an educated than to an uneducated man" (P.P., 1861, 21, pt. 3, p. 399).

70. Ibid., pt. 1, p. 243.

71. Dispute over this issue is one of the themes characterizing differences between "reformist" and "social conflict and control" historians of education noted in the sections on "Functional Accounts" and "Domination and Class-Conflict Accounts" earlier in this chapter.

72. While this argument implies that the objective of the educational reformer is to effect social change of one sort or another through the transformation of individuals, this does not exhaust the vision of some who press for educational reform. One of the arguments advanced periodically for an expansion of elementary education in the nineteenth century was that it would take the children of the poor off the streets—that is, provide some kind of custodial function.

73. Cobbett attacked the common assertion that lack of education is a

source of crime, for example, by saying that as education had increased over the first third of the nineteenth century, so had drunkenness and crime; in New York, he claimed, there were more educated than uneducated criminals (P.D., 1834, vol. 24, cols. 131–32).

## CHAPTER 3

1. *Oxford English Dictionary*, s.v. "primordial."
2. Clifford Geertz, "The Integrative Revolution: Primordial Sentiments and Civil Politics in the New States," in id., *The Interpretation of Cultures: Selected Essays* (New York: Basic Books, 1973), p. 269.
3. Edward A. Shils, "Primordial, Personal, Sacred, and Civil Ties," *British Journal of Sociology* 8, no. 2 (June 1957): 130–45.
4. This idea also dominates the writing of British history. Comparing Britain with the United States, France, and Germany, Gareth Stedman Jones, a neo-Marxist historian, remarks: "English political history has generally been thought to coincide with class alignments and . . . one of the peculiarities of England has been the pervasiveness of employment of diverse forms of class vocabulary" (Jones, *Languages of Class: Studies in English Working Class History, 1832–1982* [Cambridge: Cambridge University Press, 1983], p. 2).
5. Harold Perkin, *The Origins of Modern English Society, 1780–1880* (London: Routledge & Kegan Paul, 1969), p. 17.
6. See the section on "The Failure of Middle-Class Radical Secularism" in chapter 4.
7. Thomas Wyse, *Education Reform; or, The Necessity of a National System of Education* (London: Longman, Rees, Orme, Brown, Green & Longman, 1836), p. 359. He goes on to say that "[more] favorable dispositions cannot be desired for the universal diffusion of Education."
8. Ibid., pp. 358, 360.
9. The recent literature shows a disagreement about the social significance of the Sunday schools. Thomas W. Laqueur regards the rise of the Sunday schools in the late eighteenth century as an expression of working-class culture and an attempt to build working-class communities (Laqueur, *Religion and Respectability: Sunday Schools and Working-Class Culture, 1780–1850* [New Haven: Yale University Press, 1976]). Malcolm Dick poses the contrary argument that the Sunday school was the repository of middle-class morality, and that its major social message was to advocate the status quo (Dick, "The Myth of the Working-Class Sunday School," *History of Education*, 9, no. 1 [January 1980]: 28–29). There does not seem to be any reason to believe that both elements were not present in the Sunday school movement. In any event, by the early nineteenth century, the Sunday schools were fully assimilated into the denominational structure of British religion. See the section on "A Significant Moment of Inaction" in chapter 4.
10. Harold Silver, *The Concept of Popular Education: A Study of Ideas and Social Movements in the Early Nineteenth Century* (London: MacGibbon & Kee, 1965), p. 13.
11. P.P., 1837–38, 7, p. 167.

12. See, for example, Asa Briggs, "The Language of 'Class' in Early Nineteenth-Century England," in Asa Briggs and John Saville, eds., *Essays in Labour History* (London: Macmillan, 1967), pp. 43–73.

13. See the section on "Direct State Provision of Education" in chapter 5.

14. The movement for girls' education was mainly found among the higher classes in the nineteenth century. Girls' education in working-class institutions was an established feature. Whatever gains were made for girls' education in the nineteenth century were expressed in the establishment of institutions separate from males. For an account of the development of girls' education, see Sheila Fletcher, *Feminists and Bureaucrats: A Study in the Development of Girls' Education in the Nineteenth Century* (Cambridge: Cambridge University Press, 1980).

15. For a discussion of contemporary issues of equality and inequality, see Harold Silver, *Education and the Social Condition* (London: Methuen, 1980), ch. 3.

16. Henry James Sumner Maine, *Ancient Law: Its Connection with the Early History of Society, and Its Relation to Modern Ideas* (London: John Murray, 1861).

17. T. H. Marshall, *Citizenship and Social Class* (Cambridge: Cambridge University Press, 1950), esp. pp. 33–35.

18. R. H. Tawney, *Equality* (London: Allen & Unwin, 1931), esp. pp. 119–23.

19. R. H. Gretton, *The English Middle Class* (London: Bell & Sons, 1917), p. 220.

20. See the section on "Economic and Class Consequences" in chapter 5. For an account of the attacks on parents for their attitudes toward attendance at factory schools, see Malcolm Dick, "Industrialists and Their Factory Schools," *History of Education* 9, no. 2 (April 1980): 121–23. The obligation of industrialists to provide schools for children they employed was removed by the Education Act of 1870, which placed the obligation on the parents (ibid., pp. 125–26).

21. P.P., 1842, 16, p. 352.

22. P.P., 1843, 13, p. 204.

23. P.P., 1857–58, 45, p. 340.

24. P.P., 1861, 21, pt. 1, pp. 76–78.

25. P.P., 1867–68, 27, pt. 5, p. 19.

26. Quoted by Inspector J. P. Norris, P.P., 1854, 51, p. 409.

27. Sir James Kay-Shuttleworth, *Four Periods of Public Education* (London: Longman, Green, Longman & Roberts, 1862), p. 322.

28. P.P., 1867–68, 28, pt. 1, pp. 104–5.

29. See the section on "Educational Growth" in chapter 5.

30. C. B. Adderley, "An Address on Education," in *Transactions of the National Society for the Promotion of Social Science* (London: Longman, Green, Longman, Roberts & Green, 1859), pp. 76–77.

31. P.P., 1867–68, 28, pt. 1, pp. 15–18.

32. Mark Pattison, *Suggestions on Academical Organization, with Especial Reference to Oxford* (Edinburgh: Edmonston & Douglas, 1868), p. 326.

33. Matthew Arnold in P.P., 1861, 21, pt. 4, p. 54.

34. *A Plea for the Middle Classes* cited in G. M. Young, *Victorian England: Portrait of an Age* (1936; reprint, London: Oxford University Press, 1949), p. 88.

35. Lord Brougham, "Opening Address," in *Transactions of the National Association for the Promotion of Social Science* (London: Longman, Green, Longman, Roberts & Green, 1865), p. 2. In 1860 Arnold told the Newcastle Commission: "You must be well aware that already there are loud complaints among the lower middling classes of this country that the Committee of Council [the parliamentary governing body for the system of subsidized working-class education] is providing the poor with better schools than those to which they themselves have access; and they may be very sure that any new measure which proposes to do much for the instruction of the poor, and nothing for that of the middling classes, will meet with discontent and opposition from the latter" (P.P., 1861, 21, pt. 4, p. 56).

36. For an account of the years of great debate about the quality of middle-class education (1856–64), see David Ian Allsobrook, *Schools for the Shires: The Reform of Middle-Class Education in Mid-Victorian England* (Manchester: Manchester University Press, 1986), pp. 131–53.

37. P.P., 1867–68, 28, pt. 1, p. 655.

38. Ibid., p. 297.

39. P.P., 1857, 28, p. 50.

40. See the section on "The Disruption and Its Impact" in chapter 7.

41. P.P., 1857–58, 45, pp. 281–82. See also the section on "Economic and Class Consequences" in chapter 5.

42. Joseph Bowstead, a school inspector whose assignment covered British and Foreign Society schools, remarked that the clientele of his schools were mainly "the respectable and independent working classes" and a "few children" from the middle classes (P.P., 1859, 21, pt. 1, pp. 157–58).

43. See the section on "Origin and Nature of the System" in chapter 9.

44. P.P., 1859, 21, pt. 1, p. 150.

45. P.P., 1850, 43, p. 785.

46. P.P., 1854, 52, p. 431.

47. See the section on "Economic and Class Consequences" in chapter 5.

48. P.D., 1856, 161, cols. 797, 801–4; 1857, 144, cols. 1850–53.

49. P.P., 1856, 47, pp. 235, 521; 1857, 33, p. 250; 1859, 21, pp. 157–58; 1864, 45, pp. 169–70.

50. See the section on "Economic and Class Consequences" in chapter 5.

51. P.P., 1854, 52, p. 724.

52. Ibid. On ragged schools, see the section on "Educational Growth" in chapter 5.

53. P.P., 1861, 21, pt. 6, p. 203.

54. P.P., 1852, 7, p. 47.

55. P.P., 1861, 21, pt. 6, p. 155.

56. P.P., 1845–55, 42, p. 555.

57. P.P., 1852, 7, p. 99.

58. For additional evidence of the centrality of class divisions in education, see John S. Hurt, *Education in Evolution: Church, State, Society and Popular*

*Education, 1800–1870* (London: Rupert Hart-Davis, 1971), pp. 116–23; and id., *Elementary Schooling and the Working Classes, 1860–1919* (London: Routledge & Kegan Paul, 1979), pp. 4–23, 155–62.

59. This fear is made explicit in Bernard Mandeville, *The Fable of the Bees; or, Private Vices and Public Benefits* (London: Tonson, 1725).

60. G. Rose, in P.D., 1807, 9, col. 800.

61. See the section on "A Significant Moment of Inaction" in chapter 4.

62. Hannah More quoted in Carl F. Kaestle, ed., *Joseph Lancaster and the Monitorial School Movement: A Documentary History* (New York: Teachers College Press, 1973), p. 2.

63. Harold Silver, *The Concept of Popular Education: A Study of Ideas and Social Movements in the Early Nineteenth Century* (London: MacGibbon & Kee, 1965), p. 24.

64. P.D., 1833, 20, cols. 149–50.

65. For a historical sketch of the growth of this imagery in the wake of the Jacobin panic of the 1790s, see Richard B. Altick, *The English Common Reader: The Social History of the Mass Reading Public, 1800–1900* (Chicago: University of Chicago Press, 1957), pp. 141–43.

66. Hugh S. Tremenheere, *Notes on Public Subjects, Made during a Tour in the United States and Canada* (London: John Murray, 1852), p. 59.

67. Kay-Shuttleworth, *Four Periods of Public Education*, p. 452.

68. Ibid., p. 233.

69. See the section on "Other Religious and Political Developments" in chapter 5.

70. Henry Brougham, 1st baron Brougham and Vaux, *Letter to Lord Lyndhurst on Criminal Police and National Education* (London: James Ridgeway, 1847), p. 31.

71. W. E. Marsden, *Unequal Education Provision in England and Wales: The Nineteenth-Century Roots* (London: Woburn Press, 1987), pp. 41–46.

72. P.P., 1862, 41, p. 423.

73. P.P., 1841, 20, pp. 171–72. See a similar statement by Montague Burgoyne addressed to the governors and directors of the endowed schools in 1830, quoted in A. E. Dyson and Julian Lovelock, eds., *Education and Democracy* (London: Routledge & Kegan Paul, 1975), p. 65.

74. Kay-Shuttleworth, *Four Periods of Public Education*, pp. 232–34; for his criticism of the Lancashire Public School Association for its secularist tendencies, see Frank Smith, *The Life and Work of Sir James Kay-Shuttleworth* (London: John Murray, 1923), p. 232. For development of the argument that the teachings of the Sunday schools served the same end of social control via religious teaching, see Dick, "Myth of the Working-Class Sunday School," pp. 17–41.

75. See the section on "Primary Education and Social Mobility" in chapter 8.

76. J. F. C. Harrison, "Adult Education and Self-Help," *British Journal of Educational Studies* 6, no. 1 (1957–58): 37–50.

77. J. F. C. Harrison, "The Victorian Gospel of Success," *Victorian Studies* 1, no. 2 (December 1957): 155–64.

78. Thomas Mackay, ed., *The Autobiography of Samuel Smiles* (London: John Murray, 1905), p. 132.

79. For a corroborative view, see J. F. C. Harrison, *Learning and Living, 1799–1960: A Study in the History of the English Adult Education Movement* (London: Routledge & Kegan Paul, 1963), pp. 208–11.

80. See the section on "Primary Education and Social Mobility" in chapter 8. For the statement of a similar view that social mobility was a minor part of the imagery of working-class education in midcentury, see Hurt, *Elementary Schooling and the Working Classes*, pp. 29–34.

81. The educational views of working-class radical thinkers are summarized and discussed in Harold Silver, *English Education and the Radicals, 1780–1850* (London and Boston: Routledge & Kegan Paul, 1975), pp. 61–79.

82. See Harrison, *Learning and Living*, pp. 92–94.

83. Education was secondary to other elements in the Chartists' agenda, which was concerned mainly with constitutional and political reforms. The item *education* does not appear in the index of a recent compilation of Chartist studies, James Epstein and Dorothy Thompson, eds., *The Chartist Experience: Studies in Working-Class Radicalism and Culture, 1830–60* (London: Macmillan, 1982). Education was not among the famous six points of the Charter: equal representation, universal suffrage, annual parliaments, no property qualifications, vote by ballot, and payment to members of parliament.

84. P.P., 1867, 28, pt. 1, p. 585.

85. P.P., 1861, 21, pt. 6, p. 89.

86. Ibid.

87. P.P., 1854, 51, p. 45; 1856, 46, p. 421. The secular schools involved were the Williams Secular School in Edinburgh and the Manchester Model Secular School.

88. P.P., 1861, 21, pt. 6, p. 63.

89. W. J. C. Stewart and W. P. McCann, *The Educational Innovators, 1750–1880* (London: St. Martin's Press, 1967), pp. 188–95.

90. P.D., 1850, 112, col. 937.

91. The main ones were the Central Education League, the Lancashire Public School Association, and the Birmingham Education League. See Donald K. Jones, "The Movement for Secular Elementary Education in Great Britain in the XIXth Century," in Wilhelm Frijhoff, ed., *The Supply of Schooling: Contributions to a Comparative Study of Educational Policies in the XIXth Century* (Paris: Institut national de recherche pédagogique, 1983), pp. 83–94. For a more general review, see Edward Royle, *Victorian Infidels: The Origins of the British Secularist Movement, 1791–1886* (Manchester: Manchester University Press, 1974).

92. See the section on "A Victory for the Church" in chapter 4.

93. B. Templar, "The Religion of 'Secular' Schools, and Their Claim to Government Aid," in *Transactions of the National Association for the Promotion of Social Science* (London: John Parker & Son, 1859), pp. 407–11.

94. See the introductory section of chapter 6.

95. Hippolyte Taine, *Notes on England*, translated, with an introduc-

tion, by Edward Hyams (London: Thames & Hudson, 1957), pp. 271–72.

96. James Greenough, *The Evolution of the Elementary Schools of Great Britain* (New York: Appleton, 1903), pp. xviii–xix.

97. James Murphy, "Religion, the State, and Education in England," *History of Education Quarterly* 8, no. 1 (Spring 1968): 13–15.

98. P.D., 1807, 9, col. 1178; 1843, 67, col. 1445.

99. See the section on "Educational Growth" in chapter 5.

100. For a listing of measures that symbolize an inevitable march toward the disestablishment of the Church of England, see William H. Mackintosh, *Disestablishment and Liberation: The Movement for the Separation of the Anglican Church from State Control* (London: Epworth Press, 1972), p. xvi.

101. For the story of disestablishment in Ireland and Wales, see P. M. H. Bell, *Disestablishment in Ireland and Wales* (London: SPCK, 1969).

102. Marshall, *Citizenship and Social Class,* pp. 33–34.

103. P.D., 1835, 27, col. 308.

104. For a comment on England's failure—in contrast to the United States and Germany—to maintain either a formal or informal establishment of religion in the early nineteenth century, see W. R. Ward, *Religion and Society in England, 1790–1850* (London: B. T. Batsford, 1972), p. 3.

105. P.D., 1859, 154, col. 766.

106. Alexis de Tocqueville, *Democracy in America* (1835–39; reprint, New York: Knopf, 1987), vol. 1, "Author's Introduction," pp. 3–16.

107. P.P., 1861, 21, pt. 6, p. 62.

108. P.D., 1847, 91, col. 1024. The vulnerability of this kind of defense was underscored a few moments later when Sir C. Napier wondered why Catholics were being excluded from the provisions of the government plan for subsidizing religious societies (ibid., col. 1054).

109. See the section on "The Consolidation of Growth Under Primordial Proliferation" in chapter 5.

110. For an account of the social and cultural differences between the residents of Norfolk and Northumberland, especially with relation to class and social aspirations, see the report of J. L. Hammond, assistant commissioner of the Taunton Commission (P.P., 1867–68, 28, pt. 7, pp. 277–83).

111. Standard works tracing these developments are Marshall, *Citizenship and Social Class;* Walter Bagehot, *The English Constitution* (London: H. S. King, 1872); M. Ostragorski, *Democracy and the Organization of Political Parties* (1902; reprint, Chicago: Quadrangle Books, 1964); J. B. Conacher, ed., *The Emergence of British Parliamentary Democracy in the Nineteenth Century: The Passing of the Reform Acts of 1831, 1867, and 1884–1885* (New York: Wiley, 1971).

112. Michael Bentley, *Politics without Democracy, 1815–1914: Perception and Preoccupation in British Government* (Oxford: Blackwell, 1984).

CHAPTER 4

1. This sketch is based on Harold Perkin, *The Origins of Modern English Society, 1780–1880* (London: Routledge & Kegan Paul, 1969), ch. 2.

2. Elie Halévy estimated that in 1815 there were approximately two million Dissenters out of a population of ten million, although in some large parishes Nonconformist chapels outnumbered Anglican Churches (Halévy, *A History of the English People in the Nineteenth Century*, trans. E. I. Watkin and D. A. Barker [1924–27], vol. 1, *England in 1815* [reprint, London: Ernest Benn, 1949], p. 248).

3. A. B. Harvey argues that the evangelical activity in the late eighteenth century also invigorated the sects associated with Old Dissent, which had suffered a decline earlier in that century (Harvey, *Britain in the Early Nineteenth Century* [New York: St. Martin's Press, 1978], p. 74).

4. Ibid., p. 433. For an account of the recurrent tensions in Methodism between the authoritarian/Anglican and community/Puritan tendencies within Wesleyanism, see Robert Currie, *Methodism Divided: A Study in the Sociology of Ecumenicalism* (London: Faber & Faber, 1968), pp. 17–26.

5. In 1802 freedom of worship in the army was proclaimed by the duke of York; in 1809 the Dissenters gained the right to evangelize the slave population in Jamaica; also in 1809 they were granted the right of burial in churchyards, and were excluded, along with Anglicans, from paying tolls on their way to Sunday worship.

6. For a general picture, see Harvey, *Britain in the Early Nineteenth Century*, pp. 113–14.

7. Francis Adams, *History of the Elementary School Contest in England*, ed. Asa Briggs (Brighton: Harvester Press, 1972), p. 45.

8. W. R. Ward, *Religion and Society in England, 1790–1850* (London: B. T. Batsford, 1972), pp. 41–55.

9. For a sketch of the educational arrangements that served the middle and upper classes, see Nicholas Hans, *New Trends in Education in the Eighteenth Century* (London: Routledge & Kegan Paul, 1951), pp. 15–23.

10. Quoted in Mary Sturt, *The Education of the People: A History of Primary Education in England and Wales in the Nineteenth Century* (London: Routledge & Kegan Paul, 1967), p. 6.

11. Samuel Edwin Maltby, *Manchester and the Movement for National Education, 1800–1870* (Manchester: Manchester University Press, 1918), pp. 36–37.

12. Thomas W. Laqueur, *Religion and Respectability: Sunday Schools and Working-Class Culture, 1780–1850* (New Haven: Yale University Press, 1976), pp. 65–74.

13. For an example of the attacks on the supposedly unsettling influence of Sunday schools on the poor, see the letter signed "Eusebius" in the *Gentlemen's Magazine*, September 24, 1797, reprinted in J. M. Goldstrom, *Education: Elementary Education, 1780–1900* (New York: Barnes & Noble, 1972), pp. 22–23.

14. Halévy (*England in 1815*, pp. 526–27) gives the following rough estimates of attendance at these various types of schools: charity schools, 150,000 (1819); Sunday schools, 477,225 (1820); industrial schools, 21,600 (1806); and dame schools, 53,000 (1819). For a compilation of estimates of the growth of

Sunday schools—all criticized as unreliable in various ways—see Laqueur, *Religion and Respectability*, pp. 42–44, esp. table 5.

15. P.D., 1807, 9, col. 859.

16. Discussed in W. A. C. Stewart, *Progressives and Radicals in English Education, 1750–1970* (London: Macmillan, 1972), p. 26. Rousseau's view of education according to nature was also attacked in Anglican circles.

17. See E. G. West, "The Role of Education in Nineteenth-Century Doctrines of Political Economy," *British Journal of Educational Studies* 12, no. 2 (May 1964): 161–72.

18. This assumption of clerical control was also written into the educational clauses of the bill regulating the working of apprentices in 1802 (42 Geo III, c. 73), which constitutes the first legislation on the part of the government calling for compulsory education.

19. P.D., 1807, 9, col. 538.

20. See the section on "Muddling Through" in chapter 10.

21. P.D., 1807, 9, col. 803.

22. Ibid., col. 550. The "ecological fallacy" connected with this kind of statistical presentation was to recur repeatedly in debates throughout the century.

23. Ibid., col. 804.

24. Ibid., col. 536.

25. Ibid., cols. 853–54.

26. Ibid., col. 804.

27. Ibid.

28. Ibid., cols. 798–99.

29. In 1820, introducing his legislation for the education of the poor, Brougham noted that he was accused of wishing "the poorer classes to be taught Greek and Latin and fluxions, and other knowledge which would draw them from the cultivation of the soil, and their various humble occupations" (P.D., 1821, 2, col. 59).

30. P.D., 1807, 9, cols. 1166, 1178.

31. Ibid., cols. 1177–78.

32. For an account of the forces antagonistic to state intervention in the late eighteenth century, see A. S. Bishop, *The Rise of a Central Authority for English Education* (Cambridge: Cambridge University Press, 1971), pp. 1–4.

33. The exception to this statement is found largely with respect to Dissenters, who found the provision for vestry control of the schools proposed in the Whitbread legislation objectionable.

34. Henry Binns, the historian of the British and Foreign School Society, insists on this multiple sponsorship, complaining of the view "in some quarters that the British Society was, and is, a body of well-meaning Nonconformists of mediocre intellectual ability and narrow horizon who represent the opposition to the National Church" (Binns, *A Century of Education: Being the Centenary History of the British Foreign and School Society, 1808–1908* [London: J. M. Dent, 1908], p. vi). Binns is correct as to its sponsorship, but in subsequent years the British Society and the National Society (Church of England) fell into opposition essentially along Anglican/Dissent lines. For an indication of the tensions within the Church of England that led some of its members to join the

British and Foreign School Society, see G. F. A. Best, "The Religious Difficulties of National Education in England, 1800–1870," *Cambridge Historical Journal* 21, no. 2 (1966): 166.

35. Adams, *History of the Elementary School Contest*, pp. 53–54.

36. In this regard they differed greatly in educational philosophy from the most important alternative formulation and movement of the day, that of Robert Owen, who, under the influence of Scottish intellectual traditions, as well as of Rousseau and Pestalozzi, regarded education more in terms of self-development and the realization of personal capacities than as a mechanism for social control and discipline.

37. This last issue was one of controversy. In a debate internal to the church, the bishops argued that only children who attended Church of England services on Sunday be admitted; Low Church representatives argued that to insist on this would alienate Methodists especially, who might not object to the catechism but preferred their own chapels on Sunday. In the end, the bishops relented, for fear of losing a portion of their pupils to British and Foreign School Society schools. See Halévy, *England in 1815*, pp. 529–30.

38. For an enunciation of these principles, see the 1812 reports of the respective religious societies, reprinted in Goldstrom, *Elementary Education, 1780–1900*, pp. 47, 50.

39. Between 1809 and 1813 the British Society received £9,000 in contributions, whereas the National Society received £60,000 in the first four years of its existence (Binns, *Century of Education*, p. 81). By 1820 there existed some 1,100 day schools on the monitorial plan, but all but 235 of these were affiliated with the National Society (Carl F. Kaestle, ed., *Joseph Lancaster and the Monitorial School Movement: A Documentary History* [New York: Teachers College Press, 1973], p. 24). This kind of difference presaged an invariably recurring "tilt" in favor of the wealthier Established Church whenever voluntary support was involved. See the section on "A Victory for the Church" later in this chapter.

40. For an account of a local dispute in Nottingham in 1810–11 that resulted in the formation of two competing schools, see David Wardle, *Education and Society in Nineteenth-Century Nottingham* (Cambridge: Cambridge University Press, 1971), p. 47.

41. Kaestle, ed., *Joseph Lancaster and the Monitorial School Movement*, pp. 18–19, 21.

42. See Frank F. Rosenblatt, *The Chartist Movement in Its Social and Economic Aspects* (New York: Longmans, Green, 1916), pp. 27–32.

43. For a general description, see G. D. H. Cole and Raymond Postgate, *The British People, 1747–1946* (London: Methuen, 1961), pp. 220–26.

44. The vote of £1,000,000 was largely a Tory move to counter the proposals for popular education put forward by Brougham in 1818 (Adams, *History of the Elementary School Contest*, p. 74).

45. Arthur Aspinall, *Lord Brougham and the Whig Party* (Manchester: Manchester University Press, 1927), pp. 40–52. On Brougham's earlier legal career, marked by his defense of unpopular radical causes, see ibid., pp. 35–37.

46. Brougham was also aware of the educational strides being made in France, Switzerland, and Holland at the time; in fact he borrowed the idea of

separating general religious instruction (in schools) from sectarian indoctrination (in church and chapel) from the Dutch pattern. See Hugh M. Pollard, *Pioneers of Popular Education, 1760–1850* (London: John Murray, 1956), p. 156.

47. Chester W. New, *The Life of Henry Brougham to 1830* (Oxford: Clarendon Press, 1961), pp. 198–99.

48. P.P., 1818, 2, p. 56.

49. See the section on "The General Pattern" in chapter 8 for a summary of the evidence.

50. P.P., 1818, 4, p. 56. One witness reported that a school founded on the British and Foreign principle was referred to by the priests as "the Protestant Bible School."

51. Ibid., pp. 82–83; 113–15.

52. Ibid., p. 97.

53. Ibid., p. 150.

54. P.D., 1818, 38, cols. 589–90.

55. Incidentally, the question of the freedom of parents to determine the circumstances of their children was being debated simultaneously in Parliament in connection with the efforts of the elder Peel to restrict the hours of apprentices in cotton factories, which was to eventuate in legislation (59 Geo. III, c. 66). See the debates in P.D., 1816, 33, col. 884; 1818, 38, col. 582, 1260–63.

56. P.D., 1818, 38, cols. 1210–11. See also Adams, *History of the Educational School Contest*, p. 71.

57. Adams, *History of the Elementary School Contest*, pp. 72–73.

58. P.D., 1821, 2, col. 78. This provision presaged the famous Cowper-Temple amendment that found its way into the Education Act of 1870. See the section on "Other Religious and Political Developments" in chapter 5.

59. See Brougham's efforts to try to assure Dissenters and Catholics that his proposed legislation would not interfere with their religious freedoms. Ibid., 1821, 2, cols. 365–66.

60. P.D., 1822, 5, col. 1513.

61. David N. Hempton, "Wesleyan Methodism and Educational Politics in Early Nineteenth-Century England," *History of Education* 8, no. 3 (September 1979): 208–9.

62. P.D., 1822, 5, col. 1512.

63. In fact, Brougham seemed to have retained some bitterness over this episode. In a letter to Sir Robert Peel in 1841, Brougham spoke of the "real friends of education," but excepted "those who hate the Established Church and love their sects more than they love education" (quoted in Binns, *Century of Education*, p. 139).

64. Elie Halévy, *A History of the English People in the Nineteenth Century*, trans. E. I. Watkin and D. A. Barker (1924–27), vol. 2, *The Liberal Awakening, 1815–30* (reprint, London: Ernest Benn, 1949), p. 107.

65. Henry Craik, *The State in Its Relation to Education* (1882), rev. ed. (London: Macmillan, 1914), pp. 14–15.

66. Whitbread, Brougham, and others who pressed for educational reform in the first quarter of the nineteenth century were derogatorily called the "education-mad party."

67. Henry James Burgess, *Enterprise in Education: The Story of the Work*

*of the Established Church in the Education of the People Prior to 1870* (London: National Society and SPCK, 1958), p. 42.

68. C. K. Francis Brown, *The Church's Part in Education, 1833–1941, with Special Reference to the Work of the National Society* (London: National Society and SPCK, 1942), p. 17.

69. Binns, *Century of Education,* p. 103. Sir Robert Peel, the home secretary, to whom the appeals were addressed, declined on the grounds that a grant to the religious society would be "extremely inconvenient to Government." But it was precisely that kind of grant that was found to be the only acceptable form of intervention in 1833.

70. Reported in H. Holman, *English National Education: A Sketch of the Rise of Public Elementary Schools in England* (London: Blackie & Son, 1898), p. 44.

71. A. F. B. Roberts, "A New View of the Infant School Movement," *British Journal of Educational Studies* 20 (June 1972): 154.

72. Burgess, *Enterprise in Education,* pp. 65–66.

73. In the debate on a proposed national system of education in 1833, Roebuck stated that with respect to political enlightenment of the poor, America has "magnificent provisions . . . which surpass all that the world has seen before" (P.D., 1833, 20, col. 148). See also Adams, *History of the Elementary School Contest,* p. 88; Elie Halévy, *A History of the English People in the Nineteenth Century,* trans. E. I. Watkin and D. A. Barker (1924–27), vol. 3, *The Triumph of Reform, 1830–1842* (reprint, London: Ernest Benn, 1950), p. 106.

74. See the section on "The Solution of 1831" in chapter 7.

75. Sturt, *Education of the People,* pp. 75–76.

76. The utilitarian reformer Thomas Wyse wrote in 1836 that under conditions of religious conflict it was necessary "to separate the different persuasions, or leave the reading of the Scriptures to separate, or out-of-school, hours, under the direction of the pastors of the respective communions"; he applauded the Irish solution in this connection (Wyse, *Education Reform; or, The Necessity of a National System of Education* [London: Longman, Rees, Orme, Brown, Green & Longman, 1836], p. 158).

77. See, for example, Graham Wallas, *The Life of Francis Place, 1771–1851* (London: Allen & Unwin, 1918).

78. See, for example, E. J. Hobsbawm and George Rudé, *Captain Swing* (New York: Pantheon Books, 1968).

79. Henry Brougham, 1st baron Brougham and Vaux, *The Life and Times of Henry, Lord Brougham, Written by Himself* (New York: Harper & Brothers, 1871–72), 3:293.

80. Interestingly, however, in his catalogue of accomplishments of the first reformed Parliament, Brougham does not mention the parliamentary action in 1833 opening the door to state involvement in education (ibid., pp. 293–95).

81. Olive J. Brose, *Church and Parliament: The Reshaping of the Church of England, 1828–1860* (Stanford: Stanford University Press, 1959), pp. 22–28.

82. "Reasons for Establishing a Public System of Education in England," *Quarterly Journal of Education,* quoted in Goldstrom, *Elementary Education, 1780–1900,* p. 78.

83. Quoted in Samuel Edwin Maltby, *Manchester and the Movement for*

*National Elementary Education, 1800–1870* (Manchester: Manchester University Press, 1918), p. 41.

84. Quoted in Binns, *Century of Education*, p. 117.

85. R. E. Aldrich characterizes the situation in 1833 as follows: "In the early 1830's the leadership of the cause of popular education in the House of Commons passed from a Scotsman, Henry Brougham, to an Irishman, Thomas Wyse, and a 'Canadian born in Madras,' John Roebuck" (Aldrich, "Radicalism, National Education and the Grant of 1833," *Journal of Educational Administration and History* 5, no. 1 [January 1973]: 2).

86. P.D., 1833, 20, col. 143.

87. Ibid.

88. Ibid.

89. Ibid., col. 151.

90. Ibid., cols. 167–70.

91. Speaking before the Select Committee on Education in 1834, Brougham asserted that compulsory attendance could not be justified either on grounds of public utility or expedience. He added that "[those] who have argued in favour of such a scheme from the example of a military government like that of Prussia, have betrayed, in my opinion, great ignorance of the nature of Englishmen" (P.P., 1834, 9, p. 225). See also J. E. G. de Montmorency, *State Intervention in English Education* (Cambridge: Cambridge University Press, 1902), pp. 235–36. On Brougham's changed position on the topic of compulsory education, see Aspinall, *Lord Brougham and the Whig Party*, pp. 237–39.

92. P.D., 1833, 20, col. 173.

93. See the section on "Attendance Fees and Compulsory Attendance" in chapter 8.

94. P.D., 1843, 68, col. 1247.

95. D. G. Paz, *The Politics of Working-Class Education in Britain, 1830–1850* (Manchester: Manchester University Press, 1980), 12–13.

96. P.D., 1833, 20, col. 730.

97. Ibid.

98. Ibid., col. 734.

99. This defense, while protective of the government, proved to be a false one, in that any assistance to voluntary efforts at the time imparted an advantage to the wealthier and better-situated Established Church, as the subsequent years were to demonstrate. See the section on "Secularization and Primordialism" in chapter 10.

100. See Bishop, *Rise of a Central Authority for British Education*, pp. 10–11.

101. J. Alexander and D. B. Paz, "The Treasury Grants, 1833–1839," *British Journal of Educational Studies* 22, no. 1 (February 1974): 78–86.

102. Quoted in Adams, *History of the Elementary School Contest*, p. 106.

103. Binns, *Century of Education*, p. 124.

104. P.D., 1837, 34, col. 449.

105. P.D., 1838, 44, col. 45. The following year, Wyse also complained about the exclusion of Catholics (P.D., 1839, 45, col. 698). O'Connell's remark shows the ambiguity of usage of religious terms at the time. He apparently

equated "Protestants" with the Church of England, and erroneously so, because most Dissenters were Protestants. In addition, Catholics could from one perspective be regarded as "Dissenters" because of their relationship to the doctrines and rituals of the Church of England. In practice, however, Catholics and other Dissenters were most frequently distinguished from one another.

106. P.D., 1838, 39, col. 449; 1839, 45, col. 698.

107. Maltby, *Manchester and the Movement for National Elementary Education*, pp. 46–47. For a detailed account of the work of the Manchester Statistical Society in this decade, see P. H. Butterfield, "The Educational Researches of the Manchester Statistical Society, 1830–1840," *British Journal of Educational Studies* 22, no. 3 (October 1974): 340–57. The figures estimated for other urban centers were: Liverpool, 50 percent; York, 34 percent; Westminster, 65 percent; Birmingham, 51 percent (Adams, *History of the Elementary School Contest*, p. 95).

108. Sturt, *Education of the People*, p. 70. See also P. H. J. H. Gosden, *The Development of Educational Administration in England and Wales* (Oxford: Basil Blackwell, 1966), pp. 1–2; Paz, *Politics of Working-Class Education*, pp. 31–36.

109. For documentation of this stereotype, see the section on "Working-Class Teaching before 1846" in chapter 9.

110. P.P., 1834, 9, pp. 9, 10, 17. See also Alexander Dallas Bache, *Report on Education in Europe to the Trustees of the Girard College for Orphans* (Philadelphia: Lydia R. Bailey, 1839).

111. P.P., 1834, 9, pp. 57, 61; the religious obstacles to governmental inspection were also foreseen. P.P., 1837–38, 7, pp. 247–48.

112. For a general characterization of the complicated and often turbulent political tone of the 1830s and 1840s, see John Morley, *The Life of William Ewart Gladstone* (London: Macmillan, 1903), pp. 156–57.

113. For an account of the educational aspects of working-class radicalism in the 1830s and 1840s, see Brian Simon, *Studies in the History of Education, 1780–1870* (London: Lawrence & Wishart, 1960), pp. 253–72.

114. P.D., 1839, 48, col. 227.

115. Ibid., cols. 589–90.

116. Ibid., col. 665.

117. In 1833 the United Committee on Dissenting Grievances included a number of different dissenting denominations, but not the Wesleyans and Quakers. This was the group that led the fight for expanded Nonconformist reliefs and privileges. William H. Mackintosh believes that the Broad Church movement within the church, which was antidoctrinal and rationalistic in its criticism of ecclesiastical bodies, gave a boost to the Nonconformist efforts in the 1830s and 1840s (Mackintosh, *Disestablishment and Liberation: The Movement for the Separation of the Anglican Church from State Control* [London: Epworth Press, 1972], pp. xxi, 8–11). See also Halévy, p. 151.

118. For a discussion of hostility to the Church of England in the 1820s and the circumstances leading to the onset of the Oxford Movement, see William G. Peck, *The Social Implications of the Oxford Movement* (New York: Charles Scribner's Sons, 1933), pp. 38–39.

119. For an account of the theological and institutional sides of the Oxford Movement, see R. W. Church, *The Oxford Movement: Twelve Years, 1833– 1845* (1891), edited, with an introduction, by Geoffrey Best (Chicago: University of Chicago Press, 1970), pp. 29–69.

120. Gilbert A. Cahill, "Some Nineteenth-Century Roots of the Ulster Problem, 1829–1848," *Irish University Review* 1, no. 2 (Spring 1971): 215–37.

121. For a discussion of the religious aspects of these decades, see the sections on "A Reprise of 1820" later in this chapter and "General Features of the Period" in chapter 5.

122. The classification is taken from Sir James Kay-Shuttleworth, *Four Periods of Public Education* (London: Longman, Green, Longman & Roberts, 1862), pp. 446–47.

123. P.D., 1837, 39, col. 210.

124. Ibid., cols. 435–36.

125. Pollard, *Pioneers of Popular Education*, pp. 198–200.

126. For a general summary of the educational activity of the period, see J. L. Hammond and Barbara Hammond, *The Age of the Chartists, 1832–1854: A Study of Discontent* (1930; reprint, New York: Augustus M. Kelley, 1967), pp. 180–83.

127. P.P., 1835, 7, p. iii.

128. P.P., 1837–38, 7, p. vii.

129. Ibid., p. xi.

130. P.D., 1838, 34, col. 449.

131. Since both Lord John Russell and Lord Brougham were vice presidents of the British and Foreign School Society at the time, it is likely that that society was influential in the drafting of the Bill (Binns, *Century of Education*, pp. 128–29).

132. P.D., 1838, 39, cols. 451, 464.

133. P.D., 1838, 44, col. 1174.

134. Kay-Shuttleworth, *Four Periods of Public Education*, p. 449.

135. Bishop, *Rise of a Central Authority for English Education*, p. 21.

136. Paz, *Politics of Working-Class Education*, p. 15.

137. Quoted in Adams, *History of the Elementary School Contest*, p. 110.

138. Hempton, "Wesleyan Methodism and Educational Politics," p. 211.

139. For the extensive planning that had been done in the Committee of Council on the issue of teacher-training, see Pamela Horn, "Aspects of Education, 1839–41: The Minute Book of the Committee of the Privy Council," *Oxford Review of Education* 5, no. 1 (1979): 30–32.

140. John William Adamson, *English Education, 1789–1902* (Cambridge: Cambridge University Press, 1964), p. 126; H. F. Mathews, *Methodism and the Education of the People, 1791–1851* (London: Epworth Press, 1949), p. 33.

141. P.D., 1839, 48, col. 280.

142. Ibid., col. 300.

143. Ibid., cols. 551–52.

144. Burgess, *Enterprise in Education*, pp. 73–74.

145. This account is based on ibid., pp. 83–88; and John S. Hurt, *Educa-*

*tion in Evolution: Church, State, Society and Popular Education, 1800–1870* (London: Rupert Hart-Davis, 1971), pp. 29–35.

146. Binns, *Century of Education*, p. 130.

147. P.D., 1839, 48, col. 793.

148. Nancy Ball, *Her Majesty's Inspectorate, 1839–1849* (Edinburgh: Oliver & Boyd, 1963), p. 61.

149. P.P., 1840, 40, pp. 399–401.

150. Ibid., p. 404.

151. For an account of the inspectors' condemnatory reports, see Ball, *Her Majesty's Inspectorate*, pp. 79–81.

152. P.P., 1840, 40, pp. 395, 410.

153. Frank Smith, *The Life and Work of Sir James Kay-Shuttleworth* (London: John Murray, 1923), pp. 98–100.

154. Ball, *Her Majesty's Inspectorate*, p. 59.

155. Ibid., pp. 57–58.

156. See R. C. O. Matthews, *A Study in Trade-Cycle History: Economic Fluctuations in Great Britain, 1833–1842* (Cambridge: Cambridge University Press, 1954), pp. 141–43; see also the reports of the Poor Law Commissioners in those years (P.P., 1842, 29, pp. 10–11, and 1843, 21, p. 5).

157. P.P., 1840, 10, 40; 1841, 9; 1842, 17, 18; 1843, 13.

158. Graham is quoted in Adamson, *English Education, 1789–1902*, p. 131. For further documentation of the distress and unrest in 1841–42, see Arvel B. Erickson, *The Public Career of Sir James Graham* (Oxford: Basil Blackwell, 1952), pp. 161–62.

159. Kay-Shuttleworth, *Four Periods of English Education*, p. 232.

160. For a brief characterization of Graham's conservative political and religious views, see Erickson, *Public Career of Sir James Graham*, pp. 149, 211–12.

161. P.D., 1843, 68, col. 1440. On another occasion Graham showed less sympathy with the power of education to settle the populace. Responding to Kay-Shuttleworth's plea on behalf of training schools as helpful in the struggle to restore peace, Graham wrote in 1842 that "[these] instruments are not to be despised, and have been too long neglected; but cheap bread, plenty of potatoes, low-priced American bacon, a little more Dutch cheese and butter, will have a more pacifying effect than all the mental culture which any Government can supply" (quoted in Alexander M. Ross, "Kay-Shuttleworth and the Training of Teachers for Pauper Schools," *British Journal of Educational Studies* 15, no. 3 [October 1967]: 275–83).

162. For an account of Shaftesbury's antipathy to the manufacturers, see Georgina Battiscombe, *Shaftesbury: A Biography of the Seventh Earl, 1801–1885* (London: Constable, 1974), esp. pp. 80–81.

163. Edward Baines, Jr., *The Social, Educational, and Religious State of the Manufacturing Districts* (1843; reprint, New York: Augustus M. Kelley, 1969).

164. Edward Baines, Jr., *Letter to the Right Honourable Lord Wharncliffe* (London: Ward, 1843).

165. Hammond and Hammond, *Age of the Chartists*, pp. 191–95; Elie Halévy, *A History of the English People in the Nineteenth Century*, trans. E. I.

Watkin and D. A. Barker (1924–27), vol. 4, *Victorian Years, 1841–1895* (reprint, London: Ernest Benn, 1951), pp. 67–70.

166. Peel was cautious, however, about putting forth any general plan, and preferred instead the "cautious and gradual extension of the power and the pecuniary means of the Committee of the Privy Council" (quoted in Brose, *Church and Parliament,* p. 195). This was precisely the policy that developed a few years after the defeat of Graham's proposals.

167. P.D., 1843, 62, col. 1081.

168. Hempton, "Wesleyan Methodism and Educational Politics," pp. 213–18.

169. See the comments by Joseph Hume, John Roebuck, and T. Milner Gibson in P.D., 1843, 67, col. 1454; 1843, 69, cols. 539–40; 1843, 68, cols. 1127–28.

170. P.D., 1843, 70, col. 94.

171. Quoted in Battiscombe, *Shaftesbury,* p. 162.

172. The Congregational Union, formed in 1831, was the leading Nonconformist denomination involved in the Voluntaryist movement. As early as 1840, it had begun to entertain the idea that the union should have its own schools. See Albert Peel, *These Hundred Years: A History of the Congregational Union of England and Wales 1821–1931* (London: Congregational Union of England and Wales, 1931), p. 176.

173. For an account of the circumstances of the origin of the Voluntaryists, see Janet E. Allen, "Voluntaryism: A 'Laissez-Faire' Movement in Mid-Nineteenth Century Elementary Education," *History of Education* 10, no. 2 (June 1981): 111–24. For an estimation of the general electoral force of the Voluntaryist political group, especially in the election of 1847 and its aftermath, see Michael Bentley, *Politics without Democracy, 1815–1914: Perception and Preoccupation in British Government* (Oxford: Blackwell, 1984), p. 131.

174. See p. 134.

175. Norman Gash, *Sir Robert Peel: The Life of Sir Robert Peel after 1830,* 2d ed. (London: Longman, 1986), p. 383.

176. See pp. 302–6.

177. Smith, *Life and Work of Sir James Kay-Shuttleworth,* p. 157.

178. Paz, *Politics of Working-Class Education,* p. 128.

179. Adamson, *English Education, 1789–1902,* p. 139.

CHAPTER 5

1. Frank Smith, *The Life and Work of Sir James Kay-Shuttleworth* (London: John Murray, 1923), pp. 143–45.

2. Ibid., p. 170.

3. R. W. Church, *The Oxford Movement: Twelve Years, 1833–1845* (1891), edited, with an introduction, by Geoffrey Best (Chicago: University of Chicago Press, 1970), pp. 264–66.

4. David N. Hempton, "Wesleyan Methodism and Educational Politics in Early Nineteenth-Century England," *History of Education* 8, no. 3 (September 1979): 219.

5. For a general portrait of the growth of competing movements and the intensification of religious conflict in the 1840s, see G. I. T. Machin, *Politics and the Churches in Great Britain, 1832–1868* (Oxford: Clarendon Press, 1977), pp. 110–63.

6. See the section on "The Disruption and Its Impact" in chapter 7.

7. For a brief sketch of the political crisis of the early 1840s, and in particular of the alarming "Monster Meetings" that began to be held in the spring of 1843, see Lawrence J. McCaffrey, *The Irish Question, 1800–1922* (Lexington: University of Kentucky Press, 1968), pp. 48–57. For a discussion of the general contours of Peel's conciliatory policy, 1843–45, see Angus Macintyre, *The Liberator: Daniel O'Connell and the Irish Party, 1830–47* (New York: Macmillan, 1965), pp. 280–84.

8. Quoted in Norman Gash, *Sir Robert Peel: The Life of Sir Robert Peel after 1830*, 2d ed. (London: Longman, 1986), p. 420.

9. P.D., 1845, 79, cols. 20, 93, 1050. Gladstone actually resigned from the Peel government over the principle of the Maynooth grant (because it violated the idea of a single established church, which he had forcefully propounded in 1838, but voted for the measure as politically sound (ibid., col. 524).

10. See the petition submitted by the Scottish Presbyterians against the annual renewal in 1839 (P.D., 1839, 49, col. 170).

11. Ibid., cols. 49–50, 54, 108, 774–75.

12. For a general account of the religious array of opinions on the Maynooth issue, including the split in Dissent, see G. I. T. Machin, "The Maynooth Grant, the Dissenters and Disestablishment, 1845–1847," *English Historical Review* 31 (January 1967): 61–85.

13. See the speech representing these positions by John Bright in Parliament (P.D., 1845, 79, cols. 822–23). The British Anti-State-Church Association also took a strong stand against the Maynooth subsidy, forming an Anti-Maynooth Committee in 1845 (William H. Mackintosh, *Disestablishment and Liberation: The Movement for the Separation of the Anglican Church from State Control* [London: Epworth Press, 1972], p. 37).

14. P.D., 1845, 79, col. 941; also 80, cols. 699–700.

15. Ibid., col. 530.

16. P.D., 1845, 79, cols. 1108–9; 80, cols. 737–38 and 1367.

17. See J. B. Conacher, *The Peelites and the Party System, 1846–52* (Hamden, Conn.: Archon Books, 1972), pp. 12–14. For a general comment on Peel's difficulties in maintaining unity among the Conservatives, see G. P. Gooch, ed., *The Later Correspondence of Lord John Russell, 1840–1870* (London: Longmans, Green, 1925), 1:46.

18. For additional background to this anti-Catholicism, see the discussion by Joseph L. Altholz of the dynamic cultural, organizational, and demographic changes that contributed to a general revival of Catholicism in England in the 1840s (Altholz, *The Liberal Catholic Movement in England: The "Rambler" and Its Contributors, 1848–1864* [London: Burns & Oates, 1962], p. 2).

19. For an account of the National Society's support for the pupil scheme even before it was provided, and for the support of the British and Foreign School Society, see Henry James Burgess, *Enterprise in Education: The Story of*

*the Work of the Established Church in the Education of the People Prior to 1870* (London: National Society and SPCK, 1958), pp. 99—102.

20. Kay-Shuttleworth as much as acknowledged that this consideration was in the minds of the government in preparing the minutes of 1846. See Sir James Kay-Shuttleworth, *Public Education as Affected by the Minutes of the Committee of Privy Council from 1846 to 1852; with Suggestions as to Future Policy* (London: Longman, Brown, Green & Longmans, 1853), p. 54.

21. Walter F. Hook, *On the Means of Rendering More Efficient the Education of the People: A Letter to the Lord Bishop of St. David's* (London: John Murray, 1846).

22. Ibid., p. 21.

23. Ibid., pp. 33—34.

24. Ibid., p. 37. The scheme explicitly floated by Hook was the system of combined education then in place in Ireland. Hook was not entirely alone in his conviction that voluntary efforts could not relieve the educational situation. The Congregationalist Robert Vaughan, principal of the Lancashire Independent College in Manchester, spoke up along similar lines. See W. R. Ward, *Religion and Society in England, 1790—1850* (London: B. T. Batsford, 1972), pp. 249—51.

25. Smith, *Life and Work of Sir James Kay-Shuttleworth*, pp. 179—80.

26. See the section on "Educational Growth" later in this chapter.

27. Edward Baines, Jr., *An Alarm to the Nation, in the Unjust, Unconstitutional, and Dangerous Measure of State Education Proposed by the Government* (London: Ward, 1847), pp. 8—9.

28. Edward Baines, Jr., *Letters to the Right Hon. Lord John Russell, First Lord of the Treasury, on State Education* (London: Simpkin, Marshall, 1846), p. 109.

29. Quoted in Smith, *Life and Work of Sir James Kay-Shuttleworth*, p. 184.

30. Binns, *Century of Education*, pp. 143—45.

31. P.D., 1847, 91, cols. 950—52.

32. Hempton, "Wesleyan Methodism and Educational Politics," p. 219.

33. See *The Autobiography of Sir James Kay-Shuttleworth*, ed. B. C. Bloomfield (London: University of London, Institute of Education, 1964), p. 70.

34. D. G. Paz, *The Politics of Working-Class Education in Britain, 1830—1850* (Manchester: Manchester University Press, 1980), p. 127.

35. H. F. Mathews, *Methodism and the Education of the People, 1791—1851* (London: Epworth Press, 1949), p. 136.

36. Paz, *Politics of Working-Class Education*, pp. 27—31.

37. Ibid., p. 137.

38. Russell's biographer indicates that one factor in his determination to postpone admission of the Catholics into the scheme was his apprehension that to do so would be damaging to his party in the upcoming general election of 1847. Because this gave an impression that he had struck a bargain with the Methodists, Russell then stated publicly that he hoped to include the Catholics the following year. See John Prest, *Lord John Russell* (London: Macmillan, 1972), p. 256.

39. See Russell's explanation to Parliament on this score in P.D., 1847, 91, cols. 1217—18. See also Francis Adams, *History of the Elementary School Contest in England*, ed. Asa Briggs (Brighton: Harvester Press, 1972), p. 133.

40. Janet E. Allen, "Voluntaryism: A 'Laissez-Faire' Movement in Mid-Nineteenth Century Elementary Education," *History of Education* 10, no. 2 (June 1981): 117; see also Adams, *History of the Elementary School Contest*, p. 133.

41. Asher Tropp mentions that the pupil-teacher scheme stirred some fear among churchmen because it institutionalized the dissemination of doctrines other than its own; some apprehension among Dissenters because of the extension of government influence over their children, and some opposition on the part of working-class leaders on the same basis (Tropp, *The Schoolteachers: The Growth of the Teaching Profession in England and Wales from 1800 to the Present Day* [London: Heinemann, 1957], pp. 19–20).

42. Allen, "Voluntaryism," p. 117.

43. Mackintosh, *Disestablishment and Liberation*, p. 38.

44. P.D., 1847, 3d ser., 91, cols. 997–98, 1101, 1054, 1063, 1089–90.

45. Ibid., cols. 1227–28.

46. Gladstone, letter to Hook, quoted in Smith, *Life and Work of Sir James Kay-Shuttleworth*, p. 178.

47. Hook, *On the Means of Rendering More Efficient the Education of the People*, p. 5.

48. Ashley's comment noted in Ian Sellers, *Nineteenth-Century Nonconformity* (London: Edward Arnold, 1977), p. 72.

49. P.D., 1859, 45, col. 315.

50. Adam H. Robson, *The Education of Children Engaged in Industry in England, 1833–1876* (London: Kegan Paul, Trench, Trubner, 1931), p. 85.

51. George A. Denison, *Notes of My Life, 1805–1878* (Oxford: James Barker, 1878), p. 329.

52. P.P., 1862, 42, p. 20.

53. See, for example, Asa Briggs, *Victorian People: A Reassessment of Persons and Themes, 1851–67*, rev. ed. (Chicago: University of Chicago Press, 1970).

54. Asa Briggs, *The Age of Improvement* (London: Longmans, Green, 1958).

55. W. L. Burn, *The Age of Equipoise: A Study of the Mid-Victorian Generation* (New York: Norton, 1965), p. 18.

56. Briggs, *Victorian People*, pp. 1–3.

57. A. Abbott, *Education for Industry and Commerce in England* (London: Humphrey Milford, 1933), pp. 25–32.

58. G. F. A. Best, "Popular Protestantism in Victorian Britain," in Robert Robson, ed., *Ideas and Institutions of Victorian Britain: Essays in Honor of George Kitson Clark* (New York: Barnes & Noble, 1967), pp. 115–42.

59. Catherine Gallagher and Thomas Laqueur, eds., *The Making of the Modern Body: Sexuality and Society in the Nineteenth Century* (Berkeley: University of California Press, 1987); Stephen Marcus, *The Other Victorians: A Study of Sexuality and Pornography in Mid-Nineteenth Century England* (New York: Basic Books, 1974).

60. J. R. T. Hughes, *Fluctuations in Trade, Industry and Finance: A Study of British Economic Development, 1850–1860* (Oxford: Clarendon Press, 1960), pp. 5–8.

61. J. H. Clapham, *An Economic History of Modern Britain*, vol. 2, *Free*

*Trade and Steel, 1850–1886* (Cambridge: Cambridge University Press, 1932), pp. 155–57.

62. Briggs, *Age of Improvement*, p. 430.

63. G. Kitson Clark, *The Making of Victorian England* (London: Methuen, 1962), pp. 67–68.

64. Briggs, *Age of Improvement*, pp. 407–9.

65. J. F. C. Harrison, "The Victorian Gospel of Success," *Victorian Studies* 1, no. 2 (December 1957): 155–64.

66. Asa Briggs, "The Language of 'Class' in Early Nineteenth-Century England," in Asa Briggs and John Saville, eds., *Essays in Labour History* (London: Macmillan, 1960), pp. 69–71.

67. Machin, *Politics and the Churches*, p. 252.

68. Ian Sellers, *Nineteenth-Century Nonconformity* (London: Edward Arnold, 1977), p. 9.

69. Ibid., pp. 380–81.

70. In 1853 the British Anti-State-Church Association changed its name to "The Society for the Liberation of Religion from State-Patronage and Control" and continued its anti-establishment struggle on many fronts. The 1850s alone saw the Oxford University Act (1854), the Liberty of Worship Act (1855), the Cambridge University Act (1856), the Divorce and Matrimonial Act (1857), the admission of Jews to Parliament (1858), and the opening of the grammar schools to Dissenters (1850). See Mackintosh, *Disestablishment and Liberation*, p. 47.

71. Ibid., pp. 223–31. For an account of the theological and religious/political themes that went into this assault on the Catholics, see G. F. A. Best, "Popular Protestantism in Victorian Britain," in Robert Robson, ed., *Ideas and Institutions of Victorian Britain: Essays in Honor of Kitson Clark* (New York: Barnes & Noble, 1967), pp. 118–26. For a brief account of the Papal Aggression episode and public reaction to it, see G. P. Gooch, ed., *The Later Correspondence of Lord John Russell, 1840–1878* (London: Longmans, Green, 1925), pp. 45–46.

72. Ian Sellers, *Nineteenth-Century Nonconformity* (London: Edward Arnold, 1977), pp. 73–74; John Vincent, *The Formation of the Liberal Party, 1857–1868* (London: Constable, 1966), pp. 52–53.

73. P.P., 21, pt. 1, p. 25.

74. For a cumulative total, see table 29.

75. John Hurt, *Education in Evolution: Church, State, Society and Popular Education, 1800–1870* (London: Rupert Hart-Davis, 1971), pp. 68, 286. As Hurt points out, the formation of the Education Department was the only legislative act passed by Parliament improving elementary education before the introduction of the legislation in 1870.

76. He could have added the multidenominational British and Foreign, the Wesleyan Methodists, and the Jews, though the last did not have a full-time inspector for their few schools.

77. P.P., 1861, 4, p. 93.

78. Allen, "Voluntaryism," pp. 120–21.

79. Adams, *History of the Elementary School Contest*, pp. 136–37.

80. Smith, *Life and Work of Sir James Kay-Shuttleworth,* pp. 189–90.

81. P.P., 1847, 45, p. 9. The matter is summarized in Nancy Ball, *Her Majesty's Inspectorate, 1839–1849* (Edinburgh: Oliver & Boyd, 1963), p. 127.

82. P.P., 1847, 45, p. 21.

83. For the exchange between Lingen and the society, see P.P., 1851, 44, pp. 29–54. The issue was settled satisfactorily in 1852 (P.P., 1852, 39, pp. 376–81).

84. Burgess, *Enterprise in Education,* p. 151.

85. Ibid., pp. 156–57.

86. Denison remained embittered to the end of his life about the management clauses. He referred to 1852 as the year of the "consolidation of compulsory interference with the constitution of Church Schools." He said that the outcome of the fight on the conscience clauses "really settled the whole question *for* the Civil Power as *against* the Church" (Denison, *Notes of My Life,* p. 329).

87. See the section on "Revolutionary Fears and Open Religious Conflict" in chapter 4.

88. This connection was readily noted by observers at the time. See the testimony of Edward D. J. Wilks, secretary of the British and Foreign School Society, P.P., 1865, 6, p. 222.

89. Lord John Russell stressed this point in his testimony in P.P., 1867, 6, p. 188.

90. See the section on "Llangefni 1850–1852" in chapter 6.

91. For example, the schools sponsored by the Association Incorporated for Discountenancing Vice, and Promoting the Knowledge and Practice of the Christian Religion, founded in 1792, opened their doors to all persuasions; they taught the church catechism, but obliged only members of the Church of England to use it. See J. R. R. Adams, *The Printed Word and the Common Man* (Belfast: Institute of Irish Studies, 1987), p. 96.

92. P.P., 1818, 4, p. 58. The select committee also reported on a large number of schools investigated by it where the conscience clause was, in effect, observed (ibid.).

93. See the section on "A Reprise of 1820" in chapter 4.

94. P.P., 1840, 40, p. 395.

95. P.P., 1847, 45, p. 23.

96. Burgess, *Enterprise in Education,* p. 164. It should be noted that these actions took place at the end of the protracted struggle over the conscience clause in Llangefni. See the section on "Llangefni 1850–1852" in chapter 6.

97. Ibid., pp. 165–66.

98. See the section on "The Welsh Situation to 1870" in chapter 6.

99. Thomas W. Laqueur, *Religion and Respectability: Sunday Schools and Working Class Culture, 1780–1850* (New Haven: Yale University Press, 1976), pp. 42–61.

100. For an effort to rescue the dame schools from the harsh judgments they received at the time and in the writings of educational historians, see D. P. Leinster-Mackay, "Dame Schools: A Need for Review," *British Journal of Educational Studies* 24, no. 1 (February 1976): 33–48.

101. A presentation of the available information about these private schools

is found in Phil Gardner, *The Lost Elementary Schools of Victorian England* (London: Croom Helm, 1984). Gardner considers the figure of 135,893 returned by the Education Census in 1851 to be an undercount (pp. 58–60); his interpretation of parental motives, largely speculative, is that they sent their children to private schools because they had more control over them than they did over those provided by the religious societies and subsidized by the government (pp. 92–100).

102. See C. J. Montague, *Sixty Years in Waifdom; or, the Ragged School Movement in English History* (1904; New York: Augustus M. Kelley, 1969); Mary Carpenter, "On the Relation of Ragged Schools to the Educational Movement," in *Transactions of the Society for the Promotion of Social Science* (London: John W. Parker, 1857), pp. 226–32; Harriet Warm Schupf, "Single Women and Social Reform in Mid-Nineteenth Century England: The Case of Mary Carpenter," *Victorian Studies* 18, no. 3 (March 1974): 301–17.

103. Mary Carpenter, *Juvenile Delinquents, Their Condition and Treatment* (London: W. & F. G. Cash, 1853), pp. 15–16.

104. Eileen Yeo and E. P. Thompson, *The Unknown Mayhew* (New York: Pantheon Books, 1971), pp. 32–33.

105. John A. Stack, "The Provision of Reformatory Schools, the Lamented Class, and the Myth of the Superiority of Rural Life in Mid-Victorian England," *History of Education* 8, no. 1 (March 1979): 33–44. See also Charles A. Bennett, *History of Manual and Industrial Education up to 1870* (Peoria, Ill.: Chas. A. Bennett, 1926), pp. 231–32.

106. George C. T. Bartley, *The Schools for the People: Containing the History, Development and Present Working of Each Description of English Schools for the Industrial and Poorer Classes* (London: Bell & Daldy, 1871), pp. 270–85.

107. David Chadwick, "On Working Men's Colleges," in *Transactions of the Association for the Promotion of Social Science* (London: John W. Parker, 1859), pp. 323–35.

108. See pp. 56–57.

109. W. F. Connell, *The Educational Thought and Influence of Matthew Arnold* (London: Routledge & Kegan Paul, 1950), p. 56.

110. In Parliament the supporters of the movement were Milner Gibson, Richard Cobden, W. J. Fox, Sir Thomas Bazley, Sir John Potter, and Alexander Henry. For an account of the direct link between the work of the Anti-Corn Law League and the rise of the Lancashire Public School Association, see D. K. Jones, "The Educational Legacy of the Anti-Corn Law League," *History of Education* 3, no. 1 (January 1974): 18–36.

111. Donald Read, *Cobden and Bright: A Victorian Political Partnership* (London: Edward Arnold, 1967), p. 180.

112. Cobden quoted in Samuel Edwin Maltby, *Manchester and the Movement for National Elementary Education, 1800–1870* (Manchester: Manchester University Press, 1918), p. 81. Another leader of the LPSA, George Combe, openly applauded and modeled his views on both the Massachusetts and the Irish systems (P. N. Farrar, "American Influence on the Movement for a National System of Elementary Education in England and Wales, 1830–1870," *British Journal of Educational Studies* 14, no. 1 [November 1965]: 39–41).

113. Sir James Kay-Shuttleworth, *Four Periods of Public Education* (London: Longman, Green, Longman & Roberts, 1862), p. 510.

114. Donald K. Jones, *The Making of the Educational System, 1851–1881* (London: Routledge & Kegan Paul, 1977), p. 25; W. R. Ward, *Religion and Society in England, 1790–1850* (London: B. T. Batsford, 1972), p. 283.

115. Maltby, *Manchester and the Movement for National Elementary Education,* pp. 78–79. William Forster, who was to engineer the Education Act of 1870 through Parliament, was a member of the LPSA, and was instrumental in effecting the compromise in the 1850 debate. For an account of the ambivalence of Pakington, Adderley, and Russell toward endorsing the American system (largely because of its lack of provision for religious education), see Farrar, "American Influence," pp. 42–43.

116. P.D., 1850, 109, cols. 28, 768.

117. P.D., 1850, 110, 460.

118. P.D., 1850, 109, cols. 47–49; also col. 52. Fox's bill was opposed by the Methodists on the grounds that it promoted secular education (Mathews, *Methodism and the Education of the People,* pp. 137–38).

119. P.D., 1850, 110, col. 438; Adams, *History of the Elementary School Contest,* p. 157.

120. P.D., 1850, 109, cols. 58–59; 111, col. 768.

121. P.D., 1852, 119, cols. 1213–14.

122. Ibid., col. 388.

123. Ibid., cols. 394–95.

124. Maltby, *Manchester and the Movement for National Elementary Education,* p. 84.

125. For a broadside attack on both the LPSA and the Manchester and Salford School Committee, from a voluntaryist point of view, see John H. Hinton, *The Case of the Manchester Educationists, Part I: A Review of the Evidence Taken before a Committee of the House of Commons in Relation to the State of Education in Manchester and Salford* (Manchester: E. J. Morten, 1852).

126. P.D., 1854, 130, col. 1045.

127. Ibid., cols. 1061–65.

128. Ibid., col. 1171.

129. P.D., 1855, 137, cols. 649, 661.

130. Ibid., col. 659.

131. Ibid., cols. 2113–14.

132. Ibid., cols. 666–67.

133. Ibid., col. 2130.

134. P.D., 1856, 139, col. 1957.

135. Ibid., cols. 1969–70, 1976.

136. P.D., 1856, 141, cols. 784–88, 801–2, 832–33.

137. Ibid., 1857, 141, col. 959.

138. P.D., 1857, 144, cols. 776–78, 783.

139. P.D., 1857, 164, col. 800.

140. Ward, *Religion and Society in England, 1790–1850,* p. 285; Smith, *Life and Work of Sir James Kay-Shuttleworth,* p. 257.

141. Cited in D. W. Sylvester, *Robert Lowe and Education* (Cambridge: Cambridge University Press, 1974), p. 42.

142. P.D., 1857, 148, col. 1193.

143. Binns, *Century of Education*, p. 176. Kay-Shuttleworth wrote that this consideration, along with the spiraling cost to the government of subsidizing voluntary religious efforts, was the main motive for the formation of the Newcastle Commission in 1858; *Autobiography of Sir James Kay-Shuttleworth*, ed. Bloomfield, p. 74.

144. This phenomenon is documented extensively in chapter 9.

145. Sylvester, *Robert Lowe and Education*, pp. 42–45.

146. John Morley, *The Life of William Ewart Gladstone* (London: Macmillan, 1903), 2:42–51.

147. As shown especially in the statement in William E. Gladstone, *The State in Its Relations with the Church* (London: John Murray, 1838) and in his principled resignation over the state augmentation of the Maynooth grant in 1845.

148. Morley, *Life of William Ewart Gladstone*, 1:298–99.

149. For example, in the debate on the education budget in 1857, Pakington noted that "before the dissolution of Parliament the right hon. Gentlemen the Member for the University of Oxford [Gladstone] complained of the amount of the grant" (P.D., 1857, 146, col. 397). Gladstone openly expressed his concern in a debate of an abortive education bill in 1860 (P.D., 1860, 159, cols. 2024–25). For a general account of Gladstone's activities throughout the 1850s in relation to the education budget, see Sylvester, *Robert Lowe and Education*, pp. 44–45.

150. Tropp, *The Schoolteachers*, pp. 58–61.

151. In 1859 Sir Stafford Northcote complained that since the establishment of the Education Department in 1856, the chancellor of the exchequer had lost control over the department minutes (Hurt, *Education in Evolution*, p. 187).

152. P.D., 1857, 148, cols. 1195–96.

153. See the comment by Lowe in P.D., 1861, 144, cols. 721–22.

154. See the section on "The Welsh Situation to 1870" in chapter 6.

155. See Adderley's computation of costs and defense of the education estimates on the basis of population served (P.D., 1858, 151, cols. 137–38).

156. See the section on "Capitation Payments" in chapter 8.

157. In 1860, Lowe said: "The Education Department was overwhelmed with labour, because they were obliged to ascertain the conditions on which the money was granted, and then they were bound to see that the money was given to the exact persons for whom it was intended. It was necessary in dealing with so many bodies and individuals to act on principles of the greatest distrust. The whole of the stipends of pupil teachers and assistant teachers, the grants to the masters and mistresses instructing them, and the capitation grant, were made by means of Post Office orders. The greatest precaution was necessary in dealing with each school, and in ascertaining the locality, the denomination, and the nature of the grant, or else the Education Committee would never know what became of their money" (P.D., 1860, 160, cols. 1300–1301). For an account by Lingen of the correspondence involved simply in starting a school, see P.P., 1861, 6, question 229.

158. P.D., 1860, 160, col. 1297. For a similar complaint regarding the pro-

liferation of schools in Scotland because of competition between the Established Church and the Free Church, see P.D., 1858, 151, col. 150.

159. P.D., 1861, 144, col. 737.

160. A. S. Bishop, *The Rise of a Central Authority for British Education* (Cambridge: Cambridge University Press, 1971), p. 53.

161. The members of the Newcastle Commission were: Pakington; Sir John Coleridge, favorable to the High Church party; Nassau Senior, a political economist and past member of the Handloom Weavers' Commission; Rev. William Rogers, an Anglican clergyman from London; the universities' representatives, Rev. Charles Lake and Professor Goldwin Smith, the latter a Voluntaryist; and Edward Miall, a Dissenter and a Voluntaryist.

162. P.P., 1861, 31, pt. 1, p. 20.

163. See Mary Sturt, *The Education of the People: A History of Primary Education in England and Wales in the Nineteenth Century* (London: Routledge & Kegan Paul, 1967), p. 245.

164. Sir James Kay-Shuttleworth, "Letter to Earl Granville . . . dated July 29, 1861," in *Four Periods of Public Education*, pp. 574–75.

165. Arnold criticized the methodology of the statistics-gathering of the Newcastle Commission, and compared it unfavorably with official state methods on the Continent (*Schools and Universities on the Continent*, ed. R. H. Super [Ann Arbor: University of Michigan Press, 1964], p. 17).

166. For a methodological criticism of the Newcastle Commission's extrapolation of Inspector J. P. Norris's survey of Cheshire, Shropshire, and Staffordshire, see A. J. Marcham, "Lies and Statistics: A Note on the Newcastle Commission," *History of Education* 9, no. 3 (September 1980): 229–31.

167. Adams, *History of the Elementary School Contest*, pp. 182–83.

168. Sylvester, *Robert Lowe and Education*, pp. 49–51.

169. John Roach, *Public Examinations in England, 1850–1900* (Cambridge: Cambridge University Press, 1971).

170. For an argument that the Revised Code, advertised as consistent with the values of laissez-faire, was in fact interventionist, see Norman Morris, "State Paternalism and *laissez-faire* in the 1860's," in *Studies in the Government and Control of Education since 1860*, edited by Morris (London: Methuen, 1970), pp. 13–25.

171. Rev. David Melville, "The Educational Grant; and What Should Regulate It," in *Transactions of the National Association for the Promotion of Social Science* (London: Victoria Press, 1862), p. 28.

172. Lowe's famous remark about the Revised Code runs as follows: "I cannot promise the House that the system [under the Revised Code] will be an efficient and an economical one, but I can promise that it shall be either one or the other. If it is not cheap it shall be efficient; if it is not efficient it shall be cheap. The present is neither one nor the other. If the schools do not give instruction the public money will not be demanded, but if instruction is given the public money will be demanded—I cannot say to what amount, but the public will get value for its money" (P.D., 1862, 165, col. 229).

173. P.D., 1861, 164, col. 725.

174. Burgess, *Enterprise in Education*, pp. 177–78.

402 Notes to Pages 127–33

175. A. J. Marcham, "Recent Interpretations of the Revised Code of Education, 1862," *History of Education* 8, no. 2 (June 1979): 125.

176. Binns, *A Century of Education*, p. 179.

177. P.D., 1862, 41, col. 209.

178. P.D., 1862, 166, cols. 536–39.

179. Kay-Shuttleworth, "Letter to Earl Granville," pp. 577–79.

180. P.D., 1862, 166, cols. 140–41.

181. Laadan Fletcher, "A Further Comment on Recent Interpretations of the Revised Code, 1862," *History of Education* 10, no. 1 (March 1981): 21–31.

182. See the sections on "A Victory for the Church" and "A Reprise of 1820" in chapter 4.

183. See the section on "The Impact of the Revised Code" in chapter 9. Lowe's own hostility to teachers as a class is documented in Sylvester, *Robert Lowe and Education*, pp. 73–76. Lowe was also responding to criticisms voiced in the *Edinburgh Review* and elsewhere that pupils were taught subjects that were not needed for their station, and that teachers were being "over-educated" for the subjects required in government-supported schools for the working classes (ibid., pp. 76–78).

184. Norman Morris, "Public Expenditure on Education in the 1860's," *Oxford Review of Education* 3, no. 1 (1977): 5.

185. Ibid., p. 6.

186. P.P., 1866, 27, p. 133.

187. P.P., 1867, 22, p. 23.

188. See the section on "The General Pattern" in chapter 8.

189. P.P., 1866, 27, p. 450.

190. P.P., 1868–69, 20, pp. 237–38. Italics added.

191. P.P., 1867, 22, p. 185. C. H. Alderson made the same observation in connection with the situation in British and Foreign School Society and other non–Church of England Protestant schools in the eastern and metropolitan counties: "Payment for results unquestionably operates as a stimulus to teachers. But this stimulus is all in one direction. It is an inducement to concentrate their efforts on scholars who will yield a return in the shape of a grant of eight shillings. It is a temptation to reject those from whose inferior abilities no direct profit is likely to be derived" (P.P., 1866, 27, p. 430).

192. P.D., 1868–69, 194, col. 1205. "Any grant the amount of which is determined by individual examination after a certain attendance at School, tends to cause the neglect of the irregular, dull and migratory scholars whom *it does not pay to teach*," Kay-Shuttleworth asserted (*Memorandum on Popular Education* [London: James Ridgeway, 1868], p. 15).

193. See the section on "Segregative Tendencies" in chapter 3.

194. P.D., 1869, 194, col. 1205.

195. P.P., 1866, 27, p. 428.

196. Report of HMI W. W. Howard for Church of England Schools in Devon and Dorset; P.P., 1867, 22, pp. 252–53.

197. Laaden Fletcher has argued that the system of payment by results further exaggerated social and economic inequality because it directed resources

away from the neediest areas, but he does not, however, elaborate on the mechanisms by which this occurred (Fletcher, "Payment for Means or Payment for Result: Administrative Dilemmas of the 1860s," *Journal of Educational Administration and History* 4, no. 2 [June 1972]: 16–17).

198. P.D., 1856, 141, cols. 797, 801–2, 803–4; 1857, 144, cols. 1850–53; 1858, 49, cols. 401–4; 1860, 160, cols. 1276–77, 1283.

199. P.P., 1856, 47, p. 235; 1856, 48, p. 521; 1857, 33, p. 250; 1859, 21, pp. 157–58; 1864, 45, pp. 169–70.

200. Recording his impression of London in 1863 in his *Winter Notes on My Summer Impressions,* Dostoyevsky said, "The children of these [urban masses] almost before they are grown up, go as a rule on the streets, mingle with the crowd, and often do not return to their parents" (quoted in G. A. N. Lowndes, *The Silent Social Revolution: An Account of the Extension of Public Education in England and Wales, 1895–1965* [London: Oxford University Press, 1969], 2d ed., p. 12). See a similar comment in Hippolyte Taine, *Notes on England,* trans. Edward Hyams (London: Thames & Hudson, 1957), pp. 225–26.

201. P.P., 1852, 7, p. 99.

202. J. S. Hurt, *Elementary Schooling and the Working Classes, 1860–1919* (London: Routledge & Kegan Paul, 1979), pp. 56–59.

203. *The Victoria History of the Counties of England,* vol. 2, *Lancashire* (London: Constable, 1908), p. 390.

204. For figures showing the modest numbers in the 1830s, see Robson, *Education of Children Engaged in Industry,* p. 56.

205. See Colin M. Brown, "Industrialists and Their Factory Schools," *History of Education* 9, no. 2 (April 1980): 117–18. For the actual results of the census, see P.P., 1851, 23, pp. 297–303.

206. Keith Evans, *The Development and Structure of the English Educational System* (London: University of London Press, 1975), p. 29.

207. Eric E. Rich, *The Education Act, 1870: A Study of Public Opinion* (London: Longmans, Green, 1970), p. 50.

208. Hurt, *Elementary Schooling and the Working Classes,* p. 45. Some of the "exceptions" were found in girls' employment in lacemaking and straw plaiting; in certain areas, girls outnumbered boys as "half-timers" and this interfered in some degree with their education (Pamela Horn, "The Education and Employment of Working-Class Girls, 1870–1914," *History of Education* 17, no. 1 [January 1988]: 71–72).

209. Inspector H. M. Cabel reported in 1867 that in his district of Warwick "the percentage of idlers between seven and thirteen has, I am sorry to say, increased" (P.P., 1867, 22, p. 186).

210. The importance of the Birmingham and Manchester reports is underscored in Hurt, *Elementary Schooling and the Working Classes,* pp. 54–55.

211. P.P., 1870, 54, pp. 30–31, 167.

212. Hurt, *Elementary Schooling and the Working Classes,* pp. 60–62.

213. Hurt, *Education in Evolution,* p. 69.

214. Report of Rev. C. J. Robinson (P.P., 1866, 27, p. 248).

215. Report of Rev. H. W. Bellairs (P.P., 1869, 20, p. 23).

216. Sylvester, *Robert Lowe and Education*, p. 97.

217. Lingen summarized the substance of the conscience clause as follows: "Scriptural instruction is given to all the children in the school, but they are expressly exempted from being taught any catechism, or from being made to attend compulsorily in any place of worship on Sundays, against the wish of their parents" (P.P., 1865, 6, p. 43).

218. See the section on "The Welsh Situation to 1870" in chapter 6.

219. A. J. Marcham, "A Question of Conscience: The Church and the 'Conscience Clause', 1860–1870," *Journal of Ecclesiastical History* 22, no. 3 (July 1971): 245–46.

220. See ibid., pp. 239–42, for the story of the fight.

221. Speaking to the Select Committee on Education in 1865, Lowe reported that "wonderfully few" applicants yielded to the condition of the conscience clause (ibid., p. 54). In 1859 there were 434 grants in England and Wales, for a total of £125,000; in 1863 there were 153 grants, for a total of £35,000; and in 1866 there were 120 grants, for a total of £23,000 (P.P., 1867, 55, p. 45).

222. H. A. Bruce, who had served as vice president of the Committee of Council, said "the cases are invariably decided by myself, and are considered with very great care and anxiety. I confess that I should be very glad to be acting under a more definite system." He added that his anxiety came from the "indefiniteness of the rule" using the religious composition of communities as the criterion for requiring the conscience clause (P.P., 1865, 6, p. 67).

223. P.P., 1867, 22, p. 8.

224. Marcham, "Question of Conscience," pp. 237, 248–49.

225. Testimony of Lord Russell, Robert Lowe, C. D. Adderley, and Ralph Lingen, P.P., 1865, 6, pp. 41–43, 50, 75, 188.

226. Ibid., p. 41.

227. P.P., 1862, 43, p. 269.

228. The committee's recommendation was that "no building grant shall be made without requiring, as an indispensable condition, that a Conscience Clause shall be inserted in the trust deed" (P.P., 1866, 7, p. 129).

229. See the section on "Public Movement and Parliamentary Inaction" earlier in this chapter.

230. P.D., 1867, 188, col. 1317.

231. Ibid., cols. 1320–22.

232. Ibid., col. 1332.

233. Ibid., col. 1399. For the actual evolution of the Irish system, see the section on "The Evolution of the National System" in chapter 7.

234. P.D., 1867, 188, cols. 1346, 1366.

235. Anthony Bishop and Wilfred Jones, "The Act That Never Was: The Conservative Education Bill of 1868," *History of Education* 1, no. 2 (June 1972): 160–73.

236. On the Society for the Liberation of Religion, see n. 70 above. Clarendon is quoted in Machin, *Politics and the Churches*, p. 382.

237. Allen, "Voluntaryism," pp. 122–23. Allen also suggests that the fact that both Miall (M.P. and member of the Newcastle Commission) and Baines

(M.P. and member of the Taunton Commission) had developed close relations with the state contributed to their softening of attitude toward the role of the state in education. For an actual account of the limited institutional accomplishments of the Voluntaryists from 1846 to 1867, see Albert Peel, *These Hundred Years: A History of the Congregational Union of England and Wales, 1831–1931* (London: Congregational Union of England and Wales, 1931), pp. 177–83.

238. See the section on "The Consolidation of Growth under Primordial Proliferation" earlier in this chapter.

239. Binns, *Century of Education*, pp. 183–84. See also Keith Evans, *The Development and Structure of the English Educational System* (London: University of London Press, 1975), p. 11.

240. W. P. McCann, "Trade Unionists, Artisans and the 1870 Education Act," *British Journal of Educational Studies* 18, no. 2 (June 1970): 134–39. See also W. H. G. Armytage, "The 1870 Education Act," ibid., pp. 122–23.

241. See Hurt, *Elementary Schooling and the Working Classes*, p. 62. For a general account of the major political items on labor's agenda in the 1860s and 1870s—which did not include elementary education—see Roydon Harrison, *Before the Socialists: Studies in Labour and Politics, 1861–1881* (London: Routledge & Kegan Paul, 1965), pp. 2–4.

242. In both Manchester and Birmingham there was evidence of split between the National Education League (Nonconformist/secular) and the National Education Union (Chuch of England/religious) educational groups (see McCann, "Trade Unionists, Artisans and the 1870 Education Act," pp. 141–46).

243. *History of the Elementary School Contest*, p. 202.

244. Ibid., pp. 206–7.

245. Burgess, *Enterprise in Education*, pp. 195–97.

246. On Catholic policy between 1851 and 1870, see A. A. C. F. Beales, "The Struggle for the Schools," in George Andrew Beck, ed., *The English Catholics, 1850–1950* (London: Burns, Oates, 1950), pp. 367–38.

247. D. E. Selby, "Henry Edward Manning and the Educational Bill of 1870," *British Journal of Educational Studies* 18, no. 2 (June 1970): 197–212.

248. Keith Evans, *The Development and Structure of the English Educational System* (London: University of London Press, 1975), pp. 30–31.

249. Briggs, *Age of Improvement*, p. 435.

250. Evans, *Development and Structure of the English Educational System*, p. 29.

251. See Playfair's letter to the Taunton Commission in P.P., 1867–68, 38, pt. 17, pp. 6–7.

252. This apprehension was voiced, for example, by J. P. Norris, "Technical Instruction," in *Proceedings of the Education Department of the National Association for the Promotion of Social Science* (Belfast: Henry Greer, 1867), pp. 110–16.

253. P.D., 1867, 188, col. 1549.

254. A. J. Marcham, "Educating Our Masters: Political Parties and Elementary Education, 1867–1870," *British Journal of Educational Studies* 21, no. 2

(June 1973): 180–91; Hurt, *Elementary Schooling and the Working Classes,*
pp. 22–23.

255. P.D., 1870, 199, col. 439.

256. Ibid., cols. 443–44.

257. Ibid., cols. 465–66.

258. Ibid., col. 495.

259. Ibid., cols. 1923–25, 1934–35. The original formulation called for
local jurisdiction over religious instruction. Forster was for including only nondenominational religious instruction as in the Massachusetts model, but Gladstone insisted on either denominational religion or no religion at all. Faced with
this alternative, Forster went for local determination. See Donald K. Jones, *The
Making of the Education System, 1851–81* (London: Routledge & Kegan Paul,
1977), pp. 62–64; also Henry Roper, "W. E. Forster's Memorandum of 21 October 1869: A Re-Examination," *British Journal of Educational Studies* 21,
no. 1 (February 1973): 64–65.

260. P.D., 1870, 199, cols. 1947–48.

261. Ibid., col. 2060.

262. For accounts, see T. Wemyss Reid, *Life of the Right Honourable
William Edward Forster* (London: Chapman & Hall, 1888), pp. 502ff.; Adams,
*History of the Elementary School Contest,* pp. 219–32.

263. P.D., 1870, 202, col. 275. This formulation was a compromise between the conscience clause (permitting unwilling parents to withdraw their
children from specific denominational instruction) and the demands of Dissenters and others who were pressing for an entirely secular system.

264. W. F. Cowper-Temple, M. P., gave the following political analysis of
the course of the debate: "The truth is that those followers below the Gangway
[representatives of the National Education League and their associates] were attempting to coerce the Government. When the original measure was introduced
on the subject in February, it was received with acclamation by hon. Members
sitting below the Gangway on the Government side of the House; . . . as soon as
it was found out that the Conservatives, with the view of arriving at a settlement
of the matter, had determined to lay aside their own opinions on the subject,
and accept the measure as a compromise, then an agitation was commenced by
the Radicals, meetings were called, and articles appear in the newspapers denouncing the Bill and demanding concessions. Well, then the right hon. Gentle-
man the Vice President of the Council laid his Amendments upon the Table just
before Whitsuntide; these contained great concessions to the Radicals, such as
the Time Table Conscience Clause, the Ballot, and the abolition of the scheme of
voting in the Vestries. These concessions were, at first, deemed satisfactory by
the hon. Gentlemen below the Gangway. But again, directly it became known
that the Conservative party would not oppose them, the same tactics were repeated, agitation again arose, more meetings were held, violent speeches were
made, violent articles were written, the Government was forced to introduce
what was practically a new measure. Again the Conservative party determined
not to oppose the compromise, but to accept it, much against their desire, so as
to affect a final settlement of the question. They made no difficulty, but determined to help the Government to pass the Bill; and that was why hon. Members

below the Gangway now raised a strong opposition against it. That was a simple history of what had occurred" (P.D., 1870, 202, cols. 652–53).

265. Ibid., cols. 932–33.

266. For other government attempts to accommodate Anglican and other voluntary schools in 1870, see P. T. Marsh, *The Victorian Church in Decline: Archbishop Tait and the Church of England, 1868–1882* (London: Routledge & Kegan Paul, 1969), pp. 77–78. The House of Lords also struck out a few provisions inimical to the Church of England, which offended the Dissenters. See Emily Allyn, *Lords versus Commons: A Century of Conflict and Compromise* (New York: Century, 1931), pp. 101–2.

267. Quoted in Adams, *History of the Elementary School Contest,* pp. 231–32.

268. By 1895 the school boards provided new accommodation for 2,211,299 scholars, whereas the voluntary schools provided for 1,475,000 between 1870 and 1891 (Lowndes, *Silent Social Revolution,* p. 5).

269. Adams, *History of the Elementary School Contest,* p. 232.

270. Reid, *Life of the Right Honourable William Edward Forster,* pp. 522–42.

271. For these developments, see N. J. Richards, "Religious Controversy and School Boards, 1870–1902," *British Journal of Educational Studies* 18, no. 2 (June 1970): 180–96; Adams, *History of the Elementary School Contest,* pp. 246–96.

272. Lowndes, *Silent Social Revolution,* pp. 57–70.

CHAPTER 6

1. See H. J. Hanham, *Scottish Nationalism* (Cambridge, Mass.: Harvard University Press, 1969), ch. 1, on "the Scottishness of Scottish society"; Hanham traces "nationhood" to the twelfth century and points to persistence of a separate church, educational system, legal system, banking system, and political arrangements into the twentieth century.

2. See, e.g., William E. Gladstone, *The Church in Wales* (London: P. S. King & Son, 1871), pp. 1–2. Reference to the "Church in Wales" in contrast to the Church of Ireland indicated the subtleties of the different situations of the Established Church in each.

3. Precise quantitative comparisons are difficult, because educational conflict was fused with other types of conflict in England as well; nevertheless, the Welsh case is sufficiently striking to merit mention of this point.

4. The "both-English-and-Welsh" character of Monmouthshire illustrates this point.

5. Kenneth O. Morgan, *Wales in British Politics, 1868–1922* (Cardiff: University of Wales Press, 1980), pp. 7–8.

6. Reginald Coupland, *Welsh and Scottish Nationalism: A Study* (London: Collins, 1954), p. 217; Elisabeth Inglis-Jones, *The Story of Wales* (London: Faber & Faber, 1945), pp. 197–99.

7. Coupland, *Welsh and Scottish Nationalism,* p. 217. The official lack of sympathy with the Welsh and their distinctive culture was not uniform through-

out the Church of England and became less so in the nineteenth century. For example, the enraged outcry against the reports of the commissioners on the state of education in Wales in the late 1840s was joined by a number of English clergymen, notably John Thirlwell and Dean Cotton (ibid., p. 194).

8. David Williams, *A History of Modern Wales* (London: John Murray, 1950), pp. 166–67. The religious census of 1851 indicated that around three-quarters of the Welsh population was of Dissenting (including Methodist) persuasion.

9. John H. Clapham, *An Economic History of Modern Britain,* vol. 1, *The Early Railway Age* (Cambridge: Cambridge University Press, 1950), pp. 86, 96; W. E. Minchington, "Industrial South Wales, 1750–1914," in Minchington, ed., *Industrial South Wales, 1750–1914: Essays in Welsh Economic History* (London: Frank Cass, 1969), p. xii; A. H. Dodd, *The Industrial Revolution in South Wales* (Cardiff: University of Wales Press, 1971), p. ix; Gareth E. Jones, *Modern Wales: A Concise History, c. 1483–1979* (Cambridge: Cambridge University Press, 1984), p. 165.

10. John Davies, "The End of the Great Estates and the Rise of Freehold Farming in Wales," *Welsh History Review* 7, no. 2 (December 1974): 187.

11. Morgan, *Wales in British Politics,* pp. 1–10; Clapham, *Early Railway Age,* pp. 15–16, 106.

12. David W. Howell, "The Agricultural Labourer in Nineteenth-Century Wales," *Welsh History Review* 6, no. 3 (June 1973): 262.

13. Morgan, *Wales in British Politics,* p. 5.

14. Coupland, *Welsh and Scottish Nationalism,* pp. 173–74.

15. See Williams, *History of Modern Wales,* p. 199. For an account of the hostility expressed toward the estate agents in the chapel and in the popular literature during the nineteenth century, see Richard Colyer, "The Land Agent in Nineteenth-Century Wales," *Welsh History Review* 8, no. 4 (December 1977): 401–23.

16. Jeliger C. Symons, one of the commissioners on the state of education in Wales, commented that "the mockery of an English trial over a Welsh criminal by a Welsh jury, addressed by counsel and judge in English, is too gross and shocking to need comment" (P.P., 1847, 27.2, p. 66).

17. In the 1841 election, for instance, the Tories won nineteen of the twenty-nine seats in Wales. Only one Nonconformist was returned in the election of 1852. See David A. Bretty, "Richard Davies and Nonconformist Radicalism in Anglesey, 1837–68: A Study of Sectarian and Middle-Class Politics," *Welsh History Review* 9, no. 4 (December 1979): 439–49.

18. David W. Howell, *Land and People in Nineteenth-Century Wales* (London: Routledge & Kegan Paul, 1977), p. 11. See also the comment by Assistant Commissioner John Jenkins of the Newcastle Commission on the bifurcation of the class structure in rural Wales (P.P., 1861, 21, pt. 2, p. 443).

19. See the section on "General Background to the Educational Reforms of 1831" in chapter 7.

20. "Rebecca, when thoroughly roused and strongly encouraged by the initial success of her activities, was not long content with only redressing her economic grievances, but took advantage of the turbulent state of affairs to unmask

many of the causes of her religious dissatisfaction," Thomas Evans remarks of the Rebecca riots (*The Background of Modern Welsh Politics, 1789–1846* [Cardiff: Gomerian Press, 1936], p. 178).

21. See ibid., pp. 10–72.

22. The increase in the number of Anglican churches in the 1830s and 1840s is associated with the general reinvigoration of the Church of England following the acts of religious relief in 1818 and 1829 and the reform of Parliament in 1832, and with the church's special aggressiveness in the area of primary education, stimulated by religious polarization between church and Dissent in the 1840s. See the sections on "A Victory for the Church" and "A Reprise of 1820" in chapter 4.

23. Like most nineteenth-century figures, these must be approached with caution from a methodological point of view. For methodological examination and criticism of the 1851 religious census, see K. S. Inglis, "Patterns of Religious Worship in 1851," *Journal of Ecclesiastical History* 11, no. 1 (April 1960): 74–88; David M. Thompson, "The 1851 Religious Census: Problems and Possibilities," *Victorian Studies* 11 (September 1967): 87–97.

24. Morgan, *Wales in British Politics*, pp. 12–13.

25. See A. H. Dodd, *The Industrial Revolution in North Wales* (Cardiff: University of Wales Press, 1971).

26. Minchington, "Industrial South Wales," pp. xi–xvi; Evan J. Jones, *Some Contributions to the Economic History of Wales* (London: P. S. King & Son, 1928), pp. 49–54.

27. Clapham, *Early Railway Age*, p. 49.

28. Jones, *Modern Wales*, pp. 174–75; Minchington, "Industrial South Wales," p. xvi.

29. The parish of Trevethin, which adjoined Hertfordshire, was 44 percent English in 1840; in Blaenavon, which was further west, the proportion was 38 percent; and in 1846 the great industrial center of Merthyr Tydfil was 12.3 percent English (A. H. John, *The Industrial Development of South Wales, 1759–1850* [Cardiff: University of Wales Press, 1950], pp. 63–64).

30. Ibid., p. 68.

31. Ibid., pp. 59–60.

32. Minchington, "Industrial South Wales," p. xvi; John, *Industrial Development of South Wales*, pp. 24–27, 174–75.

33. See the section on "Variation by Sex" in chapter 8.

34. In the words of John Jenkins: "[The] only remaining sources [in addition to the clergy of the Established Church, other ministers of religion, and the middle classes, all of which were without means in Wales] are the landowners of the country, and the owners of tithes. In a large proportion of cases, the latter are either non-residents, and feel little interest in such local features as those which relate to the education of a parish or neighborhood, or otherwise they are themselves the landowners" (P.P., 1861, 21, pt. 2, p. 514).

35. Jenkins spoke of the spirit of "antiquated prejudices and narrow exclusivism" among Anglican landowners (ibid., p. 515). For an account of the financial and administrative advantages that the National Society had over the British and Foreign School Society early in the nineteenth century, see Sheila M.

Owen-Jones, "Religious Influence and Educational Progress in Glamorgan, 1800–33," *Welsh History Review* 13, no. 1 (June 1986): 72–76.

36. The commissioners on education in Wales gave eloquent testimony to the depth and intensity of class conflict in Monmouthshire and South Wales: see P.P., 1861, 27, pt. 1, p. 244, and pt. 2, p. 305.

37. The generally disadvantaged economic position of Wales in relation to England is documented in Michael Hechter, *Internal Colonialism: The Celtic Fringe in British National Development, 1536–1966* (Berkeley: University of California Press, 1975).

38. The commissioners of inquiry for South Wales cited the mismanagement of funds applicable to turnpike roads and the discrepant fees on them; tithe payments; unequal distribution of rent charges; the operation of the Poor Law Amendment Act; the administration of justice by the local magistrates, especially the amount of the fees paid to the clerks, and the progressive increase of the county rates (P.P., 1844, 16, pp. 81–82).

39. P.P., 1840, 40, pp. 614–23. Available statistics show that Monmouthshire was, in fact, one of the "lagging" regions of England and Wales with respect to educational coverage (W. E. Marsden, *Unequal Educational Provision in England and Wales: The Nineteenth-Century Roots* [London: Woburn Press, 1987], pp. 51–52).

40. P.P., 1841, 20, Minutes of the Committee of Council on Education, p. 115.

41. P.P., 1844, 16, Report of the Commissioners of Inquiry for South Wales, p. 116.

42. Cited in Welsh Nationalist Party, *The Historical Basis of Welsh Nationalism*, a series of lectures by A. W. Wade-Evans et al. (Cardiff: Plaid Cymru, 1950), p. 109.

43. P.P., 1847, 17, Reports of the Commissioners of Inquiry into the State of Education in Wales, pt. 1, pp. 7, 20, 32; pt. 2, pp. 31, 34, 54. Because of the fact that all three of the commissioners were Anglican by persuasion, and because the commission and its report were criticized by many Welsh (especially Nonconformist) spokesmen, it might be supposed that these assessments are legitimately open to doubt. It should be noted, however, that the Welsh historian David Williams, a critic of the commission, distinguishes between the taste and style of the commissioners on the one hand and the factual reports they gave on the other, which he regards as substantially accurate and confirmed by other observers of the time (Williams, *The Rebecca Riots: A Study in Agrarian Discontent* [Cardiff: University of Wales Press, 1955], pp. 97–102).

44. Brougham himself commented on this difference. See, for example, P.D., n.s., 1820, 2, col. 61. See the section on "Historical Background" in chapter 7.

45. As of 1821 these were Bedford, Berkshire, Buckinghamshire, Cambridge, Hereford, Huntington, Monmouth, Northumberland, Oxfordshire, Rutland, and Westmoreland. In the early nineteenth century, the case of Monmouthshire was a curious one, it being sometimes assigned to Wales and sometimes to England, according to the purpose of the comparison. Certainly by midcentury it showed more industrial, cultural, and religious affinity to its Welsh neighbor, Glamorganshire, than to the neighboring English counties.

46. Brecon, Denbigh, Flint, Glamorgan, Montgomery, and Radnor.

47. Anglesey, Cardigan, Carmarthen, Carnarvon, Merioneth, and Pembroke.

48. For example, E. G. West ("Resource Allocation and Growth in Early Nineteenth-Century British Education," *Economic History Review,* 2d ser., 23, no. 1 [April 1970]: 78–81) regards the Kerry figures as underestimates, in contrast to those who believe them to be overestimates.

49. Ralph Lingen, one of the commissioners, summarized the procedures as follows: "The particulars concerning each school, which appear in the tables, were collected by printing schedules, containing questions which corresponded to the headings of the columns on the tables. The schedules for day schools were filled up in the course of personal communication with the teachers, and scholars also, when present" (P.P., 1847, 27.1, p. 1). The commissioners were more satisfied with the returns of day schools than with the returns of Sunday schools. See n. 55 in this chapter.

50. For example, the information given in the educational census was completely voluntary.

51. These figures also refer to scholars of all ages. The referent of the term "private day schools" is somewhat ambiguous, but it might be inferred that these did not include the primarily middle-class proprietary and private schools, since the Newcastle Commission was charged with investigating the educational condition of the "poorer classes."

52. As late as 1869, the pattern seemed to be holding with respect to the schools of the National Society, which reported that in that year the scholars under instruction in its day and night schools on average totaled 5.5 percent of the population in England and 4.5 percent in Wales (P.P., 1868–69, 46, pp. 269–71).

53. These comparisons are difficult to interpret, because of an inevitable amount of double counting that entered into the surveys—double counting resulting from the fact that attendance at a day school did not preclude attendance at a Sunday school, and vice versa. In particular, Dissenting parents who sent their children to National Society schools may have felt obliged, in many cases, to send them to Dissenting chapels as a kind of "corrective." Henry Vaughan Johnson, the commissioner for Welsh education reporting on North Wales, made the following observation: "Where . . . the rules [of the National School] are impartially enforced, or the [Dissenting] parents too poor to purchase exemption [from learning the catechism] a compromise follows. The children are allowed to learn the Church Catechism, and to attend church, so long as they remain at school, but are cautioned by their parents not to believe the Catechism, and to return to their parental chapels as soon as they are finished schooling. A dispensation, in fact, is given, allowing conformity in matters of religion during the period required for education, provided they allow no impression to be made upon their minds by the ritual and observances to which they conform. The desired object is obtained by both parties. Outward conformity is affected for the time, and children return in after-life to the creed and usages of their parents" (P.P., 1847, 28, pt. 3, p. 54).

54. See the section on "Drawing the Battle Lines" later in this chapter.

55. Lingen complained of the difficulties involved in obtaining oral informa-

tion from superintendents and teachers of Sunday schools, many of whom kept no books. The commission printed the schedule in many English and Welsh language journals, with a request that it be filled out and returned. This method also proved to be incomplete and apparently filled with errors. Lingen concluded that "[the] Sunday-school tables . . . both in their parochial and their summed form, must be taken to be the nearest approximations to truth, which, under the circumstances, I could, by my utmost exertion, collect from the best-informed parties" (P.P., 1847, 27, pt. 1, pp. 1–2). In light of what has subsequently been learned about biases in surveys, it can be speculated that a number of factors contributed to errors in the surveys, in addition to the incompleteness of the efforts of the surveyors: (a) because the inquiry was tinged with illegitimacy in the eyes of many Dissenters from the beginning (it was regarded as decidedly both "English" and "Anglican" in stress, largely because of the national and religious backgrounds of the commissioners and their assistants), many Dissenting Sunday school teachers would have been inclined to boycott the survey, which would have led to an under-reporting of Dissenting Sunday schools and scholars; (b) on the other hand, because Anglicanism and Dissent were locked in conflict over the religious control of the Welsh population, each group had reason to inflate its estimates and claims as to the numbers attending its institutions.

56. See p. 174.

57. W. E. Marsden, *Unequal Educational Provision in England and Wales: The Nineteenth-Century Roots* (London: Woburn Press, 1987), pp. 37–40.

58. P.P., 1847, 27, pt. 1, p. iv.

59. Ibid., pt. 1, p. 3.

60. Ibid., pt. 3, p. 59.

61. Ibid., pt. 2, p. 51. For an account of the difficulties that Anglican day schools had in taking root in the "sea of dissent" in Anglesey, see D. A. Pretty, *Two Centuries of Anglesey Schools, 1700–1902* (Anglesey: Anglesey Antiquarian Society, 1977), p. 59.

62. P.P., 1861, 21, pt. 1, pp. 52–55.

63. The Education Act of 1870 permitted local authorities to enforce compulsory attendance, but general legislation on this matter was enacted only in 1876.

64. P.P., 1847, 27, pt. 2, p. 41.

65. Ibid., pt. 3, p. 54.

66. Evans, *Modern Welsh Politics*, p. 213.

67. See the introductory pages of this chapter.

68. Evans, *Modern Welsh Politics*, ch. 2.

69. For accounts of the political activities in these decades, see Evans, *Modern Welsh Politics*, chs. 3–5; Jones, *Modern Wales*, pp. 232–38; J. P. D. Dunbabin, *Rural Discontent in Nineteenth Century Britain* (New York: Holmes & Meier, 1974), pp. 21ff.; D. J. V. Jones, *Before Rebecca: Popular Protests in Wales, 1793–1835* (London: Allen Lane, 1973); id., "The Carmarthen Riots of 1831," *Welsh History Review* 4, no. 2 (December 1968): 129–42; id., "Chartism in Welsh Communities," *Welsh History Review* 6, no. 3 (June 1973): 243–61; id., "The Merthyr Riots of 1831," *Welsh History Review* 3, no. 2 (De-

cember 1966): 173–205; David Williams, *John Frost: A Study in Chartism* (New York: Augustus M. Kelley, 1969); Welsh Nationalist Party, *Historical Basis of Welsh Nationalism*, pp. 107–9.

70. Williams, *History of Modern Wales*, pp. 211–12.

71. P.D., 1846, 84, cols. 846, 855–56. Acknowledging the close connection between the "lawless proceeding in Wales" and "an entire want of anything like a system of education," the marquess of Landsdowne called for an extension of the efforts of Parliament to encourage education there, but at the same time he reiterated reluctance to consider Wales in any way separate from England, indicating that "he was not prepared to say that a different principle from that adopted in England ought to be applied to Wales" (P.D., 1846, 86, cols. 861–62).

72. P.P., 1843, 40, pp. 103–4.

73. Gwyn A. Williams, "Hugh Owen, 1804–1881," in Charles E. Gittens, ed., *Pioneers of Welsh Education* (Swansea: University College Faculty of Education, 1964), p. 66. By 1843 the Established Church had established a Welsh teacher-training college in Brecon.

74. See the section on "The Consolidation of Growth under Primordial Proliferation" in chapter 5. Reporting on Monmouthshire, Symons noted bitter opposition to the 1846 minutes on the part of Dissenting religious leaders (P. P., 1847, 27, pt. 2, p. 275).

75. Williams, *History of Modern Wales*, pp. 254–56.

76. Coupland, *Welsh and Scottish Nationalism*, p. 196.

77. Marsden, *Unequal Educational Provision in England and Wales*, p. 35.

78. HMI Joseph Fletcher noted that for North and South Wales, Monmouth, and Cornwall, "in the rural parts . . . it is yet more difficult than any other to maintain British day-schools"; he attributed this to their poverty and the dispersion of the population (P. P., 1847, 45, p. 277).

79. P. P., 1861, 21, pt. 2, p. 499.

80. Ibid., p. 501. For another brief account of the fate of Voluntaryism in South Wales, see Leslie Wynn Evans, *Education in Industrial Wales, 1700–1900* (Cardiff: Heanton Press, 1971), pp. 308–9.

81. J. D. Morell, P. P., 1854–55, 47, p. 467.

82. Williams, "Hugh Owen," pp. 66–67. For an indication of the continuing interest of the British and Foreign School Society in Wales, see Henry Bryan Binns, *A Century of Education: Being the Centenary History of the British and Foreign School Society, 1808–1908* (London: J. M. Dent, 1908), pp. 165–66.

83. As before, South Wales refers to Brecon, Denbigh, Flint, Glamorgan, Montgomery, and Radnor (along with Monmouth); North Wales refers to Anglesey, Cardigan, Carmarthen, Carnarvon, Merioneth, and Pembroke.

84. This differential was compensated for in South Wales, where industrial establishments themselves founded and supported a large proportion of the schools organized on British and Foreign principles. Evans (*Education in Industrial South Wales*, p. 317) estimates that in the early 1850s works schools eclipsed the British and Foreign schools in the south, and in 1860 half of the society's South Wales schools were works schools.

85. See the assessment of HMI J. Bowstead in P. P., 1854–55, 42, pp. 639–40.

86. Comment by Assistant Commissioner John Jenkins, P. P., 1861, 21, pt. 2, p. 525.

87. Commissioner Henry Vaughan Johnson described the private subscription schools as follows: "They are so utterly worthless, that nothing can account for their existence, except the determination on the part of Welsh parents to have their children instructed without interference in matters of conscience . . . this conclusion is confirmed by the fact that, when a British and Foreign or other neutral school is established, private-adventure schools become extinct" (P. P., 1847, 28, pt. 3, p. 54).

88. This generalization should be qualified by noting that a large part of the clientele of the Sunday schools was adult.

89. P. P., 1847–48, 50, pp. 26–29.

90. William Williams, *A Second Letter on the Present Defective State of Education in Wales* (London: James Ridgeway, 1848), pp. 14–15.

91. P. P., 1850, 44, pp. 198–99.

92. P. P., 1854–55, 42, p. 640.

93. Ibid., pp. 641–42.

94. P. P., 1856, 47, p. 461.

95. P. P., 1865, 6, p. 42.

96. Indeed, that conflict might have provided some of the evidence on which Morell based his observations in 1856.

97. P. P., 1852, 40, p. 802.

98. Ibid., p. 817; communication of October 1850 to the Committee of Council by promoters of the national school.

99. Ibid., 1852, 40, p. 807.

100. Ibid., pp. 808–9.

101. Ibid., p. 814.

102. Ibid., p. 815.

103. Ibid., p. 819.

104. Ibid., p. 820.

105. Ibid., p. 821.

106. Ibid., p. 823.

107. Surprisingly in light of Lingen's subsequent characterization of that era as one in which the policy of the Committee of Council was to encourage schools to develop in the country without detailed review of the applications. See the section on "The Welsh Situation to 1870" later in this chapter.

108. P. P., 1852, 40, p. 824.

109. This argument paralleled the opposition voiced to the idea of a multidenominational normal school put forth by the government in 1839. See the section on "A Victory for the Church" in chapter 4.

110. This argument parallels the objections of many Dissenting bodies to the proposals contained in the educational clauses of the factory legislation of 1843. See the section on "A Reprise of 1820" in chapter 4.

111. P. P., 1852, 40, p. 830. The reports referred to were those that appeared in 1847.

112. This proposal resembled the "Irish" solution of 1831 and the solution of the Education Act of 1870, both represented as separating the sectarian elements of religious instruction from other aspects of the educational process.

113. P. P., 1852, 40, p. 827.

114. Both the issue of the composition of the management committee and the issue of the amount of subscription necessary to render a candidate eligible for membership on the management committee were at once conflicts of a political, religious, and class nature. The dispute over a 20s. or 10s. limit, for example, would seem to revolve around how wealthy the subscriber would have to be to serve on the management committee (a class issue), but the wealthier members of Welsh communities also tended to be Anglican (a religious issue).

115. Ibid., p. 835. It is not certain what Owen might have been referring to in the last expression, but presumably it was the revival movement in the Church of England in the 1830s and 1840s. See the section on "A Victory for the Church" in chapter 4.

116. The prolonged dispute in the late 1840s and early 1850s between the National Society and the Committee of Council over the issue of church or lay control of the management of schools receiving state support.

117. P. P., 1857, 40, p. 837.

118. Ibid., p. 839.

119. This appears to be a threat to join the Voluntaryist effort.

120. The number of scholars in Dissenting schools in the six counties of North Wales in 1858 was 7,741 (calculated from table 17).

121. P. P., 1852, 40, p. 846.

122. Ibid., p. 857.

123. Ibid.

124. See the section on "The Consolidation of Growth under Primordial Proliferation" in chapter 5.

125. See the section on "Other Religious and Political Developments" in chapter 5.

126. P. P., 1861, 21, pt. 2, pp. 484–95; 1866, 7, p. 300.

127. P. P., 1861, 49, p. 17.

128. P. P., 1861, 21, pt. 2, pp. 517–18; 1866, 7, p. 300.

129. P. P., 1847, 45, pp. 26, 29.

130. P. P., 1857, 33, p. 16.

131. P. P., 1861, 21, pt. 2, pp. 508–11. These kinds of complaints would apply to poor agricultural districts in general, not just in Wales.

132. P. P., 1864, 45, p. 127.

133. P. P., 1857–58, 45, p. 496.

134. P. P., 1861, 21, pt. 1, p. 38.

135. Ibid., pt. 2, p. 517.

136. P. P., 1862, 43, pp. 459–547.

137. For a summary of this conflict, see John Oakley, *The Conscience Clause: Its History, Terms, Effect, and Principle. A Reply to Archdeacon Denison* (London: William Ridgeway, 1866), pp. 7–11.

138. P. P., 1868–69, 20, p. 281.

139. Ibid. For a more general discussion of the inefficiencies of proliferation

along primordial lines, see the section on "Economizing, Streamlining, Standardizing, and Secularizing" in chapter 5.

140. The proportion shows how dominant the Church of England still was in day-school education; the figure also shows why the Voluntaryists renounced their position in favor of a plan for the government to establish nondenominational national education.

141. P. P., 1867, 55, p. 43.

142. P. P., 1866, 7, p. 130.

143. P. P., 1861, 21, pt. 6, p. 66.

144. See the section on "Economizing, Streamlining, Standardizing, and Secularizing" in chapter 5.

145. For general discussion of the evolution of the conscience clause, see pp. 113–15, 135–37. See the section on "Llangefni, 1850–1852" earlier in this chapter.

146. For the impact of the franchise extension in Anglesey, see David A. Pretty, "Richard Davies and Nonconformist Radicalism in Anglesey, 1837–68: A Study of Sectarian and Middle-Class Politics," *Welsh History Review* 9, no. 4 (December 1979): 455–67.

147. John Vincent, *The Formation of the Liberal Party, 1857–1868* (London: Constable, 1966).

148. Inglis-Jones, *Story of Wales,* pp. 205–6. Liberal dominance continued throughout the century. In 1880 the Liberals won 29 seats of the 33 in Wales (including Monmouthshire), and the figure was 30 out of 44 in 1885 (P. M. H. Bell, *Disestablishment in Ireland and Wales* [London: SPCK, 1969], pp. 227–28).

149. Francis Adams, *History of the Elementary School Contest in England,* edited, with an introduction, by Asa Briggs (Brighton: Harvester Press, 1972), p. 208.

150. See Leighton Hargest, "The Welsh Educational Alliance and the 1870 Elementary Education Act," *Welsh History Review* 10, no. 2 (December 1980): 178–83. HMI J. Bowstead noted the rise in support for purely secular schools in his report on Wales in 1869 (P. P., 1868–69, 20, p. 283).

151. Hargest attributes part of this lack of success to the fact that the Nonconformists put up too many candidates in places like Merthyr and Newport (ibid., p. 178). The frustration of these efforts tended to strengthen the alliance between the Welsh and the National Education League in the several years after 1870.

152. J. S. Hurt, *Elementary Schooling and the Working Classes, 1860–1919* (London: Routledge & Kegan Paul, 1979), p. 82.

153. Hargest, "The Welsh Educational Alliance and the 1870 Elementary Education Act," pp. 204–5.

CHAPTER 7

1. John Stuart Mill, *A System of Logic, Ratiocinative and Inductive,* 9th ed. (London: Longmans, Green, Reader & Dyer, 1875), 1:449–52. See also Neil J. Smelser, *Comparative Methods in the Social Sciences* (Englewood Cliffs, N.J.: Prentice-Hall, 1976), pp. 62–64, 136–41.

2. See the section on "External Social Forces Impinging on Education" in chapter 2.

3. For a brief sketch of Irish society in the first three decades of the nineteenth century, see Lawrence J. McCaffrey, *The Irish Question, 1800–1922* (Lexington: University of Kentucky Press, 1968), pp. 12–18.

4. Thomas Wyse, *Education Reform; or, The Necessity of a National System of Education* (London: Longman, Rees, Orme, Brown, Green & Longman, 1836).

5. See the section on "The Failure of Middle-Class Radical Secularism" in chapter 4.

6. Wyse, *Education Reform*, pp. 358–60.

7. See the introductory pages to chapter 6.

8. When Palmerston, the owner of estates in Sligo, established a number of schools for peasants there, he fancied that the teachers "must be Catholics, for the people will not send their children to a Protestant" (quoted in Jasper Ridley, *Lord Palmerston* [London: Pantheon Books, 1972], p. 57).

9. Donald H. Akenson, *The Church of Ireland: Ecclesiastical Reform and Revolution, 1800–1885* (New Haven: Yale University Press, 1972), pp. 139–40.

10. See the section on "A Significant Moment of Inaction" in chapter 4.

11. These accounts are taken mainly from Norman Atkinson, *Irish Education: A History of Educational Institutions* (Dublin: Allen Figgis, 1969), pp. 69, 72; Donald H. Akenson, *The Irish Educational Experiment: The National System of Education in the Nineteenth Century* (London: Routledge & Kegan Paul, 1970), pp. 80–85; J. R. R. Adams, *The Printed Word and the Common Man: Popular Culture in Ulster, 1790–1900* (Belfast: Institute of Irish Studies, 1987), pp. 15–16, 95–99.

12. Akenson, *Church of Ireland*, p. 137.

13. Quoted in J. M. Goldstrom, *Education: Elementary Education, 1780–1900* (New York: Barnes & Noble, 1972), pp. 63–64. The quotation is from the society's tenth annual report, published in 1822.

14. H. Kingsmill Moore, a historian of the Kildare Place Society, spoke of the years of 1811–19 as those of "universal approval," "rapid development," and "uninterrupted progress" (Moore, *An Unwritten Chapter in the History of Education* [London: Macmillan, 1904], chs. 2, 4, and 5).

15. This account follows those given in Carl F. Kaestle, ed., *Joseph Lancaster and the Monitorial School Movement: A Documentary History* (New York: Teachers College Press, 1973), pp. 29–30; Henry B. Binns, *A Century of Education: Being the Centenary History of the British and Foreign School Society, 1808–1908* (London: J. M. Dent, 1908), pp. 87, 114–15; J. E. G. Montmorency, *State Intervention in English Education* (Cambridge: Cambridge University Press, 1902), p. 129.

16. This phase of Irish development—Irish religious societies searching for equal treatment with nondenominational, but predominantly Protestant, societies—also directly parallels one phase of the religious conflict over education in New York in the 1840s. See the section on "Course and Resolution of the Conflict" later in this chapter.

17. Quoted in Atkinson, *Irish Education*, p. 90.

18. Testimony of Anthony Blake, member of the commission, in 1837 (P. P., 1837, 8, pp. 59–60).

19. Akenson, *Irish Education Experiment*, pp. 97–102.

20. P. P., 1828, 4, p. 224.

21. P. P., 1830, 7, p. 50.

22. P. P., 1828, 4, p. 228. This dilemma was precisely the same stated by Hook for England in 1846: the necessity of religious instruction as part of education, but the apparent impossibility of arriving at a formula for that instruction that would not be indoctrinating, and would be acceptable to all religious persuasions, yet would remain religious. See the section on "The Consolidation of Growth under Primordial Proliferation" in chapter 5.

23. Ibid., p. 226.

24. For an account of the expression of multiple grievances in the 1820s, see James A. Reynolds, *The Catholic Emancipation Crisis in Ireland, 1823–1829* (Westport, Conn.: Greenwood Press, 1954).

25. Much of the responsibility for the ideas and preparation of the legislation lay with Thomas Wyse. For an account of his role, see James J. Auchmuty, *Irish Education: A Historical Survey* (Dublin: Hodges Figgis, 1937), ch. 4.

26. P. D., 1833, 14, col. 95.

27. P. D., 1832, 13, cols. 229, 342.

28. P. D., 1833, 14, cols. 826–27.

29. P. D., 1836, 36, col. 1160; 1838, 45, col. 757.

30. P. D., 1838, 43, cols. 269–70.

31. P. D., 1834, 18, col. 1210; 1836, 31, cols. 267–68; 1837, 26, cols. 1106–7. See also P. D., 1837, 6, pp. 355–56.

32. P. D., 1821, 4, col. 1038; 1822, 5, col. 1510; 1825, 11, col. 328; 1827, 16, cols. 1260–61; 1832, 1, col. 707; 1831, 3, col. 452; 1821, 8, cols. 184–85; 1832, 10, col. 878.

33. P. D., 1832, 7, col. 623; 1827, 15, cols. 19–20.

34. P. D., 1837–38, 7, p. 57.

35. James Biceheno, an English overseer of the poor in Ireland, reported that the dominant feeling among Catholics about the Kildare Street Society was that there was "a Protestant spirit prevailing" (P. P., 1830, 7, p. 561).

36. P. D., 1835, 7, col. 790.

37. P. P., 1830, 7, p. 603.

38. Akenson, *Irish Education Experiment*, p. 104.

39. P. D., 1818, 4, cols. 225–26; 1830, 7, cols. 50, 603.

40. P. D., 1832, 11, cols. 90–91, 1076–89, 1181–82; 12, cols. 891–92.

41. P. D., 1832, 14, col. 659.

42. P. D., 1833, 14, cols. 89, 665.

43. P. D., 1832, 10, cols. 1111–12.

44. P. D., 1832, 12, cols. 539–40; 13, cols. 306–7; 1833, 14, col. 89. There was an initial misunderstanding that the Established Church in Scotland favored the plan, but after this was clarified as being based on false information, the Kirk ended in opposing the scheme (P. D., 1833, 18, col. 1355).

45. See the section on "The Consolidation of Growth under Primordial Proliferation" in chapter 5.

46. David N. Hempton, "Wesleyan Methodism and Educational Politics in Early Nineteenth-Century England," *History of Education* 8, no. 3 (September 1979): 210. This interpretation is consistent with the Wesleyans' position on the minutes of 1846, in which they were initially reluctant to share because of their apprehension that grants would go to the Roman Catholics as well. See p. 104 above.

47. P. D., 1827, 16, cols. 1260–61.

48. See the section on "The Consolidation of Growth under Primordial Proliferation" in chapter 5. This logic was put forward by Lord Stanley (P. D., 1832, 7, cols. 611–12) and later by Peel (see p. 79 above) and Gladstone (P. D., 1845, 79, col. 524).

49. Argument by Fane, P. D., 1833, 14, col. 893.

50. P. D., 1829, 21, col. 1554; 14, col. 893; 1832, 7, cols. 610–11, 618, 620–21.

51. P. D., 1832, 10, cols. 843, 1111–12; 13, col. 299.

52. See the section on "Other Political and Religious Developments" in chapter 5.

53. See the section on "The Consolidation of Growth under Primordial Proliferation" in chapter 5.

54. A characterization of the 1831 system, including its French influences and parallels, is found in John Coolahan, "The Establishment of the National School System in Ireland," in Willem Frijhoff, ed., *The Supply of Schooling: Contributions to a Comparative Study of Educational Policies in the XIXth Century* (Paris: Institut national de recherche pédagogique, 1983), pp. 65–74. Wyse acknowledged that the plan of 1831 was influenced by the schemes of several continental countries and the United States (see Auchmuty, *Irish Education,* p. 85).

55. See the section on "The Consolidation of Growth under Primordial Proliferation" in chapter 5.

56. See the section on "Other Religious and Political Developments" in chapter 5.

57. G. P. Gooch, ed., *The Later Correspondence of Lord John Russell, 1840–1870* (London: Longmans, Green, 1925), 1:69.

58. The census of 1831 showed a total population of 13,897,000 for England and Wales, and 7,767,000 for Ireland. In 1841 the comparable figures were 15,914,000 for England and Wales and 8,178,000 for Ireland. The Irish population dropped in the 1840s, so that the total in 1851 was 6,554,000. Reported in B. R. Mitchell, *British Historical Statistics* (Cambridge: Cambridge University Press, 1988), pp. 9–10.

59. See the section on "A Victory for the Church" in chapter 4.

60. P. P., 1837, 7. The scheme for improvement is summarized in Mary Sturt, *The Education of the People: A History of Primary Education in England and Wales in the Nineteenth Century* (London: Routledge & Kegan Paul, 1967), pp. 75–76.

61. P. D., 1838, 43, col. 227; 1842, 41, cols. 411, 1026.

62. P. P., 1837, 9, p. 612.

63. Horace Mann, *Report of an Educational Tour in Germany, and Parts of*

*Great Britain and Ireland* (London: Simpkin, Marshall, 1846), p. 224. Mann's unduly rosy view—rosy in the light of the picture to be described presently—may be traceable to the fact that the Irish system appeared to be closest in structure to the U.S. system at the time.

64. Cited in David I. Allsobrook, *Schools for the Shires: The Reform of Middle-Class Education in Mid-Victorian England* (Manchester: Manchester University Press, 1986), p. 95.

65. This is reminiscent of the kind of investigation that the Committee of Council would make for small communities if apparently competitive applications came in from the National Society and the British and Foreign School Society. See the section on "The Welsh Situation to 1870" in chapter 6. The situation was not as critical in Ireland, however, because the split between "secular and literary" and "religious" associated with the national system constituted, in effect, a conscience clause, which was the bone of contention in small English communities with a majority of Dissenters.

66. Akenson, *Church of Ireland*, p. 202.

67. Akenson, *Irish Education Experiment*, pp. 151–52.

68. Ibid., p. 216.

69. Ibid., pp. 161–63.

70. Atkinson, *Irish Education*, p. 97.

71. Akenson, *Irish Education Experiment*, pp. 183–87. For a brief descriptive summary of the Presbyterians' strategies and the government concessions, see John Coolahan, *Irish Education: Its History and Structure* (Dublin: Institute of Public Administration, 1981), pp. 14–16.

72. Atkinson, *Irish Education*, p. 97.

73. Akenson, *Church of Ireland*, p. 203.

74. Ibid.

75. P. D., 1835, 26, cols. 730, 927; 1836, 31, col. 250; 32, cols. 280–90; 35, cols. 1013–14; 1838, 43, col. 223.

76. P. D., 1836, 34, col. 2223; 1837, 26, cols. 1106–7.

77. P. D., 1843, 69, col. 1181.

78. See the section on "The Consolidation of Growth under Primordial Proliferation" in chapter 5.

79. P. D., 1834, 22, col. 969; 1836, 32, col. 276; 1842, 59, cols. 669–70; 1842, 62, cols . 458–59.

80. P. D., 1839, 48, cols. 300–301; 1840, 54, col. 1165.

81. P. D., 1839, 49, col. 170.

82. P. D., 1840, 52, cols. 845–46; 1841, 63, cols. 342–43.

83. Akenson, *Irish Education Experiment*, pp. 189–90.

84. Akenson, *Church of Ireland*, p. 203.

85. The years 1839–40, it will be recalled, were the years of the significant Church of England victories over the issue of training schools and inspection that eventuated in the concordat of 1840. See the section on "A Victory for the Church" in chapter 4.

86. Akenson, *Irish Education Experiment*, pp. 197–99; id., *Church of Ireland*, p. 104.

87. P. D., 1842, 44, cols. 271–72.

88. P. D., 1844, 72, cols. 1142–43. Peel added that the number of Protestant children requiring education in Ireland was small, and that in general Protestants could afford to pay for the education of their children in that country.

89. Akenson, *Church of Ireland*, p. 204.

90. P. D., 1852, 120, cols. 1028–29; 1853, 124, col. 423; 1853, 125, cols. 1306, 1324; 1855, 137, cols. 1019–20; 1856, 141, col. 1061; 1857, 145, cols. 644–49; 1860, 156, cols. 1038–56.

91. P. D., 1857, 144, cols. 167–69.

92. P. D., 1846, 74, cols. 855–56; 1851, 118, col. 613.

93. P. D., 1848, 101, cols. 316–19; 1856, 142, cols. 1583–84; 1861, 162, col. 2224.

94. P. D., 1853, 124, col. 1163.

95. P. D., 1853, 126, cols. 559–60.

96. P. D., 1859, 155, col. 1001.

97. P. D., 1850, 112, cols. 154–55.

98. P. D., 1859, 155, col. 301.

99. P. D., 1870, 199, col. 1925.

100. P. D., 1849, 106, col. 683; 1856, 152, cols. 1582, 1596; 1859, 151, col. 1010; 1861, 164, col. 891.

101. See this pattern as described in the section on "The Consolidation of Growth under Primordial Proliferation" in chapter 5.

102. Akenson, *Church of Ireland*, pp. 204–5.

103. Akenson, *Irish Education Experiment*, pp. 269–74, 284–85.

104. Quoted in Emmet Larkin, *The Making of the Roman Catholic Church in Ireland, 1850–1860* (Chapel Hill: University of North Carolina Press, 1980), p. 400.

105. Quoted in Emmet Larkin, *The Consolidation of the Roman Catholic Church in Ireland, 1860–1870* (Chapel Hill: University of North Carolina Press, 1987), p. 115.

106. Ibid., pp. 115–33. This is not to say that the Catholics were not divided among themselves. Some bishops wanted a separate system that the church could control completely; others felt that such a system was politically unrealistic and would give Protestants more opportunity to proselytize; a third group was willing to tolerate the national system and work toward a de facto separate system subsidized by the government. See ibid., pp. 117–18.

107. Coolahan, *Irish Education*, pp. 25–27.

108. Thomas A. O'Donoghue, "Bilingual Education in Ireland in the Late Nineteenth and Early Twentieth Centuries," *History of Education* 17, no. 3 (September 1988): 209–20.

109. Akenson, *Irish Education Experiment*, pp. 215, 351–52.

110. P. P., 1860, 160, cols. 1378–79.

111. Ibid., col. 1337.

112. P. D., 1853, 127, cols. 910–11.

113. Ibid., cols. 606–7.

114. An additional measure of the magnitude of sensitivity on religious matters in Ireland is found in the intense debate in 1860 as to whether questions about religion should even be included in the census of 1861. See Malcolm P. A.

Macourt, "The Religious Inquiry in the Irish Census of 1861," *Irish Historical Studies* 21, no. 82 (September 1978): 168–87.

115. Not too much should be made of this point. In 1841 England had 289,404 Irish-born inhabitants, constituting 1.8 percent of the population; in 1851 the figures were 519,959, or 2.9 percent; in 1861, 601,634, or 3.0 percent; and in 1871, 566,540, or 2.5 percent (John Archer Jackson, *The Irish in Britain* [London: Routledge & Kegan Paul, 1963], p. 11).

116. Alexander Craig Sellar, "Scotch Education Difficulties," in Alexander Grant, ed., *Recess Studies* (Edinburgh: Edmonston & Douglas, 1870), pp. 292–93.

117. See the section on "Muddling Through" in chapter 10.

118. For a treatment of these developments as one of a number of resistances to public education, see Bruce Curtis, "Patterns of Resistance to Public Education: England, Ireland, and Canada West, 1830–1890," *Comparative Education Review* 32, no. 3 (August 1988): 318–33.

119. P. D., 1867, 188, col. 1339.

120. According to the census of 1861, 77.5 percent of the Irish population were Catholic; members of the Church of Ireland totaled 11.9 percent, and Presbyterians, 9 percent (P. M. H. Bell, *Disestablishment in Ireland and Wales* [London: SPCK, 1969], pp. 40–41).

121. See the section on "A Reprise of 1820" in chapter 4 and the sections on "The Consolidation of Growth under Primordial Proliferation" and "Other Religious and Political Developments" in chapter 5.

122. Ellwood P. Cubberly, *Public Education in the United States: A Study and Interpretation of American Educational History* (1919; rev. ed., Boston: Houghton Mifflin, 1934), pp. 62–75.

123. For a study of the impact of Jacksonian democracy on the development of the common schools in the United States, see Sidney L. Jackson, *America's Struggle for Free Schools: Social Tension and Education in New England and New York, 1827–42* (New York: Russell & Russell, 1965).

124. Diane Ravitch, *The Great School Wars: New York City, 1805–1873: A History of the Public Schools as Battlefield of Social Change* (New York: Basic Books, 1974), p. 30.

125. Ibid., p. 17.

126. Carl F. Kaestle, *The Evolution of an Urban School System* (Cambridge, Mass.: Harvard University Press, 1973), pp. 75–80.

127. Quoted in Charles E. Fitch, *The Public School: History of Common School Education in New York from 1603 to 1904* (Albany: J. B. Lyon, 1904), p. 17. This legislation expired in 1800 and was not renewed.

128. Quoted in William O. Bourne, *History of the Public School Society of the City of New York* (New York: William Wood, 1870), p. 17.

129. Vincent P. Lannie, "William Seward and Common School Education," *History of Education Quarterly* 4, no. 3 (September 1964): 181–92. For a defense of Seward's educational ideals, see Lannie, "William Seward and the New York School Controversy, 1840–1842: A Problem in Historical Motivation," *History of Education Quarterly* 6, no. 1 (Spring 1966): 52–68.

130. Kaestle, *Evolution of an Urban School System*, pp. 66–68.

131. Bourne, *History of the Public School Society of the City of New York*, pp. 3–11; Kaestle, *Evolution of an Urban School System*, pp. 162–63.

132. Bourne, *History of the Public School Society of the City of New York*, p. 27.

133. Ibid., p. 54.

134. Quoted in ibid., pp. 66–67.

135. Quoted in ibid., p. 88.

136. Ibid., p. 98.

137. See the section on "The Solution of 1831" earlier in this chapter, the section on "The Welsh Situation to 1870" in chapter 6, and "Other Religious and Political Developments" in chapter 5.

138. Kaestle, *Evolution of an Urban School System*, pp. 89–90.

139. Ibid., pp. 92–95.

140. Quoted in Bourne, *History of the Public School Society of the City of New York*, p. 140.

141. Ibid.

142. See the section on "A Victory for the Church" in chapter 4.

143. Kaestle, *Evolution of an Urban School System*, p. 146.

144. Ravitch, *Great School Wars*, p. 26.

145. Bourne, *History of the Public School Society of the City of New York*, p. 136.

146. Ibid., pp. 153–54, 175.

147. Vincent P. Lannie, *Public Money and Parochial Education: Bishop Hughes, Governor Seward, and the New York School Controversy* (Cleveland: Press of Case Western Reserve University, 1968), p. 5.

148. Ravitch, *Great School Wars*, p. 31.

149. See, for example, Vincent P. Lannie and Bernard C. Diethorn, "For the Honor and Glory of God: The Philadelphia Bible Riots of 1840," *History of Education Quarterly* 8, no. 1 (Spring 1968): 44–106.

150. Ibid., p. 30.

151. Ibid.

152. Lannie, *Public Money and Parochial Education*, p. 7.

153. Ibid., pp. 20–24. Seward had traveled to Ireland in 1833—in the earliest phases of the national school system there—and had become convinced that one of the reasons for the downtrodden condition of the population was the reactionary attitudes of the English Protestants (ibid., p. 18).

154. Ibid., p. 34; Ravitch, *Great School Wars*, p. 53.

155. See the section on "The Evolution of the Irish National System" earlier in this chapter.

156. Kaestle, *Evolution of an Urban School System*, pp. 154–55.

157. Lannie, *Public Money and Parochial Education*, p. 59.

158. Bourne, *History of the Public School Society of the City of New York*, pp. 67–68, 71, 76.

159. Lannie, *Public Money and Parochial Education*, p. 96.

160. Quoted in Ravitch, *Great School Wars*, p. 49.

161. Lannie, *Public Money and Parochial Education,* pp. 41–42.

162. Quoted in Bourne, *History of the Public School Society of the City of New York,* p. 185.

163. See the section on "A Reprise of 1820" in chapter 4.

164. Bourne, *History of the Public School Society of the City of New York,* pp. 199–201.

165. Ibid., p. 214.

166. Ibid., pp. 348–49; Lannie, *Public Money and Parochial Education,* p. 116.

167. Lannie, *Public Money and Parochial Education,* p. 96.

168. Quoted in Bourne, *History of the Public School Society of the City of New York,* p. 230. For Hook's statement, see the section on "The Consolidation of Growth under Primordial Proliferation" in chapter 5.

169. Lannie, *Public Money and Parochial Education,* p. 79.

170. This account is based on ibid., pp. 170–84.

171. Ibid., pp. 135–36.

172. Ravitch, *Great School Wars,* p. 65.

173. Ibid., p. 75.

174. Ibid., p. 80.

175. Ibid., p. 79.

176. Neil G. McClousky, ed., *Catholic Education in America: A Documentary History* (New York: Teachers College Press, 1964), pp. 23–25.

177. For a general account of the rise of parochial schools in the United States, see Robert D. Cross, "Origins of the Catholic Parochial School," in John Barnard and David Burner, eds., *The American Experience in Education* (New York: New Viewpoints, 1975), pp. 168–72.

178. See the sections on "Other Religious and Political Developments" in chapter 5.

179. R. D. Anderson, "Education and the State in Nineteenth-Century Scotland," *Economic History Review,* 2d ser., 36 (1983): 519.

180. Robert Anderson, "Education and Society in Modern Scotland: A Comparative Perspective," *History of Education Quarterly* 25, no. 4 (Winter 1985): 460.

181. P. D., 1869, 198, col. 1236.

182. For accounts of the major events of the seventeenth century, see William Boyd, *Education in Ayrshire through Seven Centuries* (London: University of London Press, 1961), pp. 19–21.

183. Ibid., pp. 35–38.

184. For a brief sketch of Knox's biography and ideas, see Alexander Morgan, *Makers of Scottish Education* (London: Longmans, Green, 1929), ch. 3.

185. In Stirlingshire, for example, "the population . . . in the first half of the eighteenth century was probably fairly stable . . . the situation in Stirlingshire was probably that of the country as a whole . . . not until the eighteenth century had got under way, did the population increase to a notable extent" (Andrew Bain, *Education in Stirlingshire from the Reformation to the Act of 1872* [London: University of London Press, 1965], p. 97).

186. See the section on "Revolutionary Fears and Open Religious Conflict" in chapter 4.

187. Boyd, *Education in Ayrshire through Seven Centuries,* pp. 56–63.

188. Ibid., p. 70.

189. Anderson, "Education and Society in Modern Scotland," p. 462. For a discussion of the democratic ideas as a "myth," and the deviations of Scottish education from that myth, see R. D. Anderson, *Education and Opportunity in Victorian Scotland: Schools and Universities* (Oxford: Clarendon Press, 1983), pp. 1–2.

190. To some degree this was true of religious developments as well. Wesleyan Methodism, for example, was relatively unsuccessful in Scotland, as compared with England and especially Wales (see William L. Mathieson, *Church and Reform in Scotland: A History from 1797 to 1843* [Glasgow: James Maclehose & Sons, 1916], p. 48). A Scottish brand of Evangelicalism was, however, of major significance. See the section on "Problems Building to 1843" later in this chapter.

191. Carl F. Kaestle, "Introduction," in Kaestle, ed., *Joseph Lancaster and the Monitorial School Movement: A Documentary History* (New York: Teachers College Press, 1973), p. 30.

192. C. G. Brown, "The Sunday School Movement in Scotland, 1780–1914," *Records of the Scottish Historical Society* 21 (1981): 3–26; Boyd, *Education in Ayrshire through Seven Centuries,* pp. 80–89.

193. Bain, *Education in Stirlingshire from the Reformation to the Education Act of 1872,* pp. 108–10.

194. Ibid., p. 111.

195. For an account of the early developments, see R. H. Campbell, *The Rise and Fall of Scottish Industry, 1707–1939* (Edinburgh: John Donald, 1980), chs. 1–3.

196. T. C. Smout, *A History of the Scottish People, 1560–1830* (New York: Charles Scribner's Sons, 1969), p. 261.

197. J. F. Grant, *The Economic History of Scotland* (London: Longmans, Green, 1934), pp. 267–68.

198. Smout, *History of the Scottish People,* pp. 468–72.

199. G. Balfour, *The Educational Systems of Great Britain and Ireland* (Oxford: Clarendon Press, 1898), p. 131.

200. The SSPCK schools were apparently a strong force in the weakening of Gaelic in the Highlands, insisting as they did on instruction in English. Charles W. J. Withers, "Education and Anglicisation: The Policy of the SSPCK toward the Education of the Highlander, 1709–1825," *Scottish Studies,* 26 (1982): 37–56.

201. Sir James Kay-Shuttleworth, *Public Education as Affected by the Minutes of the Committee of Privy Council from 1846 to 1851; with Suggestions as to Future Policy* (London: Longman, Brown, Green & Longmans, 1853), p. 395.

202. Anderson, "Education and the State in Nineteenth-Century Scotland," pp. 522–23.

203. See the section on "Revolutionary Fears and Open Religious Conflict" in chapter 4.

204. Boyd, *Education in Ayrshire through Seven Centuries,* p. 90.

205. Ibid., p. 127; Stewart Mechie, *The Church and Scottish Social Development, 1780–1870* (London: Oxford University Press, 1960), p. 139.

206. George Lewis, *Scotland, a Half-Educated Nation, both in the Quantity and Quality of Her Educational Institutions* (Glasgow, 1834).

207. For a background and critique of Lewis's pamphlet, see Donald J. Withrington, "'Scotland a Half-Educated Nation' in 1834? Reliable Critique or Persuasive Polemic," in Walter M. Humes and Hamish M. Paterson, eds., *Scottish Culture and Scottish Education, 1800–1980* (Edinburgh: John Donald, 1983), pp. 55–74.

208. Ibid., p. 61.

209. H. M. Knox, *Two Hundred and Fifty Years of Scottish Education, 1696–1946* (Edinburgh: Oliver & Boyd, 1953), pp. 23–24.

210. At the time of the extension of the Treasury grant to Scotland in 1834, Colquhoun was pressing for legislation to endow the salaries of Highlands teachers (D. G. Paz, *The Politics of Working-Class Education in Britain, 1830–1850* [Manchester: Manchester University Press, 1980], p. 15).

211. P. P., 1852, 40, pp. 660–61; 1852–53, 80, p. 763; 1854, 50, p. 406. For the continuing demands associated with the seasonal cycle in the Hebrides, see the comments of the Argyle Commission (P. P., 1867, 25, pp. 96–97).

212. P. P., 1843, 13, pp. 174–75. In 1845, HMI John Gordon detailed serious problems of early withdrawal, non-attendance, and irregular attendance for the mixed agricultural and manufacturing counties of Stirling, Clackamannan, Linlithgow, and Renfrew (P. P., 1846, 32, p. 623).

213. Ian J. Simpson, *Education in Aberdeenshire before 1872* (London: University of London Press, 1947), p. 292.

214. Sister Martha Skinnider, "Catholic Elementary Education in Glasgow, 1818–1918," in T. R. Bone, ed., *Studies in the History of Scottish Education, 1871–1939* (London: University of London Press, 1967), p. 18.

215. Bain, *Education in Sterlingshire from the Reformation to the Act of 1872,* pp. 143–44.

216. Elie Halévy, *A History of the English People in the Nineteenth Century,* trans. E. I. Watkin and D. A. Barker (1924–27), vol. 1, *England in 1815* (reprint, London: Ernest Benn, 1949), p. 525.

217. Skinnider, "Catholic Elementary Education in Glasgow, 1818–1918," p. 18.

218. Jackson, *The Irish in Britain,* p. 11.

219. Thomas A. Fitzpatrick, "Catholic Education in Glasgow, Lanarkshire and South-West Scotland before 1872," *Innes Review* 36, no. 1 (January 1985): 91–92.

220. P. P., 1818, 4, p. 58.

221. P. P., 1819, 9, p. 1300.

222. P. D., 1856, 141, col. 4.

223. Quoted from the evidence given by Patrick Cumin, an assistant commissioner of the Newcastle Commission and secretary to the Commission of

Education for Scotland before the Select Committee on Education, in P. P., 1866, 7, p. 188.

224. Andrew L. Drummond and James Bulloch, *The Church in Victorian Scotland, 1843–1874* (Edinburgh: Saint Andrew Press, 1975), pp. 75–76.

225. See the comment by D. R. Fearon in the report on Scottish education, in P. P., 1867–68, 28, pt. 5, pp. 20–22.

226. Drummond and Bulloch, *Church in Victorian Scotland*, pp. 59, 65–66, 87.

227. For a clear sketch of the complicated process of eighteenth-century secession, see George S. Pryde, *Scotland from 1603 to the Present Day* (Edinburgh: Thomas Nelson & Sons, 1962), ch. 16. For a related study interpreting these secessions in the context of the generally moderate and tolerant culture of Scottish Presbyterianism in that century, see Andrew L. Drummond and James Bulloch, *The Scottish Church, 1688–1843: The Age of the Moderates* (Edinburgh: Saint Andrew Press, 1973).

228. Drummond and Bulloch, *The Scottish Church, 1688–1843*, p. 39.

229. In 1870 Robert Wallace described Methodism as "a plant of sickly growth in Scotland. It is too elementary in its matter, and too demonstrative and unctuous in style for a Scotchman" ("Church Tendencies in Scotland," in Sir Alexander Grant, ed., *Recess Studies* [Edinburgh: Edmonston & Douglas, 1870], p. 189).

230. Smout, *History of the Scottish People*, pp. 232–38. For a brief account of the Evangelical movement, which ties it closely to the industrial and social problems of urban Scotland, see G. D. Henderson, *Heritage: A Study of the Disruption* (Edinburgh: Oliver & Boyd, 1943), pp. 54–58.

231. For the theological background of the conflict between the Evangelicals and moderates, see Drummond and Bulloch, *The Scottish Church, 1688–1843*, ch. 10.

232. See Gordon Donaldson, *Scotland: Church and Nation through Sixteen Centuries* (London: SCM Press, 1960), p. 99; A. Allan MacLaren, *Religion and Social Class: The Disruption Years in Aberdeen* (London: Routledge & Kegan Paul, 1974), pp. 26–27; Drummond and Bulloch, *The Church in Victorian Scotland*, p. 1.

233. For an account of the complicated sequence of events known as the Nine Years' Conflict, see Henderson, *Heritage*, pp. 65–101.

234. Agnes M. Mackenzie, *Scotland in Modern Times, 1720–1939* (London: W. & R. Chambers, 1941), pp. 177–79.

235. MacLaren, *Religion and Social Class*, pp. 27–30.

236. G. I. T. Machin, *Politics and the Church in Great Britain, 1832–1868* (Oxford: Clarendon Press, 1977) p. 145.

237. Ibid., p. 145.

238. John Kerr, *Scottish Education: School and University* (Cambridge: Cambridge University Press, 1913), pp. 194–95.

239. Mechie, *The Church and Scottish Social Development*, p. 247.

240. Drummond and Bulloch, *The Church in Victorian Scotland*, p. 93.

241. See the section on "The Consolidation of Growth under Primordial Proliferation" in chapter 5.

242. Lawrence Stenhouse, "Hartvig Nissen's Impression of the Scottish Educational System in the Mid-Nineteenth Century," *British Journal of Educational Studies* 9, no. 2 (May 1961): 145.

243. See the section on "Economizing, Streamlining, Standardizing, and Secularizing" in chapter 5.

244. Mechie, *The Church and Scottish Social Development*, p. 247.

245. P. D., 1869, 198, col. 1236. Playfair's periodization agrees generally with that suggested by Sellar in 1870, except that the latter calls the middle phase "Ecclesiastico-national," and dates it from 1560, the construction of the "First Book of Discipline" (Alexander Craig Sellar, "Scotch Education Difficulties," in Alexander Grant, ed., *Recess Studies* [Edinburgh: Edmonston & Douglas, 1870], p. 263).

246. P. P., 1867, 25, p. clxxiii.

247. Mechie, *The Church and Scottish Social Development*, p. 148. This spread testifies to the degree to which Scotland—by virtue of the processes of religious change described—had become thoroughly denominational. In 1870 Wallace noted fourteen distinct Christian organizations, listed according to "ecclesiastical machinery" and members: the Establishment; the Free Church; the United Presbyterian Church; the Scottish Episcopal Church; the Roman Catholic Church; the Congregationalists; the Baptists; the Evangelical Union, or Morisonians; the Reformed Presbyterians, or Cameroonians; the Wesleyan Methodists; the United Original Seceders; the Reformed Presbyterians in Scotland, or True and Original Cameroonians; unattached Episcopalians; and Unitarians (Wallace, "Church Tendencies in Scotland," p. 187).

248. P. D., 1868–69, 194, col. 289.

249. P. D., 1869, 198, col. 1237. The speaker was Playfair.

250. Balfour, *Educational Systems of Great Britain and Ireland*, pp. 134–35.

251. Comment by Leon Playfair, in P. D., 1869, 198, col. 1237.

252. P. P., 1867, 25, p. 21.

253. P. P., 1846, 32, p. 623.

254. P. P., 1867–68, 23, p. x.

255. Ibid.

256. Douglas Myers, "Scottish Schoolmasters in the Nineteenth Century: Professionalism and Politics," in Walter M. Humes and Hamish M. Paterson, eds., *Scottish Culture and Scottish Education, 1800–1980* (Edinburgh: John Donald Publishers), pp. 81–82.

257. Marjorie Cruikshank, "The Argyll Commission Report, 1865–68: A Landmark in Scottish Education," *British Journal of Educational Studies* 15, no. 2 (June 1967): 135.

258. P. P., 1867, 25, p. 145.

259. Catholics in Scotland joined Anglicans and Catholics in England in protesting that the Revised Code's emphasis on the basics constituted a threat to religious education (Skinnider, "Catholic Elementary Education in Glasgow, 1818–1918," p. 22).

260. P. P., 1866, 17, p. 113.

261. See section on "Economic and Class Consequences" in chapter 5.

262. P. P., 1867, 25, p. 135.

263. Ibid., p. cvii.

264. P. P., 1865, 18, p. 81.

265. Anderson, *Education and Opportunity in Victorian Scotland*, pp. 103–4.

266. Reginald Coupland, *Welsh and Scottish Nationalism: A Study* (London: Collins, 1954), pp. 246, 269–70, 281. H. J. Hanham dates the first modern Scottish nationalist agitation to 1850, but regards it as having been relatively dormant until the 1880s (Hanham, *Scottish Nationalism* [Cambridge, Mass.: Harvard University Press, 1969], pp. 74–82).

267. P. D., 1862, 166, col. 141.

268. P. P., 1865, 18, p. 114.

269. Cruikshank, "The Argyll Commission Report, 1865–8," p. 136. For an account of why Lowe refrained from introducing the Revised Code into Scotland, see Thomas Wilson, "A Reinterpretation of 'Payment by Results' in Scotland, 1861–1872," in Walter M. Humes and Hamish M. Paterson, eds., *Scottish Culture and Scottish Education, 1800–1980* (Edinburgh: John Donald Publishers), pp. 93–114. Wilson cites the "cultural" reasons developed here, but also suggests that the code would not have achieved as many economies in Scotland as it did in England.

270. Knox, *Two Hundred and Fifty Years of Scottish Education*, pp. 66–67.

271. P. D., 1854, 130, cols. 1166–67.

272. In 1858, Rev. James Begg indicated that one of the sources of resistance to a national system would be "an outcry about the supposed danger to religion . . . in certain quarters" (James Begg, "Obstacles to a National System of Education in Scotland," in *Transactions of the National Association for the Promotion of Social Science* [London: John W. Parker, 1858], p. 283).

273. Mechie, *The Church and Scottish Social Development*, p. 149.

274. J. C. Colquhoun, "On the Advantages which Accrue to Elementary Education in Scotland from the System of the Committee of the Privy Council on Education," in *Transactions of the National Association for the Promotion of Social Science* (London: John W. Parker, 1858), p. 357. Colquhoun judged the secularist party to be stronger than either the Catholics or the Episcopalians in Scotland.

275. Ibid.

276. Begg, "Obstacles to a National System of Education in Scotland," p. 282.

277. For a discussion of the threat to Roman Catholics of the 1869 bill for a comprehensive nondenominational school system for Scotland that made no provision for voluntary schools, see Skinnider, "Catholic Elementary Education in Glasgow, 1818–1918," p. 23.

278. Colquhoun, "On the Advantages . . . to Elementary Education," p. 357.

279. Fitzpatrick, "Catholic Education in Glasgow, Lanarkshire and South-West Scotland before 1872," p. 95.

280. P. D., 1854, 130, col. 1171.

281. P. P., 1867, 25, pp. 7–10. See also Cruikshank, "Argyll Commission Report, 1865–68," pp. 135–41.

282. P. D., 1869, 194, cols. 285–86.

283. P. D., 1854, 130, cols. 1157, 1171.

284. Ibid., col. 1190.

285. P. D., 1854, 132, col. 237.

286. Ibid., col. 146.

287. Ibid., col. 253.

288. Ibid., cols. 254, 275–76.

289. Ibid., cols. 283–84.

290. P. D., 1856, 143, cols. 374, 730–33, 1025–27.

291. Drummond and Bulloch, *The Church in Victorian Scotland,* pp. 97–98.

292. See the section on "Public Movement and Parliamentary Inaction" in chapter 5.

293. Quoted in Cruikshank, "Argyll Commission Report, 1865–68," p. 136.

294. Myers, "Scottish Schoolmasters in the Nineteenth Century," p. 89.

295. P. D., 1869, 194, col. 285.

296. Details are summarized in Cruikshank, "Argyle Commission Report, 1865–68," p. 143.

297. P. P., 1867, 25, pp. clxxiii–clxxxi.

298. P. D., 1869, 194, cols. 287–88.

299. Ibid., cols. 298–99.

300. Ibid., cols. 1766, 1768–69.

301. P. P., 1869, 196, cols. 434–51.

302. Sellar, "Scotch Education Difficulties," p. 261.

303. James Scotland, "The Centenary of the Education (Scotland) Act of 1876," *British Journal of Educational Studies* 20, no. 2 (June 1971): 122.

304. Mechie, *The Church and Scottish Social Development,* p. 149.

305. Drummond and Bulloch, *The Church in Victorian Scotland,* p. 103.

306. Ibid., p. 98.

307. Balfour, *Educational Systems of Great Britain and Ireland,* pp. 137–38.

308. Mechie, *The Church and Scottish Social Development,* p. 152.

309. Scotland, "Centenary of the Education (Scotland) Act of 1871," pp. 122–31.

310. Knox, *Two Hundred and Fifty Years of Scottish Education,* p. 63. Thus massive state intervention tended to establish a curious kind of bond between Catholics and Anglicans in Scotland as well as England. See the section on "Other Religious and Political Developments" in chapter 5. The bond was the great reluctance of both to give up control of education to the state.

311. Skinnider, "Catholic Elementary Education in Glasgow, 1818–1918," pp. 22–25. For a brief account of the economic hardships of voluntary Catholic schools between 1872 and 1918, when legislative relief was given, see Peter F. Anson, *The Catholic Church in Modern Scotland, 1560–1937* (London: Burns,

Oates & Washbourne, 1937), pp. 195–96; see also J. H. Treble, "The Development of Roman Catholic Education in Scotland, 1878–1978," *Innes Review* 29 (June 1978): pp. 111–12.

## CHAPTER 8

1. For a comment on the Owenite and Chartist educational programs, see the section on "Education as Enlightenment and an Avenue for Social Change" in chapter 3.

2. Tawney quoted in A. S. Bishop, *The Rise of a Central Authority for English Education* (Cambridge: Cambridge University Press, 1971), p. vii.

3. Lawrence A. Cremin, *American Education: The National Experience, 1783–1876* (New York: Harper & Row, 1980), pp. 2–63.

4. See pp. 45–47.

5. Eric J. Hobsbawm, "The Labour Aristocracy in Nineteenth-Century Britain," in *Labouring Men: Studies in the History of Labour* (London: Weidenfeld & Nicolson, 1964), pp. 272–315.

6. See the section on "Segregative Tendencies" in chapter 3.

7. M. Dorothy George, *England in Transition: Life and Work in the Eighteenth Century* (London: Penguin Books, 1953).

8. Neil J. Smelser, *Social Change in the Industrial Revolution* (Chicago: University of Chicago Press, 1959), pp. 52–62.

9. P. P., 1844, 12, esp. pp. 277–97.

10. The best sources for educational development in these cities are Carl F. Kaestle, *The Evolution of an Urban School System* (Cambridge, Mass.: Harvard University Press, 1973), and Carl F. Kaestle and Maris Vinovskis, *Education and Change in Nineteenth-Century Massachusetts* (Cambridge: Cambridge University Press, 1980).

11. M. G. Jones, *The Charity School Movement: A Study of Eighteenth Century Puritanism in Action* (Cambridge: Cambridge University Press, 1938), ch. 2 and pp. 85–96.

12. Quoted from a letter written by Raikes to the *Gentlemen's Magazine* in 1783, in J. M. Goldstrom, *Education: Elementary Education, 1780–1900* (New York: Barnes & Noble, 1972), p. 17.

13. P. P., 1819, 9, pt. 1, pp. 7, 423, 312, 94.

14. See, for example, P. P., 1834, 9, pp. 96, 177, 180; 1835, 7, p. 710; 1837–38, 7, pp. 267, 292–94.

15. Smelser, *Social Change in the Industrial Revolution*, p. 297.

16. Evidence of J. R. Leifchild, P. P., 1845, 16, p. 533; see also pp. 25, 803. Also P. P., 1842, 17, pp. 370–71.

17. P. P., 1843, 13, p. 201.

18. P. P., 1846, 32, p. 311.

19. Nancy Ball, "Elementary School Attendance and Voluntary Effort before 1870," *History of Education* 2, no. 1, (January 1973): 22. For an interesting bit of supplementary evidence on the link between employment and atten-

dance difficulties, see Sydney Wood, "Social History from Logbooks," *Local Historian* 14, no. 8 (November 1981): 471–76.

20. P. P., 1852–53, 80, p. 98.

21. P. P., 1850, 44, p. 492.

22. P. P., 1854, 52, p. 661.

23. P. P., 1850, 159, p. 492; 1852, 40, pp. 118, 378–79; 1857, 33, p. 263; 628–29; 1860, 54, p. 159.

24. P. P., 1861, 21, pt. 1, pp. 175, 179, 181–86; pt. 2, p. 264; pt. 6, p. 185.

25. Ibid., pt. 6, pp. 311–13.

26. David Vincent, *Bread, Knowledge and Freedom: A Study of Nineteenth-Century Working Class Autobiography* (London: Europa Publications, 1981), p. 94.

27. P. P., 1850, 43, p. 634.

28. W. F. Kalper, "Education," in *Transactions of the National Association for the Promotion of Social Science* (Liverpool: Benson & Mallett, 1858), p. 14. The year before Frederick Talbott had listed "the great demands of our manufacturers for juvenile labour" as one of the two great obstacles to the education of the working classes, the other being "the indifference of parents" ("On Some Causes of the Defective Condition of National Education," in *Transactions of the Association for the Promotion of Social Science* [London: John W. Parker, 1857], p. 194).

29. See the section on "Economic and Class Consequences" in chapter 5.

30. P. P., 1866, 34, p. xxvi. The commissioners also reported that "the means of secular and religious instruction are immensely increased, and greatly more efficient."

31. P. P., 1816, 4, p. 190.

32. P. P., 1843, 13, p. 268.

33. P. P., 1852, 40, p. 132.

34. P. P., 1853, 80, pp. 623–24.

35. P. P., 1854, 52, pp. 346, 723.

36. P. P., 1856, 47, pp. 464, 471, 492–93.

37. P. P., 1861, 49, pp. 117–18.

38. P. P., 1857, 33, p. 578.

39. P. P., 1863, 47, p. 102.

40. P. P., 1847, 45, pp. 160–61, 272–73.

41. P. P., 1852, 39, p. 52; see also 1850, 42, p. 221; 1860, 56, p. 553.

42. P. P., 1859, 21, pt. 1, p. 469.

43. Testimony of Rev. Joseph Cotton Wigram of St. James Parish before the Select Committee on Education (P. P., 1835, 7, p. 710). Some of the respondents to inquiries of the Manchester Statistical Society in 1838 mentioned want of clothes as a reason for not attending, but the society pointed out that in one parish when a wealthy woman had tried to make up this deficiency by providing clothing, the patterns of attendance were still very irregular (P. B. Butterfield, "The Educational Researches of the Manchester Statistical Society, 1830–1840," *British Journal of Educational Studies* 22, no. 3 [October 1974]: 350).

44. P. P., 1854–55, 42, pp. 521–22.

45. P. P., 1864, 42, pp. 161–62.

46. P. P., 1852–53, 80, p. 624.

47. Neil J. Smelser, *Social Change in the Industrial Revolution* (Chicago: University of Chicago Press, 1959), pp. 297–98.

48. See the testimony of Leonard Horner, a factory inspector, in P. P., 1840, 10, p. 78.

49. P. P., 1850, 44, pp. 192–93.

50. P. P., 1856, 47, pp. 472–73.

51. Brougham singled out this example in an early comment on the Midland counties (P. P., 1821, 2, cols. 63–64). As late as 1867 school inspectors were complaining about the destructive effects of lacemaking on the education of girls in the region (P. P., 1867, 22, pp. 250–55, 370).

52. P. P., 1854, 51, pp. 407–8; 1869, 20, p. 197.

53. P. P., 1843, 13, p. 172; 1847–48, 50, pp. 318–19; 1857, 12, pp. 128–29.

54. P. P., 1866, 27, pp. 362–63.

55. P. P., 1861, pt. 2, pp. 329, 336.

56. P. P., 1843, 13, p. 160.

57. Ibid., p. 202. The commissioners cited attendance at night schools by children and young persons from other trades, but added that "no children of colliers and miners attend these schools" (ibid.).

58. See, e.g., P. P., 1842–43, 20, p. 422; 1845, 21, pp. 474–75; 1845, 35, pp. 549, 559; 1846, 32, p. 219; 1834–38, 50, p. 279; 1850, 43, pp. 954–95; 1852, 40, pp. 119–20; 1852–53, 80, pp. 5–6; 1854–55, pp. 391–92.

59. P. P., 1852, 40, p. 660.

60. P. P., 1851, 44, p. 62.

61. Pamela Horn, *The Victorian Country Child* (Gloucester: Sutton, 1985), pp. 95–112.

62. P. P., 1867, 16, p. 75.

63. The initial awards of capitation payments for numbers of pupils attending 176 days annually were to communities with populations of fewer than 5,000, indicating that attendance in those communities constituted a special problem. See the section on "Capitation Payments" later in this chapter.

64. P. P., 1847, 27, pt. 1, p. 22.

65. P. P., 1816, 4, p. 197.

66. P. P., 1837–38, 7, p. 296. In 1835 Samuel Wilderspin, the champion of infant schools, complained of "seeing very near infants carrying other infants . . . they drag them about all day while the parents are at home or at work" (P. P., 1835, 7, p. 781).

67. Beryl Madoc-Jones, "Patterns of Attendance and Their Social Significance: Mitcham National School 1830–39," in Phillip McCann, ed., *Popular Education and Socialization in the Nineteenth Century* (London: Methuen, 1977), p. 47.

68. P. P., 1843, 13, pp. 274–75; 1850, 43, pp. 634–35.

69. For a survey of these arrangements in midcentury Lancashire, see Michael Anderson, *Family Structure in Nineteenth-Century Lancashire* (Cambridge: Cambridge University Press, 1971), pp. 73–74. In some areas the employment of women with young children was high; R. Burr Litchfield estimates

that in the Stockport area in the 1850s "more than half the mothers with children at home aged under one year were listed as working in the census" (Litchfield, "The Work and the Mill: Cotton Mill Work, Family Work Patterns, and Fertility in Mid-Victorian Stockport," in Anthony S. Wohl, ed., *The Victorian Family: Structure and Stresses* [London: Croom Helm, 1978], p. 192).

70. P. P., 1851, 90, p. 27. In rural areas one of the apparent motives for teachers' accepting very young children into their schools was the knowledge that if they did not, older children would be kept out of school to tend to them (Horn, *Victorian Country Child*, p. 18).

71. P. P., 1861, 21, pt. 3, p. 354–55.

72. P. P., 1861, 21, pt. 3, p. 59.

73. P. P., 1867, 22, p. 250.

74. In a survey of domestic servants for 1851, Theresa M. McBride found only 5.7 percent of them under fifteen (McBride, *The Domestic Revolution: The Modernisation of Household Service in England and France, 1820–1920* [London: Croom Helm, 1976], p. 45).

75. P. P., 1861, 21, pt. 2, p. 463.

76. A. C. O. Ellis, "Influences on School Attendance in Victorian England," *British Journal of Educational Studies* 21, no. 3 (October 1973): 316–17.

77. See *Some Habits and Customs of the Working Classes*, by A Journeyman Engineer (London: Tinsley Brothers, 1867), pp. 105–6; Mrs. Hugh Bell [Lady Bell], *At the Works: A Study of a Manufacturing Town* (London: Edward Arnold, 1907), pp. 137–40.

78. P. P., 1847–48, 50, p. 406.

79. P. P., 1857, 33, p. 263.

80. P. P., 1852, 40, p. 378.

81. P. P., 1845, 35, p. 473.

82. P. P., 1852, 40, pp. 118–19.

83. See the section on "A Victory for the Church" in chapter 4.

84. Sir James Kay-Shuttleworth, *Four Periods of Public Education* (London: Longman, Green, Longman & Roberts, 1862), p. 488.

85. Ibid., p. 490.

86. W. J. Unwin, "The Early Removal of Children from School—Suggested Remedies," in *Transactions of the Society for the Promotion of Social Science* (London: John W. Parker & Son, 1857), p. 182. For more on the status of teachers, see the section on "The Social Role" in chapter 9.

87. P. P., 1857, 12, p. 54.

88. P. P., 1852, 40, p. 118.

89. P. P., 1842, 16, p. 25.

90. P. P., 1845, 25, pp. 471–72; 1847, 45, pp. 85–86; 1848, 50, p. 306; 1850, 154, p. 492.

91. P. P., 1854, 52, pp. 79–80.

92. P. P., 1861, 21, pt. 1, p. 179.

93. Ibid., p. 188.

94. Ibid., p. 198.

95. Ibid., p. 217.

96. This statement should be qualified by pointing out that factory legisla-

tion had a compulsory aspect—making children who were employed attend manufacturers' schools—as did workhouse and reformatory education. See the section on "Economic and Class Consequences" in chapter 5.

97. P. P., 1845, 25, pp. 468–69.

98. See the sections on "Segregative Tendencies" in chapter 3 and "Economizing, Streamlining, Standardizing, and Secularizing" in chapter 5.

99. R. H. Tawney expressed the strongest skepticism about the effects of the "career open to talents" ideology, indicating that in many respects it did little for equality, because economic constraints made it impossible for all but a few to rise. "Economic realities make short work of legal abstractions," he observed. Tawney even suggested that the abstract hope held out to a few had a negative effect, namely, it served to "sharpen the edge of economic disparities with humiliating contrasts of power and helplessness." See Tawney, *Equality* (London: Allen & Unwin, 1931), pp. 149–50. Extending Tawney's logic, I would suggest that the short-term demands of children's labor and the structured "dead end" of curricula and time in school made it impossible for the expectation of mobility through the avenue of a "career open to talents" to be a realistic one for all but the tiniest minority of working-class families and their children.

100. See the section on "General Features of the Period" in chapter 5.

101. See the section on "Segregative Tendencies" in chapter 3.

102. P. P., 1852–53, 90, p. xli.

103. P. P., 1856, 47, p. 295.

104. P. P., 1861, 21, pt. 6, p. 151.

105. P. P., 1852, 40, p. 385.

106. Rev. J. P. Hastings, "The Difficulties in Promoting Rural Education," in *Transactions for the Society for the Promotion of Social Science* (London: John W. Parker & Son, 1857), p. 180.

107. See the section on "Origin and Nature of the System" in chapter 9.

108. P. P., 1861, 21, pt. 6, p. 73.

109. P. P., 1847–48, 50, p. 407.

110. P. P., 1861, 21, pt. 6, p. 24.

111. See the section on "Turbulence in the 'Closed System'" in chapter 9.

112. P. P., 1847–48, 50, p. 201.

113. P. P., 1852, 40, p. 46.

114. Ibid., p. 131.

115. P. P., 1854, 52, p. 447.

116. P. P., 1856, 47, p. 373.

117. P. P., 1854–55, 42, pp. 569–70.

118. P. P., 1857–58, 45, p. 532.

119. Ibid., p. 617.

120. P. P., 1860, 56, p. 292; 1862, 49, p. 119.

121. P. P., 1861, 49, p. 169. See also the objection raised by Matthew Arnold, p. 185.

122. See the section on "Turbulence in the 'Closed System'" in chapter 9; on the market conditions in the late 1860s, see the reports by inspectors in P. P., 1867–68, 25, p. 214; 1868–69, 20, p. 379.

123. P. P., 1856, 47, pp. 328–29, 373; 1857, 33, p. 491.

124. P. P., 1857, 33, p. 237.

125. P. P., 1857–58, 45, p. 532.

126. P. P., 1861, 49, p. 169.

127. See the section on "Turbulence in the 'Closed System'" in chapter 9. For a comment on the late 1860s, see P. P., 1868–69, 20, p. 379.

128. See the section on "The Impact of the Revised Code" in chapter 9.

129. See the section on "The Social Origins of Pupil-Teachers" in chapter 9.

130. For a general account of the rapid development of the service occupations in the late nineteenth century, see C. H. Lee, *The British Economy since 1700: A Macroeconomic Perspective* (Cambridge: Cambridge University Press, 1986), pp. 8–17. For girls, the school curriculum continued to be dominated by domestic subjects through the end of the century, on the assumption that they would be either housewives or domestic servants. The main education-related avenues of advancement for females toward the end of the century were elementary school teaching (the number of female teachers expanded from 15,075 in 1870 to 104,751 in 1899), clerical employment, and hospital nursing. See Pamela Horn, "The Education and Employment of Working-Class Girls, 1870–1914," *History of Education* 17, no. 1 (January 1988): 71–82.

131. The early history is given in David Salmon and Winifred Hindshaw, *Infant Schools: Their History and Theory* (London: Longmans, Green, 1904), pp. 8–36; and A. F. B. Roberts, "A New View of the Infant School Movement," *British Journal of Educational Studies* 20, no. 2 (June 1972): 245–55.

132. For Stow's account of his system and its applications, see David Stow, *Moral Training, Infant and Juvenile* (Glasgow: William Collins, 1834).

133. See Wilderspin's testimony before the select committee on the state of education, in P. P., 1835, 7, pp. 786–87, 797. See also Roberts, "A New View of the Infant School Movement," p. 155.

134. P. P., 1835, 7, p. 886.

135. A. F. B. Roberts, "The Development of Professionalism in the Early Stages of Education," *British Journal of Educational Studies* 24, no. 3 (October 1976): 257.

136. P. P., 1835, 7, p. 878–80.

137. P. P., 1837–38, 7, p. 187.

138. Because of these criticisms, the 1830s are described as a "crisis" for the infant school movement by Phillip McCann and Francis A. Young, *Samuel Wilderspin and the Infant School Movement* (London: Croom Helm, 1982), ch. 10.

139. Roberts, "Development of Professionalism," p. 258.

140. P. P., 1854, 52, p. 766.

141. P. P., 1861, 21, pt. 1, p. 32.

142. Eric E. Rich, *The Education Act, 1870: A Study of Public Opinion* (London: Longmans, Green, 1970), p. 50.

143. R. Szreter, "The Origins of Full-Time Compulsory Education at Five," *British Journal of Educational Studies* 13, no. 4 (November 1964): 16–28.

144. Thomas Kelly, *A History of Adult Education in Great Britain* (Liverpool: Liverpool University Press, 1962), pp. 65–79, 103–5, 112–26.

145. Henry J. Burgess, *Enterprise in Education: The Story of the Work of*

*the Established Church in the Education of the People Prior to 1870* (London: National Society and SPCK, 1958), p. 132.

146. P. P., 1852–53, 80, p. 98; 1859, 21, pt. 1, p. 91.

147. Burgess, *Enterprise in Education,* p. 133.

148. P. P., 1866, 27, p. 227.

149. Government assistance for adult education was "not acceptable or available on any considerable scale until after the 1862 Revised Code for evening schools," according to J. F. C. Harrison, "Adult Education and Self-Help," *British Journal Educational Studies* 6 (1957–58): 45.

150. P. P., 1842, 16, p. 24; 1843, 13, p. 202.

151. P. P., 1861, 21, pt. 1, p. 52.

152. P. P., 1861, 49, pp. 121–22.

153. P. P., 1861, 21, pt. 1, pp. 32, 222.

154. For a brief account of these schemes, including HMI Tremenheere's work in the mining districts, beginning in 1843, see Alec Ellis, *Educating Our Masters: Influences on the Growth of Literacy in Victorian Working Class Children* (Aldershot: Gower Publishing, pp. 33–34). See also Hugh S. Tremenheere, *I Was There: The Memoirs of H. S. Tremenheere,* ed. E. L. and O. P. Edmonds (London: Shakespeare Head Press, 1965), pp. 71–72.

155. Leslie W. Evans, *Education in Industrial Wales, 1700–1900* (Cardiff: Heanton Press, 1971), p. 272.

156. Ibid., pp. 270–72.

157. P. P., 1861, 21, pt. 1, pp. 221–22.

158. P. P., 1857, 33, p. 233.

159. See the section on "The Consolidation of Growth under Primordial Proliferation" in chapter 5.

160. See the section on "The Welsh Situation to 1870" in chapter 6.

161. See the section on "Variation by Industry and Region" in chapter 8.

162. P. P., 1852–53, 79, pp. 493–94.

163. P. P., 1854, 51, p. 30.

164. P. P., 1854–55, 42, p. 492.

165. P. P., 1856, 47, pp. 493–95.

166. P. P., 1856, 46, p. 395.

167. P. P., 1857, 33, pp. 233, 397–98.

168. See the section on "Educational Growth" in chapter 5.

169. Testimony of Rev. Frederick Temple, in P. P., 1861, 21, pt. 6, p. 378.

170. Ibid., pt. 1, p. 316.

171. John S. Hurt, *Education in Evolution: Church, State, Society and Popular Education, 1800–1870* (London: Rupert Hart-Davis, 1971), p. 85.

172. See the section on "Economizing, Streamlining, Standardizing, and Secularizing," in chapter 5.

173. P. P., 1861, 21, pt. 6, p. 370.

174. Ibid., p. 354. Temple reported that some managers told him that with the capitation grants "we have got more money from the Government than we know what to do with."

175. Ibid., pp. 14, 18.

176. P. P., 1860, 54, p. 149.

177. P. P., 1861, 21, pt. 6, p. 149.

178. See the section on "Economic and Class Consequences" in chapter 5.

179. The other major cost was the loss of earnings of school-age children who might otherwise have been working.

180. Henry Craik, *The State in Its Relation to Education* (London: Macmillan, 1914), p. 118.

181. Smelser, *Social Change in the Industrial Revolution,* pp. 210–13, 269–72, 292–94. The spirit of this sentiment is captured in the statement of the earl of Rosslyn in the debates over the cotton factories bill of 1819. He said he would "lay it down as an incontestable fact, that parents were the natural guardians of the health and prosperity of their own children, and that the legislature ought to be slow to interfere with free labour" (P. D., 1819, 40, col. 1131).

182. P. D., 1807, 9, cols. 853–54. That compulsory feature was removed by amendment after those debates.

183. P. D., 1833, 20, cols. 157–58. Roebuck's only defense against the opposition to the principle of compulsion was that compulsion was legitimate because those imposing it would be popularly chosen (col. 149).

184. Sir James Kay-Shuttleworth, "Address on Education," in *Transactions of the National Association for the Promotion of Social Science* (London: John Parker & Son, 1860), p. 93.

185. See P. D., 1807, 9, cols. 801–4, for a discussion of whether Whitbread's educational proposals would involve an increase or a decrease in the rates.

186. See the section on "Education as Prevention of Pauperism and Crime" in chapter 3.

187. P. P., 1818, 4, p. 264.

188. Ibid.

189. P. P., 1834, 9, pp. 15, 68.

190. P. P., 1852, 40, p. 380; 1857, 33, p. 300.

191. P. P., 1852–53, 90, pp. xxix–xl.

192. P. P., 1852–53, 80, pp. 671–72.

193. P. P., 1861, 21, pt. 1, pp. 73, 202.

194. P. P., 1867–68, 27, pt. 1, p. 657.

195. See the section on "Variation by Level of Economic Activity" earlier in this chapter.

196. P. P., 1854, 52, pp. 432–33.

197. P. P., 1852, 40, p. 380.

198. John Hurt, *Elementary Schooling and the Working Classes, 1860–1919* (London: Routledge & Kegan Paul, 1979), p. 71.

199. P. D., 1833, 20, cols. 149–50.

200. P. D., 1855, 137, col. 2118.

201. P. P., 1861, 21, pt. 1, p. 73.

202. See the section on "Economic and Class Consequences" in chapter 5.

203. See the sections on "Llangefni, 1850–1852" and "The Welsh Situation to 1870" in chapter 6. In 1860 Mark Pattison reflected that universal school attendance was attained easily in Germany partly because the "religious dif-

ficulty" was only a slight one there. There were only three major religious confessions—Protestants, Catholics, and Jews—even though signs of conflict between Calvinists and Lutherans were appearing. In most communities each
confession had its own school. "Compulsory attendance is only a religious
grievance where a minority of one confession is dispersed so thinly amid a
majority of the other as to be unable to have its own school" (P. P., 1861, 21,
pt. 4, p. 205).

204. For a summary of the arguments and resolution, see Rich, *Education
Act, 1870*, pp. 96–97.

205. Norman Morris, "1870: The Rating Option," *History of Education* 1,
no. 1 (January 1972): 23–24.

206. See the section on "The Failure of Middle-Class Radical Secularism" in
chapter 4. Joseph Hume described the Prussian system as an ideal solution of
the religious difficulty because of the long-standing conscience clause (P. D.,
1843, 67, col. 1455).

207. P. P., 1834, 9, p. 221.

208. Matthew Arnold, *Reports on Elementary Schools, 1852–1882* (London: His Majesty's Stationery Office, 1908), p. 117.

209. The features of the act and its effect are discussed in Michael Sanderson, "Education and the Factory in Industrial Lancashire, 1780–1840," *Economic History Review*, 2d ser., 20, no. 2 (August 1967): 267–70; see also
Smelser, *Social Change in the Industrial Revolution*, pp. 269–70.

210. Elie Halévy, *A History of the English People in the Nineteenth Century*, trans. E. I. Watkin and D. A. Barker (1924–27), vol. 3, *The Triumph of
Reform, 1830–1842* (reprint, London: Ernest Benn, 1950), p. 113.

211. Smelser, *Social Change in the Industrial Revolution*, p. 297.

212. Ibid., pp. 273–90.

213. P. P., 1852, 7, pp. 126–27.

214. See this conclusion of HMI J. P. Norris after reviewing the limited effectiveness of the Staffordshire prize scheme (P. P., 1854, 51, pp. 407–8).

215. Hurt, *Elementary Schooling and the Working Classes*, pp. 188–98.

216. John Morley, *The Struggle for National Education* (Brighton: Harvester Press, 1972), p. 133.

217. Christine Heward, "The Class Relations of Compulsory School Attendance: The Birmingham Jewelry Quarter, 1851–86," *History of Education
Quarterly* 29, no. 2 (Summer 1989): 231.

218. Morley, *Struggle for National Education*, pp. 157–58.

219. Edward Baines, Jr., *Letters to the Right Hon. Lord John Russell, First
Lord of the Treasury, on State Education* (London: Simpkin, Marshall, 1846),
p. 100.

220. Nathan Rosenberg, "Anglo-American Wage Differences in the 1820's,"
*Journal of Economic History* 27, no. 2 (June 1967): 221–29; H. J. Habakkuk,
*American and British Technology in the Nineteenth Century* (Cambridge: Cam-
bridge University Press, 1962).

221. Carl F. Kaestle and Maris A. Vinovskis, *Education and Social Change
in Nineteenth-Century Massachusetts* (Cambridge: Cambridge University Press,
1980), pp. 66–67.

222. Ibid., pp. 7–8, 116–20.

223. See the section on "Primary Education and Social Mobility" earlier in this chapter.

224. McBride, *Domestic Revolution*, p. 112, gives the following figures for the size and growth of the English servant population:

| Year | Number | Percentage Change |
|------|--------|-------------------|
| 1851 | 908,138 | |
| 1861 | 1,123,428 | +23.7 |
| 1871 | 1,387,872 | +23.2 |
| 1881 | 1,453,175 | + 4.7 |
| 1891 | 1,549,502 | + 6.6 |
| 1901 | 1,370,773 | −11.5 |

McBride adds: "The very young were no longer employed in service after 1900 since the educational system's expansion had cut into the under-fifteen population. In England . . . there were still 22,588 children under fourteen employed as servants in 1901. By 1911 less than 8,000 remained in service in this age group. Education not only kept the very young out of the labour force, but it provided them with the basic skills which expanded their occupational options" (ibid., p. 114). For a survey-based account of domestic servants and related, competitive occupations at the end of the nineteenth century, see Charles Booth, *Life and Labour of the People in London*, 2d ser., *Industry*, vol. 4, *Public, Professional and Domestic Service, Unoccupied Classes, Inmates of Institutions* (London: Macmillan, 1903), pp. 208–35.

225. W. W. Rostow, "Investment and Real Wages, 1873–86," *Economic History Review* 9 (1938–39): 144.

226. J. A. Banks, *Prosperity and Parenthood: A Study of Family Planning among the Victorian Middle Classes* (London: Routledge & Kegan Paul, 1954), p. 13. For the general downward trends toward the end of the century, see A. Newsholme, *The Declining Birth-Rate* (New York: Moffat, Yard, 1911), pp. 20–33; and John W. Innes, *Class Fertility Trends in England and Wales, 1876–1934* (Princeton: Princeton University Press, 1938), pp. 16–17.


CHAPTER 9

1. See the section on "Segregative Tendencies" in Chapter 3.

2. See the section on "A Victory for the Church" in Chapter 4.

3. Sir James Kay-Shuttleworth, *Four Periods of Public Education* (London: Longman, Green, Longman & Roberts, 1862), p. 477.

4. Ibid., p. 478. As early as 1836, Kay-Shuttleworth had connected the need for well-trained teachers with the need for social order: "In every English proprietor's domain . . . there ought to be . . . school houses with well-trained masters, competent and zealous to rear the population in obedience to the laws, in submission to superiors, and to fit them to strengthen the institutions of their country by their domestic virtues, their sobriety, their industry and aforethought" (quoted in John Hurt, *Education in Evolution: Church, State, Society*

*and Popular Education, 1800–1870* [London: Rupert Hart-Davis, 1971], p. 113).

5. Kay-Shuttleworth, *Four Periods of Public Education,* p. 478. For a summary of the difficulties in using young children as teachers, see Mary Sturt, *The Education of the People: A History of Primary Education in England and Wales in the Nineteenth Century* (London: Routledge & Kegan Paul, 1967) pp. 34–35.

6. P.P., 1847–48, 50, p. 313.

7. Kay-Shuttleworth, *Four Periods of Public Education,* p. 478.

8. P.P., 1847, 45, p. 1.

9. Sir James Kay-Shuttleworth, *Public Education as Affected by the Minutes of the Committee of Privy Council from 1846 to 1852; with Suggestions as to Future Policy* (London: Longman, Brown, Green & Longmans, 1853), p. 61.

10. Pamela Horn, *Education in Rural England, 1800–1914* (Dublin: Gill & Macmillan, 1978), p. 56.

11. Kay-Shuttleworth, *Four Periods of Public Education,* p. 483.

12. Ibid., p. 488.

13. Ibid.

14. Ibid., p. 485.

15. P.P., 1847–48, 50, p. 330.

16. Ibid., p. 406.

17. Quoted in Hurt, *Education in Evolution,* p. 125.

18. Quoted in ibid., pp. 120–21.

19. Quoted in Horn, *Education in Rural England,* p. 59.

20. Ibid., pp. 57–58.

21. P.P., 1847, 45, p. 3.

22. See Lingen's letter to inspectors in P.P., 1851, 44, pp. 87–90.

23. Horn, *Education in Rural England,* p. 64.

24. For the Newcastle Commission's catalogue of training colleges organized along religious lines, see P.P., 1861, 21, pt. 1, pp. 114–15.

25. See the section on "The General Pattern" in chapter 8.

26. P.P., 1850, 43, pp. 778–79.

27. Ibid., p. 657.

28. P.P., 1847–48, 50, p. 200.

29. Ibid., p. 676.

30. Ibid., pp. 869–71.

31. Ibid., p. 199.

32. Ibid., p. 200.

33. See Hurt, *Education in Evolution,* pp. 122–23.

34. P.P., 1861, 21, pt. 6, pp. 139, 250.

35. Horn, *Education in Rural England,* pp. 68–69.

36. For a general discussion of this issue in higher education, see Neil J. Smelser and Robin Content, *The Changing Academic Market* (Berkeley: University of California Press, 1981), chs. 1–2.

37. See the section on "Primary Education and Social Mobility" in chapter 8.

38. P.P., 1861, 21, pt. 1, p. 107.

39. Horn, *Education in Rural England*, p. 68.

40. Ibid., p. 64.

41. P.P., 1852–53, 80, p. 35.

42. In 1852 Blandford referred to "a doubt . . . expressed as to there being a sufficient number of schools for [teachers'] employment" (ibid., p. 337).

43. P.P., 1857, 33, pp. 12–13.

44. See the report of HMI Arnold in P.P., 1861, 49, p. 185.

45. This was the concern of HMI J. D. Morell in the northern counties in 1860 (ibid., p. 180).

46. Kay-Shuttleworth, *Four Periods of Public Education,* pp. 576–77. For an elaboration of Kay-Shuttleworth's complaints, see P.P., 1862, 41, p. 426.

47. P.D., 1867, 185, cols. 1162–63. A report of the Committee of Council pointed to the impact of the changed system of paying for pupil-teachers (P.P., 1866, 27, p. 129).

48. P.D., 1865, 177, col. 880.

49. P.P., 1866, 27, p. 580.

50. *The Autobiography of Sir James Kay-Shuttleworth*, ed. B. C. Bloomfield (London: University of London, Institute of Education, 1964), p. 78.

51. Reported in D. W. Sylvester, *Robert Lowe and Education* (Cambridge: Cambridge University Press, 1974), p. 99.

52. HMI J. W. D. Hernanman indicated that one of the factors that discouraged children from becoming pupil-teachers was that "the cost of training at a normal school is higher than formerly" (P.P., 1866, 27, p. 295).

53. P.P., 1863, 47, pp. 9–10; 1864, 45, p. 23.

54. P.P., 1864, 45, p. 23.

55. Statements by HMI's F. Mcyrick and G. R. Moncreiff in ibid., pp. 174, 190. For other statements regarding the diminishing supply, see also ibid., pp. 188, 224–25, 262, 391.

56. Ibid., pp. 196–97.

57. Ibid., p. 262.

58. Ibid., pp. 390–91.

59. P.P., 1866, 27, p. 625.

60. P.P., 1865, 42, pp. 112–13, 205–6, 227, 240, 268–89, 287; 1866, 27, pp. 384–85; 1867, 22, pp. 267, 278–79.

61. See the section on "Primary Education and Social Mobility" in chapter 8. For testimony on the dire situation for boys and the continuing availability of girls for the pupil-teacherships, see the comment by HMI C. F. Johnstone in P.P., 1867–68, 25, p. 159.

62. P.P., 1867, 22, p. 9.

63. HMI W. J. Kennedy reported that he had heard the fact that apprentices left by their third year as follows: "Some managers like the pupil-teachers to go away in the first three years, because by a succession of young pupil-teachers the schools are conducted more economically, as would evidently be the case, on account of the smaller pay given in the first years of apprenticeship" (P.P., 1867–68, 25, p. 170).

64. P.P., 1867, 22, p. 8.

65. P.P., 1868–69, 20, p. xxxvi.

66. P.P., 1867, 22, p. 323.

67. P.P., 1866, 27, p. 174; 1867, 22, p. 168.

68. Report of HMI E. P. Arnold in ibid., p. 201.

69. P.P., 1863, 47, p. xi.

70. P.P., 1866, 27, pp. 393–94; 1867, 22, pp. 255–56; 1867–68, 15, pp. 169–70.

71. P.P., 1867, 22, p. 9.

72. Ibid., pp. 462–63.

73. P.P., 1864, 45, pp. 163–64. HMI D. Middleton remarked that "ex-pupil-teacher assistants can be had only from the ranks of pupil-teachers, and the more these ranks are thinned the fewer assistants can be got from them" (P.P., 1867, 22, p. 462).

74. P.P., 1866, 27, pp. 581, 619–20; 1867, 22, pp. 528–29, 642–43; 1867–68, 15, pp. 494, 515, 551–52.

75. P.P., 1867–68, 25, p. xiii.

76. P.P., 1867, 22, p. 384.

77. Ibid., p. 10.

78. P.P., 1867–68, 25, p. x.

79. P.P., 1868–69, 20, p. xlv.

80. See the section on "Second Ingredient: Tracking the Forces over Time" in chapter 2.

81. It was identified as such in the section on "Economizing, Streamlining, Standardizing, and Secularizing" in chapter 5.

82. P.P., 1861, 21, pt. 1, p. 98; 1861, 21, pt. 3, p. 394.

83. P.P., 1865, 42, pp. 279–80. In the same statement, Morell also said, with some prescience, "[no] doubt things will gradually find their natural level, and the work of national education will then go on as a daily duty less affected by the ebb and flow of popular sentiments" (ibid., p. 280). Morell's observations contain a certain amount of sociological insight into the process of institutionalization.

84. Sturt, Education of the People, pp. 4–6; David Wardle, The Rise of the Schooled Society: The History of Formal Schooling in England (London: Routledge & Kegan Paul), pp. 2–5.

85. M. G. Jones, The Charity School Movement: A Study of Eighteenth Century Puritanism in Action (Cambridge: Cambridge University Press, 1938), pp. 96–109.

86. Thomas W. Laqueur, Religion and Respectability: Sunday Schools and Working-Class Culture, 1780–1850 (New Haven, Yale University Press, 1976), pp. 91–93.

87. Asher Tropp, The School Teachers: The Growth of the Teaching Profession in England and Wales from 1800 to the Present Day (London: William Heinemann, 1957), pp. 10–11.

88. Quoted in Jones, Charity School Movement, p. 102.

89. See the section on "The Failure of Middle-Class Radical Secularism" in chapter 4.

90. P.P., 1834, 9, p. 106.

91. Testimony of William Johnson, who had been clerical superintendent of

the National Society's Central School for twenty-two years (ibid., p. 9). Additional hostile comments of the same order are reproduced in Hurt, *Education in Evolution*, p. 144.

92. P.P., 1834, 9, p. 9.

93. Comment by J. T. Crossley, master in a British and Foreign School Society school for fourteen years (ibid., p. 86).

94. Evidence of Henry Dunn, secretary of the British and Foreign School Society (ibid., p. 21).

95. Ibid., p. 17; 1847, 45, p. 221.

96. Henry Dunn said in 1834 that a "very small number" of the teachers in the British and Foreign School Society schools "have been trained in our schools" (P.P., 1834, 9, p. 17). In 1844 HMI Frederick Watkins had estimated that only one in four teachers in his district had received any training, and many of those for only a very short time, but he saw the situation improving a few years later (P.P., 1847, 45, p. 221).

97. P.P., 1834, 9, pp. 89–91, 206; 1837–38, 7, 212–14.

98. Ibid., 9, p. 17.

99. Tropp, *The School Teachers*, p. 11.

100. Ibid, p. 15.

101. P.P., 1834, 9, p. 143.

102. Evidence of J. T. Crossley (ibid., p. 105).

103. Ibid., p. 106.

104. See the section on "A Victory for the Church" in chapter 4.

105. P.P., 1847–48, 50, p. 226.

106. See Kay-Shuttleworth's memorandum to instructors on these procedures in P.P., 1847, 45, pp. 33–34.

107. P.P., 1847–48, 50, p. 337.

108. For 1846, HMI Frederick Cook reported that male teachers' annual salaries in London ranged from £50 to £100, the average being £70 10s.; those of women, from £25 to £57, with the average £40 10s. Most had housing provided. In country districts, men's salaries varied from £30 to £80, the average being £63 10s.; women's, from £20 to £55, for an average of £35, with housing provided for both men and women (P.P., 1847, 45, pp. 151, 157). For the Midlands in 1845, Watkins reported the average stipend of masters to be £51 15s. 3d., and that of mistresses to be £28 19s. Mistresses of infant schools received only £18 6s. 1d. (P.P., 1846, 33, p. 367). The majority had residences supplied, rent-free.

109. P.P., 1852–53, 80, p. 146.

110. P.P., 1850, 44, p. 183.

111. P.P., 1856, 47, pp. 226–27.

112. P.P., 1850, 43, p. 774.

113. P.P., 1852, 39, p. 363.

114. P.P., 1857–58, 45, p. 30.

115. Ibid.

116. Tropp, *The School Teachers*, p. 42.

117. See the section on "Educational Growth" in chapter 5.

118. P.P., 1854–55, 51, p. 495; 1857–58, 44, pp. 322–23.

119. P.P., 1854, 51, p. 495; 1861, 49, pp. 347–48.

120. P.P., 1854, 52, pp. 14–15; 1856, 47, p. 226.

121. P.P., 1860, 54, p. 26. The Newcastle Commission's figures for certificated masters for 1859–60 were the same as the Committee's figures (P.P., 1861, 21, pt. 1, p. 64).

122. P.P., 1861, 21, pt. 1, p. 64.

123. P.P., 1857–58, 45, pp. 977–78. Speaking before the Newcastle Commission, Lingen estimated that teacher turnover was much higher in England than in Prussia (P.P., 1861, 21, pt. 6, p. 26).

124. HMI Frederick Cook reported that the proportion of students in the training colleges for schoolmistresses completing their two full years of training was decreasing (P.P., 1857–58, 45, p. 741).

125. P.P., 1861, 21, pt. 3, p. 394.

126. Ibid., pt. 1, p. 163.

127. P.P., 1854–55, 42, p. 524.

128. See the section on "Education as Avenue to Social Mobility" in chapter 3.

129. See the section on "General Features of the Period" in chapter 5.

130. See the section on "Primary Education and Social Mobility" in chapter 8.

131. Hugh S. Tremenheere, *Notes on Public Subjects, Made during a Tour in the United States and Canada* (London: John Murray, 1852), p. 57.

132. Willard S. Elsbree, *The American Teacher: Evolution of a Profession in a Democracy* (New York: American Book Co., 1939), pp. 268–83.

133. See "Postscript" in chapter 8. Also Lee Holcombe, *Victorian Ladies at Work: Middle-Class Working Women in England and Wales, 1850–1914* (Newton Abbot, Devon: David & Charles, 1973), pp. 34–35.

134. P.P., 1861, 21, pt. 2, p. 26.

135. P.P., 1861, 49, p. 74.

136. P.P., 1854–55, 42, p. 524.

137. P.P., 1861, 21, pt. 6, p. 153.

138. P.P., 1854, 52, p. 663. Italics in original.

139. *The School and the Teacher,* quoted in Sturt, *Education of the People,* p. 198.

140. P.P., 1861, 49, p. 74.

141. H. W. Bellairs, *The Teacher's Mission and Reward; an Inaugural Address to the Schoolmasters' Association for Gloucestershire* (London: Groombridge & Sons, 1855), p. 17.

142. P.P., 1860, 54, p. 37.

143. P.P., 1861, 21, pt. 6, p. 228.

144. P.P., 1857–58, 45, p. 293.

145. Ibid., p. 435.

146. P.P., 1859, 21, pt. 1, p. 149.

147. Tropp gives further evidence of the perception that teaching was a "dead-level" profession in the decades after the adoption of the minutes of 1846 (*The School Teachers,* p. 41). For further documentation of the status-consciousness of schoolteachers, see Trygve R. Tholfsen, *Working Class Radicalism in Mid-Victorian England* (New York: Columbia University Press, 1977).

148. P.P., 1857–58, 45, p. 293.

149. P.P., 1854–55, 42, p. 605.

150. P.P., 1857–58, 45, p. 323.

151. See the section on "Inspectors" later in this chapter.

152. Nancy Ball, *Her Majesty's Inspectorate, 1839–1849* (Edinburgh: Oliver & Boyd, 1963), p. 226.

153. Horn, *Education in Rural England*, pp. 218–20.

154. Ibid., pp. 217–18.

155. P.P., 1864, 45, p. 149.

156. See the section on "Economizing, Streamlining, Standardizing, and Secularizing" in chapter 5.

157. P.P., 1861, 21, pt. 4, p. 408.

158. Trygve R. Tholfsen, ed., *Sir James Kay-Shuttleworth on Popular Education* (New York: Teachers College Press, 1974), p. 28.

159. See the section on "Educational Growth" in chapter 5. For a general assessment of Lingen's poor relationships with schoolteachers and other constituencies, see A. S. Bishop, *The Rise of a Central Authority for English Education* (Cambridge: Cambridge University Press, 1971), pp. 70–74.

160. Sylvester, *Robert Lowe and Education*, pp. 76–78.

161. Tropp, *The Schoolmasters*, p. 91.

162. Bellairs, *Teacher's Mission and Reward*, pp. 13–14.

163. P.P., 1861, 21, pt. 2, p. 95.

164. Quoted from *Schoolmaster's Difficulties Abroad and at Home*, in Horn, *Education in Rural England*, p. 57.

165. "The early voluntary managers and members of school boards were 'gentlemen and ladies.' The teachers were not" (Henry B. Binns, *A Century of Education* [London: J. M. Dent, 1908], p. 172).

166. P.P., 1847, 45, p. 280. In a study of the Whitelands College for Women, Frances Widowson found a considerable number of women from lower-middle-class background among the trainees, but the number of women from these origins diminished in proportion, beginning in the 1850s (Widowson, *Going Up into the Next Class: Women and Elementary Teacher Training, 1840–1914* [London: Hutchinson, 1983], sec. 2).

167. P.P., 1861, 21, pt. 6, p. 130; 1863, 47, p. 288.

168. Report of HMI E. D. Tinling, P.P., 1860, 54, p. 65.

169. P.P., 1863, 47, p. 288.

170. P.P., 1861, 21, pt. 6, p. 153.

171. Sir James Kay-Shuttleworth, preface to "Work for Ladies in the Elementary Schools," by John Bull (January 1872).

172. P.P., 1861, 21, pt. 6, p. 131.

173. Ibid., p. 325. See also Kay-Shuttleworth, "Preface" to "Work for Ladies in the Elementary Schools," p. 2.

174. This concern with professional status appeared to continue into later decades. Around the turn of the century, James C. Greenough contrasted U.S. teachers' associations with British ones, finding that the former focused more on educational questions, such as "the principles and methods of teaching, school management, the history of education and the results of each other's experience," whereas in England the larger associations existed "for the purpose of

increasing the influence of the teachers and for securing mutual assistance and protection" (Greenough, *The Evolution of the Elementary Schools of Great Britain* [New York: Appleton, 1903], pp. 142–43).

175. HMI Frederick Watkins spoke out in favor of exclusivity on this score, arguing that the presence of clergymen would inhibit free discussion of professional subjects, but he acknowledged at the same time that teachers' organizations struggled financially because of the inability of their low-salaried members to contribute (P.P., 1856, 47, p. 284).

176. See the sections on "Economic and Class Consequences" and "Religious Consequences" in chapter 5.

177. Quoted in John W. Adamson, *English Education, 1789–1902* (Cambridge: Cambridge University Press, 1964), p. 233.

178. P.D., 1865, 177, col. 880.

179. P.P., 1856, 27, p. 703.

180. Quoted in Adamson, *English Education, 1789–1902*, p. 229.

181. See the section on "Economizing, Streamlining, Standardizing, and Secularizing" in chapter 5.

182. P.P., 1864, 45, pp. 163, 226, 245; 1865, 42, pp. 110–11, 237–38, 187; 1866, 27, p. 132; 1867, 22, pp. 212–13, 230; 1867–68, 15, p. 262.

183. P.D., 1867, 184, cols. 1348–49.

184. Matthew Arnold, *Reports on Elementary Schools, 1852–1882* (London: His Majesty's Stationery Office, 1908), p. 103.

185. P.P., 1865, 42, p. 46.

186. P.P., 1863, 47, pp. 73, 140–45.

187. Ibid., pp. 99–100, 145; 1864, 45, p. 226; 1866, 27, p. 307.

188. P.P., 1866, 27, p. 307.

189. P.P., 1867–68, 25, p. 169.

190. J. E. Dunford, *Her Majesty's Inspectorate of Schools in England and Wales, 1860–1870* (Leeds: Museum of the History of Education, University of Leeds, 1980), p. 51.

191. Asher Tropp, "Some Sources for the History of Educational Periodicals in England," *British Journal of Educational Studies* 6, no. 2 (May 1958): 151–55.

192. P.P., 1867–68, 25, p. 290. In the same year HMI W. J. Kennedy reported that "[schoolmasters'] attainments and refinement seem inferior, the aims and aspirations seem lower, and they work with less spirit and zest" (ibid., p. 169).

193. P.P., 1865, 42, p. 266. For the same complaint, see P.P., 1863, 48, pp. 136–37; 1867–68, 22, p. 168.

194. P.P., 1865, 42, p. 266; 1866, 27, pp. 130, 205–6, 327, 429; 1867, 22, p. 390.

195. P.P., 1867, 22, p. 168.

196. See the section on "Religious Consequences" in chapter 5.

197. Pamela Silver and Harold Silver, *The Education of the Poor: The History of the National School, 1824–1974* (London and Boston: Routledge & Kegan Paul, 1974), p. 101.

198. P.P., 1867, 22, p. 400.

199. P.P., 1864, 45, p. 137; 1867, 22, pp. 399–400; 1867–68, 15, pp. xcix–cv; see also Hurt, *Education in Evolution,* pp. 210–11.

200. P.P., 1867, 22, pp. 261, 398–99; 1867–68, 15, pp. 373–74.

201. P.P., 1865, 42, p. 208; 1866, 27, p. 265.

202. P.P., 1864, 45, p. 268.

203. P.P., 1867–68, 25, p. 195, and also p. 421; 1869, 20, p. 22–23.

204. For observations on mediocrity, dullness, and mechanical teaching, see P.P., 1862, 43, p. 425; 1866, 27, pp. 327, 429; 1867, 22, p. 284; 1867–68, 15, pp. 297, 333–34.

205. Matthew Arnold in P.P., 1867–68, 25, p. 296.

206. See the section on "Inspectors" later in this chapter.

207. P.P., 1867, 22, p. 197.

208. Ibid., p. 20.

209. G. A. N. Lowndes, *The Silent Social Revolution: An Account of the Extension of Public Education in England and Wales, 1895–1965* (London: Oxford University Press, 1969), pp. 10–11.

210. For developments after 1870, see Tropp, *The School Teachers,* pp. 113–34; Horn, *Education in Rural England,* pp. 240–47; H. C. Dent, *1870–1970: A Century of Growth in English Education* (London: Longman, 1970), pp. 27–31.

211. This background sketch is based on E. L. Edmonds, *The School Inspector* (London: Routledge & Kegan Paul, 1962), pp. 7–26; and Ball, *Her Majesty's Inspectorate,* pp. 2–13.

212. P.P., 1834, 9, pp. 53–57.

213. P.P., 1837–38, 7, pp. 75–76.

214. Edmonds, *School Inspector,* p. 30.

215. See the section on "A Victory for the Church" in chapter 4 and the sections on "The Consolidation of Growth under Primordial Proliferation" and "Educational Growth" in chapter 5.

216. Sir James Kay-Shuttleworth, *Four Periods of Public Education* (London: Longman, Green, Longman & Roberts, 1862), pp. 446–48. He describes the complicated lengths to which the government was willing to go in order not to interfere with religious instruction on pp. 513–14.

217. See the section on "A Reprise of 1820" in chapter 4.

218. Ibid.

219. Ball, *Her Majesty's Inspectorate,* pp. 79–81.

220. See the section on "A Reprise of 1820" in chapter 4. Generically, the issue of mixing the sexes was the same one that faced the Committee of Council with respect to the mixing of children of different denominations in small communities on grounds of economy (see the section on "Llangefni, 1850–1852" in chapter 6). The latter proved a greater point of sensitivity than the former.

221. Ball, *Her Majesty's Inspectorate,* pp. 93–100.

222. P.P., 1852, 40, p. 115. For another statement on workload, see Edmonds, *School Inspector,* pp. 51–52. Watkins's latter remark may reflect concealed hostility to Lingen, the new secretary, who early established a reputation for officiousness among the inspectors and others; see the section on "Educational Growth" in chapter 5.

223. On the proliferation of duties that led to this accommodation, see P. H. J. H. Gosden, *The Development of Educational Administration in England and Wales* (Oxford: Basil Blackwell, 1966), p. 5.

224. See the section on "The Social Role" earlier in this chapter.

225. P.P., 1851, 44, pp. 9–13.

226. See the section on "Economizing, Streamlining, Standardizing, and Secularizing" in chapter 5.

227. The representative body (religious society) for the Jewish schools was to be the London Committee of Deputies. No mention was made of veto rights over the appointment of inspectors. The Minute specified that only laymen could be inspectors, and that no stipend or augmentation would be awarded to teachers who were ministers of the Jewish religion. See P.P., 1852, 39, pp. 372–73.

228. P.P., 1854, 51, p. 41. The full rights of veto were extended to the primus bishop of the Episcopal Church in Scotland. Because of the limited number of schools to be inspected, the Committee of Council paid inspectors on a per diem basis. This arrangement showed that there were already some economy limits that the committee would not pass in the interests of religious proliferation (i.e., the appointment of a full-time inspector when the "numbers of schools would not justify . . . a separate inspector" (ibid., p. 40).

229. P.P., 1859, 21, pt. 1, p. 10.

230. Ibid., p. 9.

231. See the section on "Economizing, Streamlining, Standardizing, and Secularizing" in chapter 5.

232. David Roberts, *Victorian Origins of the British Welfare State* (New Haven: Yale University Press, 1960), pp. 152–60.

233. Hurt, *Education in Evolution*, p. 43.

234. Cited in Sturt, *Education of the People*, p. 201.

235. See the section on "The Social Role" earlier in this chapter.

236. Peter Gordon, *The Victorian School Manager: A Study in the Management of Education, 1800–1902* (London: Woburn Press, 1974), pp. xii, 9–18.

237. Hurt, *Education in Evolution*, p. 59.

238. See the section on "The Consolidation of Growth under Primordial Proliferation" in chapter 5.

239. Gordon, *Victorian School Manager*, p. 70.

240. Ibid., p. 71.

241. Dunford, *Her Majesty's Inspectorate of Schools*, pp. 60–62.

242. Quoted in Ball, *Her Majesty's Inspectorate*, p. 220.

243. Ibid., p. 222.

244. Tropp, *The School Teachers*, p. 96.

245. M. K. Ashby, *Joseph Ashby of Tysoe, 1859–1919: A Study of English Village Life* (Cambridge: Cambridge University Press, 1961), pp. 17–18.

246. Sturt, *Education of the People*, p. 201; see also *Matthew Arnold on Education*, ed. Gillian Sutherland (London: Penguin Books, 1973), p. 13.

247. P.P., 1857, 33, p. 460.

248. Dunford, *Her Majesty's Inspectorate of Schools*, pp. 50–56.

249. In 1855 Lingen made the following observation on his life with these

constituencies: "The public with which the department deals is not a political but a religious one, and a religious one in fragments. Take each fragment by itself, Church, Wesleyan, Roman Catholic, etc., and talk to any of their leading men and you see in a moment how they dread and shrink from any system which subjects the congregation to any civic and undenominational power; no matter whether that power be the Vestry, Town Council, Board of Guardians, or the House of Commons. 'Find us the money and leave us to ourselves' is the prayer of each and all of them" (quoted in Gosden, *Development of Educational Administration,* pp. 7–8).

250. A. S. Bishop, "Ralph Lingen, Secretary to the Education Department, 1849–1870," *British Journal of Educational Studies* 16, no. 2 (June 1968): 142; J. E. Dunford, "Robert Lowe and Inspectors' Reports," *British Journal of Educational Studies* 25, no. 2 (June 1977): 158.

251. For a characterization of the bases of the remote, difficult, and conflictful relations between Lingen and the inspectors, see Dunford, *Her Majesty's Inspectorate of Schools,* pp. 75–76.

252. Ibid., p. 82.

253. See the section on "The Consolidation of Growth under Primordial Proliferation" in chapter 5.

254. P.P., 1861, 21, pt. 6, p. 389. This is another manifestation of the symbiosis that characterized the relations between state and religious societies in the 1846–70 period.

255. Dunford, "Robert Lowe and Inspectors' Reports," pp. 156–58.

256. Quoted in *Matthew Arnold on Education,* ed. Sutherland, p. 50. In testifying before the select committee in 1864, Lowe remarked that "it was so notorious that the majority of the Inspectors were unfavourable to me" (P.P., 1864, 9, p. 82).

257. P.D., 1864, 174, col. 904.

258. Quoted in P.P., 1864, 9, p. 16. Dunford points out that Lowe's intervention in the inspectors' reports was not inconsistent with the general "culture" of the supervision of civil servants at the time (*Her Majesty's Inspectorate of Schools,* p. 66).

259. Dunford, *Her Majesty's Inspectorate of Schools,* pp. 72–73. Another Catholic inspector, T. W. Marshall, was dismissed in 1860 after being accused of showing pupil-teachers' examination papers to priests who were teaching them (ibid., p. 72). For an account of how these dismissals raised anxieties about job security, as well as restricting professional "freedom of expression," see Pamela Horn, "Robert Lowe and HM Inspectorate, 1859–1864," *Oxford Review of Education* 7, no. 2 (1981): 135–37.

260. P.P., 1864, 9, pp. 46, 53–54, 66–67.

261. Ibid., p. 46. The following even less offensive passage was excised from the report of HMI E. D. Tinling in 1862–63: "With regard to the schoolteachers, the withholding of the payment of any future augmentation grants has greatly loosened the hold which the country possessed over them for the continuance in the work of national education amongst the children of the poor, and this change in the future prospects of the teachers has spread still deeper amongst the pupil-teachers and candidates for apprenticeship" (ibid., p. 118).

262. P.D., 1864, 174, cols. 478–79.

263. Ibid., cols. 897, 905–6, 1182–90, 1209, 1121–28.

264. P.P., 1864, 9, p. 82.

265. P.D., 1864, 176, cols. 2072–81.

266. HMI Edward Tufnell complained about this before the Select Committee on Education in 1865 (P.P., 1865, 6, p. 81). For an account of the bitter reaction on the part of the inspectors, see Horn, "Robert Lowe and HM Inspectorate," pp. 132–33.

267. See the sections on "Economic and Class Consequences" and "Religious Consequences" in chapter 5. In the late 1860s, however, the inspectors' hostility abated, and many spoke favorably of some of the Revised Code's features (Dunford, *Her Majesty's Inspectorate of Schools*, pp. 23–24).

268. The inspectors themselves interpreted it as an assault on them (Dunford, *Her Majesty's Inspectorate of Schools*, pp. 18–19).

269. P.P., 1864, 45, p. 189.

270. Ibid., p. 8.

271. Ibid., p. 9.

272. For an account of developments in the inspectorate after 1870, see Bishop, *Rise of a Central Authority for English Education*, pp. 111–17.

CHAPTER 10

1. See chapter 2, n. 60.

2. See the section on "Public Movement and Parliamentary Inaction" in chapter 5.

3. See the section on "Obstacles to and Pressures for Reform" in chapter 7.

4. See the section on "Educational Growth" in chapter 5.

5. See the section on "Public Movement and Parliamentary Inaction" in chapter 5.

6. Weber is not normally regarded as a functionalist theorist, but his concept of "elective affinity" is close to the notion of "strain toward consistency."

7. This is not to deny the lack of fit implied by the conceptions of contradiction and dialectic change in Marxian theory.

8. See the section on "Domination and Class-Conflict Accounts" in chapter 2.

9. An early and extended statement of this position is found in Reinhard Bendix, *Nation-Building and Citizenship* (New York: Wiley, 1964).

10. John W. Meyer et al., "Public Education as Nation-Building in America: Enrollments and Bureaucratization in the American States, 1870–1930," *American Journal of Sociology* 85, no. 3 (November 1979): 591–613.

11. Ibid., p. 599.

12. John W. Meyer, John Boli, and George M. Thomas, "Ontology and Rationalization in the Western Cultural Account," in George M. Thomas et al., *Institutional Structure: Constituting State, Society and the Individual* (Newbury Park, Calif.: Sage Publications, 1987), p. 34.

13. Francisco O. Ramirez and John Boli, "Global Patterns of Educational Institutionalization," in Thomas et al., *Institutional Structure*, p. 154.

14. Francisco O. Ramirez and John Boli, "On the Union of States and Schools," in Thomas et al., *Institutional Structure,* pp. 173–97, esp. pp. 190–91.

15. Ibid., p. 190.

16. Ibid.

17. See the section on "Other Religious and Political Developments" in chapter 5.

18. Ibid.

19. See, e.g., Ferdinand Toennies, *Community and Society,* trans. and ed. Charles Loomis (New York: Harper & Row, 1963).

20. See Emile Durkheim, *The Division of Labor in Society* (1891), trans. George Simpson (Glencoe, Ill.: Free Press, 1947).

21. See Max Weber, *The Theory of Social and Economic Organization* (1922), trans. A. M. Henderson and Talcott Parsons (New York: Oxford University Press, 1947).

22. See, e.g., Robert Redfield, *The Folk Society* (Indianapolis: Bobbs-Merrill, 1947).

23. The most recent formulation of this sort is that of James S. Coleman, who posits this relationship between "purposively constructed social organization" on the one hand and "primordial institutions" on the other (see Coleman, *Foundations of Social Theory* [Cambridge, Mass.: Harvard University Press, Belknap Press, 1990], pp. xv, 652–55).

24. See, e.g., Joseph Gusfield, "Tradition and Modernity: Misplaced Polarities in the Study of Social Change," *American Journal of Sociology* 72, no. 4 (January 1967): 351–62.

25. Daniel H. Levine et al., "Religion and Political Change," in R. Duncan Luce, Neil J. Smelser, and Dean R. Gerstein, eds., *Leading Edges in Social and Behavioral Science* (New York: Russell Sage Foundation, 1989), p. 498.

26. See the summary of trade unionists' attitudes toward religion in the elementary schools in W. P. McCann, "Trade Unionists, Artisans and the 1870 Education Act," *British Journal of Educational Studies* 18, no. 2 (June 1970): 145–46.

27. This is Taine's characterization (see p. 57 above). In his discussion of the differential rates of suicide by religion, Durkheim also saw Anglicanism as intermediate between radical Protestantism and authoritarian Catholicism (Emile Durkheim, *Suicide* [1895; reprint, Glencoe, Ill.: Free Press, 1951]).

28. P.D., 1855, 135, cols. 1308–9.

29. See the section on "Problems Building to 1843" in chapter 7.

30. See the section on "Outcome and Process in Educational Development" in chapter 2 for a discussion of the dynamic relations among these ingredients.

31. As will be recalled, the league struggled over the terms implied, rejecting *secular* because of its antireligious connotations. See the section on "Other Religious and Political Developments" in chapter 5.

32. See the section on "Attendance Fees and Compulsory Attendance" in chapter 8.

33. See "Postscript" in chapter 8.

34. See Carl F. Kaestle and Maris A. Vinovskis, *Education and Social*

*Change in Nineteenth-Century Massachusetts* (Cambridge: Cambridge University Press, 1980).

35. See Michael B. Katz, *The Irony of Early School Reform: Educational Innovation in Mid-Nineteenth Century Massachusetts* (Cambridge, Mass.: Harvard University Press, 1968).

36. For an account of the historical usage and meanings of the phrase "muddling through," see Guy Chapman, "The Onus of State Action," in Harman Grieswood, ed., *Ideas and Beliefs of the Victorians: An Historic Reevaluation of the Victorian Age* (London: Sylvan Press, 1950), pp. 384–89.

# Bibliography

The research for this book included a reading of all parliamentary debates on working-class education, 1807–80; reading of the reports of parliamentary commissions on questions relating to education and other relevant topics (trades and manufacture, children's employment, mines, etc.); and reading of minutes, reports, inspectors' reports, and the correspondence of the Committee of Council and the Department of Education, 1839–70. Coverage also included books, pamphlets, and articles written by advocates and observers in the nineteenth century, as well as books and articles written by twentieth-century historians of nineteenth-century education; these are listed in the following bibliography.

Abbott, A. *Education for Industry and Commerce in England.* London: Humphrey Milford, 1933.

Adams, Francis. *History of the Elementary School Contest in England.* Edited, with an introduction, by Asa Briggs. Brighton: Harvester Press, 1972.

Adams, J. R. R. *The Printed Word and the Common Man: Popular Culture in Ulster, 1700–1900.* Belfast: Institute of Irish Studies, 1987.

Adamson, John W. *English Education, 1789–1902.* Cambridge: Cambridge University Press, 1964.

Adderley, C. B. "An Address on Education." In *Transactions of the National Association for the Promotion of Social Science,* pp. 78–86. London: Longman, Green, Longman, Roberts & Green, 1859.

Adelson, Joseph. "What Happened to the Schools." *Commentary* 71, no. 3 (March 1981): 36–41.

Akenson, Donald H. *The Church of Ireland: Ecclesiastical Reform and Revolution, 1800–1885.* New Haven: Yale University Press, 1971.

———. *The Irish Education Experiment: The National System of Education in the Nineteenth Century.* London: Routledge & Kegan Paul, 1970.

Aldrich, R. E. "H. H. Milman and Popular Education, 1846." *British Journal of Educational Studies* 21, no. 2 (June 1973): 172–79.

———. "Radicalism, National Education and the Grant of 1833." *Journal of Educational Administration and History* 5, no. 1 (January 1973): 1–6.

———. "Sir John Pakington and the Newcastle Commission." *History of Education* 8, no. 1 (March 1979): 21–31.

Alexander, J., and Paz, D. G. "The Treasury Grants, 1833–1839." *British Journal of Educational Studies* 22, no. 1 (February 1974): 78–92.

Alexander, Jeffrey; Giesen, Bernard; Münch, Richard; and Smelser, Neil J., eds. *The Micro-Macro Link.* Berkeley: University of California Press, 1988.

Allen, Janet E. "Voluntaryism: A 'Laissez-Faire' Movement in Mid-Nineteenth Century Elementary Education." *History of Education* 10, no. 2 (June 1981): 111–24.

Allsobrook, David I. *Schools for the Shires: The Reform of Middle-Class Education in Mid-Victorian England.* Manchester: Manchester University Press, 1986.

Allyn, Emily. *Lords versus Commons: A Century of Conflict and Compromise, 1830–1930.* New York: Century, 1931.

Altholz, Josef L. *The Liberal Catholic Movement in England: The "Rambler" and Its Contributors, 1848–1864.* London: Burns & Oates, 1962.

Altick, Richard D. *The English Common Reader: A Social History of the Mass Reading Public, 1800–1900.* Chicago: University of Chicago Press, 1957.

Ambrose, G. P. *The History of Wales.* Leeds: E. J. Arnold & Son, 1947.

Anderson, Michael. *Family Structure in Nineteenth Century Lancashire.* Cambridge: Cambridge University Press, 1971.

Anderson, Robert. *Education and Opportunity in Victorian Scotland: Schools and Universities.* Oxford: Clarendon Press, 1983.

———. "Education and Society in Modern Scotland: A Comparative Perspective." *History of Education Quarterly* 25, no. 4 (Winter 1985): 459–81.

Anderson, R. D. "Education and the State in Nineteenth-Century Scotland." *Economic History Review,* 2d ser., 36 (1983): 518–33.

Anson, Peter F. *The Catholic Church in Modern Scotland, 1560–1937.* London: Burns, Oates & Washbourne, 1937.

Armytage, W. H. G. *The American Influence on English Education.* London: Routledge & Kegan Paul, 1967.

———. "The 1870 Education Act." *British Journal of Educational Studies* 18, no. 2 (June 1970): 121–33.

———. *Four Hundred Years of English Education,* 2d ed. Cambridge: Cambridge University Press, 1970.

———. *The German Influence on English Education.* London: Routledge & Kegan Paul, 1969.

Arnold, Matthew. *Civilization in the United States: First and Last Impressions of America.* Boston: Cupples & Hurd, 1888.

———. *Culture and Anarchy: An Essay in Political and Social Criticism.* London: Smith, Elder, 1869.

———. *The Popular Education of France, with Notices of That of Holland and Switzerland.* London: Longman, Green, Longman, & Roberts, 1861.

————. *Reports on Elementary Schools, 1852–1882.* London: His Majesty's Stationery Office, 1908.

————. *Schools and Universities on the Continent.* Edited by R. H. Super. Ann Arbor: University of Michigan Press, 1964.

Ashby, M. K. *Joseph Ashby of Tysoe, 1859–1919: A Study of English Village Life.* Cambridge: Cambridge University Press, 1961.

Ashworth, William. *An Economic History of England, 1870–1939.* London: Methuen, 1960.

Aspinall, Arthur. *Lord Brougham and the Whig Party.* Manchester: Manchester University Press, 1927.

Atkinson, Norman. *Irish Education: A History of Educational Institutions.* Dublin: Allen Figgis, 1969.

Auchmuty, James J. *Irish Education: A Historical Survey.* Dublin: Hodges Figgis, 1937.

Bache, Alexander D. *Report on Education in Europe to the Trustees of the Girard College for Orphans.* Philadelphia: Lydia R. Bailey, 1839.

Bagehot, Walter. *The English Constitution.* London: H. S. King, 1972.

Bailyn, Bernard. *Education in the Forming of American Society: Needs and Opportunities for Study.* New York: Vintage Books, 1962.

Bain, Andrew. *Education in Stirlingshire from the Reformation to the Act of 1872.* London: University of London Press, 1965.

Baines, Edward, Jr. *An Alarm to the Nation, in the Unjust, Unconstitutional, and Dangerous Measure of State Education Proposed by the Government.* London: Ward, 1847.

————. *Letter to the Right Honourable Lord Wharncliffe, Chairman of the Committee of Council on Education on Sir James Graham's Bill for Establishing Exclusive Church Schools, Built and Supported out of the Poor's Rates and Discouraging British Schools and Sunday Schools.* London: Ward, 1843.

————. *Letters to the Right Hon. Lord John Russell, First Lord of the Treasury, on State Education.* London: Simpkin, Marshall, 1846.

————. *The Social, Educational, and Religious State of the Manufacturing Districts.* 1843. New York: Augustus M. Kelley, 1969.

Balfour, G. *The Educational Systems of Great Britain and Ireland.* Oxford: Clarendon Press, 1898.

Ball, Nancy. "Elementary School Attendance and Voluntary Efforts before 1870." *History of Education* 2, no. 1 (January 1973): 19–33.

————. *Her Majesty's Inspectorate, 1839–1849.* Edinburgh: Oliver & Boyd, 1963.

Banks, J. A. *Prosperity and Parenthood: A Study of Family Planning among the Victorian Middle Classes.* London: Routledge & Kegan Paul, 1954.

Bartley, George C. T. *The Schools for the People: Containing the History, Development, and Present Working of English School[s] for the Industrial and Poorer Classes.* London: Bell & Daldy, 1871.

Battiscombe, Georgina. *Shaftesbury: A Biography of the Seventh Earl, 1809–1885.* London: Constable, 1974.

Beales, A. F. C. "Church and State in Education: Public Support for Confessional Schools in Some English-Speaking Countries." In *History in Education: The Educational Uses of the Past,* edited by Paul Nash, pp. 256–82. New York: Random House, 1970.

———. "The Struggle for the Schools." In *The English Catholics, 1850–1950,* edited by George Andrew Beck, pp. 365–490. London: Burns, Oates, 1950.

Begg, James. "Obstacles to a National System of Education in Scotland." In *Transactions of the National Association for the Promotion of Social Science,* pp. 283–84. London: John W. Parker, 1858.

Beggs, David W., III, and McQuigg, R. Bruce, eds. *America's Schools and Churches: Partners in Conflict.* Bloomington: Indiana University Press, 1965.

Bell, Mrs. Hugh [Lady Bell]. *At the Works: A Study of a Manufacturing Town.* London: Edward Arnold, 1907.

Bell, P. M. H. *Disestablishment in Ireland and Wales.* London: SPCK [Society for the Propagation of Christian Knowledge], 1969.

Bellairs, Rev. H. W. *The Teacher's Mission and Reward: An Inaugural Address to the Schoolmasters' Association for Gloucestershire.* London: Groombridge & Sons, 1855.

Bendix, Reinhard. *Nation-Building and Citizenship.* New York: Wiley, 1964.

Bennett, Charles A. *History of Manual and Industrial Education up to 1870.* Peoria, Ill.: Chas. A. Bennett, 1926.

Bentley, Michael. *Politics without Democracy, 1815–1914: Perception and Preoccupation in British Government.* Oxford: Blackwell, 1984.

Best, G. F. A. "Popular Protestantism in Victorian Britain." In *Ideas and Institutions of Victorian Britain: Essays in Honour of George Kitson Clark,* edited by Robert Robson, pp. 115–42. New York: Barnes & Noble, 1967.

———. "The Religious Difficulties of National Education in England, 1800–70." *Cambridge Historical Journal* 12, no. 2 (1966): 155–73.

Best, John Hardin, and Sidwell, Robert T., eds. *The American Legacy of Learning: Readings in the History of Education.* Philadelphia: J. B. Lippincott, 1967.

Betts, Robin. "A. J. Mundella, Robert Wild, and Continental Systems of Education, 1884–1889: Conflicting Views on the Status of Teachers." *History of Education* 17, no. 3 (September 1988): 221–27.

Bidwell, Charles E. "The Moral Significance of the Common School: A Sociological Study of Local Patterns of School Control and Moral Education in New York, 1837–1840." *History of Education Quarterly* 6, no. 3 (Fall 1966): 50–91.

Binns, Henry B. *A Century of Education: Being the Centenary History of the British and Foreign School Society, 1808–1908.* London: J. M. Dent, 1908.

Birchenough, Charles. *History of Elementary Education in England and Wales from 1800 to the Present Day.* 3d ed. London: University Tutorial Press, 1938.

Bishop, Anthony, and Jones, Wilfred. "The Act That Never Was: The Conservative Education Bill of 1868." *History of Education* 1, no. 2 (June 1972): 160–73.

Bishop, A. S. "Ralph Lingen, Secretary to the Education Department, 1849–1870." *British Journal of Educational Studies* 16, no. 2 (June 1968): 138–63.

———. *The Rise of a Central Authority for English Education.* Cambridge: Cambridge University Press, 1971.

Booth, Charles. *Life and Labour of the People in London.* 2d ser. *Industry.* Vol. 4, *Public, Professional and Domestic Service, Unoccupied Classes, Inmates of Institutions.* London: Macmillan, 1903.

Bourne, William Oland. *History of the Public School Society of the City of New York.* New York: William Wood, 1870.

Boyd, William. *Education in Ayrshire through Seven Centuries.* London: University of London Press, 1961.

Boyd-Kinnear, John. "The Social Position of Women in the Present Age." In *Woman's Work and Woman's Culture: A Series of Essays,* edited by Josephine E. Butler, pp. 331–67. London: Macmillan, 1869.

Briggs, Asa. *The Age of Improvement.* London: Longmans, Green, 1958.

———. "The Language of 'Class' in Early Nineteenth-Century England." In *Essays in Labour History,* edited by Asa Briggs and John Saville, pp. 43–73. London: Macmillan, 1960.

———. *Victorian People: A Reassessment of Persons and Themes, 1851–67.* Rev. ed. Chicago: University of Chicago Press, 1970.

Brotherton, E. "The State of Popular Education, and Suggestions for Its Advancement." In *Transactions of the National Association for the Promotion of Social Science,* pp. 331–38. London: Longman, Green, Longman, Roberts & Green, 1866.

Brougham and Vaux, Henry Peter, 1st baron. *Letter to Lord Lyndhurst on Criminal Police and National Education.* London: James Ridgeway, 1847.

———. *The Life and Times of Henry, Lord Brougham, Written by Himself.* 3 vols. New York: Harper & Brothers, 1871–72.

———. "Opening Address." In *Transactions of the National Association for the Promotion of Social Science,* pp. 11–49. London: Longman, Green, Longman, Roberts & Green, 1860.

———. "Opening Address." In *Transactions of the National Association for the Promotion of Social Science,* pp. 1–26. London: John W. Parker, Son & Bourne, 1862.

———. "Opening Address." In *Transactions of the National Association for the Promotion of Social Science,* pp. 1–25. London: Longman, Green, Longman, Roberts & Green, 1865.

Brown, C. G. "The Sunday School Movement in Scotland, 1780–1914." *Records of the Scottish Church Historical Society* 21 (1981): 3–26.

Brown, C. K. Francis. *The Church's Part in Education 1833–1941, with Special Reference to the Work of the National Society.* London: National Society and SPCK, 1942.

Brown, Colin M. "Industrialists and their Factory Schools." *History of Education* 9, no. 2 (April 1980): 117–27.

Bruce, Maurice. *The Coming of the Welfare State.* London: B. T. Batsford, 1968.

Burgess, Henry J. *Enterprise in Education: The Story of the Work of the Established Church in the Education of the People Prior to 1870.* London: National Society and SPCK, 1958.

Burn, W. L. *The Age of Equipoise: A Study of the Mid-Victorian Generation.* New York: Norton, 1965.

Burnett, John, ed. *Destiny Obscure: Autobiographies of Childhood, Education and Family from the 1820's to the 1920's.* London: Allen Lane, 1982.

Burston, W. H., ed. *James Mill on Education.* Cambridge: Cambridge University Press, 1969.

Butterfield, P. H. "The Educational Researches of the Manchester Statistical Society, 1830–1840." *British Journal of Educational Studies* 22, no. 3 (October 1974): 340–57.

Cahill, Gilbert A. "Some Nineteenth-Century Roots of the Ulster Problem, 1829–1848." *Irish University Review* 1, no. 2 (Spring 1971): 215–37.

Campbell, R. H. *The Rise and Fall of Scottish Industry 1707–1939.* Edinburgh: John Donald, 1980.

Carpenter, Mary. *Juvenile Delinquents, Their Condition and Treatment.* London: W. & F. G. Cash, 1853.

———. "On the Education of Pauper Girls." In *Papers and Discussions on Education: Being the Transactions of the Second Department of the National Association for the Promotion of Social Science,* pp. 56–62. London: Victoria Press, 1862.

———. "On the Non-Imprisonment of Children." In *Transactions of the National Association for the Promotion of Social Science,* pp. 247–55. London: John W. Parker, 1864.

———. "On the Relation of Ragged Schools to the Educational Movement." In *Transactions of the National Association for the Promotion of Social Science,* pp. 226–32. London: John W. Parker, 1857.

———. "Our Neglected and Destitute Children, Are They to Be Educated?" In *Transactions of the National Association for the Promotion of Social Science,* pp. 313–25. London: Longman, Green, Longman, Roberts & Green, 1866.

Cartwright, Henry. "Government Treatment of Ragged Schools." In *Transactions of the National Association for the Promotion of Social Science,* pp. 325–31. London: Longman, Green, Longman, Roberts & Green, 1866.

Chadwick, David. "On Working Men's Colleges." In *Transactions of the National Association for the Promotion of Social Science,* pp. 323–35. London: John W. Parker, 1859.

Chambers, J. D. *The Workshop of the World: British Economic History from 1820 to 1880.* London: Oxford University Press, 1961.

Chambers, Thomas. "Address on Education." In *Transactions of the National Association for the Promotion of Social Science, 1865,* pp. 32–43. London: Longman, Green, Longman, Roberts & Green, 1866.

Chapman, Guy. "The Onus of State Action." In *Ideas and Beliefs of the Victorians: An Historic Evaluation of the Victorian Age,* edited by Harmon Grieswood, pp. 384–89. London: Sylvan Press, 1950.

Church, R. W. *The Oxford Movement: Twelve Years, 1833–1845.* 1891.

Church, R. W. *The Oxford Movement: Twelve Years, 1833–1845.* 1891. Edited by Geoffrey Best. Chicago: University of Chicago Press, 1970.

Clapham, J. H. *An Economic History of Modern Britain.* Vol. 1, *The Early Railway Age, 1820–1850.* Cambridge: Cambridge University Press, 1950.

————. *An Economic History of Modern Britain.* Vol. 2, *Free Trade and Steel, 1850–1886.* Cambridge: Cambridge University Press, 1952.

Clark, G. Kitson. *The Making of Victorian England.* London: Methuen, 1962.

Clarke, F. *Education and Social Change: An English Interpretation.* London: Sheldon Press, 1940.

Clarke, J. Erskine. "The Working Man's Saturday Night: Its Bane and an Antidote." In *Transactions of the National Association for the Promotion of Social Science,* pp. 805–11. London: John W. Parker, 1860.

Clifford-Vaughan, Michalina, and Archer, Margaret S. *Social Conflict and Educational Change in England and France 1789–1848.* Cambridge: Cambridge University Press, 1971.

Cohen, David K. "Loss as a Theme in Social Policy." *Harvard Educational Review* 10, no. 4 (November 1976): 553–71.

Cohen, Emmeline W. *The Growth of the British Civil Service, 1780–1939.* London: Allen & Unwin, 1941.

Cohen, Sol. *Education in the United States: A Documentary History,* Vol. 2. New York: Random House, 1974.

Cole, G. D. H., and Postgate, Raymond. *The Common People, 1746–1938.* 1938. London: Methuen, 1961.

Cole, Percival R. *A History of Educational Thought.* London: Oxford University Press, 1931.

Coleman, James S. *Foundations of Social Theory.* Cambridge, Mass.: Harvard University Press, Belknap Press, 1990.

Collings, Jesse. *An Outline of the American School System with Remarks on the Establishment of Common Schools in England.* Birmingham: Cornish Brothers, 1868.

Colquhoun, J. C. "On the Advantages Which Accrue to Elementary Education in Scotland from the System of the Committee of the Privy Council on Education." In *Transactions of the National Association for the Promotion of Social Science,* pp. 356–60. London: John W. Parker, 1858.

Colyer, Richard. "The Land Agent in Nineteenth-Century Wales." *Welsh History Review* 7, no. 4 (December 1977): 401–23.

Conacher, J. B. *The Peelites and the Party System, 1846–52.* New York: Archon Books, 1972.

————, ed. *The Emergence of British Parliamentary Democracy in the Nineteenth Century: The Passage of the Reform Acts of 1832, 1867, and 1884–1885.* New York: Wiley, 1971.

Connell, W. F. *The Educational Thought and Influence of Matthew Arnold.* London: Routledge & Kegan Paul, 1950.

Coolahan, John. "The Establishment of the National School System in Ireland, 1831." In *The Supply of Schooling: Contributions to a Comparative Study of Educational Policies in the XIXth Century,* edited by Willem Frijhoff, pp. 65–74. Paris: Institut national de recherche pédagogique, 1983.

————. *Irish Education: Its History and Structure*. Dublin: Institute of Public Administration, 1981.

Cornish, Francis W. *The English Church in the Nineteenth Century*. Vol. 1. London: Macmillan, 1910.

Coupland, Reginald. *Welsh and Scottish Nationalism: A Study*. London: Collins, 1954.

Court, W. H. B. *A Concise Economic History of Britain from 1750 to Recent Times*. Cambridge: Cambridge University Press, 1954.

Craik, Dinah Maria. *A Woman's Thoughts about Women*. London: Hurst & Blackett, 1858.

Craik, Henry. *The State in Its Relation to Education*. Rev. ed. London: Macmillan, 1914.

Cremin, Lawrence A. *American Education: The National Experience, 1783–1876*. New York: Harper & Row, 1980.

Cross, Robert D. "Origins of the Catholic Parochial School." In *The American Experience in Education*, edited by John Barnard and David Burner, pp. 168–82. New York: New Viewpoints, 1975.

Crow, Duncan. *The Victorian Woman*. London: Allen & Unwin, 1971.

Crozier, Dorothy. "Kinship and Occupational Succession." *Sociological Review* 13, n.s., no. 1 (March 1965): 15–43.

Cruikshank, Marjorie. "The Argyll Commission Report, 1865–68: A Landmark in Scottish Education." *British Journal of Educational Studies* 15, no. 2 (June 1967): 133–47.

Cubberly, Ellwood P. *Public Education in the United States: A Study and Interpretation of American Educational History*. 1919. Rev. ed. Boston: Houghton Mifflin, 1934.

Currie, Robert. *Methodism Divided: A Study in the Sociology of Ecumenicalism*. London: Faber & Faber, 1968.

Curtis, Bruce. "Patterns of Resistance to Public Education: England, Ireland, and Canada West, 1830–1890." *Comparative Education Review* 32, no. 3 (August 1988): 318–33.

Dahrendorf, Ralf. *Class and Class Conflict in Industrial Society*. Stanford: Stanford University Press, 1959.

Dalziel, Margaret. *Popular Fiction One Hundred Years Ago: An Unexplored Tract of Literary History*. London: Cohen & West, 1957.

Davies, Emily. "On Secondary Instruction, as Relating to Girls." In *Transactions of the National Association for the Promotion of Social Science*, pp. 394–404. London: Longman, Green, Longman, Roberts & Green, 1856.

Davies, E. T. *Monmouthshire Schools and Education to 1870*. Newport, Monmouthshire: Starsons, 1957.

Davis, Rev. Evan. "The Education of the Middle Classes." In *Transactions of the National Association for the Promotion of Social Science*, pp. 137–43. London: John W. Parker, 1857.

Dean of Chichester. "Address on Education." In *Transactions of the National Association for the Promotion of Social Science*, pp. 44–56. London: Longman, Green, Longman, Roberts & Green, 1866.

De Montmorency, J. E. G. *State Intervention in English Education*. Cambridge: Cambridge University Press, 1902.

Denison, George A. *Notes of My Life, 1805–1878*. Oxford: James Parker, 1878.

Dent, H. C. *1870–1970: Century of Growth in English Education*, London: Longman, 1970.

De Schweinitz, Karl. *England's Road to Social Security*. Philadelphia: University of Pennsylvania Press, 1943.

Dick, Malcolm. "The Myth of the Working-Class Sunday School." *History of Education* 9, no. 1 (March 1980): 27–41.

Digby, Anne, and Searby, Peter. *Children, School, and Society in Nineteenth-Century England*. London: Macmillan, 1981.

Dobbs, A. E. *Education and Social Movements, 1700–1850*. 1919. New York: Augustus M. Kelley, 1969.

Dodd, A. H. *The Industrial Revolution in North Wales*. 3d ed. Cardiff: University of Wales Press, 1971.

Donaldson, Gordon. *Scotland: Church and Nation through Sixteen Centuries*. London: SCM Press, 1960.

Drummond, Andrew L., and Bulloch, James. *The Church in Victorian Scotland, 1843–1874*. Edinburgh: Saint Andrew Press, 1975.

———. *The Scottish Church, 1688–1843: The Age of the Moderates*. Edinburgh: Saint Andrew Press, 1973.

Duke, Christopher. "Robert Lowe—a Reappraisal." *British Journal of Educational Studies* 14, no. 1 (November 1965): 19–35.

Dunbabin, J. P. D. *Rural Discontent in Nineteenth Century Britain*. New York: Holmes & Meier, 1974.

Dunbar, Janet. *The Early Victorian Woman: Some Aspects of Her Life (1837–1857)*. London: G. G. Harrap, 1953.

Dunford, J. E. *Her Majesty's Inspectorate of Schools in England and Wales, 1860–1870*. Leeds: Museum of the History of Education, University of Leeds, 1980.

———. "Robert Lowe and Inspectors' Reports." *British Journal of Educational Studies* 25, no. 2 (June 1977): 155–69.

Durkheim, Emile. *The Division of Labor in Society*. 1891. Translated by George Simpson. Glencoe, Ill.: Free Press, 1947.

———. *Education and Sociology*. 1903. Glencoe, Ill.: Free Press, 1956.

———. *Moral Education*. 1925. Glencoe, Ill.: Free Press, 1961.

———. *Suicide*. 1895. Translated by George Simpson. Glencoe, Ill.: Free Press, 1951.

Dyson, A. E., and Lovelock, Julian, eds. *Education and Democracy*. London: Routledge & Kegan Paul, 1975.

Eaglesham, Eric. *From School Board to Local Authority*. London: Routledge & Kegan Paul, 1956.

Edmonds, E. L. *The School Inspector*. London: Routledge & Kegan Paul, 1962.

Edmonds, E. L., and Edmonds, O. P. "Hugh Seymour Tremenheere, Pioneer Inspector of Schools." *British Journal of Educational Studies* 12, no. 1 (November 1963): 65–76.

Eisenstadt, S. N. *From Generation to Generation: Age Groups and Social Structure.* New York: Free Press, 1971.

Ellis, A. C. O. "Influences on School Attendance in Victorian England." *British Journal of Educational Studies* 21, no. 3 (October 1973): 313–26.

Ellis, Alec. *Educating Our Masters: Influences on the Growth of Literacy in Victorian Working Class Children.* Aldershot: Gower, 1985.

Elsbree, Willard S. *The American Teacher: Evolution of a Profession in a Democracy.* New York: American Book Co., 1939.

Engels, Friedrich. *The Condition of the Working Class in England.* 1845. Edited by Victor Kiernan. London: Penguin Books, 1987.

Epstein, James, and Thompson, Dorothy, eds. *The Chartist Experience: Studies in Working-Class Radicalism and Culture, 1830–60.* London: Macmillan, 1982.

Erickson, Arvel B. *The Public Career of Sir James Graham.* Oxford: Basil Blackwell, 1952.

Evans, Keith. *The Development and Structure of the English Educational System.* London: University of London Press, 1975.

Evans, Leslie Wynne. *Education in Industrial Wales, 1700–1900: A Study of the Works Schools System in Wales during the Industrial Revolution.* Cardiff: Heanton Press, 1971.

Evans, Thomas. *The Background of Modern Welsh Politics, 1789–1846.* Cardiff: Gomerian Press, 1936.

Faithfull, Emily. "Unfit Employments in Which Women Are Engaged." In *Transactions of the National Association for the Promotion of Social Science,* p. 767. London: Longman, Green, Longman, Roberts & Green, 1864.

Farrar, P. N. "American Influence on the Movement for a National Elementary Education in England and Wales, 1830–1870." *British Journal of Educational Studies* 14, no. 1 (November 1965): 36–47.

Findlay, J. J. *The Children of England: A Contribution to Social History and to Education.* London: Methuen, 1923.

Fitch, Charles E. *The Public School: History of Common School Education in New York from 1633 to 1904.* Albany, N.Y.: J. B. Lyon, 1904.

Fitch, J. G. "Educational 'Results'; and the Mode of Testing Them." In *Transactions of the National Association for the Promotion of Social Science,* pp. 28–37. London: Victoria Press, 1862.

———. "The Proposed Royal Commission of Inquiry into Middle-Class Education." In *Transactions of the National Association for the Promotion of Social Science,* pp. 380–93. London: John W. Parker, 1864.

Fitzpatrick, Thomas A. "Catholic Education in Glasgow, Lanarkshire, and South-West Scotland before 1872." *Innes Review* 36, no. 2 (June 1985): 86–96.

Fletcher, Laadan. "A Further Comment on Recent Interpretations of the Revised Code, 1862." *History of Education* 10, no. 1 (March 1981): 21–31.

———. "Payment for Means or Payment for Results: Administrative Dilemmas of the 1860s." *Journal of Educational Administration and History* 4, no. 2 (June 1972): 13–21.

Fletcher, Sheila. *Feminists and Bureaucrats: A Study in the Development of Girls' Education in the Nineteenth Century.* Cambridge: Cambridge University Press, 1980.

Foster, John. *Class Struggle and the Industrial Revolution: Early Industrial Capitalism in Three English Towns.* New York: St. Martin's Press, 1974.

Gallagher, Catherine, and Laqueur, Thomas W., eds. *The Making of the Modern Body: Sexuality and Society in the Nineteenth Century.* Berkeley: University of California Press, 1987.

Gardner, Phil. *The Lost Elementary Schools of Victorian Britain: The People's Education.* London: Croom Helm, 1984.

Gash, Norman. *Mr. Secretary Peel: The Life of Sir Robert Peel to 1830.* Cambridge, Mass.: Harvard University Press, 1961.

———. *Sir Robert Peel: The Life of Sir Robert Peel after 1830.* 2d ed. London: Longman, 1986.

Geertz, Clifford. "The Integrative Revolution: Primordial Sentiments and Civil Politics in the New States." In Geertz, *The Interpretation of Cultures: Selected Essays,* pp. 255–310. New York: Basic Books, 1973.

George, M. Dorothy. *England in Transition: Life and Work in the Eighteenth Century.* London: Penguin Books, 1953.

Gershenberg, Irving. "Southern Values and Public Education: A Revision." *History of Education Quarterly* 5, no. 4 (Winter 1970): 413–22.

Gidney, R. D. "Making the Nineteenth-Century School System: The Upper Canadian Experience and Its Relevance to English Historiography." *History of Education* 9, no. 2 (June 1980): 101–16.

Gillis, John R. *Youth and History: Tradition and Change in Europe in Age Relations, 1770–Present.* New York: Academic Press, 1974.

Ginsberg, Morris. "The Growth of Social Responsibility." In *Law and Opinion in England in the Twentieth Century,* edited by Morris Ginsberg, pp. 3–26. London: Stevens & Sons, 1959.

Gladstone, William E. *The Church in Wales.* London: P. S. King & Son, 1871.

———. *The State in Its Relations with the Church.* London: John Murray, 1838.

Glass, David V. "Education." In *Law and Opinion in the Twentieth Century,* edited by Morris Ginsberg, pp. 319–46. London: Stevens & Sons, 1959.

Goldstrom, J. M. "The Content of Education and the Socialization of the Working-Class Child, 1830–1860." In *Popular Education and Socialization in the Nineteenth Century,* edited by Phillip McCann, pp. 93–109. London: Methuen, 1977.

———. *Education: Elementary Education, 1780–1900.* New York: Barnes & Noble, 1972.

———. *The Social Content of Education, 1800–1870: A Study of the Working Class School Reader in England and Ireland.* Shannon: Irish University Press, 1972.

Gomersall, Meg. "Ideals and Realities: The Education of Working-Class Girls, 1800–1870." *History of Education* 17, no. 1, (March 1988): 37–53.

Gordon, Peter. *The Victorian School Manager: A Study in the Management of Education, 1800–1902.* London: Woburn Press, 1974.

Gosden, P. H. J. H. *The Development of Educational Administration in England and Wales.* Oxford: Basil Blackwell, 1966.

Gottlieb, David; Reeves, John; and TenHouten, Warren D. *The Emergence of Youth Societies: A Cross-Cultural Approach.* New York: Free Press, 1966.

Grant, I. F. *The Economic History of Scotland.* London: Longmans, Green, 1934.

Greenough, James, *The Evolution of the Elementary Schools of Great Britain.* New York: Appleton, 1903.

Greg, W. R. "Why Are Women Redundant?" In *Literary and Social Judgments,* edited by W. R. Greg, pp. 280–316. 2d ed. London: Trubner, 1869.

Gretton, R. H. *The English Middle Class.* London: Bell & Sons, 1917.

Gusfield, Joseph. "Tradition and Modernity: Misplaced Polarities in the Study of Social Change." *American Journal of Sociology* 72, no. 4 (January 1967): 351–62.

Habbakuk, H. J. *American and British Technology in the 19th Century.* Cambridge: Cambridge University Press, 1962.

Haines, George, IV. "German Influences upon Scientific Instruction in England, 1867–1887." *Victorian Studies* 1, no. 3 (March 1958): 215–54.

Halévy, Elie. *A History of the English People in the Nineteenth Century.* Translated by E. I. Watkin and D. A. Barker. 4 vols. 1924–27. Reprint. London: Ernest Benn, 1949–51.

Hall, Rev. John. "Intermediate Education." In *Transactions of the National Association for the Promotion of Social Science,* pp. 267–70. London: John W. Parker, Son & Bourne, 1862.

Hall, Peter Dobkin. "The Problem of Class." *History of Education Quarterly* 26, no. 4 (Winter 1986): 579–89.

Hammond, J. L., and Hammond, Barbara. *The Age of the Chartists, 1832–1854: A Study of Discontent.* 1930. Reprint. New York: Augustus M. Kelley, 1967.

Hanham, H. J. *Scottish Nationalism.* Cambridge, Mass.: Harvard University Press, 1969.

Hans, Nicholas. *Educational Traditions in the English-Speaking Countries.* London: Evans Brothers, 1938.

———. *New Trends in Education in the Eighteenth Century.* London: Routledge & Kegan Paul, 1951.

Hargest, Leighton. "The Welsh Educational Alliance and the 1870 Elementary Education Act." *Welsh History Review* 10, no. 2 (December 1980): 172–205.

Harrison, J. F. C. "Adult Education and Self-Help." *British Journal of Educational Studies* 6 (1957–58): 37–50.

———. *Early Victorian Britain, 1832–51.* London: Weidenfeld & Nicolson, 1971.

———. *Learning and Living, 1790–1960: A Study in the History of the English Adult Education Movement.* London: Routledge & Kegan Paul, 1963.

————. "The Victorian Gospel of Success." *Victorian Studies* 1, no. 2 (December 1957): 155–64.

Harrison, Royden. *Before the Socialists: Studies in Labour and Politics, 1861–1881.* London: Routledge & Kegan Paul, 1965.

Harvey, A. D. *Britain in the Early Nineteenth Century.* New York: St. Martin's Press, 1978.

Hastings, George W. "Introduction." In *Transactions of the National Association for the Promotion of Social Science,* pp. xvii–1. London: John W. Parker, Son & Bourne, 1862.

————. "Remarks on the Industrial Employment of Women." In *Transactions of the National Association for the Promotion of Social Science,* pp. 531–38. London: John W. Parker, 1857.

Hasting, Rev. J. P. "The Difficulties in Promoting Rural Education." In *Transactions of the National Association for the Promotion of Social Science,* pp. 176–81. London: John W. Parker, 1857.

Haywood, W. A. "MPs and the 1870 Education Act: A Study in Human Motivation." *Journal of Educational Administration and History* 4, no. 1 (December 1971): 20–29.

Hempton, David N. "Wesleyan Methodism and Educational Politics in Early Nineteenth-Century England." *History of Education* 8, no. 3 (September 1979): 207–21.

Henderson, G. D. *Heritage: A Study of the Disruption.* Edinburgh: Oliver & Boyd, 1943.

Heward, Christine. "The Class Relations of Compulsory School Attendance: The Birmingham Jewellery Quarter, 1851–86." *History of Education Quarterly* 29, no. 2 (Summer 1989): 215–35.

Hewitt, Margaret. *Wives and Mothers in Victorian Industry.* London: Rockliff, 1958.

Hey, Rev. Canon. "Grammar Schools." In *Transactions of the National Association for the Promotion of Social Science,* pp. 360–66. London: John W. Parker, 1864.

Hinton, John H. *The Case of the Manchester Educationists, Part I: A Review of the Evidence Taken before a Committee of the House of Commons in Relation to the State of Education in Manchester and Salford.* 1852. Manchester: E. J. Morten, 1972.

————. *The Case of the Manchester Educationists, Part II: A Review of the Evidence in Relation to a Scheme of Secular Education.* 1852. Manchester: E. J. Morten, 1972.

Hobsbawm, Eric J. "The Labour Aristocracy in Nineteenth-Century Britain." In Hobsbawm, *Labouring Men: Studies in the History of Labour,* pp. 171–315. London: Weidenfeld & Nicholson, 1964. New York: Anchor Books, 1967.

Hobsbawm, E. J., and Rudé, George. *Captain Swing.* New York: Pantheon Books, 1968.

Holcombe, Lee. *Victorian Ladies at Work: Middle-Class Working Women in England and Wales, 1850–1914.* Newton Abbot, Devon: David & Charles, 1973.

Hole, James. *The Working Classes of Leeds: An Essay on the Present State of Education in Leeds, and the Best Means of Improving It.* London: Simpkin, Marshall, 1863.

Holman, H. *English National Education: A Sketch of the Rise of Public Elementary Schools in England.* London: Blackie & Son, 1893.

Holmes, Brian. "Comparative Education as a Scientific Study." *British Journal of Educational Studies* 20, no. 2 (June 1972): 205–19.

Hook, Walter F. *On the Means of Rendering More Efficient the Education of the People: A Letter to the Lord Bishop of St. David's.* 3d ed. London: John Murray, 1846.

Hope, Louise. "Girls' Schools." In *Transactions of the National Association for the Promotion of Social Science,* pp. 397–404. London: John W. Parker, 1860.

Horn, Pamela R. "The Agricultural Children Act of 1873." *History of Education* 3, no. 4 (Summer 1974): 27–39.

———. "Aspects of Education, 1839–41: The Minute Book of the Committee of the Privy Council." *Oxford Review of Education* 5, no. 1 (1979): 29–39.

———. "The Education and Employment of Working-Class Girls, 1870–1914." *History of Education* 17, no. 1 (March 1988): 71–82.

———. *Education in Rural England, 1800–1914.* Dublin: Gill & Macmillan, 1978.

———. "The Recruitment, Role and Status of the Victorian Country Teacher." *History of Education* 9, no. 2 (June 1980): 129–41.

———. "Robert Lowe and HM Inspectorate, 1859–1864." *Oxford Review of Education* 7, no. 2 (1981): 131–43.

———. *The Victorian Country Child.* Gloucester: Sutton, 1985.

Houghton, Walter E. *The Victorian Frame of Mind, 1830–1870.* New Haven: Yale University Press, 1957.

Howell, David W. "The Agricultural Labourer in Nineteenth-Century Wales." *Welsh History Review* 6, no. 3 (June 1973): 262–87.

———. *Land and People in Nineteenth-Century Wales.* London: Routledge & Kegan Paul, 1977.

Howson, Rev. J. S. "Report on Popular Education in Liverpool." In *Transactions of the National Association for the Promotion of Social Science,* pp. 421–34. London: John W. Parker, 1859.

Hughes, J. R. T. *Fluctuations in Trade, Industry and Finance: A Study of British Economic Development, 1850–1860.* Oxford: Clarendon Press, 1960.

Hurt, John S. *Education in Evolution: Church, State, Society and Popular Education, 1800–1870.* London: Rupert Hart-Davis, 1971.

———. *Elementary Schooling and the Working Classes, 1860–1919.* London: Routledge & Kegan Paul, 1979.

———. "Professor West on Early Nineteenth-Century Education." *Journal of Economic History* 2d ser., 24, no. 4 (November 1971): 624–32.

Illing, M. J. "An Early H.M.I., Thomas William Marshall, in the Light of New Evidence." *British Journal of Educational Studies* 20, no. 1 (February 1972): 58–69.

Inglis, K. S. "Patterns of Religious Worship in 1851." *Journal of Ecclesiastical History* 11, no. 1 (April 1960): 74–86.

Inglis-Jones, Elisabeth. *The Story of Wales*. London: Faber & Faber, 1945.

Inkeles, Alex. "Convergence and Divergence in Industrial Societies." In *Modernization Theory: Research and Realities*, edited by Mustafa O. Attir, Burkhart Holzner, and Zdenek Suda. Boulder, Colo.: Westview Press, 1981.

Innes, John W. *Class Fertility Trends in England and Wales, 1876–1934*. Princeton: Princeton University Press, 1938.

Jackson, John Archer. *The Irish in Britain*. London: Routledge & Kegan Paul, 1963.

Jackson, Sidney L. *America's Struggle for Free Schools: Social Tension and Education in New England and New York, 1827–42*. New York: Russell & Russell, 1965.

Jacob, G. A. "The Professional Training and Certification of Middle Class Teachers." In *Transactions of the National Association for the Promotion of Social Science*, pp. 5–15. London: Victoria Press, 1862.

Jarman, T. L. *Landmarks in the History of Education: English Education as Part of the European Tradition*. 2d ed. London: John Murray, 1963.

Jenkins, Geraint H. *The Foundations of Modern Wales: Wales, 1642–1780*. Oxford: Clarendon Press, 1987.

John, A. H. *The Industrial Development of South Wales, 1750–1850*. Cardiff: University of Wales Press, 1950.

Johnson, Richard. " 'Really Useful Knowledge': Radical Education and Working-Class Culture, 1790–1848." In *Working-Class Culture: Studies in History and Theory*, edited by John Clarke, Chas Critcher, and Richard Johnson, pp. 75–102. London: Hutchinson, 1979.

Jones, David J. V. *Before Rebecca: Popular Protests in Wales, 1793–1835*. London: Allen Lane, 1973.

———. "The Carmarthen Riots of 1831." *Welsh History Review* 4, no. 2 (December 1968): 129–42.

———. "Chartism in Welsh Communities." *Welsh History Review* 6, no. 3 (June 1973): 243–61.

———. "The Merthyr Riots of 1831." *Welsh History Review* 3, no. 2 (December 1966): 173–205.

Jones, Donald K. "The Educational Legacy of the Anti-Corn Law League." *History of Education* 3, no. 1 (January 1974): 18–36.

———. "Lancashire, the American Common School, and the Religious Problem in British Education in the Nineteenth Century." *British Journal of Educational Studies* 15, no. 3 (October 1967): 292–306.

———. *The Making of the Education System*. London: Routledge & Kegan Paul, 1977.

———. "The Movement for Secular Elementary Education in Great Britain in the XIXth Century." In *The Supply of Schooling: Contributions to a Comparative Study of Educational Policies in the XIXth Century*, edited by Willem Frijhoff, pp. 83–94. Paris: Institut national de recherche pédagogique, 1983.

———. "Socialization and Social Science, Manchester Model Secular School

1854–1861." In *Popular Education and Socialization in the Nineteenth Century*, edited by Phillip McCann, pp. 111–39. London: Methuen, 1977.

Jones, Evan J. *Some Contributions to the Economic History of Wales*. London: P. S. King & Son, 1928.

Jones, F. "Edward Feild, Inspector of Schools, 1840–41." *Journal of Educational Administration and History* 9, no. 2 (July 1977): 8–13.

Jones, G. P., and Pool, A. G. *A Hundred Years of Economic Development in Great Britain, 1840–1940*. London: Duckworth, 1940.

Jones, Gareth E. *Modern Wales: A Concise History, c. 1485–1979*. Cambridge: Cambridge University Press, 1984.

Jones, Gareth S. *Languages of Class: Studies in English Working Class History, 1832–1982*. Cambridge: Cambridge University Press, 1983.

Jones, Ieuan G. "The Liberation Society and Welsh Politics, 1844–1868." *Welsh History Review* 1, no. 2 (December 1961): 193–224.

Jones, M. G. *The Charity School Movement: A Study of Eighteenth Century Puritanism in Action*. Cambridge: Cambridge University Press, 1938.

Journeyman Engineer, A. *Some Habits and Customs of the Working Classes*. London: Tinsley Brothers, 1867.

Judges, A. V. "Tradition and the Comprehensive School." *British Journal of Educational Studies* 2, no. 1 (February 1954): 3–18.

Kaestle, Carl F. *The Evolution of an Urban School System*. Cambridge, Mass.: Harvard University Press, 1973.

———. "Ideology and American Educational History." *History of Education Quarterly* 22, no. 2 (Summer 1982): 123–37.

———. Introduction to "Education and American Society: New Historical Interpretations." *History of Education* 7, no. 3 (October 1978): 169–72.

———, ed. *Joseph Lancaster and the Monitorial School Movement: A Documentary History*. New York: Teachers College Press, 1973.

Kaestle, Carl F., and Vinovskis, Maris. *Education and Change in Nineteenth-Century Massachusetts*. Cambridge: Cambridge University Press, 1980.

Kalper, Hon. W. F. "Education." In *Transactions of the National Association for the Promotion of Social Science*. Liverpool: Benson & Mallett, 1858.

Katz, Michael B. *The Irony of Early School Reform: Educational Innovation in Mid-Nineteenth Century Massachusetts*. Cambridge, Mass.: Harvard University Press, 1968.

Kay-Shuttleworth, Sir James P., 1st bart. "Address on Education." In *Transactions of the National Association for the Promotion of Social Science*, pp. 79–109. London: John W. Parker, 1860.

———. *The Autobiography of Sir James Kay-Shuttleworth*. Edited by B. C. Bloomfield. London: University of London, Institute of Education, 1964.

———. *Four Periods of Public Education*. London: Longman, Green, Longman & Roberts, 1862.

———. *Memorandum on Popular Education*. London: James Ridgeway, 1868.

———. Preface to "Work for Ladies in the Elementary Schools," by John Bull (January 1872).

———. *Public Education as Affected by the Minutes of the Committee of Privy*

*Council from 1846 to 1852; with Suggestions as to Future Policy.* London: Longman, Brown, Green & Longmans, 1853.

———. *The School in Its Relations to the State, The Church, and the Congregation, Being an Explanation of the Minutes of the Committee of Council on Education in August and December 1846.* London: John Murray, 1847.

Kee, Robert. *The Green Flag: A History of Irish Nationalism.* London: Weidenfeld & Nicolson, 1972.

Kelly, Edith, and Kelly, Thomas, eds. *A Schoolmaster's Notebook: Being an Account of a Nineteenth-Century Experiment in Social Welfare, by David Winstanley of Manchester, Schoolmaster.* Manchester: Printed for the Chetham Society, 1957.

Kelly, Thomas. *A History of Adult Education in Great Britain.* Liverpool: Liverpool University Press, 1962.

———. "The Origin of Mechanics' Institutes." *British Journal of Educational Studies* 1 (1952–53): 17–27.

Kerr, Donal A. *Peel, Priests and Politics: Sir Robert Peel's Administration and the Roman Catholic Church in Ireland, 1841–1846.* Oxford: Clarendon Press, 1982.

Kerr, John. *Scottish Education: School and University from Early Times to 1908, with an Addendum, 1908–1913.* Cambridge: Cambridge University Press, 1913.

Knox, H. M. *Two Hundred and Fifty Years of Scottish Education, 1696–1946.* Edinburgh: Oliver & Boyd, 1953.

Lancashire Public School Association. *A Plan for the Establishment of a General System of Secular Education in the County of Lancaster.* London: Simpkin & Marshall, 1847.

Langley, C. J. "Separate Schools in Canada." *History of Education Journal* 2, no. 1 (Autumn 1950): 48–51.

Lannie, Vincent P. *Public Money and Parochial Education: Bishop Hughes, Governor Seward, and the New York School Controversy.* Cleveland: Press of Case Western Reserve University, 1968.

———. "William Seward and the Common School Education." *History of Education Quarterly* 4, no. 3 (September 1964): 181–92.

———. "William Seward and the New York School Controversy, 1840–1842: A Problem in Historical Motivation." *History of Education Quarterly* 6, no. 1 (Spring 1966): 52–68.

Lannie, Vincent P., and Diethorn, Bernard C. "For the Honor and Glory of God: The Philadelphia Bible Riots of 1840." *History of Education Quarterly* 3, no. 1 (Spring 1968): 44–106.

Laqueur, Thomas W. "English and French Education in the Nineteenth Century." *History of Education Quarterly* 13, no. 1 (Spring 1973): 53–60.

———. *Religion and Respectability: Sunday Schools and Working-Class Culture, 1780–1850.* New Haven: Yale University Press, 1976.

Larkin, Emmet. *The Consolidation of the Roman Catholic Church in Ireland, 1860–1870.* Chapel Hill: University of North Carolina Press, 1987.

————. *The Making of the Roman Catholic Church in Ireland, 1850–60.* Chapel Hill: University of North Carolina Press, 1980.

Lawry, John R. "Australian Education 1788–1823." *History of Education Quarterly 5,* no. 3 (September 1965): 166–73.

Lawson, John, and Silver, Harold. *A Social History of Education in England.* London: Methuen, 1973.

Lee, C. H. *The British Economy since 1700: A Macroeconomic Perspective.* Cambridge: Cambridge University Press, 1986.

Lefevere, Sir John George Shaw. "Address on Education." In *Transactions of the National Association for the Promotion of Social Science,* pp. 44–60. London: John W. Parker, Son & Bourne, 1862.

Leinster-Mackay, D. P. "Dame Schools: A Need for Review." *British Journal of Educational Studies 24,* no. 1 (February 1976): 33–48.

————. "The Evolution of T'Other Schools: An Examination of the Nineteenth-Century Development of the Private Preparatory School." *History of Education 5,* no. 3 (October 1976): 241–49.

Levine, Daniel; Binder, Leonard; Bruneau, Thomas; Camaroff, Jean; Harding, Susan; Kayes, Charles; Wuthnow, Robert; and Prewitt, Kenneth. "Religion and Political Change." In *Leading Edges in Social and Behavioral Science,* edited by R. Duncan Luce, Neil J. Smelser, and Dean R. Gerstein, pp. 497–506. New York: Russell Sage Foundation, 1989.

Levy, Marion J., Jr. *The Structure of Society.* Princeton: Princeton University Press, 1952.

Lewis, George. *Scotland, a Half-Educated Nation, Both in the Quantity and Quality of Her Educational Institutions.* Glasgow, 1834.

Litchfield, R. Burr. "The Work and the Mill: Cotton Mill Work, Family Work Patterns, and Fertility in Mid-Victorian Stockport." In *The Victorian Family: Structure and Stresses,* edited by Anthony S. Wohl. London: Croom Helm, 1978.

Lowe, Right Hon. R. *Speeches and Letters on Reform.* London: Robert John Bush, 1867.

Lowndes, G. A. N. *The Silent Social Revolution: An Account of the Extension of Public Education in England and Wales, 1895–1965.* 2d ed. London: Oxford University Press, 1969.

McCaffrey, Lawrence J. *The Irish Question, 1800–1922.* Lexington: University of Kentucky Press, 1968.

McCann, Phillip. "Popular Education, Socialization and Social Control: Spitalfields, 1812–1824." In *Popular Education and Socialization in the Nineteenth Century,* edited by Phillip McCann, pp. 1–40. London: Methuen, 1977.

————, ed. *Popular Education and Socialization in the Nineteenth Century.* London: Methuen, 1977.

McCann, Phillip, and Young, Francis A. *Samuel Wilderspin and the Infant School Movement.* London: Croom Helm, 1982.

McCann, W. P. "Elementary Education in England and Wales on the Eve of the 1870 Education Act." *Journal of Educational Administration and History 2,* no. 1 (December 1969): 20–29.

———. "Trade Unionists, Artisans and the 1870 Education Act." *British Journal of Educational Studies* 18, no. 2 (June 1970): 134–50.

MacCarthy, E. F. M. "Western State Education: The United States and English System Compared." In *State Education for the People in America, Europe, India, and Australia, with Papers on the Education of Women, Technical Instruction and Payment by Results,* edited by W. Wilson Hunter. Syracuse, N.Y.: C. W. Bardeen, 1895.

McClelland, James. "National Elementary Education in the United States of America." In *Transactions of the National Association for the Promotion of Social Science,* pp. 327–35. London: John W. Parker, 1860.

McClelland, Vincent Alan. "The Protestant Alliance and the Roman Catholic Schools, 1872–74." *Victorian Studies* 8, no. 2 (December 1964): 173–82.

McClousky, Neil G., ed. *Catholic Education in America: A Documentary History.* New York: Teachers College Press, 1964.

M'Cosh, Rev. James. "On Compulsory Education." In *Proceedings of the National Association for the Promotion of Social Science,* pp. 103–9. Belfast: Henry Greer, 1867.

Machin, G. I. T. "The Maynooth Grant, the Dissenters and Disestablishment, 1845–1847." *English Historical Review* 31 (January 1967): 61–85.

———. *Politics and the Churches in Great Britain, 1823 to 1868.* Oxford: Clarendon Press, 1977.

Macintyre, Angus. *The Liberator: Daniel O'Connell and the Irish Party, 1830–1847.* New York: Macmillan, 1965.

Mackenzie, Agnes Mure. *Scotland in Modern Times, 1720–1939.* London: W. & R. Chambers, 1941.

Mackintosh, William H. *Disestablishment and Liberation: The Movement for the Separation of the Anglican Church from State Control.* London: Epworth Press, 1972.

MacLaren, A. Allan. *Religion and Social Class: The Disruption Years in Aberdeen.* London: Routledge & Kegan Paul, 1974.

Macourt, Malcolm P. A. "The Religious Inquiry in the Irish Census of 1861." *Irish Historical Studies* 21, no. 82 (September 1978): 168–87.

Madoc-Jones, Beryl. "Patterns of Attendance and Their Social Significance: Mitcham National School, 1830–39." In *Popular Education and Socialization in the Nineteenth Century,* edited by Phillip McCann, pp. 41–66. London: Methuen, 1977.

Maine, Henry James Sumner. *Ancient Law: Its Connection with the Early History of Society, and Its Relation to Modern Ideas.* London: John Murray, 1861.

Maltby, Samuel Edwin. *Manchester and the Movement for National Education, 1800–1870.* Manchester: Manchester University Press, 1918.

Mandeville, Bernard. *The Fable of the Bees; or, Private Vices and Public Benefits.* London: Tonson, 1725.

Mann, Horace. *Report of an Educational Tour in Germany, and Part of Great Britain and Ireland.* London: Simpkin, Marshall, 1846.

Mannheim, Karl. "The Problem of Generations." In *Essays on the Sociology of*

*Knowledge,* edited by Paul Kegskemeti, pp. 276–322. London: Routledge & Kegan Paul, 1952.

Marcham, A. J. "The Birmingham Education Society and the 1870 Education Act." *Journal of Educational Administration and History* 7, no. 1 (January 1976): 11–16.

———. "Educating Our Masters: Political Parties and Elementary Education, 1867–1870." *British Journal of Educational Studies* 21, no. 2 (June 1973): 180–91.

———. "Lies and Statistics: A Note on the Newcastle Commission." *History of Education* 9, no. 3 (September 1980): 229–31.

———. "A Question of Conscience: The Church and the 'Conscience Clause', 1860–1870." *Journal of Ecclesiastical History* 22, no. 3 (July 1971): 237–49.

———. "Recent Interpretations of the Revised Code of Education, 1862." *History of Education* 8, no. 2 (June 1979): 121–33.

———. "The Revised Code of Education, 1862: Reinterpretations and Misinterpretations." *History of Education* 10, no. 2 (June 1981): 81–99.

Marcus, Stephen. *The Other Victorians: A Study of Sexuality and Pornography in Mid-Nineteenth Century England.* New York: Basic Books, 1974.

Marsden, W. E. *Unequal Educational Provision in England and Wales: The Nineteenth-Century Roots.* London: Woburn Press, 1987.

Marsh, P. T. *The Victorian Church in Decline: Archbishop Tait and the Church of England, 1868–1882.* London: Routledge & Kegan Paul, 1969.

Marshall, T. H. *Citizenship and Social Class.* Cambridge: Cambridge University Press, 1950.

Marx, Karl. *Capital.* Vol. 1. 1867. New York: Penguin Books, 1976.

Mathews, H. F. *Methodism and the Education of the People, 1791–1851.* London: Epworth Press, 1949.

Mathias, Peter. *The First Industrial Nation: An Economic History of Britain, 1700–1914.* London: Methuen, 1969.

Mathieson, William L. *Church and Reform in Scotland: A History from 1797 to 1843.* Glasgow: James Maclehose & Sons, 1916.

Matthew, H. C. G. *Gladstone, 1809–1874.* Oxford: Clarendon Press, 1986.

Matthews, R. C. O. *A Study in Trade-Cycle History: Economic Fluctuations in Great Britain, 1833–1842.* Cambridge: Cambridge University Press, 1954.

May, Margaret. "Innocence and Experience: The Evolution of the Concept of Juvenile Delinquency in the Mid-Nineteenth Century." *Victorian Studies* 17, no. 1 (September 1973): 7–29.

Mechie, Stewart. *The Church and Scottish Social Development, 1780–1870.* London: Oxford University Press, 1960.

Melville, Rev. David. "The Educational Grant; and What Should Regulate It." In *Transactions of the National Association for the Promotion of Social Science,* pp. 19–28. London: Victoria Press, 1862.

———. "A Report on the Royal Commission on Public Schools." In *Transactions of the National Association for the Promotion of Social Science,* pp. 321–44. London: John W. Parker, 1864.

Meyer, John W.; Boli, John; and Thomas, George M. "Ontology and Rationalization in the Western Cultural Account." In *Institutional Structure: Constituting State, Society, and the Individual,* edited by G. M. Thomas, J. W. Meyer, F. O. Ramirez, and J. Boli, pp. 12–37. Newbury Park, Calif.: Sage Publications, 1987.

Meyer, John W.; Tyack, David; Nagel, Joane; and Gordon, Audri. "Public Education as Nation-Building in America: Enrollments and Bureaucratization in the American States, 1870–1930." *American Journal of Sociology* 85, no. 3 (November 1979): 591–613.

Meyers, Peter V. "Primary Schoolteachers in Nineteenth-Century France: A Study of Professional Socialization through Conflict." *History of Education Quarterly* 25, nos. 1–2, (Spring–Summer 1985): 21–40.

Mill, John Stuart. *Autobiography.* London: Longmans, Green, Reader & Dyer, 1873.

———. "Inaugural Address at St. Andrews." In *James and John Stuart Mill on Education,* edited by F. A. Cavenagh, pp. 132–98. Cambridge: Cambridge University Press, 1931.

———. *A System of Logic, Ratiocinative and Inductive.* 9th ed. London: Longmans, Green, Reader & Dyer, 1875.

Milne, J. D. *Industrial and Social Position of Women, in the Middle and Lower Ranks.* London: Chapman & Hall, 1857.

Minchington, W. E. "Industrial South Wales, 1750–1914." In *Industrial South Wales 1750–1914: Essays in Welsh Economic History,* edited by W. E. Minchington. London: Frank Cass, 1969.

Mingay, G. E. *Rural Life in Victorian England.* London: Heinemann, 1977.

Montague, C. J. *Sixty Years in Waifdom; or, The Ragged School Movement in English History.* 1904. New York: Augustus M. Kelley, 1969.

Moore, H. Kingsmill. *An Unwritten Chapter in the History of Education: Being the History of the Society for the Education of the Poor of Ireland, generally known as the Kildare Place Society, 1811–1831.* London: Macmillan, 1904.

Moorish, Ivan. *Education since 1800.* London: Allen & Unwin, 1970.

Morgan, A. O. "Gladstone and Wales." *Welsh History Review* 1, no. 1 (1960): 65–82.

Morgan, Alexander. *Makers of Scottish Education.* London: Longmans, Green, 1929.

Morgan, Kenneth O. *Wales in British Politics, 1868–1922.* Cardiff: University of Wales Press, 1980.

Morley, John. *The Life of William Ewart Gladstone.* 3 vols. London: Macmillan, 1903.

———. *The Struggle for National Education.* Edited by Asa Briggs. Brighton: Harvester Press, 1972.

Morris, Norman. "1870: The Rating Option." *History of Education* 1, no. 1 (January 1972): 23–42.

———. "Public Expenditure on Education in the 1860s." *Oxford Review of Education* 3, no. 1 (1977): 3–19.

———. "State Paternalism and *laissez-faire* in the 1860's." In *Studies in the Government and Control of Education since 1860,* edited by Norman Morris, pp. 13–25. London: Methuen, 1970.

Murphy, James. "Religion, the State, and Education in England." *History of Education Quarterly* 8, no. 1 (Spring 1968): 3–34.

———. *The Religious Problem in English Education: The Crucial Experiment.* Liverpool: Liverpool University Press, 1959.

Musgrave, P. W. "Constant Factors in the Demand for Technical Education, 1860–1960." *British Journal of Educational Studies* 14, no. 2 (May 1966): 173–87.

———. "A Model for the Analysis of the Development of the English Educational System from 1860." In *Sociology, History, and Education: A Reader,* edited by P. W. Musgrave, pp. 15–29. London: Methuen, 1970.

———. "The Relationship between the Family and Education in England: A Sociological Account." *British Journal of Educational Studies* 19, no. 1 (February 1971): 17–31.

———. *Society and Education in England since 1800.* London: Methuen, 1968.

Musgrove, F. *The Family, Education and Society.* London: Routledge & Kegan Paul, 1966.

———. "Middle-Class Education and Employment in the Nineteenth Century." *Economic History Review,* 2d ser., 12, no. 1 (August 1959): 99–111.

Myers, Douglas. "Scottish Schoolmasters in the Nineteenth Century." In *Scottish Culture and Scottish Education, 1800–1980,* edited by Walter M. Humes and Hamish M. Paterson, pp. 75–92. Edinburgh: John Donald, 1983.

New, Chester W. *The Life of Henry Brougham to 1830.* Oxford: Clarendon Press, 1961.

Newsholme, A. *The Declining Birth-Rate.* New York: Moffat, Yard, 1911.

Noel, Ernest. "Industrial Homes for Children." In *Transactions of the National Association for the Promotion of Social Science,* pp. 535–38. London: John W. Parker, 1859.

Norris, Rev. J. P. "The Half-Time System." In *Transactions of the National Association for the Promotion of Social Science,* pp. 42–48. London: Victoria Press, 1862.

———. "Technical Instruction." In *Proceedings of the Education Department of the National Association for the Promotion of Social Science,* pp. 110–16. Belfast: Henry Greer, 1867.

Oakley, John. *The Conscience Clause: Its History, Terms, Effect, and Principle. A Reply to Archdeacon Denison.* London: William Ridgeway, 1866.

O'Donoghue, Thomas A. "Bilingual Education in Ireland in the Late Nineteenth and Early Twentieth Centuries." *History of Education* 17, no. 3 (September 1988): 209–20.

Ostrogorski, M. *Democracy and the Organization of Political Parties.* 1902. Chicago: Quadrangle Books, 1964.

Owen-Jones, Sheila. "Religious Influence and Educational Process in Glamorgan, 1800–33." *Welsh History Review* 13, no. 2 (June 1986): 72–86.

Pakington, Sir John S. "Address on Education." In *Transactions of the National Association for the Promotion of Social Science,* 36–43. London: John W. Parker & Son, 1858.

Parsons, Talcott. *The Social System.* Glencoe, Ill.: Free Press, 1951.

Parsons, Talcott, and Smelser, Neil J. *Economy and Society.* Glencoe, Ill.: Free Press, 1956.

Paterson, Alexander. *Across the Bridges; or, Life by the South London River-Side.* London: Edward Arnold, 1911.

Pattison, Mark. *Suggestions on Academical Organization, with Especial Reference to Oxford.* Edinburgh: Edmonston & Douglas, 1868.

Paz, D. G. *The Politics of Working-Class Education in Britain, 1830–1850.* Manchester: Manchester University Press, 1980.

Peck, William G. *The Social Implications of the Oxford Movement.* New York: Charles Scribner's Sons, 1933.

Peel, Albert. *These Hundred Years: A History of the Congregational Union of England and Wales.* London: Congregational Union, 1931.

Pelling, Henry. *America and the British Left: From Bright to Bevan.* London: Adam & Charles Black, 1956.

———. *A History of British Trade Unionism.* London: Penguin Books, 1963.

———. *The Origins of the Labour Party, 1880–1900.* Oxford: Clarendon Press, 1965.

Perkin, Harold. *The Origins of Modern English Society, 1780–1880.* London: Routledge & Kegan Paul, 1969.

Peters, A. J. "The Changing Idea of Technical Education." *British Journal of Educational Studies* 11, no. 2 (May 1963): 142–66.

Phelps Brown, E. *The Growth of British Industrial Relations: A Study from the Standpoint of 1906–1914.* London: Macmillan, 1965.

Phillips, R. J. "E. C. Tuffnell: Inspector of Poor Law Schools, 1847–1874." *History of Education* 5, no. 3 (October 1976): 227–40.

Phillips, T. R. "The Elementary Schools and the Migratory Habits of the People 1870–1890." *British Journal of Educational Studies* 26, no. 2 (June 1978): 177–88.

Pillans, Professor. "A Glance at the Present Aspects of the Educational Question in the Three Great Divisions of the Empire." In *Transactions of the National Association for the Promotion of Social Science,* pp. 202–9. London: John W. Parker.

Pinchbeck, Ivy, and Hewitt, Margaret. *Children in English Society. Vol. 2, From the Eighteenth Century to the Children's Act, 1948.* London: Routledge & Kegan Paul, 1973.

Platten, Stephen G. "The Conflict over the Control of Elementary Education, 1870–1902, and Its Effect upon the Life and Influence of the Church." *British Journal of Educational Studies* 23, no. 3 (October 1975): 276–302.

Platts, A., and Hainton, G. H. *Education in Gloucestershire: A Short History.* Gloucester: Gloucester County Council, 1954.

Pollard, Hugh M. *Pioneers of Popular Education, 1760–1850.* London: John Murray, 1956.

Prest, John. *Lord John Russell.* London: Macmillan, 1972.

Pretty, David A. "Richard Davies and Nonconformist Radicalism in Anglesey, 1837–68: A Study of Sectarian and Middle-Class Politics." *Welsh History Review* 9, no. 4 (December 1979): 432–67.

———. *Two Centuries of Anglesey Schools, 1700–1902.* Anglesey: Anglesey Antiquarian Society, 1977.

Pryde, George S. *Scotland from 1603 to the Present Day.* Edinburgh: Thomas Nelson & Sons, 1962.

Pugh, D. R. "A Note on School Board Elections: Some North-Western Contests in the Nineties." *History of Education* 6, no. 2 (June 1977): 115–20.

Ramirez, Francisco O., and Boli, John. "Global Patterns of Educational Institutionalization." In *Institutional Structure: Constituting State, Society, and the Individual,* edited by G. M. Thomas, J. W. Meyer, F. O. Ramirez, and J. Boli, pp. 150–72. Newbury Park, Calif.: Sage Publications, 1987.

———. "On the Union of States and Schools." In *Institutional Structure: Constituting State, Society, and the Individual,* edited by G. M. Thomas, J. W. Meyer, F. O. Ramirez, and J. Boli, pp. 173–97. Newbury Park, Calif.: Sage Publications, 1987.

Rapple, Brendan. "Matthew Arnold and Comparative Education." *British Journal of Educational Studies* 37, no. 1 (February 1969): 54–71.

Ravitch, Diane. *The Great School Wars: New York City, 1805–1973: A History of the Public Schools as Battlefield of Social Change.* New York: Basic Books, 1974.

Raymont, T. *A History of the Education of Young Children.* London: Longmans, Green, 1937.

Read, Donald. *Cobden and Bright: A Victorian Political Partnership.* London: Edward Arnold, 1967.

Redfield, Robert. *The Folk Society.* Indianapolis: Bobbs-Merrill, 1947.

Reid, T. Wemyss. *Life of the Right Honourable William Edward Foster.* 2 vols. London: Chapman & Hall, 1888.

Reynolds, James A. *The Catholic Emancipation Crisis in Ireland, 1823–1829.* Westport, Conn.: Greenwood Press, 1954.

Rich, Eric E. *The Education Act, 1870: A Study of Public Opinion.* London: Longmans, Green, 1970.

Rich, R. W. *The Training of Teachers in England and Wales during the Nineteenth Century.* Cambridge: Cambridge University Press, 1933.

Richards, N. J. "Religious Controversy and School Boards, 1870–1902." *British Journal of Educational Studies* 18, no. 2 (June 1970): 180–96.

Ridley, Jasper. *Lord Palmerston.* London: Pantheon Books, 1972.

Roach, John. *Public Examinations in England, 1850–1900.* Cambridge: Cambridge University Press, 1971.

Roberts, A. F. B. "A New View of the Infant School Movement." *British Journal of Educational Studies* 20, no. 2 (June 1972): 154–64.

Roberts, Alan. "Churches and Children—A Study in the Controversy over the 1902 Education Act." *British Journal of Educational Studies* 8, no. 1 (November 1959): 29–51.

Roberts, Alasdair F. B. "The Development of Professionalism in the Early Stages of Education." *British Journal of Educational Studies* 24, no. 3 (October 1976): 254–64.

Roberts, David. *Victorian Origins of the British Welfare State.* New Haven: Yale University Press, 1960.

Robson, Adam Henry. *The Education of Children Engaged in Industry in England in 1833–1876.* London: Kegan Paul, Trench, Trubner, 1931.

Roderick, Gordon W., and Stephens, Michael D. *Education and Industry in the Nineteenth Century: The English Disease?* London and New York: Longman, 1978.

Roper, Henry. "Toward an Elementary Education Act for England and Wales, 1865–1868." *British Journal of Educational Studies* 23, no. 2 (June 1975): 181–208.

———. "W. E. Forster's Memorandum of 21 October, 1869: A Re-Examination." *British Journal of Educational Studies* 21, no. 1 (February 1973): 64–75.

Rosenberg, Nathan. "Anglo-American Wage Differences in the 1820's." *Journal of Economic History* 27, no. 2 (June 1967): 221–29.

Rosenblatt, Frank F. *The Chartist Movement in Its Social and Economic Aspects.* New York: Columbia University Press, 1916.

Ross, Alexander M. "Kay-Shuttleworth and the Training of Teachers for Pauper Schools." *British Journal of Educational Studies* 15, no. 3 (October 1967): 275–83.

Rostow, W. W. "Investment and Real Wages 1873–86." *Economic History Review* 9, (1938–39): 144–59.

Royle, Edward. *Victorian Infidels: The Origin of the British Secular Movement, 1791–1866.* Manchester: Manchester University Press, 1974.

Russell, Rex C. *The Foundation and Maintenance of Schools for the Poor: A History of Schools and Education in Lindsey, Lincolnshire, 1800–1902.* Lindsey: County Council Education Committee, 1965.

Russell, John, 1st earl. "The Improvement of the Law, Health, Education, and Morals of the People." In *Transactions of the National Association for the Promotion of Social Science,* 3–11. Liverpool: Benson & Mallett, 1858.

———. *The Later Correspondence of Lord John Russell, 1840–1878.* 2 vols. Edited by G. P. Gooch. London: Longmans, Green, 1925.

Saffin, N. W. *Science, Religion and Education in Britain, 1804–1904.* Kilmore: Lowden, 1973.

Salmon, David, and Hindshaw, Winifred. *Infant Schools: Their History and Theory.* London: Longmans, Green, 1904.

Samuel, Raphael, ed. *Village Life and Labour.* London: Routledge & Kegan Paul, 1975.

Sanderson, Michael. "Education and the Factory in Industrial Lancashire, 1780–1840." *Economic History Review* 20, no. 2 (August 1967): 266–79.

Schnell, R. L. "Childhood as Ideology: A Reinterpretation of the Common School." *British Journal of Educational Studies* 27, no. 1 (February 1979): 7–28.

Schupf, Harriet W. "Education for the Neglected: Ragged Schools in Nineteenth-Century England." *History of Education Quarterly* 12, no. 2 (Summer 1972): 162–83.

———. "Single Women and Social Reform in Mid-Nineteenth Century England: The Case of Mary Carpenter." *Victorian Studies* 18, no. 3 (March 1974): 301–17.

Scotland, James. "The Centenary of Education (Scotland) Act of 1872." *British Journal of Educational Studies* 20, no. 2 (June 1972): 121–36.

Selby, D. E. "Henry Edward Manning and the Educational Bill of 1870." *British Journal of Educational Studies* 18, no. 2 (June 1970): 197–212.

Sellar, Alexander C. "Scotch Education Difficulties." In *Recess Studies,* edited by Alexander Grant, pp. 261–308. Edinburgh: Edmonston & Douglas, 1870.

Sellers, Ian. *Nineteenth-Century Nonconformity.* London: Edward Arnold, 1977.

Senior, Nassau W. "Address on Education." In *Transactions of the National Association for the Promotion of Social Science,* pp. 46–71. London: Longman, Green, Longman, Roberts & Green, 1864.

Sharpless, Isaac. *The Relation of the State to Education in England and America.* Philadelphia: American Academy of Political and Social Science, 1893.

Shils, Edward A. "Primordial, Personal, Sacred and Civil Ties." *British Journal of Sociology* 8, no. 2 (June 1957): 130–45.

Shipman, M. E. *Education and Modernisation.* London: Faber & Faber, 1971.

Silver, Harold. *The Concept of Popular Education: A Study of Ideas and Social Movements in the Early Nineteenth Century.* London: MacGibbon & Kee, 1965.

———. *Education and the Social Condition.* London: Methuen, 1980.

———. *English Education and the Radicals, 1780–1850.* London and Boston: Routledge & Kegan Paul, 1975.

———. "Ideology and the Factory Child: Attitudes to Half-Time Education." In *Popular Education and Socialization in the Nineteenth Century,* edited by Phillip McCann, pp. 141–66. London: Methuen, 1977.

———. "Nothing but the Present, or Nothing but the Past?" Inaugural Lecture, Chelsea College, University of London, May 17, 1977.

———. "View from Afar: An Afterword." *History of Education* 7, no. 3 (October 1978): 237–42.

Silver, Pamela, and Silver, Harold. *The Education of the Poor: The History of the National School, 1824–1974.* London and Boston: Routledge & Kegan Paul, 1974.

Simon, Alan. "Joseph Chamberlain and Free Education in the Election of 1885." *History of Education* 2, no. 1 (January 1973): 56–78.

Simon, Brian. *Studies in the History of Education, 1780–1870.* London: Lawrence & Wishart, 1960.

Simpson, Ian J. *Education in Aberdeenshire before 1872.* London: University of London Press, 1947.

Skinnider, Sister Martha. "Catholic Elementary Education in Glasgow, 1818–1918." In *Studies in the History of Scottish Education, 1872–1939,* edited by T. R. Bone, pp. 13–67. London: University of London Press, 1967.

Sloan, Douglas. "Knowledge, Values, and Educational History: Once More unto the Breach, Dear Friends." *History of Education Quarterly* 25, nos. 1–2, (Spring–Summer 1985): 1–19.

Smelser, Neil J. "Biography, the Structure of Explanation and the Evaluation of Theory in Sociology." In *Sociological Theory and Research: A Critical Appraisal,* edited by H. M. Blalock, Jr., pp. 23–30. New York: Free Press, 1980.

———. *Comparative Methods in the Social Sciences.* Englewood Cliffs, N.J.: Prentice-Hall, 1976.

———. "The Contest between Family and Schooling in Nineteenth-Century Britain." In *Differentiation and Social Change Theory: Comparative and Historical Perspectives,* edited by J. C. Alexander and P. Colomy, pp. 165–86. New York: Columbia University Press, 1990.

———. "Evaluating the Model of Structural Differentiation in Relation to Educational Change in the Nineteenth Century." In *Neofunctionalism,* edited by Jeffrey Alexander, pp. 113–29. Beverly Hills, Calif.: Sage Publications, 1985.

———. *Social Change in the Industrial Revolution: A Study of the British Cotton Industry, 1770–1840.* Chicago: University of Chicago Press, 1959.

———. "Vicissitudes of Work and Love in Anglo-American Society." In *Themes of Love and Work in Adulthood,* edited by N. J. Smelser and E. Erikson, pp. 105–19. Cambridge, Mass.: Harvard University Press, 1980.

———. "The Victorian Family." In *Families in Britain,* edited by R. N. Rapoport, M. P. Fogarty, and R. Rapoport, pp. 59–74. London: Routledge & Kegan Paul, 1982.

Smelser, Neil J., and Content, Robin. *The Changing Academic Market.* Berkeley: University of California Press, 1981.

Smiles, Samuel. *The Autobiography of Samuel Smiles, LL.D.* Edited by Thomas MacKay. London: John Murray, 1905.

Smith, Frank. *The Life and Work of Sir James Kay-Shuttleworth.* London: John Murray, 1923.

Smith, W. O. Lester. *Education in Great Britain.* 2d ed. London: Oxford University Press, 1956.

Smout, T. C. *A History of the Scottish People, 1560–1830.* New York: Charles Scribner's Sons, 1969.

Spencer, Herbert. *Education: Intellectual, Moral, and Physical.* 1861. Reprint. London: Watts, 1903.

Stack, John A. "The Provision of Reformatory Schools, the Lamented Class, and the Myth of the Superiority of Rural Life in Mid-Victorian England." *History of Education* 8, no. 1 (March 1979): 33–43.

Stenhouse, Lawrence. "Hartvig Nissen's Impressions of the Scottish Educational System in the Mid-Nineteenth Century." *British Journal of Educational Studies* 9, no. 2 (May 1961): 143–54.

Stewart, W. A. C. *Progressives and Radicals in English Education, 1750–1970.* London: Macmillan, 1972.

Stewart, W. A. C., and McCann, W. P. *The Educational Innovators, 1750–1880.* New York: St. Martin's Press, 1967.

Stone, Lawrence. "Literacy and Education in England, 1640–1900." *Past and Present,* no. 42 (February 1969): 70–83.

Stowe, David. *Moral Training, Infant and Juvenile.* Glasgow: William Collins, 1834.

Sturt, Mary. *The Education of the People: A History of Primary Education in England and Wales in the Nineteenth Century.* London: Routledge & Kegan Paul, 1967.

Sutherland, Gillian, ed. *Matthew Arnold on Education*. London: Penguin Books, 1973.

Sylvester, D. W. *Robert Lowe and Education*. Cambridge: Cambridge University Press, 1974.

——. "Robert Lowe and the 1870 Education Act." *History of Education* 3, no. 2 (Summer 1974): 16–26.

Szreter, R. "The Origins of Full-Time Compulsory Education at Five." *British Journal of Educational Studies* 12, no. 1 (November 1964): 16–28.

Taine, Hippolyte. *Notes on England*. Translated by Edward Hyams. London: Thames & Hudson, 1957.

Talbot, Frederick. "On Some Causes of the Defective Condition of National Education." In *Transactions of the National Association for the Promotion of Social Science*, pp. 191–95. London: John W. Parker, 1857.

Tawney, R. H. *Equality*. London: Allen & Unwin, 1931.

Taylor, Brian. "Jeremy Bentham and Church of England Education." *British Journal of Educational Studies* 27, no. 2 (June 1979): 154–57.

Templar, B. "The Religion of 'Secular' Schools, and Their Claim to Government Aid." In *Transactions of the National Association for the Promotion of Social Science*, pp. 407–11. London: John W. Parker.

Theobald, Marjorie R. "The Accomplished Woman and the Propriety of Intellect: A New Look at Women's Education in Britain and Australia, 1800–1850." *History of Education* 17, no. 1 (March 1988): 21–35.

Tholfsen, Trygve R. "Moral Education in the Victorian Sunday School." *History of Education Quarterly* 20, no. 1 (Spring 1980): 77–99.

——. *Working Class Radicalism in Mid-Victorian England*. New York: Columbia University Press, 1977.

——, ed. *Sir James Kay-Shuttleworth on Popular Education*. New York: Teachers College Press, 1974.

Thompson, D'Arcy. "What Are the Best Means for Improving the Status of Teachers, and for Securing for the Public Sufficient Guarantees for the Efficiency of Their Teaching." In *Transactions of the National Association for the Promotion of Social Science*, pp. 50–61. Belfast: Henry Greer, 1867.

Thompson, David M. "The 1851 Religious Census: Problems and Possibilities." *Victorian Studies* 11 (September 1967): 87–97.

Thompson, E. P. *The Making of the English Working Class*. London: Gollancz, 1963.

Thompson, F. M. L. *English Landed Gentry in the Nineteenth Century*. London: Routledge & Kegan Paul, 1963.

Tocqueville, Alexis de. *Democracy in America*. 1835–39. New York: Knopf, 1987.

Toennies, Ferdinand. *Community and Society*. Translated and edited by Charles Loomis. New York: Harper & Row, 1963.

Treble, James H. "The Development of Roman Catholic Education in Scotland, 1878–1978." *Innes Review* 29, no. 2 (June 1978): 111–39.

——. "The Reaction of Chartism in the North of England to the Factory Education Bill of 1843." *Journal of Educational Administration and History* 6, no. 2 (July 1974): 1–9.

Tremenheere, Hugh S. *I Was There: The Memoirs of H. S. Tremenheere.* Edited by E. L. and O. P. Edmonds. Windsor: Shakespeare Head Press, 1965.

————. *Notes on Public Subjects, Made during a Tour in the United States and Canada.* London: John Murray, 1852.

Trevelyn, G. M. *English Social History: A Survey of Six Centuries, Chaucer to Queen Victoria.* London: Longmans, Green, 1945.

Tropp, Asher. *The School Teachers: The Growth of the Teaching Profession in England and Wales from 1800 to the Present Day.* London: Heinemann, 1957.

————. "Some Sources for the History of Educational Periodicals in England." *British Journal of Educational Studies* 6, no. 2 (May 1958): 151–55.

Turner, D. A. "1870: The State and the Infant School System." *British Journal of Educational Studies* 27, no. 2 (June 1970): 151–64.

Tweedie, Alec, Mrs. *America as I Saw It; or America Revisited.* London: Hutchinson, 1913.

Twining, Louisa. "Workhouse Education." In *Transactions of the National Association for the Promotion of Social Science,* pp. 331–38. London: John W. Parker, Son & Bourne, 1862.

Tyack, David. "The Common School and American Society: A Reappraisal." *History of Education Quarterly* 26, no. 2 (Summer 1986): 301–6.

Unwin, Rev. W. J. "The Early Removal of Children from School—Suggested Remedies." In *Transactions of the National Association for the Promotion of Social Science,* pp. 182–83. London: John W. Parker, 1867.

*The Victoria History of the Counties of England.* Vol. 2, *Lancashire.* London: Constable, 1908.

Vidler, Alec. "The Tractarian Movement, Church Revival and Reform." In *Ideas and Beliefs of the Victorians: An Historic Revaluation of the Victorian Age,* edited by Harman Grisewood, pp. 113–19. London: Sylvan Press, 1950.

Vincent, David. *Bread, Knowledge and Freedom: A Study of Nineteenth-Century Working Class Autobiography.* London: Europa Publications, 1981.

Vincent, John. *The Formation of the Liberal Party 1857–1868.* London: Constable, 1966.

Walcott, Fred G. *The Origins of Culture and Anarchy: Matthew Arnold and Popular Education in England.* Toronto: University of Toronto Press, 1970.

Walford, Cornelius. "An Historical and Statistical Outline of the Past and Present Position of Education in the United States of America." In *Transactions of the National Association for the Promotion of Social Science,* pp. 308–33. London: Longman, Green, Longman, Roberts & Green, 1864.

Wallace, Robert. "Church Tendencies in Scotland." In *Recess Studies,* edited by Alexander Grant, pp. 187–240. Edinburgh: Edmonston & Douglas, 1870.

Wallas, Graham. *The Life of Francis Place, 1771–1851.* London: Allen & Unwin, 1918.

Ward, Herbert. *Notes for the Study of English Education from 1860 to 1902.* London: Bell, 1929.

Ward, W. R. *Religion and Society in England, 1790–1850.* London: B. T. Batsford, 1972.

Wardle, David. *Education and Society in Nineteenth-Century Nottingham.* Cambridge: Cambridge University Press, 1971.

———. *English Popular Education, 1780–1975.* 2d ed. Cambridge: Cambridge University Press, 1976.

Weber, Max. *The Theory of Social and Economic Organization.* 1922. Translated by A. M. Henderson and Talcott Parsons. New York: Oxford University Press, 1947.

Welsh Nationalist Party, *The Historical Basis of Welsh Nationalism.* A series of lectures by A. W. Wade-Evans et al. Cardiff: Plaid Cymru, 1950.

West, E. G. *Education and the State: A Study in Political Economy.* London: Institute of Economic Affairs, 1965.

———. "Private vs. Public Education: A Classical Economic Dispute." *Journal of Political Economy* 72, no. 5 (October 1964): 465–75.

———. "Resource Allocation and Growth in Early Nineteenth-Century British Education." *Economic History Review,* 2d ser., 23, no. 1 (April 1970): 68–95.

———. "The Role of Education in Nineteenth-Century Doctrines of Political Economy." *British Journal of Educational Studies* 12, no. 2 (May 1964): 161–72.

Widowson, Frances. *Going Up into the Next Class: Women and Elementary Teacher Training, 1840–1914.* London: Hutchinson, 1983.

Williams, A. H. *The Background of Welsh History.* Cardiff: Hughes a'l Fab and the Educational Publishing Co., 1949.

Williams, David. *A History of Modern Wales.* London: John Murray, 1950.

———. *John Frost: A Study in Chartism.* New York: Augustus M. Kelley, 1969.

———. *The Rebecca Riots: A Study in Agrarian Discontent.* Cardiff: University of Wales Press, 1955.

Williams, Gwyn A. "Hugh Owen, 1804–1881." In *Pioneers of Welsh Education,* edited by Charles E. Gittens, pp. 57–80. Swansea: Faculty of Education, University College, 1964.

Williams, H. G. "The Forster Education Act and Welsh Politics, 1870–1874." *Welsh History Review* 14, no. 2 (June 1988): 242–68.

Williams, T. G. *The Main Currents of Social and Industrial Change, 1870–1924.* London: Sir Isaac Pitman & Sons, 1925.

Williams, William. *A Letter to the Right Honourable Lord John Russell, First Lord of the Treasury, on the Report of the Commissioners Appointed to Inquire into the State of Education in Wales.* London: James Ridgeway, 1848.

———. *A Second Letter on the Present Defective State of Education in Wales. Addressed to those Who Feel an Interest in Promoting the Prosperity of Wales, and the Well-Being of the People.* London: James Ridgeway, 1848.

Wills, Wilton D. "The Established Church in the Diocese of Llandaff, 1850–1870: A Study of the Evangelical Movement in the South Wales Coalfield." *Welsh History Review* 4, no. 3 (June 1969): 235–72.

Wilson, Thomas. "A Reinterpretation of 'Payment by Results' in Scotland, 1861–1871." In *Scottish Culture and Scottish Education, 1800–1980,* edited by Walter M. Humes and Hamish M. Paterson, pp. 93–114. Edinburgh: John Donald, 1983.

Withers, Charles W. J. "Education and Anglicisation: The Policy of the SSPCK toward the Education of the Highlander, 1709–1825." *Scottish Studies* 26 (1982): 37–56.

Withrington, Donald J. "'Scotland a Half-Educated Nation' in 1834? Reliable Critique or Persuasive Polemic?" In *Scottish Culture and Scottish Education, 1800–1980,* edited by Walter M. Humes and Hamish M. Patterson, pp. 55–74. Edinburgh: John Donald, 1983.

Wolstenholme, Elizabeth C. "The Education of Girls, Its Present and Its Future." In *Woman's Work and Woman's Culture,* edited by Josephine Butler, pp. 290–328. London: Macmillan, 1869.

Wood, Sydney. "Social History from School Logbooks." *Local Historian* 14, no. 8 (November 1981): 471–76.

Woodley, E. C. "The School of the Province of Quebec, with Special Reference to Religious Differences." *History of Education Journal* 4, no. 3 (Spring 1953): 97–110.

Woodson, C. G. *The Education of the Negro Prior to 1861: A History of the Education of the Colored People of the United States from the Beginning of Slavery to the Civil War.* 2d ed. Washington, D.C.: Associated Publishers, 1919.

Wright, J. S. "On the Employment of Women in Factories in Birmingham." In *Transactions of the National Association for the Promotion of Social Science,* pp. 538–44. London: John W. Parker, 1857.

———. *Some Habits and Customs of the Working Classes.* London: Tinsley Brothers, 1867.

Wyse, Thomas. *Education Reform; or, the Necessity of a National System of Education.* London: Longman, Rees, Orme, Brown, Green & Longman, 1836.

Yeo, Eileen, and Thompson, E. P. *The Unknown Mayhew.* New York: Pantheon Books, 1971.

Young, G. M. *Victorian England: Portrait of an Age.* London: Oxford University Press, 1949.

Young, G. M., and Handcock, W. D., eds. *English Historical Documents, 1833–1874.* London: Eyre & Spottiswoode, 1956.

Young, Michael. *The Rise of the Meritocracy, 1870–2033: An Essay on Education and Equality.* London: Thames & Hudson, 1958.

# Name Index

# Subject Index

Compositor: G & S Typesetters
Text: 10/13 Sabon
Display: Sabon
Printer and Binder: Edwards Brothers, Inc.